Dashboards for Excel

Jordan Goldmeier
Purnachandra Duggirala

Apress®

Dashboards for Excel

ISBN-13 (pbk): 978-1-4302-4944-3

ISBN-13 (electronic): 978-1-4302-4945-0

Managing Director: Welmoed Spahr
Lead Editor: James DeWolf
Development Editor: Chris Nelson
Technical Reviewer: Fabio Claudio Ferracchiati
Editorial Board: Steve Anglin, Mark Beckner, Gary Cornell, Louise Corrigan, Jim DeWolf, Jonathan Gennick, Jonathan Hassell, Robert Hutchinson, Michelle Lowman, James Markham, Susan McDermott, Matthew Moodie, Jeffrey Pepper, Douglas Pundick, Ben Renow-Clarke, Gwenan Spearing, Matt Wade, Steve Weiss
Coordinating Editor: Melissa Maldonado
Copy Editor: Kim Wimpsett
Compositor: SPi Global
Indexer: SPi Global
Artist: SPi Global

Distributed to the book trade worldwide by Springer Science+Business Media New York, 233 Spring Street, 6th Floor, New York, NY 10013. Phone 1-800-SPRINGER, fax (201) 348-4505, e-mail `orders-ny@springer-sbm.com`, or visit `www.springeronline.com`. Apress Media, LLC is a California LLC and the sole member (owner) is Springer Science + Business Media Finance Inc (SSBM Finance Inc). SSBM Finance Inc is a Delaware corporation.

For information on translations, please e-mail `rights@apress.com`, or visit `www.apress.com`.

Apress and friends of ED books may be purchased in bulk for academic, corporate, or promotional use. eBook versions and licenses are also available for most titles. For more information, reference our Special Bulk Sales–eBook Licensing web page at `www.apress.com/bulk-sales`.

Any source code or other supplementary materials referenced by the author in this text is available to readers at `www.apress.com`. For detailed information about how to locate your book's source code, go to `www.apress.com/source-code/`.

For Katherine.

—Jordan

To Jyosthna, of course.

—Purnachandra

Contents at a Glance

Contents

About the Authors

Jordan Goldmeier is an internationally recognized analytics professional and data visualization expert, author, speaker, and CEO. He is the owner of Cambia Factor, a data consulting agency, and a talent analyst for Ernst & Young. He is the author of *Advanced Excel Essentials*, a book on developing advanced analytics with Excel. He has consulted with and provided training for NATO Training Mission, the Pentagon, Air Force and Navy, Financial Times, University of Cincinnati, and others. His work has been cited by and quoted in the Associated Press, Bloomberg BusinessWeek, Dice News, and American Express OPEN Forum. He has held the prestigious MVP award from Microsoft since 2013 and is an owner and producer of Excel.TV, an online community devoted to sharing the stories, setbacks, and lessons from experts and practitioners in Excel, business intelligence, big data, and analytics.

Purnachandra "Chandoo" Duggirala is an author, speaker, blogger, teacher, and CEO. He is the creator of one of the most popular Excel and data analytics blogs, Chandoo.org, where he helps people become awesome in Excel. He is the author of *The VLOOKUP Book*, a book on various lookup formulas in Excel. He has worked as a consultant and trainer for many reputed organizations around the world, including Microsoft, KPMG, CapGemini, Novartis, and so on. He has held the prestigious MVP award from Microsoft since 2009. He lives in India and likes to travel, bicycle, and play with LEGOs in his free time.

About the Technical Reviewer

Fabio Claudio Ferracchiati is a senior consultant and a senior analyst/developer using Microsoft technologies. He works at BluArancio SpA (`www.bluarancio.com`) as a senior analyst/developer and Microsoft Dynamics CRM specialist. He is a Microsoft Certified Solution Developer for .NET, a Microsoft Certified Application Developer for .NET, a Microsoft Certified Professional, and a prolific author and technical reviewer. Over the past ten years, he's written articles for Italian and international magazines and coauthored more than ten books on a variety of computer topics.

Acknowledgments

This book would not exist if it weren't for the incredible Apress team. In particular, I have to thank Jim DeWolfe, whose patience and tireless efforts behind the scenes brought this book to completion. I don't even know how many times he stuck his neck out for me, but I imagine it was a lot. I also have to thank Chris Nelson, my development editor, whose intervention and wise guidance helped make this book into something great. Apress believed in the vision that is this book, and you wouldn't be reading this without them.

To the Excel bloggers, enthusiasts, analysts, accountants, and hobbyists—this book was inspired by your untiring effort to push Excel beyond its limits. This book owes so much to your imagination and creativity. Thank you, and please, never stop.

—Jordan

I must thank Jordan for inviting me to collaborate on this book. Special thanks to Chris Nelson for his patience and amazingly detailed reviews that made this book even more awesome. Thanks to Microsoft for creating Excel and helping millions of users around the world make sense of their data and for helping me to make a living from teaching people how to use Excel better. Thanks to all my readers, listeners, and students at Chandoo.org for supporting me and helping me indirectly in co-writing this book.

—Purnachandra

Introduction

This book will challenge you to think differently about Excel. *It will challenge you to think outside the cell.*

Most of us are not used to thinking differently about Excel. We're used to viewing Excel as a one-dimensional platform with a fixed set of capabilities. This myopic view has caused us to build dashboards and models, a not-so-small-number of which are perceived as being slow and clunky. Some have even accepted "slow and clunky" as the compromise to building dashboards in Excel. But it doesn't have to be this way. You can create intuitive, interactive data and analytics applications in Excel without sacrificing speed and utility, if you know how.

This book will teach you how. But it won't happen through a series of clicks or rote memorization. Indeed, memorizing everything in this book will likely not help you. To master the techniques in this book, you must learn to think creatively and differently. You must be willing and perhaps even courageous to challenge Excel's perceived limitations. You must be able to extend focused examples into your own work, adapting them to new scenarios and different problems. Luckily, as an analyst and professional, you likely already have the creative gene to get the job done. This book will show you how to apply it to Excel dashboards and development.

What to Expect

Here's what you should know. This is an intermediate to advanced-level book. We assume you are not a novice to Excel formulas and have some degree of experience with Visual Basic for Applications programming, even if it's just the macro recorder. If you are open to learning new things, this book will teach you. Remember, the most important skill is being able to think about problems differently. Chances are you already do.

This book will not help you pick the correct metrics for your dashboards, but it will help you present them in the best way possible. This is not a book dedicated to pivot tables, VBA, or formulas but rather to how you can use them appropriately, and sometimes counterintuitively, to create engaging and meaningful analytical tools.

Much of this book will focus on reverse engineering complete designs. There are many reasons we chose to present examples in this way. For one, we want to establish the use of reusable components. We'll go into reusable components later in the book, but for now, you can understand them as collections of formulas, charts, form controls, and other Excel features that allow you to repeat and implement similar design patterns across different scenarios and applications. By reverse engineering completed work, you'll see that most applications in Excel share very similar constructions that are easy to build and ready to be reused in different products.

More important, however, is that real life rarely allows you to start from scratch. More often than not, you look to the work of others for both guidance and inspiration. Perhaps you are taking over a dashboard designed by your predecessor. Or, maybe you're adapting the solution you found on an Excel forum after an Internet search. Whatever the reasons, being a good developer requires that you know how to read, understand, apply, and adapt the work of others. How to take a small concept and apply its lessons across a range of other scenarios is a skill worth developing in its own right, and to the extent possible, this book will challenge you to do just that. It's not enough to be good at Excel development; you must learn to think like a developer. This is how Excel can transcend its unfounded reputation.

How This Book Is Laid Out

This book is split into five parts.

Part I, "Dashboards and Data Visualization"

Part II, "Excel Dashboard Design Tools and Concepts"

Part III, "Formulas, Controls, and Charts"

Part IV, "From User Interface to Presentation"

Part V, "Data Models, PowerPivot, and Power Query"

Part I introduces what it takes to make an awesome Excel application: good development practices, good data visualization principles, and thinking outside the cell. "Thinking outside the cell" refers to when and how you can use Excel differently. We also review dashboards, explaining how some are successful and why many are not. Finally, we cover data visualization principles so you can understand the best ways to present your data on your dashboards and decision support systems.

Part II explains what's required for to build and design a dashboard in Excel. Specifically, we'll focus on what to do and what not to do, while applying the data visualization principles outlined in Part I. Moreover, we'll walk you through how this book uses VBA and formulas differently than you might be used to. Part II is filled with new ways to use Excel features you might already be familiar with, such as form controls and shapes.

Part III will investigate a Gantt chart dashboard used for workforce planning. This part will apply much of what was presented in Part II to implement a fully functional dashboard system with visual and interactive elements.

Part IV will investigate how to build a decision support system used to investigate different healthcare systems across different countries. The chapters in this part will go through taking in user input, storing the input in a back-end database, and displaying the final results to the user. This part also introduces some easily implemented analytics techniques from the field of management science.

Part V was written by Purnachandra, a.k.a. Chandoo, and he shows how many of Excel's new features can help build dashboards similar to those presented in the first four parts. These features include data models, slicers, and PowerPivot and Power Query. These new features make up the new Microsoft Power Business Intelligence platform.

Above all, this book will focus on thinking creatively. It will focus on showing you how to hone your skills as an analyst to use Excel to create work that will astound your boss and colleagues. Most of all, this book is about helping you take your Excel skills to the next level. This book is a journey, and you're just at the beginning. The road ahead is long, and the challenges are formidable but well within your grasp if you keep at it.

Good luck on your journey. I know it will be a good one.

—Jordan Goldmeier

PART I

Dashboards and Data Visualization

CHAPTER 1

Introduction to Dashboard and Decision Support Development

Microsoft Excel has proved itself to be a powerful development platform, and the need for material on advanced Excel development has never been greater. In recent years, however, few books have afforded developers the instruction and depth required to create advanced Excel applications. Two titles in particular, *Professional Excel Development* by Bullen, Bovey, and Green and *Excel Dashboard and Reports for Dummies* by Michael Alexander, have given serious focus to these subjects; yet a dearth of quality material still remains. Where printed material has failed to fill this gap, thriving communities and blogs have spawned on the Internet over the last few years devoted to Excel development. Naturally, the last few years have also seen growing interest in data visualization, business intelligence, and data analytics.

The Data Problem

We are so immersed in data that it's hard to make sense of it all. So far, our solution has been to rely on products and people who purportedly transform this data into something we can digest; vendors, smartphones, computers, and even the news media slice and dice this information to make it palatable for us to consume. But even these devices and people can, and often do, fail to deliver; the institutions we've entrusted for guidance through this mess have not always had our interests in mind. Where we should have met their work with skepticism, they have imbued in us a false sense of security. Intentional or not, they have led us astray.

Thus, we exist at an important and exciting time for professional Excel developers. With knowledge of Microsoft Excel spreadsheets, formulas and Visual Basic for Applications, and the desire to learn, developers can create powerful data and visualization platforms that rival the work performed by vendors. In other words, with the right tools—and the right mind-set—we can take control of our data. We can take the power back from the vendors.

However, the desire for more data visualization and analytics and the ability to create these products in Excel has not always translated into better products, especially in the last few years. Data visualization is often misunderstood by the vendors that sell it. This misunderstanding has crept its way into Excel. Some vendors and even Excel blogs sell products or instruct users on how to create fancy but useless widgets that sparkle with metallic finishes in three dimensions. But all that glitters is not gold. Just because we can add these things to our Excel spreadsheets does not mean we should.

At its core, the problem stems from a lack of clarity. At every turn we are confounded by information. When products and research fail to make us smarter, they add to our confusion. If we are to see clearly through the data storm, we must stick to what we know—what the research tells us is true. This book will not teach you how to make the newest flashy gadgets; instead, it will teach you established principles based on proven research. We will continue down the path so rarely taken by vendors: the path of research and best practices. Think of it as an adventure.

Enter Excel: The Most Dangerous Program in the World

No, really, it's possible that Microsoft's Excel is the most dangerous software on the planet.

—Tim Worstall in *Forbes Magazine*

Worstall is referring to JPMorgan's use of Microsoft Excel and its potential contribution to the global recession that began in 2008. The story is a familiar one. JPMorgan, one of the big banks, required a new way for their chief investment officer to model the risk associated with their portfolio of collateralized debt obligations (CDOs) . CDOs, as you might recall, are those complex financial instruments that are comprised of a bundle of mortgages used to speculate and manage the risk for default. In the end, many homeowners eventually defaulted on their mortgages. Yet, JPMorgan's model had not captured this at all. According to an internal report by JPMorgan, their model contained an error that "likely had the effect of muting volatility by a factor of two and of lowering the VaR [value at risk]."

What had happened? How could one of the biggest banks employ a model that was so absent from reality? According to the report, their model was "operated through a series of Excel spreadsheets, which had to be completed manually, by a process of copying and pasting data from one spreadsheet to another." The error was generated when "After subtracting the old rate from the new rate, the spreadsheet divided by their sum instead of their average, as the modeler had intended."

Worstall, like many others, blames Excel. It's too insecure, and there's no audit trail, he contends. Its flexibility is its greatest strength and Achilles heel. His argument isn't a new one, of course. Without proper internal governance and procedures regarding archiving, getting lost in a nightmare of error-ridden spreadsheets and mixed-up versions is a real possibility.

But is that really what happened in the case of JPMorgan? Are more audit controls needed? I'm not so sure.

Not Realizing How Far Spreadsheets Have Come

Many organizations still operate with the mind-set that Excel is an incredibly hard tool to use. Early versions of Excel may have required manual updates, but these days Excel provides a lot of efficient and easy ways to pull in information. As well, what reason was there to maintain many different spreadsheets? Why did they require someone to copy and paste the information with every update to back-end data? Macros easily streamline these rote activities.

It's troubling then to think a large financial institutional such as JPMorgan didn't choose to use all the capabilities available in Excel. Instead, they tended to use it in a very antiquated way. But more than that, I submit that when you don't take advantage of the features that exist to address your needs, not only are you using Excel inefficiently, you're using it incorrectly—and dangerously.

One of the main reasons I still see organizations operate with the mind-set that they need to maintain many different spreadsheets with manual updates is because they want a historical imprint of *every piece of information for every step in the process.* These files become the historical records, or in other words, the audit trail of changes. According to their internal report, JPMorgan knew that operating with several spreadsheets was foolhardy. But for many organizations—and quite possibly for JPMorgan—operating with several spreadsheets can give the appearance of having a trail of changes. JPMorgan knew they had to automate the model's process but never did. Where was the urgency?

Are more audit controls to track every change really the solution? It would have certainly helped. But I don't think it addresses the problem in full.

Garbage In, Gospel Out

Another major contributing factor was that nobody seemed interested in validating the numbers the model was spitting out. Even when their numbers seemed different from that of the other banks, JPMorgan failed to properly validate the model to verify its calculations were correct. Why? One reason might be because JPMorgan liked the numbers coming out of the model.

This is a common problem in my experience. We're less likely to double-check results that seem viscerally desirable. Often these results take the form of these three cases:

- When the models provide information that appears consistent with everyone else's numbers, we may meet the numbers with less skepticism.
- When our models provide information that is counterintuitive, we may again be less skeptical because we think we might have found a counterintuitive response.
- When our models seem to average information together, giving us a grand bargain between one or more competing ideas, we may think we have results that everyone should like.

Part of the problem is how we view models. If a lot of money and research goes into developing a model, we're less likely to turn our backs on all of the work we've performed even when we suspect there are issues. We might think we can save it, if only we had more time and resources. However, some work is just not usable when we realize it's wrong. We can try to ignore its results, but it's hard to ignore results even when we know they're bad. Think of it as an incorrect entry on a crossword puzzle written in ink: even when we want to ignore it, we often forget that the entry is wrong. Bad models affect our ability to judge in the same way.

When our model delivers results that are incorrect, however seemingly truthful, the model can be described as being "garbage in, garbage out." When management believes the results no matter what, we might describe management's behavior as "garbage in, gospel out."

■ **Remember** Think outside the cell. Excel is a great tool. I love it. But it can't do everything—and we shouldn't force it to do what we want to verify our own biases.

How Excel Fits In

The unfortunate reality is that Excel cannot make decisions for us. We cannot use it like a crystal ball to gaze for the truth into the future. We cannot pretend that disparate and conflicting information might form a real fluent idea as if we were reading tea leaves in high resolution. In fact, no program, no mechanism, and no promise however earnest can do this for us.

We should start by knowing what Excel can and cannot do for us. If we use Excel correctly, we can bring important decision-making insight to our management. If we try to turn it into something it's not, we might mistakenly misunderstand or even waste its potential. At best, if we misuse our tools, we make a mistake that is well understood and correct it immediately; at worse, we follow down a path of bad results unaware that they are bad.

What Excel Is Good For

There are several good reasons why Excel might be useful for our project. Among other reasons, Excel is

- A no-nonsense commercial-off-the-shelf (COTS) solution
- Flexible and customizable for our needs
- Inexpensive-ish
- Familiar to many in the industry
- A good return on investment
- Mostly backward compatibility

A Commercial-Off-the-Shelf Solution

Commercial-off-the-shelf (COTS) software is a common term among consumers of software and information systems. In particular, the U.S. federal government holds a special designation for COTS software packages. The reason COTS solutions are preferred is their name: they're "off the shelf." By that, we mean that COTS products are essentially ready for us to use as if we purchased them off the shelf at a retailer. Most COTS products have some assembly required, but they represent a piece of software that doesn't require a significant undertaking and investment into infrastructure to implement, train users, and maintain operations.

And this is where Excel really brings the advantage. There are many data visualization packages out there, and many of them require a certain amount of data architecture or "business intelligence" to implement. Excel doesn't require any of these technologies to begin building dashboards and powerful data visualizations.

Flexible and Customizable

Even though we can characterize Excel as an off-the-shelf solution, it still brings a strong amount of flexibility and customizability. By flexible, I mean that Excel gives you many options in which you present and visualize your data and analysis. By customizable, I mean that you are able to do things to your spreadsheet to make it indiscernible from a regular piece of software. For example, you can protect certain cells from user input. You can even remove the tab banner at the top of the screen when you send out your dashboard. These things allow you to essentially modify the user experience from looking at an Excel spreadsheet to looking at a dashboard.

Familiarity and Ubiquity

Excel is ubiquitous. Currently, Microsoft Excel is the most widely used spreadsheet platform across the world. With familiarity comes less training. Because Excel is so widely used in industry, chances are your customers don't need intense training to just pick up your work and use it right away. As well, your Excel solutions *should* work on any computer that also has Excel because the solutions are hardware independent (to a certain extent—there are notable limitations, and we'll talk about how to overcome some of them later in the book). Finally, because many users are often behind—that is, they are using versions of Excel older than the most recent one available—Microsoft, as a general rule, makes worksheets fairly backward compatible. Even if you develop in a new version, chances are most if not all of the functionality will work in the most recent previous version.

Inexpensive-ish

I say "ish" because Excel isn't incredibly cheap, especially as you move into the more expensive versions of Office, such as Professional and Professional Plus. As of this writing, the latest version of Excel, Excel 2013, was selling for $499 for the Professional Plus edition. That said, $499 is still a cheaper license than many of the full-blown data visualization packages. But chances are, you don't have to worry about buying Excel new at your local office store. You probably purchased a computer that came with a Microsoft Office Professional license—or, your company already has some license agreement with Microsoft. Whether it came with your equipment, it was purchased on your behalf, or you had to purchase it for yourself (or for your business), the purchase represents a small fixed cost to you and essentially no additional charge to carry over to your customer.

Quick Turnaround Time

In my experience, Excel solutions just don't take as long as other software solutions. On the front end, you can add and modify the format with ease and without code. As well, the coding language behind the scenes, Visual Basic for Applications (VBA), provides a high-level ability to modify the spreadsheet on the fly without tons of coding.

SPREADSHEETS AS PROGRAMMING

Many of us don't think of developing a dashboard in Excel as developing software or programming, even when we employ VBA. However, recent research suggests that a spreadsheet is a form of software programming, albeit in a less rigid environment. In *Quality Control in Spreadsheets: A Software Engineering-Based Approach to Spreadsheet Development*, the authors write the following:

The process of formula construction in spreadsheets is basically a form of computer programming.[1]

A Good Return on Investment

This should be a no-brainer at this point. When we consider all of the advantages discussed earlier, it's not hard to see why Excel could provide a much better return on investment than a big, expensive data visualization package. But the proof is in the pudding: managers will see the good work you do and see how much they've paid for it.

What Excel Isn't Good For

There are lots of things Excel cannot do (and should not be expected to do). Excel should not be used in the following ways:

- As a full-fledged database
- For enterprise-level reporting
- For replacing a full software package
- For predicting the future

In the next sections, I'll review cases in which Excel is not the best tool for the job.

[1]Rajalingham, Kamalasen, David Chadwick, Brian Knight, and Dilwyn Edwards. "Quality control in spreadsheets: a software engineering-based approach to spreadsheet development." In *System Sciences*, 2000. Proceedings of the 33rd Annual Hawaii International Conference, pp. 10. IEEE, 2000.

A Full-Fledged Database

Excel is not a database. It's a flat file that can house data that has implicit relationships like a relational database. But Excel cannot replicate the abilities that a large database provides. Excel can't learn what relational data you have. Excel can't inherently store a large amount of data effectively without some extra modifications from you, the developer. Excel can't inherently keep track of changes you've committed (you must save your work and annotate those changes—or create a macro to capture them).

For small amounts of data, Excel can provide effective storage without the bloat associated with a database. But Excel cannot replace your company's database.

Many people will use Excel like a database and not even realize it. When they need to make a report for a given month, they'll copy the tab from last month and then dump in the required table or make changes to their pivot table. I won't argue that you can do this with Excel, but it's not a good practice, and it leads to problems (see the opening to this chapter). Specifically, it requires that you disconnect the information from the copied sheet and run through a series of rote steps to update it. But to err is human, and we miss stuff. We can replace these actions with some code and formulas, and we can reduce all of those static tabs to one.

Enterprise-Level Reporting

Up until Excel 2007, you were limited to only 65,536 rows to use. But even if your data didn't seem to use all of these rows, a large amount of data in Excel 2007 and previous seemed to cause all sorts of problems like locking up for a minute or more, spontaneously crashing your spreadsheet, and long if unpredictable save and load times. In Excel 2010, Microsoft introduced PowerPivot, which allowed for much better memory management and flexibility concerning the amount of data Excel could handle.

We'll talk about PowerPivot in this book, specifically the last four chapters. You'll see it can be used to create dashboards and data visualizations very quickly. However, PowerPivot is still very new, and there's a lot to be desired from it. As of now, I do not see it as the best option for enterprise-level reporting.

A Full Software Package

In the past, I've made separate Excel applications that my clients really enjoyed. They wondered if I could combine them into one integrated tool. The original integrated tool was fast and lightweight. As time went on, they asked for more features, and the scope of the project became much larger. In the end, the final product had become much heavier and much more bloated. It was a lesson for me in Excel development.

Excel can do a lot, but if you keep dumping additions and capabilities into your files that were initially designed to do one thing, you should expect the file to become more bloated. When we develop Excel applications then, we should keep our work targeted and directed. Chances are, your Excel solution isn't objected oriented to the extent that it will allow for extensible add-ons.

Predicting the Future

I know I keep repeating myself on this point, but Excel can't solve all of your problems. Even if we make a stellar dashboard that management loves, that demonstrably saves money and time, and that provides strong insight to decision makers, we must always be concerned that what we present on our dashboard is only as strong as it is valid.

We must always be wary. A history of success isn't proof of a valid model. We could arrive at a correct conclusion on accident and not know it until our model finally spits out something incorrect. Excel is merely a tool to help us make good decisions, but good decision making happens when we view the problem holistically and not just on the screens in front of our eyes.

Buzzword Bingo: Dashboards, Reports, Data Visualization, and Others

Today, there is a lot of interest in the field of dashboards, reports, and data visualization. These terms are often used interchangeably but can and do mean different things based on context. Dashboards and reports especially are said to mean the same thing, but it would be inaccurate to say the two are equal. Dashboards are, in fact, reports, but not all reports are dashboards. You can use the terms *report* and *dashboard* interchangeably in the proper context, but please do so care.

This book will not use the terms *dashboard* and *report* interchangeably. When I say *dashboard,* I mean a very specific type of report that usually does not include a lot of interactivity, and I define it in more detail in the next section. When I say *report,* we often mean interactive screens that allow for data lookup, interactivity, and what-if analysis among others. In this book, we'll go one-step further and refer to these reports as decision support systems.

Data visualizations are often found in reports and decision support systems, especially on dashboard reports. But data visualization is simply a type of communication and nothing more. It's an important type of communication because, when used correctly, it allows us to see and understand a lot information in a moment and in a small space. But dashboards and reports are not defined by their use of data visualization. Many data products use data visualization, but it's not a requirement, and in many cases, the use might be superficial. Remember, a flashy chart, however cool looking, is wasted space if it's unnecessary.

Let's go over some definitions.

Dashboards

Dashboards are displays mainly used for monitoring what's going on in a business or organization at a given time. Some dashboards provide to the user ways to drill down into the data, filter important items, or link to information outside of the view should the user need to dig deeper. They usually contain indicators (often called *key performance indicators*) and metrics that measure and capture different areas of an organization. Dashboards, however, are limited to only one page and only report information. They do not provide the means for further analytical investigations, such as "what-if" analysis.

The dashboard guru Stephen Few was frustrated that vendors and the business intelligence community often misused the term *dashboard.* Thus, he set out to create a working definition, which has now become the widely accepted definition. Few declares the following:

> *A dashboard is a visual display of the most important information needed to achieve one or more objectives; consolidated and arranged on a single screen so the information can be monitored at a glance.*[2]

■ **Remember** A dashboard is a visual display of the most important information needed to achieve one or more objectives, consolidated and arranged on a single screen so the information can be monitored at a glance.

---

[2]From *Information Dashboard Design* (Analytics Press, 2014) by Stephen Few.

Decision Support Systems

Decision support systems provide increased analytical capability to the user to model and investigate different aspects of an organization or business. They often encompass areas of a business that go beyond monitoring its health. They may be able to generate different versions of each finding through analysis as well as save the steps required to make them.

I know these differences may seem confusing at first, but the applications serve different functions within an organization. Knowing the difference—and knowing when and how to use each—will allow you to provide better tools to your stakeholders. You can breathe easy because I'll discuss in detail how both of these different applications are made. I think it's important to understand the differences between the two, but from the standpoint of development, they're actually made using the same items and techniques.

The Excel Development Trifecta

As the beginning of this chapter pointed out (and later chapters will attest to at length), simply knowing how to use Excel isn't enough. You must know how to visualize data, you must understand best development practices, and you must learn to think critically about Excel and information. Therefore, three key elements go into good Excel development.

In this section I'll go over what I like to call the *Excel development trifecta* (see Figure 1-1). If you follow these principles, you will be well on your way to making an awesome Excel application:

- Good visualization practices
- Good development practices
- Critically thinking about development, or "thinking outside the cell"

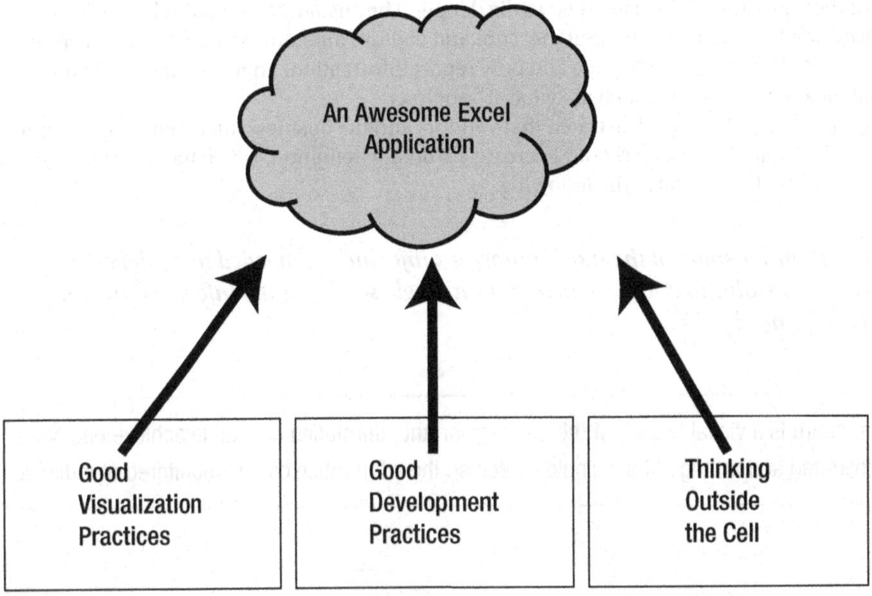

Figure 1-1. *The Excel development trifecta will help you develop great Excel applications*

Good Visualization Practices

Good visualization is the cornerstone of a good Excel application product. If you are not presenting information in a way that is understandable to your audience, you communicate little, if anything. Bad visualization design will surely hinder your work. Therefore, this book will only endeavor into good visualization practices and design. We will leave what doesn't work on the shelf—or in the bin—to where it belongs.

Many online analytical applications and Excel dashboards feature dials and gauges in a vein similar to what can be found in your car. While building these instruments in Excel may prove to be beneficial from a learning perspective, dials and gauges are notoriously bad at conveying information. That these designs have become popular on dashboards is an unfortunate turn of events and is the result of dashboard vendors whose interest in marketing the dashboard metaphor reaches further than their ability to comprehend the underlying research behind their products. Consider the following data and charts.

THE INFAMOUS PIE CHART

Let's say you want to investigate the performance of each of your products over the last year. Table 1-1 lists how each product performed.

Table 1-1. *Percentage of Sales for Each Product*

Product	Percent of Overall Sales (%)
Product A	25%
Product B	14%
Product C	38%
Product D	23%

How might you present this information visually? On first glance you might be tempted to present the information as a pie chart, like in Figure 1-2.

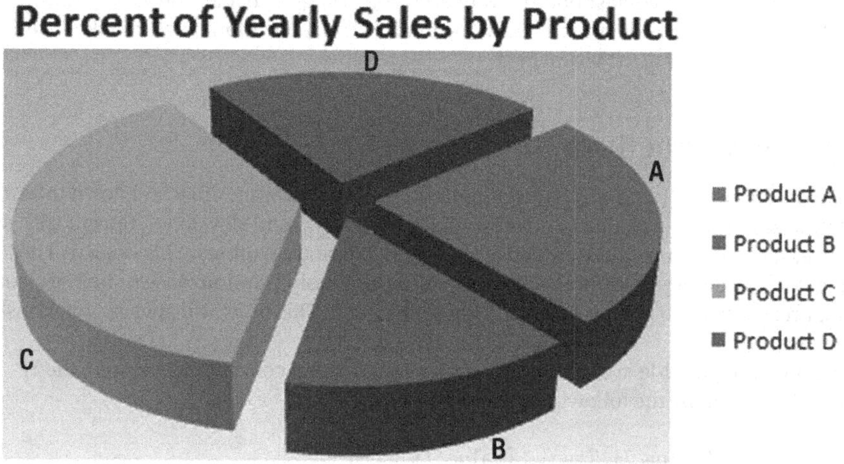

Figure 1-2. *Percent of yearly sales by product presented in a pie chart*

As it turns out, research on data visualization suggests this isn't the best way to present the data when we want to compare proportions. We have more trouble comparing differences when they are encoded in area than we do when they encoded as lines. Consider the chart in Figure 1-3.

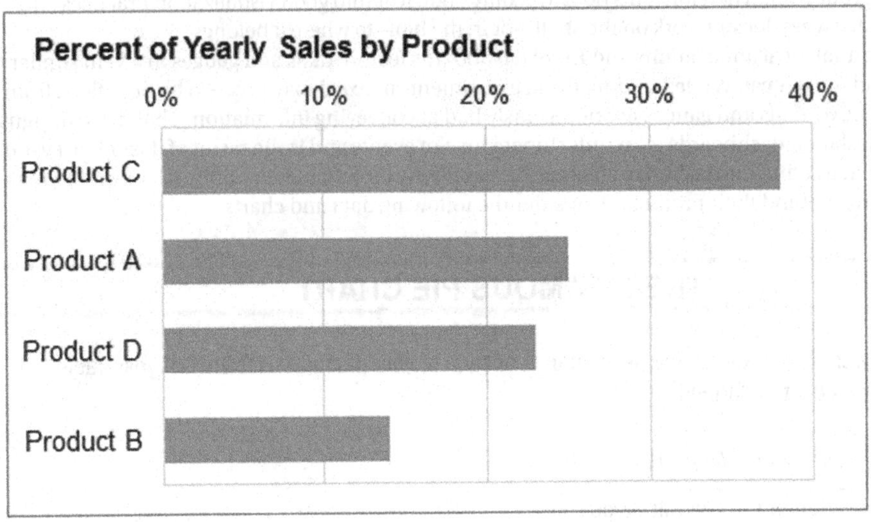

Figure 1-3. *Percent of yearly sales by product presented in a bar chart*

Clearly the bar chart in Figure 1-3 does a better job of allowing us to compare what proportion of overall sales each product sold represents. In addition, the bar chart shows the information by greatest to least proportion. Presenting information in a sorted order would be impossible with a pie chart.

Not only does good visualization practice make your work effective, it places your work ahead of what's already available. When your managers and clients see your work, they'll instantly know what you've produced is better. A great feature of good visualization is that it takes advantage of "preattentive" cognitive processes in our brain. When dashboards and reports are designed to communicate, information is transferred seamlessly from the screen into the viewer's mind. Bad visualization quickly makes itself apparent by taxing and overwhelming the visual field.

Good Development Practices

Excel is a flexible environment providing to the developer many different avenues to travel down to complete similar tasks. Yet this flexibility can also lead to traveling down dark alleys and slow lanes. Specifically, some development practices are better than others. Some formulas are better than others. This book will not prefer every method but instead prefer those that use less storage memory (random access memory), use fewer processor resources, and have proven to work faster than others. This book will always prefer best practices to any practice.

To demonstrate different possible avenues, consider the simple Excel conditional formula, the `IF` formula. If you recall, `IF` is given by the following:

```
IF(Condition_To_Evaluate, [Value_If_True], [Value_If_False])
```

The IF formula is pretty straightforward. The three parameters of the IF formula break down as follows:

- *Condition_To_Evaluate*: For this first parameter, you supply to Excel an expression that evaluates to either TRUE or FALSE. For example, if you wanted Excel to evaluate whether cell A1 was greater than 9, you would supply this parameter with A1 > 9 as an argument.
- *Value_If_True*: Whatever you supply to this parameter is what Excel will return should the condition in the former parameter result in TRUE.
- *Value_If_False*: Whatever you supply to this parameter is what Excel will return should the condition in the former parameter result in FALSE.

If you have a scenario with multiple conditions, that is, a scenario in which you wanted to evaluate another condition when the first evaluates to TRUE or FALSE, you could use *nested* IF statements. Consider the following example.

Say your organization sells widgets for $3 when a buyer purchases 100 or less, $2 when a buyer purchases more than 100 but less than or equal to 200, and $1 when a buyer purchases more than 200. You could use nested IF statements, as shown in Figure 1-4.

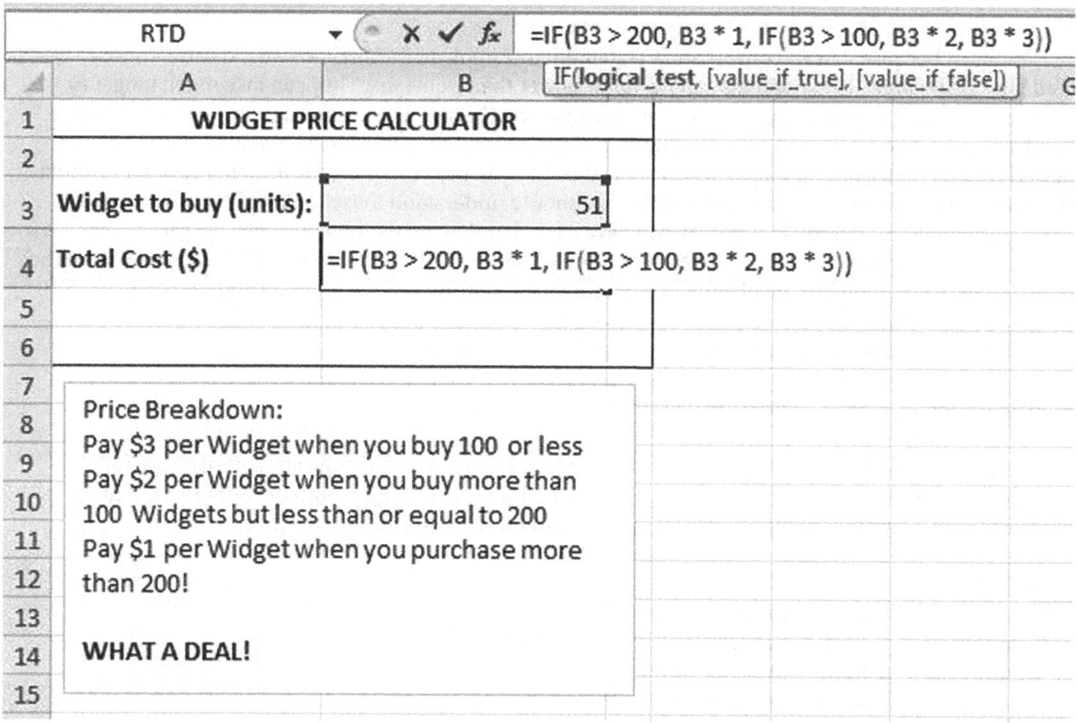

Figure 1-4. *Nested IF-statement formula for calculating the price of a widget based on quantity*

At first glance, nested IF statements may appear to be the best and only solution to this problem. But there is indeed another way to do this problem. You could, for example, use Boolean logic. Boolean logic employs a set of binary symbols, TRUE and FALSE, exactly like the Condition_To_Evaluate from the previous IF formula. The great thing about Excel is that TRUE and FALSE and the numbers 1 and 0 can represent both Boolean logic and numbers. From the nested IF statements shown earlier, we could convert that formula from this:

```
=IF(B3 > 200, B3 * 1, IF(B3 > 100, B3 * 2, B3 * 3))
```

to the following:

```
=B3 * ((B3 <= 200)  + (B3 <= 100)   + 1)
```

How does the new formula work? Let's say the number 51 is in cell B3; then we have this:

```
=B3 * ((B3 <= 200)  + (B3 <= 100)   + 1)
=51 * ((51 <= 200)  + (51 <= 100)   + 1)
=51 * ((TRUE)  + (TRUE)   + 1)
=51 * (1 + 1 + 1)
= 51 * $3.00 = $153.00
```

Now just because we can convert an IF statement to a Boolean formula like we did earlier, should we? Well, that all depends. IF statements can be much slower than Booleans. They can take much longer to process, especially when they must branch to other nested IF statements. Boolean formulas, on the other hand, are quick and execute as a single equation. Not only are using Boolean formulas much faster than nested IF statements, but they also provide to us the ability to use conditional tests in many other formulas. When choosing how to construct our formulas, we should understand these trade-offs.

Consider another problem. Let's say you have a label update on the screen displaying the sentence "Displaying x programs," where x is the current number of programs in viewing. Most likely, you'll want the screen to say something like "displaying 1 program" when there's only one program and say "displaying 10 programs" when there is more than one.

To do this without an IF statement, you would write the following:

```
= "Displaying " & B1 & " program" & Left("s", B1 > 1)
```

Remember that the LEFT() formula takes in a given string and returns the amount of characters specified in the second argument. Earlier, we place a conditional statement into the number of characters field instead of a constant number. Now let's play around with what can go into B1:

```
If B1 = 7 then,
= "Displaying " & B1 & " program" & Left("s", 7 > 1)
= "Displaying " & B1 & " program" & Left("s", TRUE)
= "Displaying " & B1 & " program" & Left("s", 1)
= "Displaying " & B1 & " program" & "s"
= "Displaying " & B1 & " programs"
```

```
=Displaying 7 Programs
```

Now consider if B1 = 1, then we have this:

```
= "Displaying " & B1 & " program" & Left("s", 1 > 1)
= "Displaying " & B1 & " program" & Left("s", FALSE)
= "Displaying " & B1 & " program" & Left("s", 0)
= "Displaying " & B1 & " program"
= "Displaying 1 program"
```

Good development practices go beyond what's doable on the spreadsheet. Indeed, good development practices extend into our Visual Basic for Applications code. Writing a large matrix of information to a spreadsheet, for example, can be completed several ways. We could iterate through every line in the array like the code here:

```
For i = 1 To 10

    Sheet1.Range("A" & i).Value = vArray(i)

Next i
```

Or we could do it in one pass:

```
    Sheet1.Range("A1:A10").Value = vArray
```

The difference between these methods is substantive. When Excel iterates through every line of the array, it must execute each instruction inside the loop. That is, Excel must read the value from the array, print the array to the screen, and update the spreadsheet (since writing to the screen will trigger updates in certain functions known as *volatile functions*)—and it must do this *n* amount of times, which, in this example, is 100 times. So, that's three actions per each iteration, or 3 * 100, so it's 300 actions.

Now consider the second example. The entire process is handled in only one action. Rather than calling for Excel to update the screen 100 times, this code updates the screen only once—but it yields the same results as the previous code. For complex spreadsheets filled with many interactions, the second code snippet is clearly the better choice.

Thinking Outside the Cell

Above all, this book will encourage you to think differently, if not critically. You've been told before, I'm sure, to "think outside the box." The phrase unfortunately has become a trite marketing gimmick of personal coaches and inspirational speakers. Yet, if we remove the hype surrounding its use, we find a tangible and important instruction. Specifically, we must become aware of the limitations we've constructed for ourselves and remove them when they hinder our work.

Were you surprised to find Boolean formulas could substitute for IF statements? Did you know that pie charts do not effectively convey information? These revelations merely scrape the surface of what is possible if we think about spreadsheet development differently, when we think outside the cell.

Because when we do, we no longer see Excel as just a boring spreadsheet, in other words, a perfunctory drawing board for the listless accountant, the engineer, or the basement dwelling nerd (well, maybe I'm still one of those at heart). Instead, we see a rich canvas upon which to paint complex pictures; a flexible landscape whose curvature can be molded into mountainous regions in which we can see everything; or simple terrains that stand in for the larger picture. We can achieve much in Excel if we take a step back from our cell walls and give our imagination some time to hold the reigns.

When we "think outside the cell," we concentrate on what is and isn't possible in Excel. We evaluate the distinction between conventional wisdom and hype, implementing and disregarding each accordingly. We blur the line between what we've been told is possible and what we've been told isn't, but we also draw distinct lines between what we've previously thought to be hazy. We add nuance to the simple and clarity to the complex. We don't just rely on the authority of books like this; we balance knowledge with other expertise and experience, synthesizing intuition and expert information into a holistic paradigm.

Consider what constructions keep you locked into a certain way of thinking. Why do you think the way you do? What certainties do you have about spreadsheet development, about business, about life?

More than developing quality spreadsheets, thinking outside the cell is a personal experiment. At this auspicious time, words like *dashboards, reports*, and *visualization* are at risk of becoming virtually meaningless, proffered by vendors that do not imbue these words with meanings. Already, businesses are becoming weary of those that sell these things. And yet, these words do have meaning. When we understand them and use them correctly, we can provide rich data to businesses to help them make decisions. But we only do this when we remove our work from the world of confusion in which it is born.

■ **Note** Throughout this book, we'll return to the idea of "thinking outside the cell." When we think outside the cell, we tap into our creative resources and think about Excel, our work, and our projects differently. We can harness this new way of thinking to do some really cool stuff.

Available Resources

In this section, I'll talk about what kinds of resources are available to help guide you through your journey.

Google

Google...Google...Google! Google is your best friend. If you're ever stuck on a problem, simply ask Google the same way you might your friend. Usually, you'll see the results of Excel forums with folks asking the very same questions.

`www.google.com`

Chandoo

This site, by Purna "Chandoo" Duggirala, is a phenomenal resource for every Excel developer, from novice to professional. Chandoo covers many topics including dashboards, VBA, data visualization, and formula techniques. His site is also host to a thriving online forum community. Chandoo also is a contributing author of this book (Part V).

`www.chandoo.org`

Clearly and Simply

Clearly And Simply is a site by Robert Mundigl. The site is mainly focused on dashboards and data visualization techniques with Excel and Tableau.

`www.ClearlyAndSimply.com`

Contextures

Debra Dalgleish runs the Contextures web site that focuses on Excel development and dashboards, particularly with PivotTables. Her approach to dashboards and the use of PivotTables is different from mine but well worth a read. She is also the author of these Apress books: *Excel 2007 PivotTables Recipes, Beginning PivotTables in Excel 2007,* and *Excel Pivot Tables Recipe Book.*

`www.contextures.com`

Excel Hero

Excel Hero was created by Daniel Ferry. While his blog is not very active anymore, you will find his older content incredibly useful. Several of his articles have served as the inspiration of the content found in these pages.

`www.ExcelHero.com`

Peltier Tech

Jon Peltier is a chartmaster. His web site is full of charting tutorials and examples. He provides sage wisdom on data visualization and proper data analysis. His web site covers every conceivable thing you might want to do with a chart in Excel.

`www.peltiertech.com`

The Last Word

The most important skill this book will require of you, however, is the desire to learn. Some of the material may appear challenging at first. You may even find yourself frustrated at times. In these moments it's best to take a break for a moment, find your bearings, and start from the beginning of the section in which you left off. The material is complex but well within your grasp. I urge you to push through to the end of the book. The material is worth it, but more important, you're worth it. What will you learn in this book will distinguish you.

CHAPTER 2

A Critical View of Information Visualization

We are drowning in information, while starving for wisdom.

—E. O. Wilson

In this chapter, first I will go into more detail about the differences between dashboards and business analytical applications. I go through the history of these applications. I then go into some detail on the confusion surrounding each, specifically as it relates to data visualization. Next I'll talk about what makes for a bad visualization.

Understanding the Problem

When I talk about dashboards in this book, I'm specifically referring to the *i*nformation *d*ashboards used by businesses, nonprofits, and government organizations, among others, to monitor one or more organizational objectives. Dashboards found inside one's car—or, say, on a panel in the International Space Station—are another type of dashboard altogether. These dashboards are often mechanical in nature and are primarily used to monitor physical systems. There are key differences between the dashboard you might find on your computer and the one you might find in the control panel of a mechanical device. The metaphor, as I'll explain in what follows, is useful to the extent that both communicate necessary information quickly and efficiently. But the differences between the two are also noteworthy, so let's discuss them further.

Mechanical dashboards are designed very differently than their informational dashboard counterparts. Consider the airplane—where you would find a mechanical dashboard—in which the pilot is the operator of the vessel. The pilot relies on important information presented in the small area right in front of his or her eyes, called a *flight instrument panel*. However, the instrument panel isn't the only source of help and information available to the pilot. The pilot must also rely on other devices and people including what he or she can see outside the windows of the cockpit, the copilot, and communications from control towers, among others. If any one or more of these resources fails—if, say, the flight dashboard blacks out or the communication system malfunctions—the pilot relies on training, experience, and intuition. In this sense, the dashboard then is but one important resource available to help an operator move something—a plane, a car, even an organization—safely to its destination.

The previous distinction is often misunderstood by dashboard vendors and popular visual designers who argue that we should rely solely on devices such as dashboards for decision making. Part of this is hype: as we are able to create applications quickly, we can model and display data better than we ever could before. Vendors have attempted to draw our attention to their work with flashy and sparkly metallic finishes for pie charts. But with that attention, these gimmicky devices do little to inform. In this way, they fail to deliver on their fundamental reason for existing. As you'll see throughout this book, a primary reason dashboards and business applications fail is because they employ superficial visualizations not based on research.

But another, significant part of the misunderstanding involves the privilege status we as a society give to devices—to anything really—that purport to process and subsequently present information. Think about this way: the original deliveryman of our data was the news, which was an institution that we came to trust (for better or for worse) to vet the veracity of what was presented. In our present day, data comes to us from virtually everywhere, not just the news. The ubiquity of data around us has, in many ways, given us a false sense of security. The decisions we make give the impression that we have a clear view of all the facts, but this is not always the case. In truth, while the sheer volume of information has undoubtedly increased, the channels through which we receive this information are dominated by a few key players.

Think about information in your own daily life. How many different search engines do you consult to find something on the Internet? Probably not many. How many different news companies do you browse to find about what's going in the world? You probably have a preferred source—and many news services share stories. This book is no different: I prefer Microsoft Excel for spreadsheet development (for good reason), but, for the sake of argument, how many other spreadsheet applications exist to this level of popularity?

We impart a great degree of trust in our information delivery systems, as we should. When they meet our needs, they are invaluable. But with this trust comes great responsibility to do the job and to do it well. What you develop in this book will seek to present information to meet this level of trust. Many organizations and institutions have been all too quick to take advantage of our trustworthiness of their data, encouraging myopia with regard to decision making. They are hoping we won't cast a critical eye to their work, but unfortunately for them, that's exactly what you'll do later in this chapter.

Of Pilots and Metaphors

Let's return to the airplane example. What pilots use in their cockpits is an evolving set of tools resulting from new technology and continuous research. Analog controls and dials were the norm prior to the mid-1970s (Figure 2-1). Growing demand for flying, however, would soon turn the skies into a congested highway. More information was required for the pilot, and before the advent of advanced digital systems, cockpits were filled with tons of indicators and signals competing for space and attention. In response, NASA studied cockpits in an attempt to develop a new system to encapsulate all the information surrounding pilots and to increase situational awareness of their environment. The result is what's called a glass cockpit, as shown in Figure 2-2, which is an advanced digital representation of the most important information to pilots. Since its implementation, our skies have become safer with fewer accidents. Glass cockpits are mandated in all commercial flights by the NTSB.

Figure 2-1. *Older type of cockpit on a Hornett Moth, 193.7*[1]

Figure 2-2. *Glass cockpit*[2]

[1]Produced by "Arpingstone." Released into public domain. `https://commons.wikimedia.org/wiki/File:Hornet_moth_dh87b_g-adne_arp.jpg`.

[2]Photograph taken by "Naddsy." Reused in accordance with Creative Common Attribution 2.0 Generic License. `https://creativecommons.org/licenses/by/2.0/deed.en`.

And here's the point I want to drive (fly?) home: compared to information visualization products on the market, pilot dashboards are drab and ugly. They exist to help pilots make decisions, but they don't dictate such decisions to them. In fact, a real problem for glass cockpits is they can—and sometimes do—black out. In response, recent studies by the United States' General Accountability Office have encouraged more training to pilots in the event that this happens. But what's interesting is that even without the glass cockpit, pilots rely on their other information channels so as not to fly blind. This is a different direction than the visualization industry has taken us.

But what if aircraft had followed this trajectory? What if the view outside the window, the controls, and the copilot were replaced with one dashboard and then that dashboard was blacked out? Who would want to fly that aircraft? Would you? Would you choose to be a passenger on that flight? Would you want to be in the same sky as that aircraft? That flight instruments have followed a path different from information dashboards is because traversing our skies safely is far too important for our pilots to rely on colorful nonsense. In fact, glass cockpits don't flash or sparkle, but they have a great safety record because they were designed using research.

A Metaphor Too Far: Driving Down the Information Superhighway

At its core, the problem stems from a world of vague definitions. This is not a new problem to technology development.

For a moment, let's take a trip down memory lane. Growing up, I heard much talk about the *i*nformation *s*uperhighway. I heard this term in the mid-1990s, at a time when I was just a child, when the home personal computer was taking off, modems still made crazy telephone sounds, and the idea that information could be transferred at anything greater than kilobytes per second seemed like a pipe dream. That term *information superhighway* seemed everywhere—on radio, on television, and in magazines. Even our first computer had the phrase printed on everything from the installation discs to its nascent pamphlets. Yet the definition of this term always seemed different depending on who you asked.

For now, I'll ask the *Oxford English Dictionary*:

> *A route or network for the high-speed transfer of information; esp.*
>
> *a) a proposed national fiber-optic network in the United States;*
>
> *b) the Internet.*

So, what was it? An abstract concept? A physical structure of a proposed fiber-optics network? The Internet? How could the definition of something so ubiquitous be so hard to pin down?

And here we find the same problem with dashboards. When hype surrounds a product, we hear terms for the product everywhere but care little of its definition. Today, many people are still confused about a dashboard is.

For many, real definitions aren't required. What mattered then—and what matters now—is the metaphor. For the information superhighway, the idea that rapid information could traverse distance quickly was an exciting prospect. But more than that, in the middle of the 1990s, the superhighway became a national symbol of driving into yet unexplored territory. The information age would soon be upon us, and from our vantage point we needed to drive only a short distance down that superhighway to warm ourselves in the sunlight ahead. We would be able to shine a light on the new information. The sun ahead, we assured ourselves, would surely illuminate hidden truths.

And we may be no farther down that highway than we were a decade ago. Indeed, we may just be driving in circles. Today's information visualization products are meant to illuminate, but they still carry the bloated metaphor of their mechanical brethren so far as to hinder the process of data sensemaking. They feature radial dials and gauges that dazzle, but research suggests these gadgets inform little.

What's clear, however, is that if we are to keep our heads above water, how we come to understand and digest data cannot be ambiguous. The information superhighway was more than just a signal of the information to come down its road; indeed, its prolific use in the face of a vague definition is the manifestation of the data storm that now surrounds us with confusion. So too, if today's information dashboards do not provide us with shelter from the data storm, then they work against us. When they add to our confusion, they are indiscernible from the storm itself.

A Brief History of Dashboards and Information Visualization

The original visual communication products that first appeared in the 1980s were commonly referred to as *executive information systems*—they represent what we likely today call dashboards. These initial systems were often unreliable and, for many businesses, expensive and impractical. Yet, nearly two decades later, they have become the hallmark of business intelligence packages. Several factors contributed to this rise.

Specifically, initial hardware problems were overcome by the middle of the 1990s when advances in data warehousing made implementing the necessary hardware and software to monitor system metrics more practical and cost efficient. A new way of querying data, online analytic processing (OLAP), played an important role in allowing analysts to quickly pull and report aggregated information from their data stores to executives.

At the same time, a new way to monitor business was being advanced by David Norton and Robert Kaplan, called *balanced scorecards*. This new way called for the development of metrics called *key performance indicators* that could monitor and measure the success of a business. This was part of a new way to measure business called *total performance management*. The synthesis of new technology and new ideas about measuring business carved the desire from executives to monitor more.

Yet it would not be until the Enron scandal—and the executive scandals that followed suit—that the need for computer based metrics took off. In response to Enron, the United States implemented a set of rigid standards to companies concerning their reporting requirements and information assurance standards. The new set of rules required a level of corporate governance that visual communication products, like dashboards, could help achieve.

Finally, the prominence of spreadsheet software in corporations and Internet technologies like Adobe Flash gave developers the means to more easily visualize complex ideas through charts and graphics in a short amount of time. As organizations began to fill their data stores, the need for ad hoc analysis was more necessary than ever. Such cheaper methods brought the idea of visualization to the fore. Organizations such as the United Nations Development Program and General Electric began to emphasize the ways in which data could help the world. Businesses and governments struggled to make sense of what they called *big data*. Social networking provided a new type of data based entirely around the consumer that organizations sought.

And yet, in many ways, the requirements of these systems—to quickly convey important information and to help analysts quickly divine meeting from data—have changed little if at all since their inception. Indeed, the skepticism that existed in the 1980s surrounding the ability for technology to truly improve business performance still remains in the minds of business executives today. While businesses embrace new technology, they are still hesitant to what they perceive as offshoring business decisions to a computer. Throughout the history of dashboards, those at the top of the company have relied on and blame their information technology for the inability for their technology to deliver. At the same time, business leaders have argued in newspapers and magazines that if the dashboard wasn't working for a company, the executives needed to take a look at their metrics; it was their fault for measuring the wrong indicators. While companies argued internally over why their technologies and metrics weren't good enough, visualization expert Stephen Few found fault in work not based in grounded research. In 2005, Few wrote the following:

> *Information technology hasn't delivered what it promised us. Yes, we live in the information age, and yes, much has changed—but to what end? Do you know more today than before? Are you smarter? Do you make better decisions? We often still make the same bad decisions, but now we make them much faster than before, thanks to technology's questionable gift of "more and faster" This is hardly the better world that we imagined and hoped for.*

But not all is doom and gloom. When we take a step back, we can remove ourselves form the swarm of information around us. We can look at key parts of the storm and organize them for data sensemaking. Indeed, this is what information communication helps us do.

A Quick Summary Before Taking a Critical Look

Looking back through everything presented so far, you may have noticed a few key themes. Don't worry about looking back through everything; I'll save you the time and trouble and summarize what I feel are the important parts.

- Beware not to take any visualization metaphor too far.
- Just because it's information presented in a seemingly professional way, don't trust it outright.
- Technology isn't the problem, though it often receives the blame.
- Dashboards and business analytics applications help make good decisions, but you shouldn't rely on them such that your view of other information becomes obscured.
- At the end of the day, it's all about communication.

Dashboards by Example: U.S. Patent and Trademark Office

In 2010, the U.S. Patent and Trademark Office (USPTO) released several dashboards reflecting its internal operations and requirements. Figure 2-3 shows part of an older version of its patent dashboard, a large colorful series of radial dials and gauges. (When this text was original written, the USPTO was using the older dashboard shown in Figure 2-3. It has since updated the dashboard to follow many of the principles outlined in this book. However, I will use its previous iteration for illustrative purposes.) Take a moment to analyze the following figures. As you go through each one, consider the following: How well does this information communicate? Does this dashboard include extra "ink"—that is, does the dashboard include extra stuff not really required?

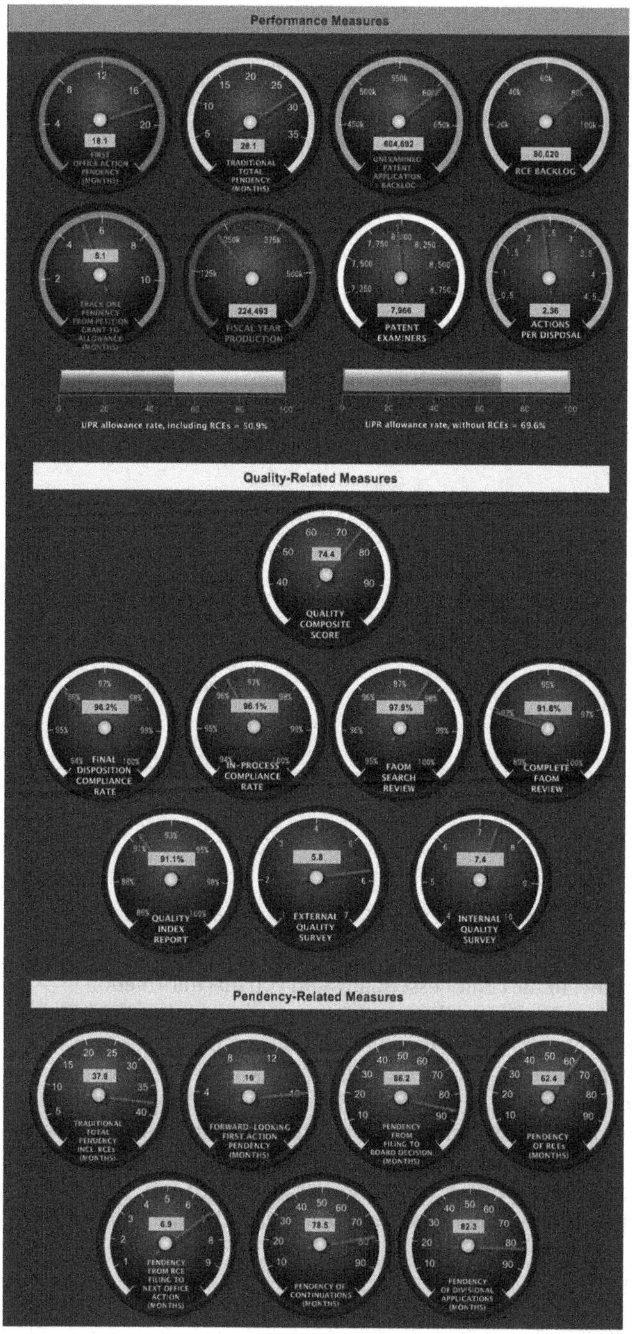

***Figure 2-3.** A snapshot of the USPTO's dashboard*

■ **Note** To view the new, updated, and better USPTO dashboard, visit `www.uspto.gov/dashboards/patents/main.dashxml`.

What did you notice? The following sections are my thoughts.

Radial Gauges

Gauges are a favorite among dashboard and visualization vendors despite communicating information poorly. Consider Figure 2-4 from the USPTO's dashboard. What information do you gain from the graphic? Well, you can ascertain that there were 28.1 months of traditional total dependency.

Figure 2-4. *A radial dial showing traditional total pendency from the USPTO's dashboard web site*

But how did you figure this out? Well, the label in the center essentially told you this information. Putting your finger over the label for a moment, would you have been able to guess the number 28.1 or even 28 months? Not likely. Gauges and radial dials do not allow for precision in visualization.

Now, consider that only the label helped you out; then what is the point of the visualization? What do you gain from the radial gauge metaphor? The developer certainly spent a lot of time ensuring the gauge has a drop shadow, gradiating light source, and cool neon car colors. But none of these additions does anything to convey information. As you will see in Chapter 3, these extra colors and doodads amount to extra ink that services their function little. Information visualization expert Edward Tufte calls this *chartjunk*.

All the extra ink and junk gauges fill a disproportionate amount of space compared to the information they convey.

Now, consider the series of gauges in Figure 2-5.

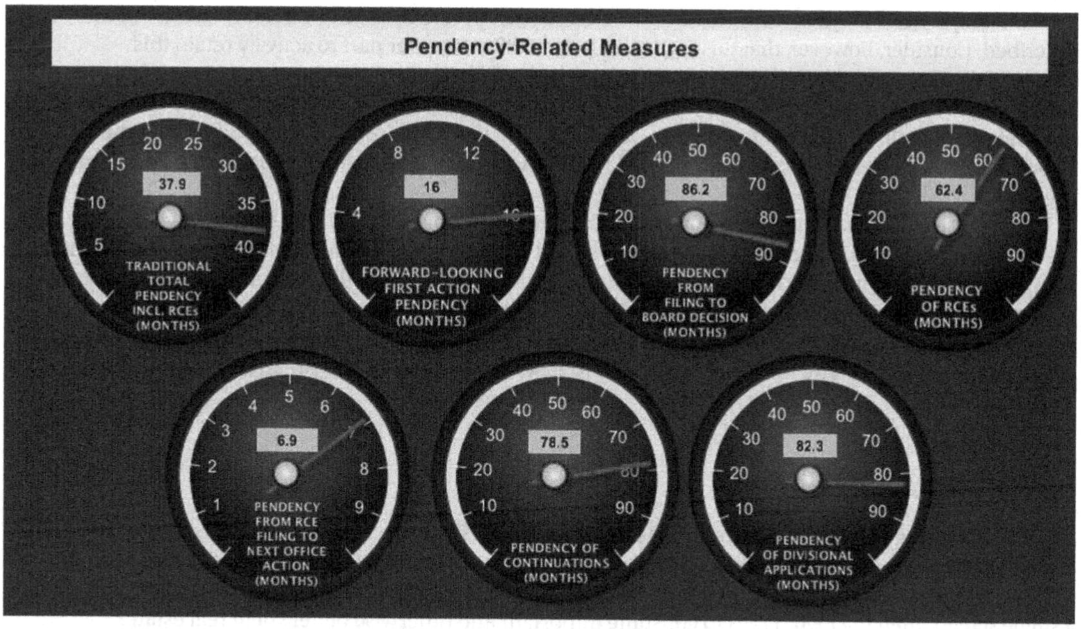

Figure 2-5. *A series of radial gauges found on the USPTO's dashboard*

Is the information in each metric compared easily across? Not really. They might be better understood presented as bullet charts, which I talk more about in Chapter 3.

So Many Metrics, So Little Working Memory

This dashboard is filled with many, many metrics for you to scan and analyze. What are the most important of these metrics? Does the dashboard let you know which have more importance than the others?

In many ways, this dashboard does not summarize as much as it could. The metrics are grouped together logically, but the long-page format means you must remember what you've read at a higher section if you need to compare it to a section below. At first thought, you may not realize there is anything wrong with this.

The problem comes from our own limitations in working memory. Research has shown that our working, or short-term, memory can hold a small amount of information for not very long. In most of our daily routine, our working memory serves us faithfully to remember thoughts when moving from one associated activity to the next and to remember the steps of a daily routine, such as brushing our teeth. Our working memory fills with the steps of what we must do: (1) grab the toothpaste, (2) grab the toothbrush, and (3) go on to shave after this activity.

However, we know from research that our working memory can hold about two or three "chunks" of data at any one time. This limitation affects how we interpret information, such as pie charts, graphs with legends, and radial gauges like those featured earlier.

The gauges display two pieces of information each: (1) the name of the metric presented and (2) the value of the metric presented. But, some of the gauges on the dashboard will display three pieces of information with an added goal metric. Returning to what we know about working memory, these pieces of information fill in the slots available to hold such chunks of data. If you must actively store this information and then scan the rest of the page, it's likely to be not an easy task without trying to commit this information to your long-term memory. Further, when you find the metric against which you want to compare, the information in this metric will also likely need to fill its information into one of the slots of working memory. If all the slots are taken, your working memory will dump some information to make room.

You may try this for yourself; you may even find success at retaining information for longer than described. Consider, however, that this is the result of an effort on your part to actively retain this information. That is, it's likely that by simply being aware of the limits of working memory, you are attempting to commit the information to more long-term storage, such as thinking about the information, repeating it yourself, or even writing it down. If you must do this in an information visualization, then consider whether the data presented in a visual manner is as illuminating as its visualization configuration suggests.

There are solutions to the limits of our working memory; one way is to take advantage of our preattentive processes. These processes are activated when we are looking at visual patterns. When we compare values in a bar chart, preattention comes to life. We don't need to commit a visual shape size to memory; the mere act of placing it next to another similar shape that is taller, shorter, or the same size conveys simple information that does not require us to commit it to working memory in a way that we may lose it before using it. I'll use Chapter 3 to discuss how best to use preattentive processes in your work.

Is the Logo Necessary?

Often it's tempting to create a nice logo at the top of our work. I'm not a graphic designer, so I cannot weigh in on the design effectiveness of the logo in Figure 2-6. However, on the function of a dashboard, the logo serves little purpose but to take up space. If the end goal of a dashboard, as described in Chapter 1, is to use a single screen, then the logo serves to consume important and otherwise better spent real estate.

Figure 2-6. *What point does this logo serve?*

The top of the screen will be the first thing you see when you scan this dashboard, and the top-left corner of the screen is where, as I'll demonstrate, the most important information should reside. The dashboard's title, a logo, or its owner is important information, but if you are to feature it prominently, you must ask yourself what data it conveys. As a general rule, if the item of the dashboard does not convey data or information, it should be featured with less, not more, prominence.

Returning to the idea of privileged information, notice the language and images used to describe the dashboard. The logo says "Your window to the USPTO," yet does this dashboard, as a whole, truly contribute to a better informational understanding into the government bureaucracy or into its goals or progress? I don't think it does. But the trope of having a clearer view into the process by merely invoking the use of information visualization is readily seen.

While likely unintentional, the pair of binoculars with a view clouded by data seemingly reiterates the suggestion by vendors that all we must see is data. In reality, the poor viewer of the binoculars may be looking at too much data from afar while not realizing what information is available to him at hand. The image is a just another reflection of the myopia that diving into a sea of information can create.

The author Stephen Few lists 13 common pitfalls found on dashboards, which you can apply to your work as well.

- Exceeding the boundaries of a single screen
- Supplying inadequate context for the data
- Displaying excessive detail or precision
- Expressing measures indirectly
- Choosing an inappropriate media of display
- Introducing meaningless variety
- Using poorly designed display media
- Encoding quantitative data inaccurately
- Arranging the data poorly
- Ineffectively highlighting what's important
- Cluttering the screen with useless decoration
- Misusing or overusing color
- Designing an unappealing visual display

When you consider the definition of a dashboard given in Chapter 1, you see that the USPTO's dashboard violates some of the original guidelines outlined. For one, you don't really know what the most important information is for you to consume. Second, while the information can be said to be visualized, the processes used in delivering this information to you aren't ideal. You're left wondering if visualizing in this case has really brought a significant benefit to simply presenting the information in, say, a report or another form. Finally, the information was not presented in a single view but rather was spread across an entire horizontal column.

In many ways, the USPTO dashboard may lend itself to commendation for encouraging transparency of their process. However, you must remember the privilege data is given when evaluating the performance of the information visualizations themselves.

Visualizations That Look Cool but Just Don't Work

The unfortunate reality is that many visualization efforts fail to live up to a high standard in which the organizations that house them promote their effectiveness. On the one hand, like any field, visualization research is growing. Recent interest in the field, however, has encouraged work that is more hype than useful. Consider the dashboard in Figure 2-7, which is inspired by style that is seen commonly in corporate dashboards.

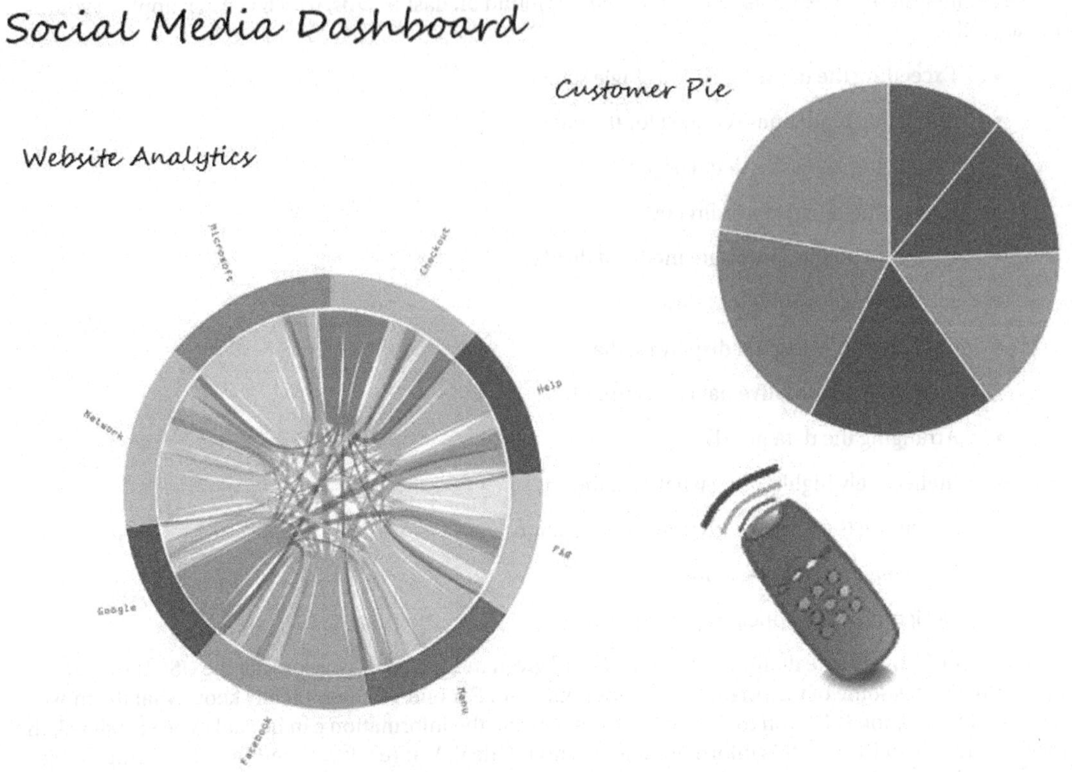

Figure 2-7. An example dashboard style that is used in various companies' dashboards

Perhaps the first thing you notice is the part shown in Figure 2-8.

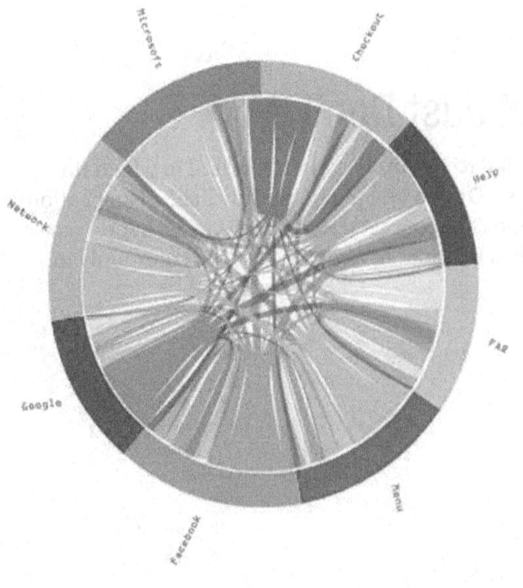

Figure 2-8. This chart seems to steal all of the attention. What is it?

It's true that the company that made this dashboard presented it as a proof-of-concept and not from a real dashboard. But this graphic is featured prominently in its libraries; indeed, it's a piece of eye candy meant to draw your attention to its work. In a real business application, it strains the imagination to see how a chart like this might ever be useful. Sure, it might have your attention, but it offers little in the way of its intended use: to communicate information quickly and effectively.

The chart in Figure 2-8 was not born in insolation; rather, it is a product of the hype that surrounds information visualization. Vendors add this type of chart to their chart libraries promising a variety of ways to present information. But no amount of variety will fill a need if it cannot do what it was born to do. But how did this hype begin? For that we turn away from private business and focus on data journalism.

Data Journalism

Data journalism is relatively new. Just as interest in using data for better business decisions has grown in the past few years, data journalism—using data to tell a journalistic story in new and novel ways—has grown in parallel. One notable example is the journalist David McCandless, who is known for his data visualization work in the mass media. Among other things, he is a contributor to the *Guardian*'s data blog, and his work has been featured in the Museum of Modern Art in New York. You can check out his work at `www.davidmccandless.com/`.

His work exists more in the colorful world of the chart of Figure 2-8. It's not that his work is uninteresting—far from it. In presentations on data visualization I've done, I pass around his book along with books from other data visualization experts. His book almost always receives the most attention. That's because his work is colorful and flashy. But if you take a close look at his work at the link provided, you'll see concepts presented in a way that stress art over communication. In this book, I'll draw a distinction between this type of data visualization (more appropriately described as data journalism or data art) and the business data visualizations presented here.

And yet it's important to understand the business world hasn't yet drawn the distinction. McCandless, for instance, isn't alone in communicating art over facts. Other outlets, like the *Washington Post*'s Wonk Blog, feature work that's overly complicated, communicates little, or is repurposed without enhancements from other outlets. You can see one of my favorite examples of overly complicated data journalism graphics at this article from FlowingData.com, which uses a Wonk Blog chart: `https://flowingdata.com/2012/05/18/is-the-filibuster-unconstitutional/`. Compare that to the simplified chart in Figure 2-9, which would be considered too boring by a data journalist. Which do you think is easier to read?

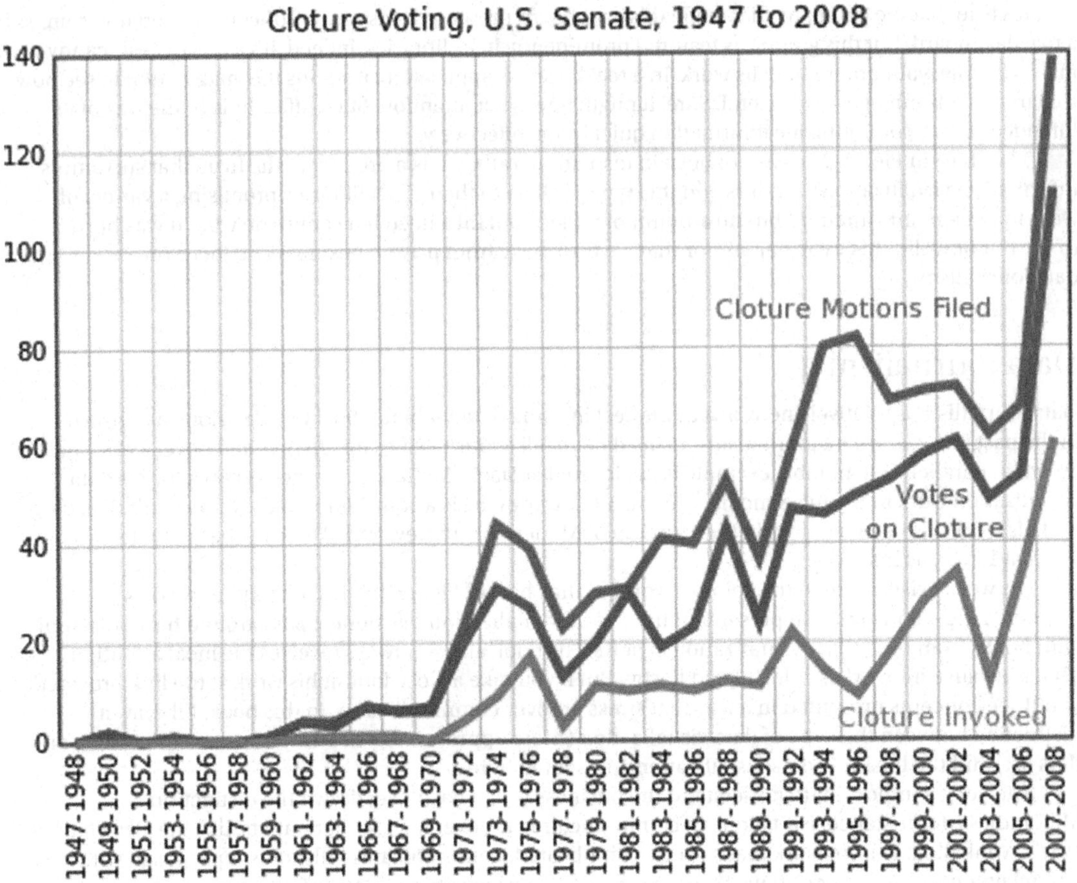

Figure 2-9. *A much better cloture chart from Wikipedia*[3]

But aside from this work being a poor communicator, much of this work suffers from underlying confirmation bias built in. This is not hard to understand; the author's personal conclusions and opinions compensate for data stripped of its ability to tell a story. You must remember that data art is often created with an agenda already in mind. Infographics, a type of data art, often exist to promote a product or provide stats for an organization convincing you to donate to them. In data art, the author's narrative shapes the data presented rather than letting the data tell its own story.

As you develop your applications, you should let the data speak for itself. If you're not careful, you can design applications that allow managers and stakeholders to create results they already agree with. It's sometimes hard to identify this confirmation bias because, by its nature, the feeling of validation comes with a visceral feeling of pleasurable affirmation. In reality, confirmation bias works against you; rather than illuminating new insights, it provides you with what you already believe to be true. In that sense, it provides you with nothing of new value.

[3]Created by Randy Schutt. Reprinted here under Creative Commons Attribution-Share Alike 3.0 Unported license.

Why These Examples Are Important

The previous examples aren't trivial visualizations found randomly on the Internet made by nobodies. For example, David McCandless has given talks about information design and data visualization at well-known conferences and to vendors. The point I want to underscore is not that McCandless or any other designer's work is bad from an artistic standpoint—I readily admit that I am not equipped with the expertise to make this sort of evaluation. I want to note instead how interest in visualization has driven work unsuitable for decisions to be preferred by businesses. In reality, what is praised outside our offices does not and cannot deliver this to us. When you consider the influence McCandless et al. has had on the business side of information visualization, are you at all surprised by this type of chart (see Figure 2-10), whatever it is?

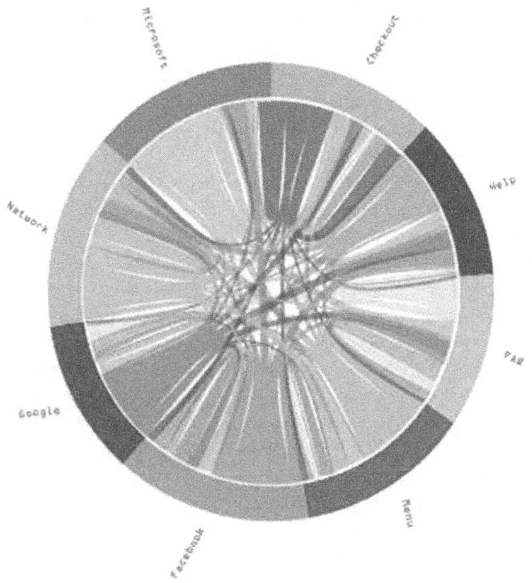

Figure 2-10. *Again, what are you looking at?*

The Last Word

The world of information may at first appear daunting and dizzying. Information surrounds everything we do, and the information channels we've come to rely on to be our guides aren't always using the best methods to communicate with us. However, learning about information visualization and data interpretation can arm us with the ability to understand our world more correctly. You should remember that information visualization is part of the decision-making process, but it shouldn't replace your own decision-making faculties. You need to rely on data, but you also need to rely on personal experience, intuition, and those around you that you trust. When you prefer data to everything else, you become myopic, but if you understand where data interpretation sits with everything else, a real, true big picture is within your grasp. In the next chapter, I'll go through the principles of visualization and discuss how you can use them to your advantage.

CHAPTER 3

The Principles of Data Visualization in Microsoft Excel

To my knowledge, there is little in the current spreadsheet literature discussing best practices with data visualization. There are many books on how to create pie charts, three-dimensional charts, and spider-charts, but few discuss why for each of these charts there is always a better choice available. I see why tutorials on these subjects are at first appealing; after all, the former charts are part of the Excel core package library. Therefore, to perhaps pass the Expert Microsoft Excel certification, knowing how to create these charts may be of service to you. However, for us, the developers and data consumers, these charts do more harm than good.

They harm because they inhibit our ability to make sense of the data. When we have a good understanding of the data, we can make good decisions. A bad, misleading, or short understanding of the data will encourage misinformed decisions. Thus, good data visualization will help explore the data, it will help us communicate properly to others, and it will inevitably foster good decisions. Therefore, understanding best practices is a worthy endeavor.

This is where Microsoft Excel comes in. I don't have to tell you that Excel can allow you to create many types of charts and present data in many different ways. But Excel's default presentations of data—that is, the chart defaults in format and color—are not always the best for displaying data. However, as later chapters will demonstrate, creating good-quality charts is not hard, but it may take patience when first moving through the steps.

The chart images in this chapter will all be produced in Microsoft Excel.

What Is Visual Perception and How Does It Work?

In this section, I'll talk about the fundamentals of visual perception and how we can best take advantage of it. By end of this chapter, you'll find that good visualization builds from the science of how perception works.

Note Good visualization builds from the science of how perception works.

Perception and the Visual World

There are three different objects in perception. They are light, objects in our visual field, and us.

- First, visible light reflects off every surface in the known universe.
- Our eyes capture this light from within our surrounding environment, turn it into information, and then send it to our brains using the optic nerve as a channel.
- At the end of the optic nerve is the optic chiasm, where the optic nerves from both eyes meet. Here, the information is sent into our brains to be processed.

The result of this process is what we refer to as *visual perception*. Although the world outside our eyes is read in as light, how we understand that world—that is, how we perceive the world—is a product of our brain's processes. Experience, psychology, and intuition all play an important role in our visual perception. Indeed, as discussed in Chapter 2, our own personal biases contribute to our perceptions of all things, not just those that are visual. What we can divine from this is that visual perception is the *interpretation* of *processed information* we receive from the visual world.

But in the visual world, as you shall see, we have our own preference for certain patterns. When lines look like they should be connected, our brains will attempt to connect them. This process is not too different from how we interact with other things in our life. The phrase "connect the dots" refers to our human ability to take disparate pieces of information and link them together into a fluent idea; it's no mistake that the phrase parallels how we consume, construct, and interpret visual patterns.

Our Bias Toward Forms: Perception and Gestalt Psychology

In the 1930s and 1940s, several German psychologists set out to understand how we perceive shapes in terms of the patterns of grouping we do through our eyes. This study is referred to as Gestalt psychology, and its principles provide an interesting window through which we can understand objects in our visual world. These principles are called the *Gestalt laws of grouping*. They allow us to perceptively predict the sensation of shapes. Here I discuss a few of them germane to our work in Microsoft Excel:

- Similarity
- Proximity
- Closure
- Common grouping
- Continuation

Similarity

Similarity states that elements of the same form—that is, elements that share similar characteristics like shape, color, or size—will be perceived as being part of a group. For example, consider the set of shapes in Figure 3-1, representing a banquet hall design made in Excel.

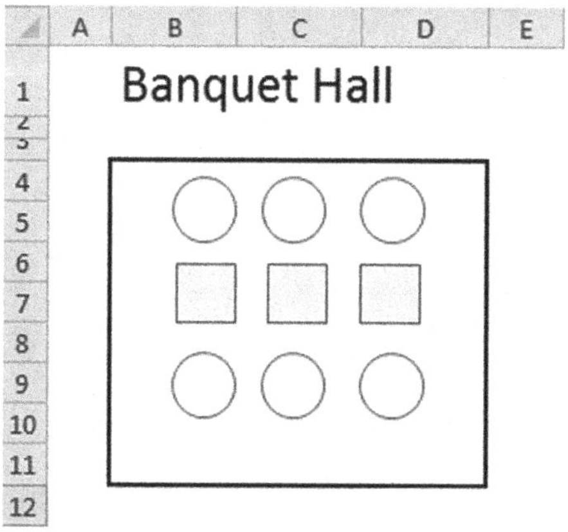

Figure 3-1. *The grouping of shapes demonstrates the concept of similarity*

How many groups of shapes do you see? Most of us will answer three groups. In Figure 3-1 we see first a group of circles, next a group of squares, and finally a group of circles again. The overall pattern appears to be a square, but our eyes can process both the shapes as groups and the shape that those shapes form.

Our ability to group shapes by color is the same pattern we see in tables of information, like in Figure 3-2.

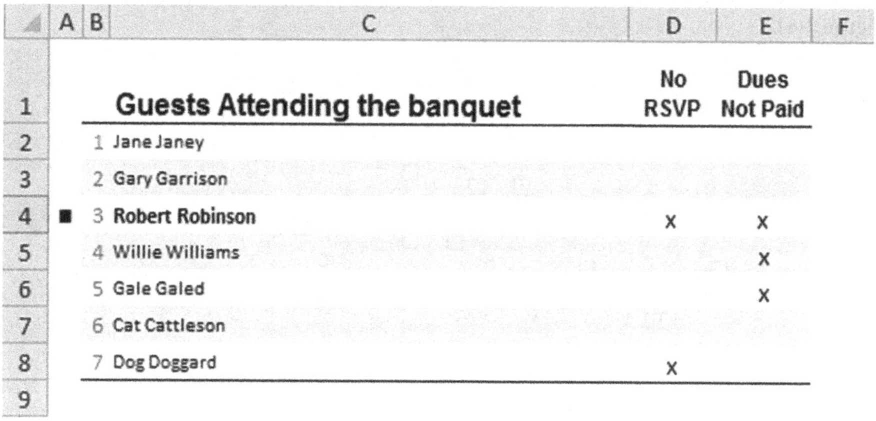

	Guests Attending the banquet	No RSVP	Dues Not Paid
1	Jane Janey		
2	Gary Garrison		
3	Robert Robinson	X	X
4	Willie Williams		X
5	Gale Galed		X
6	Cat Cattleson		
7	Dog Doggard	X	

Figure 3-2. *The alternating color pattern creates contrast and breaks up group similarity*

In Figure 3-2 we see that a repeating gray highlight allows our eyes to see the differences in the rows of the table.

Proximity

Proximity concerns our ability to discern different groups based on distance. Shapes that appear closer together will be perceived as their own groups. We can call these groups of shapes *clusters*. We can perceive series of clusters when dots clump together in one area but form patterns separate from other dots. In Figure 3-3, the scatterplot appears to show one group (some might argue two groups) of dots trending upward.

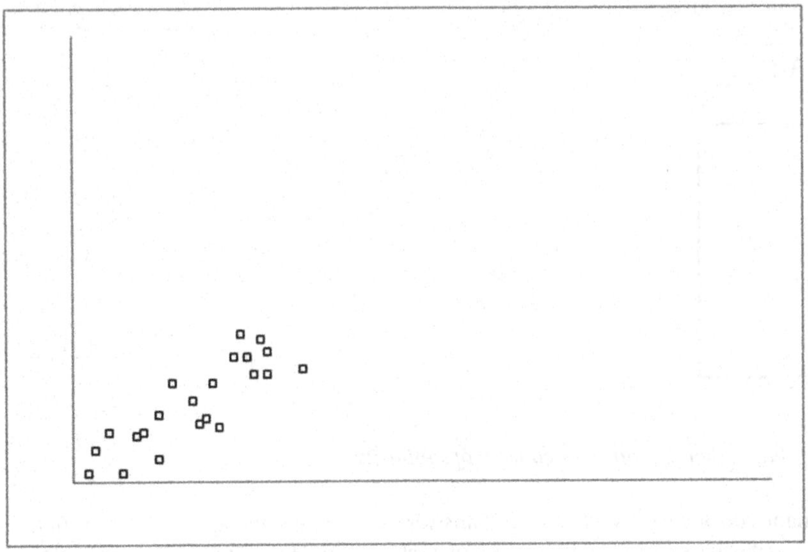

Figure 3-3. *How many groups or clusters of dots to you see?*

However, what we perceive as distance can change when we zoom in. The dots now appear to show several groups (see Figure 3-4).

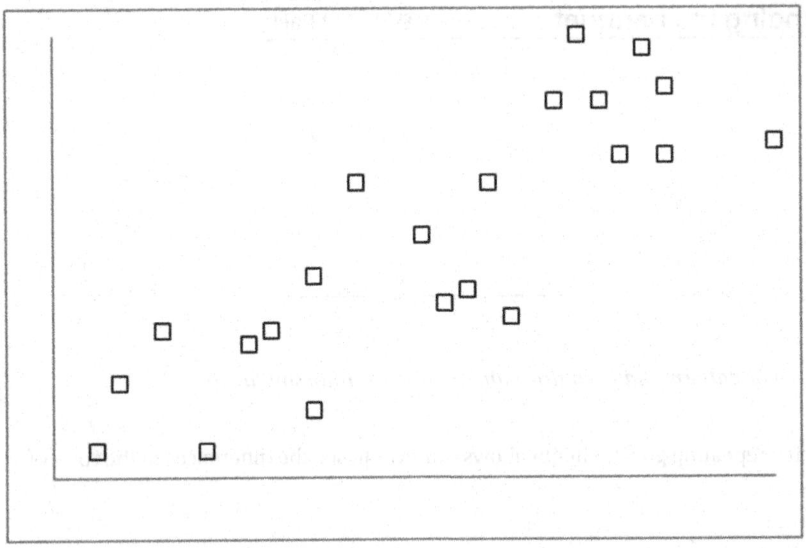

Figure 3-4. *How does zooming in on the dots change our perception of clusters?*

I asked some of my colleagues to find out how many groups they perceived at this level of zoom. Some said they saw four groups (Figure 3-5).

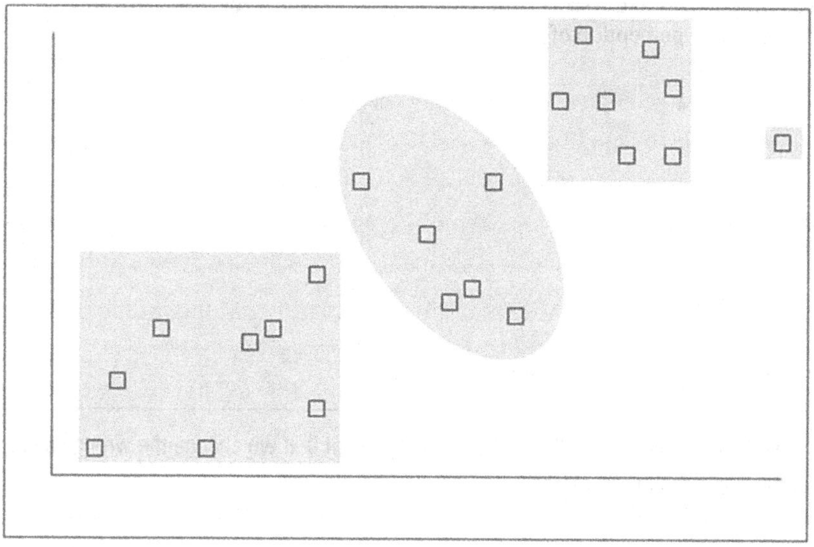

Figure 3-5. *Some people see four groups of dots*

Some said three (Figure 3-6).

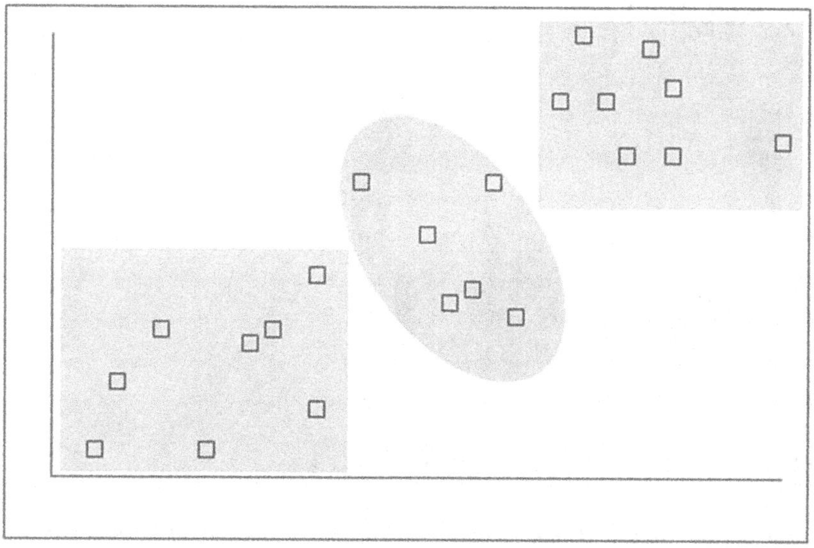

Figure 3-6. *Some said they saw only three groups of dots*

And still others said they saw two. But whether zoomed out or in, we are looking at the same series of dots. Therefore, how we choose to scale the data will affect our perception of it. If we choose the wrong scale, we risk displaying the data ineffectively and inaccurately.

In Figure 3-7, we can see how changes to the size of dots (A), the scale height of the x-axis (B), and the scaled height of the y-axis (C) can affect perception of groups.

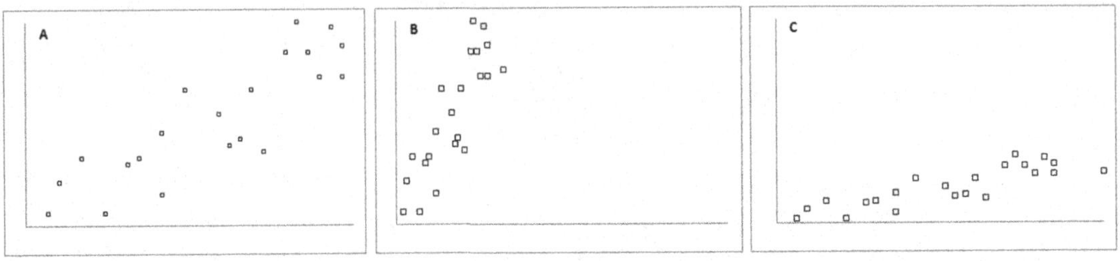

***Figure 3-7.** Changing the scale affects the perception of groups*

■ **Remember** How we choose to scale the data will affect our perception of it. If we choose the wrong scale, we risk displaying the data ineffectively and inaccurately.

In Figure 3-8, we see a plot of regions, grouped by the quarter of a year and units sold for a business. I've added labels to aid in our understanding, but even labels can't provide the visual information to adequately separate the data by region.

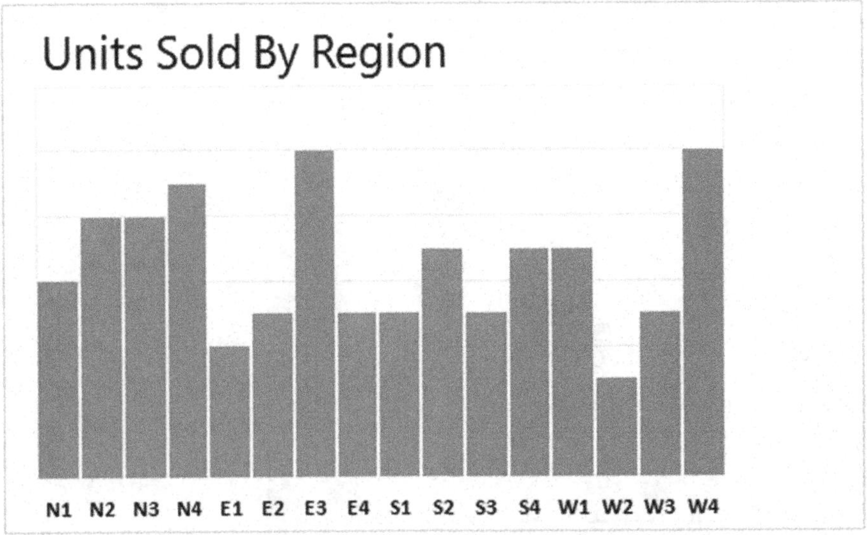

***Figure 3-8.** Using the same color scheme throughout makes it appear as if all the bars are part of the same group*

We could apply what we've learned from the principle of similarity and change the colors for each region (see Figure 3-9).

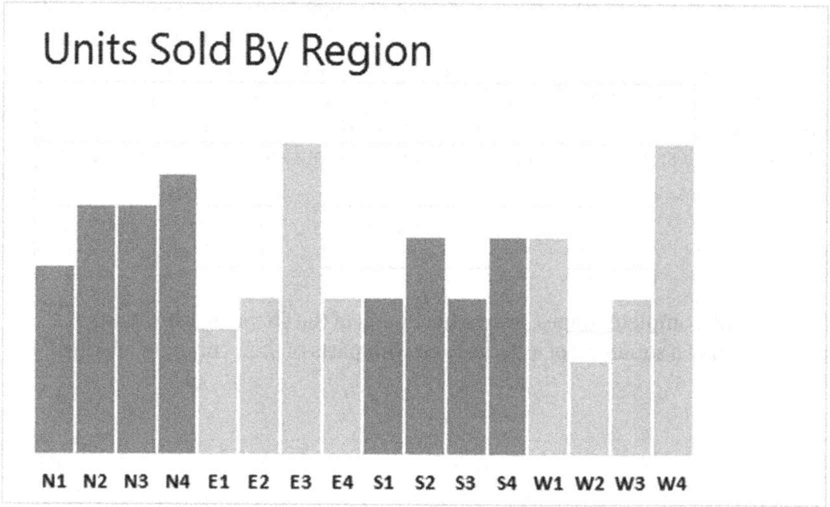

***Figure 3-9.** Similarity aids in our ability to differentiate the bar chart groupings*

We're getting closer, but remember that these regions can represent a data cluster. Let's try adding some space instead (Figure 3-10).

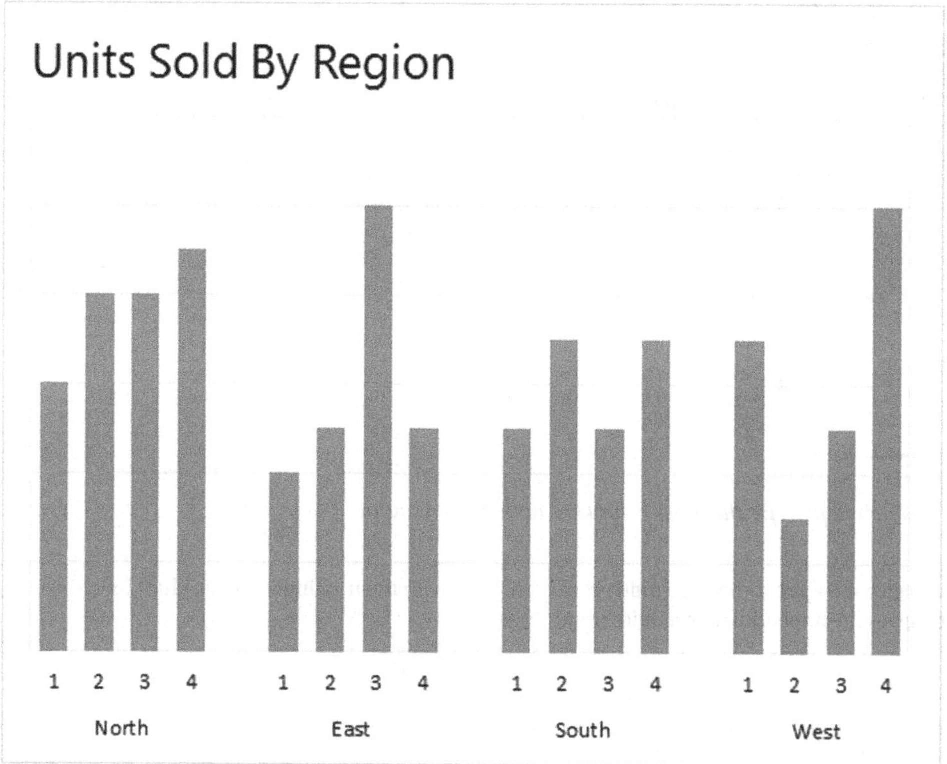

***Figure 3-10.** Adding space gives the visual depth required to make the distinction between each region*

Now we have it. Proximity, when used correctly, allows us to visually combine and separate pieces of data into groups. There are a few ways to achieve the effect described earlier in Excel. In Figure 3-10, I've used a simple method of adding a piece of data called a *spacer*. The spacer essentially acts as the fifth data point in a series of North, East, South, but not West. The spacer contains no data, so when we view it in a graph, it appears to separate—to act as a buffer—between each series. By default, Excel does not provide the ability to add these spaces between series; but, with a little configuration on our side, we can style the chart accordingly.

Closure

Closure concerns our ability to create complete shapes, even where parts of the shape may be missing. We can, for example, see the outlines of a square or of a circle, even with parts of their contours missing (Figures 3-11 and 3-12).

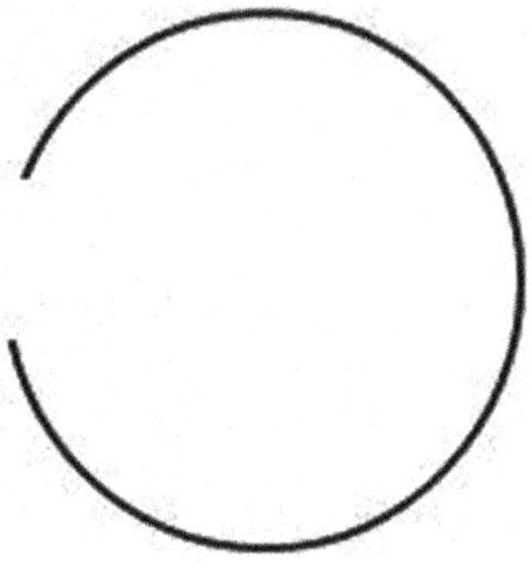

Figure 3-11. *This looks like a circle, doesn't it?*

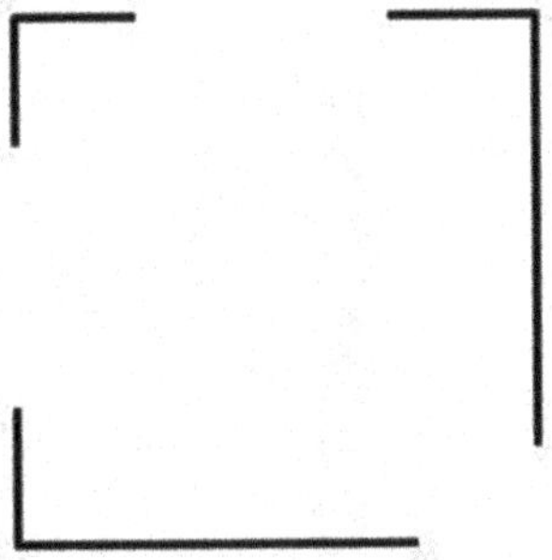

Figure 3-12. *You should perceive the series of broken contours as a square*

Closure can give the appearance of a fluid set of data. Even with the missing data, the chart in Figure 3-13 still gives the appearance of a fluid, trending series.

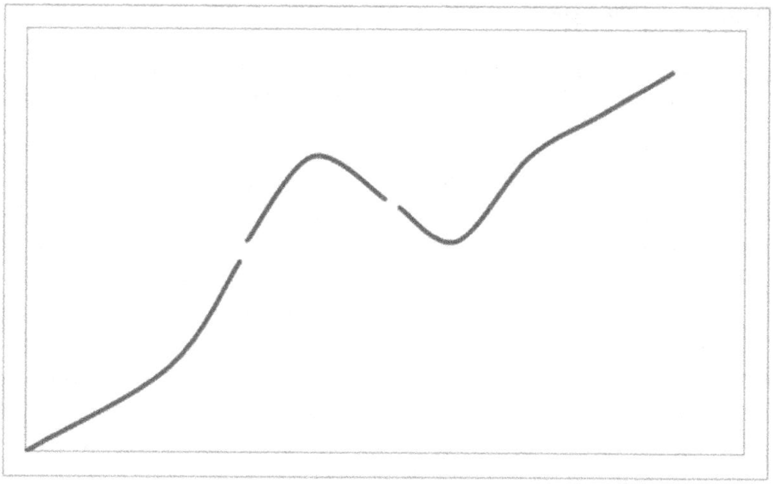

Figure 3-13. *An example of closure*

In other words, closure allows us to perceive shapes, or objects, as complete forms when enough information about an object is already present. Our predispositions to shapes we see all around us—circles, squares, lines—allow us to fill in the missing information and infer a complete shape. You can see how this principle might work to our advantage and also to our disadvantage. By using the principles of closure, we can view patterns in data that might otherwise be lost in a table. On the other hand, this connection that our mind creates potentially results in misleading inferences if we don't take more time to look at the data and confirm our inferences.

A common illusion is that of Kanizsa's triangle, as shown in Figure 3-14. It's worth noting here that the contours of the triangle are never truly drawn. Rather, they are created by our brains as we interpret the white space to form contours and area. This is an immediate example of our brains using the features of closure.

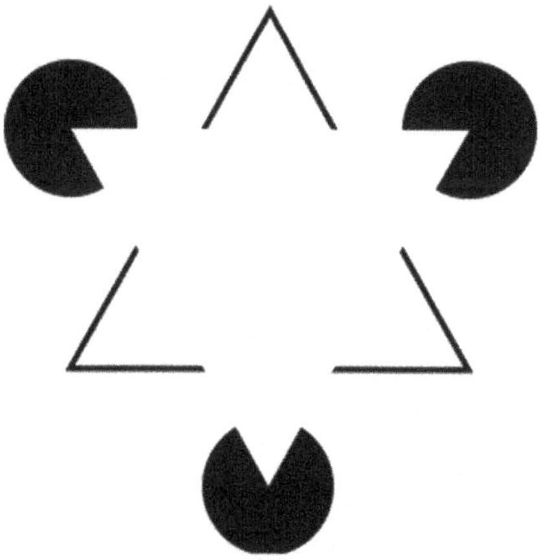

Figure 3-14. *Kanizsa's triangle*[1]

[1]By Fibonacci (Own work) [GFDL (`www.gnu.org/copyleft/fdl.html`) or CC-BY-SA-3.0 (`http://creativecommons.org/licenses/by-sa/3.0/`)], via Wikimedia Commons.

Common Groups of Shapes and Points

Common grouping concerns the mind's ability to perceive connected objects as single, uniform shapes. The crisscross pattern in Figure 3-15 is perceived as two lines crossing one another and not as four lines meeting at a single, shared center point.

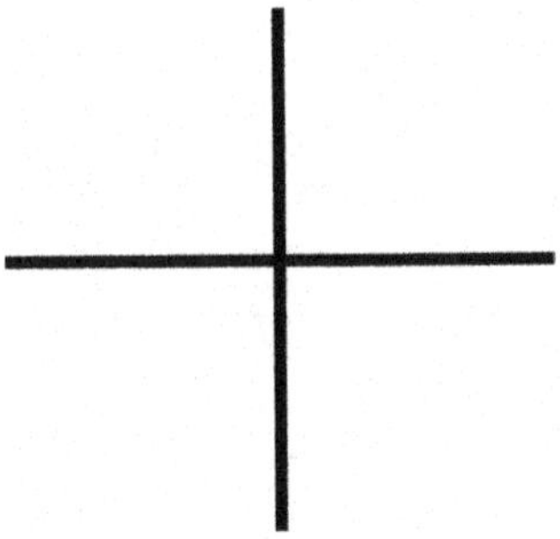

Figure 3-15. *Most people perceive this crisscross as two bisecting lines*

Similarly, we can also see common groups of data when they are enclosed by some boundary. In the previous example about proximity, these boundaries were perceived by the distance of the data points to each other. The ensuing discussion highlighted certain points on the graphs by surrounding them with a rectangle and varying the hue of the background behind them.

Figure 3-16 demonstrates an example of *enclosure*. Our minds create a common grouping for these data points because they appear to exist in a space with shared boundaries and color. This principle will prove important as a means to highlight and separate data.

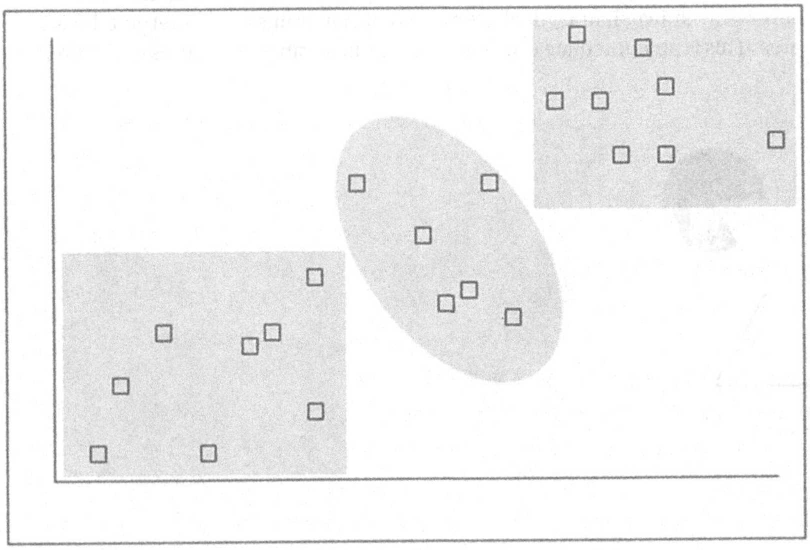

Figure 3-16. *Closure creates groupings of objects that appear to exist within shared boundaries, even when such contours are not drawn*

Continuation

Continuation concerns our minds' ability to perceive continuation of overlapping shapes and forms as being uninterrupted. The line through the triangle in Figure 3-17 is perceived as one continuous line and a complete triangle.

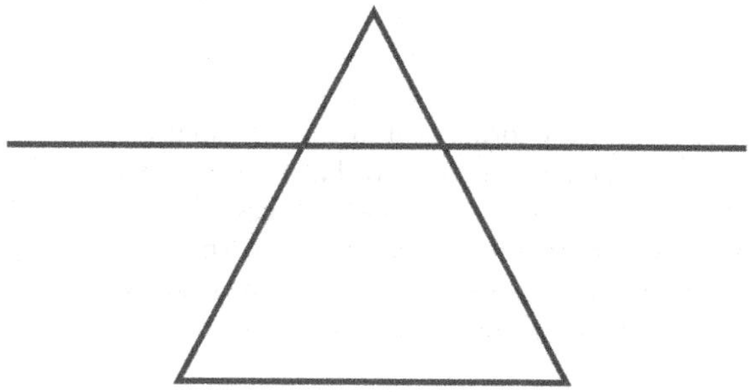

Figure 3-17. *The line is perceived as one continuous line through the triangle*

We don't perceive the triangle as shown in Figure 3-18.

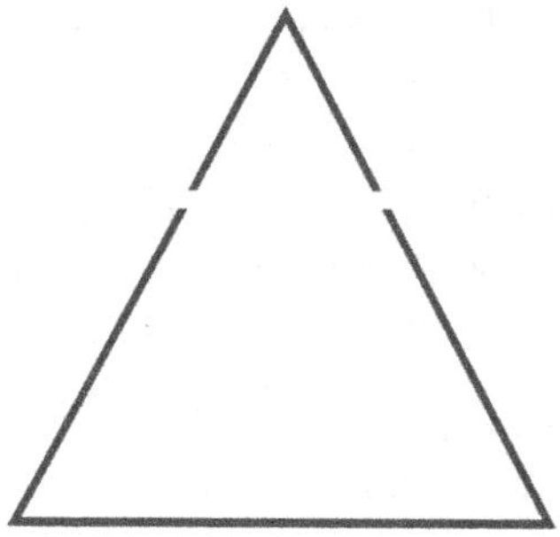

Figure 3-18. *Continuation says we don't perceive breaks through intersecting shapes*

And we don't perceive the line as shown in Figure 3-19.

Figure 3-19. *A broken-up line*

Continuation is important because it suggests we understand lines and shapes as whole figures. Even though a line chart may just be several data points for each month, we interpret the connects between each point as part of an overall trend. This is important when we consider the differences between a line chart and a bar chart. The data points on a bar chart are presented as discrete without connection. On the other hand, that same data could be plot on a line chart with the data points connected. How this information is presented to us will affect how we interpret it. Therefore, we must choose the correct charts to reflect the underlying data.

The preceding sections provided a summary of these grouping principles:

- Similarity
- Proximity
- Closure
- Common grouping
- Continuation

From this reading, we learn how our minds perceive shapes and forms as grouped. We can use these principles to understand how best to organize our presentation data in such a way that informs instead of misleads. When used correctly, these shapes will allow us to see a bigger picture more easily. However, we are not yet finished with the discussion of how our minds organize and perceive shapes. This section provided insight into how we complete and infer information not necessarily presented. The next section will discuss how we highlight and alert data that differs—that is, stands out—from the group.

The Preattentive Attributes of Perception

Preattentive attributes are the patterns we recognize immediately, before we're even consciously aware of them. They work to our advantage, in this way, by presenting patterns we can interpret immediately without taxing our short-term memories. Preattentive attributes are particularly useful for representing quantitative values. In his book *Now You See It* (Analytics Press, 2009), Stephen Few quotes Colin Ware[2] on preattentive attributes.

> *We can do certain thing to symbols to make it much more likely that they will be visually identified even after very brief exposure. Certain simple shapes or color 'pop out' from their surroundings. The theoretical mechanism underlying pop-out is called pre-attentive processing because logically it must occur prior to conscious attention. In essence, pre-attentive processing determines what visual objects are offered up to our attention. An understanding of what is processed pre-attentively is probably the most important contribution that visions science can make to data visualization.*

In Table 3-1, I've summarized the preattentive attributes important to our discussion with Excel.

[2]Colin Ware, *Information Visualization: Perception for Design*, Second Edition (Morgan Kaufmann, 2004)

Table 3-1. *The Preeattentive Attributes of Perception*

Color Attributes			
Hue		Intensity	
Spatial Attributes			
Position	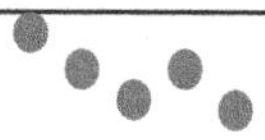		
Grouping	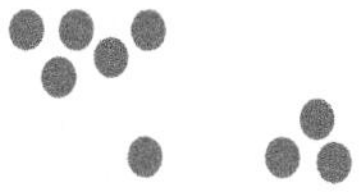		
Form Attributes			
Length		Width	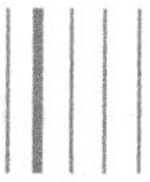
Orientation		Shape	
Size		Curvature	

Color Attributes

Both hue and intensity are useful for creating distinctions in quantitative values. Hue can be useful to signify which projects may be high risk, as in Figure 3-20. The project with the darker hue signifies that it has a higher associated risk than the other projects being evaluated. While the points themselves are plotted in two dimensions, cost and return on investment, the ability to show different color attributes on a scatterplot introduces a third dimension.

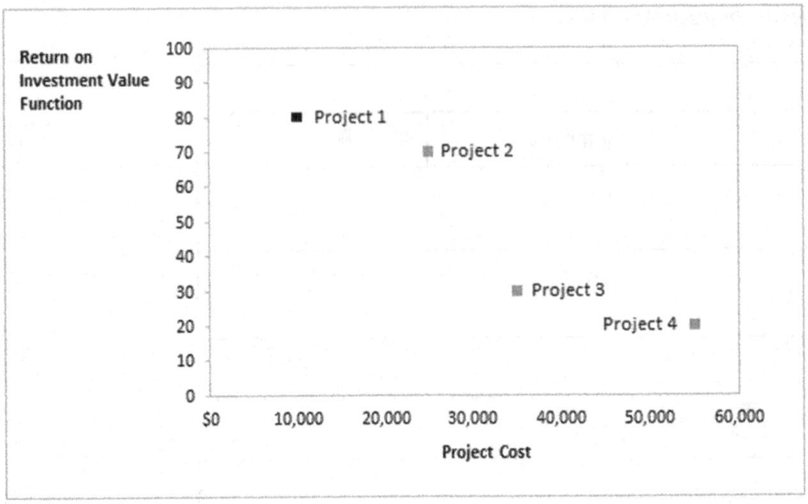

Figure 3-20. *An example of showing three dimensions with a scatterplot*

Changing the intensity of a color can show a difference in quantitative degrees. Figure 3-21 shows a screenshot of the map-coloring tool ColorBrewer 2.0 (`colorbrewer2.org`). I'll talk about using ColorBrewer in Chapter 20.

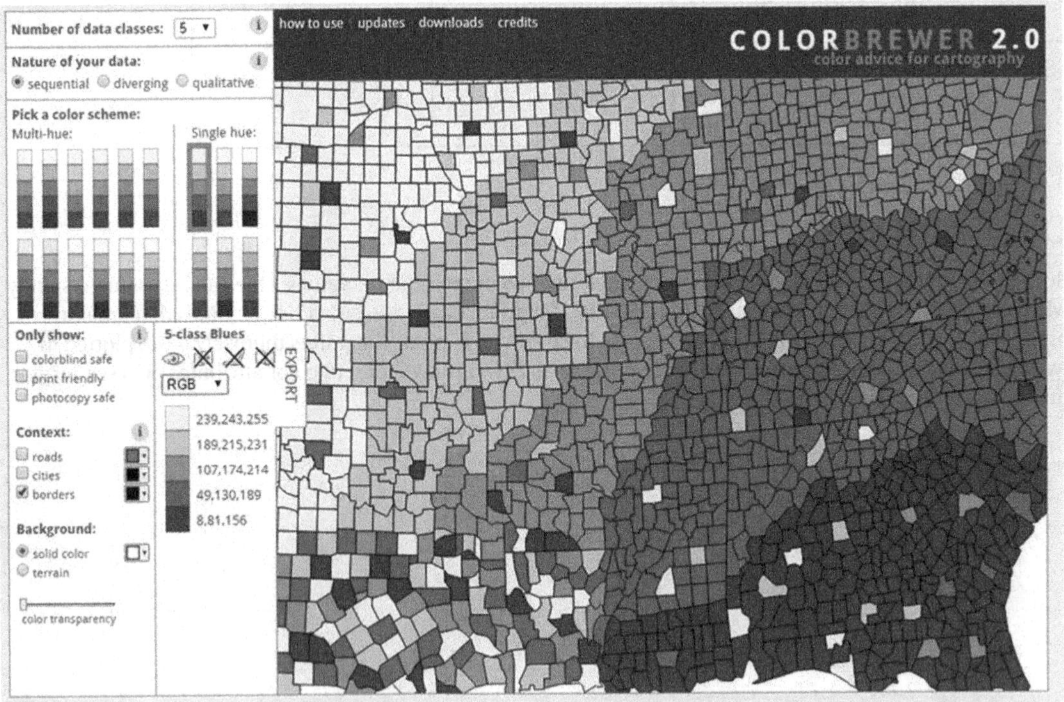

Figure 3-21. *Color Brewer 2.0*

Intuitively, we interpret a darker intensity as representing greater values, especially when it is contrasted against a lighter intensity, which may be interpreted as representing a lesser quantity. Such techniques of encoding color into quantitative scales are familiar to us in weather maps. Charts that employ the same techniques are often called *heatmaps*. In Excel, heatmaps can be created with some conditional formatting (see Figure 3-22).

Correlation Analysis

	x1	x2	x3	x4	x5
x1	0.00	0.79	0.30	0.20	0.10
x2	-0.65	0.00	0.05	0.92	0.03
x3	-0.90	0.50	0.00	0.50	-0.70
x4	0.60	0.90	0.90	0.00	0.80
x5	0.60	0.60	0.75	0.65	0.00

Figure 3-22. *A heatmap created in Excel with conditional formatting*

However, showing colors with varying degrees may be useful when viewing maps but may be less so for tables like the one shown earlier. We could improve upon the table in Figure 3-22 by simply highlighting only the important numbers, as in Figure 3-23.

Correlation Analysis

	x1	x2	x3	x4	x5
x1	0.00	0.79	0.30	0.20	0.10
x2	-0.65	0.00	0.05	**0.92**	0.03
x3	**-0.90**	0.50	0.00	0.50	-0.70
x4	0.60	**0.90**	**0.90**	0.00	0.80
x5	0.60	0.60	0.75	0.65	0.00

Figure 3-23. *An improved heatmap*

High-Precision Judging

Two types of preattentive attributes allow for a high degree of precision when viewing them: special positioning and length. While these two attributes fall under different categories, they aren't really so different when our eyes judge them. Consider the scatterplot in Figure 3-24.

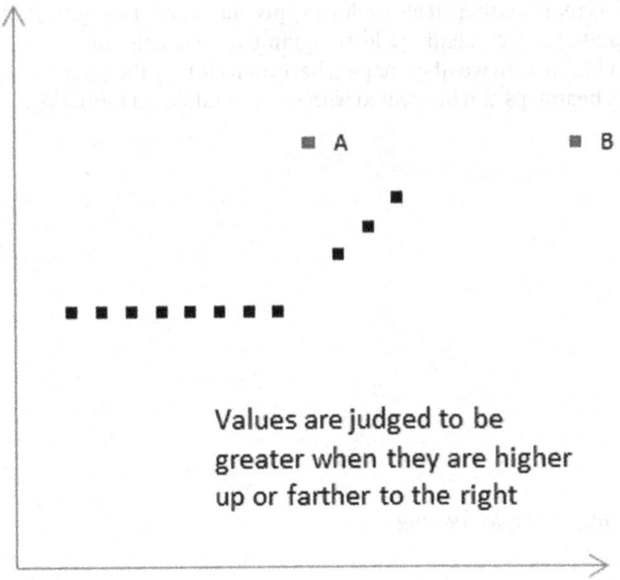

Figure 3-24. *We intuitively perceive values as being greater when they are higher up and farther to the right*

With a high degree of precision, our eyes can plainly see which values are greater (or lesser) than the other plotted values. In particular, the two highlighted (A and B) points manifest this phenomenon. Both dots, A and B, appear to have greater values than the points around them. Both are at the same height incidentally, but because of the points around them, A's value seems to highlight its distance above the rest of the dots, while B highlights the significant distance of its placement to the right of the points. Thus, we see that how our brain perceives the points A and B happens within the context of the points surrounding them.

It should be no surprise then that column charts allow for a similar degree of high precision. The chart in Figure 3-25 shows the same values from Figure 3-24 but encoded as columns. In Figure 3-25, I've also added category labels representing dates for each point. The additional labels ground the axis into a familiar date reference. That the column on the right bar represents April seems intuitively correct given its distance from the other data points, and its correctness is confirmed through the addition of labels.

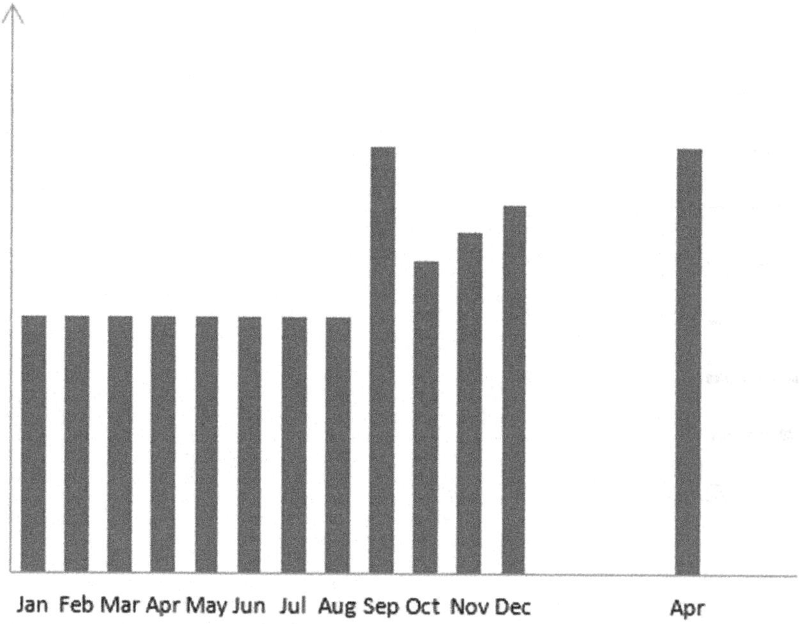

Figure 3-25. *Labels confirm our visual spatial reasoning*

What both charts have in common is that they use Cartesian two-dimensional, coordinate planes. Where the other preattentive attributes manipulate the data points themselves, variations in length and spatial position show their visualization prowess by taking advantage of the canvas upon which they are painted. Not only are our eyes good at judging the different points within a bunch, but they work well at interpreting the distances among groups of values. Plots that take advantage of the two-dimensional coordinate plane are among the strongest visual communicators.

Lower Precision, but Still Useful

Form preattentive attributes are similar to color attributes in that they modify the representation of data at a specific point. They are, however, less precise in their representation of differing quantities. The increase of width, for example, seems to encode a great quantity. A good demonstration of this point—although not a chart itself—is Excel's line width selection pane (Figure 3-26).

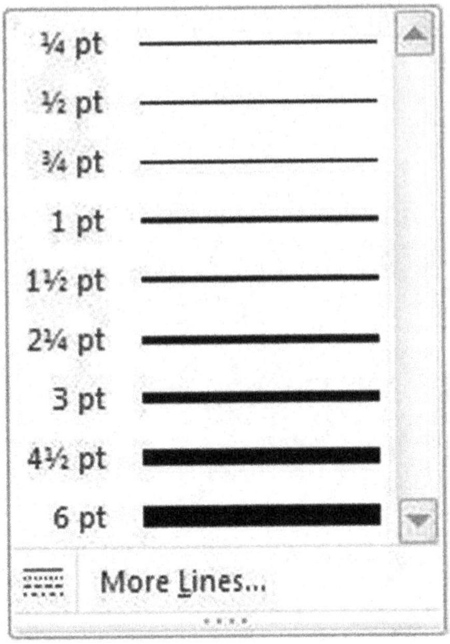

Figure 3-26. *Excel's line selection pane demonstrates our ability to perceive greater widths as greater values*

The other preattentive attributes are best used to show a difference in category instead of quantity, as shown in Figure 3-27.

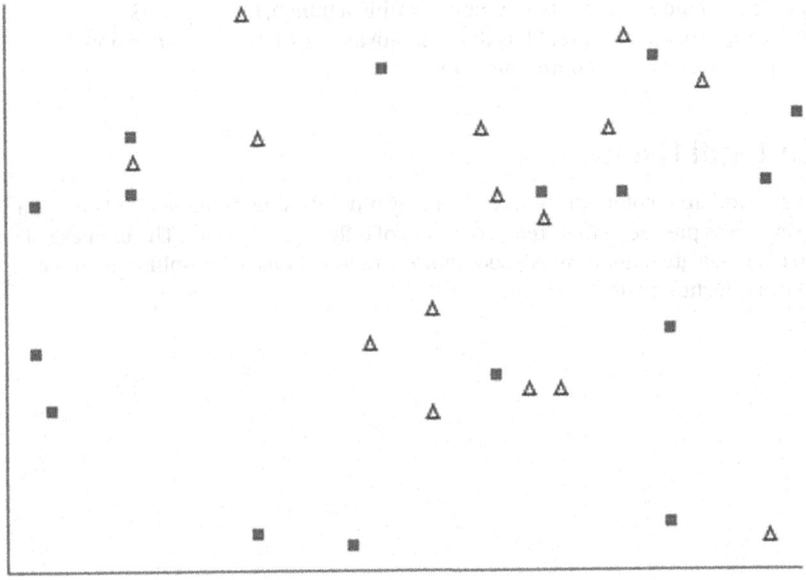

Figure 3-27. *A scatterplot demonstrating different categorical values*

The Last Word

At this point, you should have some familiarity with how our eyes receive and perceive visual information. These concepts work to our advantage by allowing information to be known to us immediately. By taking advantage of these, we can design charts and informational layout that are immediately insightful and do not strain the reader's memory and attention. Some may argue that these charts have become boring. From the standpoint that they are not overly flashy and do they include additional dimensions —if the absence of these items makes these charts boring—then such proclamations will give rise to no argument from me. However, if the data is meant to tell a story, then the patterns and properties that enhance understanding and build on our perception tendencies will provide a much richer, and more interesting, story. In the next chapter, we'll take a look at the library available for representing data with Microsoft Excel.

CHAPTER 4

The Excel Data Presentation Library

As you can imagine, there are many ways to present your data to the world. However, some ways are better than others. Excel gives you the flexibility and choice of how to present your data, but not every default chart or recommendation by Excel is worth heeding. In this chapter, you'll move through the list of data presentation and chart types that I particularly like...and the ones that I don't like. This list is by no means comprehensive, but you should get an idea of what kind of data visualization technologies are worth presenting in your work.

Tables

The most basic of these types of representations is the table. We're all pretty familiar with tables, I'm sure—like the one shown in Figure 4-1.

	A	B	C	D	E	F
1		TYPE	PW	PL	SW	SL
2		0	2	14	33	50
3		1	24	56	31	67
4		1	23	51	31	69
5		0	2	10	36	46
6		1	20	52	30	65
7		1	19	51	27	58
8		2	13	45	28	57
9		2	16	47	33	63
10		1	17	45	25	49
11		2	14	47	32	70
12						

Figure 4-1. *A typical Excel table*

There is a tendency today to create zebra lines on a table. The visualization guru Edward Tufte does not like zebra lines. In the message board for his web site, he has summed them up.

> *Strips are merely bureaucratic or designer chartjunk; good typography can always organize a table, no stripes needed.*
>
> Edward Tufte

I bring this up because there is some disagreement on this, especially among designers. In my own work, I don't often employ zebra lines. But I haven't found them distracting, either—especially when paired with a light color. You should stay away from harsh, contrasting colors both for the table rows and for the table's header. The chart shown in Figure 4-2 uses zebra lines to the extreme.

H	I	J	K	L
TYPE	PW	PL	SW	SL
0	2	14	33	50
1	24	56	31	67
1	23	51	31	69
0	2	10	36	46
1	20	52	30	65
1	19	51	27	58
2	13	45	28	57
2	16	47	33	63
1	17	45	25	49
2	14	47	32	70

Figure 4-2. *Extreme and unnecessary zebra lines*

Tables are an important part of data representation. Often, they are overlooked by designers who try to create a chart out of information that would better be placed in a table.

Line and Bar Charts

However, sometimes tables aren't good enough. For example, if you wanted to understand how sales have changed over time, a table might give you specific points, but it won't give you the entire story. This is where data visualization comes in. In this section, I'll discuss data visualization in the context of line and bar charts.

Let's begin with the table shown in Figure 4-3.

	Jan	Feb	Mar	Apr	May	Jun	July	Aug	Sept
Widget Revenue	2221	2334	2523	2100	2400	3100	2500	2777	3294

Figure 4-3. *A table showing widget revenues*

If you wanted to understand the direction of the data, the numbers presented by themselves won't do a lot for you. Perhaps you could try to see the direction in your head, but this isn't an easy feat. By plotting these numbers on a chart, a much clearer picture is illuminated. Figure 4-4 shows how charts present a much broader picture.

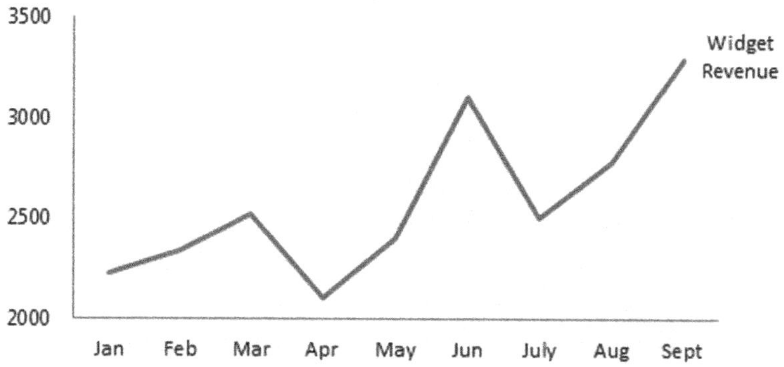

Figure 4-4. *The widget revenue line chart shows a much richer story than the numbers do by themselves in a table*

From Figure 4-4, the full story becomes clear. You can see immediately the following:

The lowest point happened in April.

The highest point happened at the end of the series, but there was a peak in June.

There appears to be some seasonality about every fourth month, starting in January.

Line charts are great for showing the trend of data, especially through time. However, they should not be used for categorical data. The chart shown in Figure 4-5, for example, is *categorically* incorrect. This is because line charts are used to show trends. There is no inherent underlying trending relationship between independent categories of fruit. Indeed, the order of fruits in the x-axis is truly arbitrary. Compare this to a time-series chart where the order of data points in the x-axis increases in time from left to right.

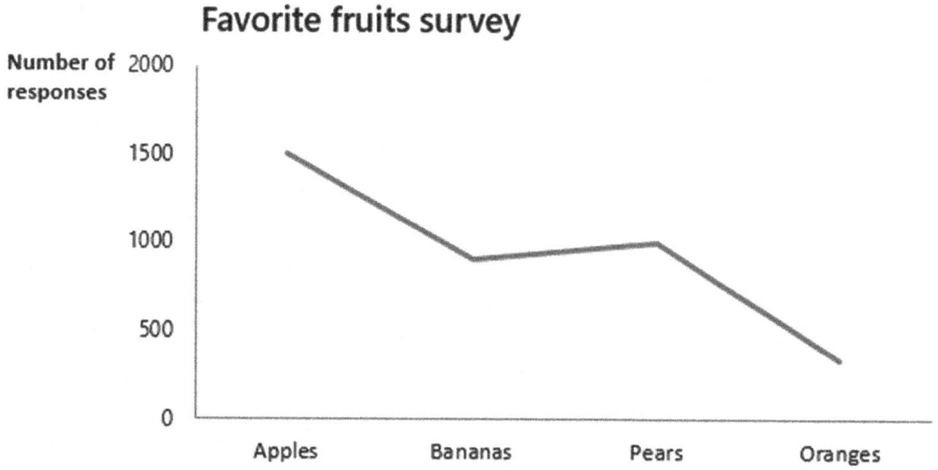

Figure 4-5. *Lines that show trends should be used to imply categorical variables have an inherent trend*

When no underlying connection exists between independent data points, you should not contrive such a connection with a line chart. Figure 4-6 shows the correct way to display this type of data with a column chart.

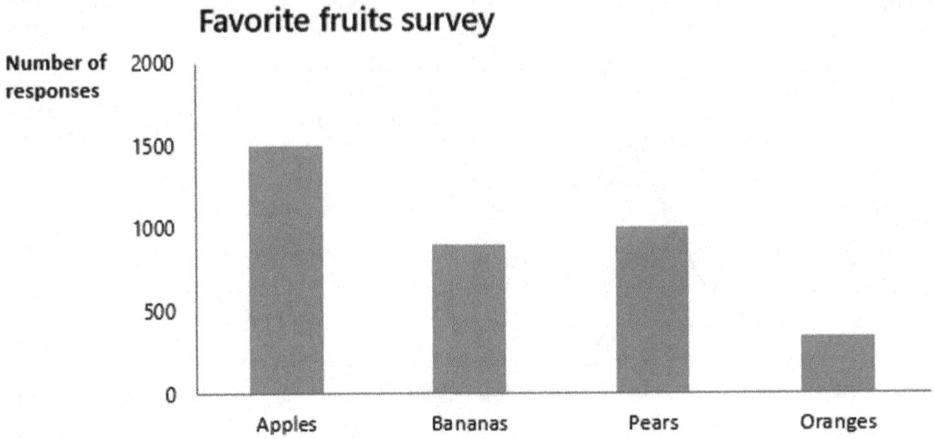

Figure 4-6. *A column chart is the more appropriate choice to show this type of data*

Bar and column charts are essentially the same thing but with different orientations. Where there exists a lot of information to display, using a bar often allows for better scanning of the data. Take a look at the bar chart shown in Figure 4-7.

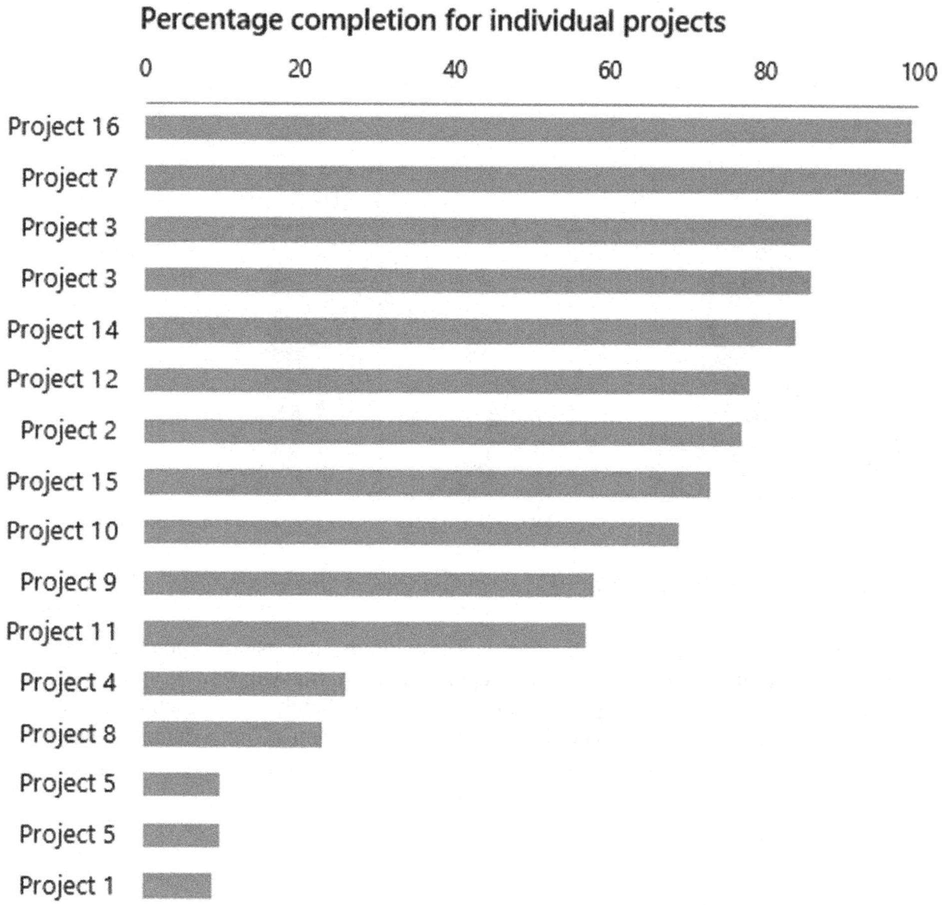

Figure 4-7. *Using bar charts allows for scanning of differences in data*

Though technically the same as bar charts, just flipped, column charts do well (and perhaps better than bar charts) when comparing different groupings of common categories. Figure 4-8 shows an example of this.

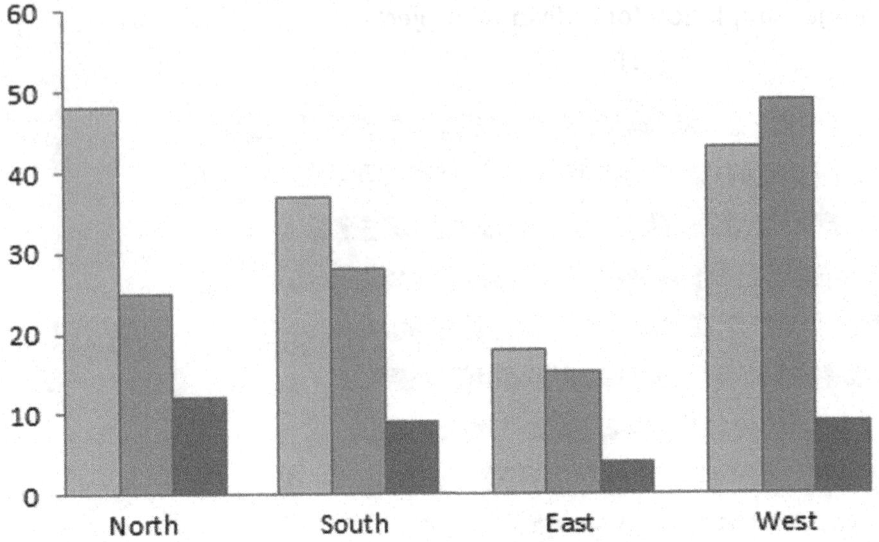

Figure 4-8. *Column charts do well when presenting different groupings of common categories*

When you are plotting distinct categories, using either bars or columns, it's a usually a good idea to list the categories in either ascending or descending order, depending upon what you want to emphasize. Listing each category in ascending or descending order allows you to immediately show which values are greatest and least and which categories are smaller or larger among similar values. This is demonstrated in Figure 4-9.

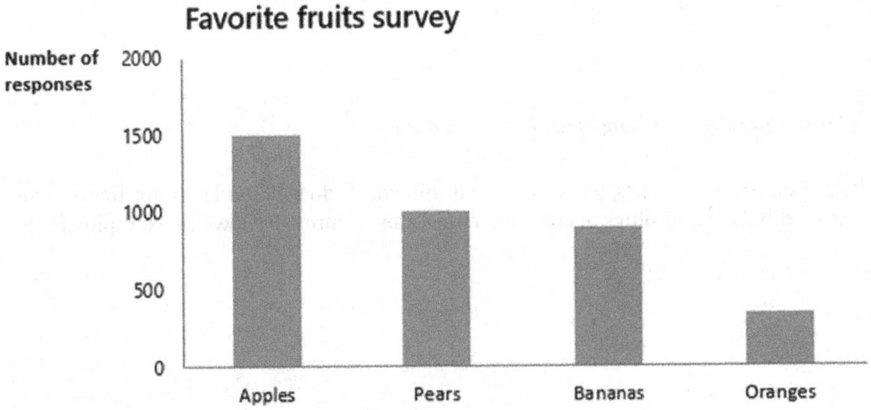

Figure 4-9. *Results shown in descending order*

Scatter Charts

Scatter charts are useful to visualize relationships between variables. The process of analyzing this relationships is called *correlation analysis*. I'll go into that in a moment.

Scatter Charts vs. Line Charts

But before moving on to discussing the process of correlation, I will take a moment to identify the differences and similarities between scatter charts and line charts. I will do this because scatter charts and line charts can produce similar output, and it might be unclear when to use one over the other. Figure 4-10 shows two similar charts, one a line chart (on top) and the other a scatter chart (on the bottom).

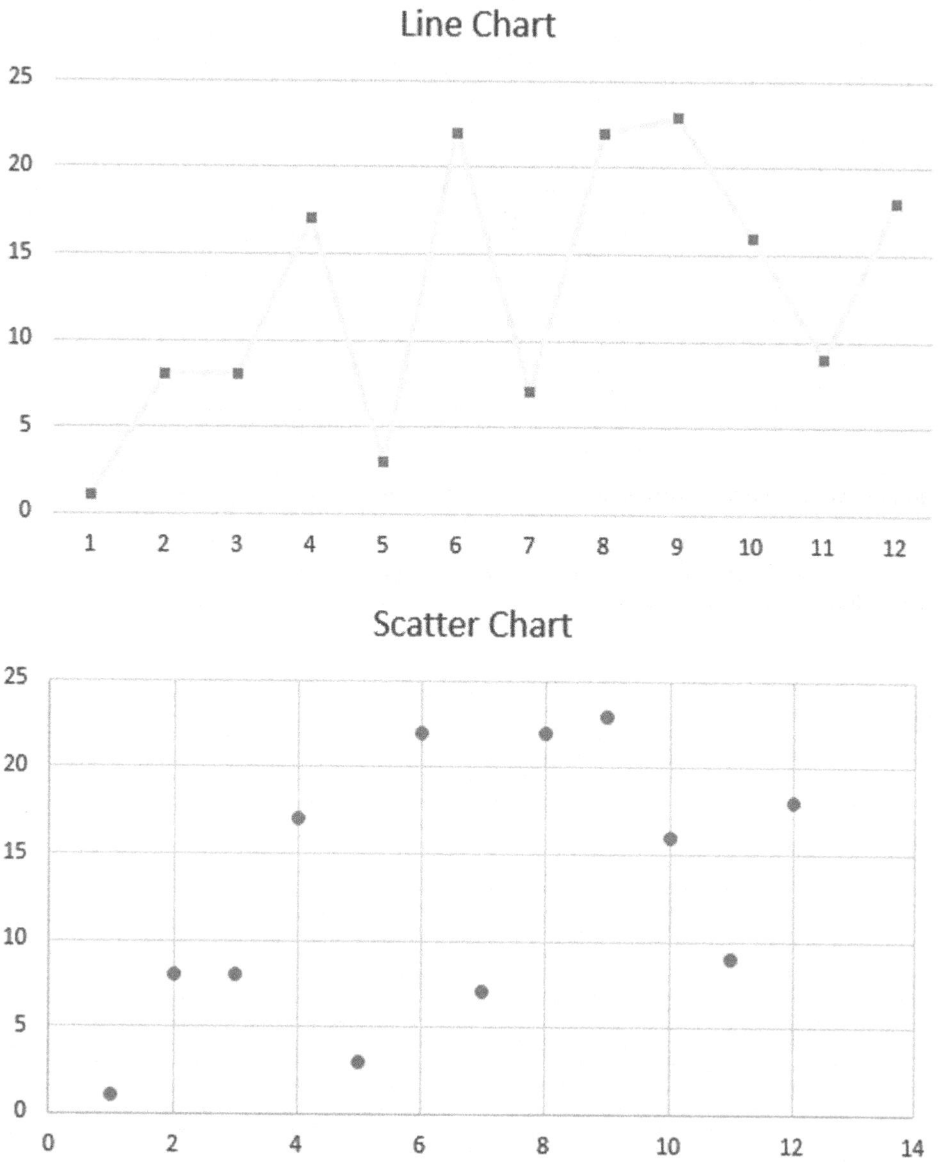

Figure 4-10. *A line chart and a scatter chart showing the same data*

To understand the difference, you must investigate how each chart treats spreadsheet data. Line charts plot data with respect to the order in which the data appears. For instance, Figure 4-11 shows a chart plotting data from the spreadsheet. The spreadsheet lists numbers 1 to 7 in ascending order.

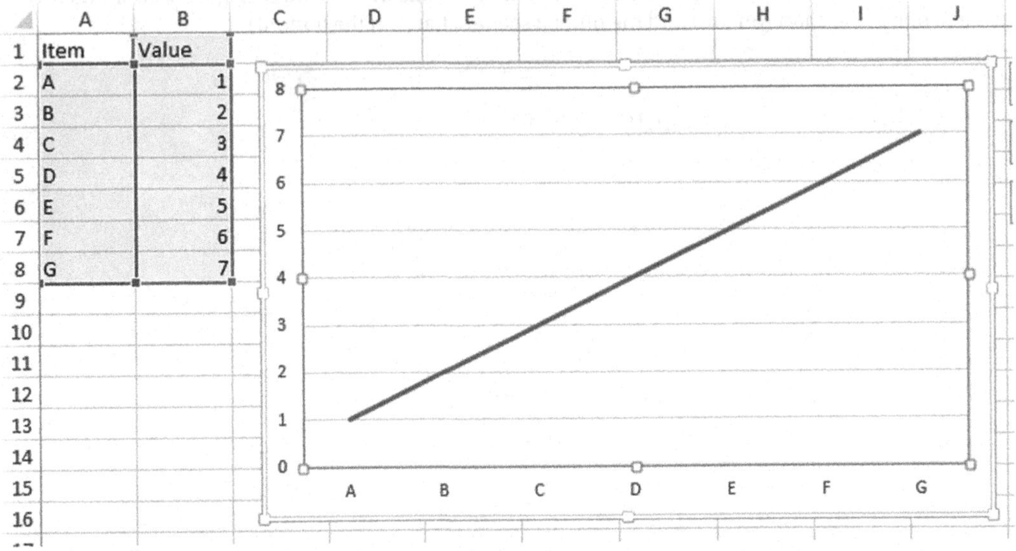

***Figure 4-11.** The line chart plots data points that the spreadsheet has listed in ascending order*

If you change the order of these values, the chart changes in parallel (Figure 4-12). In Figure 4-12, I've swapped the locations for numbers 3 and 4.

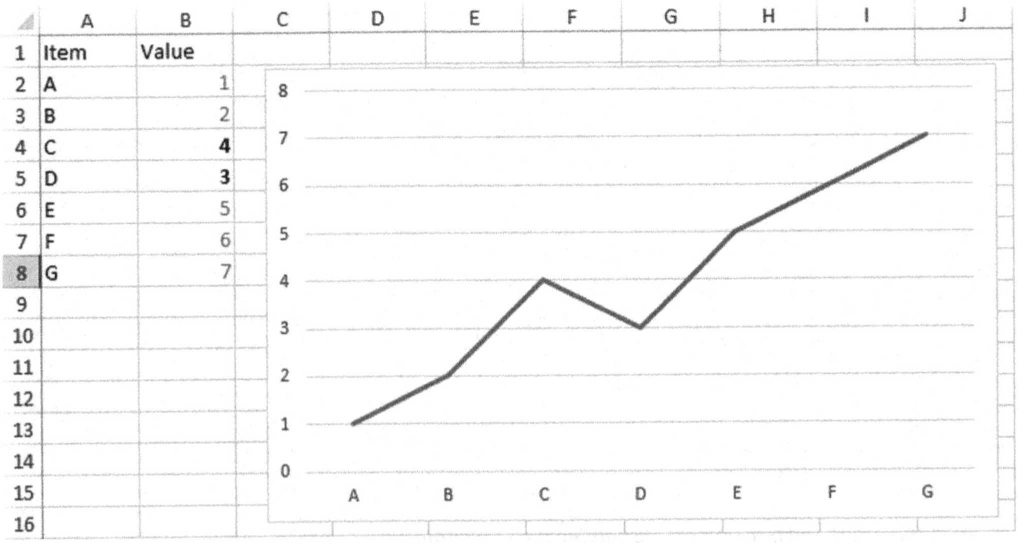

***Figure 4-12.** The numbers 3 and 4 have swapped positions, and the chart updates accordingly*

This happens with line charts because you are plotting only one set of variables. On the other hand, scatter charts plot two sets of variables (x- and y-coordinates) to define where they are placed on a chart. Figure 4-13 now shows a scatterplot. Notice that the chart relies on two series of data points representing respective x- and y-coordinate values. Changing the order of this series (Figure 4-14) does not change the data as it's presented on the chart. This is because data points are plotted with respect to one another.

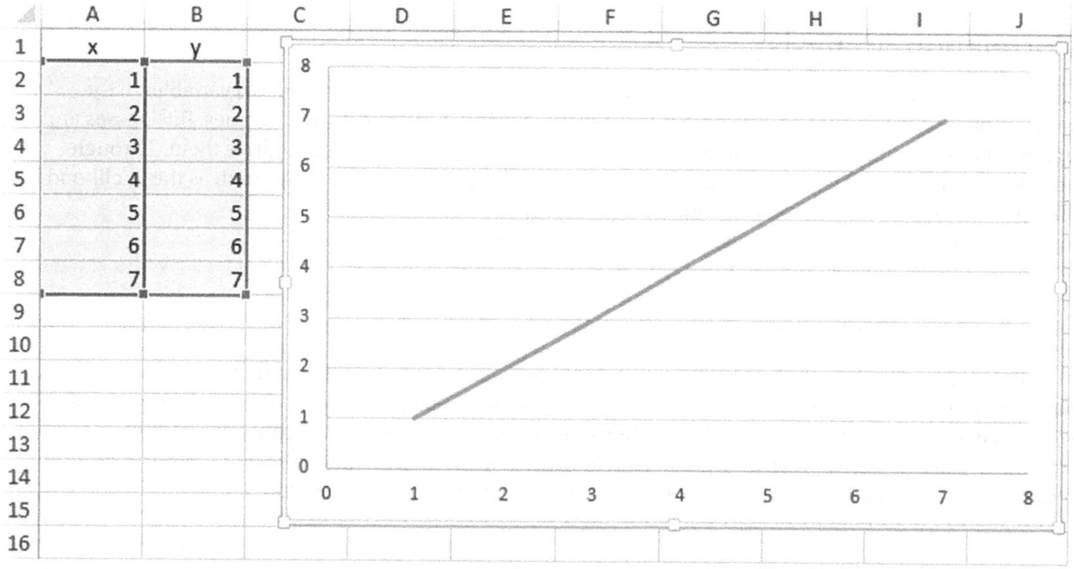

Figure 4-13. *A scatterplot requires two series of data points representing x- and y-coordinate values*

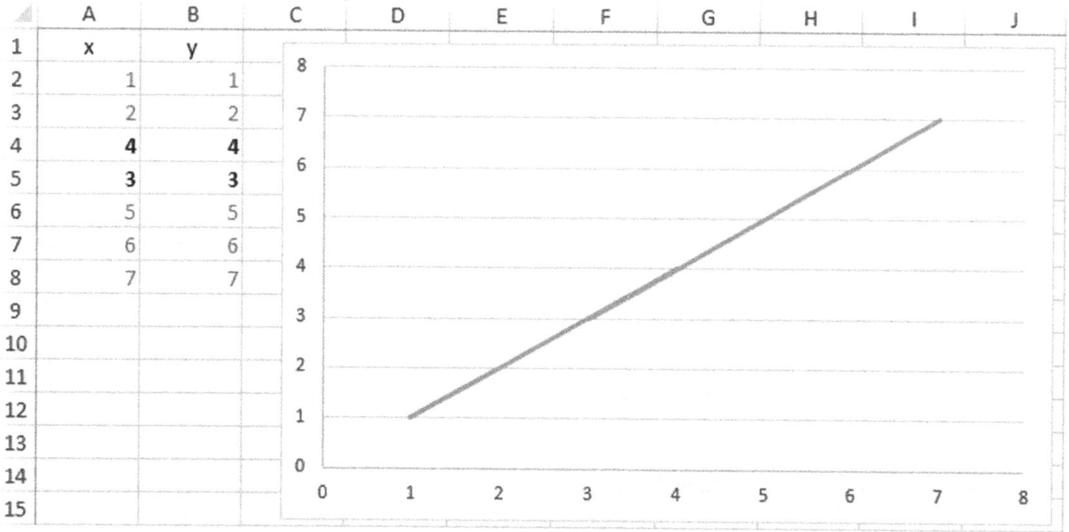

Figure 4-14. *Switching the data points does not change what's plotted on the chart*

The difference between these two is not arbitrary. Scatterplots require two sets of variables because they are particularly useful for understanding what relationship, if any, exists between two variables. While line charts and scatter charts can create similar, often identical, charts, you should pick the one that best reflects (or is perhaps a natural extension of) what you are trying to model. And indeed, scatter charts are best used for correlation analysis. Trying to use them for simple time-series analysis may add more complication than necessary.

Correlation Analysis

Correlation analysis seeks to understand a cause-and-effect relationship between two variables, if the relationship exists. Correlations are particularly useful to understand effects or outcomes. Businesses and organizations can take advantage of these items by understanding the inputs that drive them. Through correlation analysis, businesses can understand what inputs affect certain outputs, such as the likelihood a shopper is to buy a certain product given their other preferences.

The two moving parts to correlation analysis are as follows:

The independent variable: This is the cause or input.

The dependent variable: This is the effect or output.

The most common type of correlation analysis measures the linear relationship between two variables. For example, Figure 4-15 shows a positive linear relationship between two variables: years of work experience and annual salary. This relationship is a *positive* correlation because an increase in work experience leads to a positive increase in salary. For Figure 4-15, a survey asked several professionals how much they make per year and how many years of work experience they had acquired.

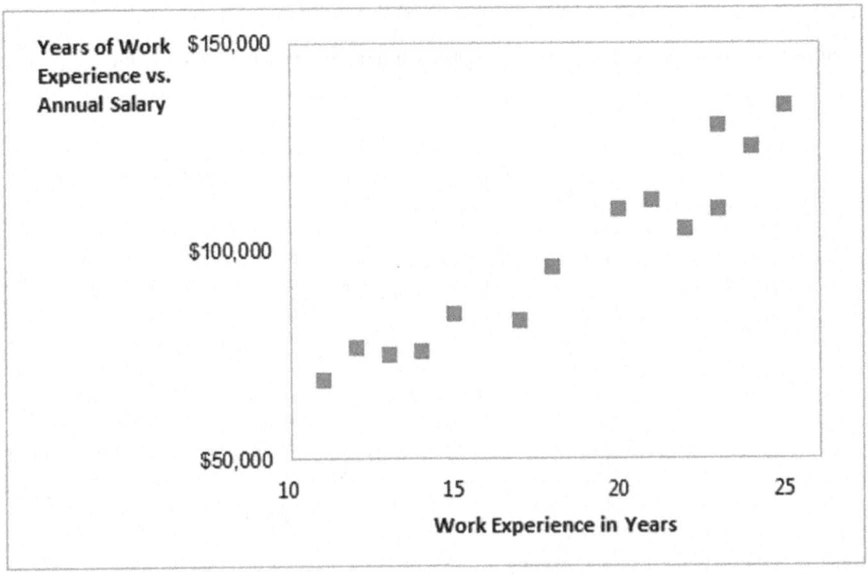

Figure 4-15. *An example of a hypothetical correlative relationship*

On the other hand, you might find that there are some *negative* correlation relationships. For example, Figure 4-16 shows one such relationship. For Figure 4-16, a group of students were asked how many hours they spent reading each week and how many hours they spent watching television.

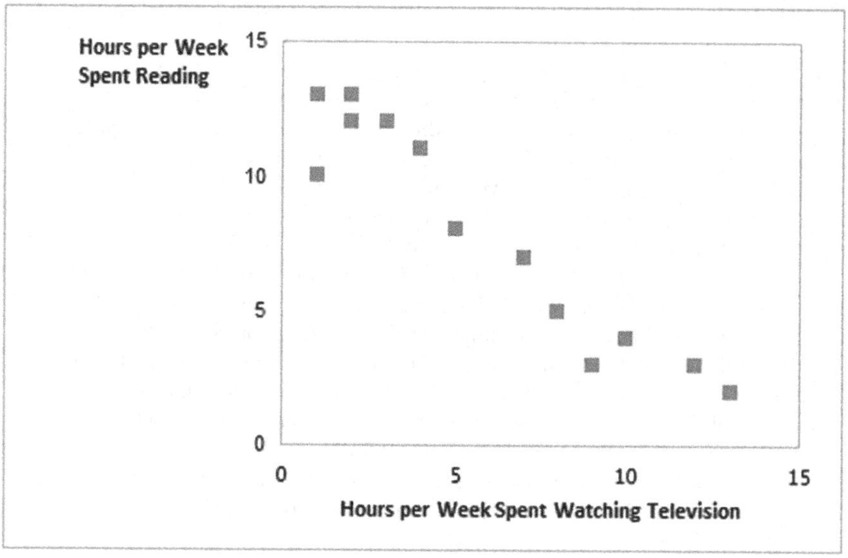

Figure 4-16. *An example of a possible negative correlation relationship*

Correlation Fit and Coefficient

A common measurement of the "strength" of the positive or negative linear relationship between two variables is the called the *coefficient of determination.* The first step to using this measurement is to impose a *line of best fit* onto the data, like that in Figure 4-17. Excel allows you to apply such a line. The best way to understand the line of best fit is to consider the relationship you are looking for. In Figures 4-15 and 4-16, you are looking to see whether an increase or decrease in one variable leads to a proportional increase or decrease in the other.

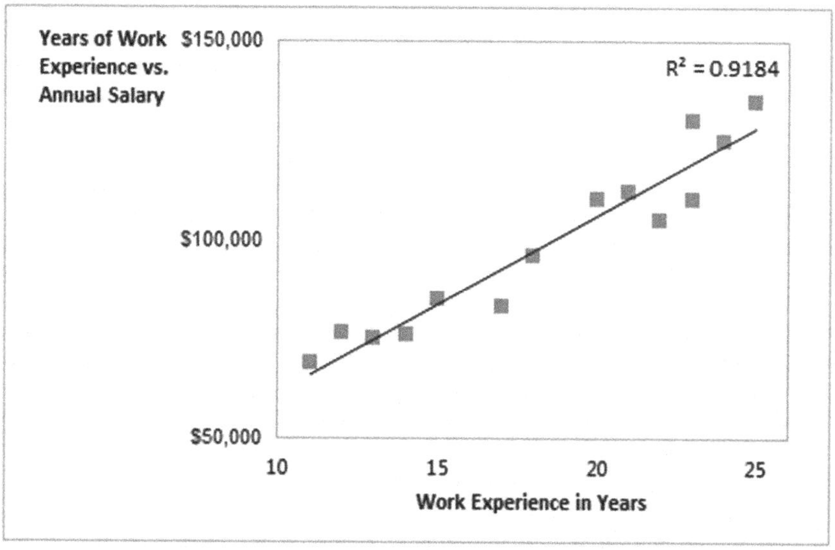

Figure 4-17. *Using Excel's trendline feature to create a line of best fit*

In a world where an increase of two years of work experience always leads to adding a fixed amount to one's salary, you could expect two points below to form a perfect line. However, our world is much noisier. Work experience doesn't always lead to making exactly a certain amount of money; in addition, there are no guarantees that you will make more than someone else with the same amount of work experience. However, what you can do to understand the general relationship between these two variables is to try to impose their relationship onto a simple trend. This is what the line of best fit does in the previous example.

A quality line of best fit would allow you a good, predictive approximation of the relationship. For example, you don't have a point in the previous example to represent 19 years of work experience and the salary a person with that much experience might receive. But, based on the data, you can still draw an estimate of what someone with 19 years of experience might make a year. To do this, you could find the place on the black line that intersects with the 19 years of experience and match that point to the yearly salaries. As you can see, according to the data, someone who has worked for 19 years might expect to make about $100,000.

The R^2 in Figure 4-17 is the coefficient of determination. It's a measurement of how well the data fit onto the line of best fit in Figure 4-17. The closer R^2 is to 1.0, the better the line of best fit can be said to approximate the linear underlying relationship of the data, if it exists. An R^2 closer to zero is not likely to be accurately approximated with a line of best fit. Alternatively, allowing R^2 might suggest a faint relationship between two variables with other unknown factors contributing more strongly to the relationship. Knowing what the R^2 suggests is more art than science. However, so long as you interpret this coefficient correctly, you'll be on your way to making good decisions.

Linear Relationship and Using R^2 Correctly

The coefficient of determination is useful for understanding how well the data can be modeled as a linear correlation, but it's not without its pitfalls. The existence of outliers—data points that significantly deviate away from the trend of the rest of the data points—can skew the R^2 to look better or worse than it should. The four datasets in Figure 4-18, known as *Anscombe's quartet*, all have the same R^2 value, but each demonstrates a different distribution of data.

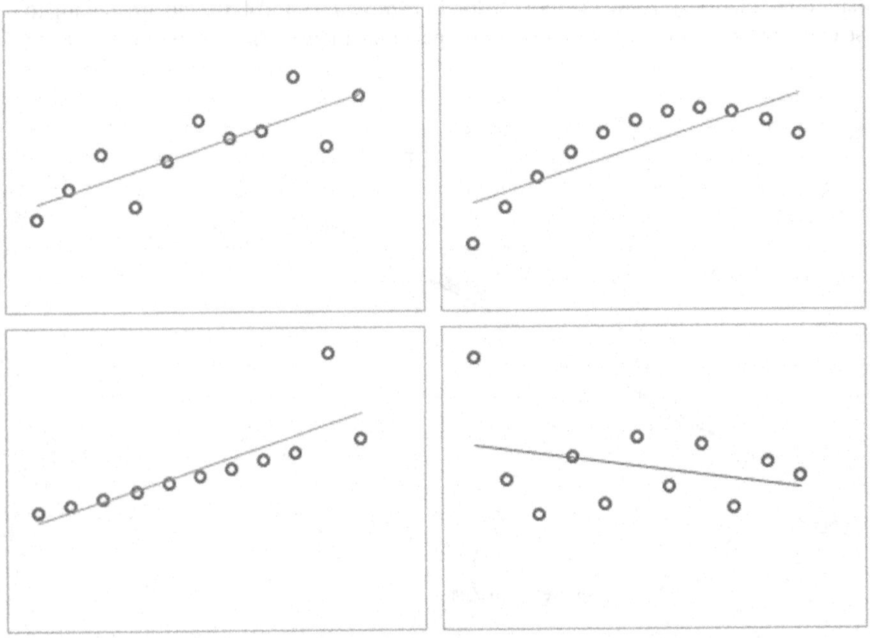

Figure 4-18. *Anscombe's quartet: despite the scatter of the data, each line of best fit has the same R^2 value*

This is why visualizing the data is so important. You could find the R^2 value independent of any visualization by just applying some statistical analysis to the data, but then you might accidently think you are capturing a relationship that doesn't necessarily exist.

The coefficient of determination also has another area of concern. A strong R^2, a value close to 1.0, should not be used to confirm the existence of a statistical relationship, if it can be said to exist. In other words, *correlation doesn't mean causation.* You could find random albeit independent variables and present them visually such that they appear to form a linear relationship. A common example is to plot ice cream sales and frequencies of drownings in a small town during a summer. As time goes on and the summer months become hotter, you might see that both appear to increase in tandem. In reality, the two variables have virtually no cause-and-effect relationship between each other. That they increase respectively has more to do with the weather: people like to eat ice cream and go swimming when it's really hot outside.

■ **Caution** R^2 can be misleading if not used correctly.

Bullet Graphs

Stephen Few first developed bullet charts as a replacement to the radial gauge charts that he and I despise. He writes the following:

> *The bullet graph was developed to replace the meters and gauges that are often used on dashboards. Its linear and no-frills design provides a rich display of data in a small space, which is essential on a dashboard. Like most meters and gauges, bullet graphs feature a single quantitative measure (for example, year-to-date revenue) along with complementary measures to enrich the meaning of the featured measure. Specifically, bullet graphs support the comparison of the featured measure to one or more related measures (for example, a target or the same measure at some point in the past, such as a year ago) and relate the featured measure to defined quantitative ranges that declare its qualitative state (for example, good, satisfactory, and poor). Its linear design not only gives it a small footprint, but also supports more efficient reading than radial meters.*
>
> —Stephen Few, *Bullet Graph Design Specification*, March 2010

Take a look at the bullet graph in Figure 4-19 and its specification by Stephen Few.

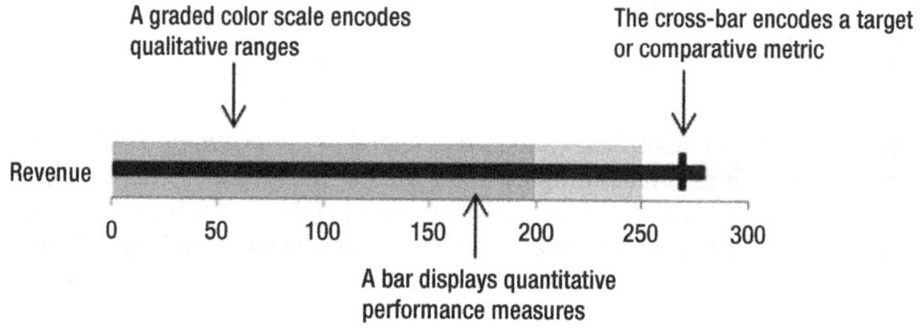

Figure 4-19. *The specification of bullet graphs*

Bullet graphs can be displayed horizontally, vertically, and in a series. Stephen Few particularly likes bullet graphs because they can be packed together with other charts in a small space. For instance, in Figure 4-20, bullet charts display a significant amount of information despite their small size.

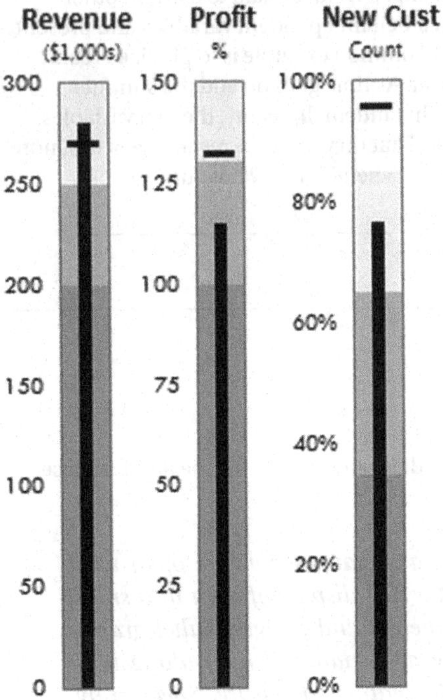

Figure 4-20. *Compact bullet charts in a small space*

Bullet graphs are not part of the default chart package in Excel. The chart like the one in Figure 4-20 requires some cleverness to build in Excel, as you will see in Chapter 12. However, pushing Excel beyond its limitations is what "thinking outside the cell" is all about.

Bullet graphs allow for a lot more advanced visualization than is displayed in Figure 4-20. You can have multiple targets and several qualitative scales. It's unfortunate they are not included in Excel's default charting package because they bring a significant amount of visual information in such a contained space. Consider how much information is displayed in a single bullet graph. Do radial gauge charts from Chapter 2 provide for the same amount of visual analysis?

Small Multiples

Small multiples go by several names. You may hear them called *trellis charts* or *panel graphs*. Each of these different names, I believe, accurately describes small multiples, and I will use these names interchangeably throughout the book. Indeed, small multiple charts are powerful. They employ the same chart design many times but across different variables. For example, take a look at the small multiple charts in Figure 4-21.

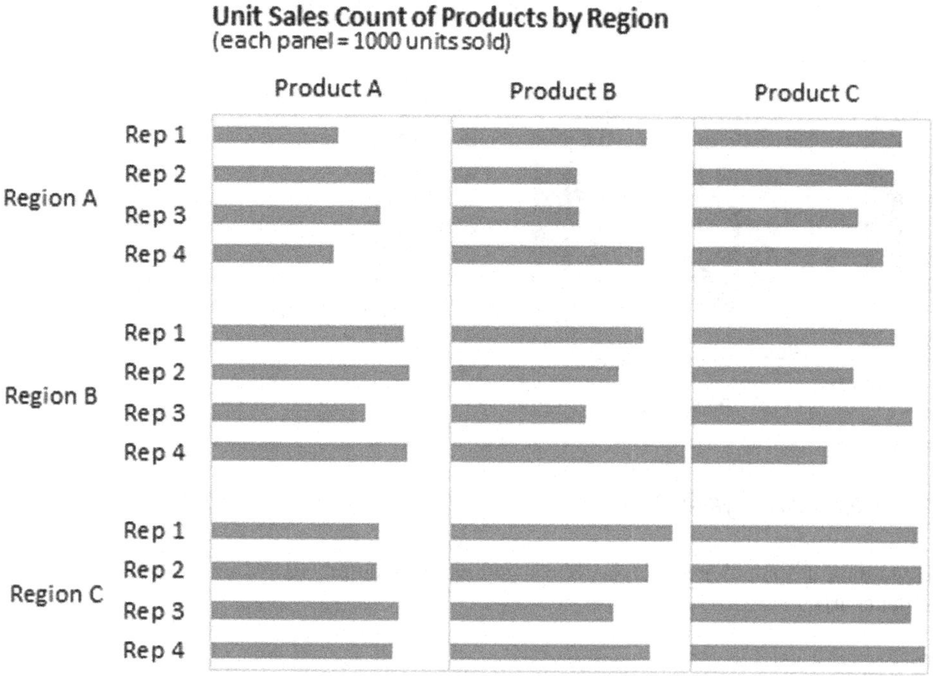

Figure 4-21. *An example of small multiple charts*

In Figure 4-21, the intersection of the region and product can be thought of as a panel. Consider how much information is displayed. Two variables effectively make up the x- and y-axes. Additionally, each panel displays one dimension of information. Therefore, you've displayed three dimensions but without resorting to visualizing in three dimensions. This is one of the great advantages to small multiples. In *The Visual Display of Quantitative Information,* Eduard Tufte says the following about them:

> *Small Multiples are economical: once viewers understand the design of one slice, they have immediate access to the data in all the other slices. Thus, as the eye moves from one slice to the next, the constancy of the design allows the viewer to focus on changes in the data rather than on changes in graphical design.*

Charts Never to Use

I have reviewed the best charts for relaying visual perception and data sensemaking. Compared to the charts available in Excel and perhaps to other chart packages, the list may seem small. However, what makes these charts different from the others is that they are based on research. They have proven their worth repeatedly.

In this section, I will review charts that you should really never use.

Cylinders, Cones, and Pyramid Charts

These charts are similar to bar charts, except they are much harder to read. Cylinders appear to offer your data a gradient color from a hidden light source, but this is not the way to make your data shine. Take a look at the three-dimensional cylinder chart in Figure 4-22.

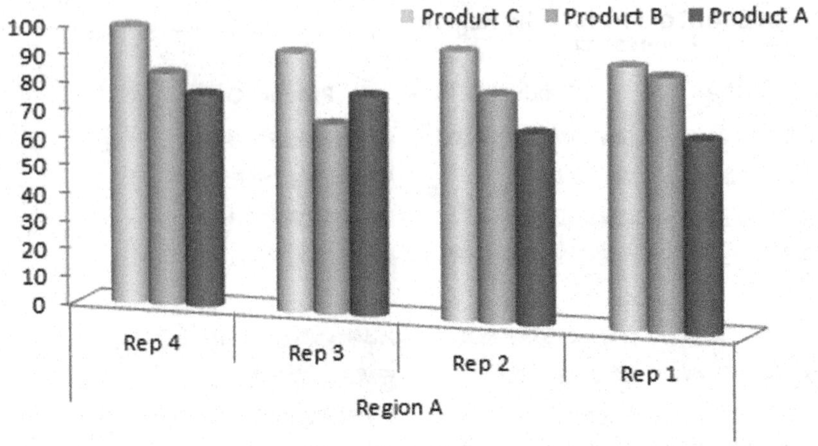

***Figure 4-22.** A three-dimensional cylinder chart*

Cones and pyramids, despite their spikes, are bad at getting to the point. Figures 4-23 and 4-24 show these other offender charts.

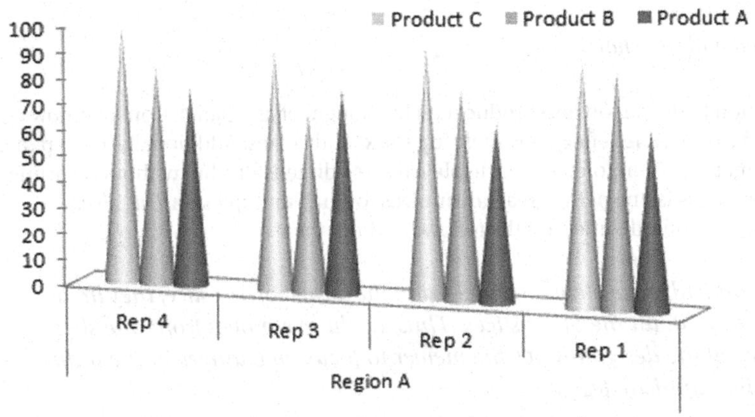

***Figure 4-23.** Pointy cone charts don't aid in understanding*

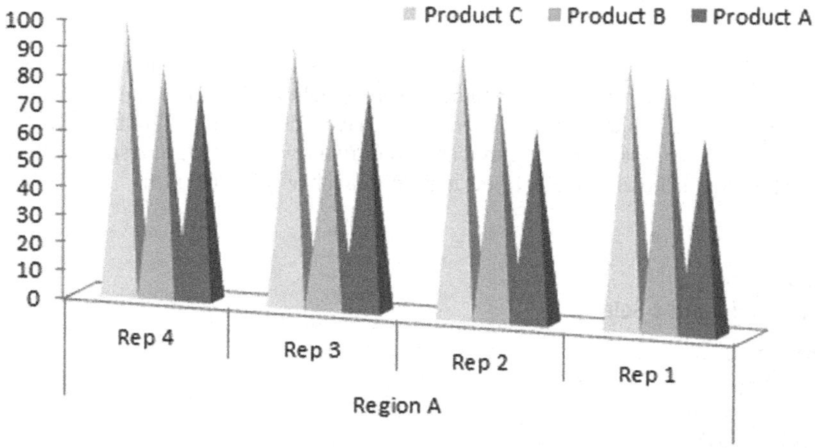

Figure 4-24. *More pointy, pyramid charts that show the same data while not aiding in visual understanding*

Having viewed far too many of these types of graphs, I've come up with the following guiding principle:

There are very few, if any, good reasons data should take the form of stalagmites.

Pie Charts

Pie charts are among the most used charts on dashboards, in reports, and in presentations. However, if you look to the data visualization principles presented in Chapter 3, you can see why they fail. Our ability to judge precision among areas (the wedges of the chart) is not as strong as our ability to judge differences in height. That is, the data shown in pie chart is often better suited for a column or bar chart. Furthermore, the extent to which you understand the data being conveyed in a pie chart is often because other information (like labels or a table) is presented in conjunction with the chart (as, perhaps, a tacit admission that such charts by themselves are largely ineffective). For a more detailed explanation, refer to the "The Problem with Pie Charts" sidebar in Chapter 1.

I've been asked when they're ever OK to use, so I created Figure 4-25 to help answer the question.

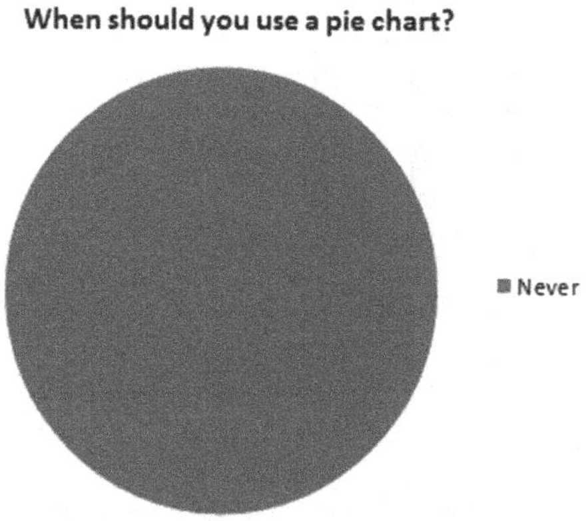

Figure 4-25. *One of the few pie charts allowed in this book*

Doughnut Charts

Doughnut charts are glorified pie charts (see Figure 4-26). Unlike real doughnuts, which often feature delicious filling, doughnut charts are filled with nothing of the sort. For some reason, doughnut charts have become popular on the Web and in magazines. The publication *The Economist* even used one to show countries with increasing weight problems in their populations using doughnut charts complete with frosting and sprinkles, taking the doughnut chart metaphor quite literally (see `www.youtube.com/watch?v=yGHC8dRYrlM`).

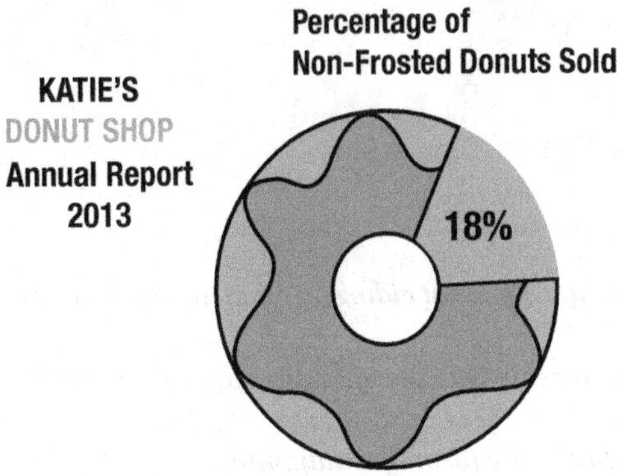

Figure 4-26. *Doughnut charts are simply glorified (or, arguably, unglorified) pie charts*

Charts in the Third Dimension

Charts that employ the third dimension often suffer from data *occlusion*, as discussed in Chapter 2. Consider what Figure 4-27 might look like when plotted into the third dimension. Figure 4-22 shows this three-dimensional plot.

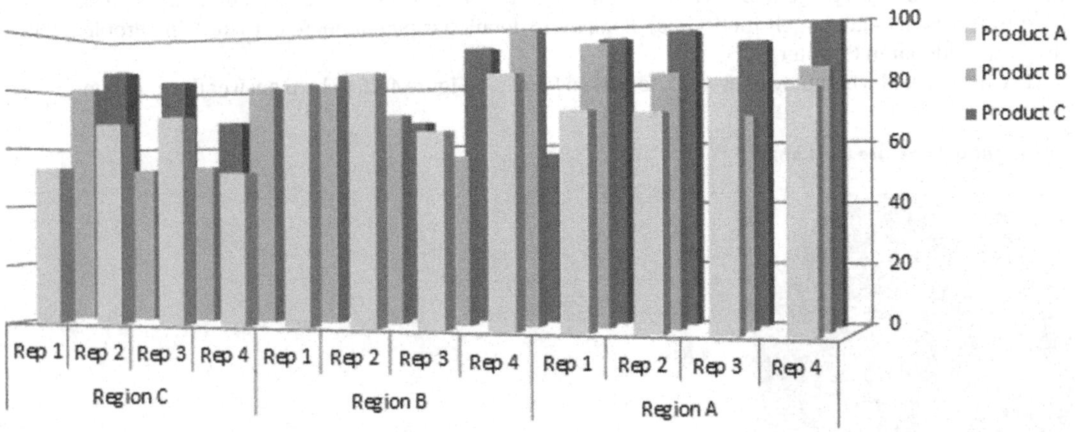

Figure 4-27. *The data from Figure 4-21 now in the third dimension*

Looking at Figure 4-27, how easy do you find it to view the values for product C? How easy is it to compare the different product values? Not easy at all, I imagine.

This is because our eyes are not good at comparing anything in the third dimension. Consider the pie charts shown in Figure 4-28. Depending upon your perspective, you might think there are more yes than no answers. When you pull away from the third dimension, though, you see that they are equal, as shown in Figure 4-29.

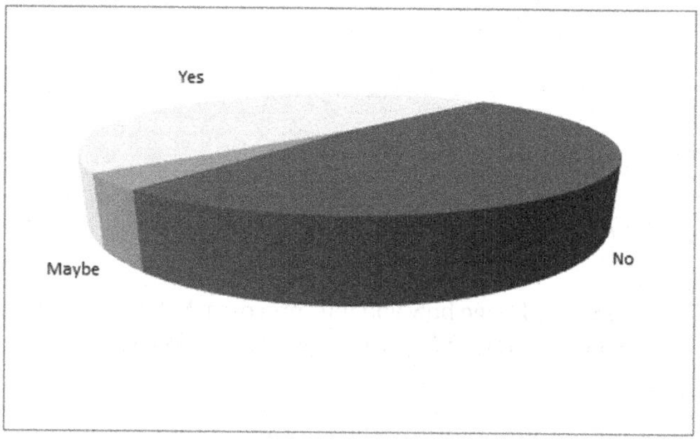

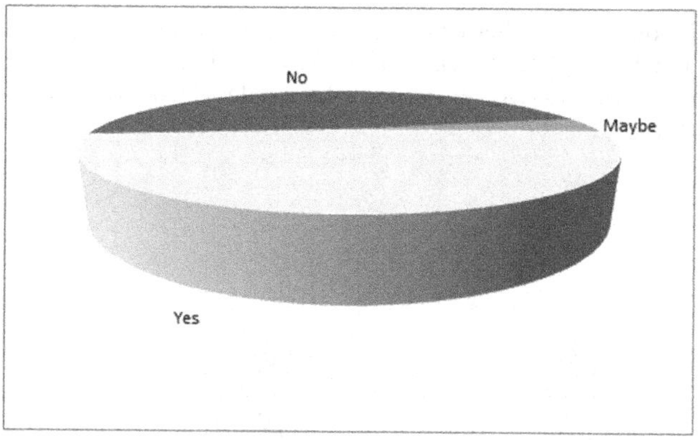

Figure 4-28. *The same values are shown in the three-dimensional pie chart with differing dimensions*

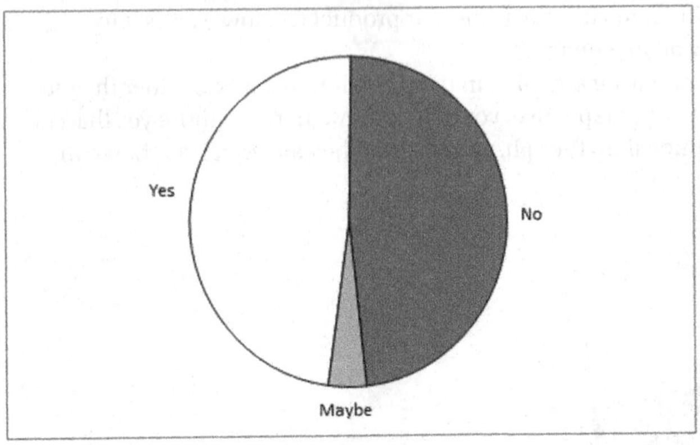

Figure 4-29. *When you look with no three-dimensional perspective, the data is no longer distorted*

What you learn from this is that perspective does in fact change how you interpret data. You should be keen to use data visualization methods that help transmit and not confuse the underlying message.

Surface Charts

Surface charts are glorified line charts in the third dimension. They look like rough terrain when viewed. Perhaps if you want to show management how much your data looks like the world's most impossible golf course (see Figure 4-30), surface charts could be useful. Otherwise, they should be avoided. I have yet to find a reasonable use for them in the regular business world.

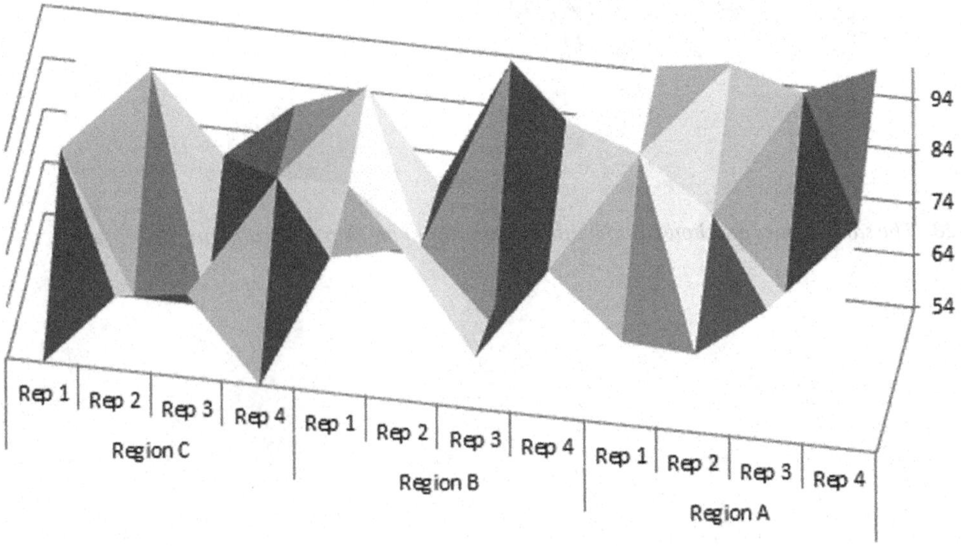

Figure 4-30. *Surface charts are not easily interpreted*

Stacked Columns and Area Charts

Stacked columns and area charts may seem like a good idea at first glance, but they run into a similar problem as pie charts: they suffer from inconsistent baselines. Continuing with the theme, Figures 4-31 and 4-32 plot the same data, in a stacked area chart and bar chart separated by region, respectively.

Looking at Figure 4-31, you can evaluate the values for product A without much difficulty. However, when you attempt to evaluate the other products—especially as your eyes move up to product C—the differences in values become less perceptible. Figure 4-32 does a much better job of persisting these differences across all product lines.

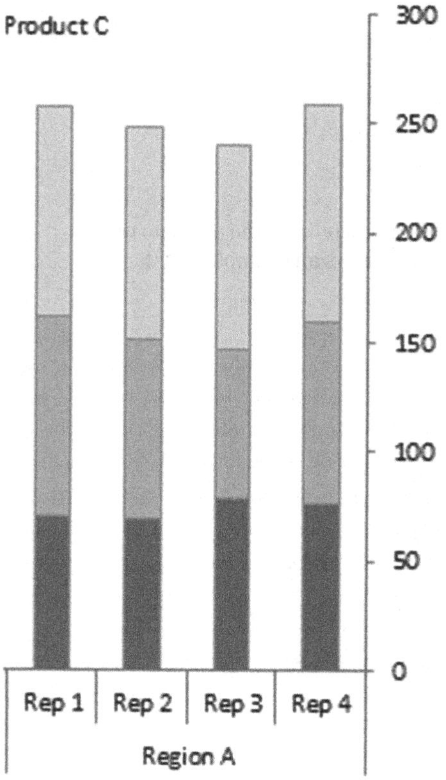

***Figure 4-31.** An example of a stacked column chart*

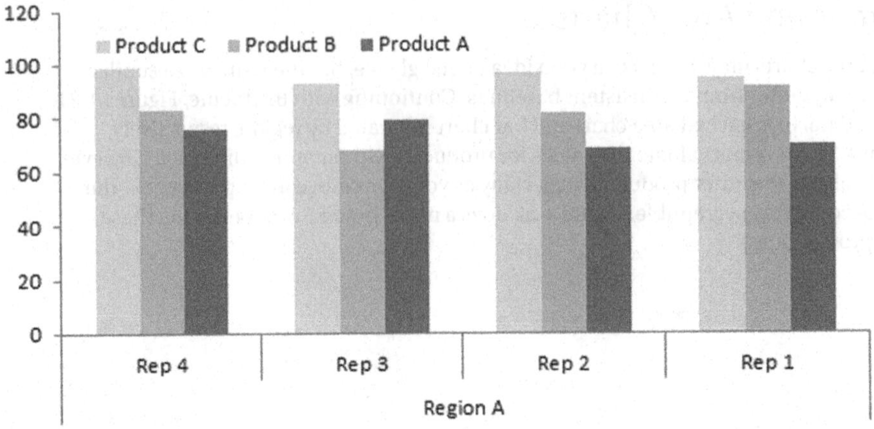

Figure 4-32. *The same data used in Figure 4-26 but separated by category*

Additionally, surface charts, stacked or otherwise, don't provide much relief to the problem of obfuscation or inconsistent baselines for the same dataset. Figure 4-33 shows an example of data obfuscation by using an area chart.

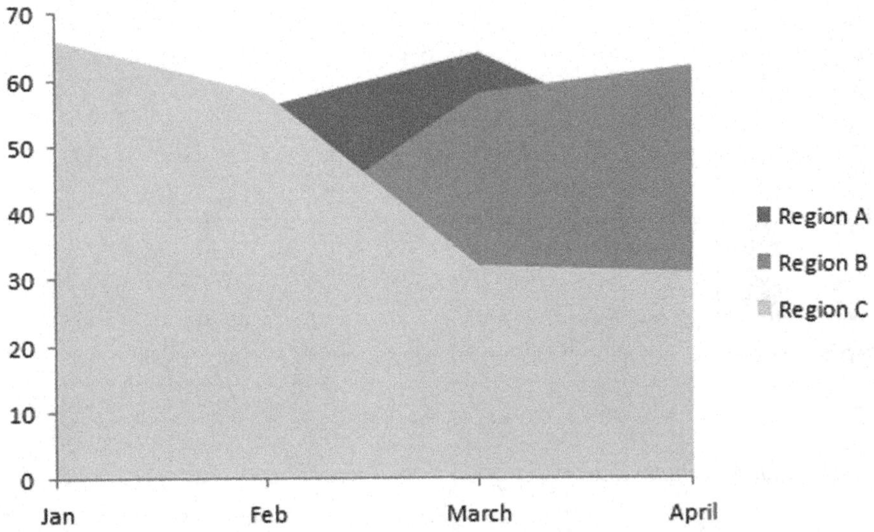

Figure 4-33. *Overlapping areas obfuscate the data behind them*

You could stack the data as you did for the previous stacked column chart, but you still run into the same problem of changing baselines (Figure 4-34). In particular, imagine you changed the order of the regions shown in Figure 4-34. This would actually change the shape of how they are shown in the chart. In other words, while the underlying data would stay the same, their presentation and how you would interpret the results would be affected.

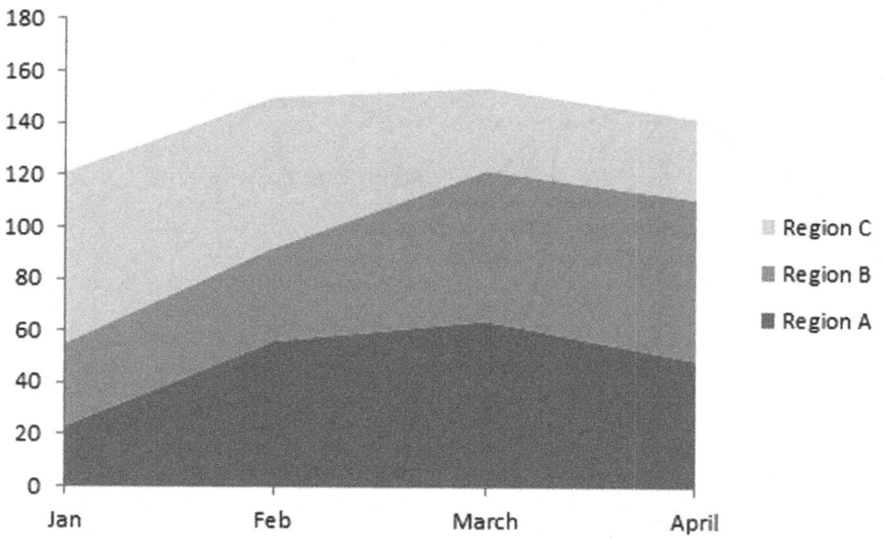

Figure 4-34. *Changing baselines with area charts has the similar problem of changing baselines*

Radar Charts

Radar charts are line charts that connect data around in a circle rather than from left to right as you might expect. Except to make one's data appear like a spider web or bird's nest, they offer little advantage. Often it's argued they highlight certain extremes in the values they are measuring. However, they don't do this any better than a typical bar or column chart might. In addition, they violate the rule of connecting categorical data via lines. Figure 4-35 shows an example radar chart. Again, you should compare this chart to that of Figure 4-21—which does a better communicating data?

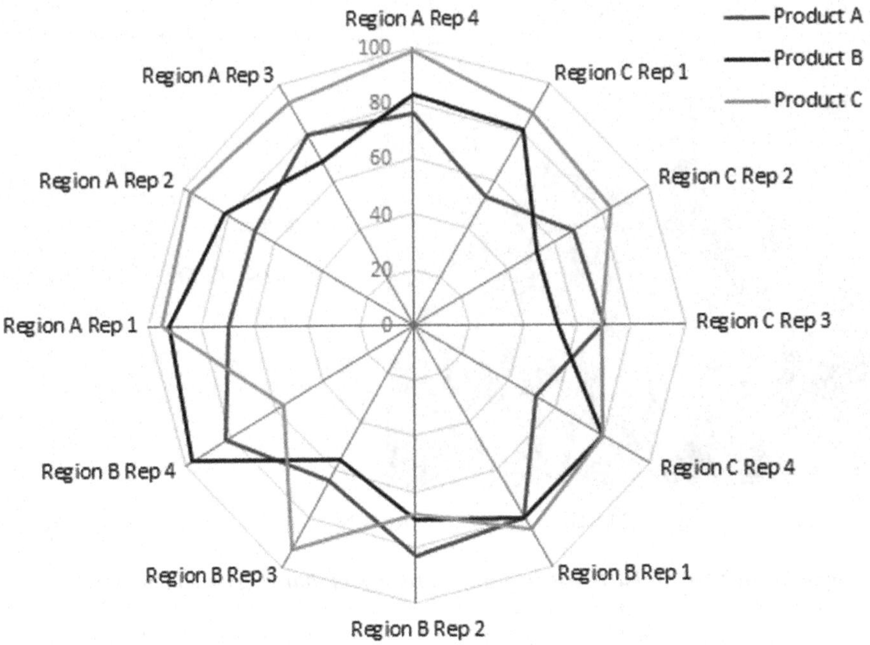

Figure 4-35. *An example of a radar chart using the same data from Figure 4-21*

The charts you should avoid all suffer from the same problems. Specifically, they either obfuscate data or rely on imprecise visual perception, predominantly that of evaluating an area. The charts you should use, on the other hand, rely on a proven understanding of how our minds perceive the world. Armed with this information, you're ready to use techniques that work. When your audience is not caught up in trying to understand a complex or less than useful data visualization, they are spending more time and energy on understanding the presentation of the problem and not the underlying problem. Whether it's with data visualizations or anything else, how you present your data should be a natural extension of the underlying thing being modeled.

The Last Word

I realize some of my recommendations of charts to avoid might come as a shock to you. You've likely used these charts before and thought, what's the harm? In truth, the harm is hard to quantify by itself. But if you place the directive to use proper data visualizations in context, you find the wrong choice does more than communicate poorly; it takes the reader's attention from the underlying message and goal of your work. If you can't bring yourself to stop using some of these charts, I understand. But it's worth asking yourself, in your own work, whether you are presenting information in the best way possible.

PART II

Excel Dashboard Design Tools and Concepts

CHAPTER 5

Getting Started: Thinking Outside the Cell

In this chapter, I'll talk about some misconceptions concerning Excel development. It's quite often heard that Visual Basic for Applications (VBA) is where all "advanced" Excel takes place. The thought is VBA can do everything, and if you want your data to be sorted, manipulated, and so forth, you'll need VBA. But you should think of Excel formulas and VBA not as separate entities but as tools that should work in tandem to present the best result.

It's true that many of the capabilities presented in this book will require knowledge and use of VBA, but it would inaccurate to describe everything as macro coding. This misconception, I believe, stems from the idea that a certain level of programming mastery is required to make Excel do fancy things. The macro recorder has played a strong role in this misconception because many believe that macros are seemingly the only way to make Excel perform automated tasks or create dynamic capabilities.

That this misconception is widely believed is not hard to understand when you consider Excel's spectrum of users, from accountants who probably don't think of their work as being too technical to engineers who might view their work as being a lot closer to coding. But, as Chapter 1 established, using Excel in any way is a type of unstructured computer programming. Perhaps you never thought of yourself as a coder, but the way you use Excel to construct solutions is similar to the processes that computer programmers use when they develop their work.

Consider this example. I could describe Rory McIlroy as a good putter, which is true, but it's only part of the story. *Rory McIlroy is a terrific golfer.* VBA can help you do a lot in Excel, but knowing all the features of Excel—and knowing when they should be used—will make you terrific with Excel. You can be good at just VBA, but there's more to developing terrific programs than just VBA. Don't get me wrong, I love VBA. And if VBA is something you've always wanted to master, I say go ahead. But when it comes to Excel development, VBA is only half the story.

The other half of the story is all of the Excel capabilities at your disposal. In particular, there are formulas, custom formatting, conditional formatting, and form controls, among others. Indeed, you could create a capable, dynamic dashboard with all of these things without ever having touched any VBA.

In my opinion, the distinction between VBA and everything else isn't very useful for what we want to do. If you rely purely on VBA for everything, your spreadsheets might not be as great as they could be. As you'll see in this chapter, choosing VBA, formulas, or a mixture of both brings its own set of challenges and advantages.

In the following sections, I'll go through some common scenarios and talk about the different ways to solve the problems presented.

HOW MY WORKSHOP SUDDENLY CHANGED ITS NAME

On one occasion, I was invited to give a workshop on developing dashboards with Excel. I had planned to deliver a presentation on all the cool things you could do without VBA since I had only an hour set aside for instruction. When I arrived to the presentation room, the organizers had changed the name of my class from Advanced Excel Development to Advanced VBA. It's not uncommon for people to assume doing anything outside the normal use of Excel must be Visual Basic for Applications at work.

House Hunters: Excel Edition

In this section, I'll go through three different ways to build a simple application. The application allows the user to switch between several different properties. When the user moves to the next property, a new property is shown. In all, you're dealing with only three properties, but you can extend the underlying functionality to more complex dashboards and Excel applications. There will be instances in which users must switch between pictures and information. As I go through three different ways to solve this problem, you should consider the benefits and costs for each. Figure 5-1 shows one such attempt at solving this problem in Excel.

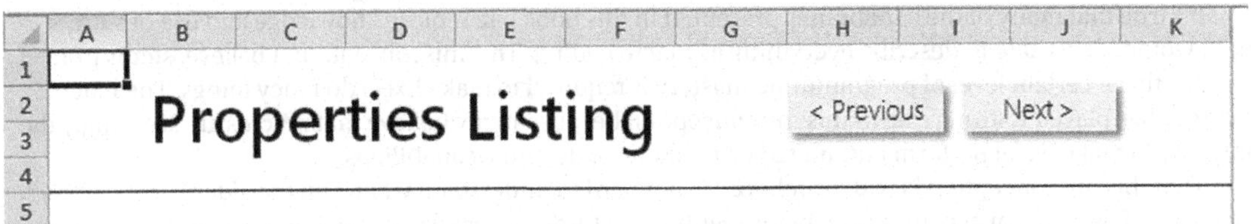

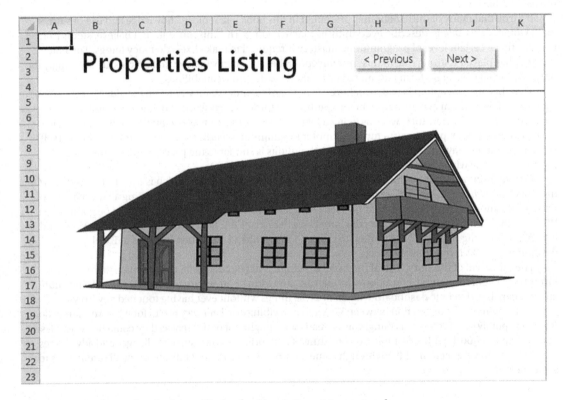

***Figure 5-1.** Implementing the image display for the rotating picture example*

The following are the three methods you'll consider in this section:

- **A purely VBA method**: This method largely relies on coding.
- **The semi-VBA method**: This method uses some spreadsheet functionality in conjunction with code.
- **The no-code method**: This method uses no code at all but instead relies solely on formulas and features.

In the next subsections, I'll go through these methods and talk about the different ways to attack this problem. You can follow along on your own by downloading `Chapter5HouseHunters.xlsm` from the chapter files.

The Purely VBA Method

In this section, I'll discuss the purely VBA method. You can get a copy of this method implemented in full from Properties List Example 1 in the `Chapter5HouseHunters.xlsm` chapter file.

In this first method, most of the mechanics are performed through code. I present this method as a lesson in what not to do. The code may seem innocuous at first—and to a certain extent it is—but in many ways, it's also unnecessary (and annoying, as you'll see in Chapter 6). It represents the rut many Excel developers find themselves in, offloading important features to VBA when it needn't be this way.

Figure 5-2 shows this implementation in action.

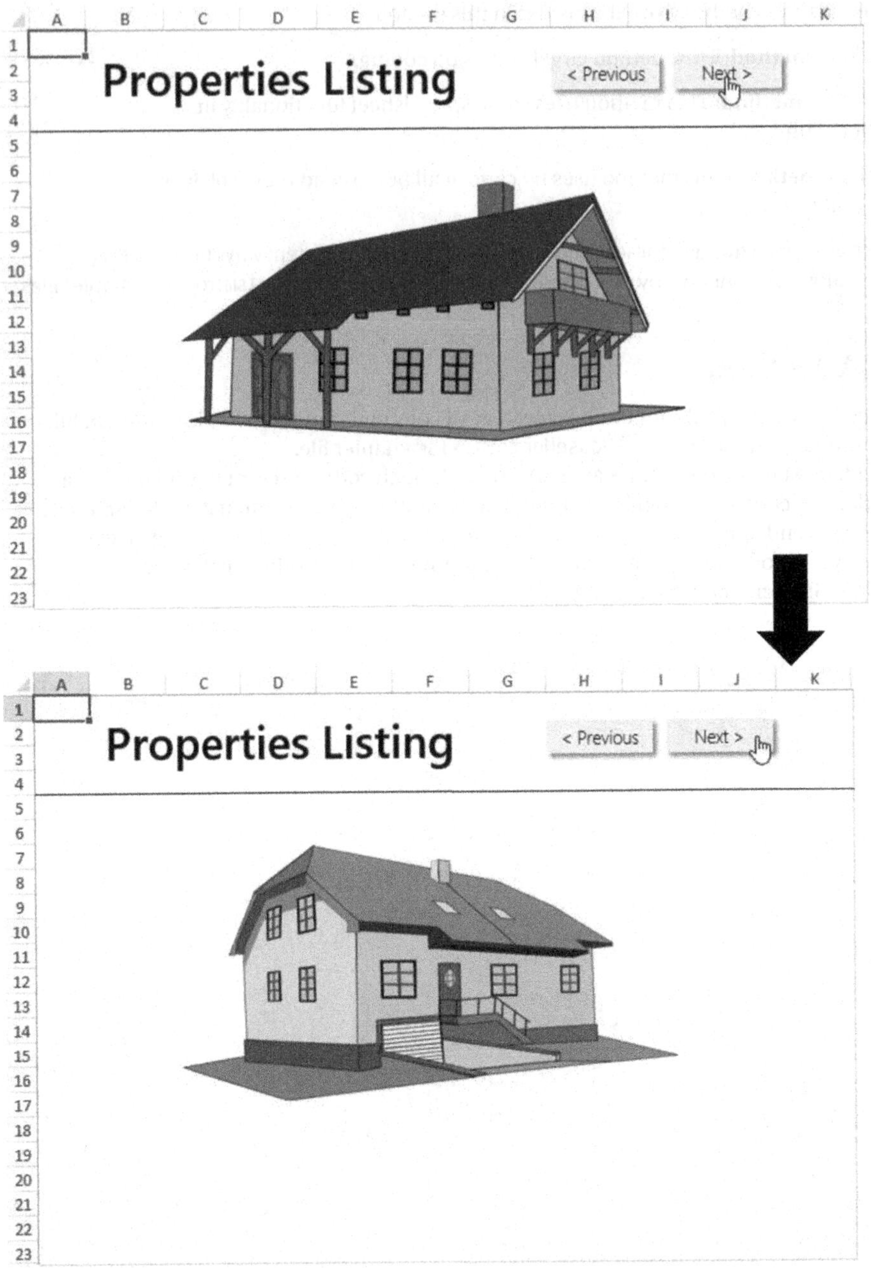

Figure 5-2. *Clicking the Next button moves to the next house available to the program. The mechanics are largely driven by VBA*

Figure 5-2 features a simple Excel application. Users can switch between properties by using the Previous and Next buttons. Both the Previous and Next buttons are simply text boxes with macros assigned to execute on a click. When the Next button is clicked, `GoNext` is called; when the Previous button is clicked, `GoPrevious` is called. Listing 5-1 displays the code for both of these methods.

I say this method is "*largely driven by VBA*" because VBA is used to upload, store, and ultimately present each picture of the house. The spreadsheet is used as a place to lay out the application, but few spreadsheet features (for example, formulas and functions, conditional formatting, and cells) are used.

Listing 5-1. The GoNext and GoPrevious Methods

```
Private CurrentHouseIndex As Integer

Public Sub GoNext()
    'Test if CurrentHouseIndex has been reset
    If IsEmpty(CurrentHouseIndex) Then CurrentHouseIndex = 0
    'Increment
    CurrentHouseIndex = CurrentHouseIndex + 1
    'Check to if the third house is already being displayed
    If CurrentHouseIndex <= 3 Then
        'Send the current index into the new image handler
        Call InsertNewImage(CurrentHouseIndex)
    Else
        CurrentHouseIndex = 3
    End If
End Sub

Public Sub GoPrevious()
    'Test if CurrentHouseIndex has been reset
    If IsEmpty(CurrentHouseIndex) Then CurrentHouseIndex = 1
    'Decrement
    CurrentHouseIndex = CurrentHouseIndex - 1
    'Check to if the third house is already being displayed
    If CurrentHouseIndex > 0 Then
        'Send the current index into the new image handler
        Call InsertNewImage(CurrentHouseIndex)
    Else
        CurrentHouseIndex = 1
    End If
End Sub
```

Notice how this code works. There are three files stored in the chapter directory that can be displayed in this program. They're `House1.png`, `House2.png`, and `House3.png`. A private variable, `CurrentHouseIndex`, keeps track of the current index of the house to be displayed. Both procedures call `InsertNewImage`, as shown in Listing 5-2.

Listing 5-2. The InsertNewImage Method

```
Private Sub InsertNewImage(Index As Integer)

    Dim OldTop      As Integer
    Dim OldLeft     As Integer
    Dim OldWidth    As Integer
    Dim OldHeight   As Integer
```

```
    Dim ShapeName   As String
    With Me.Pictures(1)
        OldWidth = .Width
        OldHeight = .Height
        OldTop = .Top
        OldLeft = .Left
        .Delete
    End With

    ShapeName = Me.Pictures.Insert(ThisWorkbook.Path & "\House" & Index & ".png").Name

    With Me.Shapes(ShapeName)
        .LockAspectRatio = False
        .Height = OldHeight
        .Width = OldWidth
        .Top = OldTop
        .Left = OldLeft
    End With

End Sub
```

The `InsertNewImage` uses the current index to decide which picture file to show. It then replaces the shape shown on the spreadsheet with the desired uploaded image. It also sets the height and width to ensure uniformity across all presented images.

It may not be so obvious, but there are several problems with this code. First, take note of the `.Delete` and `.Insert` actions in the code. There is, in fact, no method to simply select the picture as an object and link it to a new source image. You have to first delete the old image and then insert the new one. In addition, that also means you have to set the picture height, width, left, and top properties every time you change pictures.

The code also relies on the pictures being exactly where you expect them to be. In practice, you can't always be so confident this spreadsheet won't be run from a different folder.

Finally, you might also have noticed `IsEmpty(CurrentHouseIndex)` in the `IF` conditions of both the `GoNext` and `GoPrevious` subroutines. You have to do this because the variable, `CurrentHouseIndex`, is a variable created in the code. These types of variables created outside procedures are a huge pet peeve of mine (and I hope of yours by the time you're finished with this book). The problem is that these variables are essentially cleared out when Excel runs into errors (or when you open the spreadsheet for the first time). They must be initialized, and you test whether it's empty in an attempt to initialize it if hasn't already been initialized. Placing this variable in the code also prevents you from immediately seeing what the current index is at any time. In the next method, you'll see a much better alternative.

The Semi-code Method

Declaring variables outside of procedures isn't the only way to keep track of important data while still allowing for it to be exposed to other procedures. In this section, you'll see an alternative to the one presented previously, which relied largely on code.

In this section, you'll be working on the Semi-VBA tab from within the `Chapter5HouseHunters.xlsm` chapter file.

Figure 5-3 shows one of the major changes employed by this method. If you select cell A1 in the example image, you'll see that it isn't actually blank. (Sneaky, right?) The formula bar shows that it contains a value. If you move your eyes to the left of the formula bar just a few pixels, you'll see that I've given cell A1 the name `Example2.HouseIndex`. `Example2.HouseIndex` actually does what the coded variable did in the previous example: it tracks the current index of the selected property.

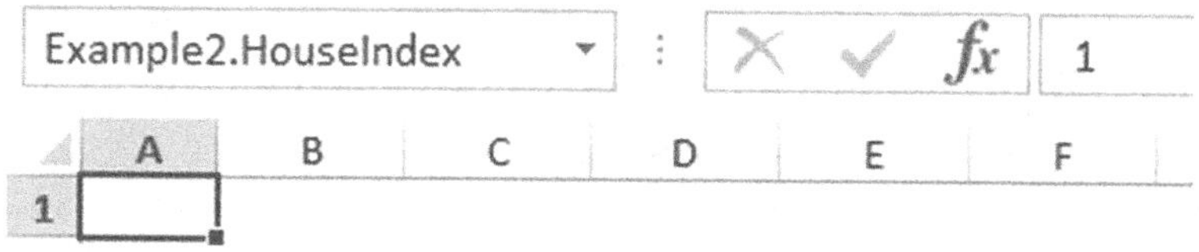

Figure 5-3. *You now use a named range to store the variable instead of a variable in the code*

This method also replaces another annoying constraint from the previous method. As you might recall, the previous method required separate images stored in a folder. But there's a way around that in Excel. And to take advantage of that workaround, you'll need to employ a rather old yet overlooked Excel feature—the Camera tool.

Say Cheese: Introduction to the Camera Tool

The Camera tool is one of the coolest features in Excel that many have not heard of. For some reason, Microsoft has tucked this little gem away from its standard toolbars. To gain access to the Camera tool button, you'll have to add it manually. First, you'll add it to your Quick Access Toolbar.

Here's what you need to do:

1. Click the File tab at the top right of the screen and select Options.
2. Click Quick Access Toolbar in the tab list.
3. In the "Choose commands from" drop-down, select Commands Not in the Ribbon.
4. Scroll down the list until you find the Camera tool, as shown in Figure 5-4. It might help your search to click the top of the list and type **C** to skip to where items starting with *C* begin.

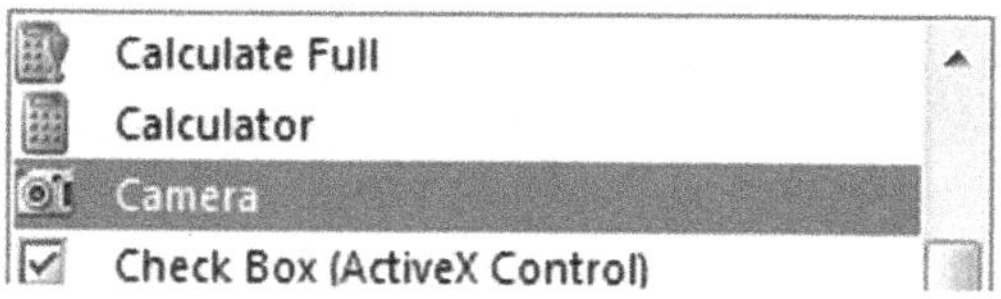

Figure 5-4. *The Camera tool shown among the list of Excel features available*

5. Click the Add ➤ button to add it to your Quick Access Toolbar list. Then click OK.

The Camera tool allows you to view any part of your workbooks as a picture. In Figure 5-5, I have a series of random numbers.

	A	B	C	D	E	F
1	1	4	5	5	4	1
2	1	5	1	4	4	2
3	5	3	1	5	1	2
4	2	5	5	3	4	1
5	1	1	1	3	3	2
6	3	3	4	5	5	4
7	3	3	3	3	5	2
8	4	5	2	4	1	1
9	2	2	3	2	4	3
10	2	4	2	2	3	5
11	4	5	2	3	3	2
12	4	3	4	4	2	2
13	2	5	4	3	5	5
14	2	5	1	4	1	4
15	1	4	3	2	1	2

***Figure 5-5.** A series of random numbers*

With the Camera tool, you can view this section of numbers anywhere else on the spreadsheet. Figure 5-6 shows a section of this series of numbers as a picture. You simply select the desired cells, click the Camera tool to take a snapshot (the desired cells will now have a border around them similar to what happens when you copy a range), and then click anywhere on the spreadsheet where you would like the desired picture of your range to appear.

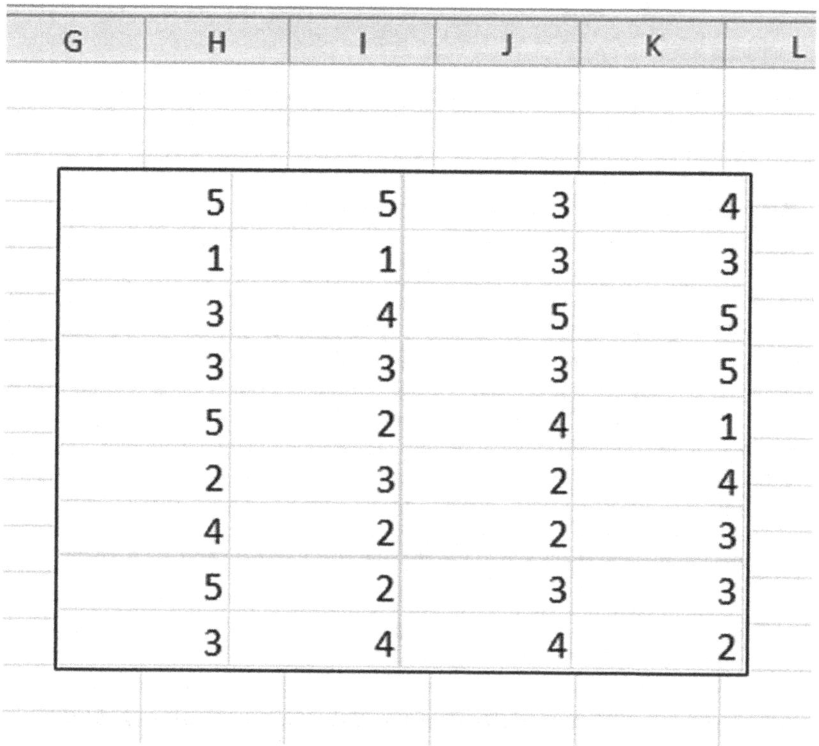

G
H
I
J
K
L
5 5 3 4
1 1 3 3
3 4 5 5
3 3 3 5
5 2 4 1
2 3 2 4
4 2 2 3
5 2 3 3
3 4 4 2

Figure 5-6. *The series of numbers shown as a picture*

Figure 5-7 shows how this works behind the scenes. The Camera tool creates a picture that's connected to the spreadsheet in a way similar to that of other formulas. The picture, as shown in Figure 5-7, is actually connected to a cell range. If you were to make changes to the numbers in that cell range, the connected picture would update immediately, similar to what would happen if the data were summed and you changed a number.

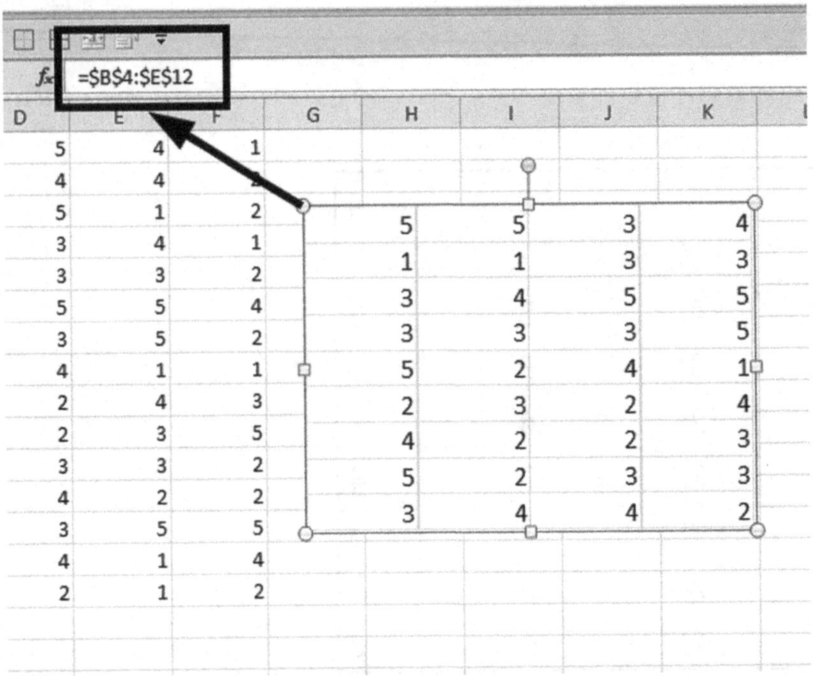

Figure 5-7. *The Camera tool allows you to create pictures of anything on the spreadsheet and works like Excel formulas*

MORE ABOUT THE CAMERA TOOL

Incredibly, the Camera tool always provides a real-time view. If you modify anything in the viewed region, the Camera will update its view automatically. You don't need to reset the connection or perform a recalculation. This makes it a versatile, plug-and-play tool.

Actually, I'll let you in on a little secret about the Camera tool, but don't tell anyone. The Camera tool and an Excel image object are actually…*the same object*. If you insert an image into your spreadsheet, you can use it just like the Camera tool! Simply select the image object and then use the formula bar to set its reference.

Using the Camera Tool

In this section, you'll take what you just learned about the Camera tool and apply it your spreadsheet. In `Chapter5HouseHunters.xlsm`, there is a worksheet tab called Pictures (Figure 5-8). Figure 5-8 shows borders around these images so that you can see their clearly defined cell regions, which represent defined named ranges. (The borders won't be in your download file because they're here for demonstration purposes only.) Figure 5-9 shows the first house and its defined region.

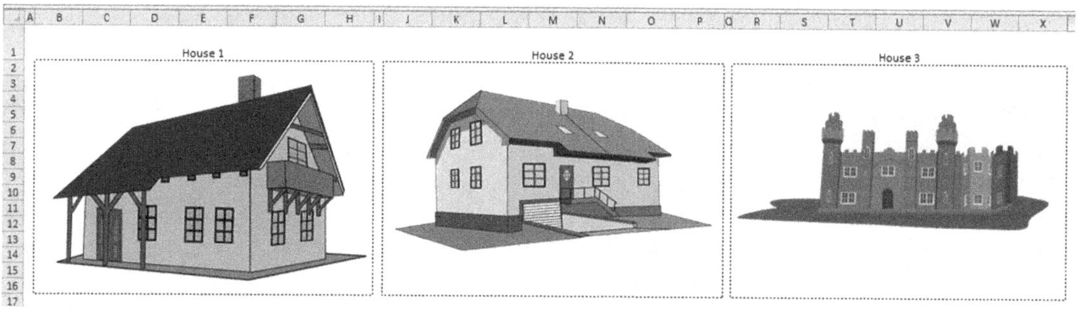

Figure 5-8. *A modified image of the Pictures worksheet tab*

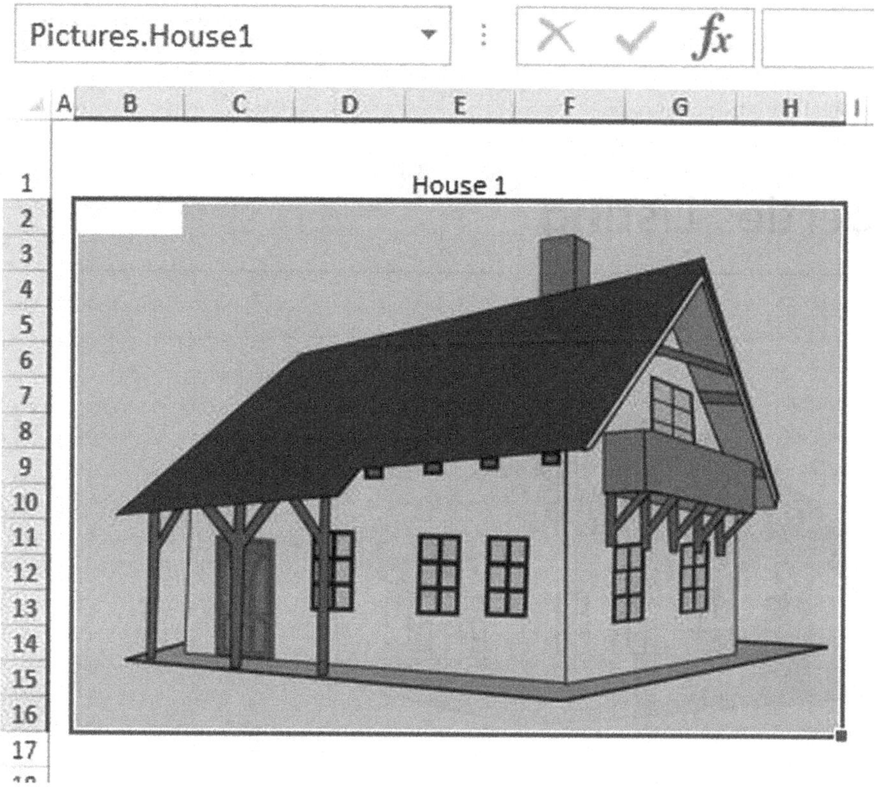

Figure 5-9. *The defined region for the first house is Pictures.House1. You can see it as a named region in the drop-down box*

To make life easier, I've gone through and named each range surrounding a house. In fact, you can also see these named ranges in the named range drop-down box (Figure 5-10). The pictures are named `Pictues.House1`, `Pictures.House2`, and `Pictures.House3`, respectively.

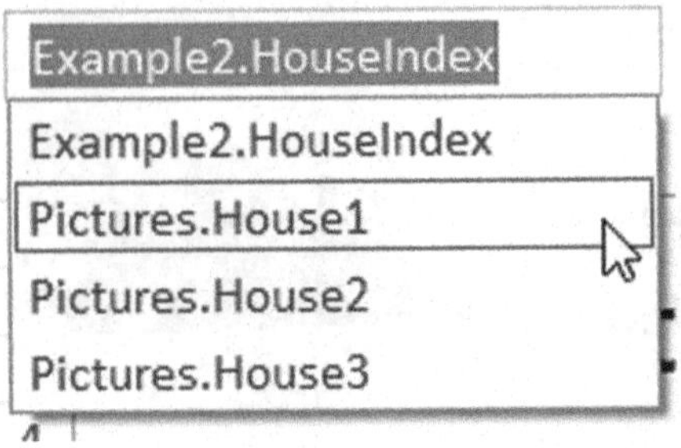

Figure 5-10. A listing of each named range

If you select the picture, you'll see in the formula bar it points to a named range mentioned previously (Figure 5-11).

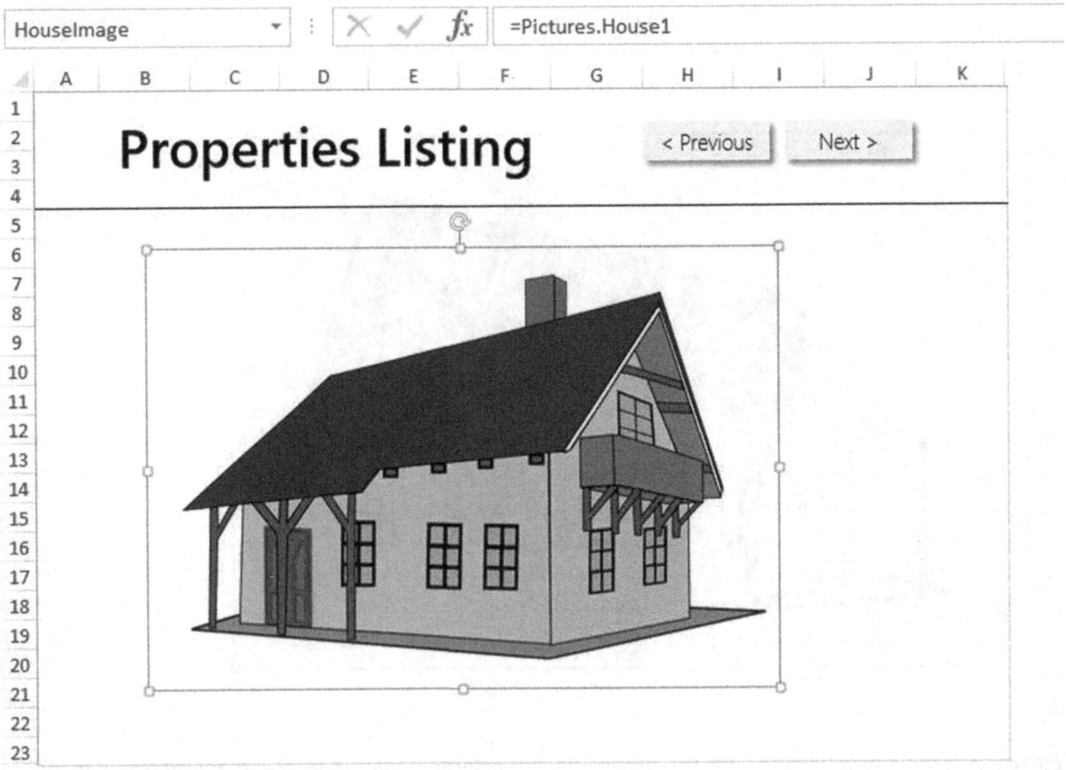

Figure 5-11. The selected image points to Pictures.House1

Notice the picture points to the ranges created around each house. In fact, this picture is simply the result of using the Camera tool. To create this effect, you add the Camera tool to this worksheet tab and then replace its formula with a desired named range. You can do this manually by typing it by hand, as shown in Figure 5-12, or you can set the range via VBA.

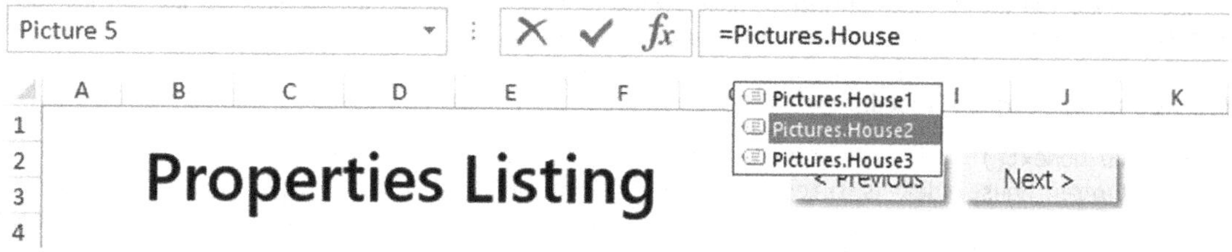

***Figure 5-12.** Setting the Camera tool formula manually by typing in the desired range*

In fact, if you click Next, you can see the image update to Pictures.House2 (Figure 5-13). This update happens using VBA. The VBA code replaces the formula used by the picture tool—you'll see this in a moment.

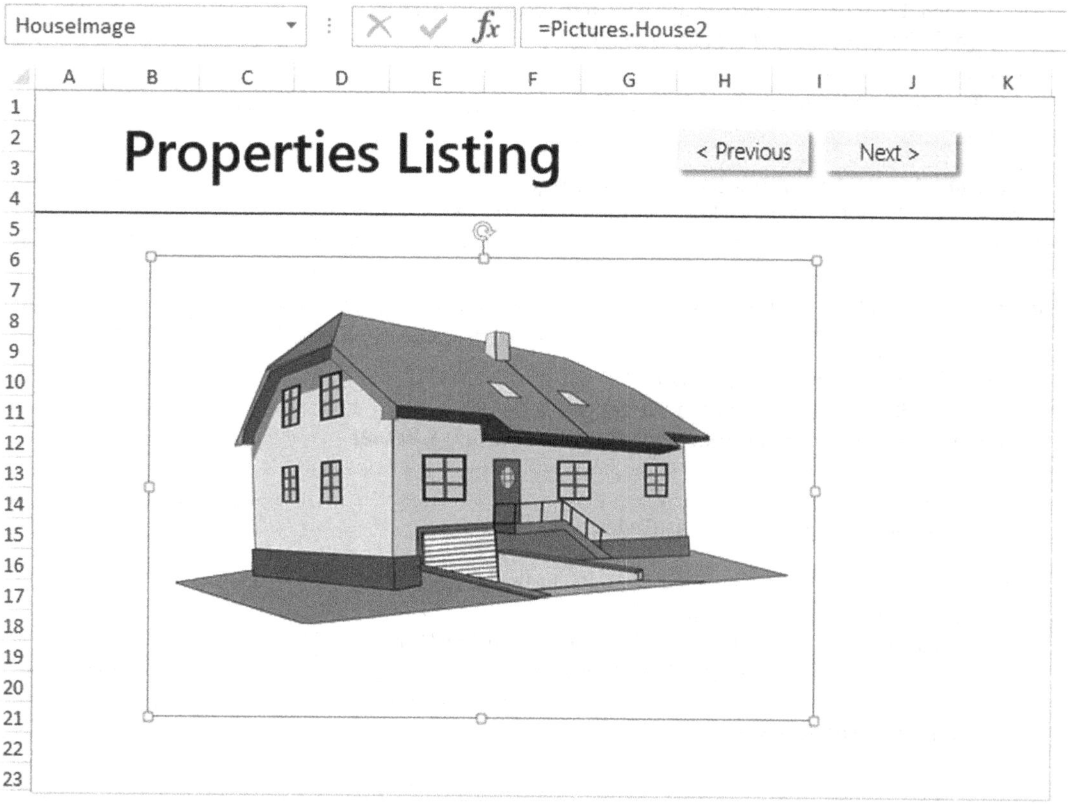

***Figure 5-13.** Upon hitting Next, the image now points to Pictures.House2*

Let's jump to the code (which is considerably smaller than the previous example). Listing 5-3 shows the GoNext procedure; Listing 5-4 shows the GoPrevious procedure.

Listing 5-3. The GoNext Procedure

```
Public Sub GoNext()
    Dim CurrentHouseIndex As Integer

    'Pull in the value from the named range
    CurrentHouseIndex = Me.Range("Example2.HouseIndex").Value2

    'Increment
    CurrentHouseIndex = CurrentHouseIndex + 1

    'Check to if the third house is already being displayed
    If CurrentHouseIndex <= 3 Then
        'Send the current index into the new image handler
        Call InsertNewImage(CurrentHouseIndex)
    Else
        CurrentHouseIndex = 3
    End If

    'Assign the updated value back to the range
    Me.Range("Example2.HouseIndex").Value2 = CurrentHouseIndex
End Sub
```

Listing 5-4. The GoPrevious Procedure

```
Public Sub GoPrevious()
    Dim CurrentHouseIndex As Integer
    'Pull in the value from the named range
    CurrentHouseIndex = Me.Range("Example2.HouseIndex").Value2

    'Decrement
    CurrentHouseIndex = CurrentHouseIndex - 1

    'Check to if the third house is already being displayed
    If CurrentHouseIndex > 0 Then
        'Send the current index into the new image handler
        Call InsertNewImage(CurrentHouseIndex)
    Else
        CurrentHouseIndex = 1
    End If

    'Assign the updated value back to the range
    Me.Range("Example2.HouseIndex").Value2 = CurrentHouseIndex
End Sub
```

These two procedures are fairly similar. They both pull in the value stored in the cell named `Example2.HouseIndex`. Like I talked about previously, this stores the current index of the house shown. The value is stored in a spreadsheet cell rather than as a private variable. This allows you to see the value at any given time—and, if the spreadsheet hits a runtime error, the value won't be cleared should you have to restart everything.

The most significant changes from the previous implementation is the InsertNewImage procedure (Listing 5-5). Let's take a look.

Listing 5-5. The InsertNewImage Procedure

```
Private Sub InsertNewImage(Index As Integer)
    Me.Shapes("imgHouse").DrawingObject.Formula = "Example2.HouseIndex" & Index
End Sub
```

Compare this code listing with that of the pure-VBA method. Here I've replaced several lines of code with just one. You form a string representing the desired range by concatenating the supplied index number with the string "Example2.HouseIndex" to form one of three named ranges defined earlier. The field DrawingObject.Formula is actually what you're setting when you manually assign an image to a specified range.

This implementation definitely addresses disadvantages presented by the first method. For one, you no longer need to keep track of where the required images are stored. Since you've loaded them on to your spreadsheet, you can feel safe knowing that they will always be within reach where you left them. However, you did have to carve out another part of the spreadsheet to store them. Specifically, because the Camera tool will show exactly what's within the defined cell region, ideally the images would be stored beyond the reach of someone who might accidentally edit or delete them.

Moreover, up until now, you haven't really considered the impact of using code on your spreadsheets. But this is a real problem to consider because some organizations prevent the transmission (and downloading) of Excel spreadsheets that contain code. At one of my previous jobs, we weren't able to send workbooks containing macros through our organization's firewall.

Might there be a way to create the desired functionality without using any VBA code? The next implementation allows for just that.

The No-Code Method

In the no-code method, you'll build upon your previous work; however, as you will see, this method may actually be the easiest to implement compared to two previous examples.

To get started, click the No-Code tab in the Chapter5HouseHunters.xlsm chapter file. At the top, you'll see I've replaced the Next and Previous buttons with a form control scroll bar (Figure 5-14). The scroll bar isn't the most elegant replacement for the sharp-looking buttons of the previous examples, but those buttons work only when they are connected to macros. (I'll go into form controls in more detail in Chapter 12.) The scroll bar, as you will see, doesn't require you to connect it to any macro.

***Figure 5-14.** The Next and Previous buttons have been replaced by a form control scroll bar*

Right-click the scroll bar and select Format Control. The Format Control dialog box appears, as shown in Figure 5-15.

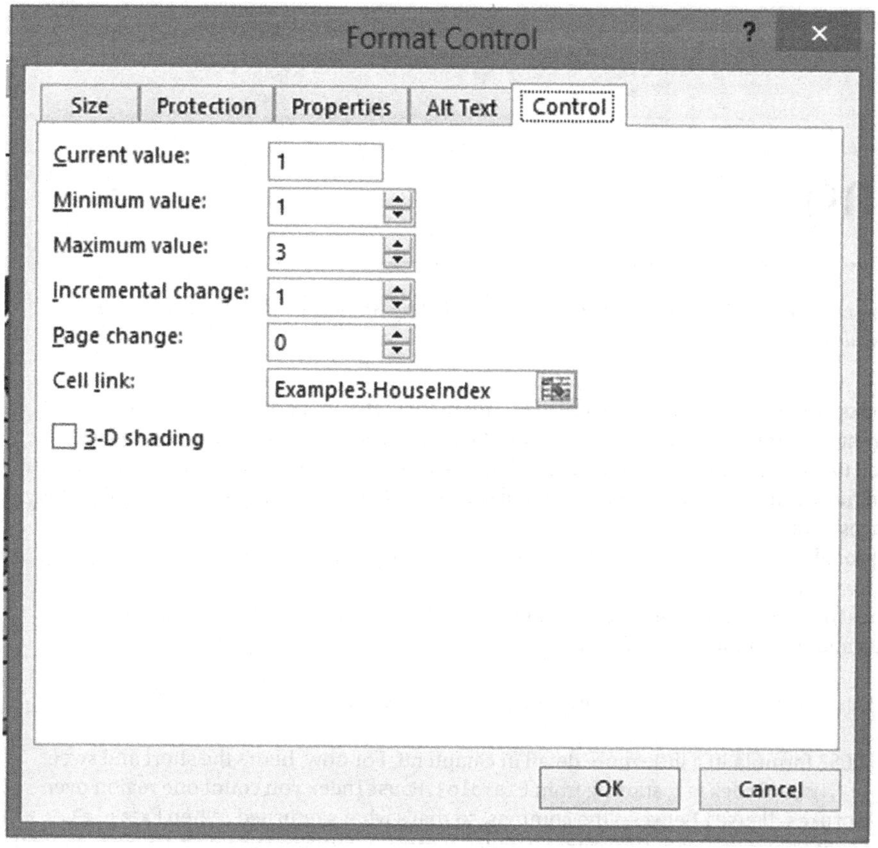

Figure 5-15. *The Format Control dialog box*

Here you can set the properties of your form control scroll bar. Minimum Value is set to 1, and Maximum Value is set to 3. This makes sense because you have only three houses to choose from. Incremental Change is set to 1 because you want the scroll bar to increase or decrease by 1 when the left and right paddles are clicked. For now, let's skip Page Change and focus on "Cell link." This is similar to a reference used with the Camera object. Just as the Camera object allows you to view the part of a spreadsheet to which it refers, likewise the form control scroll bar can "present" the value given by the named range.

Unlike the Camera tool, however, you can actually modify the value given in "Cell link" using the left and right paddles of the form control scroll bar. When you click the paddles, `Example3.HouseIndex` will actually automatically increment and decrement. Remember how you used VBA for that before?

Click OK to exit the dialog box, but don't deselect the scroll bar quite yet. Take a look at what's in the formula bar (see Figure 5-16).

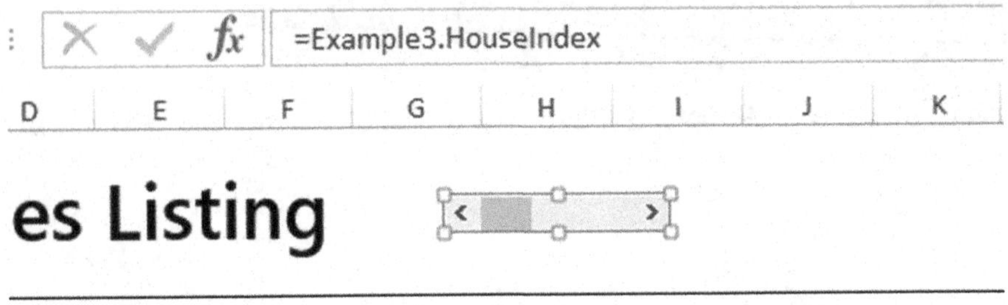

Figure 5-16. The form control scroll bar connects to the spreadsheet the same way the pictures from the Camera tool and formulas do

Hey now, that looks familiar! Like I said, the way the Camera tool references other areas of your Excel workbook is no different from the cell link mechanism found within the form control scroll bar. In fact, if you want to set the cell link quickly, simply select the scroll bar with a right-mouse click and then set the reference from within the formula bar. Nifty right? As you'll see, many Excel components work by allowing you to supply references to them.

But now you're probably wondering how you connect changes to `Example3.HouseIndex` to changing the picture of the house shown.

The answer comes in two parts. The first part is that I used the following formula to test the value of `Example3.HouseIndex` and return the correct range.

```
=CHOOSE(Example3.HouseIndex, Pictures.House1, Pictures.House2 , Pictures.House3 )
```

I'll go over the `CHOOSE` formula in a little more detail in Chapter 6. For now, here's the short and sweet version. When `Example3.HouseIndex` is 1, starting from `Example3.HouseIndex` you count one region over. In this case, you see `Pictures.House1` between the commas, so that's what's returned. When `Example3.HouseIndex` is 2, you count two regions over; `Pictures.House2` is returned. When `Example3.HouseIndexis` 3, you count three regions over...and so forth.

If you click any of the unused cells in the Example 3 tab and type the previous formula, the result will be a `#VALUE` error. So, where on the spreadsheet did I write this formula? Well, that's the thing—it's actually not stored anywhere on the sheet. Instead, I've stored it as a named range. That's the second part of the answer.

If you open the Name Manager from the Formulas tab, you can find it listed under `SelectedHouse` (see Figure 5-17).

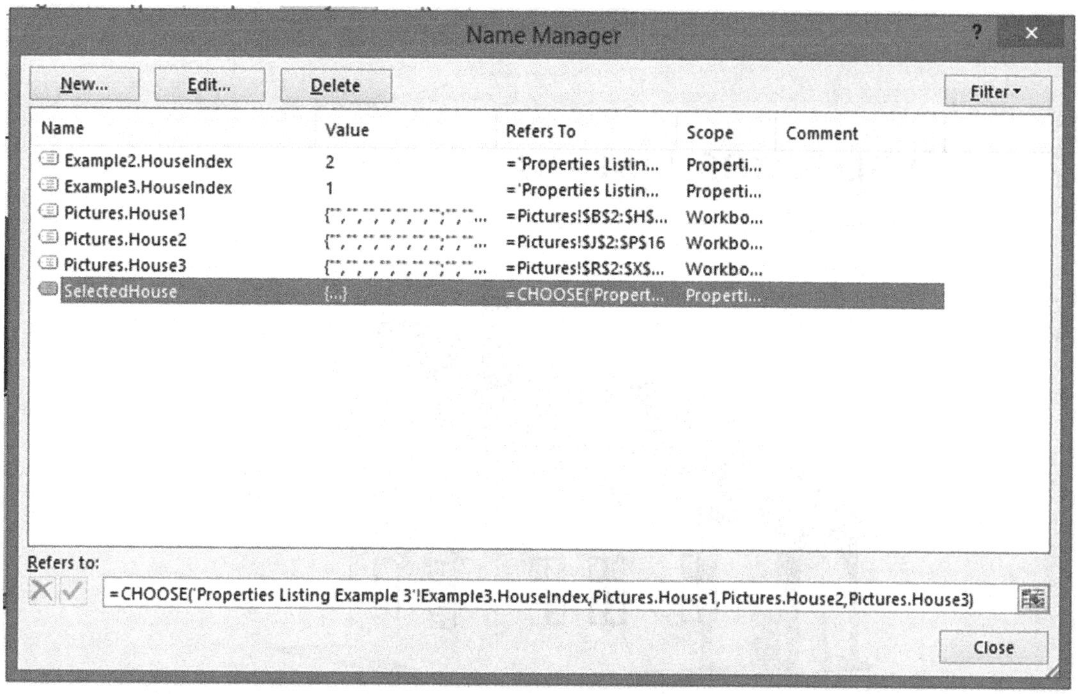

Figure 5-17. *The Name Manager shows all the named ranges on the sheet. It's where you store the CHOOSE formula*

So, now that you know the formula is stored as the named range `SelectedHouse`, guess how you change the reference for the image object? You simply tell the image to reference `SelectedHouse` (Figure 5-18). You do this by selecting the image with your mouse, going up to the formula, and typing `=SelectedHouse`.

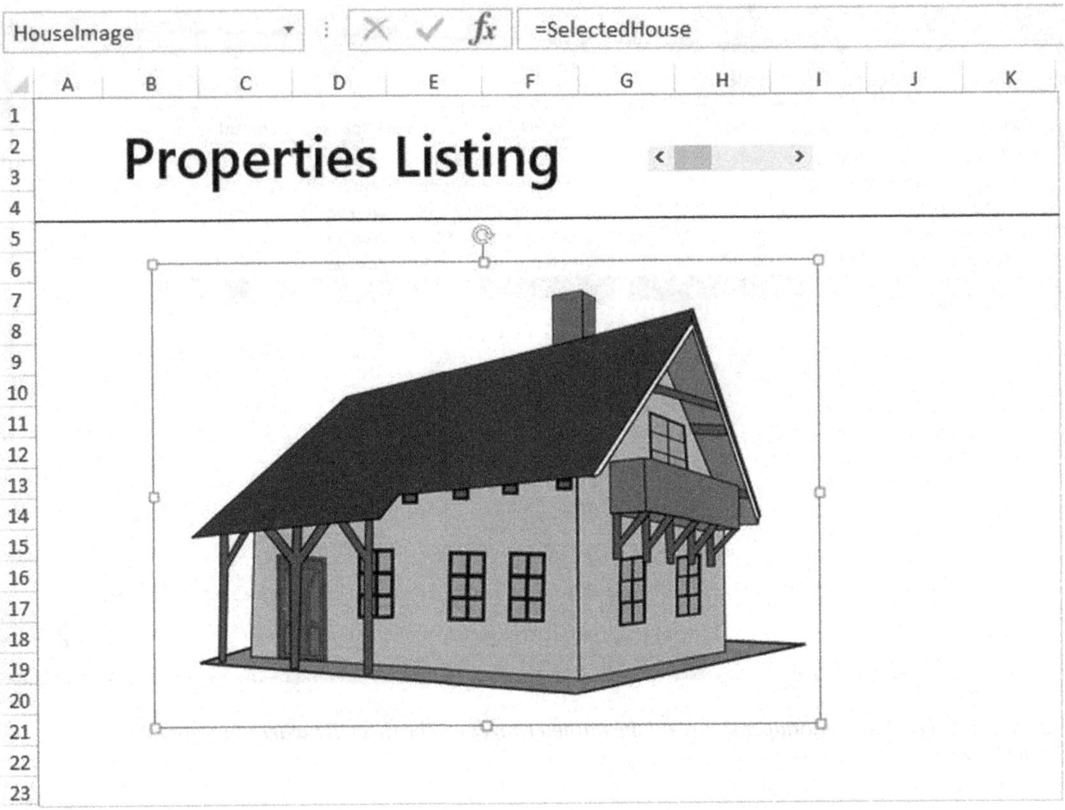

Figure 5-18. *The image now references the named range SelectedHouse, which has the CHOOSE formula telling the image which house picture to return*

To recap, these are the steps:

1. You link a form control scroll bar to the named range `Example3.HouseIndex`. Because the scroll bar is "scrolled," the change in value is reflected in `Example3.HouseIndex`.
2. You use a formula that references `Example3.HouseIndex`. A reference to a named range is returned in the formula dependent upon the value of `Example3.HouseIndex`.
3. The formula is stored as a named range, but it's not linked to any cell. Instead, the formula itself *is* the value of the named range. You call this named range `SelectedHouse`.
4. Finally, the image is set to reference `SelectedHouse`. Because the formula returns different ranges, the ranges are fed into the image.

The "no-code" method successfully delivers the capability you need at the expense of the cleaner, button-based aesthetic. Still, you should prefer the functional to the flashy; in the grand scheme, I don't believe the buttons will be missed so long as the use of the scroll bar is adequately explained. Some might even prefer the scroll bar because it effectively doubles as a progress meter from the house at the beginning of the list to the one at the end.

The "no-code" method may appear confusing at first, but in truth, you can turn it around much more quickly than that of the coding methods demonstrated prior. There are, in fact, fewer moving parts, and it won't take long to get them working. However, there isn't a good method for inline documentation when strictly using formulas. Excel's Visual Basic editor allows you to include documentation right next to your code. The no-code method does not include a mechanism by which you can annotate what's going on for yourself or for others. But, with more practice, reading exactly what a formula is doing will come easily. As well, you can still create documentation independently of your work. I don't have a specific opinion on the best way to document formulas, but sometimes I create separate file with notes like the recap previously to document what my formulas do.

The no-code method is also technically faster functionally than the other methods. If you go to one of the pervious examples, you might notice your mouse momentarily turning into a busy icon as each new picture is processed. In the no-code method, there isn't really any processing required.

Consider this example. If there were a larger list of houses, the difference would become clear as you move down the list. In the code-based methods, each mouse click on a button fires a macro to move forward. If you need to move forward five houses, you will inevitably fire the `GoNext` and `InsertNewImage` procedures five times. With a scroll bar, when you hold down one of the paddles, the value will increment and decrement as you hold it, but it won't fire any changes until you release your mouse. So, if you hold down the increase-paddle and let go once you've increased the house index by five, Excel will be given only one direction to return the range given by the index when you mouse is released.

Effectively, you've optimized the process. If there is *n* number of houses to choose from, in the worst-case scenario you'll have to fire *n* number of procedures to view the desired house using the code-based method. With the no-code method, no matter how many houses there are, there will always be one direction called. Finding ways to optimize how often Excel must process a direction or calculate a formula is essential to thinking outside the cell.

In the next section, I'll discuss novel ways to deal with sorting data on a spreadsheet.

Sorting

There are occasions where you may need to pull from a sorted list whose values are subject to change at any given moment. For example, you might have the range shown in Figure 5-19. The problem is that you need to be able to change any of these values but require that the list automatically sort each value upon a change.

	A	B	C
1	Chris	1	
2	Cathy	3	
3	Karol	3	
4	Matt	4	
5	Steve	5	
6	Mark	5	
7	Mary	9	
8	Alex	10	
9	Sam	15	
10	Joe	20	
11	Ben	22	
12	Carl	24	
13			
14			

Figure 5-19. *An example of data that would need to be sorted*

Sorting isn't a hard problem for Excel, and VBA can easily accommodate your needs. For example, to sort the previous list upon a value change, you could write something like Listing 5-6 into the `Worksheet_Change` method of the sheet.

Listing 5-6. Implementing a Sort in the Worksheet_Change Event

```
Private Sub Worksheet_Change(ByVal Target As Range)

    Application.ScreenUpdating = False

    With Me.Sort
        .SetRange Range("A1:B13")
        .Header = xlGuess
        .MatchCase = False
        .Orientation = xlTopToBottom
        .SortMethod = xlPinYin
        .Apply
    End With

    Application.ScreenUpdating = True

End Sub
```

This method basically addresses the issue, but there are caveats. For one, you need to set the `ScreenUpdating` properties to false to keep Excel from moving the selector back to the sorted range every time there is a change to the sheet. As well, you may need to use the `Worksheet_Change` event to handle other spreadsheet interactivity—do you really want your list to be sorted every time a cell is changed for the entire workbook?

Alternatively, you could employ a sorting mechanism that uses no code at all and instead relies purely on formulas. You would do this by using the `SMALL()` formula to sort ascending and the `LARGE()` formula to sort descending. The `SMALL` and `LARGE` formulas are basically the same mechanism but in reverse. You'll be using `SMALL` for this example (more on both formulas in later chapters), so for reference, the formula works like this:

```
=Small(Array, k)
```

- `Array`: An array or range of numerical data for which you want to determine the kth smallest value
- k: The position (from the smallest) in the array or range of data to return

So for the previous range, you could write `=SMALL(B1:B13, 2)`, and the result would be as follows since 3 is the second smallest value in the array:

```
3
```

Let's take a look at a new set of values, which you can find in `Chapter5SortingExample.xlsm` from the chapter files. In Figure 5-19, I've sorted the list of values in column B into column E by simply using the `SMALL` formula. For the array, I've supplied the array of values (highlighted in Figure 5-20) B2:B13. For the kth values to pull out, I've used `ROW() -1. ROW()` pulls back the current row number in which the formula resides. Since you start on row 2, you subtract 1 from it. When dragged down, the `ROW()` - 1 becomes the numbers 1 through 12. Therefore, `SMALL($B$2:$B$13, ROW() - 1)` returns the first smallest number in the series in the first row and the 12th smallest—or the largest value in the series—in the last row.

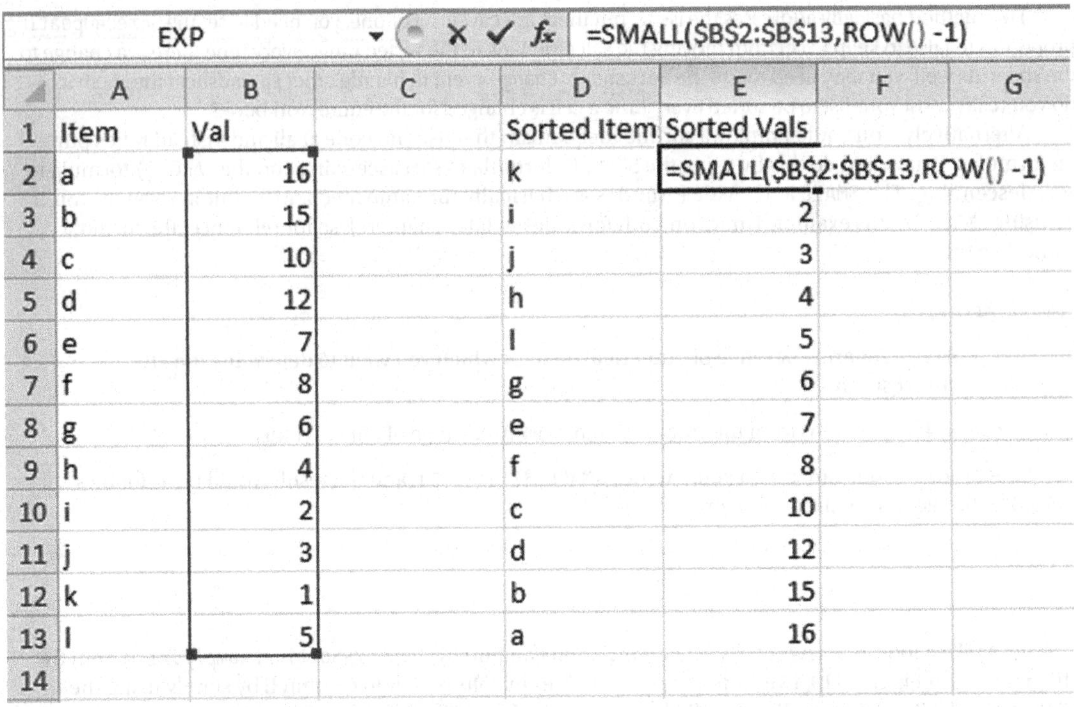
EXP =SMALL($B$2:$B$13,ROW() -1)

	A	B	C	D	E	F	G
1	Item	Val		Sorted Item	Sorted Vals		
2	a	16		k	=SMALL($B$2:$B$13,ROW() -1)		
3	b	15		i	2		
4	c	10		j	3		
5	d	12		h	4		
6	e	7		l	5		
7	f	8		g	6		
8	g	6		e	7		
9	h	4		f	8		
10	i	2		c	10		
11	j	3		d	12		
12	k	1		b	15		
13	l	5		a	16		
14							

Figure 5-20. *Using SMALL to help create a sorted listed*

However, that takes care of only the sorted values—you still need the associated item labels. To do this, you'll have to look up the locations of those values with yet more formulas. First, you'll need to find where the values in the sorted series (Column E) match up to their original placement in the unsorted series (Column B). You can do this using the `MATCH()` formula. For example, the formula `MATCH(E3,$B$2:$B$13,FALSE)` will return a location of 9. If you take a look at Figure 5-21 and start counting down nine rows from the start of B2, you'll arrive at the location of where the 2 resides. If you look to the column to the left, you'll see the item label you want.

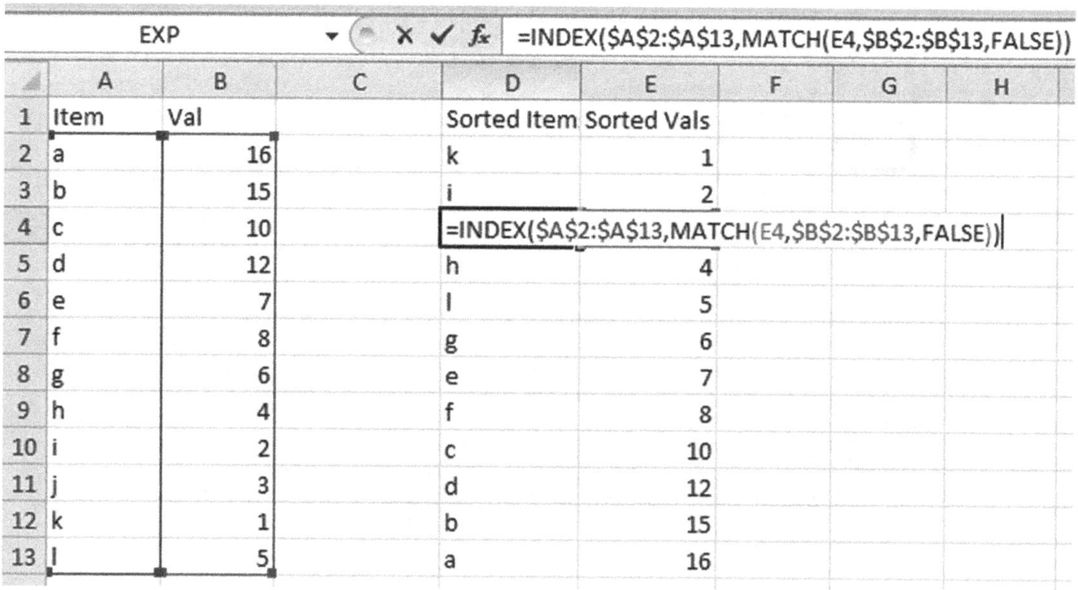
EXP
=INDEX($A$2:$A$13,MATCH(E4,$B$2:$B$13,FALSE))
Item
Val
Sorted Item
Sorted Vals
a 16 k 1
b 15 i 2
c 10 =INDEX($A$2:$A$13,MATCH(E4,$B$2:$B$13,FALSE))
d 12 h 4
e 7 l 5
f 8 g 6
g 6 e 7
h 4 f 8
i 2 c 10
j 3 d 12
k 1 b 15
l 5 a 16

Figure 5-21. *Using INDEX and MATCH to create a formula-based sorted list*

To grab this label, you'll use the `INDEX` formula, which allows you to return a value form within an array by supplying a specific location—a perfect partner to the `MATCH` formula. I've done just that in Figure 5-20.

If you're not used to using formulas in this way, this second method might appear daunting. In the first example of rotating pictures, the formula-based method had fewer moving parts—here, the formula-based method has more parts than its code-based counterpart. As well, it employs the `MATCH` formula, which is a type of lookup formula and can become costly over time to use.

There are, however, occasions in which you might prefer using only formulas. For example, by using formulas, the resulting sorted lists are separate from the initial raw data. Conversely, the first, code-based sorting method makes direct changes to the series list. Sometimes, it's a good development practice to not make direct changes to the raw data. Formulas, then, can provide the buffer to transform the original raw data without modifying it.

Now that you've seen the power of formulas, let's take a look at a novel use of both formulas and VBA code together. Enter the "Rollover Method."

The Rollover Method

I don't claim a lot of originality in my life, but as far as I know, I was the first to have discovered and written about the mechanism that serves for the basis of the Rollover Method (which I've also uncreatively titled). The Rollover Method allows for what had been previously thought impossible in Excel: the ability to run macro code upon a mouse rolling over a cell.

As far as I can tell, the Rollover Method may just be a bug, an unintended consequence that I've figured out how to exploit (which, admittedly, was entirely accidental on my part). Yet, with the Rollover Method, you can create a lot of powerful stuff. For my blog, I created the periodic table of elements shown in Figure 5-22 that allows users to roll over certain elements to see information about them. As well, users can roll over the selections on the side to highlight element classifications.

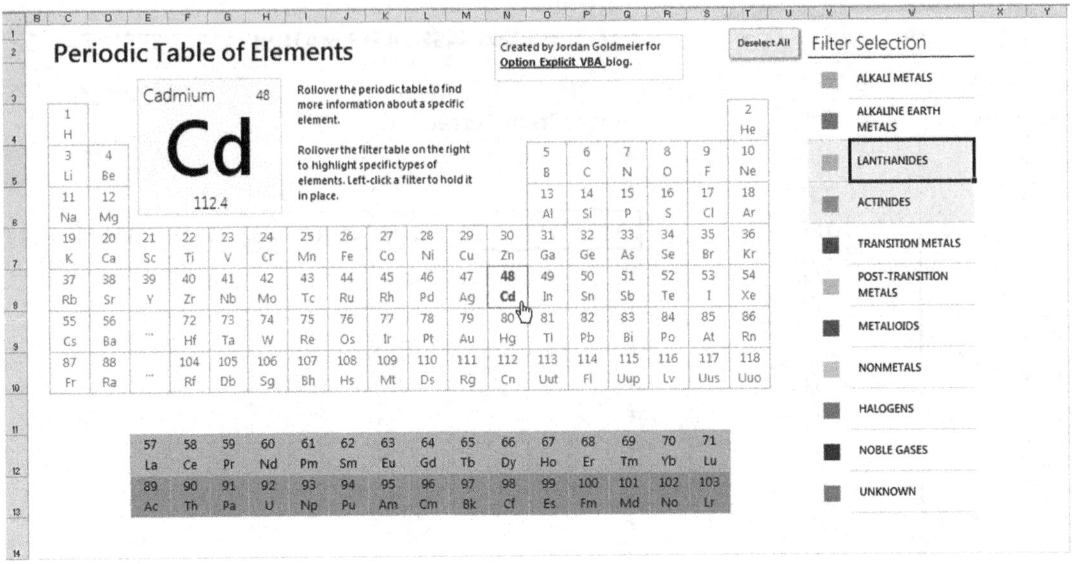

Figure 5-22. *An interactive periodic table of elements in Excel that uses the Rollover Method*

My friend Robert Mundigl of ClearlyAndSimply.com used the Rollover Method to create a dashboard that creates a pop-up bubble when a user rolls their mouse over different regions of a map of Oktoberfest (see Figure 5-23).

Figure 5-23. *When the user hovers over certain parts of the map, a pop-up is displayed with relevant details*

Rollover Method Basics

The Rollover Method uses two key components: user-defined functions (UDFs) and the hyperlink formula.

Here's a refresher on the hyperlink formula:

```
=Hyperlink(location, [Friendly Text])
```

- `location` : Here you write the intended address of your hyperlink. This can be a web page (for example, `http://www.google.com`) or a file on your computer.
- `[Friendly Text]`: This is an optional field that provides a caption to your hyperlink. If you leave it blank, it will simply display the address in the previous parameter.

As you might recall, user-defined functions are the functions that you can write within VBA modules and then use in your spreadsheet. For example, you could use the user-defined function in Listing 5-7 in your spreadsheet like in Figure 5-24.

Listing 5-7. An Example of a User-Defined Function

```
Public Function AddTwoNumbers(a As Integer, b As Integer) As Integer
    AddTwoNumbers = a + b
End Function
```

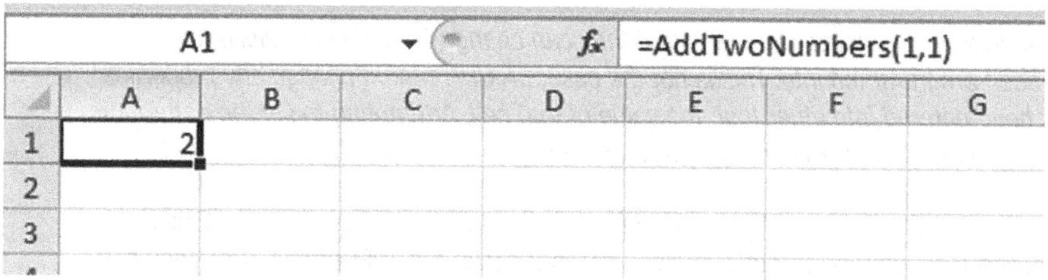

Figure 5-24. *User-defined functions can be used much like standard Excel functions*

Rollovers work by treating user-defined functions as macros that fire when your mouse moves over a cell; it's similar to how you can assign a macro to a button or shape to be fired when the user clicks it. To use one, you place the user-defined function within the `HYPERLINK` formula , like this:

```
=HYPERLINK(MyMouseOverEvent(),"Click here")
```

Although, as you will see, this is still only half the picture.

Implementing the Rollover Method

To implement the method, complete the following steps:

1. Open a new instance of Excel.
2. You're going to write a user-defined function as described earlier. So, open the Visual Basic editor from the Development tab.

3. Create or find a free module and insert a UDF that looks like this:

```
Public Function MyMouseOverEvent()
    Sheet1.Range("A1").Value = "Event Fired!"
End Function
```

4. Now, go to Sheet1 of your Excel spreadsheet and, in cell A2, type the following:

```
=HYPERLINK(MyMouseOverEvent(),"Click here")
```

Upon hitting Enter, you should get a #VALUE! error, but ignore it for a second. Roll your mouse over cell A2—and *voila*! —cell A1 should now say "Event Fired!"

WAIT, WHAT'S THE DEAL WITH THE #VALUE! ERROR?

Well, this is where life gets tricky. You see, using a UDF you were able to change the value of another cell. Technically, that's not allowed; in fact, Excel shouldn't have even let you do it. Most experts thought using a UDF to change the value of another cell was impossible. For example, in *Professional Excel Development*, the authors wrote the following:

> *One of the most common beliefs about UDFs is that they can change the value of cells other than the one they've been programmed into. This is not the case....A UDF cannot change any properties of the cell it has been entered into other than the value of that cell. Attempting to set the pattern or border of a cell from within a UDF, for example, will not work.*

And yet, that's exactly what the Rollover Method allows you to do! I suspect, however, that Excel knows that it wasn't supposed to let you do it. That's why you get that pesky #VALUE! error. Luckily, you can handle that error easily, using the `IFERROR` formula.

5. So, in cell A2, rewrite the formula to look like this:

```
=IFERROR(HYPERLINK(MyMouseOverEvent(),"Click here"), "Click here")
```

The Rollover Method turns cells into hotspots that can fire macros when your mouse rolls over them. The prototype for it is as follows:

```
=IFERROR(HYPERLINK(UserDefinedFunction, text_to_display), text_to_display)
```

The Rollover Method is useful for implementing functionality that can provide the user with details on demand. For instance, when the user hovers over a certain cell, the Rollover Method can signal a macro that will display specific information. You'll implement the Rollover Method into a dashboard later in this book.

The Last Word

I'll expound upon the previous examples at length throughout this book. Ideally, this chapter has whet your appetite for what you can build in Excel. In Chapter 1, I talked about Excel development as a journey, so let's reflect on how far you've come.

Remember the three pillars to making an awesome Excel application? I discussed optimization and using formulas to separate your work from raw data. These items fall into the area of good development practice. In the chapters previous, I talked about makes for quality data visualization. In this chapter, and throughout the book so far, I've talked about thinking outside the cell. But the journey has only just began and there's still so much more to learn.

In the next chapter, I'll delve deeper into VBA coding, once again challenging long-held conventions.

CHAPTER 6

Visual Basic for Applications for Excel, a Refresher

Of course, no advanced book on developing anything in Excel would be complete without a chapter on the interpreter language housed within Excel, Visual Basic for Applications (VBA).

This chapter won't be an introduction to VBA but rather a review of VBA programming techniques and development principles found in this book and practiced throughout most of my career. What follows may appear unconventional at first. Indeed, it may differ somewhat from what you've been previously taught. However, I don't leave you with a few instructions and no guidance. Instead, I'll explain in detail why I believe what I believe—and why you should believe as I do. If you find that you don't (and I certainly welcome disagreement), consider the other important—actually, more important—takeaway from this chapter: the code choices and styles you use should always follow from a set of principles, guidelines, and convention. When you code, do so with structure and meaning. Know *why* you believe what you believe.

But, the most important thing to do right now is to ready yourself to begin coding. This requires that you set the right conditions in your coding environment.

Making the Most of Your Coding Experience

I tend to get more done when I'm less frustrated. I'll be so daring to suggest you're probably the same way. And let's not kid ourselves: coding in VBA can be a frustrating experience. For instance, have you ever been halfway through writing an `IF` statement and then realized you needed to fix something on another line? So, you click that other line and Excel stops everything to pop up a message box saying that you've written a syntax error, like in Figure 6-1. Chances are, you already knew that. In fact, you wanted to change an earlier line in the code to prevent another error from happening.

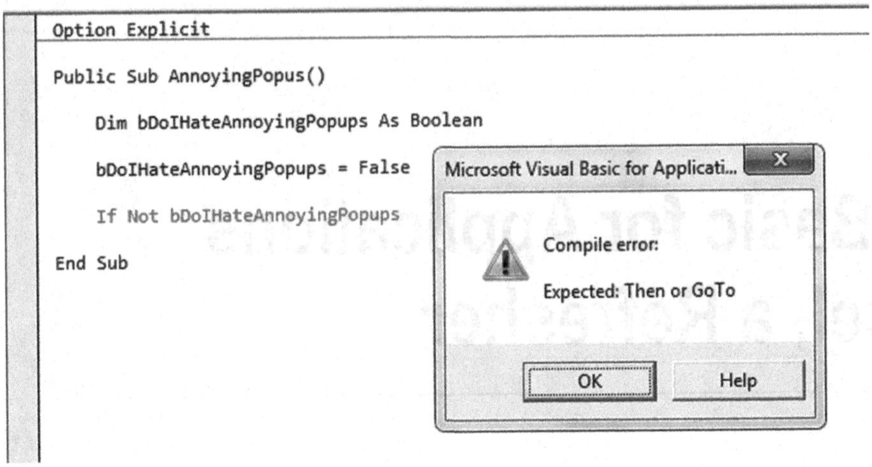

Figure 6-1. *That all-too-annoying pop-up error box telling you what you likely already know*

Tell Excel: Stop Annoying Me!

I mean, nobody's perfect, but you don't need this pop-up ruining your coding flow every time you click to another line. So, save yourself from unnecessary pop-ups by disabling Auto Syntax Check from the Options dialog box, which you access by selecting Tools ➤ Options (see Figure 6-2). This will only disable the pop-up. The offending syntax error is still highlighted in red; in other words, you don't lose any functionality, just the annoyance.

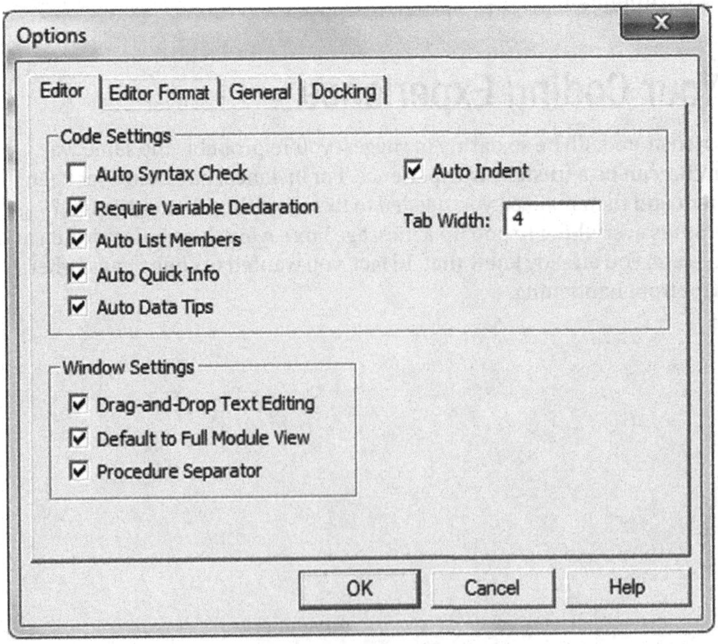

Figure 6-2. *Clear the Auto Syntax Check box for distraction-free coding*

Make Loud Comments

If you comment your code regularly—and you should—you've probably noticed comments don't "stand out" very much. In fact, I'll be the first to admit I've gone through code and missed comments because they've "blended in" with their surroundings. Figure 6-3 shows perhaps a more extreme example involving rather busy code, but the point remains: the two comment markers (') I've placed in the routine are not easily or immediately found.

```
Public Sub CommentTest()
    MsgBox "1"
    MsgBox "2          "
    MsgBox "3     "
    MsgBox "4                 "
    MsgBox "         5  "
    MsgBox "6  " '
    MsgBox "    7  "
    MsgBox "       8  "
    MsgBox "                9  "
    MsgBox "   10  "
    MsgBox "     11  "
    MsgBox "      12  "
    MsgBox "14       " '
    MsgBox "    15  "
    MsgBox "16  "
End Sub
```

Figure 6-3. *Comment markers at 6 and 14 blend in with the code*

Luckily, you don't have to use the preset colors. In fact, you can make the comments stand out. Go back to the Options dialog box from the Tools menu. Click the Editor Format tab and select Comment Text from the Code Colors list box. Below the list box you can specify the foreground and background colors, which are the text color and highlight properties, respectively (see Figure 6-4). Personally, I like using a dark blue foreground and light blue background (see Figure 6-5). You'll have to try this on your own to get the full effect; to that end and to preserve the formatting guidelines of this book, the highlight does not appear in the code listings throughout the book.

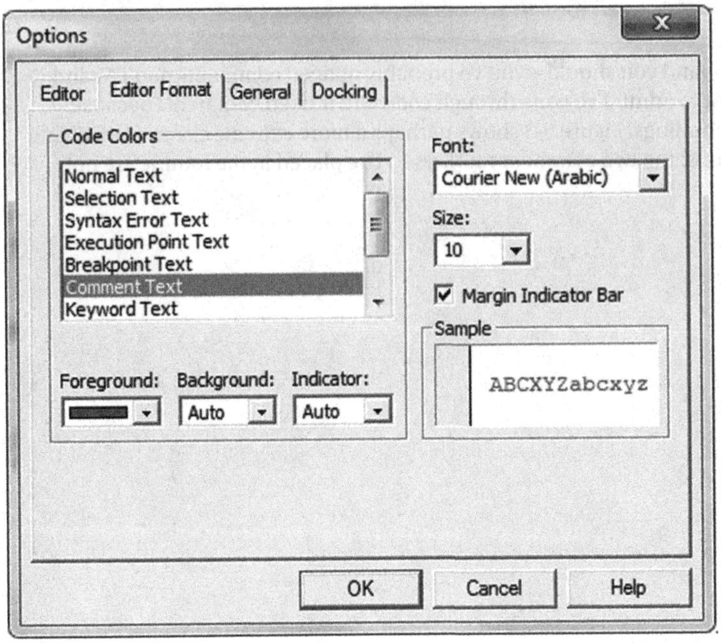

Figure 6-4. *The Editor Format tab of the Options dialog box*

```
Public Sub CommentTest()
    MsgBox "1"
    MsgBox "2          "
    MsgBox "3    "
    MsgBox "4                   "
    MsgBox "        5  "
    MsgBox "6  " '
    MsgBox "   7  "
    MsgBox "     8  "
    MsgBox "              9   "
    MsgBox "   10   "
    MsgBox "     11   "
    MsgBox "      12   "
    MsgBox "14      " '
    MsgBox "    15   "
    MsgBox "16   "
End Sub
```

Figure 6-5. *Let your comments be heard with bold colors*

Pick a Readable Font

Leave the Options dialog box open because you'll need it once more. By default, Excel uses Courier New (Figure 6-6) as its default coding font. Again, this font, like the comment style defaults, doesn't emphasize the clear readability. I prefer the font Consolas shown in Figure 6-7 because I think it does a much better job in this regard.

```
Option Explicit

Public Sub CommentTest()
    MsgBox "Try Reading this Font."
End Sub
```

Figure 6-6. *Sample code with Courier New as the font*

```
Option Explicit

Public Sub CommentTest()
    MsgBox "Try Reading this Font."
End Sub
```

Figure 6-7. *More readable text with Consolas*

You can change the font by selecting Normal Text from the list box (Figure 6-4) and using the font drop-down on the side of the dialog box. Excel gives you lots of fonts to choose from, but the best fonts with which to code are those of fixed width. So if you choose something other Consolas or Courier New, make sure to pick a readable, fixed-width font.

Start Using the Immediate Window, Immediately

The Immediate window is like a handy scratchpad with many uses. If the Immediate window is not already open, go to View ➤ Immediate Window in the Visual Basic Editor. You can type calculations and expressions directly into the Immediate window using the `print` keyword. Figure 6-8 provides some examples of typing directly into the Immediate window.

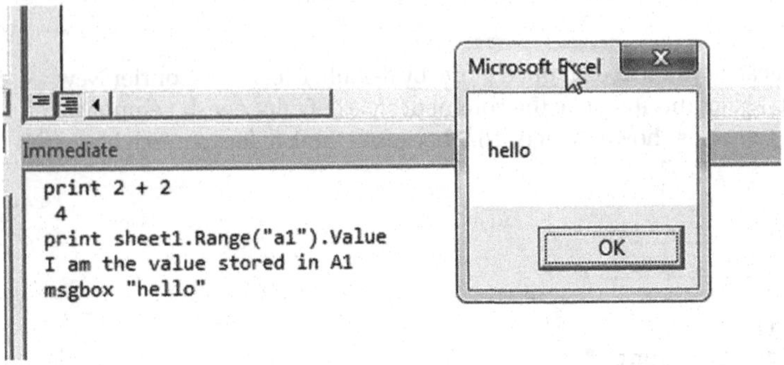

Figure 6-8. *The Immediate window*

In addition, you can also print the response of a loop or method directly into the Immediate window. To do this, use `Debug.Print`. Listing 6-1 shows you how.

Listing 6-1. Using Debug.Print to Write to the Immediate Window While in Runtime

```
For i = 1 to 100
    Debug.Print "Current Iteration: " & i
Next i
Debug.Print "Loop finished."
```

Opt for Option Explicit

VBA doesn't require you to declare your variables before using them—that is, unless you place the words `Option Explicit` at the top of your code module. Without `Option Explicit`, the `For` loop from Listing 6-1 would run without problems. When you use `Option Explicit`, you must declare all variables before they are used. In Listing 6-2, I've used the `Dim` keyword to declare the integer `i`.

Listing 6-2. A For-Next Loop with Declared Variables

```
Dim i as Integer
For i = 1 to 100
    Debug.Print "Current Iteration: " & i
Next i
Debug.Print "Loop finished."
```

If you forgo `Option Explicit`, as I did in the first instance, Excel will simply create the variable `i` for you. However, that `i` won't be an integer; rather, it will be of a *variant* type. This may not sound like such a bad thing at first, but letting Excel simply make variables for you is a recipe for trouble. What if you misspell a variable, like `RecordCount`, as I've done in Listing 6-3?

Listing 6-3. An Example of a Variable Created on the Spot Because Option Explicit Wasn't Used

```
RecordCount = 1
Msgbox RecordCout
```

Excel won't alert you to an error. Instead, it will simply create `RecordCout` as a new variable. Do you trust your ability to find misspellings in your code quickly?

In practice, I've found using `Option Explicit` alleviates many potential headaches. So, do yourself a favor; in the Option dialog box (Tools ➤ Options), set Require Variable Declaration to Excel to automatically (and proudly) display `Option Explicit` at the top of every module. And when the error in Figure 6-9 appears, give yourself a pat on the back for not having to scour your code to find your misspellings.

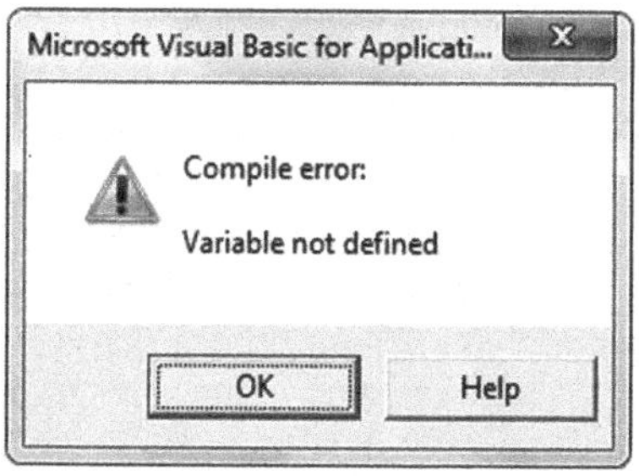

Figure 6-9. *Breathe a sigh of relief! You have Option Explicit on the case!*

Seriously, I can't tell you how important `Option Explicit` is. I'd repeat "Always use `Option Explicit`!" 1,000 times here if I could. But I'll just let Excel do it for me instead. Paste the following formula into an empty cell before moving to the next section:

```
=REPT("Always use Option Explicit! ",1000)
```

Naming Conventions

A naming convention is a common identification system for variables, constants, and objects. By definition, then, a good naming convention should be sufficiently descriptive about the content and nature of the thing named. In the next subsections, I'll talk about two naming conventions. The first, Hungarian Notation, is the most common notation used for VBA coding. Indeed, I'm unaware of any book that has argued against its use—that is, until now. The second, my preferred notation, is what I call "loose" CamelCase notation, and it's been the standard for just about all modern object-oriented languages.

Hungarian Notation

In this section, I'll talk about Hungarian Notation. In this notation, the variable name consists of a prefix—usually an abbreviated description the variable's type—followed by one or two words describing the variable's function (for example, its reason for existing). For example, in Listing 6-4, the `s` before `Title` is used to indicate the variable is of the `String` type. The term *title*, as I'm sure you can guess, describes the string's *function*—in other words, its reason for existing.

Listing 6-4. An Example of Hungarian Notation

```
Dim sTitle as String
sTitle = "The new spreadsheet!"
```

Table 6-1 shows some suggested prefixes for common variables and classes.

Table 6-1. *Prefixes Suggested by Hungarian Notation*

Prefix	Data Type
B	Boolean
D	Double
I	Integer
S	String
V	Variant
Rng	Excel.Range
Obj	Excel.Object
Chrt	Excel.Chart
Ws	Excel.Worksheet
Wb	Excel.Workbook

In this book, I will discourage the use of Hungarian Notation in your code. I'm not here to tell you that Hungarian Notation is terrible because it does have its uses. For instance, VBA code isn't known for having strict data type rules. This means you can assign integers to strings without casting from one type to the other. So, including the type in a variables name isn't a terrible idea at all.

But much of this type confusion can be resolved by using descriptive and proper variables names, as you'll see in the next few pages. For now, however, it's a good idea to at least familiarize yourself with Hungarian Notation if you haven't done so already. Hungarian Notation is still widely used in VBA to this day, so it's important that you can read it proficiently even if you decide in this moment to never use it again. (Good choice!)

The fact is, Hungarian Notation is old. Indeed, in many ways, it's a relic of a bygone era—namely, the era in which people still used Visual Basic 6.0. (Those were the days, right?) In fact, Microsoft's Design Guidelines for .NET libraries has discouraged its use for more than decade. So, what I'm proposing in this next section might feel new, but it's actually been around for quite some time.

"Loose" CamelCase Notation

In this section, I'll talk about CamelCase notation as my preferred alternative. CamelCase notation begins with a description (with the first letter in lowercase when it's a local, private variable) and usually ends with the object type *unabbreviated*. For example, the variable in Listing 6-5 refers to a chart on a worksheet for sales.

Listing 6-5. A Demonstration of CamelCase Notation

```
Dim salesChart as Excel.Chart
Set salesChart = Sheet1.ChartObjects(1).Chart
```

I'll be honest and admit I'm not always such a stickler about that lowercase descriptor, which is why I call my use of this notation "loose." The important takeaway when using this notation is to use *very descriptive names*. It's unlikely a variable name like `ChartTitle` will be confused for an integer in your code. Whether it's `recordCount` or `RecordCount`, you'll likely understand that count refers to a non-negative integer. Variables that represent objects should end with the object name *unabbreviated*. Notice in Listing 6-5 that the variable name ends with `Chart`. Ranges should end with `Range`, and so on.

Descriptive names are important. Use a variable name that describes what the variable does so that when you come back to it later, you can remember what you did. If you have a test variable, then (please, for the love of God) call it `test`; don't just call it `t`. It's OK to use `i` in a `For/Next` loop where the `i` is simply an iterator and is not used later in the code, but don't name variables used to count objects with short names like `i`, `j`, `k`, `a`, `b`, or `c`. Finally, there's really no good reason to use an underscore in your variable names. They're not easier to read.

Named Ranges

As I said, naming convention goes beyond just VBA. Indeed, a proper naming convention should be applied to all Excel objects, including those that reside on a spreadsheet. Therefore, in this section, I'll talk about naming objects on the spreadsheet in the form of named ranges.

It's rather common to see Excel developers use the prefix `val` to refer to named cell ranges. This prefix is an attempt to extend the Hungarian Notation principles into the physical spreadsheet (as if you haven't already had enough of it!). However, I still prefer a more modern approach. Specifically, what I like to do is combine the name of the tab and the function of the variable to be more object-oriented. Figure 6-10 shows a good example of what I mean.

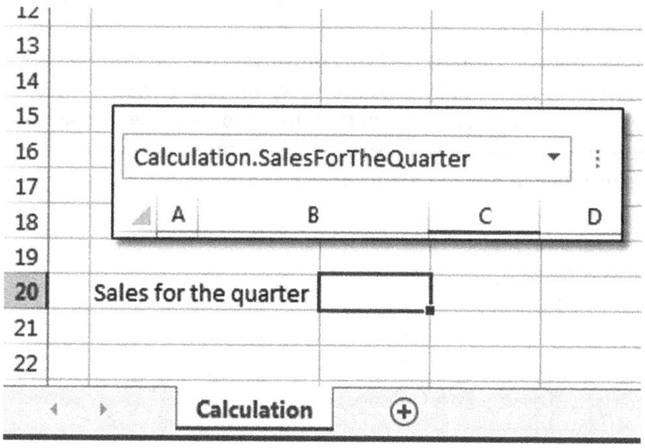

Figure 6-10. *An object-oriented-like naming convention for named ranges*

In Figure 6-10, the name of the tab is combined with the variable. Aside from being more object-oriented-ish, this type of naming brings other distinct advantages. For one, you can more easily and logically group named ranges that exist on the same worksheet tab. In addition, as you'll see in the next section, this type of convention works well when interfacing between named ranges and VBA.

Sheet Objects

In this section, I'll focus on naming conventions for sheet objects. There's one property of the sheet object that I'm a big fan of changing, and it's the name of the object itself. When you change the name of a worksheet tab on the spreadsheet, you're actually changing the name of the tab (think of it as changing a caption); you are not, in fact, changing the name of the worksheet object.

If for nothing else, changing the name of the worksheet object is a great way to clear up confusion when looking at the Project Explorer window. For example, Excel seems to have a problem keeping the names of worksheet tabs and the names of the objects themselves straight, as I'm sure you've noticed before. Take a look at Figure 6-11 to see what I mean.

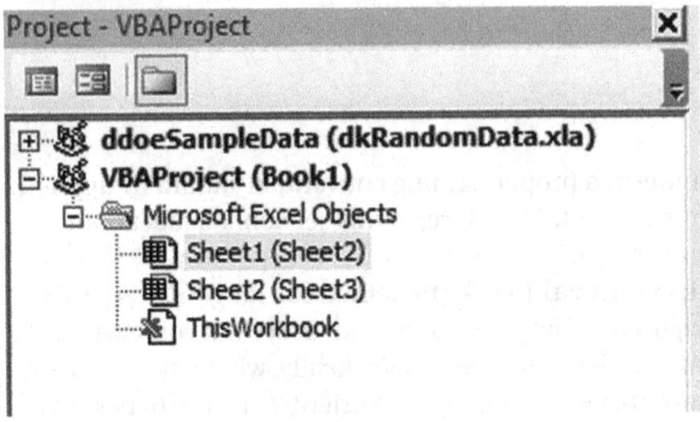

***Figure 6-11.** The Project Explorer demonstrating a lack of consistency when it comes to worksheet object and tab names*

The *object* name is the item outside the parentheses; the tab name is the one inside the parentheses. If I were to write `MsgBox Sheet1.Name` in the Immediate window, I would see a response of "Sheet2."

To change the name of the object, go to the Properties window from within the editor (View ➤ Properties Window, if it's not already visible) and change the line that says (Name). In Figure 6-12, my worksheet tab's caption is Financial Data, so I'm going to change its object name to FinancialData.

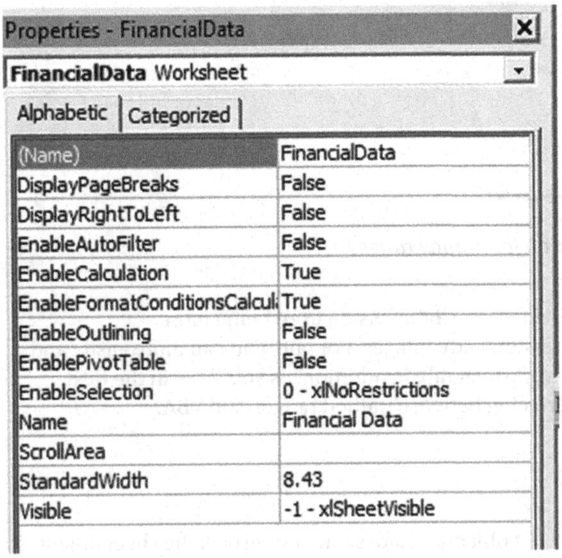

***Figure 6-12.** The Properties window showing how to change the worksheet object's name*

YES, I KNOW IT'S CONFUSING

If you look at the Project Explorer (Figure 6-11), you'll see that the worksheet object name comes first and the tab name follows in parentheses. The Properties window appears to do just the opposite; the first name in parentheses, "(name)", refers to the object's name, while the second name item (under Enable Selection) refers to its name as it appears on the tab. Why did Microsoft choose to do it this way? Your guess is as good as mine.

Referencing

In this section, I'll talk about referencing. *Referencing* refers to interacting with other worksheet elements from within VBA code and also on the worksheet. This is where a good naming convention and a proper coding style really make the difference.

Let's take a made-up named range concerning cost of goods sold. Hungarian Notation proponents would give the named range something like `valCoGS` (CoGS = cost of goods sold). The notation I suggest would combine the tab name with a nicely descriptive title (you could make it shorter if you'd like, but I like long titles), something like `IncomeStatement.CostOfGoodsSold`. So, let's take a look at why you might prefer a long named range such as this.

Shorthand References

This section discusses shorthand references, a syntax you can use in your code to refer to a named range on a sheet. Here is where the advantage of the latter notation proves its worth. As you know, you can refer to a named range through the sheet object where the name resides (technically, you can refer to it through any sheet object, but only on the worksheet in which it was created will it return the correct information). So, the typical way to read from or assign to the COGS named range mentioned earlier using Hungarian Notation might look like this:

```
Worksheets("Income Statement").Range("valCoGS").Value
```

On the other hand, if you use my method, you can employ the shorthand range syntax as follows:

```
[IncomeStatement.CostOfGoodsSold].Value
```

That's right! These two lines of code mean and do the same thing. Now, which do you think is easier to read and is more descriptive of what it represents? Which more easily captures the worksheet in which it resides? Which would you rather use in your code?

So, before you go off using the shorthand notation for everything, I should point out a significant caveat. Using the shorthand brackets method can become, in certain situations, slow. Technically, it's a slower operation for Excel to complete than using a worksheet object. However, you would really notice this only if you used the shorthand notation during a long and computationally expensive loop. For typical code looping, you're not likely to see the difference, but if you're looking to speed things up in a loop, it's best to forgo the shorthand.

Worksheet Object Names

In the previous section, I showed you how to change worksheet object names. In this section, you'll see why I think it's such a good idea.

Think about what you can do with this change. Because the new name reflects some descriptive information about the worksheet tab, you can use the object instead of the `Worksheets()` function to return the one you're interested in. Confused? Let's take a look. Here's the old way, which takes in the worksheet's tab name to return the worksheet object:

```
Worksheets("Income Statement").Range("A1")
```

And here's what you can do instead:

```
IncomeStatement.Range("A1")
```

Again, which do you think easier to understand and work with?

Procedures and Macros

In this section, I'll talk about the benefit of changing sheet names on procedures. Once you've changed the procedure name, you can also place your macro into the sheet object.

Take a look at how cleanly these procedures appear in the Macro dialog box versus the ones housed in a sheet object with a default name in Figure 6-13. In addition, if you want to call a public procedure stored in a sheet object, you can simply write `IncomeStatement.CalculateNetTotal` from within the code of another sheet object (or module) in Excel. I'll talk about the benefits of storing a procedure in a sheet object (versus a module) in the next section.

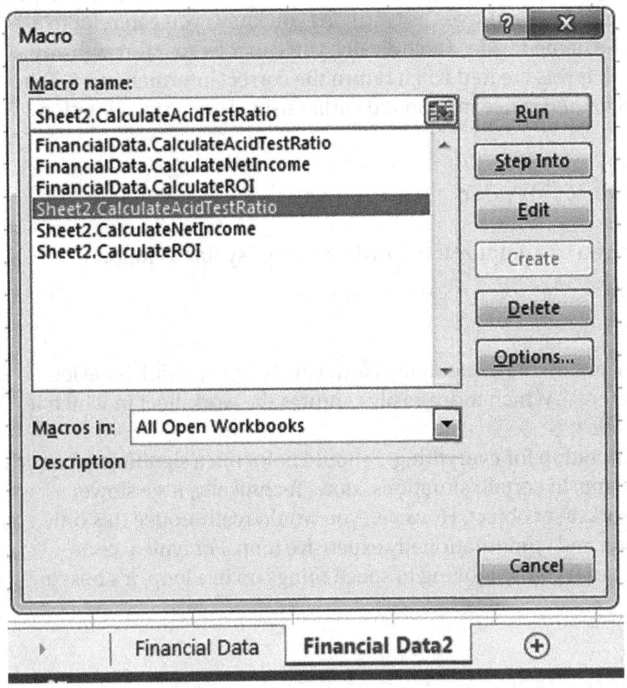

Figure 6-13. *A demonstration of changing worksheet tab names and storing procedures therein*

Development Styles and Principles

Now that you've set up your coding environment and I've talked about naming conventions, I need to talk about development styles and principles. The following sections cover simple coding guidelines that if you stick to, you'll be creating self-contained, easy-to-follow code and designs in no time. The first principle follows naturally from the previous section.

Strive to Store Your Commonly Used Procedures in Relevant Worksheet Tabs

If you're an avid user of the macro recorder, you know that Excel writes what you do to an open module. In many ways, a module feels like a natural place for a procedure. But ask yourself, is there any real reason why you're storing the procedure there?

The problem with storing your procedures in a module is that it creates really sloppy code. I know what you're thinking: how dare I say that! You separate your modules into different logical pieces. The items inside each of your well-named modules are relevant to one another. Chances are, though, the procedures in your model are used by only one or two spreadsheets. If that's the case, why not store the procedures in the worksheet objects themselves?

Consider this example I've seen time and time again. You have a Main worksheet tab that acts as a menu to direct users to several other worksheet tabs. Then, in each of these tabs, you have a button that takes users to the Main worksheet. Let's use the tabs from Figure 6-14 for this example.

Figure 6-14. *A common spreadsheet layout in which Main acts a menu to take users to each tab*

If you create this direction mechanism via the module method, you get ugly navigational code like in Listing 6-6. I also assume in Listing 6-6 that you're doing some type of processing work where the user goes from a different worksheet tab back to Main.

Listing 6-6. Ugly Navigational Code

```
' Links from Main screen
Public Sub From_Main_Goto_Config()
    Worksheets("Config").Activate
End Sub
Public Sub From_Main_Goto_Edit()
    Worksheets("Edit").Activate
End Sub
Public Sub From_Main_Goto_View()
    Worksheets("View").Activate
End Sub
Public Sub From_Main_Goto_Options()
    Worksheets("Options").Activate
End Sub
```

```
'Link back to Main from each screen
Public Sub From_Config_Goto_Main()
    .
    .
    .
    Worksheets("Main").Activate
End Sub
Public Sub From_Edit_Goto_Main()
    .
    .
    .
    Worksheets("Main").Activate
End Sub
Public Sub From_View_Goto_Main()
    .
    .
    .
    Worksheets("Main").Activate
End Sub
Public Sub From_Option_Goto_Main()
    .
    .
    .
    Worksheets("Main").Activate
End Sub
```

What do I mean by ugly? Well, creating this mechanism in a module requires you to use funky procedure names to differentiate one from the other. And just take a look at what each of these procedures look like in the Macro dialog box (Figure 6-15). Each of these names looks so similar. It would be easy to accidentally assign the wrong macro. (Are you nodding your head because you've done it before? I know your pain.) In addition, even if you store procedures in separate modules, there's nothing in the Macro dialog box to differentiate this type of organization.

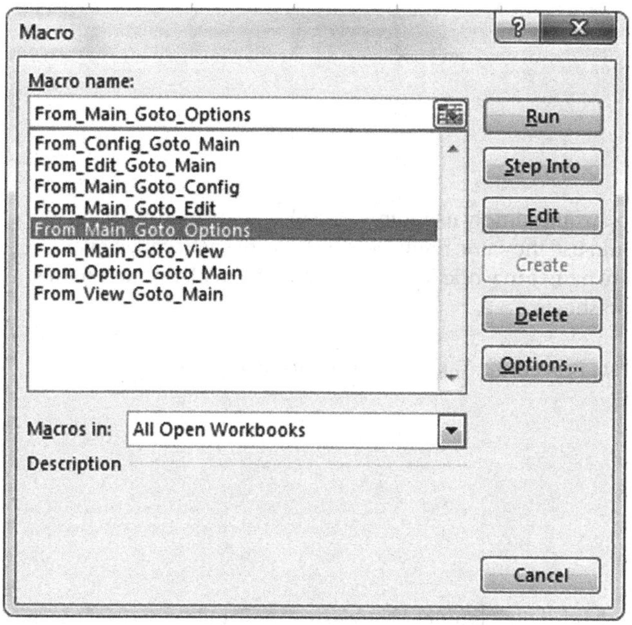

Figure 6-15. *A mess in the Macro dialog box*

But now, let's take a look at my suggested improvements (including changing the worksheet names shown previously). You can store the procedures that take you from the Main tab to other worksheet tabs in the Main worksheet object (Figure 6-16).

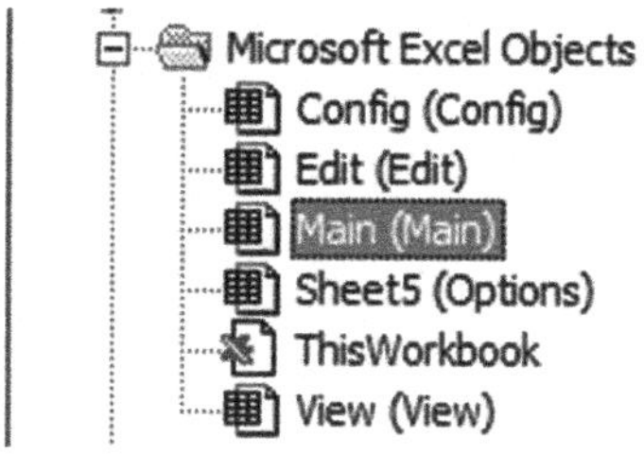

Figure 6-16. *A view from Project Explorer when the worksheet object names are changed*

As well, you can use much cleaner-looking procedure headings, as shown in Listing 6-7.

Listing 6-7. Cleaner Code Now Stored in the Main Worksheet Object

```
Public Sub SendToConfig()
    Config.Activate
End Sub
Public Sub SendToEdit()
    Edit.Activate
End Sub
```

```
Public Sub SendToView()
    View.Activate
End Sub
Public Sub SendToOptions()
    Options.Activate
End Sub
```

Next, in each separate worksheet object you would simply use something like the procedure in Listing 6-8. As a matter of proper style, you should use the same name, `BackToMain`, in each worksheet object. Remember, unlike in modules, procedure names in worksheet objects aren't global. Because of this, you can use the same name across different worksheets.

Listing 6-8. BackToMain Stored in Each Separate Procedure; Takes the User Back to the Main Page

```
Public Sub BackToMain()
.
.
.
    Main.Activate
End Sub.
```

Take a look at Figure 6-17. As you can see, each procedure is much easier to read and understand right away from within the Macro dialog box. In addition, notice how you've made the code more object-oriented-like. Each tab to which you can navigate from Main shares the same procedure. It's as if they are of a similar class. When you add extra procedures to the worksheet (but keep the one sending users back home), you are *inheriting* the features of each sheet and then adding new ones to it.

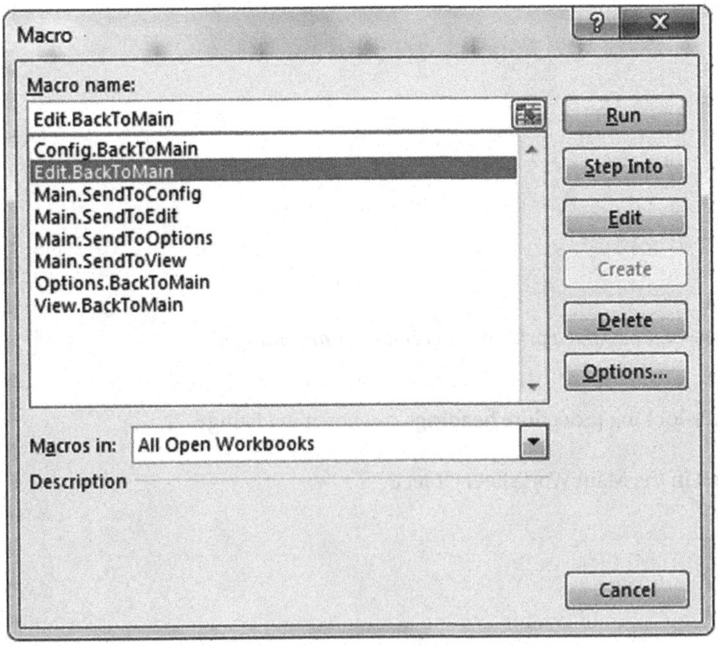

Figure 6-17. *The Macro dialog box showing a much cleaner presentation and organization of code and procedure names*

And another thing . . .

You thought I was done complaining about putting procedures in modules, didn't you? Well, I'm not. There's another problem I need to address head-on in this section. So, let's do that by taking a quick survey. Grab a pen to mark down your answers. If this is a library book, upon returning the book, tell them you found it this way.

THE ACTIVE OBJECT STRESS TEST

Circle all that apply.

I ran a macro that uses the `Selection` object. However, I (or the user) selected the *wrong* worksheet item (either manually or in the code) and accidentally made undoable changes to everything. This makes me feel

a. Annoyed
b. `REPT("I want to scream!", 1000)`
c. Like I never want to use the `Selection` object again

I ran a macro that uses the `ActiveSheet` object, but accidentally I was looking at the wrong sheet before running the macro. Also, I forgot to save everything before running the macro, so now I have start over. I feel

a. Exhausted
b. `REPT("I want to scream!", 1000)`
c. Totally done using `ActiveSheet`, forever

I ran a macro that uses `ActiveCell`, but the wrong cell was selected for some unforgivable reason. The code made changes to that cell and a whole bunch of cells around it. Unwittingly, I ended up making incorrect and undoable changes to the entire spreadsheet. I feel

a. Terrible
b. `REPT("I want to scream!", 1000)`
c. So over using `ActiveCell`

Now take a look at your answers. If you circled C for any of the previous questions, you're in luck. I have some really great news for you in the next section.

No More Using the ActiveSheet, ActiveCell, ActiveWorkbook, and Selection Objects

You don't need these objects; in this section, you'll see why. It's often the case that coding inside a module encourages you to use these objects since the procedures themselves aren't worksheet-specific. But if you're already working inside the procedure (as I suggested earlier), you can use the `Me` object. `Me` is always the container object in which your code is housed. For example, if the following code were in Sheet1, the `Me` object refers to Sheet1.

```
Me.Range("A1").Value = "Hello, Me!"
```

That's not all, either. You can use `ThisWorkbook` instead of `ActiveWorkbook` to ensure you are always modifying the workbook in which your code resides. If you want to modify a cell, address it directly like I've done in the previous code. If you want to refer to a chart or shape, why select it first? Which gets to the point more easily, Listing 6-9 or Listing 6-10?

Listing 6-9. Using Selection and Active Objects

```
ActiveWorkbook.Worksheets("Sheet1").Activate
ActiveSheet.Shapes("Shape1").Select
Selection.Fill.ForeColor.RGB = RGB(0, 0, 0)
```

Listing 6-10. Referencing Objects Directly

```
Me.Shapes("Shape1").Fill.ForeColor.RGB = RGB(0, 0, 0)
...
Dim salesChart As Excel.Chart
Set salesChart = [SalesChart].Chart
```

Isn't VBA great? It sure is but not for everything. That brings me to the next principle.

Render Unto Excel the Things That Are Excel's and Unto VBA the Things That Require VBA

VBA lets you do a lot, but it's not a great idea to do everything in VBA, especially when it involves reinventing the wheel. For instance, it's tempting to store all your program's global variables in a module. This method brings the advantage of total and complete accessibility: the variables can be accessed anywhere at any time by any procedure.

However, these variables are also "freed" from memory whenever your code errors out or whenever you tell Excel to "reset" (Figure 6-18). When this memory is dumped, you must start over—those variables once again become zeros or blanks. Often those who use this method must create an `Initialize` or `Restore` procedure to restore the correct values to these variables before you can do anything else in the spreadsheet.

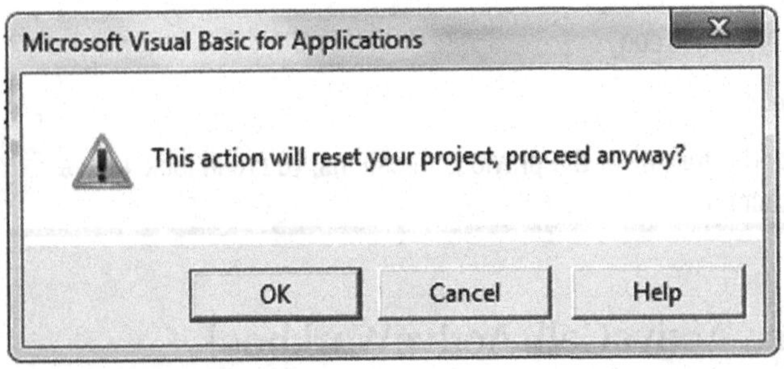

Figure 6-18. *Hitting OK will reset the values of all those public variables stored in procedures*

There's a better way, people. I don't need to tell you that Excel is a giant storage closet. It's a much better idea to store your application models *on the spreadsheet* instead of in the module where they are susceptible to being cleared out every time there's an error. Just create a new tab to hold your backend variables. Name it something like Calculations, Variables, Constants—you get the picture. Then use the shorthand range syntax discussed earlier to access these ranges. It couldn't be simpler. And it brings an additional benefit worth mentioning in my next principle.

Encapsulating Your Work

Encapsulation is a tenant of object-oriented programming that argues (1) associated data and procedures should be organized together and (2) access to and manipulation of the former items should be restricted or granted in only certain circumstances. By coupling together relevant procedures into a relevant worksheet tab, you fulfill the first item.

The second item is fulfilled when you store application variables on the worksheet. This is because the only way to change these variables is by either writing to them with code or updating them manually behind the scenes. Let's say you have a named ranged called `Calculate.Input`. I can change this variable's value in the code (see the following code), which requires I run a macro:

```
[Calculate.Input] = 1
```

Or I can change its value by finding it on the spreadsheet and typing in something new, as in Figure 6-19.

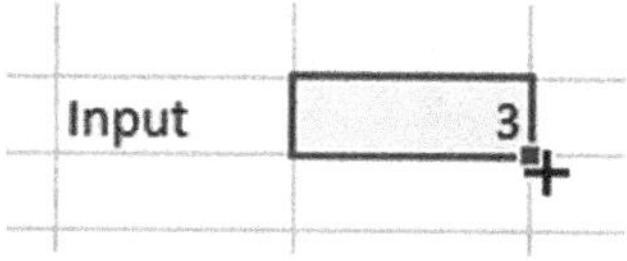

Figure 6-19. *A worksheet named range variable called Calc.Input*

However, if I want to access this variable somewhere else on the worksheet, I must access it through a formula, like this:

```
= Calc.Input - 1
```

Notice that this simply accesses the value stored in `Calc.Input`—it doesn't change the value itself. However, it's impossible with a formula to change the value of `Calc.Input`. Like I said earlier, there are only two ways to change its value, a macro or a human. This is an example of encapsulation.

The Last Word

In this chapter, I talked about how to set up your coding experience to make the most of it, proper naming conventions, and development styles and principles. Some of these suggestions were counterintuitive to what is commonly taught, but I explained why they were useful. I don't expect you to leave this chapter entirely convinced, but ideally you see the value in developing good coding practices—and why sometimes doing things differently makes sense.

CHAPTER 7

Avoiding Common Pitfalls in Development and Design

There are two areas in which I find common pitfalls: in development and in design. The development side concerns the overuse and inefficient use of certain formulas and VBA code. The design side concerns ineffective use of layout.

Your goal for a finished dashboard should be an Excel file that runs quickly, uses less memory and processing, and requires less storage. Sometimes moving toward this goal will call for enhancements in design that come at the expense of development, or vice versa. In these instances, you'll need to understand the trade-offs for each. I'll go through those trade-offs as you make your way through the next two chapters.

For most software projects, optimization comes in at the end, when everything works as it's supposed to. Things aren't so simple with Excel. Some enhancements are best added at the end, but you can save yourself considerable headache by planning for those enhancements early on. Other areas, such as the layout of the display screen, might require that you pursue a little planning on the front end before diving into developing your work. The good news is that Excel's flexible environment allows you to make changes easily, and you can usually test those changes immediately.

Pitfalls happen simply because you don't know they're there. You've learned how to do something one way in Excel but haven't properly understood its ramifications. You've accepted, among other things, slow spreadsheets and wonky design as the status quo. For instance, there's no reason your user should have to wait several minutes for the spreadsheet to load or for the spreadsheet to complete a calculation. But many people have accepted these items as part of development in Excel.

I say, no more.

In the next few sections, you'll take a look at a few of the common pitfalls in development and design—and how they manifest. Specifically, you'll look at calculation pitfalls and see how the choice of formula makes a considerable difference on speed. Next, you'll turn your attention to how the use of VBA code can both speed up and slow down your spreadsheets. You'll return to volatile actions to see how you can limit them in your code. Finally, you'll take a look at file-naming conventions, an often overlooked but no less important part of the development and design of your work.

Calculation Pitfalls

One of the most common pitfalls, and reasons for spreadsheet slowness, involves Excel's calculation process. Calculations, as you might have guessed, are a fundamental part of Excel. Microsoft puts it this way:

> ***Calculation** is the process of computing formulas and then displaying the results as values in the cells that contain the formulas. To avoid unnecessary calculations, Microsoft Excel automatically **recalculates** formulas only when the cells that the formula depends on have changed.*

In other words, when a cell or series of cells must be updated because of changes on a spreadsheet, Excel performs a recalculation. The order in which to update each cell is an internal process handled by Excel. Using an algorithm, Excel determines the complexity of each calculation and its dependents—and creates an optimized calculation chain. Potentially, a cell could be updated multiple times through the recalculation process depending upon how Excel creates the calculation order.

Compared to earlier versions of Excel, this internal process is pretty efficient. However, poor design on the development side can cause recalculations that fire too often or take too long to complete. To optimize your spreadsheets, you can limit the triggers that cause recalculation and limit the amount of time Excel spends performing a recalculation.

The most common triggers of recalculation are *volatile functions* and certain actions that cause the spreadsheet to recalculate, which I'll call *volatile actions*. Having too many volatile functions and actions can seriously slow down spreadsheet calculation. Another common reason for slow calculation involves the choice of formula. Some formulas, as you will see in the examples that follow, can be faster than others. Last, persistent unhandled formula errors also cause significant calculation slowdown. I'll go through each of these items in the following subsections.

Volatile Functions and Actions

Typically, Excel will recalculate only the formulas that depend on values that change. However, some formulas are always triggered for recalculation regardless of whether their value has changed or the value of a cell they depend on has changed. These functions are called volatile functions because they and their dependents will always recalculate with every change made to a spreadsheet. For some volatile formulas, the trigger is obvious. For example, `RAND` and `RANDBETWEEN` are volatile because you would want and should expect them to continuously generate new, random data. They'd be useless otherwise. `NOW` and `TODAY` are volatile because what they return depends on a constantly changing unit, in this case, time. But other functions are not as obvious; specifically, `OFFSET`, `INDIRECT`, `CELL`, and `INFO` are volatile. The `OFFSET` and `INDIRECT` functions help you look up information from different parts of the spreadsheet (much like `VLOOKUP` and `INDEX`). Why these last four functions are volatile is a mystery.

In any event, you should attempt to curb the use of volatile functions. In most cases, the functionality they bring can be replaced by safer, nonvolatile formulas or by using VBA instead (but not too much VBA because that brings on its own set of issues).

For the presentation of dashboards and reporting applications, you're not likely to require the continual generation of random data. When you require today's date, you might be better off using a macro to write the day's date to the sheet when it's first activated. However, the volatility of `OFFSET` and `INDIRECT` is somewhat tragic because they are both functions that could otherwise be useful.

The good news is that using volatile functions sparingly (and only when necessary) will have negligible effects on your spreadsheet. In the case of `OFFSET` and `INDIRECT`, `INDEX` is almost always a suitable replacement. The results of `NOW`, `TODAY`, `CELL`, and `INFO` can all be replicated easily and written to the spreadsheet with VBA. Rarely will a dashboard require that you use these formula functions specifically. The good news is that you can greatly lessen the impact of volatile functions recalculating by also limiting volatile actions.

Here are the most common volatile actions:

- Modifying the contents of a spreadsheet
- Adding, deleting, filtering, and hiding/unhiding rows
- Disabling and then enabling the calculation state

Let's go through these items.

Modifying the Contents of a Spreadsheet

When you select any cell on a sheet and change its value, you're modifying the sheet's contents. Obviously, this type of action is largely unavoidable for what you're doing in this book and how you use spreadsheets in general. A spreadsheet wouldn't be useful to you if you couldn't make changes to it!

However, there are ways to avoid making unnecessary and redundant changes to a spreadsheet's contents. For instance, let's say you're using a VBA macro to iterate through a series of cells. When a cell has a certain value, perhaps you want to write a value to the cell right next to it to as a signal. Figure 7-1 shows an example of where you have a series of values and want to place an *x* next to the values that fit the criteria of being greater than 1,000.

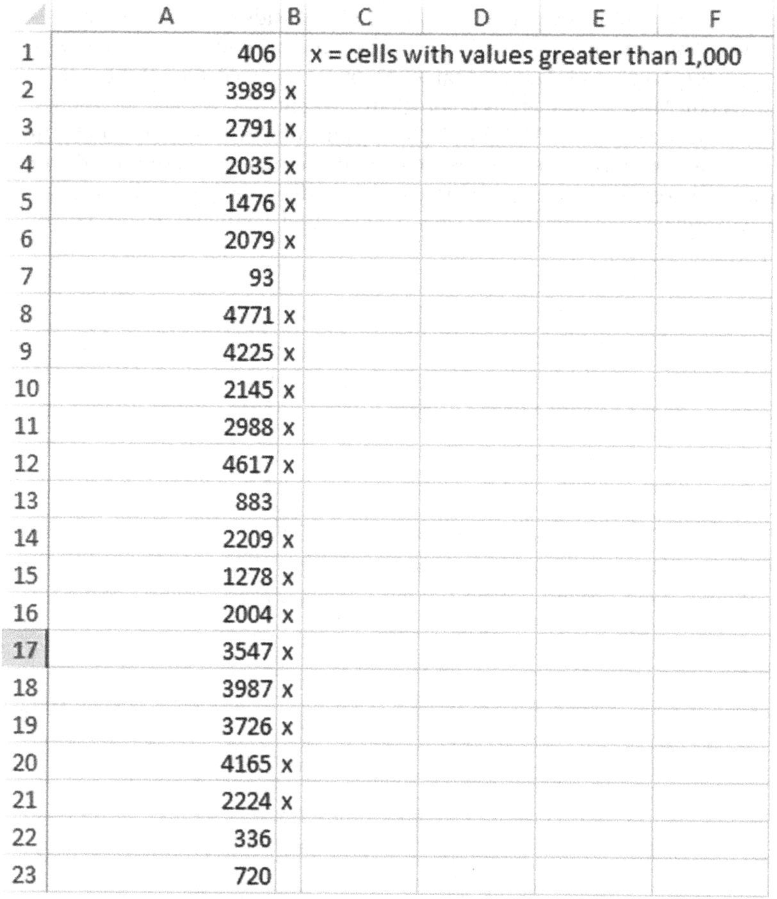

	A	B	C	D	E	F
1	406		x = cells with values greater than 1,000			
2	3989	x				
3	2791	x				
4	2035	x				
5	1476	x				
6	2079	x				
7	93					
8	4771	x				
9	4225	x				
10	2145	x				
11	2988	x				
12	4617	x				
13	883					
14	2209	x				
15	1278	x				
16	2004	x				
17	3547	x				
18	3987	x				
19	3726	x				
20	4165	x				
21	2224	x				
22	336					
23	720					

Figure 7-1. *An example of where I'm using a signal, in this case an x, to identify values greater than 1,000*

You can use the code shown in Listing 7-1.

Listing 7-1. VBA Code to Test Whether Values in Column A Are Greater Than 1,000

```
Public Sub SignalValuesGreaterThan1000()
    Dim CurrentCell As Range
    Set CurrentCell = Me.Range("A1")

    While Len(CurrentCell.Value) > 0
        If CurrentCell.Value > 1000 Then
            'Test if an 'x' has already been placed
            If CurrentCell.Offset(0, 1).Value <> "x" Then CurrentCell.Offset(0, 1).Value = "x"
        End If

        'Move to the next row
        Set CurrentCell = CurrentCell.Offset(1)
    Wend
End Sub
```

In particular, notice the code section in bold. Rather than simply setting the value to an *x*, you're first testing whether it's already been set (perhaps from a previous iteration). If it's already been set, you're not going to set it again. Remember, every time you change the value of the cell, you're committing a volatile action. Simply testing whether a property has already been set can help you limit such actions. I'll go into this in more detail later in the subsection "Testing Properties Before Setting Them."

In the meantime, you can limit such actions altogether by employing formulas instead. For instance, in the cells next to each value, you can employ a formula to test the values of the numbers. You simply add the formula in cell B1 and drag down. Then every update made to these numbers does not require the code in Listing 7-1 because the formulas will update the signals in real time. This method completely avoids volatile actions to set the signal (Figure 7-2).

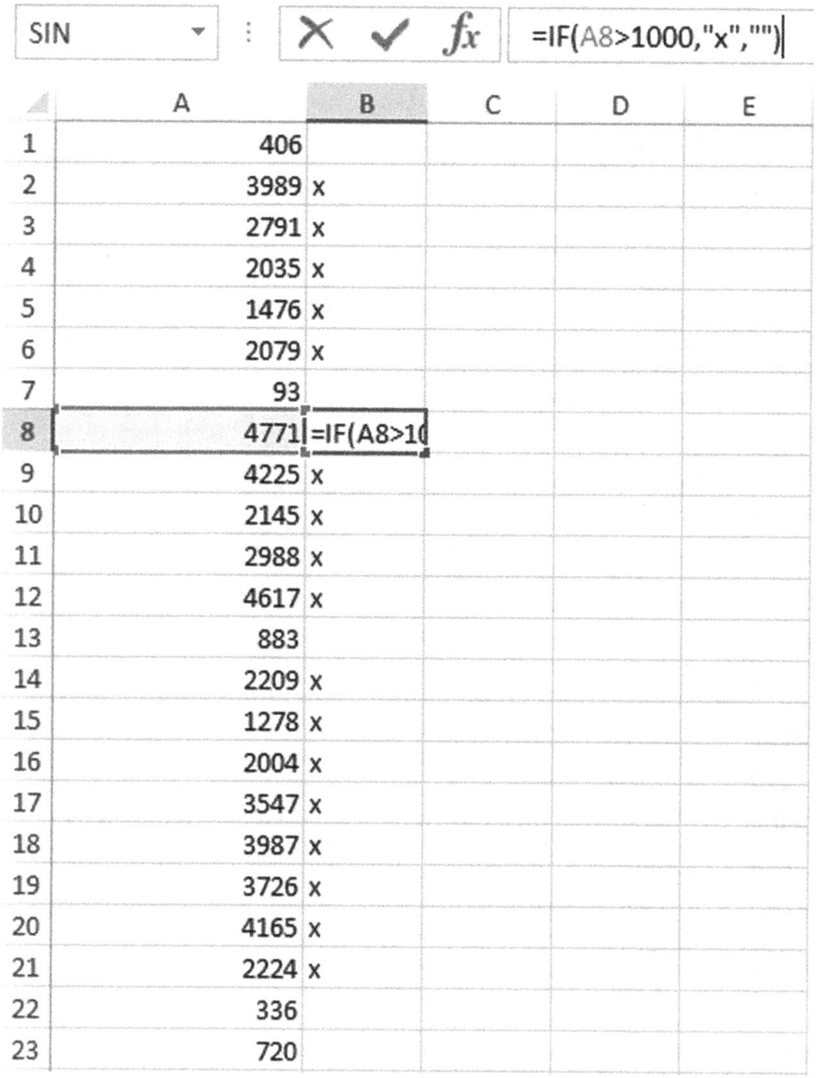
SIN
=IF(A8>1000,"x","")
A
B
C
D
E
1 406
2 3989 x
3 2791 x
4 2035 x
5 1476 x
6 2079 x
7 93
8 4771 =IF(A8>1(
9 4225 x
10 2145 x
11 2988 x
12 4617 x
13 883
14 2209 x
15 1278 x
16 2004 x
17 3547 x
18 3987 x
19 3726 x
20 4165 x
21 2224 x
22 336
23 720

Figure 7-2. *Using formulas next to each number is a way to bypass using VBA to write an x every time*

Finally, you can employ custom formats, which allow you to bypass formulas altogether. For instance, in Figure 7-3, I've first set each cell in B1 to be equal to the cells in A1.

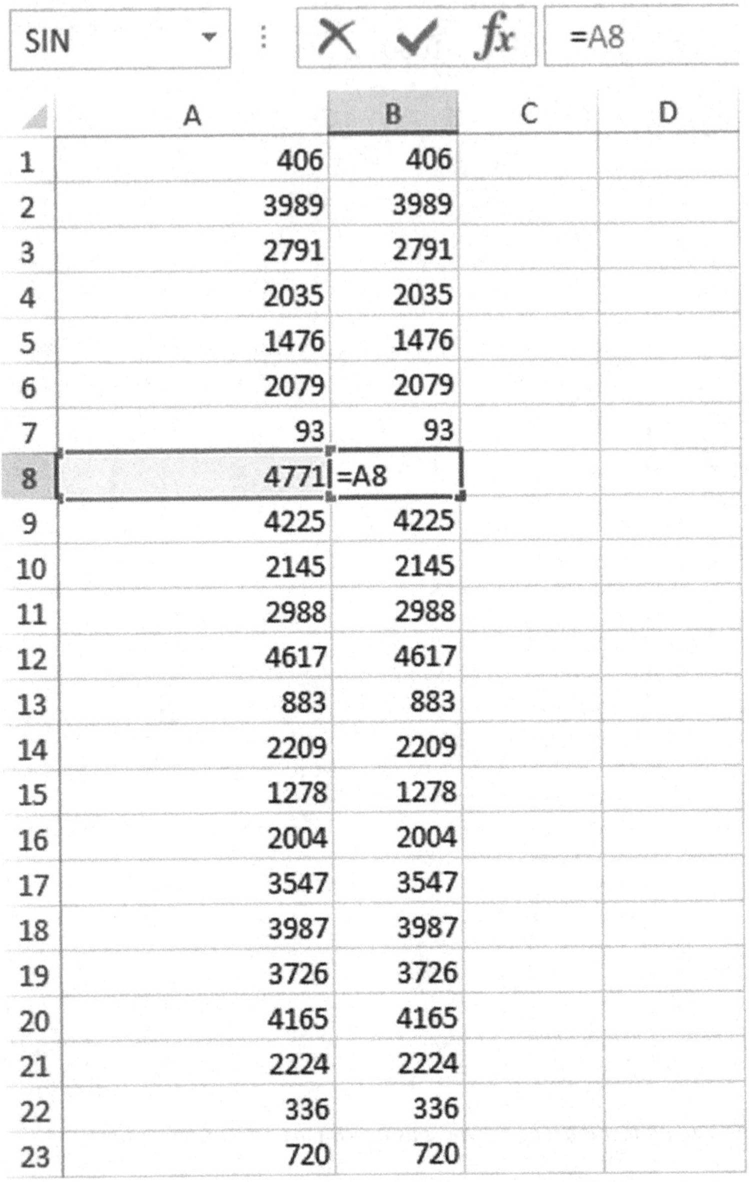

	A	B	C	D
1	406	406		
2	3989	3989		
3	2791	2791		
4	2035	2035		
5	1476	1476		
6	2079	2079		
7	93	93		
8	4771	=A8		
9	4225	4225		
10	2145	2145		
11	2988	2988		
12	4617	4617		
13	883	883		
14	2209	2209		
15	1278	1278		
16	2004	2004		
17	3547	3547		
18	3987	3987		
19	3726	3726		
20	4165	4165		
21	2224	2224		
22	336	336		
23	720	720		

Figure 7-3. *The first step in applying custom formats to signal which cells are greater than 1,000*

You can then highlight the entire range created in column B, right-click, and select Format Cells. Within the Format Cells dialog box that appears (Figure 7-4), you can use the custom formatting code `[>1000]"x";""` to set any value that is greater than 1,000 to x and leave all other potential values in the series as a blank string. (I'll go into using these custom format conditions in later chapters.)

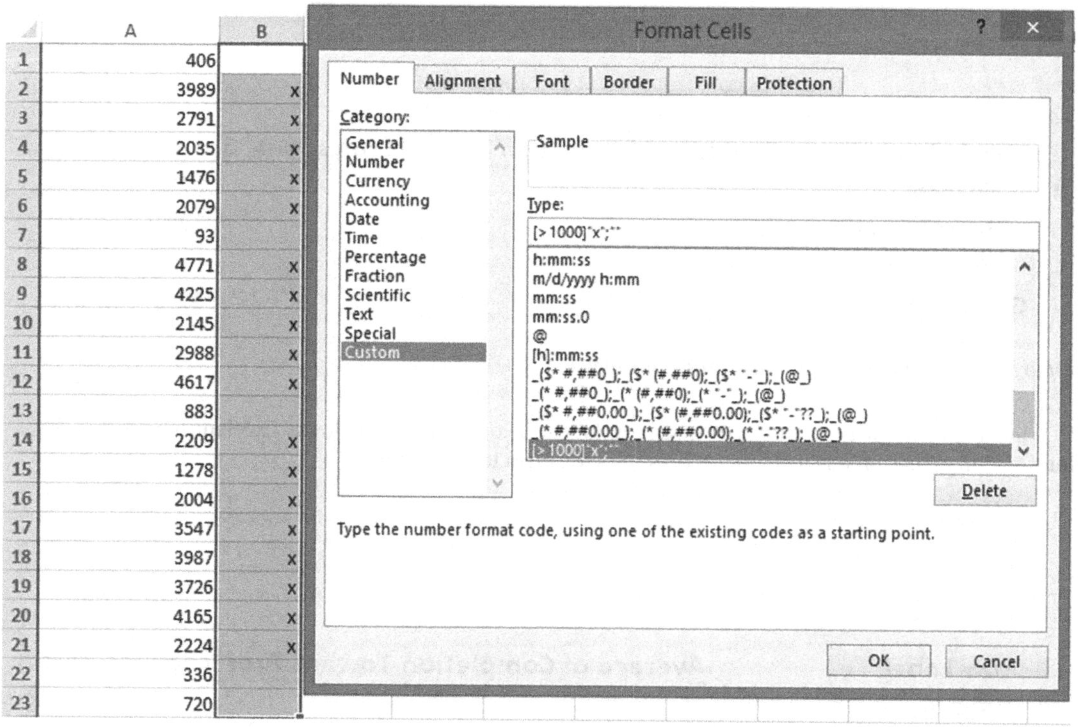

***Figure 7-4.** Applying a custom format to the cells in the list*

Applying this custom format will achieve the same results as the other examples presented. And each example presents its own costs and benefits. The VBA code method is easy to follow and understand. The formula method is faster, but when you have a lot of data and a more complex example of setting a signal (or even a series of signals), the VBA method might prove faster. The custom format method wins on speed over all the other methods (since it requires virtually no calculation to assign from one cell to another), but custom formats aren't commonly used in this way, and some spreadsheet users without familiarity with the custom format might look at the series of *x*'s in puzzlement.

What you choose to use in your work must be weighed against these factors. It's important that you are continuously looking for ways to achieve the same results while committing the fewest volatile actions as possible. This will allow you to perform complex calculations and display complex data without grinding your spreadsheet to a halt.

Adding, Deleting, Filtering, Hiding/Unhiding Rows and Columns

Another volatile action involves making changes to the design of the spreadsheet. Specifically, telling Excel to add, delete, filter, or hide a row will cause a recalculation.

Pivot tables are among the worst offenders in this regard. I break from my colleagues on the use of pivot tables for many of the types of dashboards you're building here. They seem like an obvious choice for dashboards because of their ability to summarize data. But their drill-down and filtering capabilities result in volatile actions.

Figures 7-5 and 7-6 show how pivot tables cause volatile actions.

	A	B
1		
2		
3	**Row Labels**	**Average of Completion Toward Professional Goals**
4	⊞**Finance**	**57%**
5	⊞**Human Resources**	**52%**
6	⊞**Marketing**	**85%**
7	**Grand Total**	**58%**

Figure 7-5. *A pivot table with a collapse row label*

In Figure 7-5, you see several collapsed row labels. If you want to drill down, Excel must write that new information to the spreadsheet. Figure 7-6 shows the pivot table expanded.

	A	B
1		
2		
3	**Row Labels**	**Average of Completion Toward Professional Goals**
4	⊞**Finance**	**57%**
5	**Human Resources**	**52%**
6	Aline Rojas	40%
7	Martin Rocha	90%
8	Melyssa Mcmahon	80%
9	Quyn Rivera	40%
10	Randall Sanders	90%
11	Shannon Cardenas	50%
12	Stewart Everett	40%
13	Tiger Shaw	10%
14	Vielka Zamora	30%
15	⊞**Marketing**	**85%**
16	**Grand Total**	**58%**

Figure 7-6. *The same pivot table with Human Resources expanded*

This innocuous action causes the inevitable recalculation. In fact, you can test this for yourself by placing the following code into the worksheet object code:

```
Private Sub Worksheet_Calculate()
    MsgBox "Calculation Initiated!"
End Sub
```

There is one caveat, however, and that's using pivot tables in conjunction with much of the new capabilities implemented in Excel 2010 and expanded upon in Excel 2013. Pivot tables, when used in conjunction with slicers and other tools, such as power queries, can be rather powerful. However, again, you must gauge the use of this power in the context of unwanted volatile actions. Previous books on dashboards and interactive reports have presented pivot tables as a great feature for dashboards. However, in practice, pivot tables often overwhelm dashboards and become so large and unwieldy that they are a major cause of slowdown. That is why we will hold off on using pivot table capabilities until the final chapters of this book. I want to show you how you can achieve much of the same capabilities with formulas and code while greatly minimizing volatile actions.

Disabling and Then Enabling the Calculation State

In this section, I'll talk about how changing the calculation state can cause volatile recalculations, negatively affect spreadsheet speed, and create wonky errors.

It's common practice, much to my dismay, to disable calculation when a spreadsheet has become unwieldy. There are certain instances, especially when you are using Excel to explore a problem, when you must disable calculation but only temporarily (for instance, you receive a spreadsheet with unclean data and the process to clean it requires you to temporarily suspend calculation just to set up formulas to get the data in good condition). Dashboards and reports, however, deal with the presentation of data and not its exploration. Let me say this rather definitively: there is no good reason your dashboards, reports, and applications should ever have to disable calculation.

For the uninitiated, there are two ways you can disable (and subsequently enable) automatic recalculation. You can disable automatic recalculation yourself through Excel's ribbon by going to the Formulas tab and clicking Calculation Options ➤ Manual (see Figure 7-7).

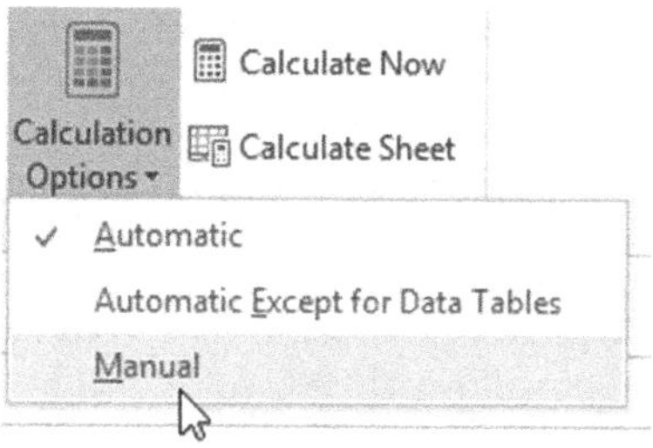

Figure 7-7. *Manually setting the calculation state*

This method of disabling calculation, that is, manually through the ribbon system, often happens when you must clean data. Again, I'm not against turning off manual calculation temporarily. As well, you can disable automatic recalculation within VBA, using the following code to turn it off:

```
Application.Calculation = xlCalculationManual
```

You can use the following code to flip it back on:

```
Application.Calculation = xlCalculationAutomatic
```

However, this second form of disabling calculation through VBA is both common and terrible. From a functional standpoint, there's no difference between changing the calculation state either in the code or manually on the ribbon. However, in practice, when calculation is turned off in the code, it's often because the programmer is asking too much of Excel (that is to say, they haven't read this chapter yet).

The problem with turning on manual calculation, especially before doing some complex calculations in VBA that must interface with the spreadsheet, is that things can become screwy quickly. Here's why: it's common practice to turn off manual calculation right before some intensive process. However, the programmer will still require some cells to calculate. In these instances, the programmer will select a few active cells and have them calculate the formulas stored therein.

When a cell's value has changed (remember, this is a *volatile* action), Excel will mark that cell in its calculation algorithm as becoming "dirty." The process of recalculating every cell in the calculation chain is what makes it clean again. But if an intensive loop were to error out, there may be a series of cells that are clean having been calculated and still some that are dirty. There's no way to tell of course which is which. That information is stored internally. If you've messed with the calculation state before in this way, you probably know what I'm talking about. Some cells may have correctly calculated values; others not. It's just not worth the headache.

The long and short of it is this: when you select Manual in the set Calculation Options drop-down list, you lose control of the calculation process, which you should be in control of. If you plan correctly and avoid (or, at least, mitigate the unavoidable) volatile functions and actions, you won't run into a situation in which manual calculation feels like a viable option. But you might be relying on certain calculations to be performed on your spreadsheet that setting the calculation to manual will prevent from executing. And it's often forgotten that when you once again set the calculation to automatic, *a full recalculation is executed.* Full recalculations recalculate everything on the spreadsheet. And if you have complicated formulas, the result might express itself similar to Figure 7-8.

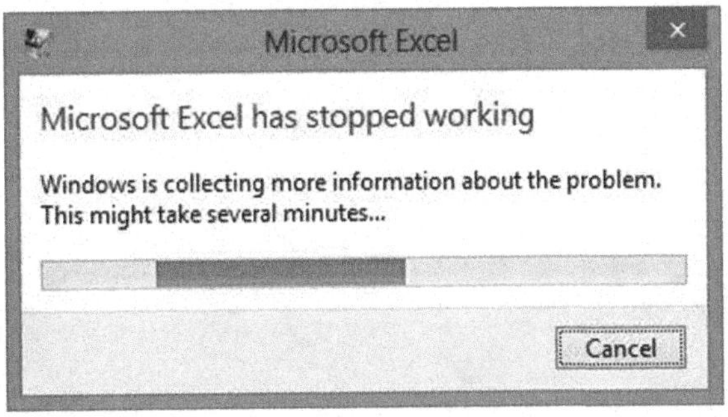

Figure 7-8. *Don't let unruly calculations do this to your spreadsheet*

So, I strongly recommend against changing the calculation state. If your spreadsheet is moving slowly, this chapter (and the rest of the book) will contain optimization tips that might help.

■ **Caution** Don't use `Application.CalculationState = xlCalculationManual`. There's almost always a better way.

Understanding Different Formula Speeds

In this section, I'll discuss how the choice of formula can affect the speed of calculations. This subject is rather vast, and the subsection here won't do it justice. For an example, you'll look at how speed differences manifest in the process of data lookups. But for a more lengthy explanation and too see advancements in this area, see the work of Excel MVP Charles Williams and his blog, "Excel and UDF Performance Stuff," at `https://fastexcel.wordpress.com/`.

Lookups refer to finding relevant data from different parts of the spreadsheet. Lookups are important to dashboards because they're used to report results among other capabilities. Common lookup functions include `VLOOKUP` (naturally), `INDEX`, and `MATCH`. The next two subsections discuss advantages and common pitfalls in using `VLOOKUP` and why `INDEX` and `MATCH` sometimes prove to be a better choice.

VLOOKUP

The most common lookup formula is probably `VLOOKUP`. One advantage of `VLOOKUP` is that it's pretty easy to use and understand. `VLOOKUP` searches through each possibility in the first column to match the supplied lookup value. In the worst-case scenario, it must look through every element to make a match if the desired value is at the bottom of the list or to discern that it's not even in the list at all. Therefore, in terms of performance on large lists, many `VLOOKUP`s can become slow.

And, in many instances, `VLOOKUP` might be better replaced by using the `INDEX` function. These instances exist where there is some inherent ordered list structure in the data to be traversed. For example, in the example in Figure 7-9, you can get by without using `VLOOKUP`. Since the program list is in order and the last character of each item is a number, you could use `INDEX` to pick out the program in the third row instead of using `VLOOKUP` to find "Program3." (See Figure 7-9.)

	A	B	C	D
1		Name	Status	Budget
2		Program1	Funded	4 Mil
3		Program2	Funded	5 Mil
4		Program3	Over Budget	41 Mil
5		Program4	Funded	30 Mil
6		Program5	On time	98 Mil
7		Program6	Funded	51 Mil
8		Program7	Over Budget	17 Mil
9		Program8	On time	5 Mil
10		Program9	On time	84 Mil

Figure 7-9. *An example of an inherently ordered list*

And, assuming the example holds true in the real world (that is, all the programs include some number at the end of their name that identifies where they might fall in a list), you could use that information for the `INDEX` function. For instance, let's say "Program3" was input into cell A1; you could then use the function `RIGHT(A1,1)` to return the first rightmost character in the string. This would return the number 3—the row number you're interested in. In full, you could then use the function `=INDEX(D2:D10, RIGHT(A1,1))` instead of `VLOOKUP` to reference directly the cell you're interested in.

Another example is where you have used a list of sequential numbers to encode rows or tables. Take a look at the table in Figure 7-10.

	A	B	C	D	E
1		id	Phases	$ per Month	
2		1	Planning	$250	
3		2	Execution	$300	
4		3	Maturity	$400	
5					

Figure 7-10. *A table of planning phases organized by ID*

You could use this information to define the per-month cost of a project, like in Figure 7-11.

	JAN	FEB	MAR	APR	MAY	JUN	JUL	AUG
Project 1	1	1	2	2	2	3	3	3

Figure 7-11. *An intermediate table to aid in the process of lookups*

This information would could then serve as an index lookup to create the table in Figure 7-12.

	JAN	FEB	MAR	APR	MAY	JUN	JUL	AUG
Project 1	250	250	300	300	300	400	400	400

Figure 7-12. *The final table after using the intermediate table to look up values for each phase*

It may be tempting to write "Planning" instead of 1 in Figure 7-12, but you don't need to do this because `INDEX` works with an ID number. You can also use `VLOOKUP` on numbers, but `INDEX` really is the better option. Remember, be on the lookout for when `INDEX` might do a better job than `VLOOKUP`.

The examples here are small. It's not a big deal for `VLOOKUP` to traverse a small number of values. But as stated previously, `VLOOKUP` must go through each item in the list to find a match (hence the traversal). Again, in a worst-case scenario, `VLOOKUP` must go through each item in the list to find a match. To the extent you can minimize traversal, you should.

However, the real world contains messy data that does not always formulate itself so neatly in the previous two examples. `VLOOKUP` then is particularly useful when data in a list contains no additional information inherent to each data point about its location in the list. The example shown in Figure 7-9 did contain such information, but names in the next example (Figure 7-13) do not.

And, it's often forgotten that `VLOOKUP` can return multiple cells at once. Take the table in Figure 7-13, for example. Here you see representatives on the left side of the table and information about their job performance in the fields thereafter.

	A	B	C	D
1	**Rep**	**Sales Figures**	**Targets**	**Targets Beat?**
2	Jeremy	$34,534	$30,000	Y
3	Mark	$12,321	$15,000	N
4	Carol	$21,232	$20,000	Y
5	Steve	$1,000	$9,000	N
6	Gordon	$2,323	$4,500	N
7	Billy	$89,732	$75,000	Y
8	Marissa	$3,544	$10,000	N

***Figure 7-13.** A table showing representative performance data*

Let's consider the table in Figure 7-13. If you wanted to know Jeremy's performance but only wanted to return his sales figures and whether these figures beat his target, you might be tempted to create two different lookups, as shown in Figure 7-14.

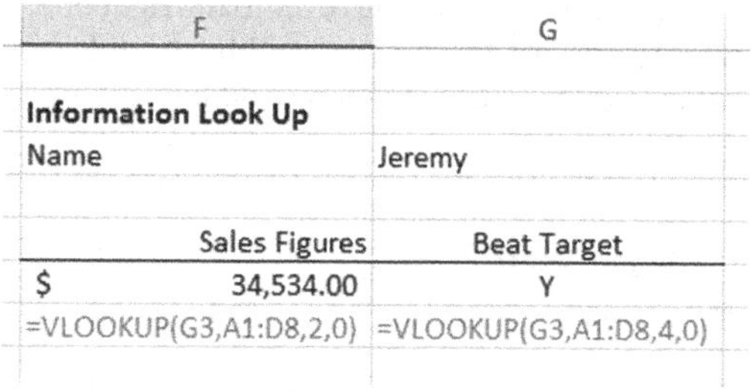
F
G
Information Look Up
Name
Jeremy
Sales Figures
Beat Target
$
34,534.00
Y
=VLOOKUP(G3,A1:D8,2,0)
=VLOOKUP(G3,A1:D8,4,0)

***Figure 7-14.** Two different lookups to pull back the different associated fields*

But VLOOKUP provides a way around this. You could use an array formula instead that stretches across the two cells. You simply need to fill that column parameter with an array of the columns you'd like to pull back. This is shown in Figure 7-15.

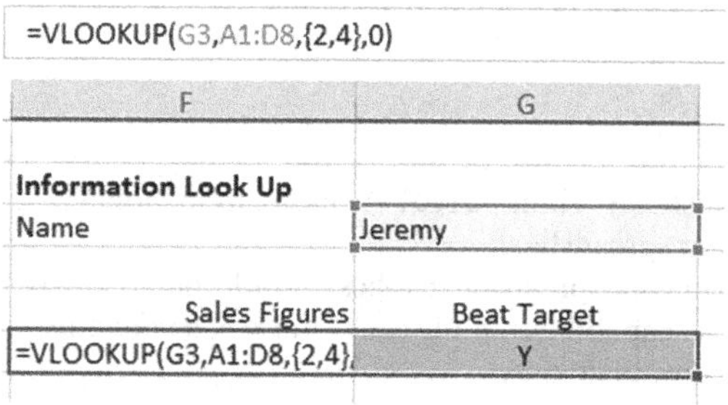
=VLOOKUP(G3,A1:D8,{2,4},0)
F
G
Information Look Up
Name
Jeremy
Sales Figures
Beat Target
=VLOOKUP(G3,A1:D8,{2,4}
Y

***Figure 7-15.** Using an array formula to return columns 2 and 4*

Notice I've used those curly brackets to denote an array formula. Also, notice, that the columns to be returned need not be adjacent to one another. Here, returning multiple items at once provides the immediate advantage of turning two (but it could be several, in your case) lookups into one.

■ **Note** Remember array formulas always require you press Ctrl+Shift+Enter to return multiple items across multiple cells.

INDEX/MATCH

There's actually a pretty interesting argument out there *against* using `VLOOKUP`. Charlie Kyd, of ExcelUser.com, has run the numbers, and using a combination of `INDEX` and `MATCH` is faster than `VLOOKUP` in most cases and still slightly faster in its worst case. Instead of `VLOOKUP`, your formula would look like this:

```
=INDEX(range, MATCH(row_index_num, lookup_array, 0), column_index_num)
```

The most obvious advantage to using `INDEX/MATCH` is that the lookup can go in any direction. Remember how `VLOOKUP` was used in Figure 7-14? Well, `VLOOKUP` can pull information that belongs only to the right of the first column. But what if you wanted to search who had sales figures of $21,232? You wouldn't be able to do this with `VLOOKUP`, but you can easily do this with `INDEX/MATCH`. Figure 7-16 shows how to do this.

	A	B	C	D
1	**Rep**	**Sales Figures**	**Targets**	**Targets Beat?**
2	Jeremy	$34,534	$30,000	Y
3	Mark	$12,321	$15,000	N
4	Carol	$21,232	$20,000	Y
5	Steve	$1,000	$9,000	N
6	Gordon	$2,323	$4,500	N
7	Billy	$89,732	$75,000	Y
8	Marissa	$3,544	$10,000	N
9				
10	Who had sales of $21,232?		Carol	=INDEX(A2:A8,MATCH(21232,B2:B8,0))

Figure 7-16. *Using INDEX/MATCH to look up information to the left of the lookup column*

Spreadsheet Errors

Spreadsheet errors are a major cause of slowdown for spreadsheets. Think `#DIV0!` errors are innocuous? Think again! They can contribute to major bottlenecks in your spreadsheet.

Often spreadsheet errors are lurking in parts unknown of your spreadsheet, relics of work you no longer need. You can hunt them down by using Excel's Go To Special capability. Simply click Find & Select on the Home tab and then select Go To Special. Figure 7-17 shows how to do this.

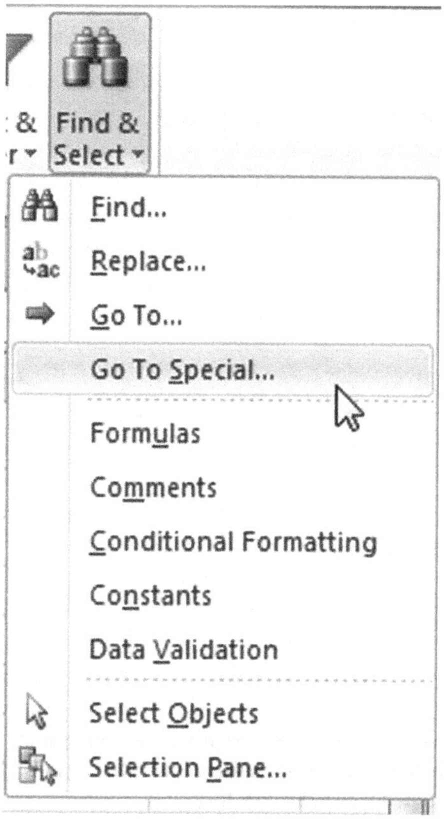

Figure 7-17. *You can find the Go To Special feature under Find & Select on the Home tab*

Once you see the Go To Special dialog box (Figure 7-18), select the Formulas option and clear every check box except for the Errors box. This will take you to the errors on your spreadsheet.

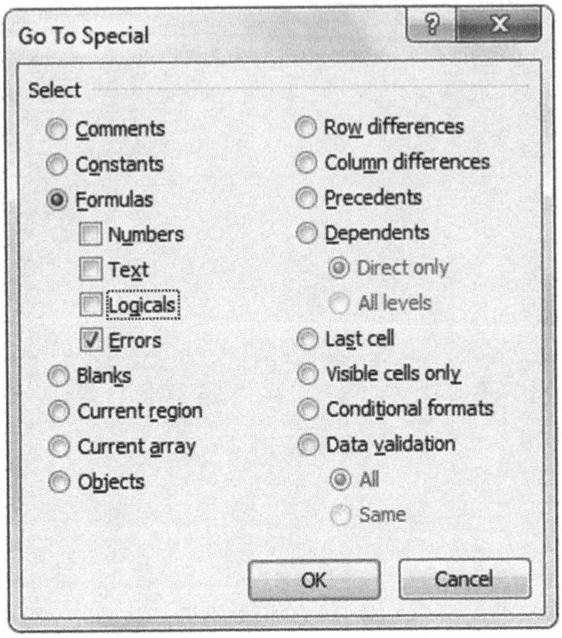

Figure 7-18. *The Go To Special dialog box*

After clicking OK, all spreadsheet errors will be highlighted. What you want to do with those highlighted pieces is largely up to you. If they are an integral to your model, the easiest way to fix them is by placing an `IFERROR` around the formula. The following code shows the prototype for the `IFERROR` formula:

```
IFERROR(value,value_if_error)
```

The first parameter, `value`, is where you place the original formula to be evaluated. The second parameter, `value_if_error`, is where you place what you want the function to return only if an error results in the first parameter. This is a great way to capture error-prone cells in your worksheet.

Alternatively, I've found errors like these abound in forgotten and no longer used sections of spreadsheets. Using the Go To Special directive as I've done here might especially helpful for finding parts of the spreadsheet that are no longer necessary. Consider deleting them in addition to the `#DIV/0!` Table 7-1 shows spreadsheet errors to look out for.

Table 7-1. *Common Formula Errors*

Formula Error Name	Description
`#DIV/0!`	This is returned when a zero is supplied as the divisor in a quotient.
`#VALUE!`	This is returned when the wrong type is supplied to a formula. For instance, `=SUM(1,"2")` would return this error.
`#REF!`	This is returned when the range referenced no longer exists. For instance, if column A is deleted, then a cell with the formula `=A1` would return the `#REF!` error.
`#NAME?`	This is returned when a formula function is misspelled.
`#NUM!`	This is returned when you supply numbers into a mathematical function like `IRR` or `NORM.DIST` that violate underlying mathematical properties.

I bring all of this up to demonstrate that formulas can and do slow down spreadsheets. However, you can go too far in making your formulas super speedy, realizing only small gains while making unreadable formulas. Therefore, there will always be some consideration you'll have to go through when choosing which formulas to use. Ultimately, however, if you build with speed in mind, then taking a few liberties with formulas won't kill a spreadsheet, but a lot of liberties will.

Code Pitfalls

Of course, formulas are only part of the problem. In this section, I'll talk about coding pitfalls. It's worth revisiting here an example that was shown in both Chapters 1 and 5. Specifically, you should attempt to avoid as much iteration as necessary.

You could use the following code that iterates ten times:

```
For i = 1 To 10

    Sheet1.Range("A" & i).Value = ReturnArray(i)

Next i
```

or you could use one line of code, as shown here:

```
Sheet1.Range("A1:A10").Value = ReturnArray
```

The speed gain here is significant when the examples become nontrivial. In the first iteration example, Excel must write to the screen ten times. Each of these writes is a volatile action that will command a recalculation. On the other hand, the second line of code requires only one write action (and only one recalculation). In other words, the one line in the second example code can complete the same amount of work in one-tenth the time as the first example. Indeed, if the iteration in the first example was for 100 items, the second code line (properly updated to reflect 100 items) would take 1/100th the time to complete as the iteration method.

Copy/Paste Iterations

What should be absolutely key to avoid is the use of copying and pasting via VBA. It's common for those simply starting out with Excel to record a macro of a copy-and-paste action. Listing 7-2 shows such code I recorded with a macro.

***Listing** 7-2.* A Recorded Macro Showing Copy-and-Paste Code

```
Sub Macro1()
'
' Macro1 Macro
'

'
    Range("A3:A4").Select
    Selection.Copy
    Range("D3").Select
    ActiveSheet.Paste
End Sub
```

Often, this code is edited and then placed into a loop to re-create the action many times. However, each paste is a volatile action. Moreover, the clipboard—where the information that's been copied is stored—is not controlled within Excel. It's not uncommon for it to be cleared out when an intervening process—sometimes a process you've instantiated with Excel and sometimes a Windows process—to clear out the clipboard. You can't rely on the clipboard to store information. For that, as I'll talk about this book, there are variables and the spreadsheet as a storage device.

Testing Properties Before Setting Them

In this section, I'll discuss a technique of testing properties before setting them. I first read about this technique in *Professional Excel Development*. Given that it requires some extra code, it may feel out of place. One would think it less efficient. For instance, let's say you have some loop that runs through a series of cells and sets specific cells in those series to be bold. Testing whether a cell is already bold before turning it bold would look something like this:

```
If CurrentCell.Font.Bold <> True then CurrentCell.Font.Bold = True
```

This setup may look awkward, but it proves to be much faster for certain types of problems. Often you'll have situations where you must iterate through a series of cells that will already have the changes (such as making a cell bold) applied the last time you ran the code. You're simply rerunning the code to reflect updates made when data was updated in the list. You don't need to set a cell to a specific format if that format was already set previously. The action of testing whether a format has been set is actually must faster than changing the format itself. So, by not repeating redundant actions, you can greatly speed up the code.

Let's see this in a larger example. Let's say you have a spreadsheet with a series of columns with numerical values in them. Figure 7-19 shows what I'm talking about. You can see this file in action: download `Chapter7TotalExample.xlsm`.

	A	B	C	D	E	F	G	H	I
1		**KPI 1**		**KPI 2**		**KPI 3**		**KPI 4**	
2		4177		4315		783		1997	
3		3335		4233		685		2575	
4		400		3565		64		3160	
5		2004		636		1179		1495	
6		3874		3939		321		543	
7		24		2913		1037		2427	
8		1453		961		3389		479	
9		1041		1779		2825		1247	
10		2733		**Total**		3456		1595	
11		682		22341		1641		2985	
12		359				1034		2393	
13		1360				**Total**		3186	
14		2584				**16414**		**Total**	
15		1163						**24082**	
16		**Total**							
17		25189							

Figure 7-19. *Columns of numerical values with different size columns*

This example was inspired by a question I saw proposed on an Excel forum. The poster had a spreadsheet similar to this but with many, many more KPIs. Their goal was to highlight in yellow and make bold the numbers under each Total. As you can see in Figure 7-18, some of the numbers are already highlighted and bold, but not all.

The typical way to solve this problem with VBA is to find the Total cell and then make each cell underneath yellow and bold. Listing 7-3 shows a code example that can do this.

Listing 7-3. Code Used to Highlight Total Values

```
Public Sub HighlightTotals()

    Dim FindRange As Range
    Dim FirstRange As Range

    With Me.Cells
        Set FirstRange = .Find(What:="Total", _
            After:=Me.UsedRange.Cells(Me.UsedRange.Cells.Count), _
            LookIn:=xlValues, _
            LookAt:=xlPart, _
            SearchOrder:=xlByRows, _
            SearchDirection:=xlNext, _
            MatchCase:=False, _
            SearchFormat:=False)
```

```
        Set FindRange = FirstRange

        Do
            Dim BelowTotalCell As Range
            Set BelowTotalCell = FindRange.Offset(1)

                BelowTotalCell.Font.Bold = True
                BelowTotalCell.Interior.Color = vbYellow

        Set FindRange = .FindNext(FindRange)

        Loop While Not FindRange Is Nothing And _
            FirstRange.Address <> FindRange.Address

    End With

End Sub
```

Take a look at the bold code in Listing 7-3. Notice that it sets the cells to yellow and bold every time. But, as Figure 7-19 demonstrates, there may be occasions when these cells are either already bold, yellow, or both. It would make more sense to test each cell first before making the change. Listing 7-4 shows these updates.

Listing 7-4. Updated Code Testing Properties Before They Are Set

```
Public Sub HighlightTotals()

    Dim FindRange As Range
    Dim FirstRange As Range

    With Me.Cells
        Set FirstRange = .Find(What:="Total", _
            After:=Me.UsedRange.Cells(Me.UsedRange.Cells.Count), _
            LookIn:=xlValues, _
            LookAt:=xlPart, _
            SearchOrder:=xlByRows, _
            SearchDirection:=xlNext, _
            MatchCase:=False, _
            SearchFormat:=False)

        Do
            Dim BelowTotalCell As Range
            Set BelowTotalCell = FindRange.Offset(1)

            If BelowTotalCell.Font.Bold <> True Then _
                BelowTotalCell.Font.Bold = True
                If BelowTotalCell.Interior.Color <> vbYellow Then _
                    BelowTotalCell.Interior.Color = vbYellow
```

```
            Set FindRange = .FindNext(FindRange)

        Loop While Not FindRange Is Nothing And _
            FirstRange.Address <> FindRange.Address

    End With

End Sub
```

Again, this may seem inefficient at first because it involves extra code. However, changing the property of an Excel object, like a cell, is a much more intensive process for Excel. Simply testing common properties before setting them will cut down on repetitious changes that Excel could avoid. Indeed, this idea can be extended beyond cell formats. It applies to all objects in Excel that have properties you can set. For instance, perhaps you are iterating through a series of shapes or through a series of worksheet tabs. The same principles hold.

Bad Names

In the previous chapter, I talked about correct naming conventions for variables. In this section, I'll extend that concept to file names and worksheet tab names. You may be wondering whether this section even belongs in this chapter or in this book. File names and worksheet tab names are often left to the preferences of the user or to organization policy. In my experience, however, such policies (or, alternatively, such lack of *good* policies) have led to file names that are incomprehensible to other users and clients. Not only do good names help you understand what's going on, but in the case of spreadsheet file names, they also help you understand how your work has evolved over time.

Let's direct our focus to file names first.

Different organizations might have policies directing you to how you should name your files—or perhaps you have preferences you've developed over the years that guide how you name files. However you choose to name files, the names should be descriptive and understandable to more than just you. This simple point is often forgotten. Figure 7-20, for example, shows several versions of dashboards. Can you tell which file is the most recent version?

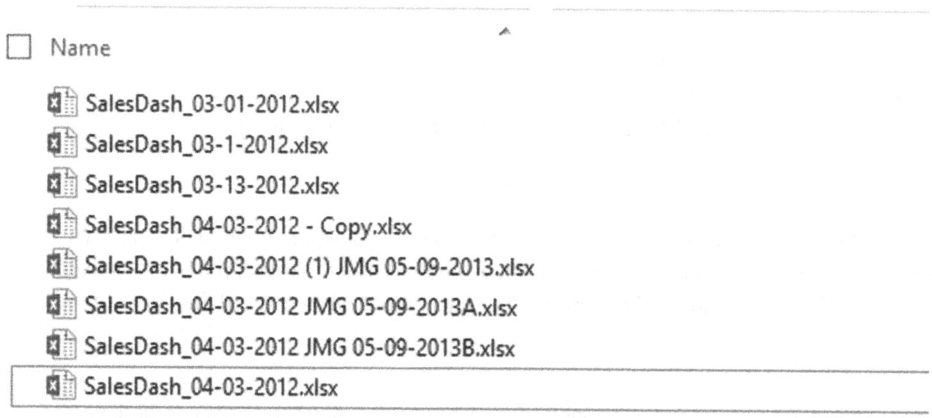

Figure 7-20. *A common-looking list of files*

The most recent file in this list is `SalesDash_04-03-12 JMG 05-09-2013B.xlsx`. Now let's compare the list in Figure 7-20 to the same files renamed in the list shown in Figure 7-21.

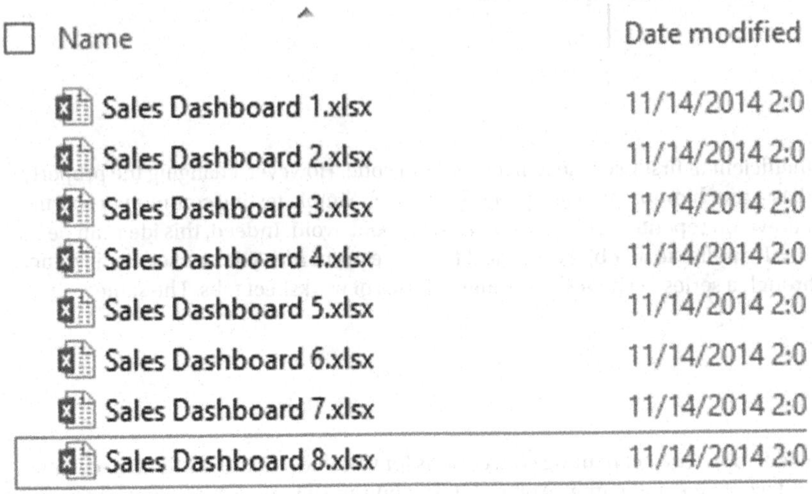

Figure 7-21. *Better file names help with organization and file archiving*

This may seem trivial, but proper file names will help you keep track of your progress. In the "Proper File Name Style" sidebar, I've outlined some common rules to name your files.

PROPER FILE NAME STYLE

What follows are five style rules that should help you have more descriptive file names.

Use Your Words

An ideal Excel file name should be two or three succinct words and contain few numbers. Current operating systems no longer constrain file name character length, so there is no excuse for or cleverness in using shorthand. Capitalize each word as you would a document title.

Abbreviate Only Proper Nouns

If your file is an example to someone, it should have the full word "Example," not "ex," in its title. If your Excel dashboard is the second version of the "Cost Analysis and Reporting System," you may abbreviate your file name to "CARS v2.xlsx," but a VBA Chart Tutorial should never be named "VB ChrtTut.xlsm."

Always Connect Words with a Space and Nothing Else

The name of your file is not a programming variable or engineering quantity. The words in your file name should not be connected with underscores (_) or dashes (-).

Use Clear Dates, but Don't Include Dates in Every File Name

Unless your file is a report that comes out on a specific, periodic schedule, there's likely not a good reason to put today's date in your file name. If you must put a date in your file, place the date at the beginning, left side of the file name so it appears first. This ensures the date is not cut off when viewed in a file explorer. Dated files are likely to be stored with similar files in the same folder, so cutting off the last bit of each file name on the right is less harmful than cutting off the date.

Numbers Are Preferable to Dates

If you have several iterations of a file, use a numbering system instead of dates. Using dates leads to the horrible practice of adding extra numbers at the end of the file name, for example `InventoryList 22 Feb 2001_1.xlsx`, `InventoryList 22 Feb 2001_2.xlsx`, and so on. Moreover, using dates and the former practice will not instantly make clear which is the latest version of your file when viewed in a file directory. However, placing a number at the end of your file name (`Inventory List 1.xlsx`, `Inventory List 2.xlsx`) always will make clear the latest (and first) iteration of the file whether sorted by file name, file type, or date modified when viewed in a directory (these files will always be either first or last). Numbers always should appear as the last character on the right.

You can extend this idea to worksheet tab names. You should just be mindful of undescriptive names creeping into your work. Compare Figure 7-22 to Figure 7-23.

Figure 7-22. *A worksheet with terrible tab names*

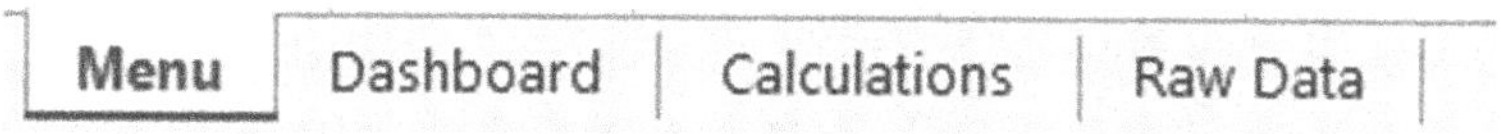

Figure 7-23. *A worksheet with terrific tab names*

I don't have specific guidelines for tab names except to follow the theme presented so far. Use spaces to separate words, use descriptive names as much as possible, and keep others in mind as you work. You never know who else might take up your work after you've left. Or, perhaps several weeks, months, or even years later you'll have to revisit your old work—you'll thank yourself for using descriptive and commonly understood titles in place of retired acronyms and jargon no longer in vogue.

The Last Word

In this chapter, I discussed many of the pitfalls of development. They come in several forms: calculation, code, and design. The concepts presented are not hard-and-fast rules. Rather, they are principles to keep in mind as you develop. Sometimes you will have to break a rule or toss out convention. But keeping convention in mind is what allows you to know when to break a rule. When you develop with intention, the work you create is far superior.

In the next chapter, you'll delve more deeply into dashboard layout.

CHAPTER 8

The Elements of Good Excel Dashboards and Decision Support Systems

In this chapter, I'll discuss what makes for a good dashboard and what I even mean by the term. As you go through the chapter, you should pay particular attention to the many examples presented by Microsoft and others. I will critique this work and explain why you might choose something different. At times, it might feel I'm challenging common wisdom. But I'll do that for good purpose: many misconceptions of creating applications in Excel have led to poor design.

Types of Dashboards

Before moving forward, let's talk about the dashboards commonly found in the business community. You should use these categories to help you shape what you would like to build. But don't feel as if you should have to hold fast to them. What you choose to build often depends on your functional needs. The categories themselves help aid you in understanding how your work ought to be used. And, according to the experts, there are three main types of dashboards commonly used in business.

- Strategic
- Operational
- Analytical

Strategic

In this section, I'll discuss tactical or strategic dashboards. These dashboards provide information to managers and decision makers about the underlying health of the business or organization. Because these dashboards are strategic in nature, they do not typically contain complicated metrics or key performance indicators. Instead, they offer simple information at a high level and at an aggregate level. Often the information provides insight into a problem that would require further analysis.

Operational

Operational dashboards provide insight into specific company operations. They are often more complex than strategic dashboards. The information presented often requires a timely response, so they are more likely to highlight problems and alert their core audience to take action. Operational dashboards often contain drill-down capabilities that allow users to gain insight both from a high level and from a lower level. This allows users to understand how factors at the lowest levels affect metrics at the higher levels.

Analytical

Analytical dashboards are often more dense than the former two presented. They allow for comparison of multiple factors and trends. They offer the greatest amount of detail compared to the former two. Where tactical dashboards are often concerned with a reporting period (for instance, they are updated each month) and operational dashboards monitor processes often in real time, analytical dashboards allow for multiple comparison across varying dimensions.

These descriptions should help you think about what you want to get out of your dashboards. Many, like Stephen Few, would argue that little interactivity should exist on dashboards, except to the extent the interactivity enhances understanding. I don't disagree with this idea at all, but I do wonder if Stephen Few might disagree with some of the additions that follow. Indeed, I used to be a hardliner on this, but as time goes on, I find that dashboards in Excel go great with Excel's interactivity, which is why I would like to bring up a fourth type of dashboard-type product that is common in Excel but doesn't technically qualify as a dashboard—*the decision support system*.

Decision Support Systems

At their core, interactive reports provide for decision support. They are sometimes referred to as *spreadsheet decision support systems* when built in Excel. In this book, I refer to them as either interactive reports or decision support systems. For these spreadsheets reporting is often dynamic, changing to reflect user input and interactivity. I do believe that there is significant overlap between decision support systems and dashboards.

In any event, decision support systems differ from dashboards in that they go beyond monitoring and help support organizational-level decision making. They generally employ different elements than dashboards (more on this from a data perspective in Chapter 11); for instance, they use charts for data sensemaking, and both require proper execution of design to deliver. As well, they may be model driven. That means they are presenting information in the abstract.

In their purest form, dashboards help you monitor a process. But if you extend the idea behind analytical dashboards, you can easily incorporate what-if analysis. Excel allows you to do this easily. Figure 8-1 shows a hybrid that allows for both monitoring and investigation. The two charts on the left help you to monitor what's going on, while the selection capability on the right allows the user to drill down to understand what's going on behind the scenes.

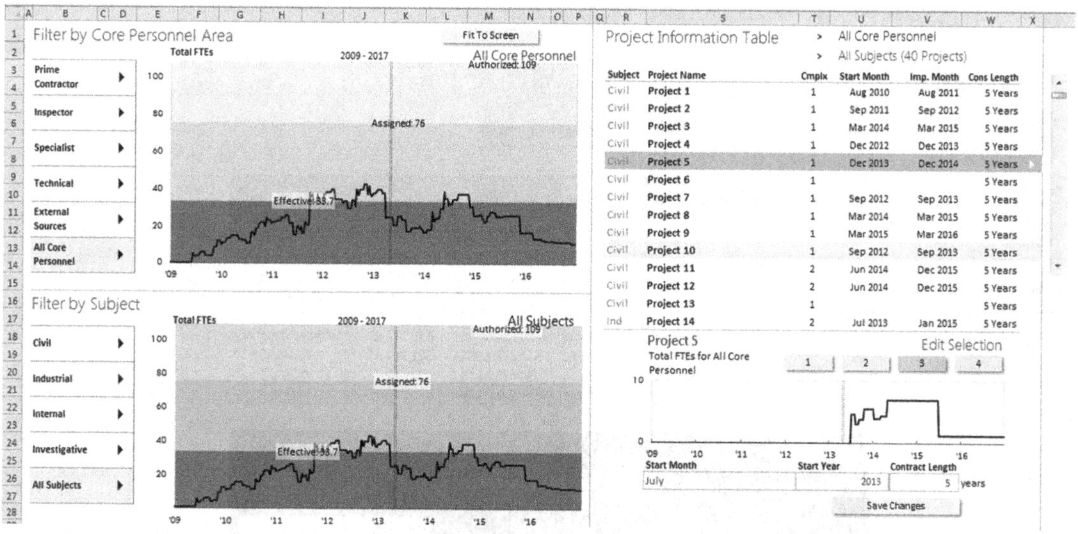

***Figure 8-1.** A dashboard that also allows you to perform decision analysis*

In the report in Figure 8-1, the user is able to change certain properties of each project to see how these changes affect the needs in the aggregate. Often these interactive capabilities are coupled with extra areas for user input. The buttons in the Edit Selection and drop-down boxes are types of input blocks. For the most part, your work will provide some level of monitoring or some level of decision support—or both. You'll take some liberties here and refer to this work as a dashboard, Excel application, or decision support system. Luckily in terms of developing for Excel, the differences between the two aren't all that important. What's important are the underlying principles. Let's go through them.

Simplified Layout

The backbone of a good dashboard in Excel is good layout and back-end design. In this section, I'll go through the tenets of good layout, which I've coined *simplified layout*.

Both dashboards and interactive reports ought to employ what I like to call a simplified layout, by which I mean that they both make efficient and optimal use of the screen. However, most work you might run into today do not follow a simplified layout. For instance, it's not uncommon for developers to break up the pieces of their analysis across many different worksheet tabs. But simplified layout would dictate you should always show relevant data together and not make the process of ascertaining the story from the data more complex by needlessly separating it. Simplified layouts make use of the principles of visualization outlined in Chapters 3 and 4: space is devoted to content, and meaningful data isn't separated.

To wit, Microsoft's built-in features do not always encourage simplified layout. In the example dashboard in Figure 8-2, otherwise available screen space is devoted to slicers. (You can download this file, `Chapter8ContosoDashboard.xlsx`, from the chapter files folder.) This example shows a complex layout.

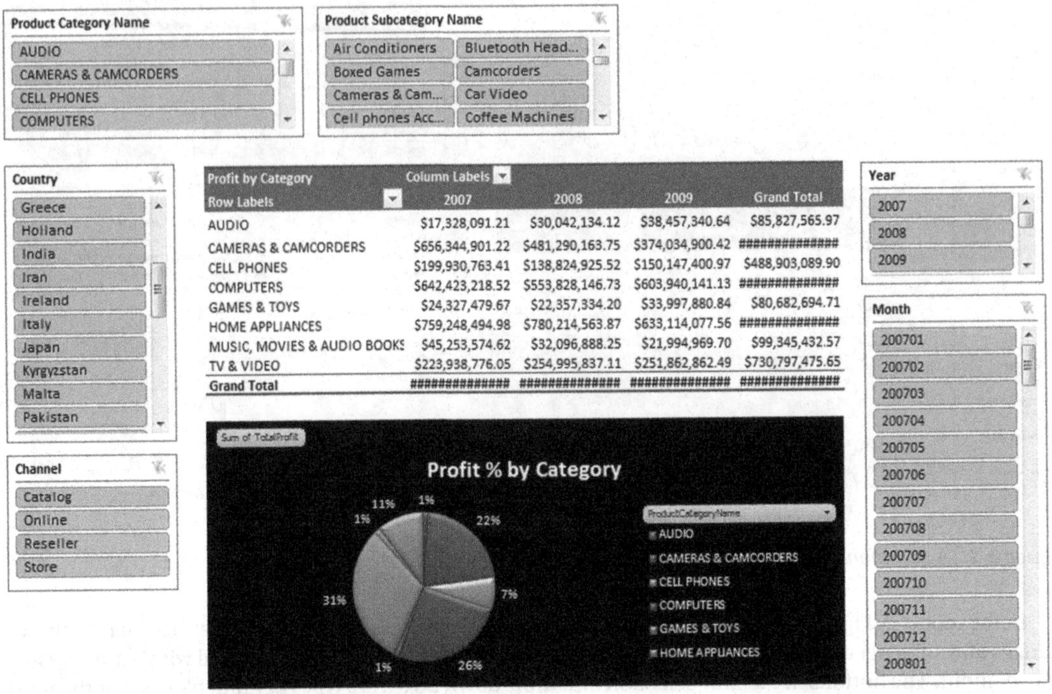

***Figure 8-2.** A dashboard created with Power Pivot that is big on controls and low on information*

This result is an overly complicated screen that makes it hard to connect what's in view and what has been filtered. While the slicers do allow for drill-down capability, with the available screen space, you might have been better off creating several smaller charts that you already know you're interested in. Moreover, you could redesign this report to present alerts to show you which areas require attention. You could click those alerts to find out more about them, as needed. As it stands, this spreadsheet allows you to slice and dice the data but at the expense of conveying good information.

Figure 8-3 shows an example of an application with a common design theme. It sections off certain areas to help organize the information you'd like to present. However, a good portion of this information lies beyond the viewpoint of the screen. The effect is to globally disconnect the information being presented.

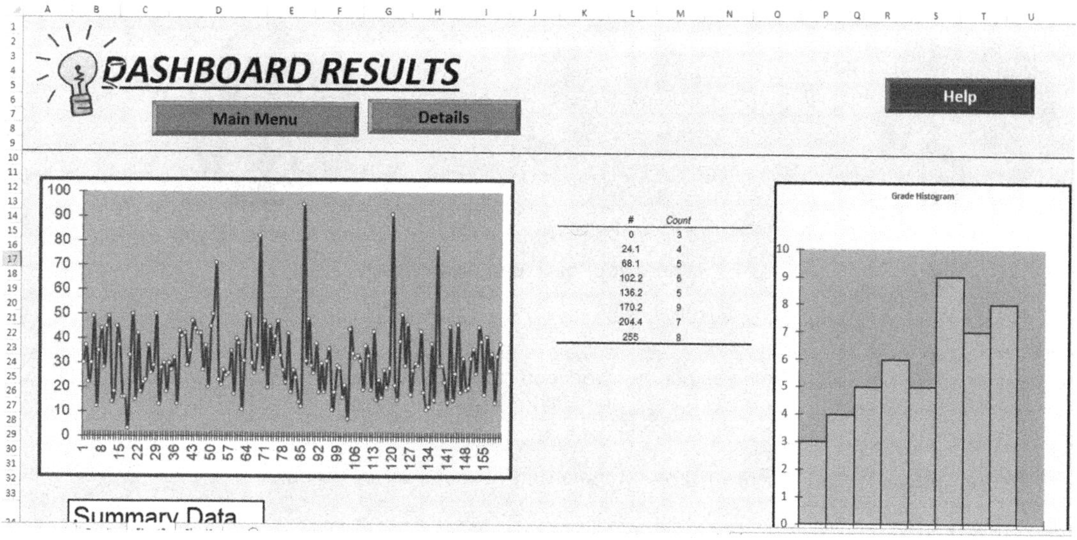

Figure 8-3. *An example decision support system*

Both of these examples demonstrate a common problem in Excel development and information presentation. Often developers build more interactivity or provide more information than the project requires. You should make it a goal in your work to never present information in such a way that it requires the user to scroll all over the spreadsheet to see the information. Furthermore, you should not segment results and reports into different tabs. In other words, everything you want to present should be clearly visible in one view. Therefore, the tenets of simplified layout are as follows:

- Present all information in one view, without scrolling.
- Use only one tab to present information.

Perhaps you now see the challenges that lay ahead. If you want to increase your information density—that is, the amount of information presented onscreen—you can't fill it with copious controls or separate it across spreadsheets and tabs.

Information-Transformation-Presentation

Good dashboards and decision support systems use a concept I call *information-transformation-presentation* (ITP). (Hey! That rhymes!) This is a common design type similar to n-tier design in the field of business intelligence. As part of ITP, you separate the back-end data from the calculations you do to it (transformation) and its presentation (that's where you show the information). Figure 8-4 shows this idea conceptually.

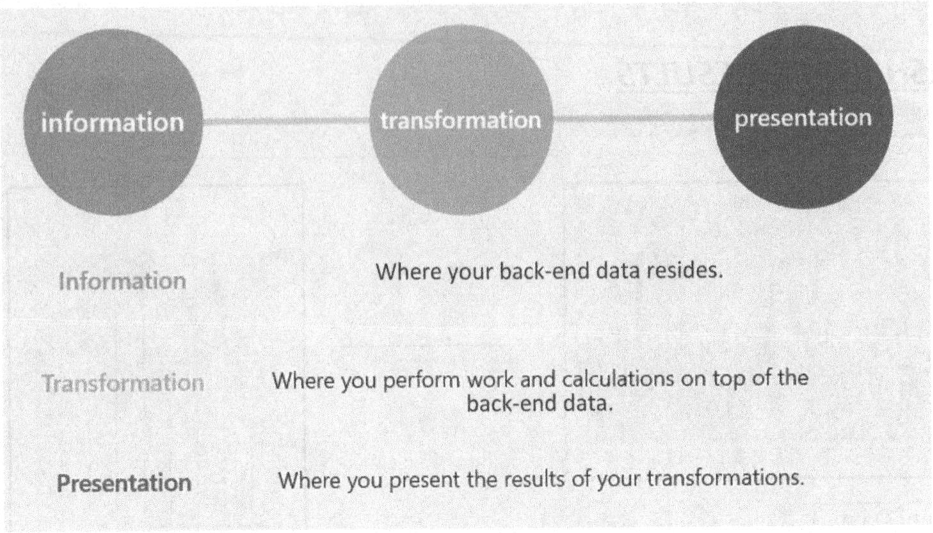

Figure 8-4. *A conceptual description of information-transformation-presentation*

The basic idea behind ITP is to separate the various elements of your work. In the information section, you store the back-end data that is usually in its raw form. As new information is added to the dashboard, this is where the information is stored. You never change this data on the spreadsheet. However, you will perform calculations on this information to transform it into something you want to present. The transformation section is where these calculations take place. Finally, once you are happy with your transformations, this information is presented in the visual layer, which is the presentation section. Figure 8-5 shows this process in detail using graphics from a spreadsheet application you'll create in Chapters 17 to 20.

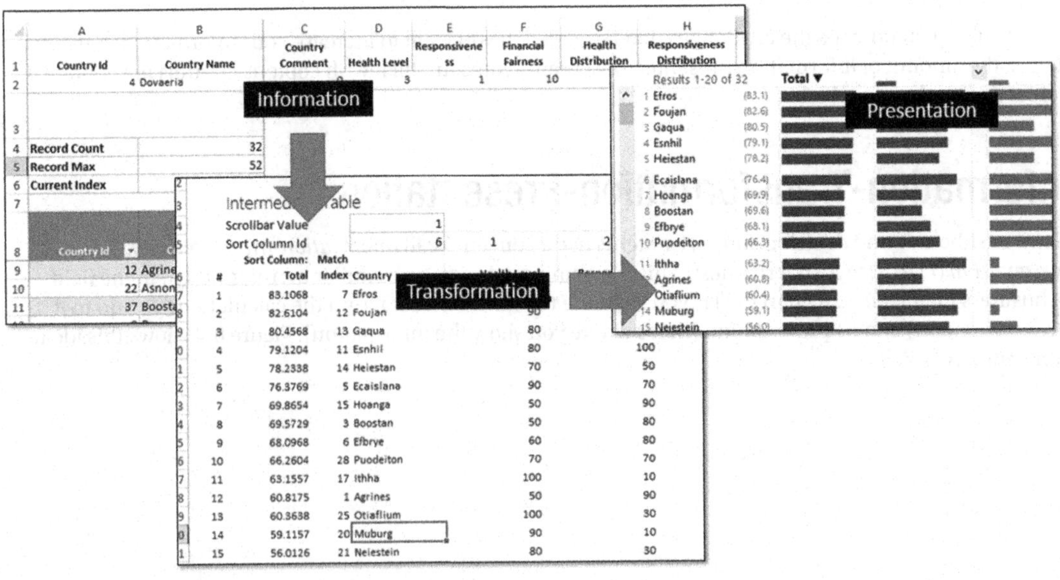

Figure 8-5. *The healthcare analysis decision support system you'll create later in the book uses ITP*

The most important feature of this design pattern is that *the information is always connected*. For instance, the layout shown in Figure 8-5 is entirely connected by way of formulas. When data on the back end is changed, it automatically changes this information on the presentation layer. In other words, changes are ramified through the entire construction. This is what helps you keep the data consistent across each layer. This terrific dynamic doesn't work if the data is disconnected.

Here's what I mean by *disconnected*: It is common practice in many Excel applications to create a report on the fly based on the back end. This information is often disconnected from the underlying data. Often this report is initiated by a RUN button similar to the one shown in Figure 8-6.

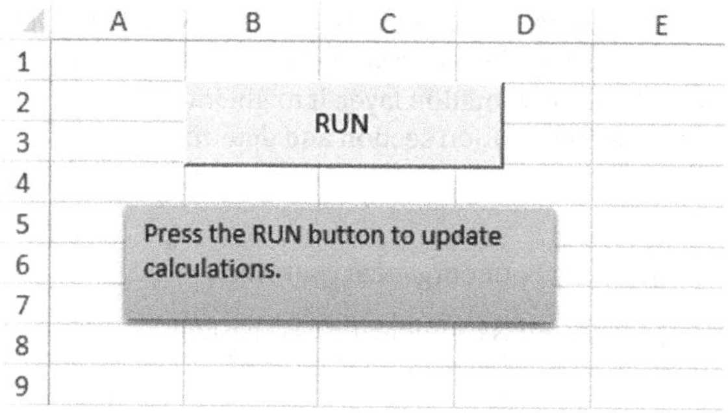

Figure 8-6. *The RUN button—a common dashboard mistake*

This dynamic violates ITP because the information doesn't flow from the information layer on its own to the presentation layer. In Figure 8-6, each layer is part of the spreadsheet. However, you should try as best as possible to avoid using code that does the transformation work when it can be done on the spreadsheet. Doing this work in VBA prevents you from being able to understand the calculations throughout the entire process. As updates are made to the back-end data, the resultant information isn't automatically updated on the chart. The different layers are easily disconnected at each turn.

In fact, it's this underlying connectivity that proves the robustness of ITP. As the introduction to this book lays out, spreadsheet errors are ubiquitous and unavoidable. If you accept that you live in a world where errors are unavoidable, then you should construct your work in a way that will help errors rise to the surface immediately. In the RUN button dynamic, it's much harder to understand where errors take place. (Is it an error in the code? Is it in error in how the code interacts with the spreadsheet? Is the data incorrect because the user forgot to hit the RUN button before preceding?)

In some instances (and I have seen more than enough instances of this during my years), the RUN button setup might not even let users know that errors exist. This is because complex calculations have been incorporated into complex VBA code. For many developers, going back through the code is a tedious task that they would prefer and more often than not avoid. In going through their work, it becomes enough for the developer that the model can generate output as expected. The test for error-free work shifts from evaluating whether the results make sense to ensuring the VBA code can run without generating annoying runtime errors. Indeed, this overuse of code has conditioned us to believe that model errors can take the form only of runtime errors, and we often forget the calculations themselves might be incorrect.

And incorrect calculations must break the model. By keeping everything connected through ITP, you can immediately evaluate whether your model is presenting data correctly. Because as you change data on the front end, the changes are quickly ramified through to the resulting presentation. Therefore, you don't have to go through the calculations looking for the potential of miscalculation because you can judge miscalculation in real time. Simply consider the common process of looking up the location of an item with VBA. You could write code to iterate through a list, but the code might never make the match, and yet it appears to work as expected because you forgot to compensate for a situation when no match was found.

You could use the `Application.Match()` function in your code. But if no match is found, a Type Mismatch error will result. The problem is Type Mismatch is also the same error that would result if a match was found but the variable it assigns the result to is of the incorrect type. It's the same error that results if you place the wrong arguments into the Match function. In other words, you're going to have to dig a little bit to figure out exactly what caused the runtime error.

In ITP, however, you don't have these issues. If you use a `MATCH` worksheet function—and no match is found—an `#NA` error will result. Everything that relies on that data field will result in an `#NA`. If a chart relies on the data point, no data will be shown. You immediately see there is an issue. And ITP helps you understand where the error takes place.

That's because errors are propagated up through to the presentation layer. So, when you encounter an error on the presentation layer, your first step is to check whether the error exists on the transformation layer. If the transformation layer calculates correctly, then you can reasonably conclude the error is originating in the presentation layer. Similarly, if the error appears on the transformation layer, it might indicate an underlying problem with your information. You can check the information section and determine from there whether it's where the error originates.

For brevity, let's summarize the benefits of ITP.

- ***Separation of concerns***: By separating each area, you better organize your work.
- ***Auditing transparency***: You can better audit your models by following a consistent logical pattern of development.
- ***Error propagation***: Because of this design, you can easily start from the presentation and work backward to find errors.
- ***Integrity of back-end data***: The back-end data stays "raw" with minimal changes to it.

Common Dashboard Problems

As you did in the previous chapter, you'll place some focus on common problems in Excel dashboards. You can summarize them as follows:

- Using too much formatting and embellishments
- Employing far too many tabs than is necessary
- Bad layout
- Needless protection
- Unnecessary instructions and documentation

Let's go through each item.

Too Much Formatting and Embellishment

In this section, I'll talk about formatting and embellishment. I don't really need to hammer this point too much anymore, but it's worth demonstrating the differences here. Figure 8-7 shows a dashboard with lots of color, clip art, name attribution, and three-dimensional charts.

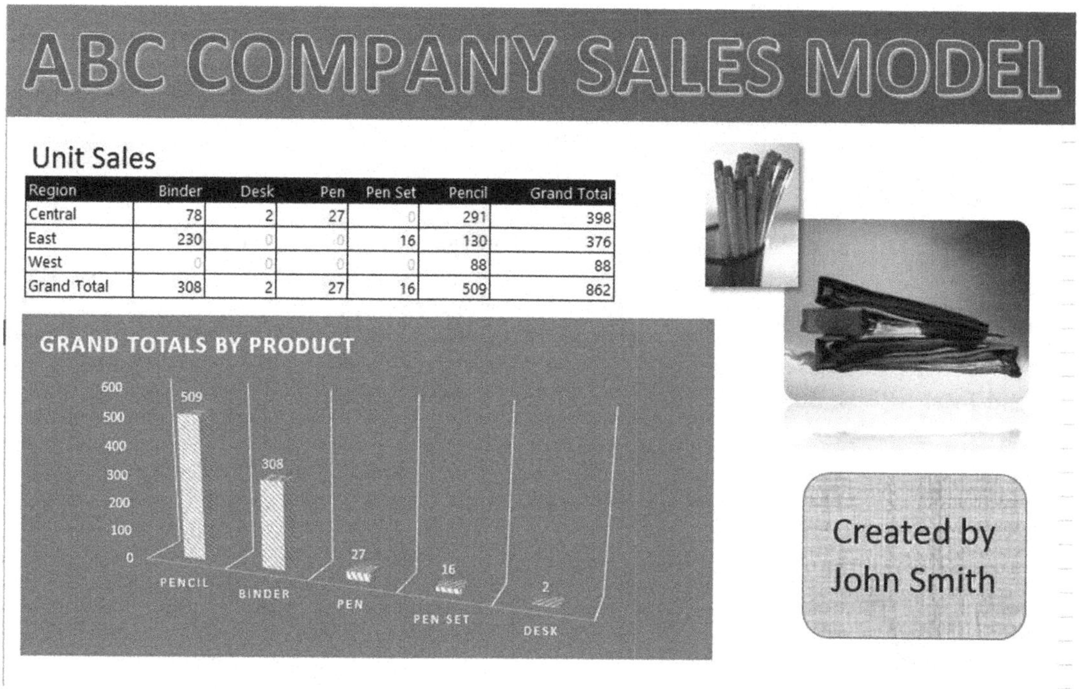

Figure 8-7. *A dashboard crowded by nonsense*

Again, if you are to achieve your goal, you must be more judicious with what you present. There is no reason for the clip art; it certainly doesn't make the work more interesting to read. Worse, it's distracting. Figure 8-8 presents a much needed revision.

ABC Company Sales Model

Unit Sales

Region	Binder	Desk	Pen	Pen Set	Pencil	Grand Total
Central	78	2	27	0	291	398
East	230	0	0	16	130	376
West	0	0	0	0	88	88
Grand Total	308	2	27	16	509	862

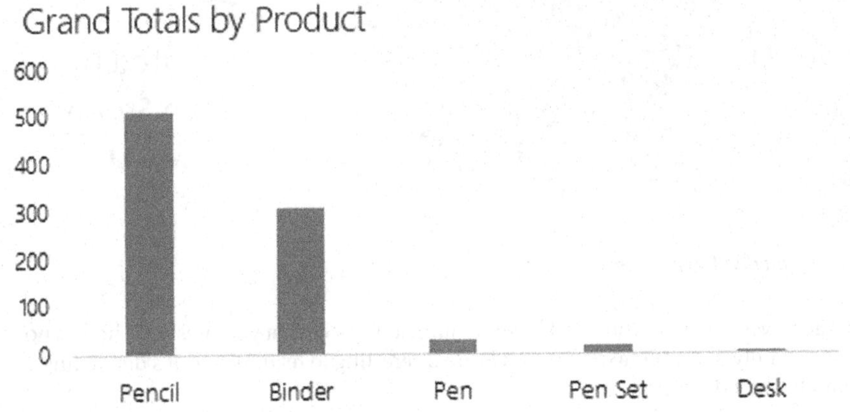

Figure 8-8. *A cleaner, more elegant presentation of information*

To make things look spiffy, it's also not a bad idea to remove the gridlines wherever you present information. You can hide gridlines by deselecting the Gridlines option in the Show group on the View ribbon tab (see Figure 8-9).

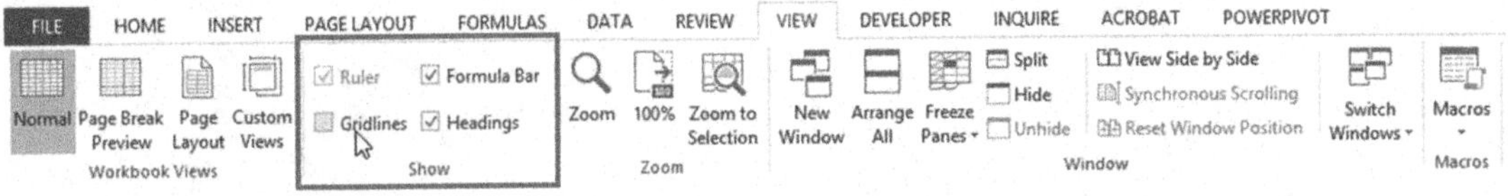

Figure 8-9. *You can remove gridlines by deselecting Gridlines on the View tab*

Too Many Tabs

Another common development structure I've seen concerns separating information across different tabs. Each tab then usually has one chart on it. Figure 8-10 shows the welcome screen of such a dashboard. The user would click a link on this spreadsheet and be taken to one of corresponding charts. In Figure 8-10, if the user were to click "Go to" next to Quarter 1 Sales, the user would arrive at the Quarter 1 tab, as shown in Figure 8-11.

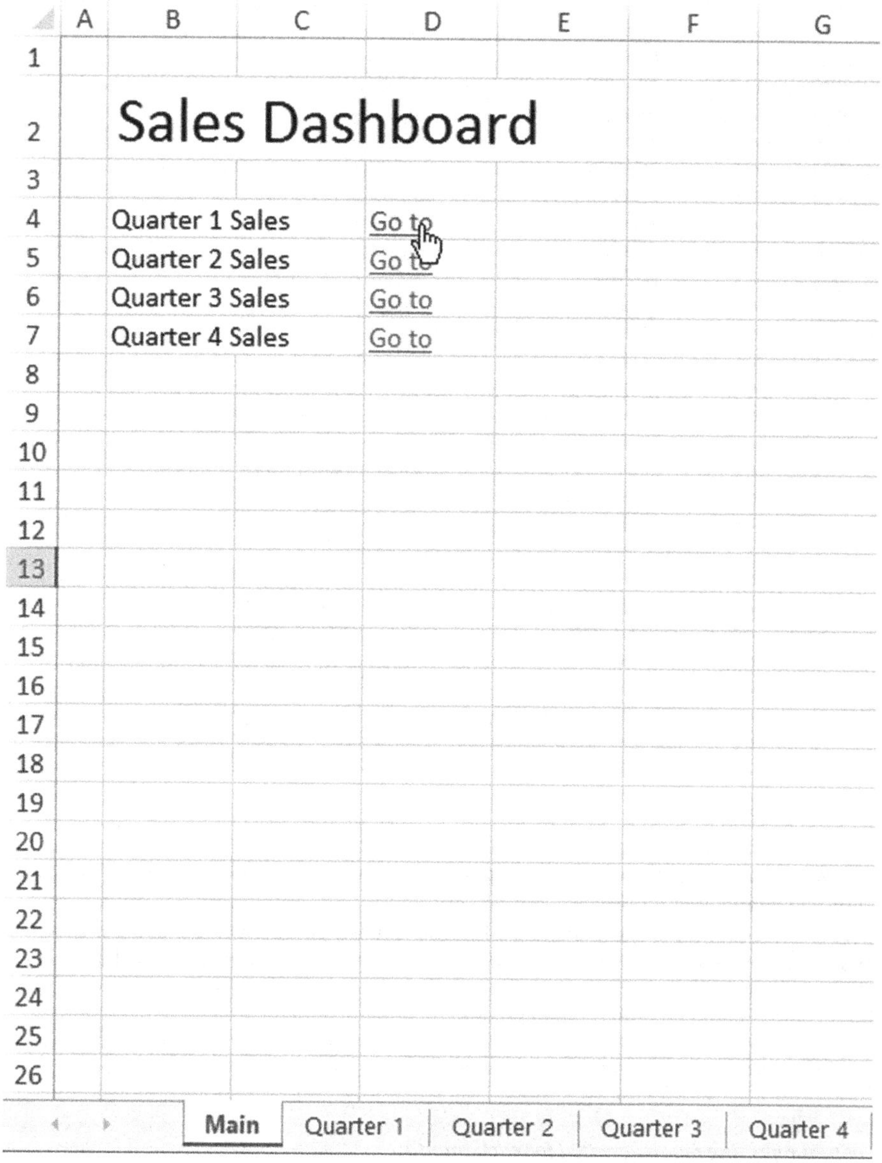

Figure 8-10. *A welcome screen that separates information*

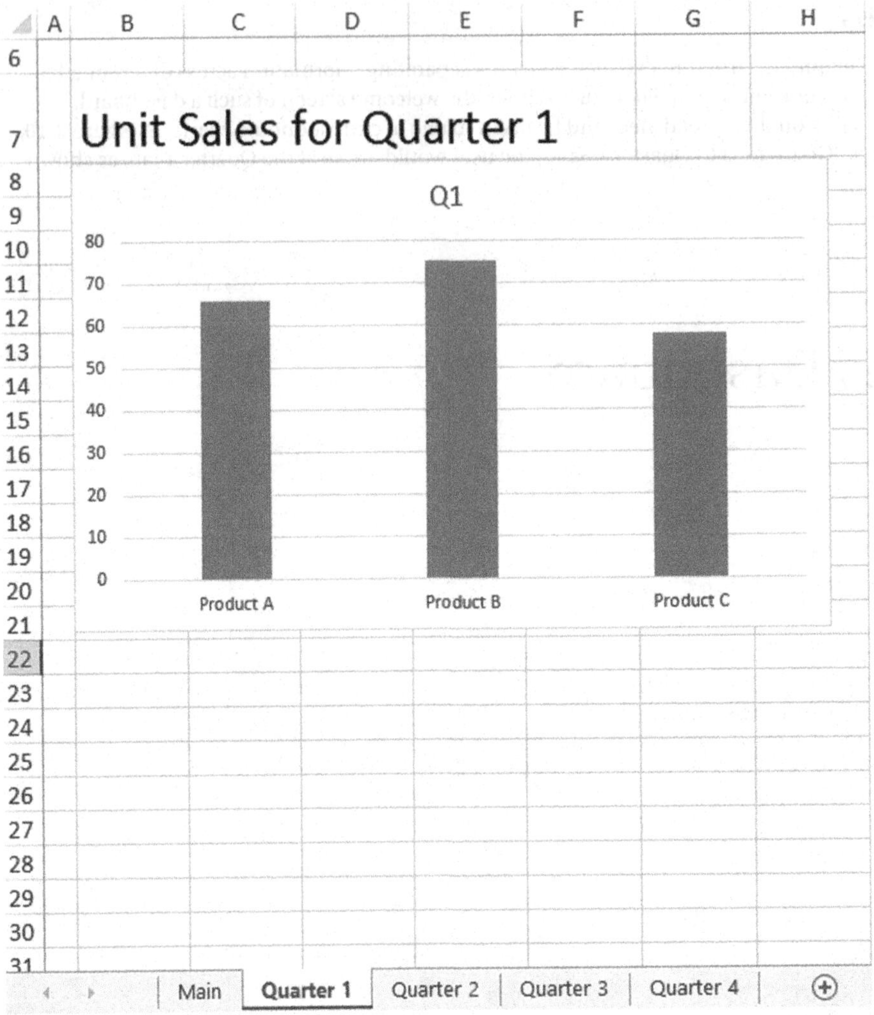

Figure 8-11. *Results for Quarter 1 sales*

However, there's no reason to show only one chart per page. Following the tenets of simplified layout, all information should be shown together if possible.

Another common reason for tabs filling up a dashboard or decision support system is that the tabs represent historical versions. For instance, Figure 8-12 shows several tabs with the names of months. Each month has a new report created for it.

Figure 8-12. *A series of tabs reflecting reports created for each month*

The only reason someone might use this setup is if they aren't following the information-transformation-presentation construct. If they are using a RUN button, they have to generate a new report. And the only way to keep the report is by archiving it as a copy of a new tab. However, if you employ ITP, then everything is connected.

Figure 8-13 shows a simplified version of ITP compensating for new reports. As a user changes the month of interest, that information is used by the transformation layer to look up the month of interest. Then, the presentation layer uses these results to update the chart. It all happens instantaneously. And previous information is archived (and retrievable) by virtue of its storage in the information section.

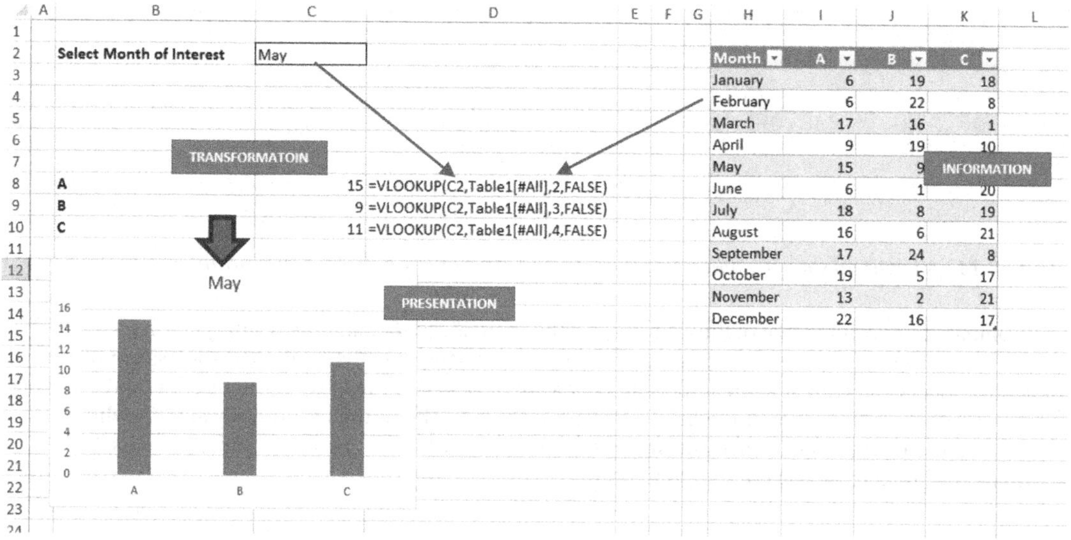

Figure 8-13. *A simplified presentation of ITP*

Bad Layout

In this subsection, I'll discuss how layout affects the usefulness of a dashboard. Some examples of bad layout were presented in Figures 8-2 and 8-3, in the "Simplified Layout" section.

In particular, Figure 8-2 places the most important information in the center of the screen. However, research performed by data visualization gurus like Stephen Few and others have argued the most important information should be placed highest up and leftmost. This is the true focal point of where your eyes expect to see information. Figure 8-14 presents a shaded guide to help understand how to distribute information across the screen. The darkest shade is where you should expect the most important pieces of information. The lighter shades—at the bottom and to the far right—are where controls and filters should go.

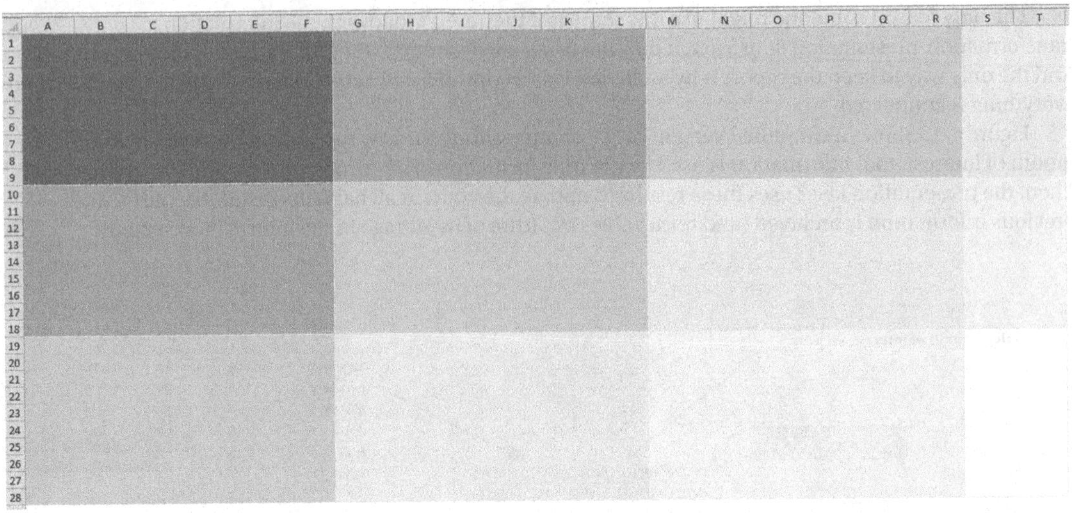

Figure 8-14. *A heatmap showing where your eyes should expect to find the most important information*

Compare this layout to that of the example dashboard in Figure 8-2 and the results page in Figure 8-3. In the former, the data is shown in the center of the screen, leaving the other real estate for less important things, like slicers. In Figure 8-3, the important charts are relegated to the lower portions of the spreadsheet. Figure 8-15, on the other hand, immediately presents a chart that helps the user quickly identify which dates are problematic (you'll be investigating this dashboard in Chapters 13 to 15). And it presents this information without requiring the user to scroll.

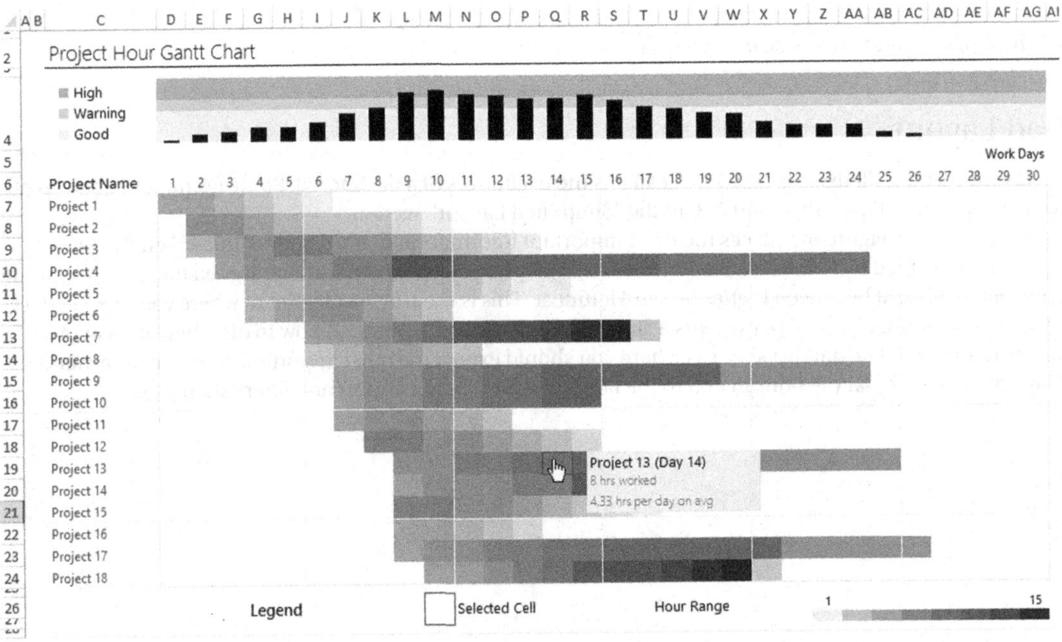

Figure 8-15. *An example dashboard that presents the most important information immediately*

As I've stated already, you should not expect the user to have to scroll off the screen to find the most important information. Where information might spill off the screen, I've found it common practice to zoom out the spreadsheet beyond Excel's standard 100 percent. For instance, a spreadsheet at 90 percent might provide more screen real estate.

To the extent possible, I would strongly urge you not to change Excel's regular zoom settings. How your work appears on other monitors is a function of DPI, font size, and those zoom settings. In the past, spreadsheets appearing differently on different screens and environments was a much more significant problem than today. However, many desktop users have standard monitor sizes. As of this writing, you should expect most of your work to be on a wide-screen monitor with a resolution of 1900×600—or similar. Most screens today are of similar resolutions and aspect ratios. If you will be working on a screen that deviates from the usual standard, you should plan for that ahead of time if possible.

ACCOMMODATING DIFFERENT SCREENS

Sometimes you can't get around the fact that everyone at the office has different screen settings. In these instances, you should still aim to keep your zoom level to 100 percent if you can. However, you might find you must zoom out or in slightly on different monitors.

I have a solution that works about 80 percent of the time, assuming the variation across these different machines isn't significant (and giving common standards for monitors, it shouldn't be).

Figure 8-16 shows a hypothetical example of a dashboard where the content fills most of the area in view. Above the box representing the content, I've selected the region A1:U1.

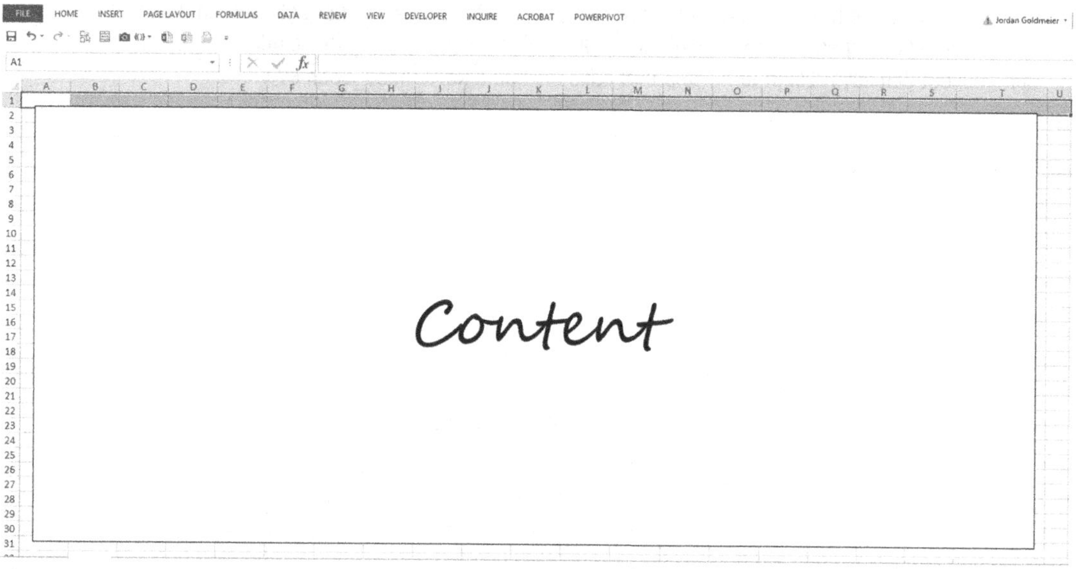

Figure 8-16. *A hypothetical dashboard with content that fills the viewing area*

In Figure 8-17, I've named the region A1:U1 `Dashboard.ContentWidth`.

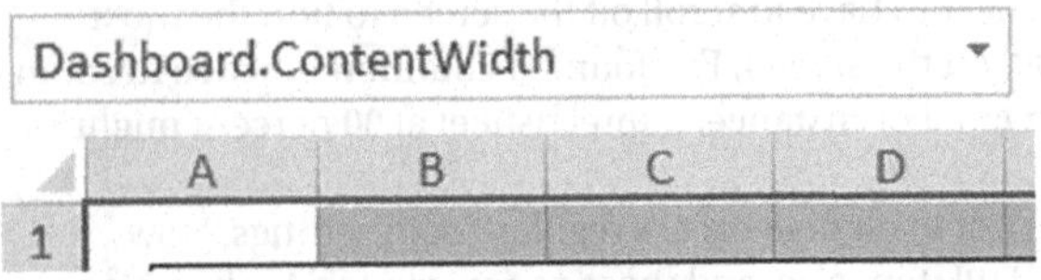

Figure 8-17. The selected region has been named Dashboard.ContentWidth

Now, you can use this information in the `Workbook_Open` event to automatically size the spreadsheet to fit everything within the width specified by `Dashboard.ContentWidth`.

Check out Listing 8-1. When the worksheet is opened, Excel is told to zoom to fit the region given by `Dashboard.ContentWidth`. So, regardless of the monitor or resolutions used, Excel will always zoom to fit the width specified by the region. If there are only slight differences in resolution between monitors, this solution does a pretty good job.

Listing 8-1. This Code Will Automatically Zoom to Fit the Region Given by Dashboard.ContentWidth

```
Private Sub Workbook_Open()
  [Dashboard.ContentWidth].Select
  ActiveWindow.Zoom = True
End Sub
```

Be forewarned, however, there is a small quirk with this code. If Excel is improperly shut down in a previous use, the Document Recovery pane will appear when you next open an Excel file. This will shrink the viewing area available to see the spreadsheet. Because of this, this zoom feature doesn't always work (Figure 8-18). Luckily, there are two easy workarounds: (1) instruct users to deal with the recovered documents and then exit the file and return once again or (2) include a button on the spreadsheet that says "zoom to fit" and that calls the same `Worksheet_Open` event.

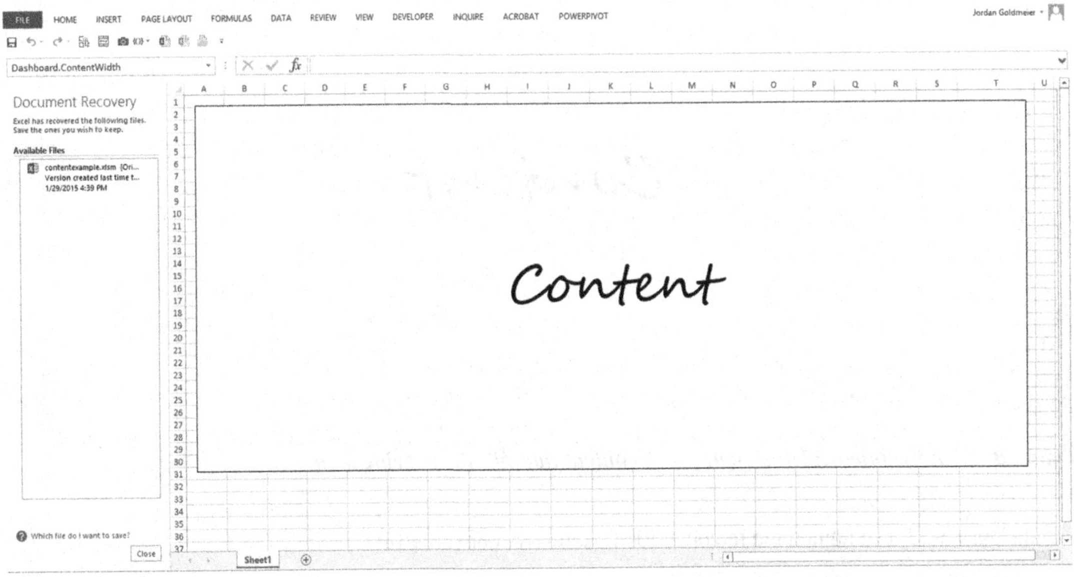

Figure 8-18. An example of the Document Recovery pane preventing this functionality to work as intended

Lastly, I want to point out a design consideration not mentioned earlier. In Figures 8-16 and 8-18, the rightmost portion of the content region ends partway through column T. However, I set the content width to include column U. I did this because I want there to be a small buffer between the end of the content region and the end of what you can see on the spreadsheet. In fact, I've tried to size column U accordingly to fit the distance between Column T and the scroll bars. This assures there is always a buffer between the content and the end of the viewing area when using this technique.

In general, I use the additional space created when the ribbon is hidden. Figure 8-18 in the preceding sidebar provides an example of the ribbon being hidden with extra space provided. I generally hide the ribbon manually and instruct users in my included instructions to do the same. Code exists to automatically hide the ribbon when the worksheet is opened, but I'm not a fan of it. Such code often creates problems when other spreadsheets are open at the same because it affects all instances of the same Excel window.

In addition, I would avoid all commands that completely remove functionality from Excel. For instance, it's somewhat common for developers to hide everything in the Excel windows, including worksheet tabs, the ribbon, the formula bar, and the headings. With respect to the formula bar and headings, you can hide these items as they appear on the worksheet using the View tab (refer to Figure 8-9). But you should avoid hiding these items automatically via code when the workbook is opened. Again, if the workbook is opened after another workbook has already been opened, this code will remove the formula bar across all spreadsheets sharing the same instance of Excel. It's an easy way to have your client call you up asking why they no longer see their formula bar.

Needless Protection

This section deals with protecting the spreadsheet through Microsoft Excel's built-in mechanism. What I've found is that people are perhaps a bit too overzealous in their desire to protect everything.

Indeed, what I'm about to say is sacrilegious, *but you shouldn't develop with the assumption that your client is a complete idiot who will undoubtedly break everything in your spreadsheet.* Using worksheet protection, hiding worksheet tabs, removing menus—these almost always cause other issues. For instance, if a dashboard instructs Excel to remove the ribbon tab menu and worksheet tabs, this change will happen across other open instances of Excel. The same clients who insisted that such protection was needed will scratch their heads when the ribbon menu tab has unexpectedly disappeared from their other opened Excel instance. And worksheet protection often causes other unforeseen issues. For instance, protecting certain areas of the spreadsheet might require you to unprotect it momentarily in the code to make changes (remember, protection can cut both ways). Turning protection on and off constantly to debug and figuring out which of Excel's protection features cover which spreadsheet elements is an incredible hassle. I don't believe it's worth it, and I think it causes many more problems than it truly solves.

The fact is *you will never prevent the user from every error imaginable.* Indeed, it's not even worth your time attempting to prevent such hypothetical scenarios. Every time you lock something up from the client, you make it that much harder for you to fix any underlying issues. If you work with the mutual trust of your client in mind, you won't need to invest so much time in preventative maintenance.

I'm not saying you should completely avoid any level of protection in your work. I am saying, however, that common methods, such as hiding the worksheet tabs, will make a larger headache for you while providing almost no value to your stakeholders. You can get by with the following methods, which I would call "good enough protection."

Hiding Unused Rows and Columns

You can prevent users from scrolling off into the great unknown by hiding the unused portion of your spreadsheet. In Figure 8-19, I've selected all the columns to the right of the unused portion of my work. You can easily do this in your work by selecting the first unused column after your content area. Then, with that column selected, use the keyboard combination Ctrl+Shift+Right Arrow.

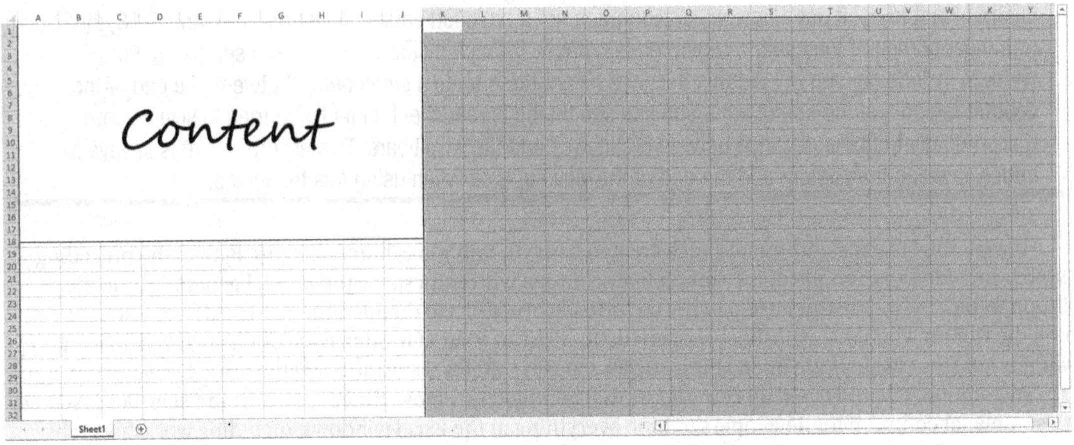

***Figure 8-19.** All columns to the right of my content region have been selected*

Then, on the Home tab, select Format ➤ Hide & Unhide ➤ Hide Columns (Figure 8-20).

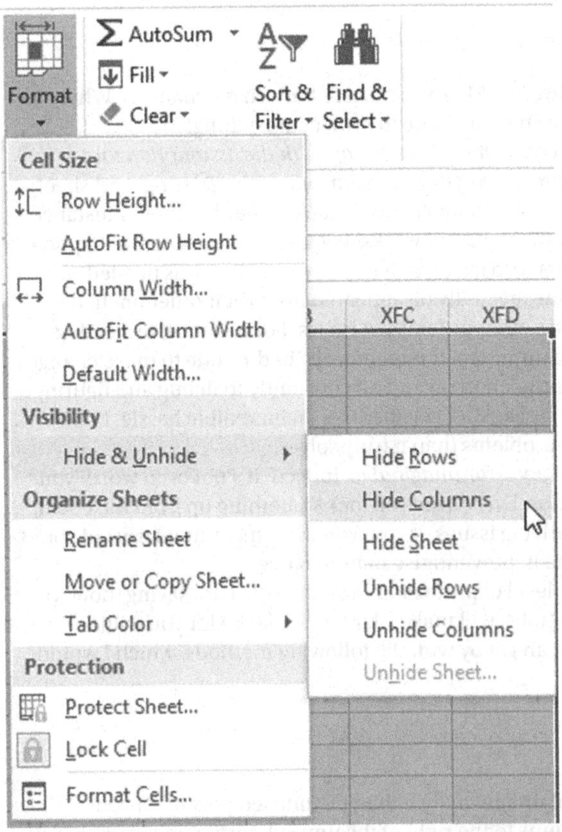

***Figure 8-20.** You can hide selected columns by selecting these options*

You can do the same by selecting the unused row portions (select the first row and press Ctrl+Shift+Down Arrow) and selecting Hide Rows from the menu shown in Figure 8-20. This will create a compact spreadsheet similar to the one shown in Figure 8-21.

Figure 8-21. *The unwanted regions are now removed from view.*

Controlling the Scroll Area

Another alternative is to control the worksheet property called the scroll area. In Figure 8-22, I've set the scroll area to C3:F9 (Excel automatically adds the $) in the Properties windows for the worksheet (Developer ➤ Controls Groups ➤ Properties). If you try this on your own spreadsheet, you'll see that the worksheet scroll bar no longer works. It won't let you scroll beyond the scroll area! Additionally, you won't be able to select any cell outside the region given by the scroll area! This is a great way to prevent users from selecting cells they shouldn't—and keeping them from scrolling beyond the designated viewing area.

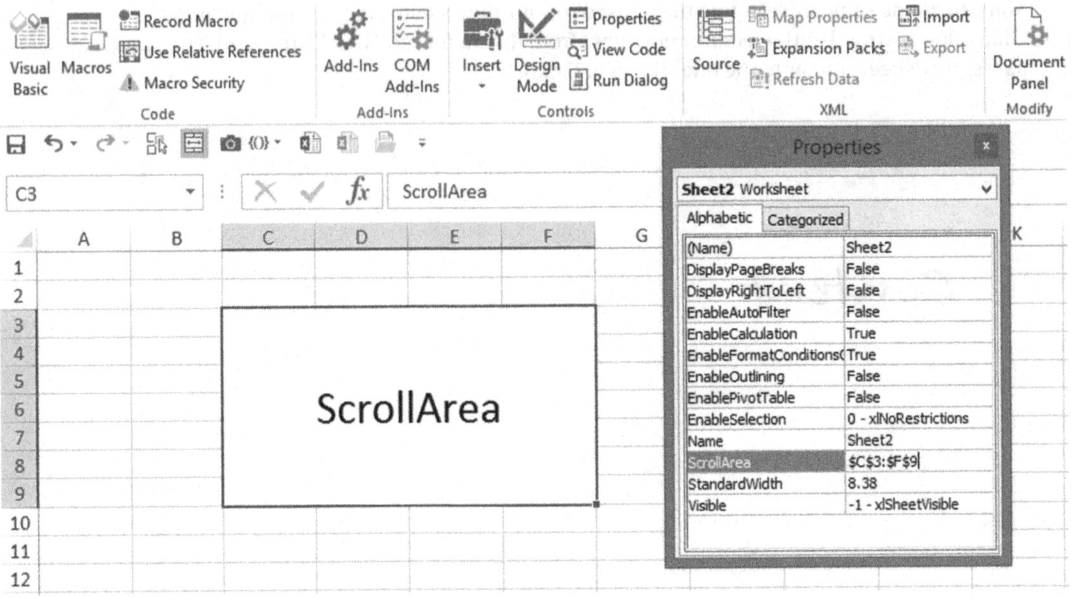

Figure 8-22. *Once the scroll area is set to the region C3:F9, the user will not be able to click outside that region*

Alas, changing the scroll area from the Properties window isn't permanent. Your settings won't be saved the next time you open the spreadsheet. However, you can get around this with a little code. Take a look at Listing 8-2.

Listing 8-2. Setting the Scroll Area Upon Opening a Worksheet

```
Private Sub Workbook_Open()
  Dashboard.ScrollArea = [Dashboard.ScrollArea].Address
End Sub
```

Ultimately, neither of these methods can fully protect your worksheet. But full protection is a pipe dream that cannot be achieved. Instead, both of these methods provide good enough protection for most users. Indeed, they present the added advantage of being easily set and reversed. So when you need to make changes to update your work, you can access these protected areas quickly.

Instructions and Documentation

You should not place full instructions on how to use the dashboard inside the Excel file. If you build work that is intuitive, complete instructions are not required. You should include enough instructions to let the users know where to input information. But a complete reference manual does not belong in the spreadsheet at all.

Save such work for Microsoft Word. Excel is not a word processor. Attempts at including full instructions on spreadsheets often require cramming an incredible amount of information into Excel text boxes. But this is now how text boxes were meant to be used. More often than not, instructions do not fit fully in these text boxes and information is cut off. In addition, many of these instructions are filled with screen grabs of the tool and associated shapes to show users where to click. All of these extra shapes, images, and text boxes add up. They can increase the file size of your work by several megabytes. I'm not against large Excel files per se—but you should devote additional storage to presenting information, not storing instructions.

Furthermore, Microsoft Word is just a better tool for this. With Word, you can create a table of contents. You can organize your screenshots and labels figures. There's a reason I used Word to write this book and not Excel! There's absolutely zero reason to believe or academic research to support including copious instructions within your tool has any effect on how people use it.

I don't want to make any accountants or auditors reading this book too anxious with what I'm about to say. From within these worlds, I've seen directives that suggest every spreadsheet—including dashboards—should have a living record of every update, when the updates were made, and who the intended audience of the work is for. The Spreadsheet Standards Review Board (`www.ssrb.org/`), for instance, recommends a number of items to include within the spreadsheet itself. I've read documents from financial consulting agencies that argue the spreadsheet should include a living record of who used the work last, what changes were made, and so on. While I believe these requirements are well intentioned, my experience suggests they don't help. Indeed, they take attention away from the true goal of the dashboard or decision support system. They become a burden over time as users become tired of filling in the required information.

I will be the first to argue that you should do things according to convention. But I don't think every sheet in your workbook requires a section with stated assumptions and purpose. If you design intuitively, these items aren't needed. I realize these standards have been developed to combat spreadsheet errors that have historically caused problems for many in the financial industry. But little research has justified their existence on the spreadsheet itself. If you feel compelled to record this information—or if company policy dictates that it be recorded—then open a separate Word document or Excel spreadsheet and record updates there.

The Last Word

In this chapter, I described what I mean by an Excel dashboard and decision support systems. While the goal of these tools differs, from a development perspective in Excel, the underlying concepts are the same. In particular, I discussed simplified layout and the ultimate goal to display on the relevant information in one view. Finally, I challenged common dashboard requirements and discussed why many don't use Excel correctly.

You may disagree with some of the advice presented in this chapter. Or, you may agree but might be constrained in your ability to follow through because of organizational policy. In either case, this should have you thinking about why you do what you do. I don't believe it's enough to follow certain guidelines that have not proven themselves useful. You should look to your own work to consider how certain layout choices, design, or processes you've taken for granted might actually go against your ultimate goal.

You goal is to make the most of Excel by dedicating as much real estate, storage, and processing to delivering critical data to the user.

PART III

Formulas, Controls, and Charts

CHAPTER 9

Introducing Formula Concepts

Q: What does every newborn spreadsheet need?

A: Formula

Spreadsheet formulas hold a unique place in advanced Excel development. Most of us are familiar with formulas as a means to produce results more quickly than with manual calculation. For example, if we want to find the arithmetic sum of a range, does it make sense to pull out the Burroughs Adding Machine and punch in each item one by one? No. The very nature of a spreadsheet provides a built-in means to manipulate its elements.

Most of us are used to this type of manipulation with formulas; that is, we use formulas as a means to find and return results. Spreadsheet formulas, when used for Excel development, however, do much more. They form the infrastructure upon which much of our work is based.

Throughout this book we will be working with formulas. Some of these formulas will be very complex. When you first start, they may appear daunting. However, practice makes perfect, and experience is your greatest teacher. The more you use them, the more you develop a formula literacy. What may have appeared hard to read at first glance should become easier. But more important than knowing the formulas themselves is understanding the concepts behind what drives them.

And, of course, Excel includes a few tools and features to help you understand your formulas. Let's go through a few of them you can start using now.

Formula Help

In this section, I'll talk about making the most of your formula experience. The following tips should make your life easier, especially when working with complex formulas.

F2 to See the Formula of a Select Cell

Chances are you're already pretty familiar with F2. But for the uninitiated, pressing the F2 key on a cell containing a formula will highlight the portions of a spreadsheet upon which the formula depends. If you're trying to evaluate a formula, F2 is a good first start to your investigation.

F9 for On-Demand and Piecewise Calculation

F9 is the shortcut key to tell Excel to recalculate. If you type `=RANDBETWEEN(1,2)` in an empty cell on an Excel worksheet and then press F9 continuously, you will see that cell update to 1 or 2 at random. (In addition, if you have any other volatile formulas, those will update too).

F9 can also provide a piecewise, or partial, calculation of a long formula. Take the seemingly complex formula shown in Listing 9-1.

Listing 9-1. An Example of a Long, Complex Formula

```
=IF(SUMPRODUCT(A1:A3*(B1:B3>2))>7, CONCATENATE(A2 & L3), IFERROR(C6, "An error occurred."))
```

Let's say you want to evaluate only a part of this formula, specifically the highlighted portion of the same formula but now in Excel's formula bar (Figure 9-1).

Figure 9-1. *You can select a portion of the formula to be evaluated immediately*

In fact, you can tell Excel to evaluate just that easily. If you highlight the portion as I've done in Figure 9-1, you can press F9 to see what it evaluates to (see Figure 9-2).

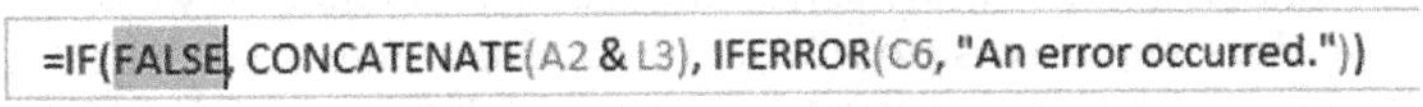

Figure 9-2. *Pressing F9 on the highlighted portion evaluates the highlighted portion immediately*

You now see this portion evaluates to False. In the formula bar, Excel just rewrites this portion of highlighted text to read "FALSE." And you can do this to any portion of the formula. If you click outside the formula bar or press the escape key, the formula will return to its original, unevaluated text. F9 then, when used with formulas, is the ultimate on-demand approach for quick formula evaluation.

Evaluate Formula Button

The Evaluate Formula button allows you to step through an entire formula. Here's how it works. First, click the cell you're interested in investigating. Then, click the Formulas tab on the ribbon. Go to Evaluate Formulas in the Formula Auditing group. Take a look at Figure 9-3.

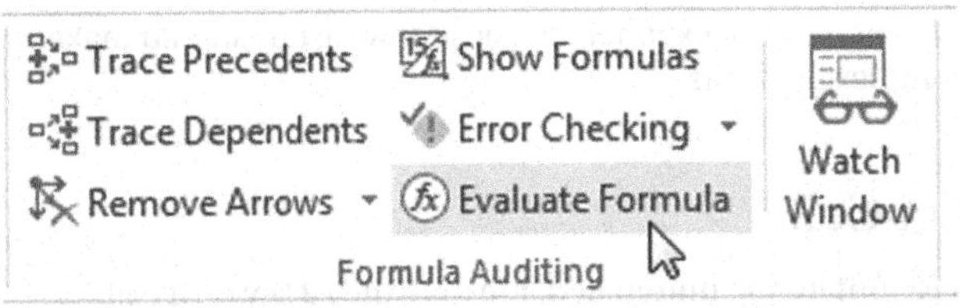

Figure 9-3. *The Evaluate Formula button*

A dialog box similar to the one shown in Figure 9-4 should appear. The underlined portion is the current expression to be evaluated. If available, you can go deeper into the formula by pressing the Step In button. You can Step Out if that level of granularity is no longer need. For formulas that resolve to an error, the Evaluate Formula tool can be very helpful to understand the conditions right before the error. I find Evaluate Formula an indispensable part of my Excel Development toolkit.

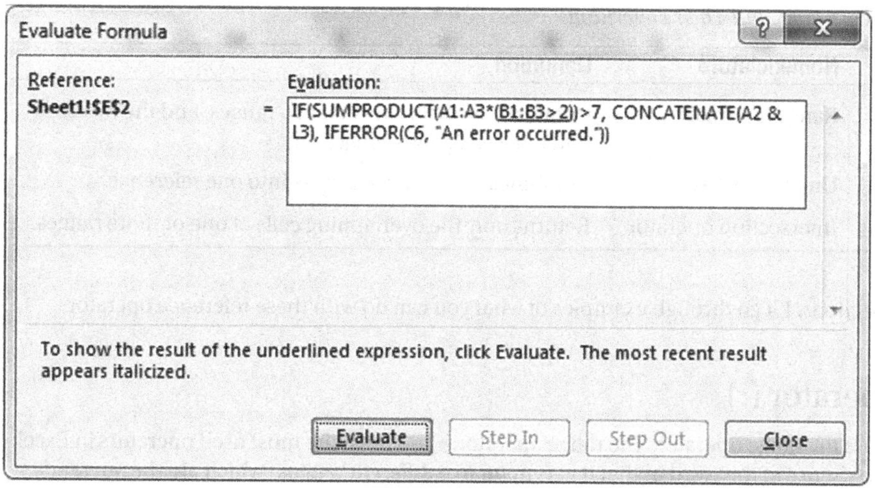

Figure 9-4. *The Evaluate Formula dialog box*

Excel Formula Concepts

In this section, I'll talk about formula concepts you'll be using throughout the rest of this book. To begin, Excel formulas are made up of four main types:

- Functions, such as `AVERAGE()`, `SUM()`, `IF()`
- Constants and literals, such as number, string, and Boolean values like 2, 100, 1E7, "Hello world", and FALSE
- References, such as A1 or A1:A20
- Operators, such as +, -, /, >, :

You're probably already familiar with several of these types. Obviously, functions make up a huge part of formula use. Constants that are numbers are also probably familiar. However, did you know that Boolean values like TRUE and FALSE are also constants? Finally, you've probably used references and operations many times by now, but did you know the colon (:) that forms the range A1:A20 is also an operator?

Operators, in Depth

This section will discuss Excel operators. You're probably familiar with Excel's arithmetic operators, plus (+), minus (-), times (*), and divide (/). But besides arithmetic operators, Excel has a *text* and three *reference* operators.

Excel's text operator is the ampersand (&), which stands in for the `CONCATENATE` function. For instance, the formulas `=A1&B1` and `=CONCATENATE(A1,B1)` do the exact same thing. You've probably also used Excel's reference operators many times, the colon (:) in particular, without thinking of them as operators. Excel's two other reference operators are the comma (,) and space ( ) characters. Table 9-1 talks about what they do.

Table 9-1. Reference Operators and Their Descritions

Reference Operator	Nomenclature	Definition
: (colon)	Range operator	Combines all cells between two ranges, and the two cells into one contiguous range.
, (comma)	Union operator	Combines multiple references into one reference.
(space)	Intersection operator	Returns *only* the overlapping cells of one or more ranges.

In the next few sections, I'll go through examples of what you can do with these reference operators.

The Range Operator (:)

In this section, I discuss the range operator. The range operator (:) is one of the most used operators in Excel. It's an operator in every sense of the word in that it acts upon two different ranges (which are the operands, if you want to get technical) and returns a contiguous range. What's so great about the range operator is that you can actually combine functions, like

```
= A1:INDEX(A:A, COUNTA(A:A))
```

and

```
= B1:OFFSET(B:B, COUNTA(B:B), 0)
```

So let's take a look at an example that shows the power of the range operator.

EXAMPLE: DYNAMICALLY SIZED RANGES

Using the range operator, you can create dynamically sized ranges. This means you can create a range that can grow and shrink as the list they represent is added to or subtracted from. Both the `INDEX` and `OFFSET` formulas can help you with this mechanism. In this example, they both work about the same way. Consider the range in Figure 9-5.

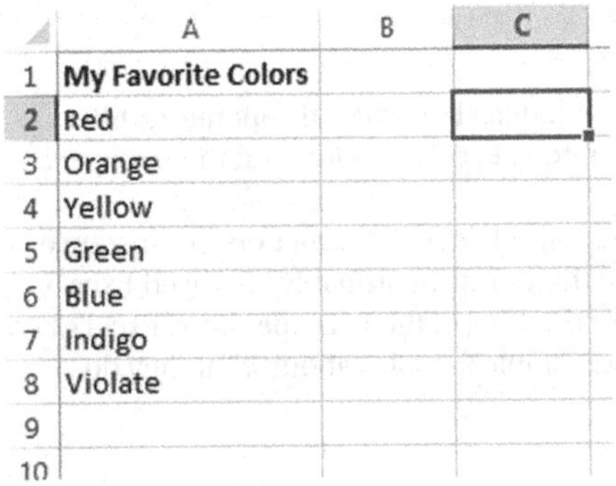
A
B
C
1 My Favorite Colors
2 Red
3 Orange
4 Yellow
5 Green
6 Blue
7 Indigo
8 Violate
9
10

Figure 9-5. A sample set of data upon which you will create a dynamically sized range

If I want a count of all my favorite colors in this example (in real life, I have only one favorite color, and *it's black*), I can use the COUNTA function on the range A2 to A8. But what if I want to add to the list? In that case, I must reapply my formula to accommodate the next color in cell A9. Alternatively, I can just say something like `A2:A1000`, where the second range is an arbitrarily large number. Neither the former's formula reapplication nor the latter's arbitrarily high number are very good fixes.

The best solution is to use a dynamically sized range. To do this with the INDEX formula, you can write `=$A$2:INDEX($A:$A,COUNTA($A:$A))` like in Figure 9-6.

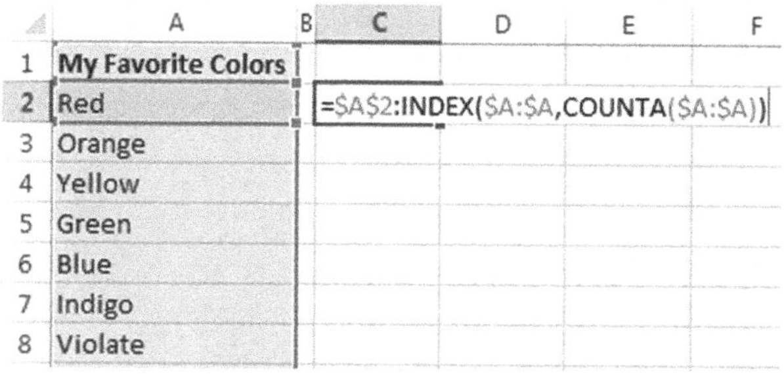

Figure 9-6. *A demonstration of the formula that will ultimately help you create a dynamically sized range*

Here's how it works. You supply the entire column range A:A to the INDEX formula. In the row argument of the INDEX formula, you're interested in the last row of content in the column range of A:A. COUNTA, which counts every filled cell in the range supplied to it, will return an 8, since the last row of content is the eighth row down. When you use INDEX, you're probably used to its returning values. If you hadn't added that A1 at the beginning of the formula, the INDEX function by itself would have simply returned the word "Violate." But behind the scenes, Excel is actually returning a *reference* to the cell containing "Violate," not just its value. So, effectively, Excel is returns A8, which becomes A1:A8 in the formula.

When you press Enter, you'll probably see the formula return the value Red. This is because it's returning the top of the range. If you continue to drag the formula down, you'll see that it returns the other cells in the range too (if it doesn't, select the entire range and press Ctrl+Shift+Enter). But to really use dynamically sized ranges to your advantage, you can assign them to a named range as I've done in Figure 9-7. Make sure when you do it the cell references are absolute.

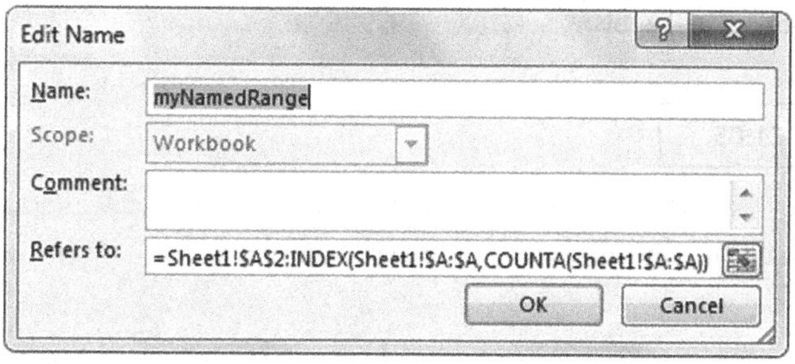

Figure 9-7. *Creating a new named range out of the formula*

You can then use that named range elsewhere on your spreadsheet. For example, in cell C8 in Figure 9-8, I've used the formula `=COUNTA(myNamedRange)`. As you can see, I've added to my list, and the count has updated automatically. Just imagine using these dynamically sized ranges in charts, dropdowns, and formulas! You'll get to do that in the next chapter.

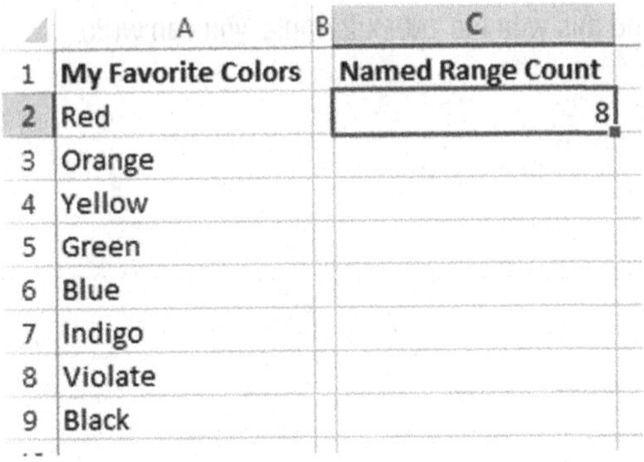

	A	B	C
1	My Favorite Colors		Named Range Count
2	Red		8
3	Orange		
4	Yellow		
5	Green		
6	Blue		
7	Indigo		
8	Violate		
9	Black		

Figure 9-8. *Using the Name Range elsewhere*

You can do the same with `OFFSET`, using this formula:

```
=$A$2:OFFSET($A$1,COUNTA($A:$A),0)
```

Experiment a little and see if you can figure this one out. Remember, if you need help, use the formula help suggestions from the beginning of the chapter.

A final note is in order. There's also some argument on whether `INDEX` is faster than `OFFSET`, since `OFFSET` is a volatile function (that means it will recalculate every time the sheet recalculates) and `INDEX` is not. In general, I prefer `INDEX` for this reason.

The Union Operator (,)

The union operator (,) is also likely familiar to you. The formula `=SUM(A1:A10,C1:C5)` employs the union operator to combine the two disparate ranges into one range upon which to take the sum. Unlike the range operator, which forms a contiguous range between two cells, the union operator essentially turns the two noncontiguous ranges into one long range. Think of it like this:

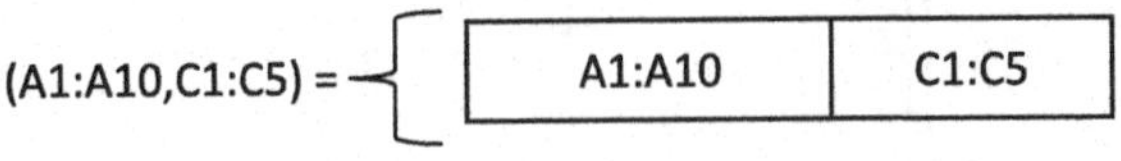

In this next section, I'll talk about how you can use the union operation to your advantage.

EXAMPLE: PULLING RANK

Let's say you wanted to find where a certain number ranks within a series of numbers, when they're ordered. For example, if you have an unsorted series of numbers (8,4,6,1, and 2), you can use Excel's `RANK` function to find where the number 6 resides in a descending list of these numbers. (,)

In Figure 9-9, I have the formula `=RANK(D2,$A$2:$A$6)` in cell D2.

	A	B	C	D
1	Number Series			
2	8		Input Num	6
3	4		Rank	2
4	6			
5	1			
6	2			

Figure 9-9. *A demonstration of finding the rank of a given number within an unsorted list*

`RANK` will automatically turn the range in the given series in descending order (by default, descending is selected; however, this can be changed in `RANK's` third, optional parameter). The rank of the number 6 then is 2, as shown in Figure 9-10.

8 **6** 4 1 2

Six is highlighted and is in the second place in the region

Figure 9-10. *A visual representation of how this example works*

This function only works when the input number (in D2 above) is a number in the set of the five given numbers. But what if you want to find where the number 4.4 resides in the ordered series? The formula, left as is, will return an `NA()` error if D2 is set to 4.4. To get around this, you need to add the input number to the set of numbers. You can do this with the union operator, like so:

```
=RANK(D2,($A$2:$A$6,D2))
```

If D2 = 4.4, the series `($A$2:$A$6,D2)` becomes `8, 6, `**`4.4`**`, 4, 1, 2`, which returns the number 3. Consider how this formula might be useful. If you have a list times, dates, or temperatures and want to return certain information when an input value is between two boundaries, you can do that with this formula. (,)

The Intersection Operator ( )

The intersection operator ( ), demonstrated as one space, returns one or more cells from overlapping ranges. Figure 9-11 shows that the intersection of range D2:D6 and B4:F4 is 3. You can verify that both of the ranges intersect, or overlap, at cell D4.

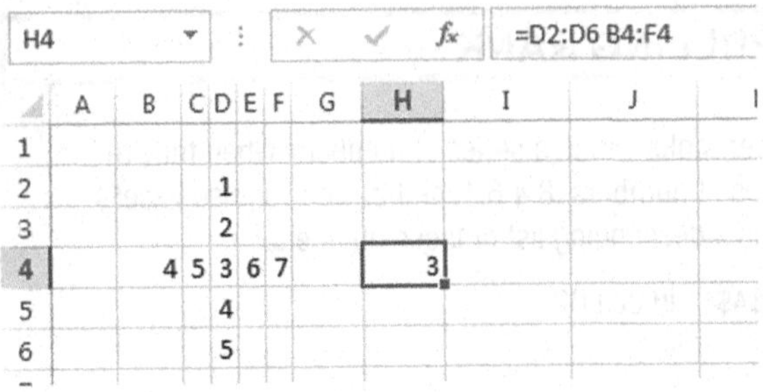

Figure 9-11. *The intersection operator in action*

You'll learn a creative use for the intersection operator in this next example.

INTERSECTING REGIONS AND MONTHS

Let's say you have a table of units sold by month and region, like in Figure 9-12.

	A	B	C	D	E	F	G	H
1		Jan	Feb	Mar	Apr	May	Jun	Jul
2	North	326	880	42	59	745	621	960
3	South	974	830	414	462	670	551	60
4	East	201	747	388	748	163	135	32
5	West	413	914	560	331	277	639	685

Figure 9-12. *A sample set of regional and monthly data*

To save time, you've had a macro assign columns B through H to be the named ranges Jan, Feb, Mar, etc. You've done the same thing for each region, assigning the row ranges to North, South, East, and West.

Then, if you're interested in the sum total of units sold in the East region on January and March, you can use the formula `=SUM(East Jan:March)`, as shown in Figure 9-13.

EXACT =SUM(East Jan:March)

	A	B	C	D	E	F	G	H
1		Jan	Feb	Mar	Apr	May	Jun	Jul
2	North	326	880	42	59	745	621	960
3	South	974	830	414	462	670	551	60
4	East	201	747	388	748	163	135	32
5	West	413	914	560	331	277	639	685

Figure 9-13. *An application of the union operator on sample regional and monthly data*

The formula returns 1366, which is the sum of 201, 747, and 388. If you want to see the performance for the eastern region for just the months of January and March but not February, you can use the following formula:

```
=SUM(East Jan + East March)
```

If you're particularly mathematically minded, and hopefully you will be somewhat by the end of the next chapter, you can simplify this formula like so:

```
=SUM(East  (Jan, March))
```

Note that `East Jan + East March = East (Jan, March)`, which parallels the Distribution Laws of algebra. I'll go into this in a little more detail later in the next chapter.

When to Use Conditional Expressions

In this section, you're going to dive deeper into conditional expressions. If you've used `IF`, then you've used a *conditional expression* before. Conditional expressions are all about testing things. For example, in the formula `=IF(AB>2, "Yes", "No")`, the first argument, `AB>2`, is the conditional expression. Any expression that uses the logic operators, =, <, >, etc., is a conditional expression.

So you want to test the value of a cell and return a result if it passes a test or another result if it fails. Quick: *which function should you use?*

Was your answer `IF`? *If* it was, then you're not alone. The `IF` function feels like a natural choice, especially because the first parameter of the `IF` function calls for a logical expression. But there are also some instances where `IF` isn't the best choice. The Excel MVP, Daniel Ferry, has gone so far as to argue that the `IF` function is the most overused function of all. And, as this chapter will demonstrate, there's good reason to believe this.

Deceptively Simple Nested IF Statements

One supposed advantage to using the `IF` function is the ability to make use of nesting conditions. For example, if I have multiple compounding conditions, I can place `IF` statements inside the `value_if_true` and `value_if_false` parameters (Listing 9-2). In my experience, however, `IF` statements are nested far more often than they need to be.

Listing 9-2. A Prototype of the IF Function

```
IF(logical_test, value_if_true, value_if_false)
```

Even I have to admit that nested `IF` statements are unavoidable. But I like to save them for formulas that exhibit natural branching conditions. Consider

```
=IF(ProjectStatus = "Stopped", IF(Err_Code=1, "Halted by internal error.","Uknown error."),
"Project has NOT finished.")
```

I would argue this is a good example of the problem with using nested IF statements. Its inherent logic naturally represents a branching condition (see Figure 9-14).

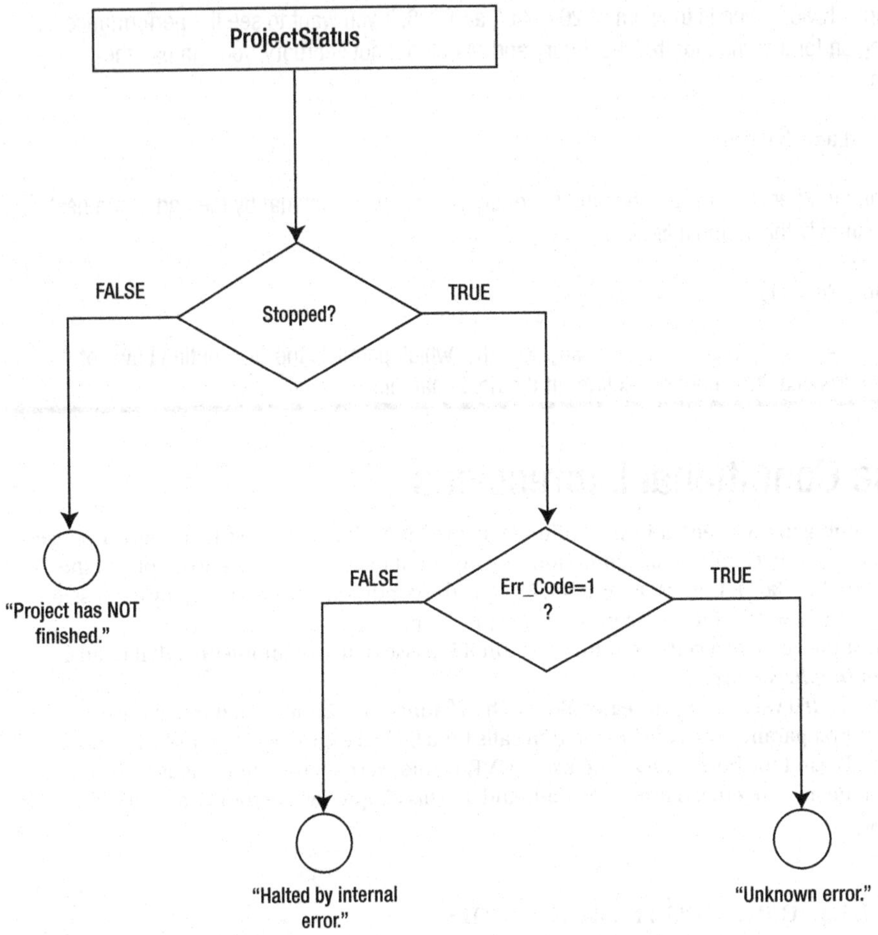

Figure 9-14. *A flowchart showing the branching conditions of your IF statement*

Sometimes it's not always so clear whether the problems represent a compound branching condition. A good rule of thumb is to start from one of the possible results and work backwards. Ask yourself: does the result naturally follow from the test condition? In other words: does this result make sense given the conditions?

Confused? I hear you. Well, let's consider the following example from Microsoft's very own help guide, shown in Listing 9-3.

Listing 9-3. An Example of Nested IFs from Microsoft's Excel Help

```
=IF(A2>89,"A",IF(A2>79,"B", IF(A2>69,"C",IF(A2>59,"D","F"))))
```

This formula returns a letter grade based on a student's raw grade stored in A2. It's a good example of a problem that makes for a poor branching condition. The grade you receive isn't the result of *not receiving another grade*. (I know you're scratching your head here but bear with me for a moment). Your letter grade is the result of where your score falls within one of five different numerical boundaries. If anything, this is a lookup problem. You could easily employ the `RANK` function example from above or use the `MATCH` function. But if you were to frame this problem organically, the reason a student receives an F is not because they didn't receive a D, C, B, or A. The IF function above turns this lookup problem into a branching condition problem when it needn't be.

Another common example involves using states as numbers. Consider the formula in Listing 9-4.

Listing 9-4. Another Example Using IFs That Isn't a Branching Condition

```
=IF(A2=1, "Small",IF(A2=2,"Med", "Large")).
```

In this example, A2 holds an encoded Id or state. For an example like this, the states could be anything, but they usually form some natural *ordinal* scale. In the example above, the Ids map to the following results: 1=**Small**, 2=**Medium**, and 3=**Large**. We call these categories ordinal because they can be ordered naturally. Here again, IF is not a good choice. The problem presented is not a branching condition but rather a test of scale. Indeed, for formulas like these, the CHOOSE function is a much better choice.

CHOOSE Wisely

In this section, I'll go through how to use CHOOSE, and why for some situations it makes for a better choice than IF. CHOOSE is much like IF, but it can more naturally deal with ordinal data. Listing 9-5 includes the prototype for CHOOSE.

Listing 9-5. CHOOSE() Prototype

```
CHOOSE(index_num, value1, value2,...)
```

CHOOSE analyzes the argument supplied to the index_num parameter and returns the value at the given index number. In the example above, when index_num is 1, value1 is returned; when index_num is 2, value2 is returned, and so forth.

In the previous instance, you could simply write =CHOOSE(A2, "Small", "Med", "Large"). This appears to be more closely align with the way this example is naturally formulated. Because of this, CHOOSE makes the data arrangement more easy to read and understand at first glance. Compare the two arrangements:

IF arrangement

```
=IF(A2=1, "Small",IF(A2=2,"Med", "Large")).
```

CHOOSE arrangement

```
=CHOOSE(A2, "Small", "Med", "Large")
```

GENERATING RANDOM DATA WITH CHOOSE()

CHOOSE is also great for generating random categorical or nominal data. This type of random data generation is particularly useful to create test data for your dashboard backend database. All it takes is the addition of the RANDBETWEEN function. Say you have categorical data of Big, Medium, and Little. You could generate data with the following formula:

```
=CHOOSE(RANDBETWEEN(1,3), "Big", "Medium", "Little")
```

Why This Discussion Is Important

Like the IF statement, CHOOSE can be useful for elements that appear on your next spreadsheet dashboard, decision support tool, or application.

A nested IF condition will attempt to evaluate every condition until a true value results or terminates to the end of the nest. CHOOSE makes one evaluation and goes to the specified index. On its face, CHOOSE would seem superior for scenarios in which a nested condition isn't necessary. Fewer evaluations means fewer instructions for Excel to complete. In previous versions of Excel and on older machines, conserving machine processing by using optimal formula structures really did seem to make a difference. However, now that we've entered the age of multithreaded processers, I must admit the performance differences have become less noticeable.

So then why have I made the distinction? Well, using the formula that best matches what you're trying to accomplish just makes sense. In addition, and perhaps more importantly, when you come back to your formula later after having been away from your spreadsheet for a while, a formula that better matches your test conditions will ultimately be easier to once again comprehend, especially if it's complex in nature.

Ok, you're not convinced. I wasn't at first, either. In the end, there may not be a noticeable difference between using IF or CHOOSE, I admit. But in previous chapters I turned conventional coding on its head. And I'll keep doing so throughout this book.

And if you're tempted to keep using IF, read on. Chances are you'll find it at least one example in which IF isn't necessary.

Introduction to Boolean Concepts

In this section, I'll talk about concepts surrounding Boolean expressions. For the unfamiliar, Boolean formulas use a type of mathematical logic called Boolean algebra and they're the natural result of *conditional expressions.*

The most important feature of a Boolean expression is that it always returns one of two mutually exclusive values: either it returns TRUE, or it returns FALSE. Excel, however, brings another important twist to the TRUE/FALSE dynamic. *Sometimes* TRUE can also mean the number one, and FALSE can also mean the number zero. Let's take a look in the following example.

FILTERING ODD OR EVEN VALUES

Booleans are great for filtering. Take a look at Figure 9-15. In this example, I've created a mechanism to only show either odd or even values in the accompanying chart.

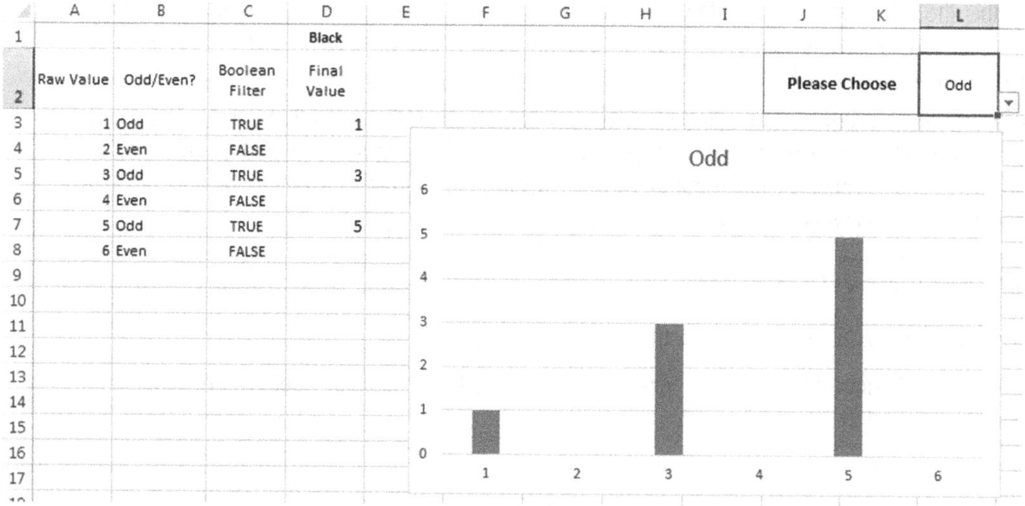

Figure 9-15. *Booleans used for filtering*

I provide the user a dropdown box to select between either showing odd values or even values. On the left, I've included a table that helps evaluate what the final chart will show. Figure 9-16 shows this table in more detail.

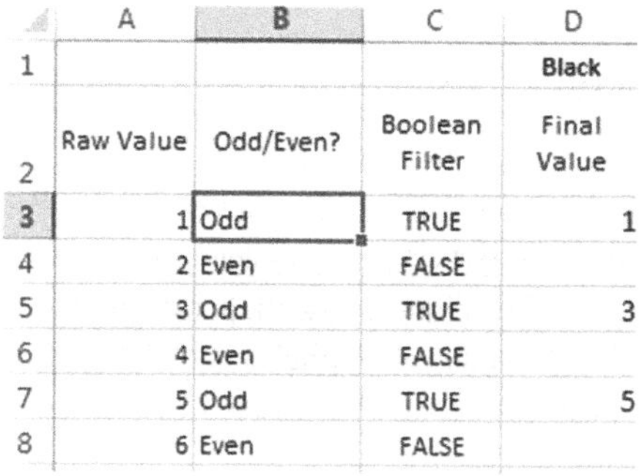

	A	B	C	D
1				Black
2	Raw Value	Odd/Even?	Boolean Filter	Final Value
3	1	Odd	TRUE	1
4	2	Even	FALSE	
5	3	Odd	TRUE	3
6	4	Even	FALSE	
7	5	Odd	TRUE	5
8	6	Even	FALSE	

Figure 9-16. *The table that allows for chart filtering*

In column B, I use the following formula:

```
=CHOOSE(MOD(A3,2)+1,"Even","Odd")
```

So let's break this down.

Nested inside the `CHOOSE` conditional is the `MOD()` formula. `MOD` performs *modulo division*, which is a technical way of saying it performs division like a third grader. Remember when you first started learning how to divide, *3 divided by 2* would equal *1 remainder 1*? Well, modulo division performs this same operation but only returns the remainder part. In the case of `MOD(A3,2)` you're simply testing whether the list of numbers given in column A is odd or even. As you might recall, when even numbers are divided by two, there is never a remainder (think of it as a reminder of zero); for odd numbers there's always a remainder of one.

What you run into is that you're using the `CHOOSE()` formula to tell Excel whether to return the word "Odd," or to return the word "Even." `CHOOSE()`, however, can't take in numbers that are less than one, and so far, it's possible this could return a zero. So, my solution is to add the one at the end. So going back to the original `CHOOSE` formula,

```
=CHOOSE(MOD(A3,2)+1,"Even","Odd")
```

...you can see how all the parts fit together.

Moving on to Column C (Figure 9-17), you're simply testing if the contents in Column are equal to the contents of your dropdown.

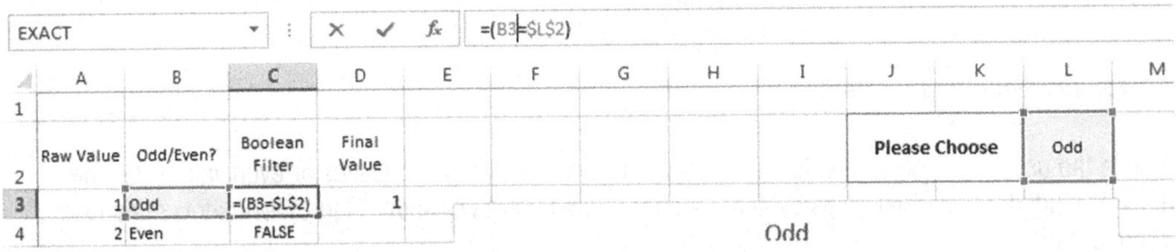

Figure 9-17. Testing whether the contents of the boolean filter are equal to the dropdown

This is achieved by writing the following Boolean formula from cell C3:

```
=(B3=$L$2)
```

The parentheses surround the test condition telling Excel to either return a TRUE or FALSE value. When there's only one test case, the parentheses are optional. However, it's good practice to keep parentheses anyway, keeping in line with the idea presented above that you should match your formulas to manifest the conditions you're developing. And, specifically, note that the following two formulas are not equal:

```
=(B3=$L$2)+1  =\=  =B3=$L$2+1
```

Finally, in Column D you multiply columns A and C (Figure 9-18). When the number in Column A is multiplied by a TRUE value, it's the same as multiplying it by the number one. When multiplied by a FALSE value, it's the as multiplying it by zero. The chart is linked to column D so the outcomes in column D are automatically updated on the chart.

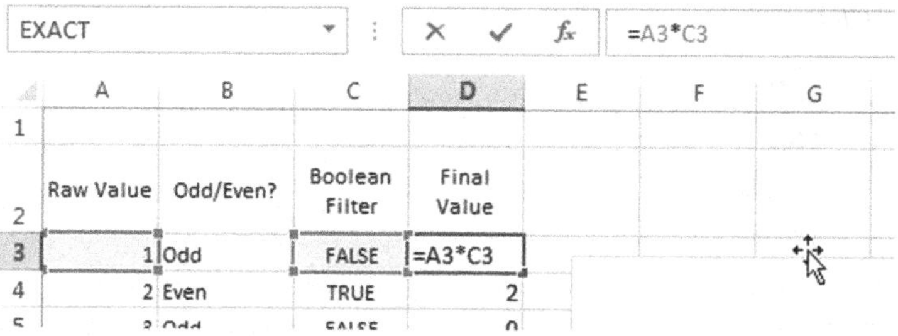

***Figure 9-18.** The Final Value column of your table*

I have to admit: CHOOSE wasn't the best function for the example above. By all accounts, if you were thinking I should have used IF instead, you wouldn't have been off base. The values of "Even" and "Odd" aren't ordinal. Numbers are either only *even* or *odd*. And I'm usually of the belief that the more natural the function mirrors the problem, the easier it is to comprehend. What makes the example above such a good IF problem is because the Boolean dynamic, that TRUE/FALSE = 1/0, goes both ways. Recall in your test for an even or odd value, the MOD function was returning either a zero or a one. You could have written =CHOOSE(MOD(A3,2)+1,"Even","Odd") as =IF(MOD(A3,2),"Odd","Even") which is reasonably easier to read, and it's probably easier to comprehend when you come back to it later.

Condensing Your Work

What makes =IF(MOD(A3,2),"Odd","Even") so readable is because there are no nested conditions. Once you add more conditions, it becomes much harder to comprehend at first glance. And, when you represent information on your spreadsheet, you'll sometimes have to condense formulas from different cells into one to save space. In the example above, if you want to condense your work, you can do something like this in column D:

```
=IF(MOD(A3,2),IF($L$2="Odd",A3,0),IF($L$2="Even",A3,0))
```

But now the IF function is long and harder to understand. Maybe it's time you dispense with the IF function altogether. But how can you recreate the same conditions without using IF? Well, you can use the exclusive-or function, XOR, like this:

```
=XOR($L$2="Even",MOD(A3,2))*A3
```

■ **Note** XOR is available only in Excel 2013.

The Legend of XOR()-oh

Technically, XOR is not pronounced "zore," but rather as "ex-or," which as you've likely figured is shorthand for exclusive-or. So what the heck does XOR do? Well it's a type of truth-testing conditional function. You're probably somewhat familiar with Excel's cousin truth functions, AND and OR.

Let's review them first. AND tests if all the supplied conditional expressions are TRUE. If they are, AND returns TRUE. If one condition is not true, as in FALSE, AND returns FALSE. OR tests if *only one* argument is TRUE and returns TRUE when at least one conditional expression evaluates to TRUE. If all arguments passed to OR evaluate to FALSE, OR returns FALSE. Table 9-2 shows the outcomes for AND and OR formulas when supplied with only two arguments, x and y.

Table 9-2. A Truth Table for AND and OR Functions

X	Y	=AND(x,y)	=OR(x,y)
TRUE	TRUE	**TRUE**	**TRUE**
TRUE	FALSE	FALSE	**TRUE**
FALSE	TRUE	FALSE	**TRUE**
FALSE	FALSE	FALSE	FALSE

XOR adds an extra constraint: *only one of the arguments can contain a value of TRUE.* That's what makes it so *exclusive.* It's like a club where everyone is invited but only one person is allowed to come in—and that person is you, you lucky dog! You can think of `OR()` as being *all inclusive* because it does not constrain the amount of TRUE values required to return TRUE. It's like a club that everyone can get into (but then everyone leaves because I decide to show up). The truth table is for XOR is shown in Table 9-3.

Table 9-3. The Truth Table for XOR

X	Y	=XOR(x,y)
TRUE	TRUE	FALSE
TRUE	FALSE	**TRUE**
FALSE	TRUE	**TRUE**
FALSE	FALSE	FALSE

Going back to your condensed formula, let's see how `XOR()` works by examining this formula: `=XOR($L$2="Even",MOD(A3,2))*A3`.

Recall, `MOD(A3,2)` will return a one when A3 is odd and a zero when A3 is even. In the example above, you're always testing if the dropdown has "Even" selected. So, let's say A3 equals an odd value, like the number 3. Listing 9-6 shows a step-by-step evaluation when L2 is even. Listing 9-7 shows a step-by-step evaluation when L2 is odd.

Listing 9-6. Formula Evaluation When L2 Is Even

```
If $L$2="Even" then
=XOR($L$2="Even", MOD(A3,2))*A3
=XOR(TRUE, 1)*A3
=FALSE*A3
=0 * 3
=0
```

Listing 9-7. Formula Evaluation When L2 Is Odd

```
If $L$2="Odd" then
=XOR($L$2="Even", MOD(A3,2))*2
=XOR(FALSE, 1)*A3
=TRUE*A3
=1 * 3
=3
```

So, think about this way: you're actually interested in the inverse relationship between your two conditions. If `$L$2` has `"Even"` selected, for the value in A3 to show, it must also be even. For even values, `MOD(A3, 2)` will return a zero (which is the opposite result of the test `$L$2 = "Even"`). If `$L$2` has `"Odd"` selected, the first argument will return FALSE, but `MOD(A3, 2)` will actually return a one.

Do We Really Need IF?

For this section, I'll combine everything you've learned so far to answer the question: do we really need `IF`? The fact is, many problems that feel like they need `IF` probably don't need it. Let's go through a few quick examples.

Need to test if a cell is blank so you can return a blank instead of a zero?

Use:

```
=--REPT(A2, LEN(A2)>1)
```

Instead of:

```
IF(LEN(A2) > 0, A2, "")
```

Note: "–" is shorthand to convert a string into a number.

Need to return a certain range based on a dropdown select?

Just add the numbers 1, 2, 3, and 4 to the beginning of your dropdown items (see Figure 9-19).

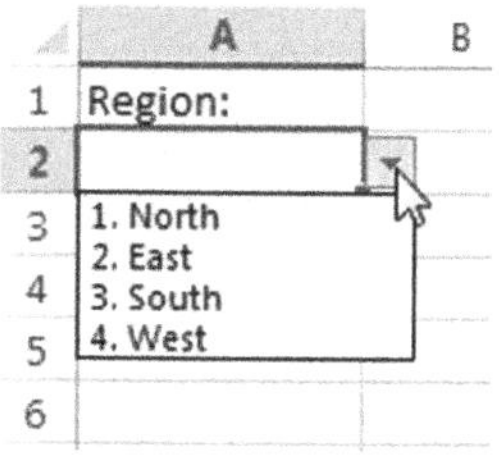

Figure 9-19. *Adding numbers to the dropdown items can help you quickly ascertain which item was selected without using an IF statement*

Use:

```
=CHOOSE(--LEFT(A2, 1), NorthRange, EastRange, SouthRange, WestRange)
```

Instead of:

```
IF(A2 = "North", NorthRange, IF(A2 = "East", EastRange, IF( A2 = "South", SouthRange, WestRange)
```

Want to know what grade you got?

Figure 9-20 shows a grade letter calculator.

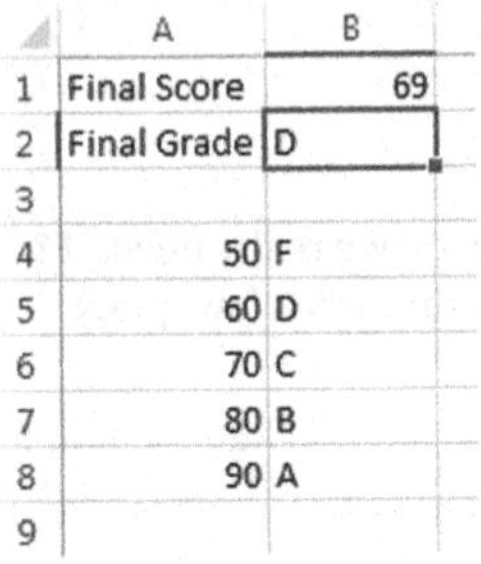
A
B
1 Final Score 69
2 Final Grade D
3
4 50 F
5 60 D
6 70 C
7 80 B
8 90 A
9

***Figure 9-20.** A grade calculator that uses INDEX and MATCH instead of nested IFs*

Use:

```
=INDEX($B$4:$B$8, MATCH(B1,$A$4:$A$8,1))
```

Instead of:

```
=IF(B1>89,"A",IF(B1>79,"B", IF(B1>69,"C",IF(B1>59,"D","F"))))
```

Need to return a -1 whenever a test condition is zero; otherwise return the value?

This example uses Figure 9-21 as an example.

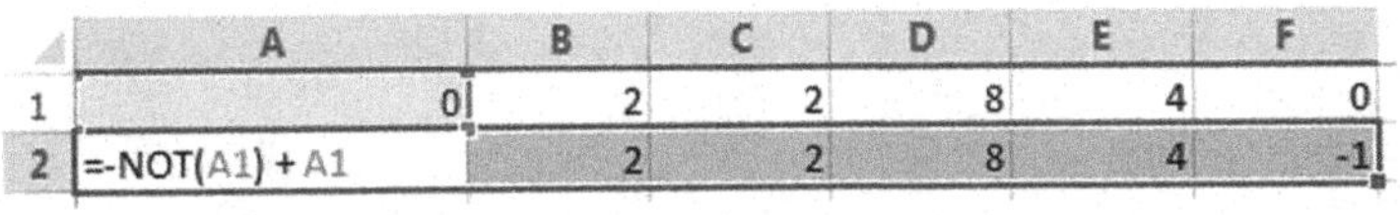
A B C D E F
1 0 2 2 8 4 0
2 =-NOT(A1) + A1 2 2 8 4 -1

***Figure 9-21.** You can use Boolean functions instead of IF*

Use:

```
=-NOT(A1) + A1
```

Instead of:

```
=IF(A1=0, 0, A1)
```

The Last Word

I realize some of the material in this chapter might be new for you. And perhaps you're not yet ready to turn your back on IF. Fair enough; although don't expect me to use it much from here on out! The point of this chapter is to get your mind to think differently about certain problems. IF is a common convention, but the popular choice isn't always the best. This chapter introduced you to formula concepts you've used many times before but might not have realized what they were or what they meant. Empowered with new knowledge, I'm confident you'll be able to think about formulas differently.

The best formulas fit somewhere on a spectrum of performance, readability, and design simplicity. If the formula you're using to model your problem feels like a *good fit,* chances are—it is. I firmly believe that formulas that are a natural fit to a problem give you that "intuitively pleasing" feeling when you look at them. If this chapter has you thinking how you might do some of your own formulas differently, then my work is done here.

CHAPTER 10

Advanced Formula Concepts

The previous chapter's formula examples may have appeared complicated at first, but you should be able to use them with time, practice, and patience. If you followed the advice at the start of Chapter 9, which was to work through formulas with techniques like Excel's Evaluate Formula feature, you should find them easier to understand.

In this chapter, you will investigate how these formulas are applied. Specifically, I will cover the following:

- Filtering and highlighting
- Selection
- Aggregation

Filtering and Highlighting

Following what you learned about ones and zeros in Chapter 9, you can use formulas for filtering results. In Chapter 9, you employed a mechanism to filter even and odd values using Booleans. Highlighting, as it turns out, isn't much different than filtering. Let's take a look.

Filtering with Formulas

Figure 10-1 shows the tables I've set up for the example (download `Chapter10Example1.xlsx` from the project files to follow along). On the left is the raw data. In the middle is the criteria that you want to filter, and on the right are some conditional tables to help know which items fit the criteria you would like to display.
The information in the middle is linked to the front screen, which I'll get to in a moment.

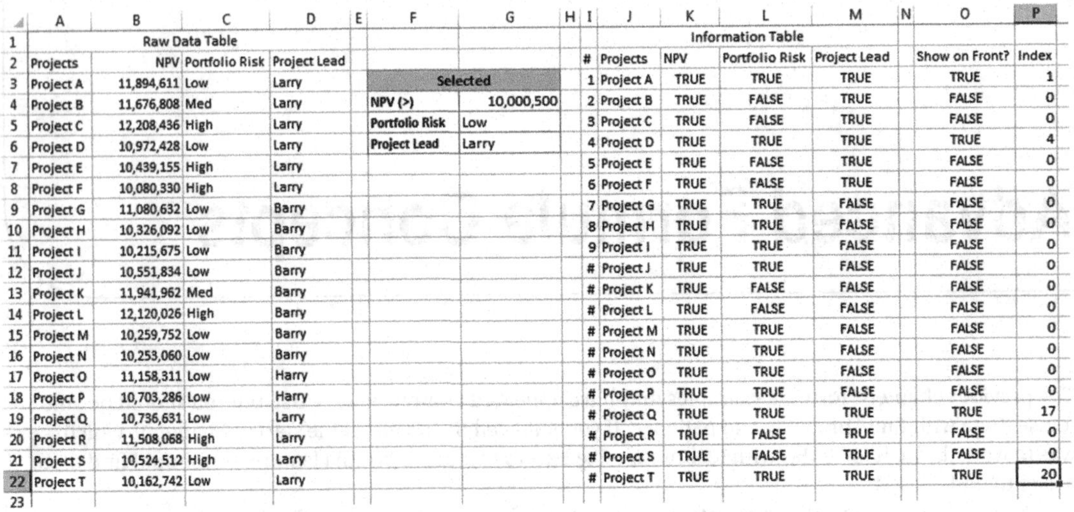

	A	B	C	D	E	F	G
1	Raw Data Table						
2	Projects	NPV	Portfolio Risk	Project Lead			
3	Project A	11,894,611	Low	Larry		Selected	
4	Project B	11,676,808	Med	Larry		NPV (>)	10,000,500
5	Project C	12,208,436	High	Larry		Portfolio Risk	Low
6	Project D	10,972,428	Low	Larry		Project Lead	Larry
7	Project E	10,439,155	High	Larry			
8	Project F	10,080,330	High	Larry			
9	Project G	11,080,632	Low	Barry			
10	Project H	10,326,092	Low	Barry			
11	Project I	10,215,675	Low	Barry			
12	Project J	10,551,834	Low	Barry			
13	Project K	11,941,962	Med	Barry			
14	Project L	12,120,026	High	Barry			
15	Project M	10,259,752	Low	Barry			
16	Project N	10,253,060	Low	Barry			
17	Project O	11,158,311	Low	Harry			
18	Project P	10,703,286	Low	Harry			
19	Project Q	10,736,631	Low	Larry			
20	Project R	11,508,068	High	Larry			
21	Project S	10,524,512	High	Larry			
22	Project T	10,162,742	Low	Larry			
23							

	H	I	J	K	L	M	N	O	P
1			Information Table						
2		#	Projects	NPV	Portfolio Risk	Project Lead		Show on Front?	Index
3		1	Project A	TRUE	TRUE	TRUE		TRUE	1
4		2	Project B	TRUE	FALSE	TRUE		FALSE	0
5		3	Project C	TRUE	FALSE	TRUE		FALSE	0
6		4	Project D	TRUE	TRUE	TRUE		TRUE	4
7		5	Project E	TRUE	FALSE	TRUE		FALSE	0
8		6	Project F	TRUE	FALSE	TRUE		FALSE	0
9		7	Project G	TRUE	TRUE	FALSE		FALSE	0
10		8	Project H	TRUE	TRUE	FALSE		FALSE	0
11		9	Project I	TRUE	TRUE	FALSE		FALSE	0
12		#	Project J	TRUE	TRUE	FALSE		FALSE	0
13		#	Project K	TRUE	FALSE	FALSE		FALSE	0
14		#	Project L	TRUE	FALSE	FALSE		FALSE	0
15		#	Project M	TRUE	TRUE	FALSE		FALSE	0
16		#	Project N	TRUE	TRUE	FALSE		FALSE	0
17		#	Project O	TRUE	TRUE	FALSE		FALSE	0
18		#	Project P	TRUE	TRUE	FALSE		FALSE	0
19		#	Project Q	TRUE	TRUE	TRUE		TRUE	17
20		#	Project R	TRUE	FALSE	TRUE		FALSE	0
21		#	Project S	TRUE	FALSE	TRUE		FALSE	0
22		#	Project T	TRUE	TRUE	TRUE		TRUE	20
23									

Figure 10-1. *An example table to demonstrate applied formula concepts*

Let's take a better look at the table on the right. For the NPV column, let's set up a conditional to compare whether the selected NPV is greater than the item in the current row of the Raw Data Table (Figure 10-2).

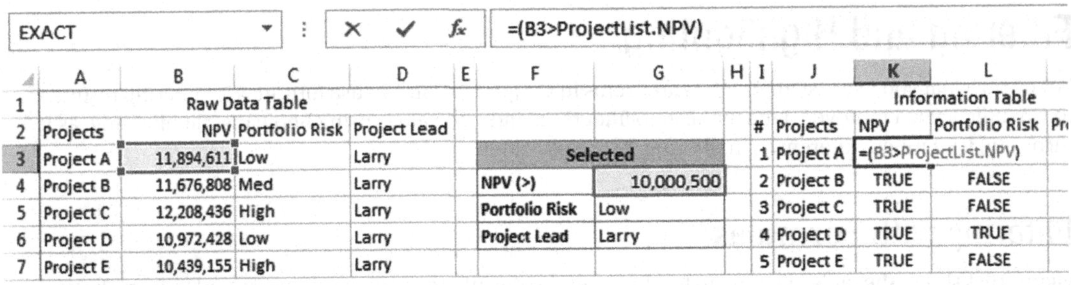

EXACT | =(B3>ProjectList.NPV)

	A	B	C	D	E	F	G	H	I	J	K	L
1	Raw Data Table										Information Table	
2	Projects	NPV	Portfolio Risk	Project Lead					#	Projects	NPV	Portfolio Risk
3	Project A	11,894,611	Low	Larry		Selected			1	Project A	=(B3>ProjectList.NPV)	
4	Project B	11,676,808	Med	Larry		NPV (>)	10,000,500		2	Project B	TRUE	FALSE
5	Project C	12,208,436	High	Larry		Portfolio Risk	Low		3	Project C	TRUE	FALSE
6	Project D	10,972,428	Low	Larry		Project Lead	Larry		4	Project D	TRUE	TRUE
7	Project E	10,439,155	High	Larry					5	Project E	TRUE	FALSE

Figure 10-2. *The Raw Data Table*

Then do the same comparisons for Portfolio Risk and Project Lead. See Figures 10-3 and 10-4.

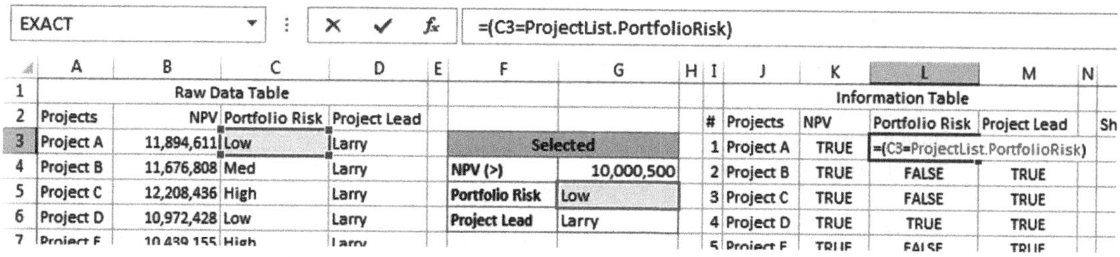

Figure 10-3. *You're testing for what level of Portfolio Risk is selected*

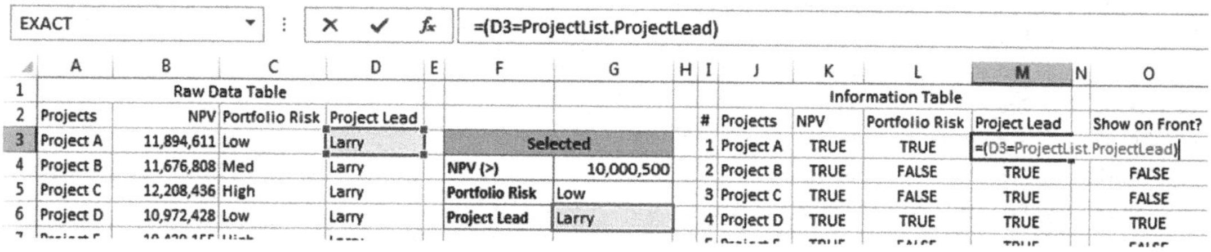

Figure 10-4. *You're testing for which Project Lead has been selected*

In the last two columns, you identify which projects you want to be highlighted. Since you're looking for projects whose values come at the *intersection* of your criteria, you'll test if each condition is met, and you'll use AND for that (Figure 10-5).

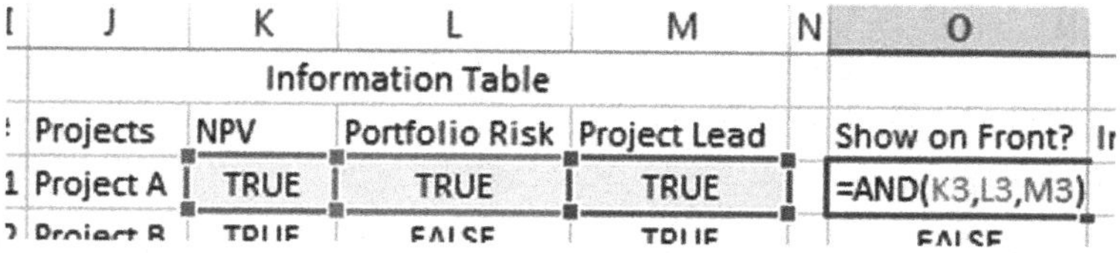

Figure 10-5. *Testing when all three conditions are met*

Finally, for extra help, you'll include the Project's index in column P. This isn't itself necessary to complete your work, but sometimes an extra column of information can help, provided you have enough room for it.

All of this work goes to help the highlighting mechanism developed on the front screen. Click the Dashboard (incomplete) tab in example file to see what I'm talking about (shown in Figure 10-6).

	A	B	C	D	E
1					
2					
3			NPV (>)	$10,000,000	
4			Portfolio Risk	Low	
5			Project Lead	Larry	
6					
7			Project Name	NPV($)	Risk
8	TRUE	1	Project A	11.9M	L
9	FALSE	2	Project B	11.7M	M
10	FALSE	3	Project C	12.2M	H
11	TRUE	4	Project D	11.0M	L
12	FALSE	5	Project E	10.4M	H
13	FALSE	6	Project F	10.1M	H
14	FALSE	7	Project G	11.1M	L
15	FALSE	8	Project H	10.3M	L
16	FALSE	9	Project I	10.2M	L
17	FALSE	10	Project J	10.6M	L
18	FALSE	11	Project K	11.9M	M
19	FALSE	12	Project L	12.1M	H
20	FALSE	13	Project M	10.3M	L
21	FALSE	14	Project N	10.3M	L
22	FALSE	15	Project O	11.2M	L
23	FALSE	16	Project P	10.7M	L
24	TRUE	17	Project Q	10.7M	L
25	FALSE	18	Project R	11.5M	H
26	FALSE	19	Project S	10.5M	H
27	TRUE	20	Project T	10.2M	L

***Figure 10-6.** The Dashboard (incomplete) tab*

Now take a look at Column A. Column A tests whether the current index in Column B is the same as the index returned from the Project List tab. Essentially, the result is the same as the Show on Front field in Column O on the Project List tab (Figure 10-7).

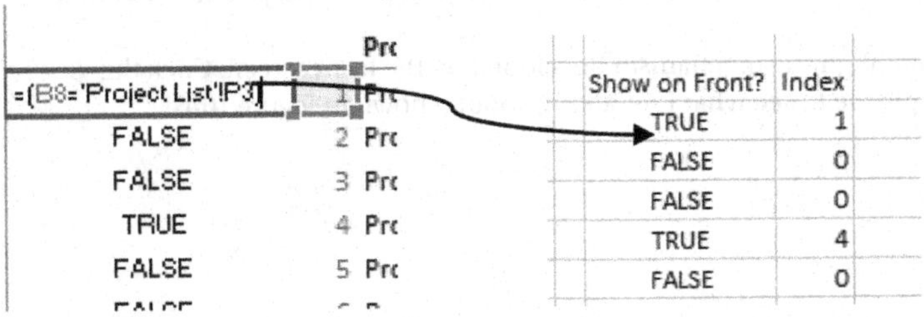

***Figure 10-7.** TRUE/FALSE on the dashboard corresponds to backend calculations*

Conditional Highlighting Using Formulas

In this section, I'll talk about how to add condition highlighting to the spreadsheet. Let's do the following steps.

1. Highlight the project table, as I have done in Figure 10-8 by selecting cells C8:C27.

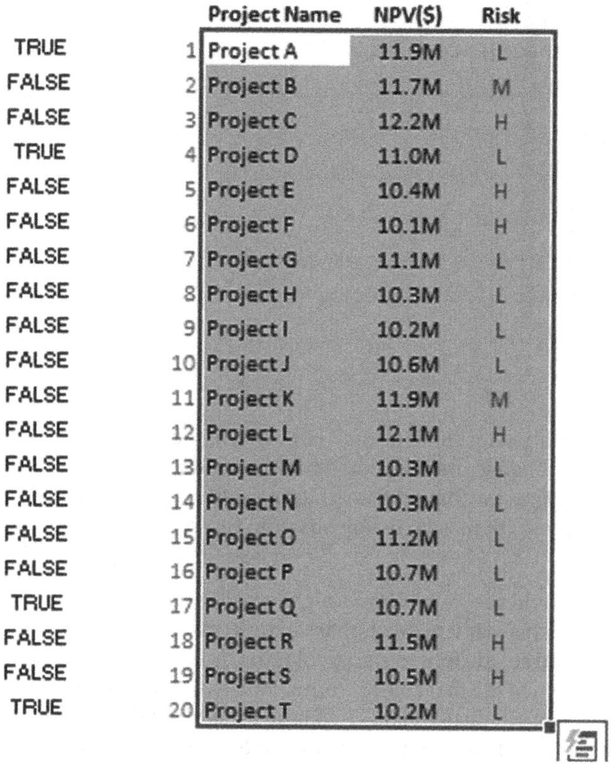

		Project Name	NPV($)	Risk
TRUE	1	Project A	11.9M	L
FALSE	2	Project B	11.7M	M
FALSE	3	Project C	12.2M	H
TRUE	4	Project D	11.0M	L
FALSE	5	Project E	10.4M	H
FALSE	6	Project F	10.1M	H
FALSE	7	Project G	11.1M	L
FALSE	8	Project H	10.3M	L
FALSE	9	Project I	10.2M	L
FALSE	10	Project J	10.6M	L
FALSE	11	Project K	11.9M	M
FALSE	12	Project L	12.1M	H
FALSE	13	Project M	10.3M	L
FALSE	14	Project N	10.3M	L
FALSE	15	Project O	11.2M	L
FALSE	16	Project P	10.7M	L
TRUE	17	Project Q	10.7M	L
FALSE	18	Project R	11.5M	H
FALSE	19	Project S	10.5M	H
TRUE	20	Project T	10.2M	L

Figure 10-8. *Selecting cells C8:C27*

2. From the Home tab, go to Conditional Formatting ➤ New Rule ➤ Use a formula to determine which cells to format.

3. Click in the address box titled Format Values where this formula is true. In the formula box, type `=(` and then click on cell A8, which is the top of the condition list.

4. A8 will appear as the absolute reference $A$8. However, you do not want every row to test only this cell. Rather, you want each row to test against the cell for the row. So press F4 twice to toggle through the absolute reference options until you reach $A8. Then finish the formula by typing `=TRUE)`. Figure 10-9 shows the correct formula.

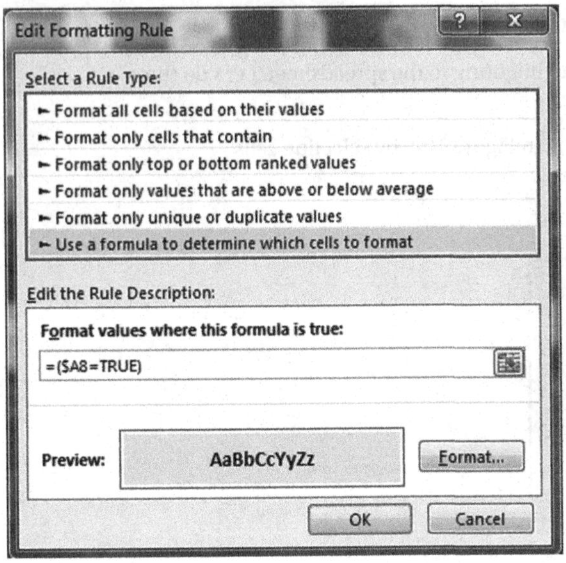

Figure 10-9. *The Edit Formatting Rule dialog box*

5. Click the Format button. Under the Font tab, select Bold under Font Style. In the Color dropdown, select the Black color to change the selection from Automatic. On the Fill tab, choose a light color to serve as the filtered item's background. I've chosen a light peach color. Finally, press OK in each dialog box until you've returned to the spreadsheet.

If you've performed these steps correctly, you should see several items highlighted in your list (see Figure 10-10). To bring more emphasis to these items—and to deemphasize the items outside your selection—highlight the table range again, C8:C27, and set the font to a gray color that is lighter than black but still readable. I chose the darkest gray at the bottom of the first color column. Finally, you'll want to get rid of those conditional formulas in Column A. The easiest way to do this is to hide the entire column by right-clicking Column A and selecting Hide. Alternatively, I've simply set the font of the condition formulas to white. Personally, I like having the extra margin of white space on the left side of the screen.

		Project Name	NPV($)	Risk
7		Project Name	NPV($)	Risk
8	1	Project A	11.9M	L
9	2	Project B	11.7M	M
10	3	**Project C**	**12.2M**	**H**
11	4	Project D	11.0M	L
12	5	**Project E**	**10.4M**	**H**
13	6	**Project F**	**10.1M**	**H**
14	7	Project G	11.1M	L
15	8	Project H	10.3M	L
16	9	Project I	10.2M	L
17	10	Project J	10.6M	L
18	11	Project K	11.9M	M
19	12	Project L	12.1M	H
20	13	Project M	10.3M	L
21	14	Project N	10.3M	L
22	15	Project O	11.2M	L
23	16	Project P	10.7M	L
24	17	Project Q	10.7M	L
25	18	**Project R**	**11.5M**	**H**
26	19	**Project S**	**10.5M**	**H**
27	20	Project T	10.2M	L
28				

Figure 10-10. *A list of highlighted items*

One last thought before moving on: I could have created another conditional format formula testing if A8=FALSE and then colored everything gray based on that. To me, that's extra work. Conditional formats are volatile actions. Consider this: no instruction is executed to set the table items that are FALSE to be grayed out if you've already set them to gray by default. Remember to always be on the lookout for shortcuts.

Selecting

Selection is the process of returning only certain information (thinking of selecting from a group). Selecting is similar to filtering and highlighting, except that selecting only returns the information you're interested in. Filtering, for example, simply hides the information you're not interested in. Highlighting does the same as filtering through emphasizing and deemphasizing certain items. Selection, on the other hand, always contains **only** the complete set of information you're interested in. Nothing more or less.

Open example file `Chapter10Example2.xlsx`. In this example, you're going to create a range that can grow and shrink dynamically based on what you want to return. In this way, you'll be creating the mechanism that selects the portion to return. Go to the Project List tab, and note the column of zeros you've created, as shown in Figure 10-11.

N	O	P	Q	R	S	T
	Show on Front?	Index		Count-non 0s		
	FALSE	0				
	FALSE	0				
	FALSE	0				
	FALSE	0				
	FALSE	0				
	FALSE	0				
	TRUE	7				
	TRUE	8				
	TRUE	9				
	TRUE	10				
	FALSE	0				
	FALSE	0				
	TRUE	13				
	TRUE	14				
	FALSE	0				
	FALSE	0				
	FALSE	0				
	FALSE	0				
	FALSE	0				
	FALSE	0				

Figure 10-11. *The Project List tab*

If you recall from the previous chapter, the zeros indicate projects you don't want to return. Alternatively, the numbers indicate projects you DO want to return. So, what you need to do now is count those projects. I've already laid out a spot for this count in cell R3. So go ahead and put this formula into R3:

```
=COUNTIF($P$3:$P$22,">0")
```

In the columns next to the box labeled Count-non 0s, set up the column headers as I have in Figure 10-12.

Q	R	S	T	U	V	W	X
			Selecting				
	Count-non 0s		Index Location	Project Name	NPV	Portfolio Risk	
	6						

Figure 10-12. *Column headers that you will use in the process of developing a selecting mechansim*

Now, follow these steps.

1. In cell T3, type in the following formula (shown in Figure 10-13):

```
=LARGE($P$3:$P$22,I3)
```

	Information Table								Selecting	
#	Projects	NPV	Portfolio Risk	Project Lead	Show on Front?	Index	Count-non 0s		Index Location	Project
1	Project A	TRUE	TRUE	FALSE	FALSE	0	6		=LARGE($P$3:$P$22,I3)	

Figure 10-13. *Using the LARGE function in the Index location*

Note what what's happening here. You're using the index you created in column I to pull out the nth largest value from within the range indices that aren't zero. When you drag down, you'll have grouped all the indices you're interested in at the top of the range (Figure 10-14). You should find there are six non-zero items at the top—exactly as the formula predicted.

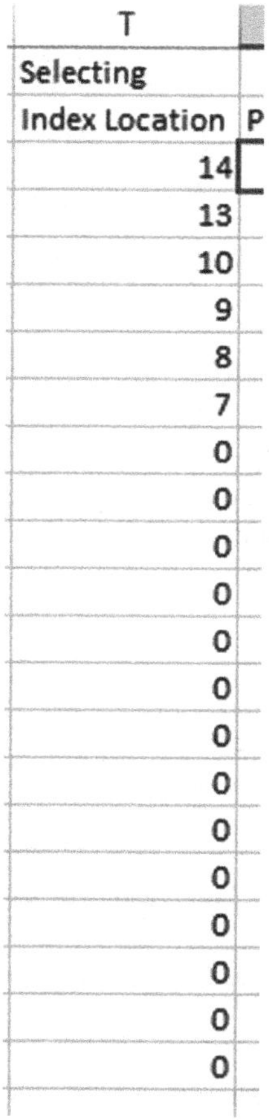

T	
Selecting	
Index Location	P
14	
13	
10	
9	
8	
7	
0	
0	
0	
0	
0	
0	
0	
0	
0	
0	
0	
0	
0	
0	

Figure 10-14. *The LARGE function returns the indices of the items you're interested in at the top of the range*

2. Now, in cell U3, type `=INDEX($A$3:$B$22,T3,)`, as shown in Figure 10-15.

	A	B	C	D	S	T	U	V	W
1		Raw Data Table				Selecting			
2	Projects	NPV	Portfolio Risk	Project Lead		Index Location	Project Name	NPV	
3	Project A	11,894,611	Low	Larry		14	=INDEX($A$3:$B$22,T3,)		
4	Project B	11,676,808	Med	Larry		13			
5	Project C	12,208,436	High	Larry		10			
6	Project D	10,972,428	Low	Larry		9			
7	Project E	10,439,155	High	Larry		8			
8	Project F	10,080,330	High	Larry		7			
9	Project G	11,080,632	Low	Barry		0			
10	Project H	10,326,092	Low	Barry		0			
11	Project I	10,215,675	Low	Barry		0			
12	Project J	10,551,834	Low	Barry		0			
13	Project K	11,941,962	Med	Barry		0			
14	Project L	12,120,026	High	Barry		0			
15	Project M	10,259,752	Low	Barry		0			
16	Project N	10,253,060	Low	Barry		0			
17	Project O	11,158,311	Low	Harry		0			
18	Project P	10,703,286	Low	Harry		0			
19	Project Q	10,736,631	Low	Larry		0			
20	Project R	11,508,068	High	Larry		0			
21	Project S	10,524,512	High	Larry		0			
22	Project T	10,162,742	Low	Larry		0			
23									

Figure 10-15. *Adding the INDEX formula to the Project Name column*

3. When you press Enter you should immediately get a #VALUE! error. But don't worry about that for now. Using the cell anchor in the lower right of the selected cell, drag the formula over to V3 to copy it into that cell. Now, with both U3 and V3 selected, click the formula bar and press Ctrl+Shift+Enter. You should see a full row returned of the project name and NPV values. Now drag down.

   In case you're wondering why you need to do this, remember that `INDEX` allows you to return one or more cells from within an array; all you must supply are the row(s) or columns(s) you'd like to grab. Because you returned more than a single cell, you had to use Ctrl+Shift+Enter.

■ **Note** Remember, any time you return more than a single cell, you have an array formula. When you have an array formula, you must use Ctrl+Shift+Enter.

---

4. Now for some fun! You're going to use a dynamic range formula you learned about in the previous chapter. Remember, dynamic ranges requires two things: (a) a contiguous range; and (b) the total amount of items in the range. Luckily, the first thing you did was create that count of non-zeros!

In a cell off to the side (I've chosen X3), type =OFFSET($V$3,0,0,$R$3), as shown in Figure 10-16.

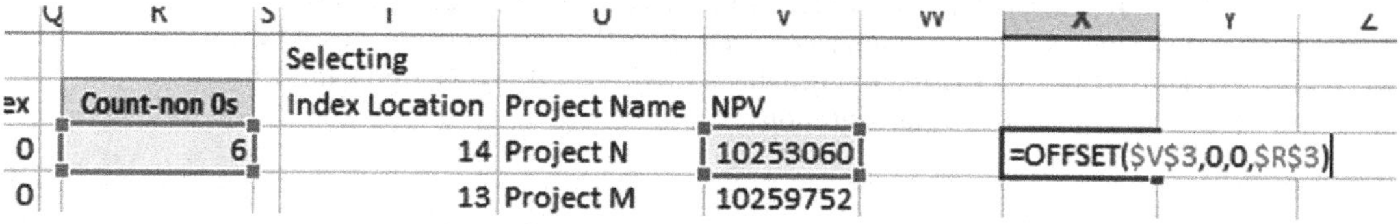
Q
R
S
T
U
V
W
X
Y
Z
Selecting
ex
Count-non 0s
Index Location
Project Name
NPV
0
6
14
Project N
10253060
=OFFSET($V$3,0,0,$R$3)
0
13
Project M
10259752

Figure 10-16. *Using OFFSET to create a dynamic side function*

Remember how OFFSET works. That fourth argument specifies the height of the offset range to be returned. Here, you don't actually want the returned range to be moved from cell V3 (which is why you supply a zero in the first two arguments); you simply want V3 to be the starting point and to have the range "grow" (or expand) downward from there.

5. When you press Enter, the result returned should be the same value as in V3. If you drag X3's anchor downward, you should see all six values returned, and you'll start getting errors thereafter. At this point, you're simply testing the formula. Now that you know it works, you're going to assign it to a named range.

   So, click on X3 and copy the formula now that you know it's working. Go to Name Manager from the Formulas tab. Click on New. Give it a name like "ProjectList.ReturnSelection" and paste the formula you copied into the Refers To box. Press OK until you're back at the spreadsheet screen.

6. Go to the dashboard worksheet.

7. From the Insert tab, insert a column chart. If the chart automatically selects data, right-click the chart and go to Select Data and remove any preloaded data.

8. Now, click the Add button and press OK for whatever default data is loaded. Series1 with a value of 1 should be the only series in the Select Data dialog, as shown in Figure 10-17.

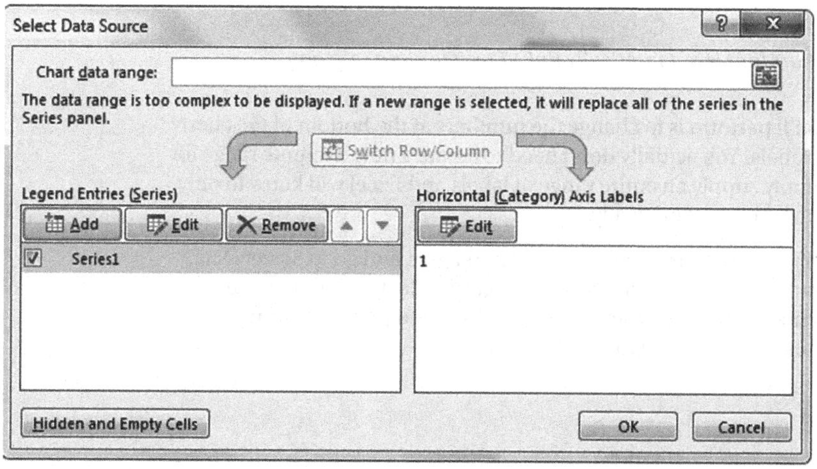

Figure 10-17. *The Select Data Source dialog box*

9. Click OK to return to the spreadsheet. Now click the single column displayed to see its formula in the formula bar.

10. Now you're going to replace the "{1}" with a reference to the named range you just created. For this series, *you must include the workbook name,* as shown in Figure 10-18, otherwise this mechanism won't work. Why? Not sure: that's just what Excel wants. I don't ask questions.

```
=SERIES(,,'Chapter 10 Ex3 .xlsx'!ProjectList.ReturnSelection,1)
```

Figure 10-18. *The SERIES function that appears when you click on a chart*

Viola! If it worked correctly, you should see a series of columns like in Figure 10-19.

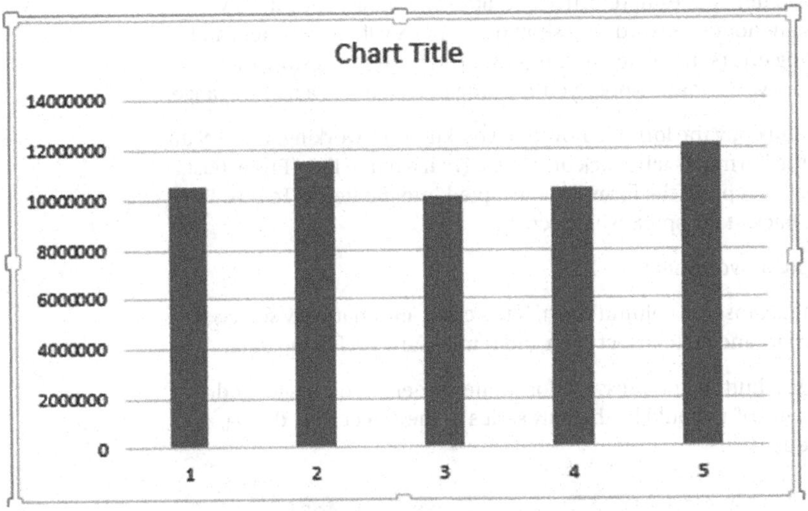

Figure 10-19. *A dynamic chart that is automatically linked to your data selections*

11. The last step you'll perform is to change the numbers at the bottom of the chart to their correct labels. You actually don't need to create a new dynamic range for this. You can simply supply an entire range of labels and Excel will know to only pull back the top labels automatically.

    To see what I'm talking about, right-click the chart again and go to Select Data. Press the Edit button under the Horizontal category. Select the entire range of projects in column U from the Project List worksheet and press OK until you reach the spreadsheet screen (Figure 10-20).

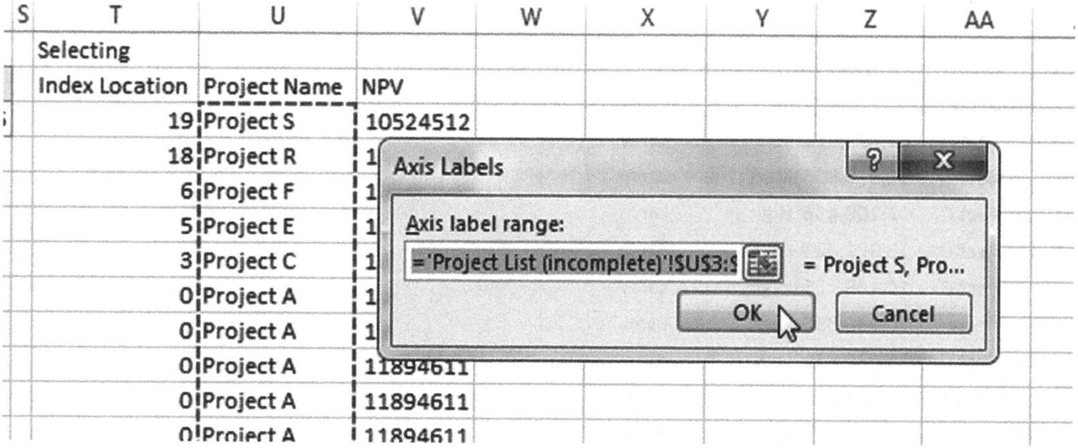

Figure 10-20. *The Axis Labels selection box*

Now the labels are automatically assigned! Go ahead and mess with the dropdown boxes to see it work in action.

Okay, one last piece before moving on. Go ahead and click one of those columns again in the chart and look at the formula bar. You should see that the range you've entered for your labels is now the second argument in the formula box. Just like for the series values, you could have simply entered the label range directly in the formula box. In case you're interested, here's how the series formula breaks down:

```
=SERIES(series_title , series_label_range , series_value_range , series_index)
```

If you'd like to supply this chart a title directly, go ahead and type a string into that `series_title` parameter. That last parameter, `series_index`, holds the current index of the series. If you have multiple series in your chart, setting the `series_index` will change the series order by inserting the series you're currently editing at the index you give.

Aggregating

In this section, I'll talk about aggregation, particularly the formulas you can use for aggregation. I'll also take a detour into some algebra, but nothing terrible. I promise.

Using SUMPRODUCT for Aggregation

Aggregation is the process of grouping similar items and presenting them as a whole. Excel has several aggregation formulas that you might already use every day including `SUM`, `AVERAGE`, and `COUNT`. If you want to get even more complicated—as if life isn't already complicated enough!—you could use the `SUMIF`/`SUMIFS` functions or `COUNTIF`/`COUNTIFS` functions to find the sum and count of multiple ranges of the same length satisfying certain criteria.

Let's say for the information in Figure 10-21, you were interested in all projects by Larry or Barry in which NPV is greater than 11,000,000 *or* portfolio risk is low.

	A	B	C	D
1	Raw Data Table			
2	Projects	NPV	Portfolio Ris	Project Lead
3	Project A	11,894,611	Low	Larry
4	Project B	11,676,808	Med	Larry
5	Project C	12,208,436	High	Larry
6	Project D	10,972,428	Low	Larry
7	Project E	10,439,155	High	Larry
8	Project F	10,080,330	High	Larry
9	Project G	11,080,632	Low	Barry
10	Project H	10,326,092	Low	Barry
11	Project I	10,215,675	Low	Barry
12	Project J	10,551,834	Low	Barry
13	Project K	11,941,962	Med	Barry
14	Project L	12,120,026	High	Barry
15	Project M	10,259,752	Low	Barry
16	Project N	10,253,060	Low	Barry
17	Project O	11,158,311	Low	Harry
18	Project P	10,703,286	Low	Harry
19	Project Q	10,736,631	Low	Larry
20	Project R	11,508,068	High	Larry
21	Project S	10,524,512	High	Larry
22	Project T	10,162,742	Low	Larry

Figure 10-21. *The Raw Data table containing projects, NPV, portfolio risk, and the project's lead*

To do that, you could use this formula, which isn't very pretty:

```
=COUNTIFS(ProjectLead,"Larry",NPV,">11000000")+COUNTIFS(ProjectLead,"Larry",PortfolioRisk,"
Low")+COUNTIFS(ProjectLead,"Barry",NPV,">11000000")+COUNTIFS(ProjectLead,"Barry",
PortfolioRisk,"Low")
```

This is because SUMIFS and COUNTIFS test for the intersection of data by themselves. There's no room for an OR condition in these formulas. But you have alternatives. For example, you could use the SUMPRODUCT formula for this problem, which would look like this:

```
=SUMPRODUCT(((ProjectLead="Larry")+(ProjectLead="Barry"))*((NPV>11000000)+
(PortfolioRisk="Low")))
```

I know you're scratching your head, so let's dig deeper. SUMPRODUCT by its name suggests it was designed for matrix algebra operations. To wit, Microsoft's definition of SUMPRODUCT is pretty mathematical. Specifically, SUMPRODUCT "multiplies corresponding components in the given arrays, and returns the *sum* of those products" (my emphasis). But this exactly what's so great about SUMPRODUCT.

When you write something like `(ProjectLead="Barry")` you're turning the range given by `ProjectLead` into array of TRUE/FALSE based on the supplied condition. That's from Chapter 9. So something like `(ProjectLead="Larry")*(NPV>11000000)` is calculated as shown in Figure 10-22.

L	M	N	O	P	Q	R	S	T	U	V
(ProjectLead="Larry")*(NPV>11000000)				Dot Product Calculation						
Project Lead		NPV		Project Lead		NPV		Result		
Larry		11,894,611		1	*	1		1		
Larry		11,676,808		1	*	1		1		
Larry		12,208,436		1	*	1		1		
Larry		10,972,428		1	*	0		0		
Larry		10,439,155		1	*	0		0		
Larry		10,080,330		1	*	0		0		
Barry		11,080,632		0	*	1		0		
Barry		10,326,092		0	*	0		0		
Barry	*	10,215,675	=	0	*	0	=	0	=	4
Barry		10,551,834		0	*	0		0		
Barry		11,941,962		0	*	1		0		
Barry		12,120,026		0	*	1		0		
Barry		10,259,752		0	*	0		0		
Barry		10,253,060		0	*	0		0		
Harry		11,158,311		0	*	1		0		
Harry		10,703,286		0	*	0		0		
Larry		10,736,631		1	*	0		0		
Larry		11,508,068		1	*	1		1		
Larry		10,524,512		1	*	0		0		
Larry		10,162,742		1	*	0		0		

Figure 10-22. *A visual represetation of what's happening when you use SUMPRODUCT*

In a certain sense, you're performing a query on the data. If you know SQL, the arrangement above could also be written as

```
SELECT COUNT(ProjectLead)
WHERE ProjectLead = "Larry" AND NPV > 11000000
```

You're About To Be FOILed!

OK, I know what you're thinking, *how the heck am I ever going to remember how to write one of those fancy* SUMPRODUCT *formulas?* Well, it all comes down to FOILing, which you might recall from your early days of learning algebra.

At first glance, the series of COUNTIFS functions appears easier to write and understand, even if the formula ends up being much longer. But I'm here to tell you that if you can write a series of COUNTIFS functions, you're already writing the same formula. No, seriously: I can prove this to you with some simple algebra. So let's talk FOILing (First, Outside, Inside, Last) from your algebra class. Let's do it on an expression inside the SUMPRODUCT formula.

So

```
((ProjectLead="Larry")+(ProjectLead="Barry"))*((NPV>11000000)+(PortfolioRisk="Low"))
=
    (ProjectLead="Larry")*(NPV>11000000)
+   (ProjectLead="Larry")*(PortfolioRisk="Low")
+   (ProjectLead="Barry")*(NPV>11000000)
+   (ProjectLead="Barry")*(PortfolioRisk="Low")
```

Now compare that FOILed expression to series of COUNTIFS functions.

```
=
    COUNTIFS(ProjectLead,"Larry",NPV,">11000000")
+   COUNTIFS(ProjectLead,"Larry",PortfolioRisk,"Low")
+   COUNTIFS(ProjectLead,"Barry",NPV,">11000000")
+   COUNTIFS(ProjectLead,"Barry",PortfolioRisk,"Low")
```

Here's the kicker: the plus symbol (+) acts as your OR condition and the multiplication symbol acts as your AND condition. If you think you'll have trouble remember the plus's + and multiplication's *, remember that these symbols aren't arbitrary, they represent algebraic operations.

■ **Note** Remember, for SUMPRODUCT queries, + = OR, * = AND.

If you open Chapter10Example3.xlsx, I've placed a summary table on the front page that employs SUMPRODUCT (Figure 10-23).

Project Breakdown

	NPV	
	<11M	>12.0M
High	=SUMPRODUCT((NPVRange<11000000)*(ProjectList.PortfolioRiskRange='Dashboard (incomplete)'!$G21))	
Med	0	0
Low	9	0
	12	2

Figure 10-23. *A demonstration of SUMPRODUCT on your dashboard*

Reusable Components

In this section, I'll take a few moments to go through a concept I call *reusable components*. Take a look at the outlined components in Figure 10-24.

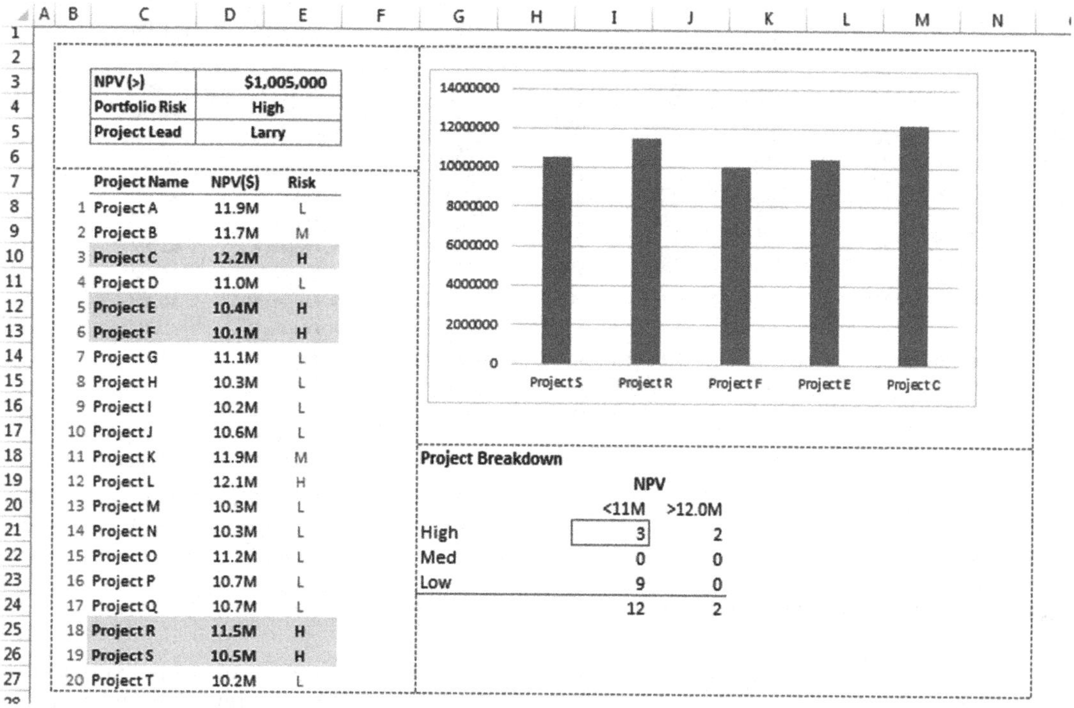

Figure 10-24. An example of reusuable componants

Admittedly, these components were not placed with any specific care. I did this on purpose to demonstrate how easily these components can be moved around, as shown in Figure 10-25.

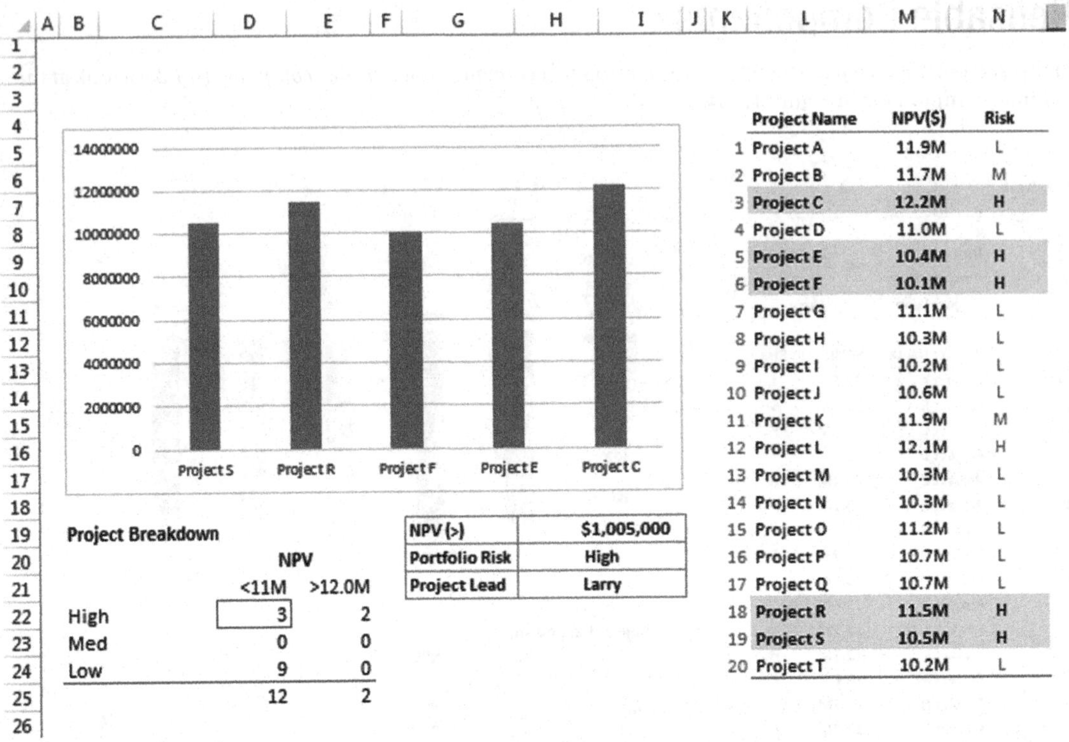

Figure 10-25. *A demonstration of how componants can be easily moved around*

There was some reformatting required, of course. But if I select the entire region of a table, I'm able to move it somewhere else on the screen without having to update any code or other formulas that refer that area. In addition, if I want to create another table similar to the one above, I can copy and paste the table into another free area on the spreadsheet and update the formulas that make it refer to another desired location. This is what is meant by *reusability*. And developing reusable components really helps down the road.

The Last Word

In this chapter, you build upon the formulas presented in the previous chapter. You applied what you learned to create the processes of filtering, highlighting, selecting, and aggregation. Finally, you learned about the usefulness of reusable components.

CHAPTER 11

Metrics: Performance and Context

Purna "Chandoo" Duggirala, who created and writes for Chandoo.org, is a strong advocate of data context. Consider his article "Never use simple numbers in your dashboards." In it, he argues for including additional information about single data points. For example, the sales data for a single month can tell only that month's story. However, including last month's sales, last year's sales, and how sales have trended can provide for a much richer story. This is because, in Chandoo's words, several data points can present a "better story than a simple number alone."

Telling the Whole Story Like a Reporter: An Introduction to Analytics

A good dashboard report or interactive decision tool does more than just provide information; it *tells a story*. And a good story requires description, setting, and context. In my high-school journalism class, we liked to talk about the five *w*'s and one *h*: who, what, where, when, why, and how. Dashboards aren't much different than a good newspaper article or a well-researched magazine article. Your dashboard should tell a story, and you should present all the details sufficient to tell that story.

Thinking back to the introductory chapters of this book, you'll recall the reasons why some dashboards and data visualizations fail. I had argued that data applications cannot make decisions for you, nor should you expect them to. Instead, they can provide you with the necessary information to make good decisions. This confusion results from a misunderstanding of the purpose of the data displayed.

Dashboards and decision tools can easily provide a *descriptive* context. For example, they can easily address the who, where, and when, even in exhaustive detail if need be, provided the data necessary to present this information is available. However, the what to some extent (arguably, what has some overlap into descriptive context), why, and how are not as easily presented, in part because a good description of *what has happened*, the root causes behind *why it has happened*, and the context required to sufficiently describe *how it has happened* are harder to capture. For example, the reason *why* one department performs better than another may require some research into an organization's processes, and for that matter, it may be the subject of intense debate within an organization.

Decision tools should contain the who, when, and where, which you can think of as descriptive analytics. In addition, the what, why, and how aid in the development of *prescriptive action*. That is, they help alert you to and potentially inform the best decision. A metric that does not meet its goal or department that is performing better than another can encourage you to investigate the reasons for these phenomena and how to replicate or avoid them. This is a key area where dashboards and decision tools differ. A dashboard can inform you to take prescriptive action. A decision tool, like a decisions support system, can provide recommendations through *prescriptive analytics*.

Finally, there's one more *w* to the mix—that of the "what if." The what-if forms the *predictive* analytics of the dashboard. Prediction speaks to what you think will happen given certain preconditions. For example, the easiest precondition is that you will continue to perform next month as you did this month. See Figure 11-1.

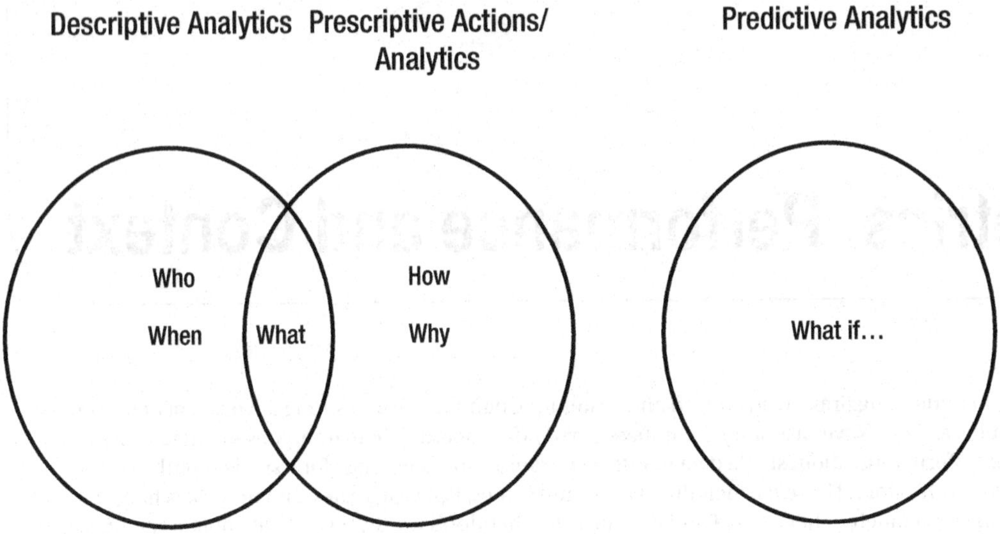

***Figure 11-1.** A description of the different types of analytics*

Let's go through these.

Who and Where

The who or where in this case could be a person or a department. In a certain sense, they aren't very different. Consider the table in Figure 11-2. The table answers the question, how well have the departments under my purview provided quality customer service?

	A	B	C	D
1				
2		**Average Grade for Customer Service by Department**		
3		Key: 1=Worst, 5=Best		
4		**Department**	**Grade**	
5		Customer Service	2.4	
6		Technical Support	4.0	
7		Accounts	4.5	
8		Online Help	4.2	
9		**Average**	**3.8**	

***Figure 11-2.** A demonstration of a dashboard answering the who and where questions of descriptive analytics*

This table answers the where, which refers to a particular department, but it doesn't answer the who, which refers to a person. For example, you might be interested in your representatives who support the Customer Service department. It's tempting then to include the entire list of staff and their corresponding scores on the dashboard. I've excerpted part of this list in Figure 11-3.

	A	B	C
1	First Name	Last Name	Customer Satisfaction
2	Elizabeth	Hunt	1.0
3	Anna	Cole	1.0
4	Jackson	Cole	1.0
5	Dominic	Green	1.0
6	Landon	Young	1.0
7	Hailey	Price	1.1
8	Kylie	Kelly	1.1
9	Jordan	Warren	1.1
10	Joseph	Kelley	1.1
11	Jackson	Warren	1.1
12	Robert	Boyd	1.1
13	Isabella	Campbell	1.1
14	James	Knight	1.2
15	John	Reynolds	1.2
16	Gianna	Clark	1.2

Figure 11-3. *A table that answers the where question of descriptive analytics but not the who*

But the full list is much bigger (100 names in fact). And that's just my sample data. Real data, as you probably know, can be much bigger than that. So, excerpting a list for the user is probably not the best idea. Furthermore, excerpting the list puts the responsibility of finding the problem on the user. Instead, you must think in terms of telling a story; specifically, you want to communicate relevant context quickly, providing accurate descriptions to bring the narrative to life. As such, the who you are interested in are probably the worst performers. See Figure 11-4.

(Arguably, you might also be interested in the best performers, but to the extent dashboards alert you to problems requiring action, you are definitely *more interested* in the worst performers.)

	Bottom 10 Performers in Cust Serv Dept		
9	**Rep Name**	**Cur Grade**	**Rnk**
10	Hunt, Elizabeth	1.0	100
11	Cole, Anna	1.0	99
12	Cole, Jackson	1.0	98
13	Green, Dominic	1.0	97
14	Young, Landon	1.0	96
15	Price, Hailey	1.1	95
16	Kelly, Kylie	1.1	94
17	Warren, Jordan	1.1	93
18	Kelley, Joseph	1.1	92
19	Warren, Jackson	1.1	91
20	Boyd, Robert	1.1	90

Figure 11-4. *A table that helps you communicate the worst performers quickly*

When

Answering the when always deals with time. For example, answering when can be as simple as supplying the previous month's rank in addition to the current rank (see Figure 11-5). This provides context for the current performance. Is there an underlying trend or perhaps an unexpected aberration?

Bottom 10 Performers in Cust Serv Dept

Rep Name	Cur Grade	Cur Rnk	Last Month
Hunt, Elizabeth	1.0	100	100
Cole, Anna	1.0	99	98
Cole, Jackson	1.0	98	99
Green, Dominic	1.0	97	82
Young, Landon	1.0	96	89
Price, Hailey	1.1	95	96
Kelly, Kylie	1.1	94	93
Warren, Jordan	1.1	93	94
Kelley, Joseph	1.1	92	92
Warren, Jackson	1.1	91	88
Boyd, Robert	1.1	90	90

Figure 11-5. *A table that helps answer the who, where, and when of descriptive analytics*

The when can be much more in depth than this, of course. A timeseries chart is often a good way to present the when.

Why, How, and What

In this section, I'll discuss the why, how, and what that make up the components of prescriptive analytics. In particular, the way prescriptive analytics is used actually differs in the context in which it takes place. In the next two subsections, I'll discuss the differences of how analytics exist on dashboards and in other decision tools.

Dashboards

You may recall from earlier in the book that there are inherent differences between dashboards and other decision support tools. To wit, dashboards don't make prescriptive recommendations; rather, they alert users to areas that need attention. They can, for instance, measure current performance against a selected target. In a sense, the target is a type of "ideal." By placing a metric on a dashboard with an ideal value to be attained, there is a prescriptive argument being made about how what is being measured ought to perform. Bullet charts, introduced in Chapter 4, are great examples of comparing how you're doing against what you think you should be doing. Figure 11-6 shows an example bullet chart you can make in Excel.

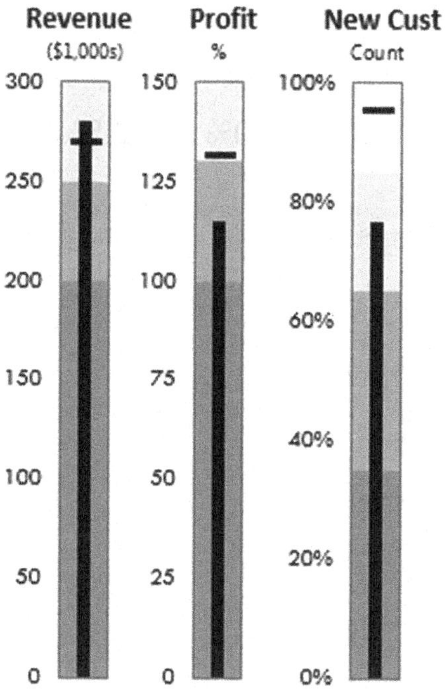

Figure 11-6. *Bullet charts show how you're actually doing against how you think you should be doing*

On the other hand, when a measurement comes in significantly under an ideal, the dashboard is signaling that some intervention ought to be taken. Ideally, it will also provide other descriptive measurements important to why the measure is coming in under the ideal. With this information, the dashboard user can take the necessary actions or investigations to rectify the problem. Dashboards don't usually present prescriptive analytics by themselves, but they can prescribe action to be taken when necessary.

Decision Tools

Decision support systems, on the other hand, employ full prescriptive analytics. For example, the analysis in Figure 11-7 shows an example decision support system that lists countries with the best healthcare systems based on a set of a metrics.

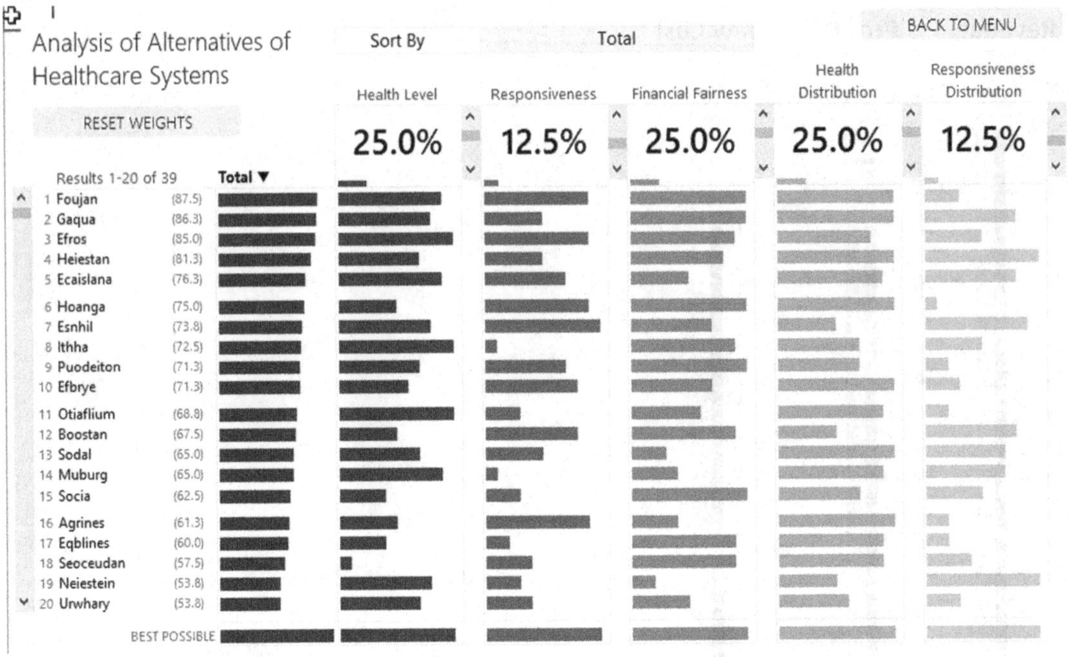

Figure 11-7. An example of a decision support system using prescriptive analytics

This decision support system allows you to change the weights the model uses. This is called *sensitivity analysis*. With sensitivity analysis, you can change the weights to see which countries are still the top performers (that is, you're testing how sensitive the model is to changes in weights). This is different from a regular dashboard because it allows you to change how the results are calculated. In other words, the result is making a prescriptive recommendation based on the decisions made by the user. This is different from a dashboard, which can only recommend intervention and investigation.

You'll investigate in greater detail the decision support system shown in Figure 11-7 in Chapters 17 through 20.

What If?

In this section, I'll talk about the "what-if" question predictive analytics helps answer. "What-if" analysis asks questions about the data, given certain conditions, to make an educated guess about what happens as a result. "What-if" analysis often takes the form of regression on a dashboard, but it needn't always. For example, the chart in Figure 11-8 (from Chapter 3) makes a prediction about years of experience and salary. It assumes two key conditions: that salary and years of experience are inherently related and that the relationship between the two can be expressed accurately by a linear equation.

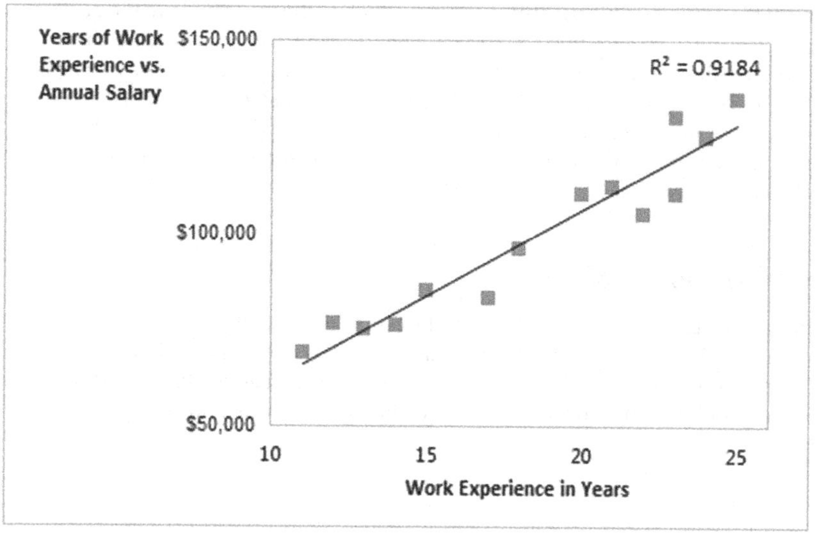

Figure 11-8. *An example of predictive analytics. Using the regression line, you can predict how much one might make based on the years worked*

Predictive analytics plays roles on both dashboards and decision support systems. On dashboards, regression can help predict what sales in the next quarter might look like. On a decision support tool, the user might specify a set of interactive assumptions before the model results are generated. Often these assumptions help test prescriptive actions ("What if our company sells this type of product that would result in a better gross margin?"). Whether on a dashboard or decision support tool, you must always remember that predictions follow from a series of assumptions. Their results are true only to the extent their underlying assumptions hold true.

Metrics, Metrics, Metrics

At the end of the day, your dashboard or decision tool will produce some data to display. That data presented together with context—a signal, a performance indicator, a goal, or a target—is a metric. What metrics you choose to display will depend ultimately on what you want to convey to the user, and that decision will be manifest regardless of whether the problem you must solve takes the form of a dashboard or decision support application.

Knowing what information to collect and ultimately display is half the battle. The other half is deciding how to present the information. As discussed earlier, dashboards are more descriptive in nature; decision support systems are more prescriptive and predictive. Here some examples of metrics commonly found on dashboards and in decision tools:

- *Financial*: Revenues, expenses, profits, financial ratios
- *Marketing*: Satisfaction surveys, return on investment, audience engagement
- *Information technology*: Downtime, transfer rate
- *Healthcare*: Wait times, occupancy rate, length of stay, lab turnaround time

As I said in the beginning of the book, I won't attempt to tell you which of these metrics are the best to display. There are many good books and web sites that can help you on this path. At the same time, there are equally as many resources that claim certain KPIs are the best. A simple Internet search of the *best KPIs to use* will return many results with contradictory information. With that in mind, I feel I should take a few moments to tell you what criteria I use to evaluate metrics. I call this my "working criteria" because they make for a good rule of thumb, but they are only a starting point for evaluation. Remember, what may be the best for you depends on what you want to display.

Working Criteria for Choosing Metrics

The following criteria were in fact suggested for another domain altogether, specifically that of Value Focused Thinking, a decision support tool used in the field of management science and operations research.[1] However, I found them appropriate for helping analyze criteria to be placed on dashboards and decision tools. Specifically, you can judge metrics by their ability to fulfill the following criteria:

- Mutual exclusivity
- Common interpretation
- Sufficiency

Mutual Exclusivity

Metrics should not overlap in what they measure and present as best as possible. For example, profit margin is net profit divided by net income. There may indeed be good reason to place the net profit, net income, and profit margin on the same dashboard. But there also may be other cases where profit margin is the only thing of interest. In this case, the addition of net income with a profit margin measure adds nothing. Ratios are susceptible to this problem. Often you're interested only in the resulting ratio but not its components. Be on the lookout for instances in which metrics with shared components merely repeat the same information.

Figure 11-9 provides a good example of mutual exclusivity being violated.

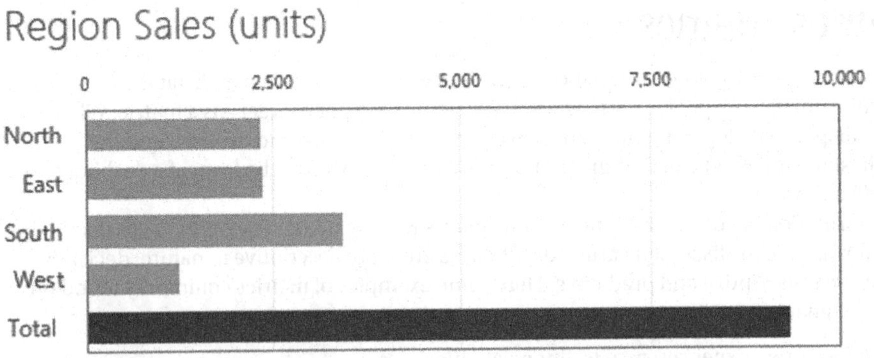

***Figure 11-9.** An example where mutual exclusivity is not being followed*

[1]See Parnell, G. S., Chapter 19, *Value-Focused Thinking Using Multiple Objective Decision Analysis, Methods for Conducting Military Operational Analysis: Best Practices in Use Throughout the Department of Defense*, Military Operations Research Society, Editors Andrew Loerch and Larry Rainey, 2007.

The total bar simply reintroduces the unit sales values for each region. However, how much does it actually add to the intracomparison of one region to the other? The total value may still be important, but the visualization in Figure 11-9 merely reintroduces the same information. Figure 11-10 includes the same information as before but in a way that doesn't visually repeat data already presented.

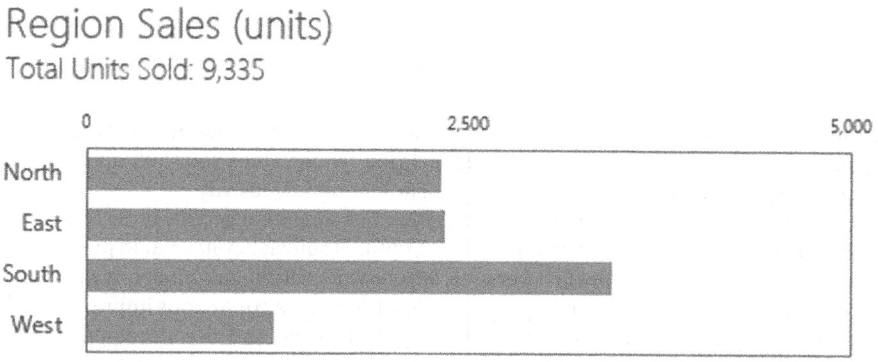

Figure 11-10. *Data is not repeated and therefore mutual exclusivity is maintained*

Common Interpretation

Common interpretation is the assurance that the metric presented is interpreted in the same way by everyone within the organization. Most financial ratios aren't subject to disagreement. However, constructed metrics may bring about confusion. Consider the benefit value function in Figure 11-11: 0 has the least benefit; 1 has the most. It's not clear, however, what a 1 or a 0 really means. You simply know that a greater number is better.

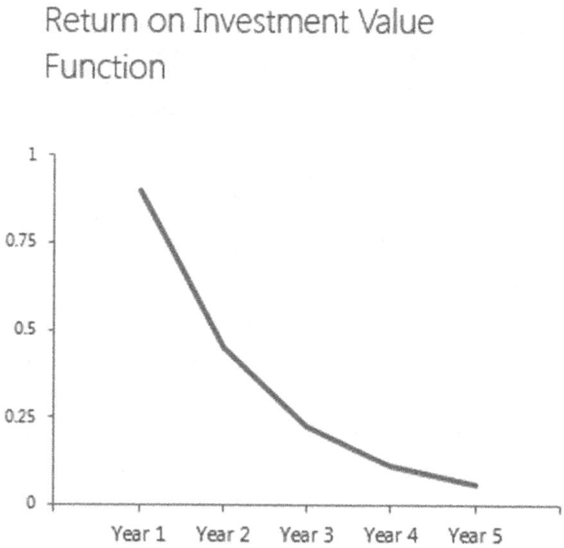

Figure 11-11. *An example where common interpretation is violated; you don't really know what a one or zero means in this context*

The chart shown in Figure 11-11, unfortunately, is adapted from a real one I came across during my career. I knew that a 1 was better than a 0, but it wasn't clear what that might mean. One might interpret a value of .5 to return half the value of a year with a 1. Others might interpret a year with a .5 to be half as good ("good" could mean anything here) as a year with a 1. These interpretations and so many more are all valid when the metric has not been clearly defined. Common interpretation suggests we should all have the same understanding of metrics presented our way.

Sufficiency

Sufficiency deals with the number of metrics being displayed. On the one hand, you shouldn't waste screen real estate by showing only a few metrics while leaving lots of whitespace. On the other, you shouldn't display data just to fill space, especially if the data overlaps and violates mutual exclusivity.

I used to tell developers to display "as few metrics as possible," but I've since changed my tune. Less isn't always more when it comes to presenting information. Finding optimal sufficiency in what to present is a goal rather than a task to be completed. Often the first iteration of your work will fail to sufficiently present all of your ideas. This is to be expected; achieving sufficiency happens through the continuous improvement of your work. Rarely will you get it right the first time, but if you are open to change and view development as an evolution, then you will converge upon a highly sufficient display over time.

In all cases, you should be wary of dumping every piece of data, metric, and chart on your display. Often you display everything because you want your bosses, managers, and clients to be happy. In organizations where there is disagreement about what to display, putting everything on a dashboard feels like a positive compromise. But you shouldn't do this. As developers, it's your job to help tell the correct story in the most effective way possible. If your work attempts to be all things to all people, it gives more weight to the personalities attempting to shape the story in their own way than to the actual underlying story (which should be told by the data). You should push back against the interests that would have your work become a cluttered patchwork of the opinions and ideas that ineffectively present what's really going on.

The Last Word

In the previous several chapters, you learned layout, formulas, and how to present data to your users. In this chapter, we looked at the different ways dashboards and decision support tools help you answer questions. In particular, I focused on the differences between descriptive, predictive, and prescriptive analytics. Next, I covered the principles to help you present information well. I showed that data presented should be mutually exclusive to the other data being presented (that is, you should eliminate redundancies). I established you should maintain a common and consistent interpretation of the information presented. Finally, I established you should strive to show the required amount of information necessary to tell the correct story.

CHAPTER 12

Charts with Heart (or, How to Avoid a Chart Attack)

You may have noticed the charts throughout this book have not been all quite the same, at least not in terms of format; I have several mainstay designs from which I pull, but I don't always use the same design each time. And I will argue to you there is no exact format you should follow. There is no problem with your data visualizations being formatted to reflect your personality and tastes so long as the visualizations naturally reflect the underlying problem being modeled and follow data visualization principles. In this chapter, I'll through some principles to help ensure your work does just that.

Challenging the Defaults

Excel has a lot of default settings that will work against you. The good news is that you can save your chart designs as templates once you're happy with your creations. However, creating a good design sometimes requires a few clicks, some trial and error, and, most importantly, patience.

Data-Ink Density

One test of good chart design is to measure the data-ink density. The measure was created by Edward Tufte and first written about in his book *The Visual Display of Quantitative Information* (Graphics Press, 1983). Tufte made a distinction between data-ink—that is, the "ink" used to encode and convey data and information—and non-data-ink, which he described as embellishments and redundant. He outlined five principles to this end:

- Above all else show data.
- Maximize the data-ink ratio.
- Erase non-data-ink.
- Erase redundant data-ink.
- Revise and edit.

Figure 12-1 shows one such example of a default Excel chart. Take a look and consider what elements appear extraneous to the chart's effectiveness.

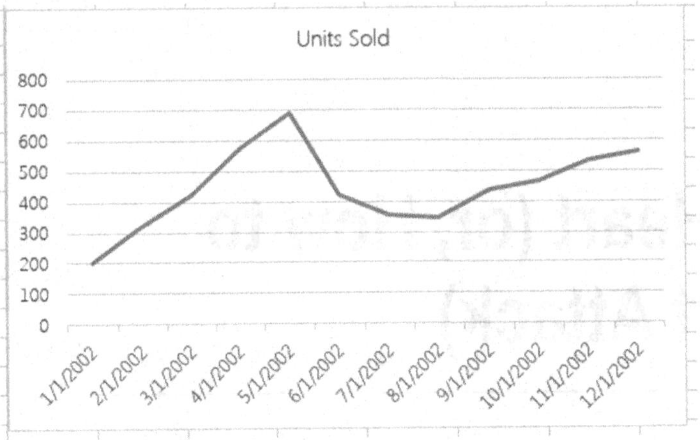

Figure 12-1. *A line chart created using Excel's defaults*

Well, one item I notice right away is that we're interested only in months across an entire year epoch—there is no need for either the day of the month or even the year. Instead, we could add the information about the year to the title. And, we could do some custom formatting to clean up the dates. Next, we could remove the plot lines because that isn't necessarily what we are looking for when using a chart (for true precision, a table is the best choice). Finally, we can shrink the axes of the chart—and resize the chart to better show the trend of the data. Figure 12-2 presents the result.

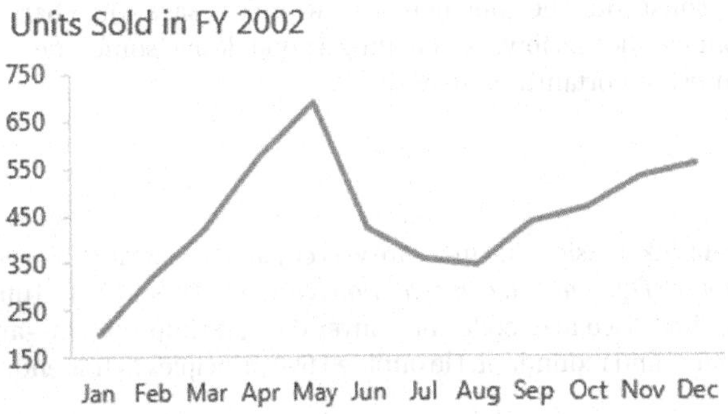

Figure 12-2. *The chart from Figure 12-1 has been redone to show only the most important elements required to effectively communicate data*

Charts: More Art Than Science, in Some Ways

Figure 12-2 is what I call a *Few-esque* design because it appears similar to the designs in Stephen Few's books. However, there have been other terrific chart designs that apply the same research that vary from his design. Indeed, my own designs don't mimic his entirely. For what it's worth, Few's work differs in design from Edward Tufte and Cleveland Williams, to name a few data visualization experts. I bring this up to challenge the notion that good data visualization requires you to follow only one proper formula or set of instructions.

Rather, the sequence you follow will be defined by your experience. Making a high-quality chart is often more of an art than a science (especially in Excel). Tufte knew this when he prescribed his instructions. As you can see, his instructions don't offer a specific terminus at which a chart has been perfectly designed. Instead, he left the judgment up to you. To those who've argued that the work of Tufte and Few offers rote and humorless charts, I'm here to turn this perspective on its head. There is a great deal of creativity required to create *effective* charts.

But not all creativity is useful. For instance, the chart in Figure 12-3 shows a nifty trick[1] where an image (in this case, that of barrels) stands as the backdrop of the column values in the column charts. One might think this image is relevant given the focus of the chart is oil production. But what we know from Tufte, the addition of embellishments and color do nothing to help our understanding of what the chart exists to convey.

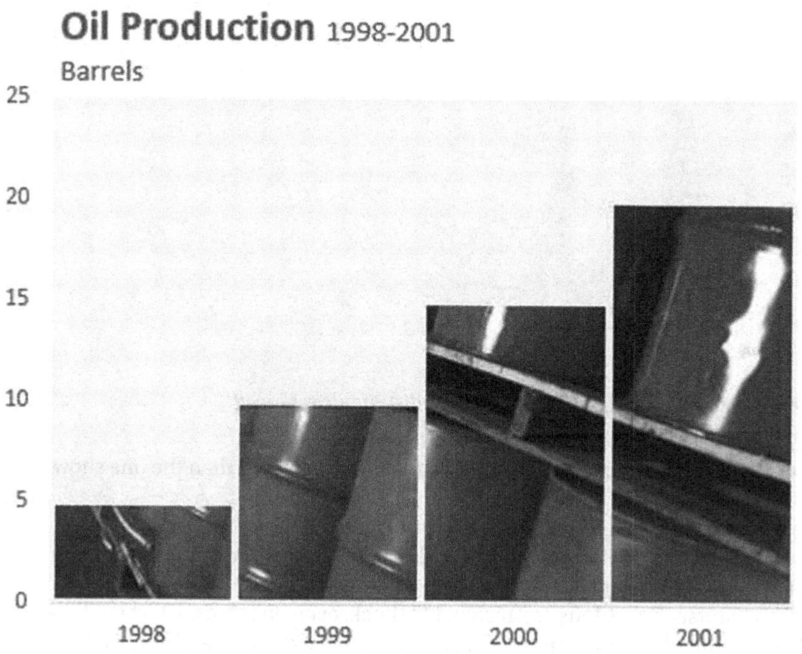

Figure 12-3. *The image of barrels stands in the background of the column values. While it may seem like a nifty addition to the chart, the image itself adds little to our understanding*

Contrast the chart shown in Figure 12-3 with the same chart presented more simply in Figure 12-4.

[1]Against my better judgment I'll provide you with a link of how this nifty trick is achieved: `http://chandoo.org/wp/2013/05/06/column-chart-with-background-image/`.

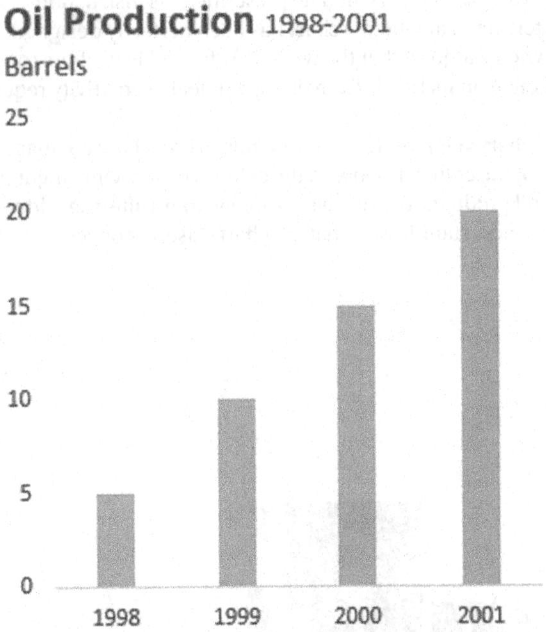

Figure 12-4. *The same data presented in Figure 12-3 but with embellishments removed*

The chart shown in Figure 12-4 is far less busy and easier to read and understand than the one shown in Figure 12-3.

This approach may appear too reductionist or minimalist, but truly it isn't. It's not promoting the principles of the architect, Ludwig Mies van der Rohe, who famously said, "Less is more." Instead, it's simply a principle of sufficiency. When an element doesn't add value, remove it. When more is required, add it. This is not a hard-and-fast rule, of course. Deviations are acceptable (heck, even encouraged) when they add to understanding. You should remember, as Few puts it, "what works, what doesn't, and why." When you understand the concepts of data visualization, only then do you know when deviations help and not hurt.

Chart Formats for Simple Comparison

Column and bar charts are among the most widely used chart type in this book. However, as established, Excel's default formatting often gets in the way of our ability to make sense of them. In the next subsections, I'll go through how best to make use of column and bar charts.

Column and Bar Charts

Some have argued that bar (and column) charts are boring and ugly. It's true that bar charts are used a lot—perhaps even more than necessary—but they are, at the same time, incredibly versatile. The trick is getting them to communicate effectively. Figure 12-5 represents a default chart created in Excel 2013. There's nothing wrong with it per se, but you can make a few more additions to make it communicate more effectively.

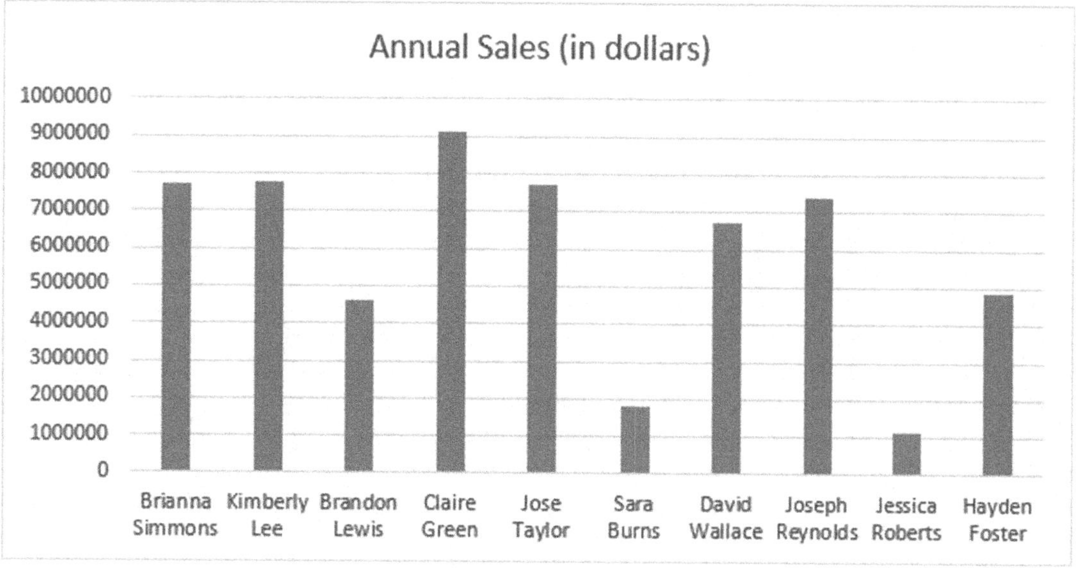

Figure 12-5. *An example column chart*

1. The first thing you can do is sort the individuals from highest to lowest in terms of annual sales. Chapter 5 talked about one such way to do it dynamically. Ideally, this method would always be employed so that the data is always sorted on the graph.
2. Second, you can make the y-axis easier to understand by simplifying its units. Excel provides a way to simply chart units in the formatting properties of the y-axis for the chart. However, I find this mechanism cumbersome and somewhat contradictory in its representation of numbers. So, instead, you'll use a custom format to describe these numbers.
3. Finally, you can erase the lines that do not help you for comparison and change some of the layout. Figure 12-6 shows the final result.

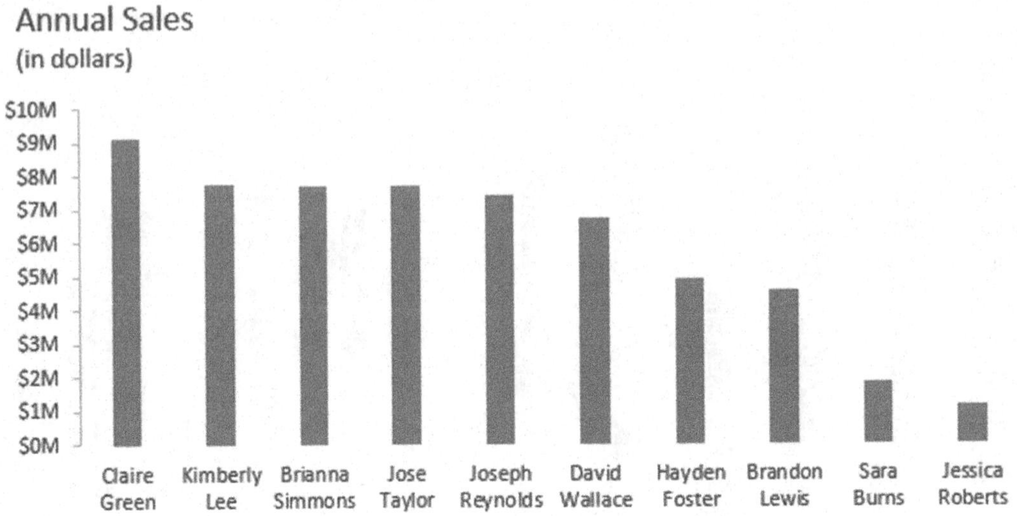

Figure 12-6. *When sorted and with other unnecessary data elements removed, the chart becomes much easier to read*

Layout Constraints

Sometimes you don't have the space to show the labels cleanly as I've done in Figure 12-6. Excel will attempt to convince you there's nothing wrong with craning your neck by tilting the labels to uncomfortable angles (see Figures 12-7 and 12-8).

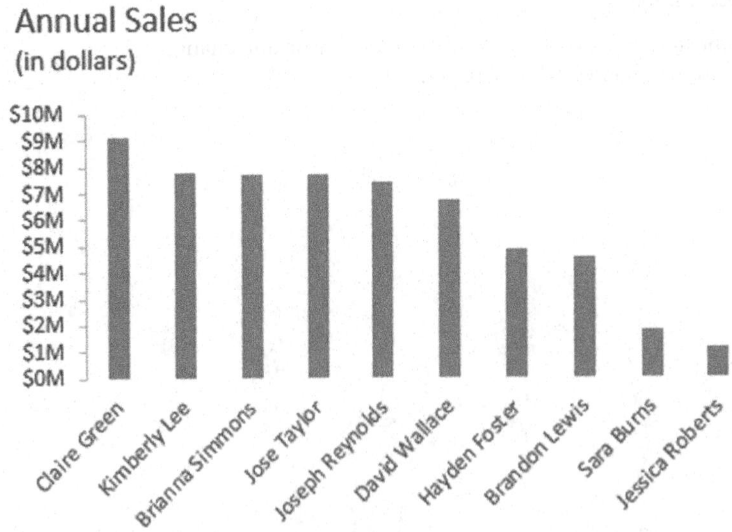

Figure 12-7. *By default, chart labels will often be set at an angle by Excel*

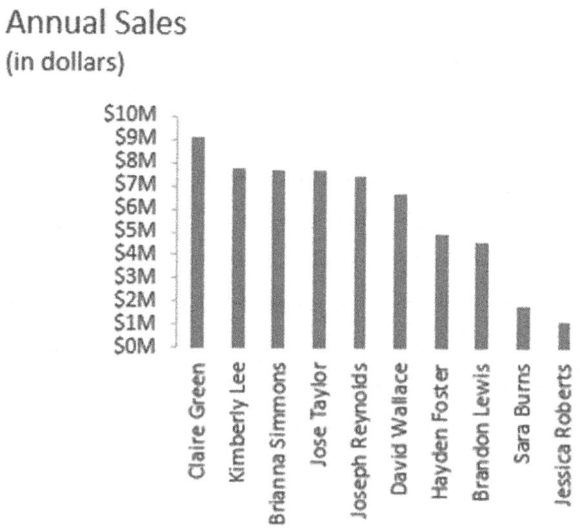

Figure 12-8. *Sometimes Excel will rotate labels by 90 degrees with the belief they are now easier to read*

You're much better off in these instances changing the chart type. In Figure 12-8, I used a column chart. In Figure 12-9, I've switched the data to a bar chart. You can easily change the type of chart by selecting Change Chart Type on the Chart Format tab.

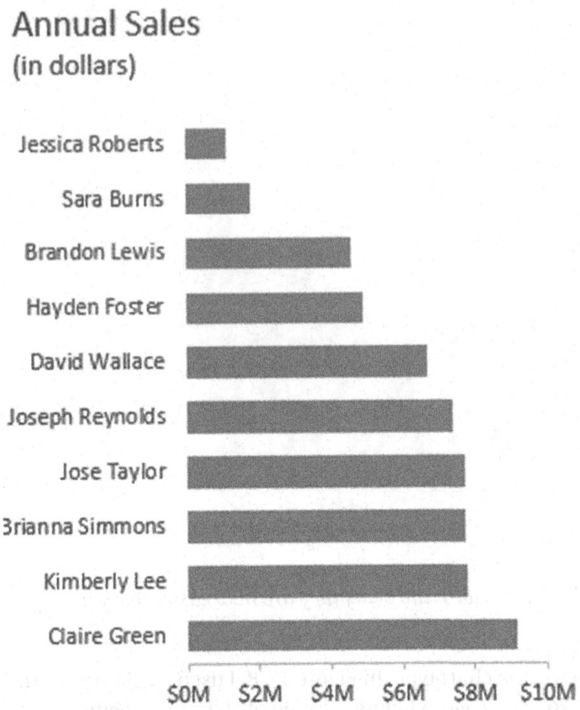

***Figure 12-9.** Sometimes it's a good idea to look to other chart types to compensate for readability*

Banding

Banding is the process of highlighting certain regions of chart. The region always represents some form of range. This range can be historical observations, tolerance levels, or some other type of bounded region. The chart in Figure 12-10 shows banding that provides the historical high and lows for temperature in a region. You can work with a version of this chart yourself by opening `Chapter12ChartExamples.xlsm` in the book chapter files.

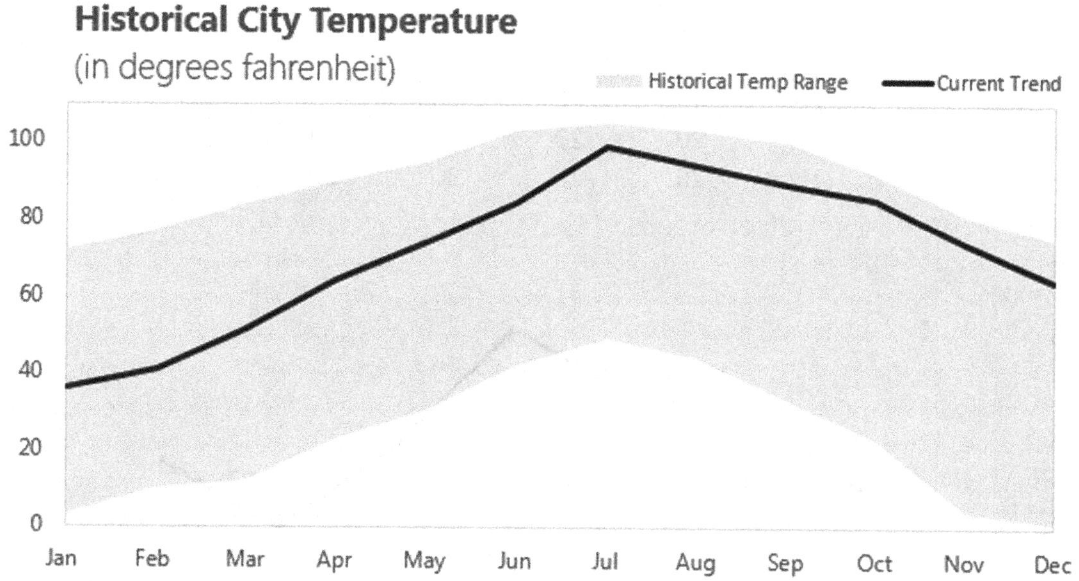

Figure 12-10. *An example of a chart with banded regions*

There are many, many types of chart you can create with banding. I'll go through a few in this chapter, but it will be by no means exhaustive. Luckily, creating bands in charts isn't particularly hard once you get the hang of it. There are two basic ways to create them, and each has its benefits.

Let's start with the first way. To begin, you'll need to start with a regular line chart. You'll need three different series to work with. First, you'll need to know the lower region of your band. Next, you'll need to know the upper region of the band. Finally, you'll need to know your current values to plot against the banding. In Figure 12-11, I've plotted my trend line in black representing the current values against which to compare the band. Mya desired tolerable region is between 10 and 30. You'll notice in the figure, however, the high end of my region shows 20 instead 30. You'll see why in the second. You can also see in the figure the boundaries of these regions appear as flat lines across the chart. In the table in Figure 12-10, each data point represents the boundary fixed across the time horizon. The trick here is to turn these two flat lines into stacked bar charts.

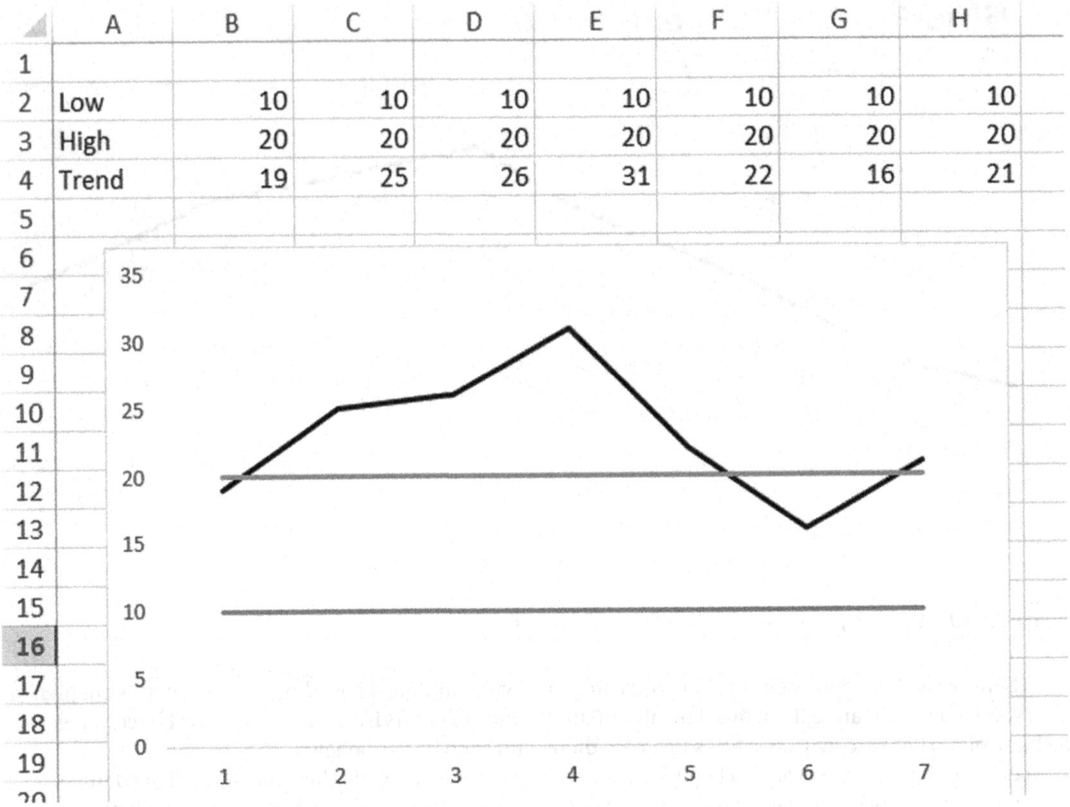

***Figure 12-11.** The beginning stages of a banded region chart*

I can do that by right-clicking each line and selecting Change Series Chart Type, as shown in Figure 12-12.

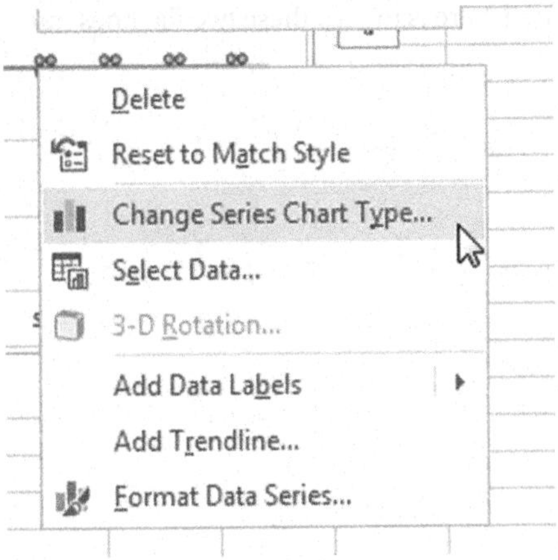

***Figure 12-12.** Changing the series chart type*

From there, you can change each high and low line to a stacked bar (Figure 12-13).

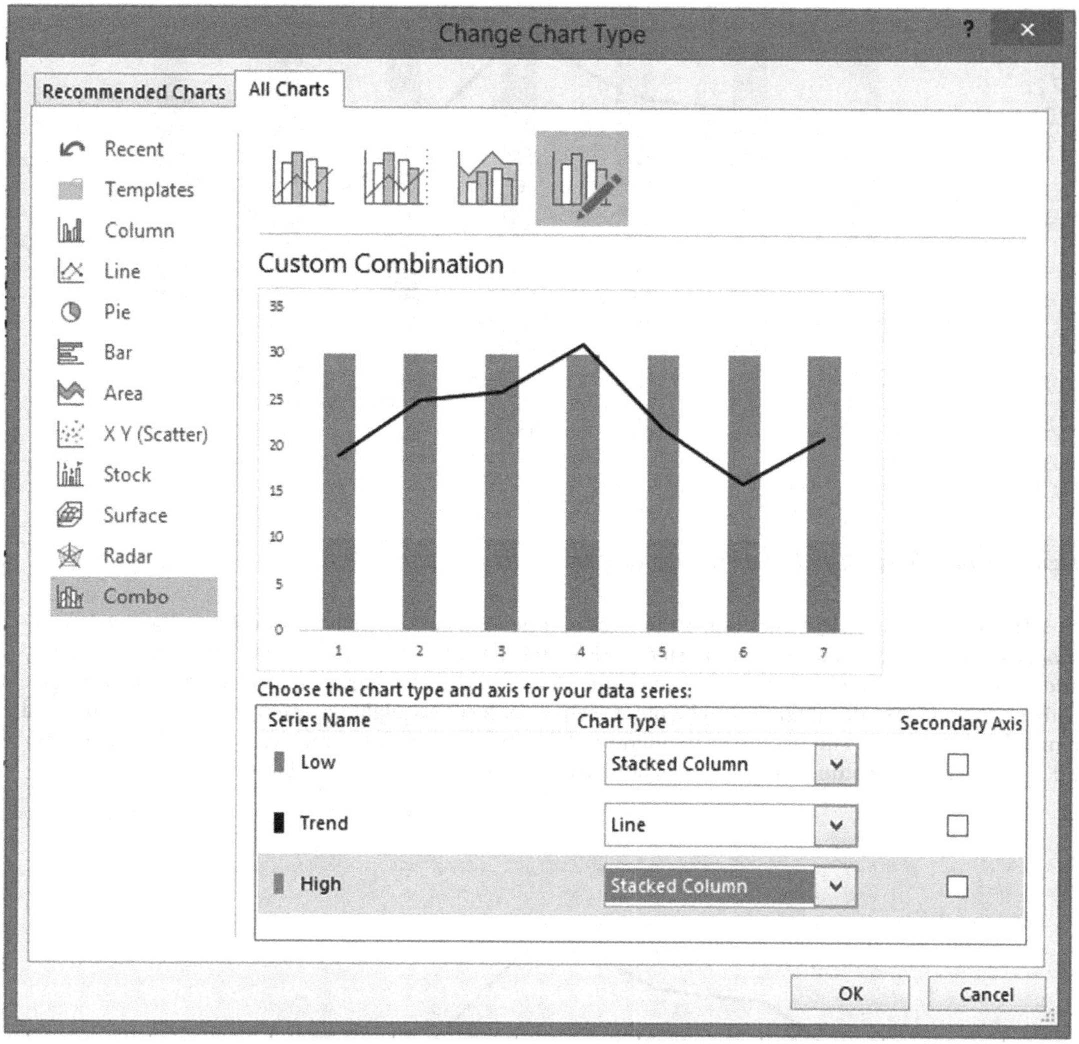

Figure 12-13. *The Change Chart Type dialog box*

Once complete, you should see a chart similar to that in Figure 12-14.

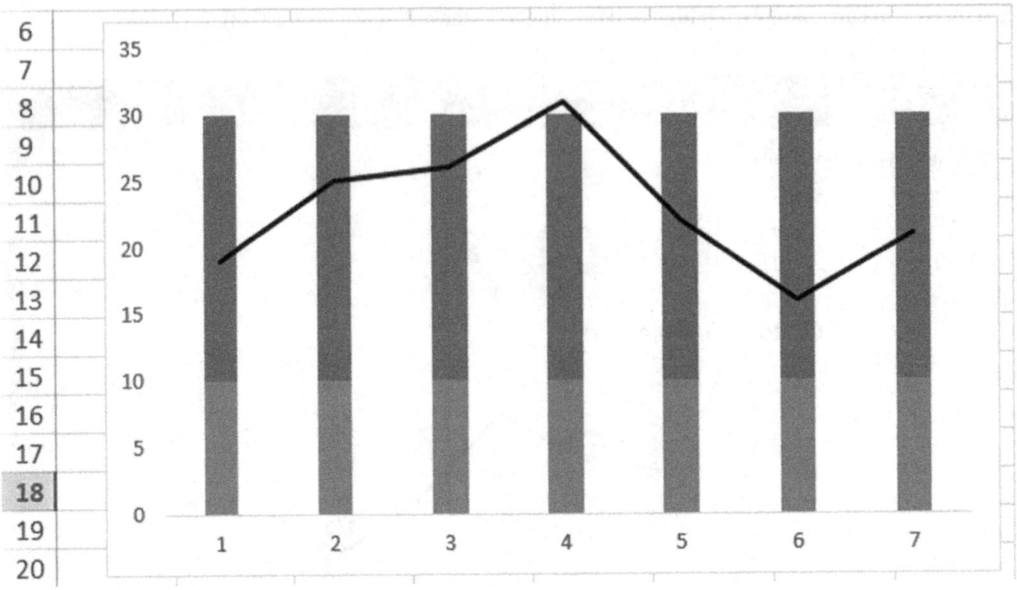

Figure 12-14. *Changing the line charts to stacked bar charts*

At this point, you'll right-click one of the stacked series and click Format Data Series. In the Gap Width property, you'll set the value to zero so that there is no result width. Finally, you'll select the bottom series and set its fill color to no fill. And that's it. In Figure 12-14, I've gone a few extra steps and painted the range with a lighter color so that it doesn't stand out. Excel's default colors might be a poor color for the range, and remember, you want to emphasize the trendline and deemphasize the band relative to it. (Make sure to get rid of any default formatting not mentioned here to ensure your chart looks similar to Figure 12-15.)

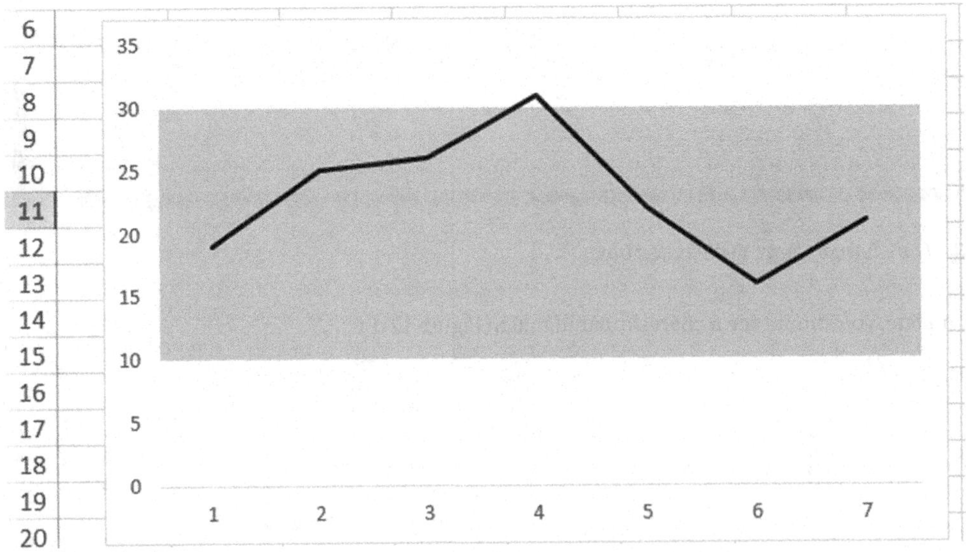

Figure 12-15. *How the final banded chart looks using stacked column charts*

Before moving on, I would like to direct your attention back to Figure 12-10. Remember previously I pointed out that the desired banded range would be from 10 to 30? Because you inevitably switch from line charts to stacked column charts, the values must add up to the top range of the desired region. That's because the columns are stacked.

The other method for creating bands in Excel requires the use of area plots. The concept, however, is similar to the previous. Figure 12-16 shows the two area plots required to create banding. The "high" plot is another area plot that sits on top of the "low" plot. The "low" plot is then recolored to be white, which gives the effect the remaining area in the "high" area series not covered by the "low" series is a region.

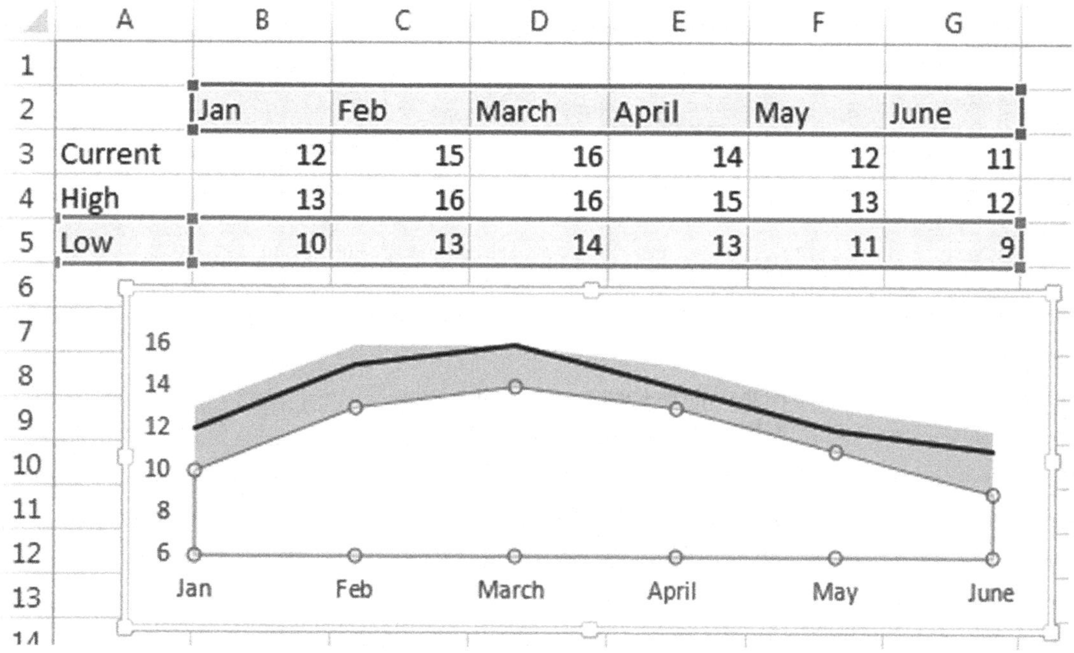

Figure 12-16. *Banding created using area charts*

Figure 12-17 shows this chart is simply a combination of a line chart and two stacked area charts.

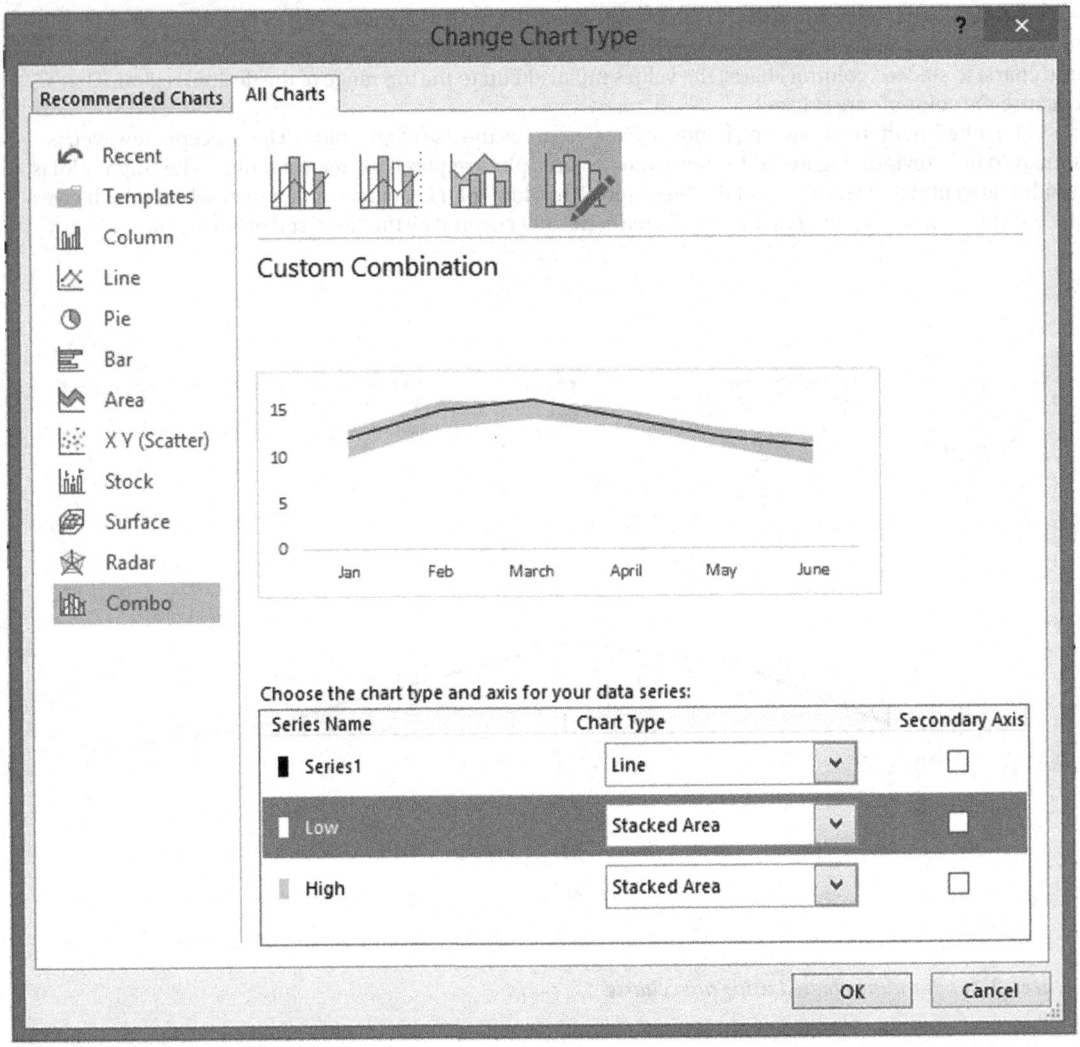

Figure 12-17. *The Change Chart Type dialog box showing the region is created using two stacked area series and a one line chart*

I find using area charts is best for when the banded region is not uniform across the series. Figure 12-18, for instance, shows the awkward representation of a banded region when stacked column charts are used.

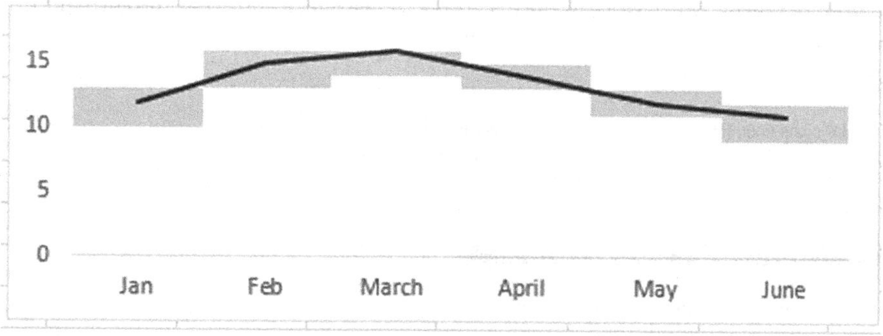

Figure 12-18. *Using column charts to create banding for a nonuniform region*

On the other hand, Figure 12-19 shows the stacked column chart method for a uniform banded region using the oil production data from Figure 12-3 earlier in the chapter.

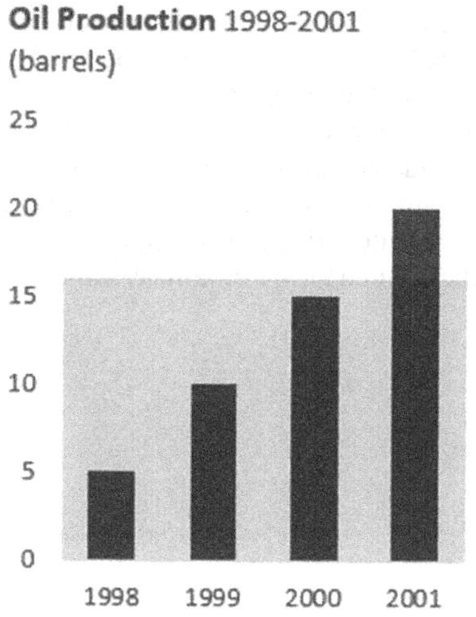

Figure 12-19. *Column charts are used here to create the banded region*

Bullet Charts

Before finishing this chapter, I will talk about how to create bullet charts in Excel. These charts are among the most important charts for dashboard developers in Excel. They were originally invented by the dashboard expert Stephen Few. They are prized for their ability to encode many types of comparative measurements in a small plot. They aren't part of Excel's standard chart library, but with only a few steps, you can make them yourself. In fact, bullet charts in many ways represent a combination of the examples presented previously in this chapter.

Recall from previous chapters the specification and layout of bullet charts. They are comprised a current value, usually a bar-line; a target value, usually another comparative that runs perpendicular to the bar measure; and graded color ranges, which serve as the backdrop against which you gauge the current value (Figure 12-20). Revisit Chapters 4 and 11 for a refresher on bullet charts.

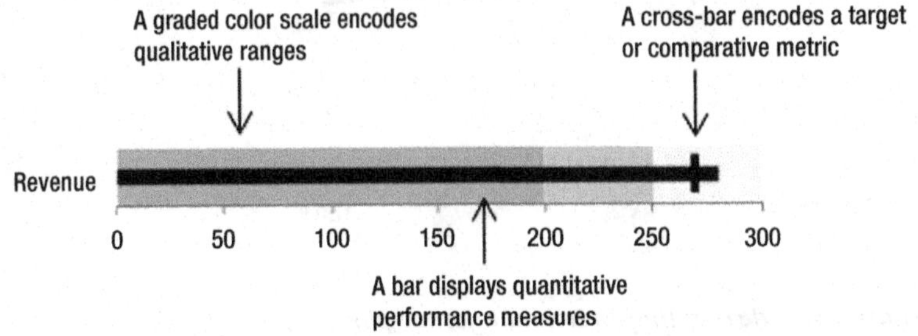

***Figure 12-20.** An example bullet chart with descriptions on how best to understand it*

Bullet charts can be displayed either vertically or horizontally. In Excel, as it turns out, vertical bullet charts are in fact easier to create than horizontal charts. This is because, for vertical charts, you can basically create the entire thing with stacked bar charts. On the other hand, horizontal charts require the use of the scatterplot and stacked bar charts and some spacing calculations. There is a trick to get around the problems associated with horizontal charts, and I'll show you how to do it before the chapter ends.

Let's go through how to make a bullet chart. I've taken the first few steps to creating a bullet chart in Figure 12-21. The Bad, Med, and Good quantities will become the shaded region behind the current value. Figure 12-21 is the result of highlighting each of these quantities and selecting the stacked bar chart. However, Excel has accidentally thought that each of these items is a separate series. If this happens to you, you'll want to right-click the chart, go to Select Data, and then click Switch Row/Column, as shown in Figure 12-22.

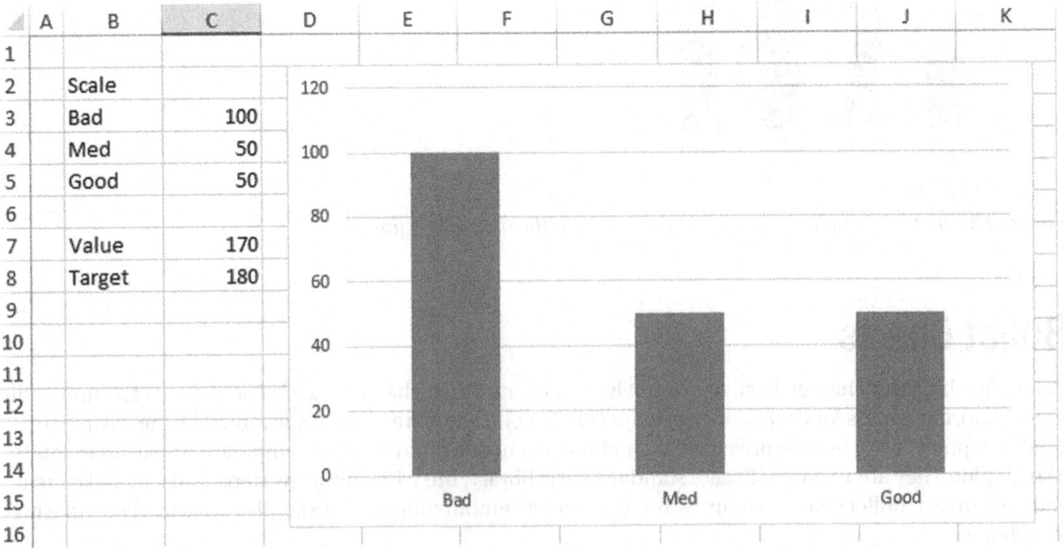

***Figure 12-21.** The first step for creating the bullet chart is to start with three series*

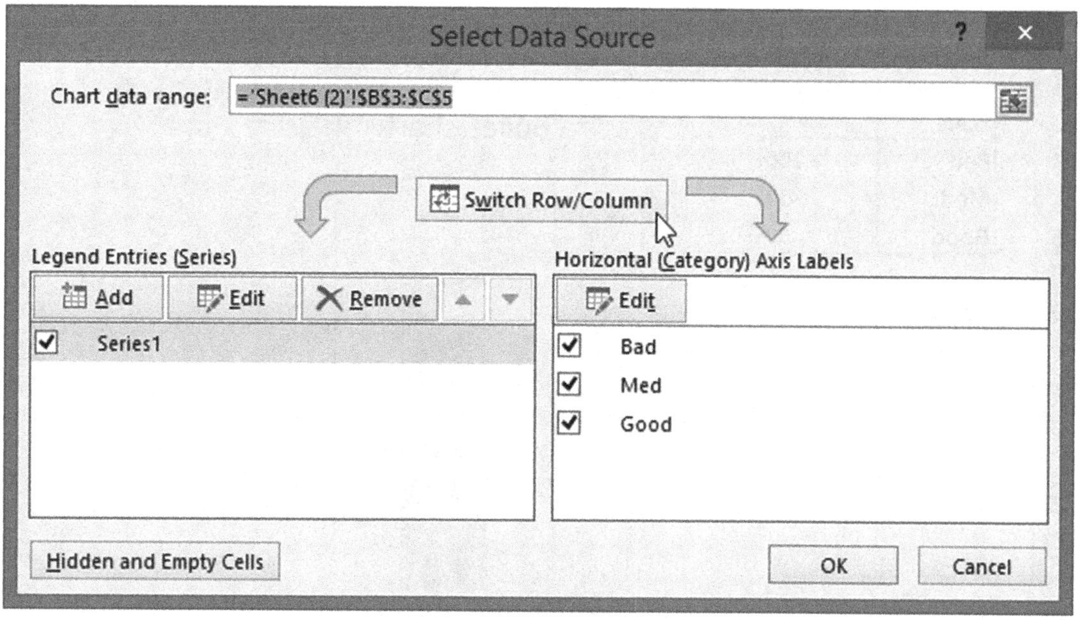

Figure 12-22. *Use the Switch Row/Column button to combine the three different series into one*

This will result in the correct layout. Take a moment to recolor each bar so they are part of the same scheme and vary in hue from most intense at the bottom to least intense at the top. You can use Excel's color palette in the color picker to help with shading in this configuration. Figure 12-23 presents the results.

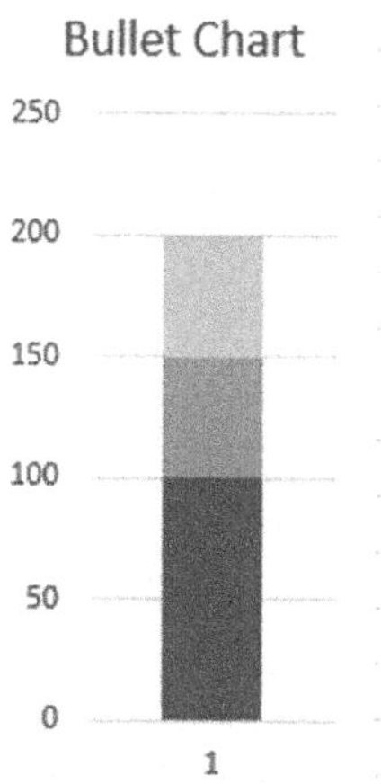

Figure 12-23. *Bullet chart with colors reformatted*

At this point, you're ready to plot the chart's current value. The easiest way to do this in this example is to copy the target value, using Ctrl+C, and then paste it into the chart, using Ctrl+V. In Figure 12-24, I've taken a snapshot of my completing this process. Figure 12-25 shows the result of this process.

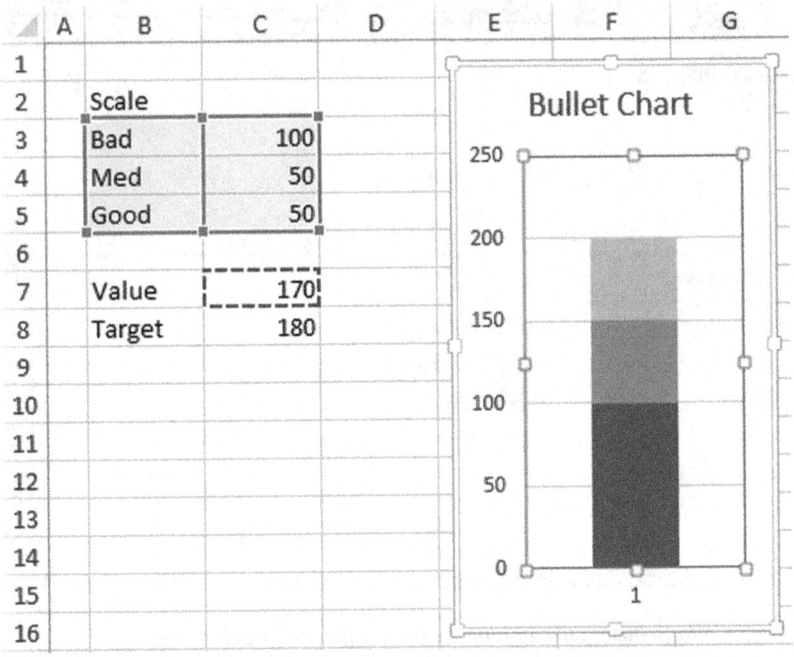

Figure 12-24. *You can place the target value into the bullet chart by selecting the cell containing the current value, pressing Ctrl+C to copy, and then selecting the chart and pressing Ctrl+V to paste*

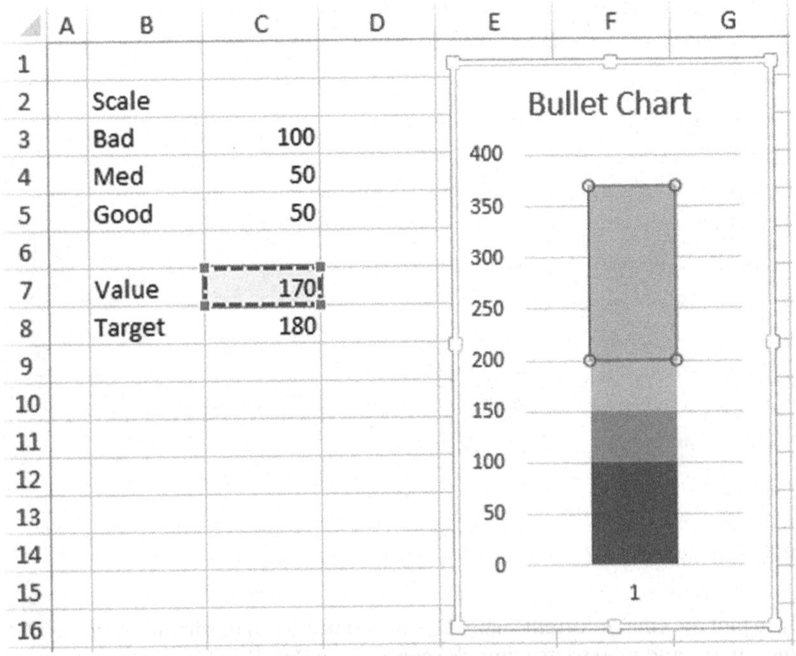

Figure 12-25. *The result of pasting the target value into the bullet chart*

At this point, you'll select the current value that has just been plotted on top of the stack. You'll want to place this series onto the secondary axis. To do this, you'll right-click the top of the stack and select Format Data Series. In the Series Options tab, you'll select the Plot on Secondary Axis option. Immediately, the target value will obscure all or part of the stacked chart behind it. You'll also notice that another scale has appeared on the right of the chart representing the secondary axis. The first thing you'll want to do is resize both scales so that they are equal. In this case, since the total of the Bad, Med, and Good series is 200, you'll resize both to be in the range of 0 to 200.

Next, you'll select the stacked series behind the current series. If you can't click one of these series because the current value is obscuring it, you can select a series from the Current Select drop-down on the Format tab. Select any of the stacked series. You'll want to change the gap width from within the Series Options again in the Format Data Series menu. Set Gap Width to 0%. Figure 12-26 shows the current progress.

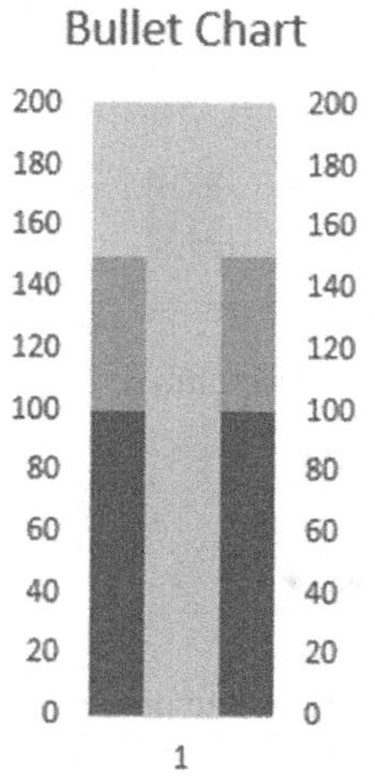

Figure 12-26. *The current progress in the bullet chart*

So far so good. Now you'll do the same as you did for the current value and paste the target value onto the chart. Again, the new series will appear at the top of the stack. Select this series and change it to an XY scatterplot. The target value should appear as a marker, as shown in Figure 12-27.

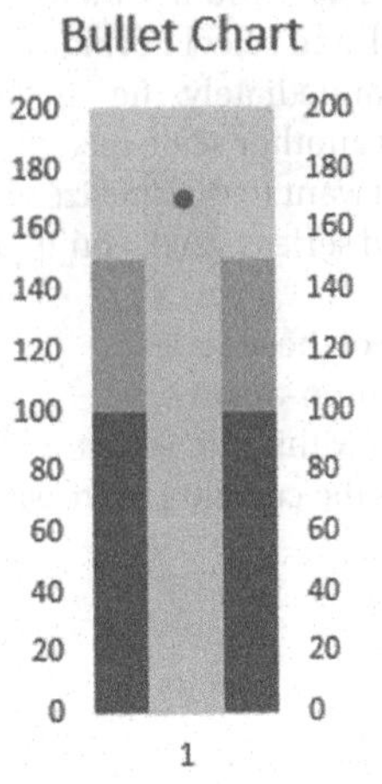

Figure 12-27. The target value marker added

At this point, you'll create the cross-bar target effect by adding Excel error bars to the new point.

- In Excel 2007 and 2010, go to the Layout tab and select Error Bars ➤ More Error Bar Options.
- In Excel 2013, go to the Design tab and select Add Chart Element ➤ Error Bars ➤ More Error Bar Options.

This will add error bars to the point. The default values in the error bars is usually too large and does not look good in the bullet chart. In my example, I've selected the Fixed Value option for the error and set it to .25. In addition, select No Cap for End Style (see Figure 12-28).

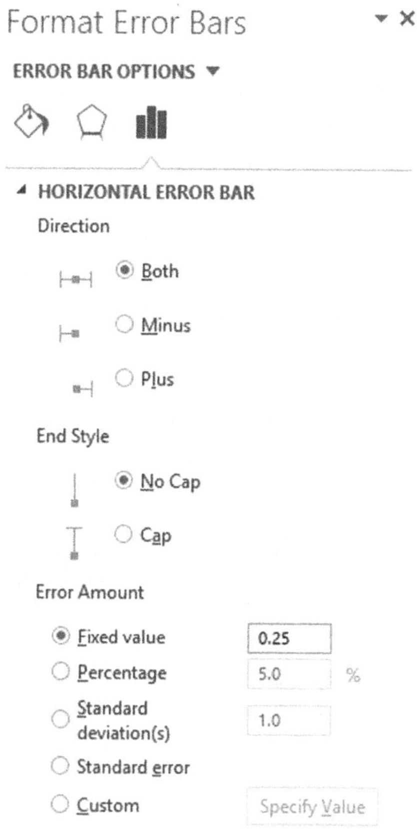

Figure 12-28. *The Format Error Bars context pane displaying the settings made to the error bar to achieve the cross-bar effect for bullet charts*

Now, it's time to do some formatting to clean up. For this example, I've set the error bars to be black in color and 2.00 thickness. I then selected the point that the error bars cross through and went to Format Data Series and chose Marker ➤ Marker Options ➤ None. Next, I went to the Format tab and selected Y Error Bars. If you're following along, these might have a name of something like Series XX Y Error Bars, where XX is some number in the series. Once selected, press Delete. You don't need them. I then selected the current value bar and set its fill color to black. Finally, I changed the gap width of the current value bar to make it fit nicely within the banded region. Figure 12-29 shows the results.

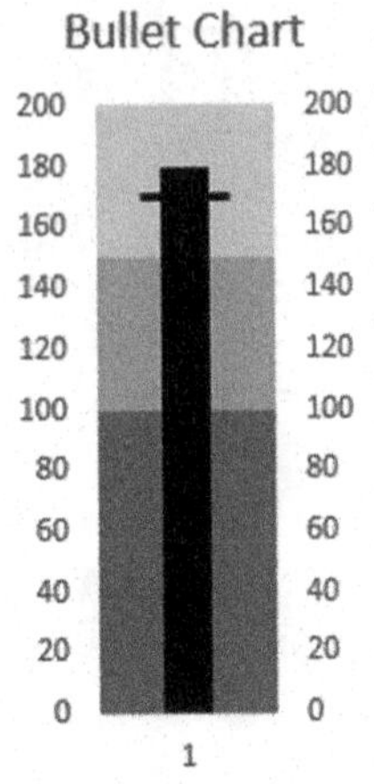

Figure 12-29. *A completed bullet chart after formatting cleanup*

The last steps will be to remove one of the axes and add more information about the plot. There are several things you can do at this point. You could change the gap width once again to accommodate an axis, as I've done in Figure 12-30, but this isn't necessary.

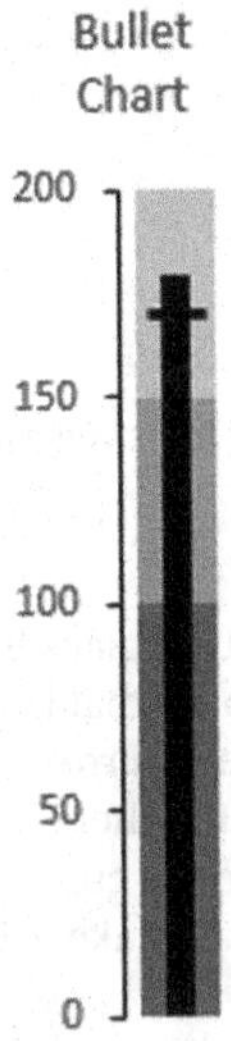

Figure 12-30. *A completed bullet chart*

Now let's say you want to create horizontal bullet charts instead of vertical bullet charts. You can use the following technique I learned from my colleague, Michael Alexander. First, create the bullet chart following the instructions laid out in this chapter. Next, rotate all the labels of text on the bar chart. In Figure 12-31, I've selected the primary y-axis and right-clicked to get to Format Axis. In the Text Box options, I've selected to rotate all text 270 degrees.

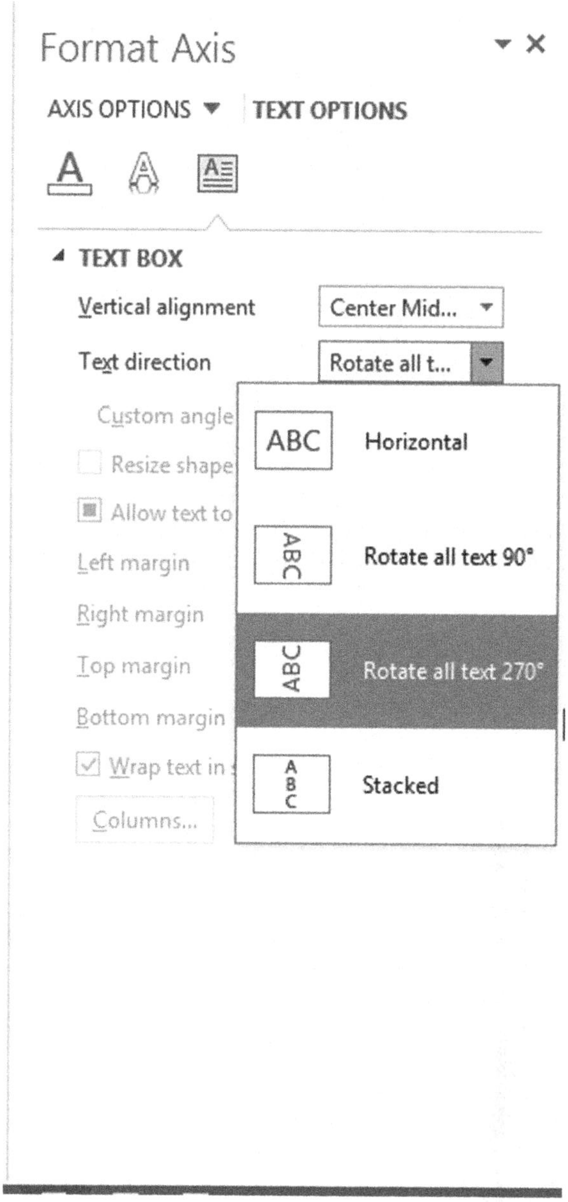

Figure 12-31. *Setting the labels to rotate the text 270 degrees*

The result appears in Figure 12-32.

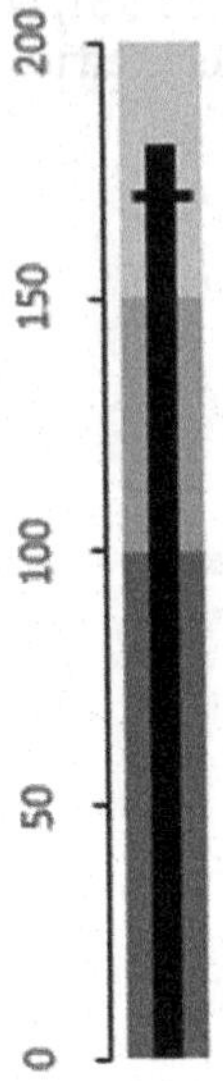

Figure 12-32. The bullet chart with rotated text

Next, I used the Camera tool to capture an image of the chart. (See Chapter 5 for a Camera tool refresher.) The original chart and Camera tool results appear next to another in Figure 12-33.

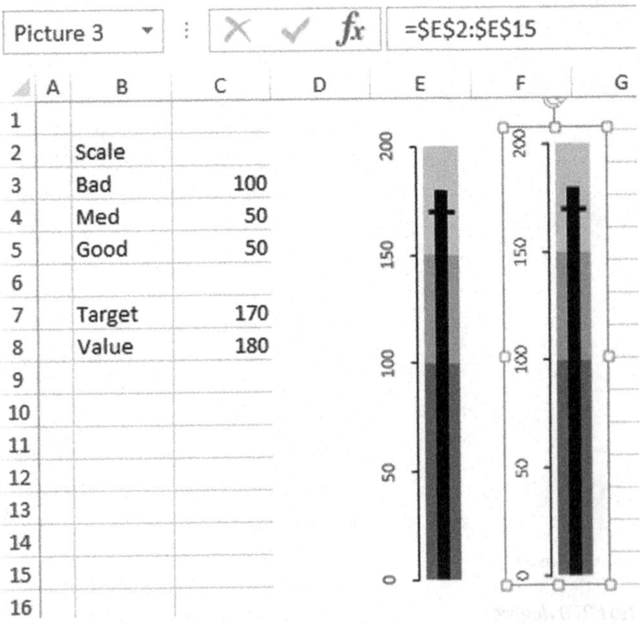

Figure 12-33. The bullet chart and result from the Camera tool appearing side-by-side

Finally, using the Camera tool's rotation anchor, I rotated the bullet chart 90 degrees (see Figure 12-34).

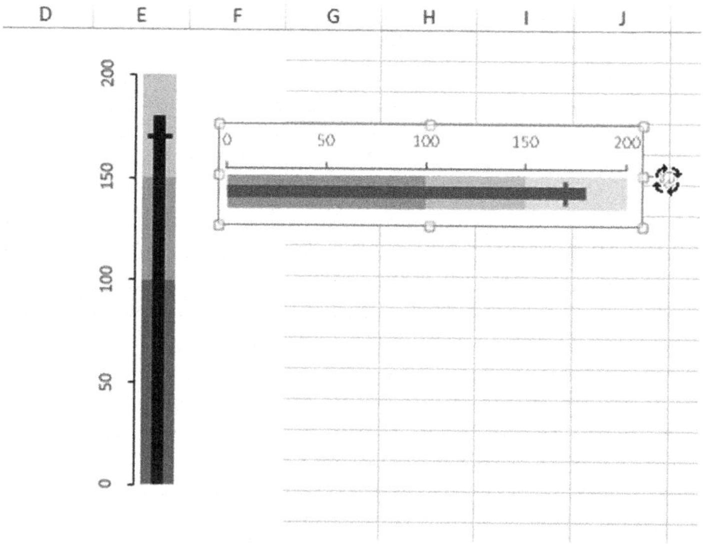

***Figure 12-34.** Rotating the bullet chart*

That's all that's required to create a vertical bullet chart.

The Last Word

In this chapter, I discussed some guidelines to making high-quality charts in Excel. You applied some of these principles to develop bar and column charts, banded regions, and, finally, bullet charts. In the following chapters of this book, you'll apply many of the principles outlined in this chapter.

CHAPTER 13

Creating an Interactive Gantt Chart Dashboard

In the next three chapters, I'll discuss how to create a Gantt chart dashboard. In this chapter, I'll take you on a tour of the dashboard so you can become familiar with its mechanisms from a high level. As is the case with most of this book, you'll reverse engineer what's already been created. This allows you to divide the underlying mechanics into different sections. Moreover, it should drive home a salient point about reusable components: your work can be broken in disparate pieces. What you build is the sum of its parts, and those parts can exist independently on their own or together in unison.

Figure 13-1 shows what you'll be investigating in this chapter. You can follow along by opening `Chapter13GanttChart.xlsm`, shown in Figure 13-1.

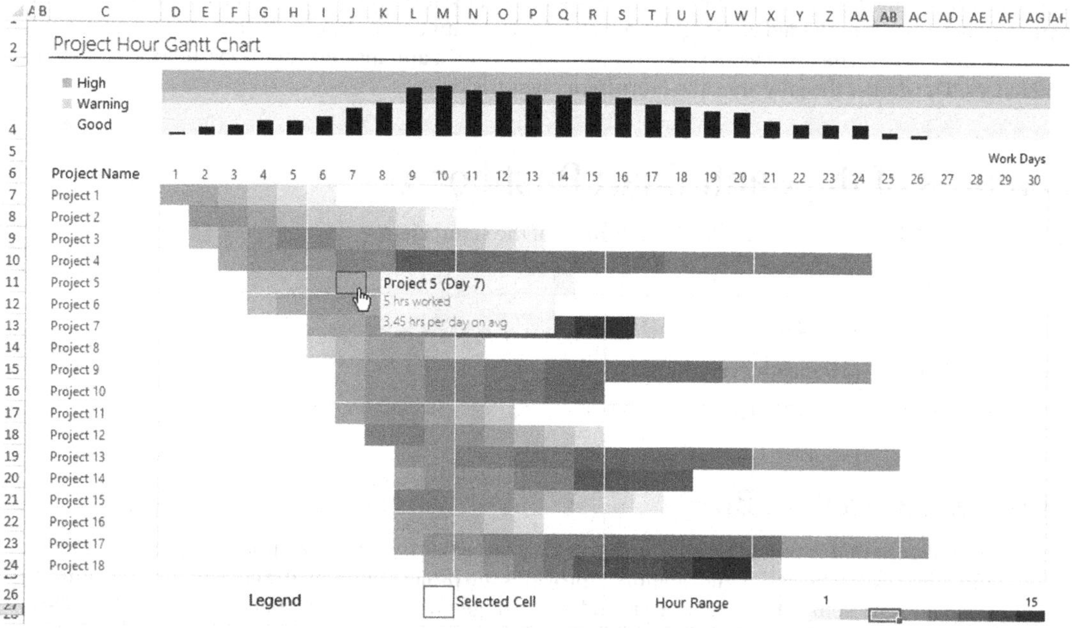

Figure 13-1. The interactive Gantt chart you'll be building in this chapter

If you're new to Gantt charts, here's a brief refresher. Gantt charts were created by Henry Gantt in the early 1900s. Their goal is to communicate a project's schedule using data visualization. Gantt charts can get complicated quickly, showing everything from project changes to dependencies and including multiple projected end dates based on different scenarios, among other things. I'll keep things simple here and attempt to show three different dimensions for each project record. Figure 13-2 breaks down what we want to show.

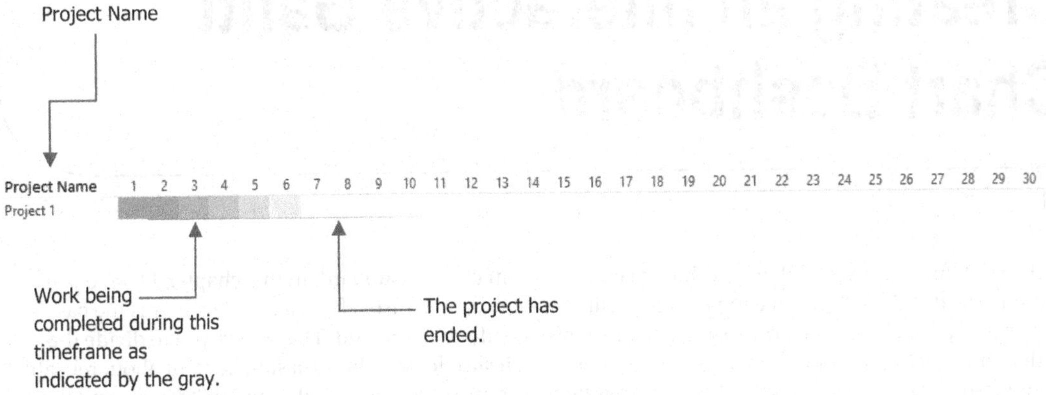

Figure 13-2. *An example project record from the Gantt chart*

For this Gantt chart, the project's date begins when you start seeing some gray area. If it's simply white, as you can see by the records in Figure 13-1, the project hasn't started yet. Similarly, the end date is the last date shown in gray. The shaded gray regions are essentially heatmaps for how many hours are required to complete the project. The exact values aren't shown within the heatmaps, but you can visually ascertain the differences. The darker the gray area, the more hours required.

Features of the Gantt Chart Dashboard

In this section, I'll go through three different features of the Gantt chart.

- The pop-up information box
- The banded region chart
- The legend beneath everything

Let's go through each of these items.

Pop-up Information Box

If you look at Figure 13-1, you'll see a pop-up. I provide a larger version of this pop-up in Figure 13-3. The pop-up provides several pieces of information. It provides the project number, the current day, the number of hours visually represented by the gray area, and the average number of hours per day for a given project.

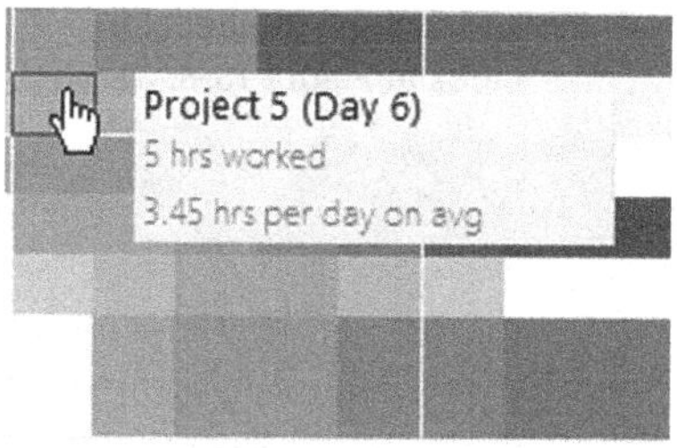

Figure 13-3. *Pop-up providing information on demand about a given day for a given project*

The pop-up feature is driven by the rollover mechanism described in Chapter 5. That means to see information for a given day and given project, the user simply needs to roll their mouse over a given cell. They do not to need to click anywhere.

Banded Region Chart

The Gantt chart also provides a graded chart across the top (Figure 13-4). I'll talk about it in this subsection.

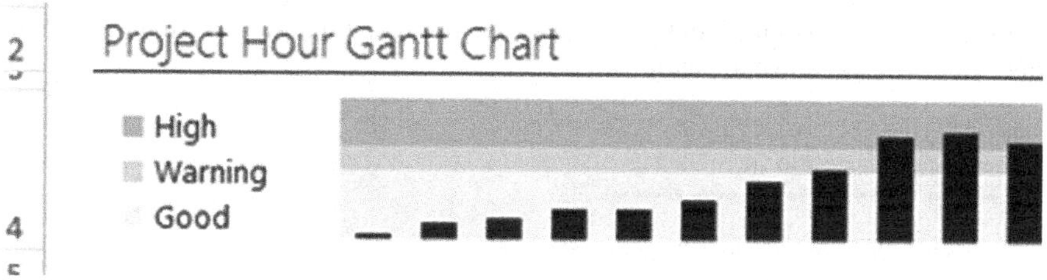

Figure 13-4. *A banded region chart shown at the top of the dashboard*

The bar charts represent the culmination of all hours worked on a specific date. Some days the project might have too many hours assigned to work on it. There are graded regions to help the user judge when too many hours have been assigned. At the top of the chart, the darkest region signifies that far too many hours have been assigned to a specific day to work. If you saw this on your real-life dashboard, you would know to take corrective action. Below the High region, the Warning region provides a small margin of extra hours that can be considered a cushion before moving into the High region. A warning region is not ideal but may be tolerable. Below the Warning region is the Good region. Cumulative hours within this region indicate the number of hours to work is well within tolerable limits.

Dynamic Chart Legend

In this subsection, I'll talk about the dynamic chart legend shown in Figure 13-5.

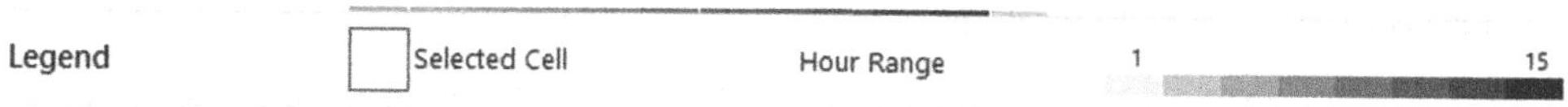

Figure 13-5. *A legend that will automatically visually calibrate to the back-end data supplied*

What makes this legend dynamic is its ability to calibrate to whatever back-end data is supplied. I'll get to the back-end data used in this dashboard in a moment. But for now, take a look at Figure 13-6, which shows that the legend is actually based on a series of formulas.

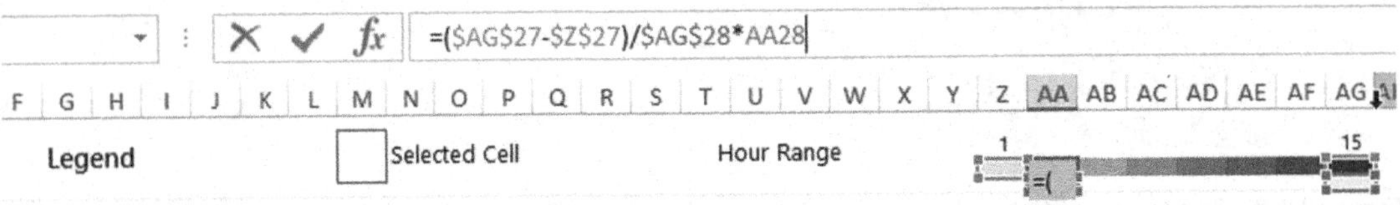

Figure 13-6. *The legend is based on a series of formulas*

The reason I bring this up is to drive home that the legend is not static. As the back-end data of this model changes, the legend can easily adjust to this information. You need make this legend only once, and further changes in data will automatically adjust to accommodate the new minimum and maximum data. This legend is just another example of a reusable component.

Behind the Scenes

In this section, I'll go into the back-end elements of this dashboard to understand how it all comes together. The dashboard includes three tabs, as shown in Figure 13-7.

Figure 13-7. *The three worksheet tabs in this dashboard workbook file*

These three tabs are as follows:

- *Dashboard*: This is the main page of your work. It includes the information that will ultimately allow you to understand how hours are allocated among your days and projects.
- *Calculation*: This is an "intermediate" tab, which you'll use to transform the raw back-end data so you can present it on the dashboard. It includes several calculations that will enable you to present this information.
- *Data*: This is where the dashboard's back-end data resides. This data is used by the Calculation tab and then ultimately by the dashboard to present information to the user.

Notice the design pattern here. The Data tab informs the Calculation tab, which then informs the Dashboard tab. This follows the information (Data tab) a ➤ transformation (Calculation tab) ➤ presentation (Dashboard tab) dynamic presented in Chapter 8. The Dashboard tab never refers directly to the Data tab. Instead, it uses the Calculation tab as an intermediary.

I'll go through each of these tabs from right to left (see Figure 13-7).

The Data Worksheet Tab

In this section, I'll talk about the Data worksheet tab. Figure 13-8 shows an excerpt from the tab starting from the top.

	A	B	C	D
1	Id	Project Name	Day Number	Hours Require
2	1	Project 1	1	5
3	2	Project 1	2	5
4	3	Project 1	3	4
5	4	Project 1	4	3
6	5	Project 1	5	2
7	6	Project 1	6	1
8	7	Project 1	7	0
9	8	Project 1	8	0
10	9	Project 1	9	0
11	10	Project 1	10	0
12	11	Project 1	11	0
13	12	Project 1	12	0
14	13	Project 1	13	0
15	14	Project 1	14	0
16	15	Project 1	15	0
17	16	Project 1	16	0

Figure 13-8. *A snapshot of the Data tab*

The Data tab contains one thing—an Excel table. There's nothing fancy you do with it except store your back-end data. The table consists of four different columns. Let's go through each of them.

- *Id*: This column simply includes a unique identifier for each record.
- *Project Name*: This column tracks the project name a given record refers to.
- *Day Number*: This column tracks the day a given record refers to.
- *Hours Required*: This column tracks how many hours were required for a given project and day.

I can understand if you're confused. But the best way to think about this data is that for each project and for each day displayed on the dashboard there is a given record detailing the hours required. If there are 18 projects and 13 expected workdays, then there would be 18*30, or 540, total records.

The Calculation Worksheet Tab

The Calculation worksheet tab is where you do work (that is, perform calculations) on the back-end data (from on the Data tab). This pattern (the back-end data feeding into the Calculation tab, which then feeds into the presentation layer) is part of the framework presented in previous chapters. Figure 13-9 shows a snapshot of the Calculation worksheet tab.

	A	B	C	D	E	F	G	H	I	J	K	L	M	N	O	P	Q	R	S	T	U	V	W	X	Y	Z	AA	AB	AC	AD	AE	AF
1																																
2																	Days															
3	Location	Project Name	1	2	3	4	5	6	7	8	9	10	11	12	13	14	15	16	17	18	19	20	21	22	23	24	25	26	27	28	29	30
4	0	Project 1	5	5	4	3	2	1	0	0	0	0	0	0	0	0	0	0	0	0	0	0	0	0	0	0	0	0	0	0	0	0
5	30	Project 2	0	6	6	5	4	3	3	3	2	1	0	0	0	0	0	0	0	0	0	0	0	0	0	0	0	0	0	0	0	0
6	60	Project 3	0	4	5	6	7	7	6	6	5	4	3	2	1	0	0	0	0	0	0	0	0	0	0	0	0	0	0	0	0	0
7	90	Project 4	0	0	5	6	6	6	7	7	10	10	9	9	9	9	9	9	9	8	8	8	8	8	8	8	0	0	0	0	0	0
8	120	Project 5	0	0	0	4	4	5	5	5	4	4	3	2	1	1	0	0	0	0	0	0	0	0	0	0	0	0	0	0	0	0
9	150	Project 6	0	0	0	4	5	6	6	5	4	3	0	0	0	0	0	0	0	0	0	0	0	0	0	0	0	0	0	0	0	0
10	180	Project 7	0	0	0	0	0	5	5	6	7	8	10	11	11	12	14	15	3	0	0	0	0	0	0	0	0	0	0	0	0	0
11	210	Project 8	0	0	0	0	0	3	4	5	5	4	3	0	0	0	0	0	0	0	0	0	0	0	0	0	0	0	0	0	0	0
12	240	Project 9	0	0	0	0	0	0	5	6	6	7	7	8	8	9	9	9	9	9	9	6	6	6	6	6	0	0	0	0	0	0
13	270	Project 10	0	0	0	0	0	0	5	6	6	7	7	8	8	9	9	0	0	0	0	0	0	0	0	0	0	0	0	0	0	0
14	300	Project 11	0	0	0	0	0	0	5	6	6	5	4	3	0	0	0	0	0	0	0	0	0	0	0	0	0	0	0	0	0	0
15	330	Project 12	0	0	0	0	0	0	0	7	7	6	6	5	4	3	2	0	0	0	0	0	0	0	0	0	0	0	0	0	0	0
16	360	Project 13	0	0	0	0	0	0	0	0	6	6	7	7	8	8	9	9	9	9	9	9	6	6	6	6	6	0	0	0	0	0
17	390	Project 14	0	0	0	0	0	0	0	0	5	6	6	6	7	7	10	10	10	10	0	0	0	0	0	0	0	0	0	0	0	0
18	420	Project 15	0	0	0	0	0	0	0	0	7	7	6	6	5	4	3	2	1	0	0	0	0	0	0	0	0	0	0	0	0	0
19	450	Project 16	0	0	0	0	0	0	0	0	5	5	4	3	2	0	0	0	0	0	0	0	0	0	0	0	0	0	0	0	0	0
20	480	Project 17	0	0	0	0	0	0	0	0	5	6	6	7	7	8	8	9	9	9	9	9	9	6	6	6	6	6	0	0	0	0
21	510	Project 18	0	0	0	0	0	0	0	0	0	5	5	6	7	8	10	11	11	12	14	15	3	0	0	0	0	0	0	0	0	0
22			5	15	20	28	28	36	51	62	90	94	86	83	78	78	83	74	61	57	49	47	32	26	26	26	12	6	0	0	0	0
23																																
24		Chart Setup																														
25		Cushion	60	60	60	60	60	60	60	60	60	60	60	60	60	60	60	60	60	60	60	60	60	60	60	60	60	60	60	60	60	60
26		Warning	20	20	20	20	20	20	20	20	20	20	20	20	20	20	20	20	20	20	20	20	20	20	20	20	20	20	20	20	20	20
27		Take Action	120	120	120	120	120	120	120	120	120	120	120	120	120	120	120	120	120	120	120	120	120	120	120	120	120	120	120	120	120	120

Figure 13-9. *The Calculation worksheet tab*

The Calculation worksheet tab is divided into two sections. The top section is a tabular view of the back-end data. The bottom section is used to create the banded region chart shown in Figure 13-4. I'll hold off on talking about the banded region chart until later in the chapter. For now, focus your attention on that top section.

You can think of this top section as laying out the data in much the same that a pivot table might. Figure 13-10 shows how the back-end data is mapped onto this tabular table. The name of each project becomes the row key and the corresponding day number becomes the column header. The hours required, which appear to be listed vertically in the table on the Data worksheet tab, are now listed horizontally at the intersections of their corresponding project name and date.

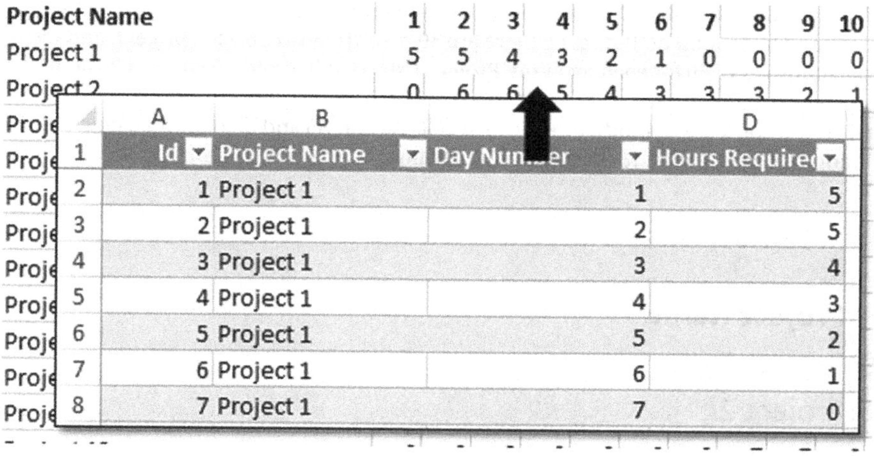

	Id	Project Name	Day Number	Hours Required
2	1	Project 1	1	5
3	2	Project 1	2	5
4	3	Project 1	3	4
5	4	Project 1	4	3
6	5	Project 1	5	2
7	6	Project 1	6	1
8	7	Project 1	7	0

Figure 13-10. *The back-end data is mapped onto the Calculation tab in tabular form. The layout is similar to a pivot table*

This layout is similar to a pivot table, but it's specifically not a pivot table. As I mentioned at the beginning of this book, I'll try to avoid using pivot tables to the extent possible (except for when you are employing their functionality as part of Microsoft's new Power BI tools), and here is no exception. If you were to implement a pivot table, you would lose the ability to have live updates in the back end of your data automatically populate your dashboard. That's because pivot tables require you to refresh the connection to the source data for each and every update.

Because you're not using pivot tables, you'll have to use formulas to create the same schema. As explained previously, each project has 30 associated records representing the 30 days available to be worked. Since your data is in sorted order, you know the location of the records associated with each project. For instance, the first 30 records deal with Project 1, records 31 to 60 deal with Project 2, records 61 to 90 deal with Project 3, and so on.

As means to help you look up the locations of the records you're interested in, I've created a Location column (Figure 13-11) that sits to the left of the tabular data.

3	Location	Project Name
4	0	Project 1
5	30	Project 2
6	60	Project 3
7	90	Project 4
8	120	Project 5
9	150	Project 6
10	180	Project 7

Figure 13-11. *The Location column that will help you look up the corresponding data for each project*

Notice the locations follow what I described previously, although the location numbers are off by one, which you'll understand in a moment. But recall there are 30 records between each project, and in Figure 13-11, you see multiples of 30 for each location. Project 1 starts at 0, Project 2 starts at 30, and Project 3 starts at 60.

To create this list, I simply started by typing a 0 and a 30 in cells A4 and A5 and then dragged down to include the required amount of cells. Figure 13-12 shows this in action.

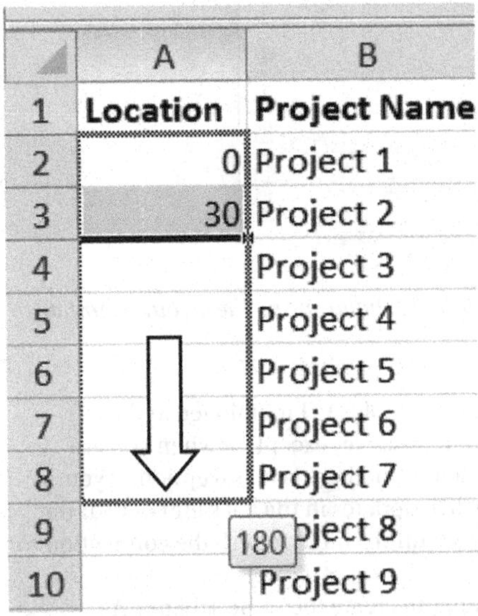

A
B
Location
Project Name
0
Project 1
30
Project 2
Project 3
Project 4
Project 5
Project 6
Project 7
180
Project 9

***Figure 13-12.** The list of multiples of 30 is easily created using Excel's autonumbering features*

Once you have the locations set, you can look up the hours required for a given day. Since the day numbers are listed across the top, you can use this information for the lookup. In cell C4 (Figure 13-14), you are looking for the hours required for Project 1 on Day 1—the first record from the back-end data. In Figure 13-13, you are using the `INDEX` function to find that record. Recall that `INDEX` works by returning a designated row (and optionally, a designated column) from a given array or range of data. Whatever record you're interested in, you can find it by using the location for a given project and then adding the given day number across the top. In Figure 13-13, `C$3 + $A4` would return a 1, for the first record in the project table. You can achieve this lookup based on `INDEX` by dragging the formula across.

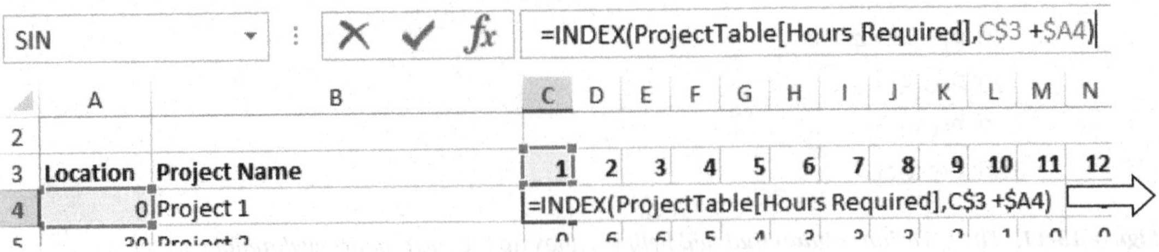

***Figure 13-13.** You can find the hours required for a given project by adding the day number to a specific project number's location in the back-end database*

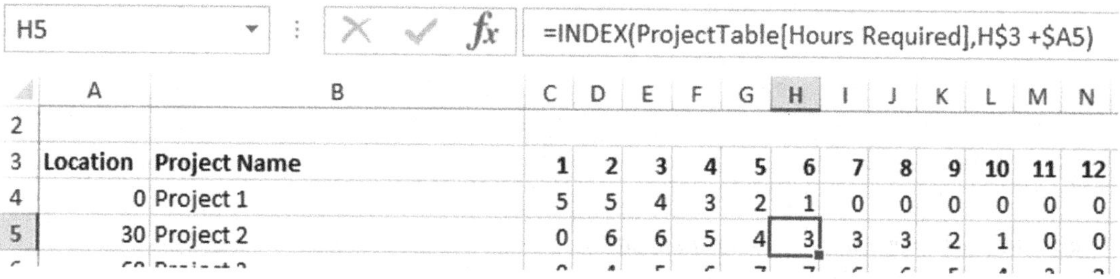
H5 =INDEX(ProjectTable[Hours Required],H$3 +$A5)

	A	B	C	D	E	F	G	H	I	J	K	L	M	N
2														
3	Location	Project Name	1	2	3	4	5	6	7	8	9	10	11	12
4	0	Project 1	5	5	4	3	2	1	0	0	0	0	0	0
5	30	Project 2	0	6	6	5	4	3	3	3	2	1	0	0

***Figure 13-14.** The formula to find the hours required for the sixth day uses INDEX and both the beginning record location and day number*

Similarly, the hours required to work on the sixth day for Project 2 (Figure 13-14) would be found in location 36 (the result of adding H$3 and $A5) on the project table (Figure 13-15).

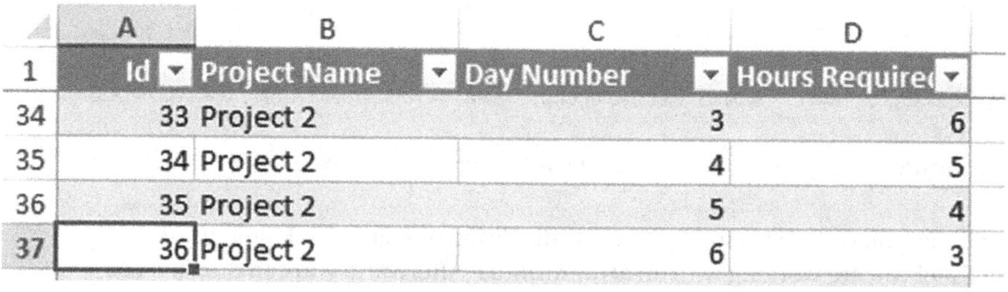

	A	B	C	D
1	Id	Project Name	Day Number	Hours Required
34	33	Project 2	3	6
35	34	Project 2	4	5
36	35	Project 2	5	4
37	36	Project 2	6	3

***Figure 13-15.** The data point highlighted in Figure 13-14 exists at record 36, or 30 + 6, from the formula in Figure 13-14*

I hope you now understand the underlying mechanics of this table, which shows the back-end data in tabular form. But, before moving on, I should note a problem I ran into in its setup. In Figure 13-16, I've once again highlighted the first data point on the table. Notice that the formula in the formula bar is an array formula (you can tell by the curly braces shown at the beginning and end of the formula).

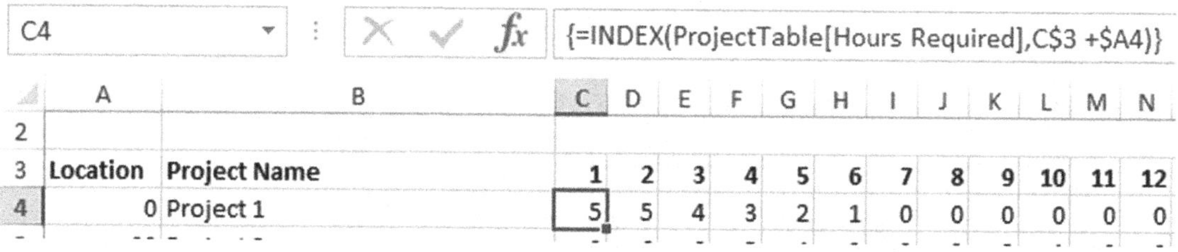
C4 {=INDEX(ProjectTable[Hours Required],C$3 +$A4)}

	A	B	C	D	E	F	G	H	I	J	K	L	M	N
2														
3	Location	Project Name	1	2	3	4	5	6	7	8	9	10	11	12
4	0	Project 1	5	5	4	3	2	1	0	0	0	0	0	0

***Figure 13-16.** An array formula is used to pull information from the back-end database*

Since you are not returning multiple cells or working with arrays, an array formula may feel like an odd, if unnecessary, choice. However, to make the setup of this table easier, an array formula is necessary.

Here's why. Let's clear everything out and start from scratch. In Figure 13-17, I've started over and skipped the array formula formulation.

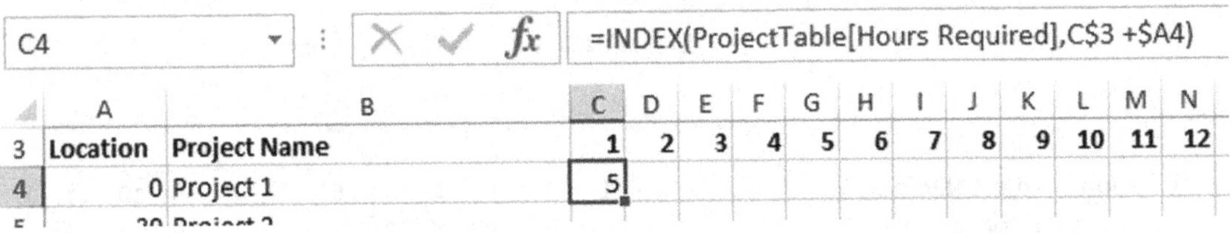

C4 | =INDEX(ProjectTable[Hours Required],C$3 +$A4)

	A	B	C	D	E	F	G	H	I	J	K	L	M	N
3	Location	Project Name	1	2	3	4	5	6	7	8	9	10	11	12
4	0	Project 1	5											

Figure 13-17. *The same formula but not as an array*

If you use the anchor and drag to the right, you would expect the formula shown in Figure 13-17 to populate similarly across the cells. However, when you don't use an array formula, a strange thing happens. The table header you're interested in, Hours Required, isn't technically an absolute reference. As you drag to the right, the formula begins to cycle through each header name (similar to what would happen if you dragged a formula reference and relative cell reference). This is shown in Figure 13-18 with the resulting formulas displayed.

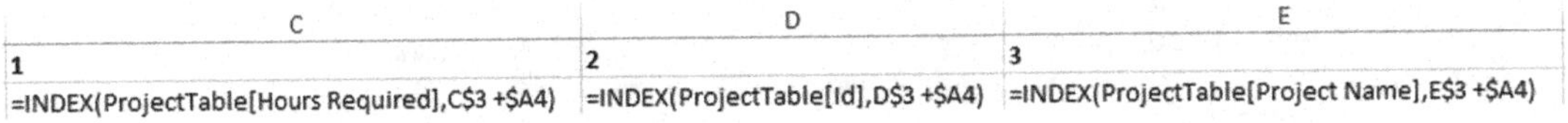

C	D	E
1	2	3
=INDEX(ProjectTable[Hours Required],C$3 +$A4)	=INDEX(ProjectTable[Id],D$3 +$A4)	=INDEX(ProjectTable[Project Name],E$3 +$A4)

Figure 13-18. *The table headers are cycled through when no array formula is used*

To get around this issue, you can start with the formula displayed in Figure 13-17 and press Ctrl+Shift+Enter to tell Excel you are working with an array formula. Afterward, you can drag the cell containing the formula without fear the column you're interested in will change in tandem.

At the bottom of the tabular data, there is a row marked Total. This row simply displays the sum total of hours required for each day across all projects. Figure 13-19 shows the formula required.

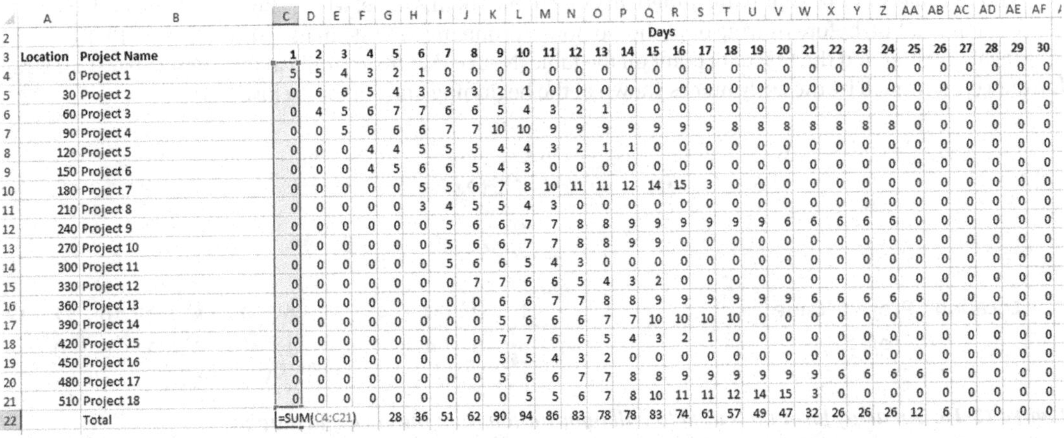

	A	B	C	D	E	F	G	H	I	J	K	L	M	N	O	P	Q	R	S	T	U	V	W	X	Y	Z	AA	AB	AC	AD	AE	AF
2																	Days															
3	Location	Project Name	1	2	3	4	5	6	7	8	9	10	11	12	13	14	15	16	17	18	19	20	21	22	23	24	25	26	27	28	29	30
4	0	Project 1	5	5	4	3	2	1	0	0	0	0	0	0	0	0	0	0	0	0	0	0	0	0	0	0	0	0	0	0	0	0
5	30	Project 2	0	6	6	5	4	3	3	3	2	1	0	0	0	0	0	0	0	0	0	0	0	0	0	0	0	0	0	0	0	0
6	60	Project 3	0	4	5	6	7	7	6	6	5	4	3	2	1	0	0	0	0	0	0	0	0	0	0	0	0	0	0	0	0	0
7	90	Project 4	0	0	5	6	6	6	7	7	10	10	9	9	9	9	9	9	9	8	8	8	8	8	8	8	0	0	0	0	0	0
8	120	Project 5	0	0	0	4	4	5	5	5	4	4	3	2	1	1	0	0	0	0	0	0	0	0	0	0	0	0	0	0	0	0
9	150	Project 6	0	0	0	4	5	6	6	5	4	3	0	0	0	0	0	0	0	0	0	0	0	0	0	0	0	0	0	0	0	0
10	180	Project 7	0	0	0	0	0	5	5	6	7	8	10	11	11	12	14	15	3	0	0	0	0	0	0	0	0	0	0	0	0	0
11	210	Project 8	0	0	0	0	0	3	4	5	5	4	3	0	0	0	0	0	0	0	0	0	0	0	0	0	0	0	0	0	0	0
12	240	Project 9	0	0	0	0	0	0	5	6	6	7	7	8	8	9	9	9	9	9	9	6	6	6	6	6	0	0	0	0	0	0
13	270	Project 10	0	0	0	0	0	0	5	6	6	7	7	8	8	9	9	0	0	0	0	0	0	0	0	0	0	0	0	0	0	0
14	300	Project 11	0	0	0	0	0	0	5	6	6	5	4	3	0	0	0	0	0	0	0	0	0	0	0	0	0	0	0	0	0	0
15	330	Project 12	0	0	0	0	0	0	0	7	7	6	6	5	4	3	2	0	0	0	0	0	0	0	0	0	0	0	0	0	0	0
16	360	Project 13	0	0	0	0	0	0	0	0	6	6	7	7	8	8	9	9	9	9	9	9	6	6	6	6	6	0	0	0	0	0
17	390	Project 14	0	0	0	0	0	0	0	0	5	6	6	6	7	7	10	10	10	10	0	0	0	0	0	0	0	0	0	0	0	0
18	420	Project 15	0	0	0	0	0	0	0	0	7	7	6	6	5	4	3	2	1	0	0	0	0	0	0	0	0	0	0	0	0	0
19	450	Project 16	0	0	0	0	0	0	0	0	5	5	4	3	2	0	0	0	0	0	0	0	0	0	0	0	0	0	0	0	0	0
20	480	Project 17	0	0	0	0	0	0	0	0	5	6	6	7	7	8	8	9	9	9	9	9	9	6	6	6	6	6	0	0	0	0
21	510	Project 18	0	0	0	0	0	0	0	0	0	5	5	6	7	8	10	11	11	12	14	15	3	0	0	0	0	0	0	0	0	0
22		Total	=SUM(C4:C21)				28	36	51	62	90	94	86	83	78	78	83	74	61	57	49	47	32	26	26	26	12	6	0	0	0	0

Figure 13-19. *The total row contains the sum of hours worked for each day across all projects*

The Dashboard Worksheet Tab

The Dashboard worksheet tab is the place where all the information created in the Calculation tab feeds into. You already looked at the Dashboard worksheet tab at the beginning of the chapter. Right now, I would like to point you toward an intermediate table placed below the dashboard to be interested in. Figure 13-20 shows an excerpt of what is actually a much larger section.

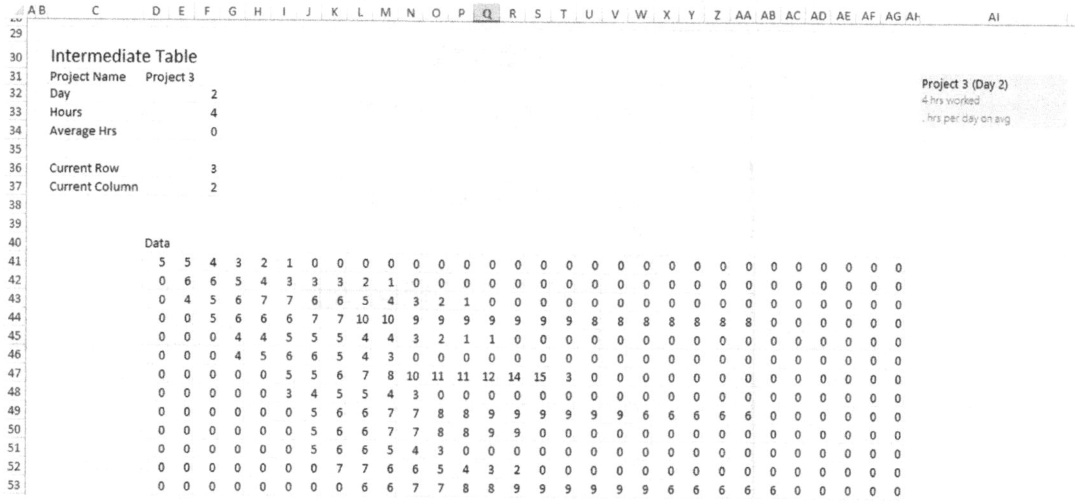

Figure 13-20. *The intermediate table—where a good portion of the dashboard mechanics are calculated*

I'll return to intermediate tables later in this book, but you can think of them as an extension of the transformation layer presented as part of the information-transformation-presentation framework mentioned earlier in this book. I could have easily placed this on the Calculation worksheet tab, but for what we're trying to do, sometimes it makes more sense to keep pertinent information on the same tab—even if that requires some redundancy.

For instance, the data in the intermediate table is actually just pulling from the tabular data in the Calculation tab (Figure 13-21).

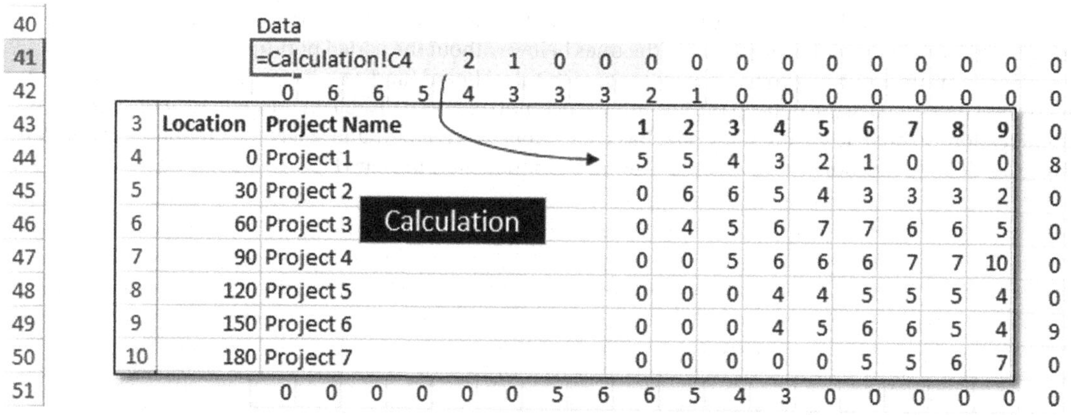

Figure 13-21. *Data in the calculation table feeds into the dashboard table*

That data is then fed into the dashboard front end. In Figure 13-22, you see the formula for one of the cells of the dashboard refers to its corresponding cell (I45—shown twice at the end of the formula) in the intermediate table.

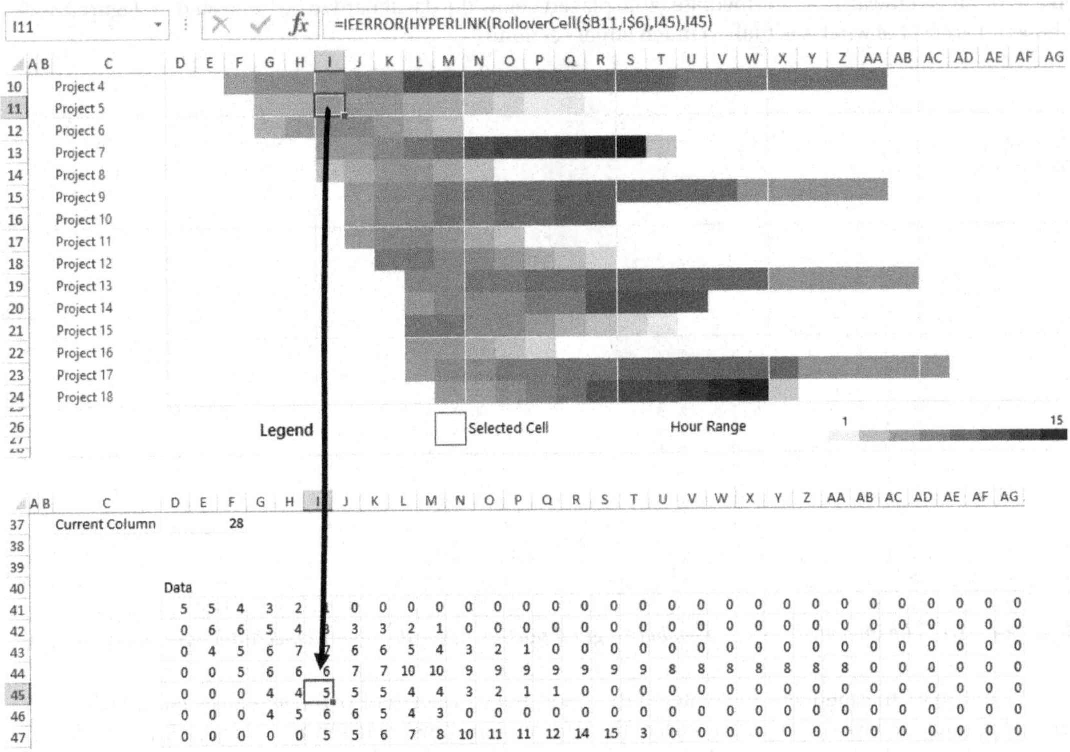

Figure 13-22. *The results of the calculation table feed into the dashboard*

You may be wondering what's going on with that `IFERROR` and `HYPERLINK` stuff at the beginning of the formula. These functions are actually part of the rollover method discussed in Chapter 5. As mentioned at the start of this chapter, rollover interactivity was implemented on this dashboard, and these functions are required to make it work. I'll go into them in more detail in the next chapter. For now, it may be helpful to imagine these cells are simply referencing the ones below without the added pop-up.

If the pop-up is bugging you as you investigate this dashboard (and, yes, it can do that—sometimes it's a good idea to make the pop-up the last thing you build), you can disable in the code to help your investigation. To do that, go into the Visual Basic for Applications editor and select the module ScenarioUDF. The user-defined function, `RolloverCell`, should be immediately in view (Figure 13-23).

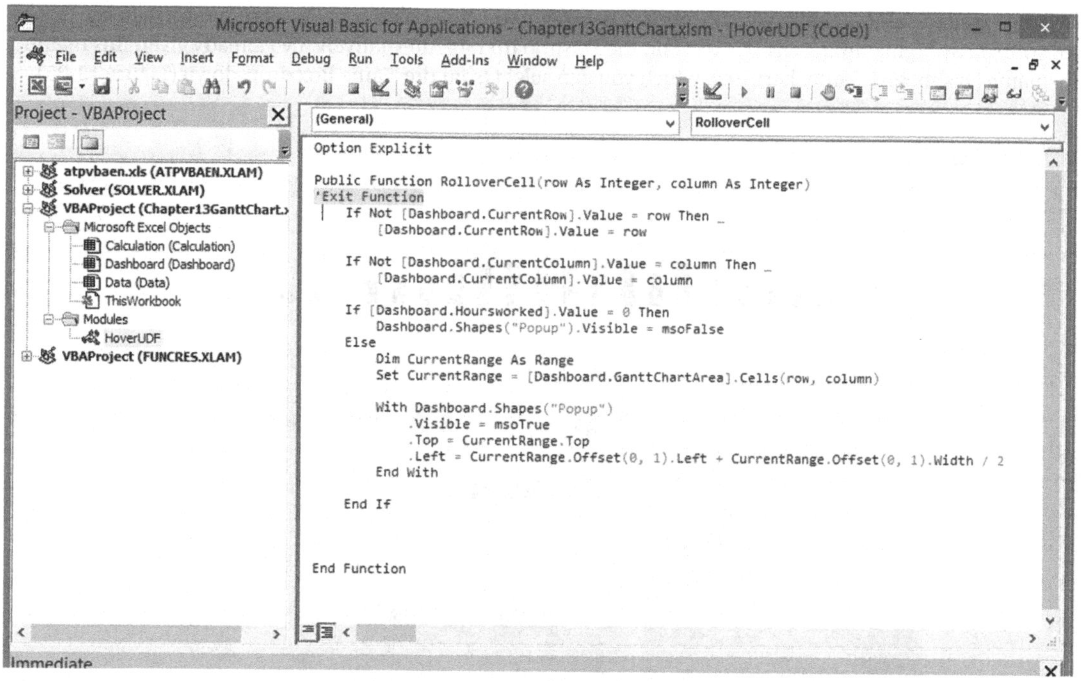

Figure 13-23. *A snapshot of the RolloverCell function*

There is a commented line after the function definition that says `Exit Function`. For testing and debugging, you can remove the apostrophe right before `Exit` to turn it into a VBA command (Figure 13-24). This will tell Excel to immediately leave the rollover function without executing the remaining code. Just remember to add the apostrophe back in when you're done with your investigations or code debugging.

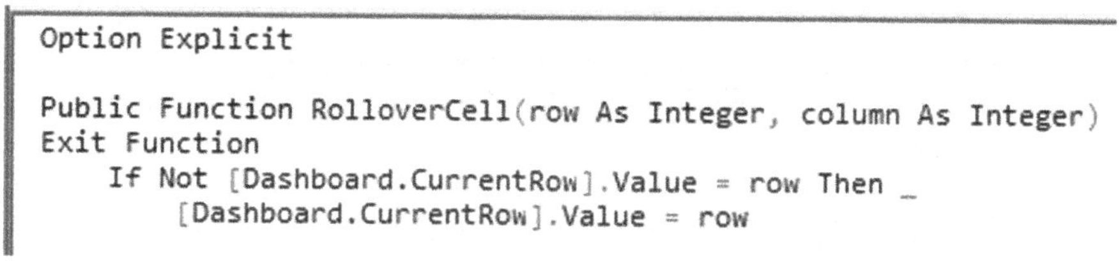
Option Explicit
Public Function RolloverCell(row As Integer, column As Integer)
Exit Function
If Not [Dashboard.CurrentRow].Value = row Then _
[Dashboard.CurrentRow].Value = row

Figure 13-24. *Exit Function is no longer commented out—Excel will now leave the User Defined Function without executing the rest of it*

If you're still following along (and you should be!), go ahead and remove the apostrophe so you can continue your investigation. You should now be able to move your mouse around the dashboard area without the pop-up box following suit. Depending upon where your mouse was when you removed the comment symbol in front of `Exit Function`, the pop-up box might still be showing. The way the function is set up, if there is no data in the region highlighted, the pop-up box will disappear. However, if your mouse was previously hovering over a cell project data in it, the pop-up box will remain over that cell, even if it no longer follows your cursor. Feel free to click the pop-up box and simply move it to the side. (Don't delete it! You'll need it later.)

The graded color region on the dashboard is generated using conditional formatting. You can see this for yourself by highlighting cells D7:AG24 on the Dashboard tab. Alternatively, I've already given this region the name Dashboard.GanttChartArea, which you can select from the Name Box drop-down (Figure 13-25).

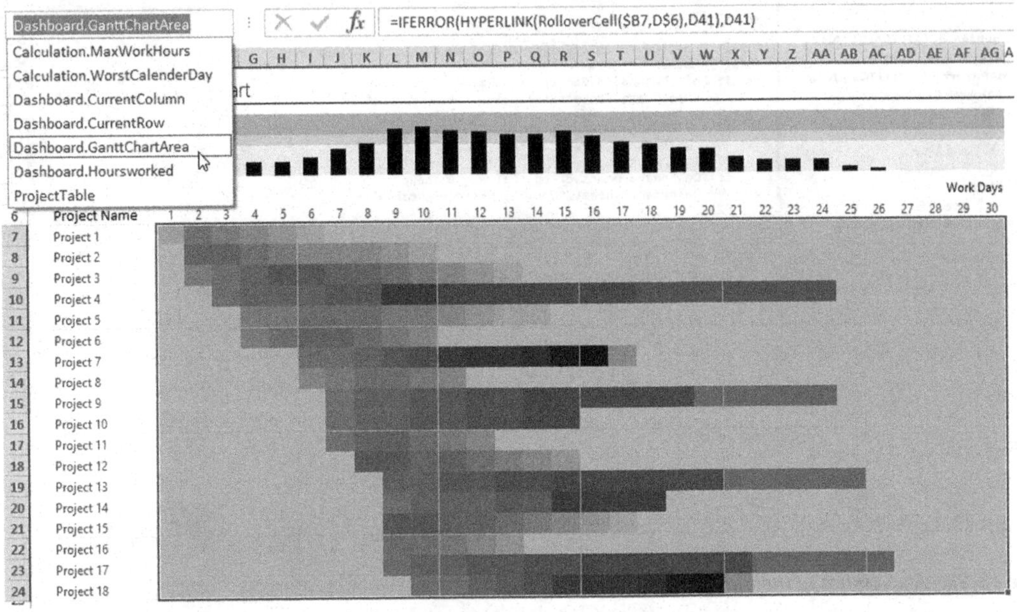

Figure 13-25. Selecting the Gantt chart area on the dashboard

With the region selected, you can view the conditional formatting set by clicking Conditional Formatting on the Home tab and going to Manage Rules. The Conditional Formatting Rules Manager dialog box will pop up (Figure 13-26). As shown in the figure, select the second rule and then click Edit Rule.

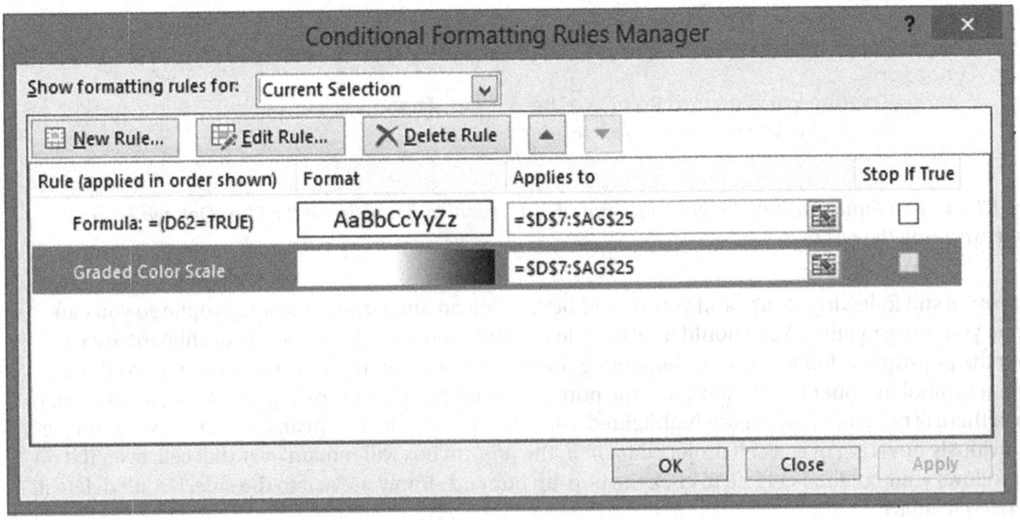

Figure 13-26. The Conditional Formatting Rules Manager dialog box

Clicking Edit Rule will bring up the Edit Formatting Rule dialog box (Figure 13-27).

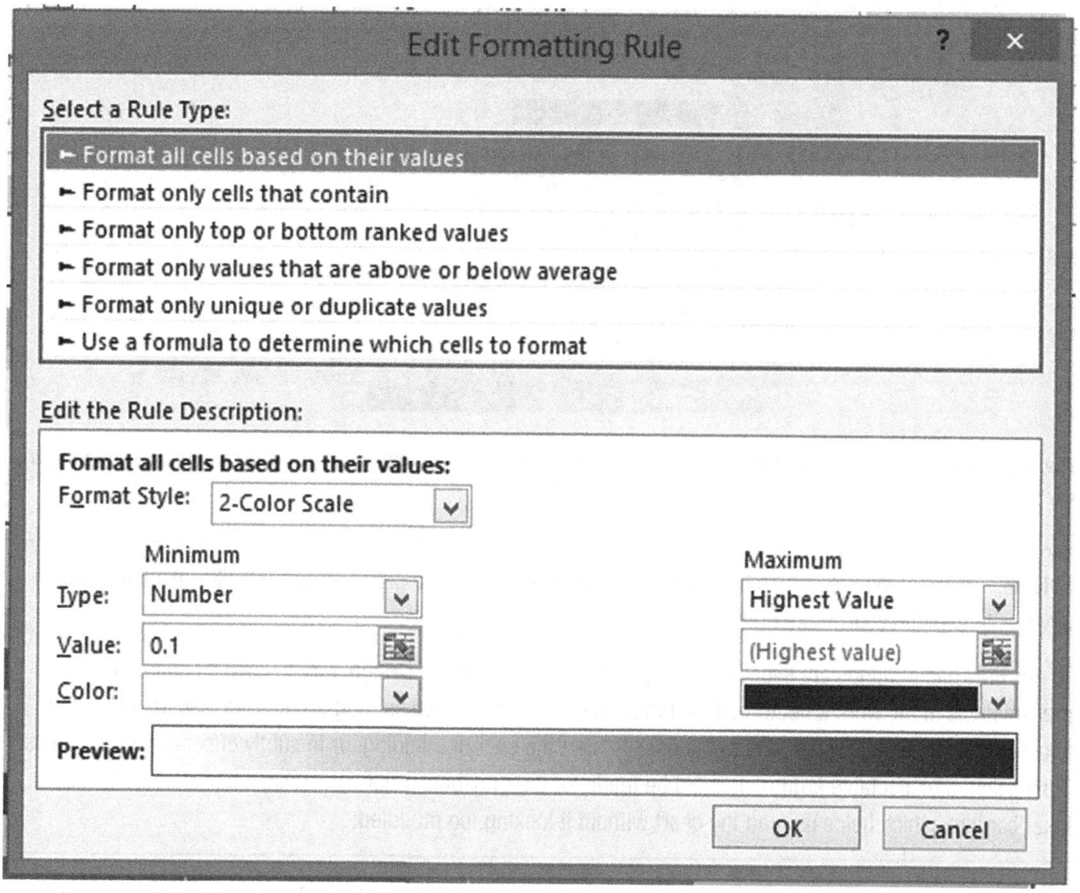

Figure 13-27. *The Edit Formatting Rule dialog box*

The Edit Formatting Rule dialog box contains rules associated with the data region. Notice in Figure 13-27, I've selected "Format all cells based on their values" as my rule. Under Format Style, I've selected 2-Color Scale. This tells Excel I'm interested in formatting the range of cells based on two different colors at the extremes. For Minimum, I've told Excel I want to use a specific number by selecting Number in the Type drop-down. Technically, the lowest value available in the data range is zero, which indicates no hours required for that project for a specific date—such values are found either before the project has started or after it has ended. You want these zeros to remain white and not be colored. Therefore, you set the rule to a number arbitrarily small and close to zero but not at zero—in this case, .1. On the other hand, you won't always know what the maximum will be, so I've let Excel analyze the data presented to figure this out. I've done this by selecting Highest Value in the Type drop-down under the Maximum label.

Next, you set the colors desired to be shown at your extremes. For the lowest value, select a pure-white color. The effect of this is that zeros in the dashboard will be white. If you were to set it to a light gray instead, everything less than .01 would also be light gray. Figure 13-28 shows the effect of this. On the other hand, if you start with a solid white, Excel will know to keep cells holding numbers less than .1 white and shade cells with greater numbers.

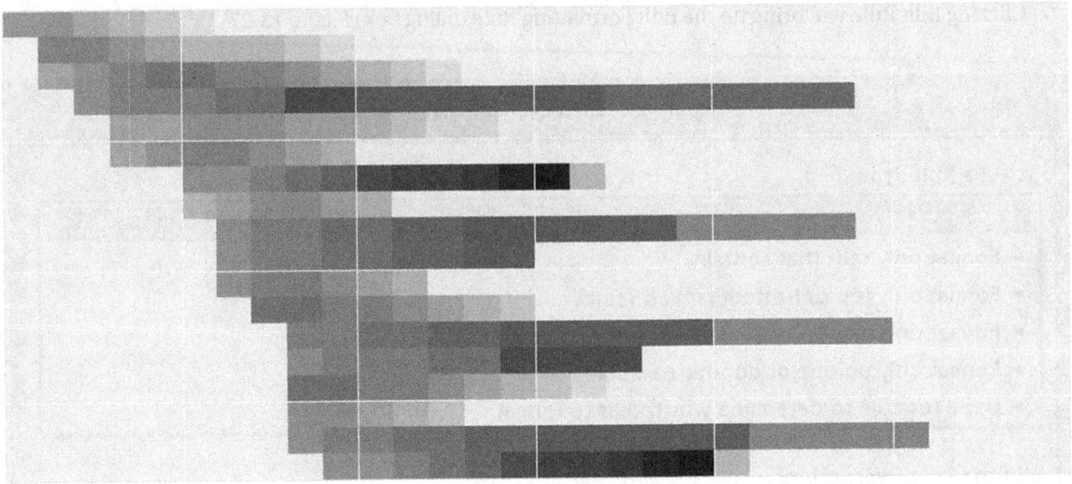

Figure 13-28. A light gray background appears when you start the custom formatting bands with a light gray color

---

■ **Note** Some of my colleagues have said to me they rather like the gray background. I'll leave the decision whether to use it in your future endeavors up to you.

To me, gray backgrounds are evocative of old and ugly user interface design. I try to keep all nondata presentations in my work a neutral white. I think color should be used sparingly, only with discern and when necessary, such as to present data to the user, to alert the user of a finding, or to subtly offset different regions. Then again, a respectable argument could be made for the gray background because it helps brings focus to inner borders, which helps us read the chart without it looking too muddled.

Once you are finished looking at the Conditional Formatting dialog box, click OK until you get back to the dashboard. Typically when you apply conditional formatting rules to cells, the numbers inside the cells remain. Yet, in this dashboard, you can see that no numbers are shown; rather, only their fill colors as defined by the conditional formatting rules remain. I was able to remove the numbers from view by using a custom formatting trick.

Once again, you can go ahead and select the shaded data region either by highlighting cells D7:AG24 or by selecting Dashboard.GanttChartArea from the Name Box drop-down (shown earlier in Figure 13-25). With this region once again selected, take a look at the Number group on the Home tab. In the Number Format drop-down, you'll see Custom has been selected (Figure 13-29). That's because I've defined a custom format to hide the numbers. In the lower-right corner, there is a button to click that will present the Format Cells dialog box (Figure 13-30). Go ahead and click where the cursor is present in Figure 13-29.

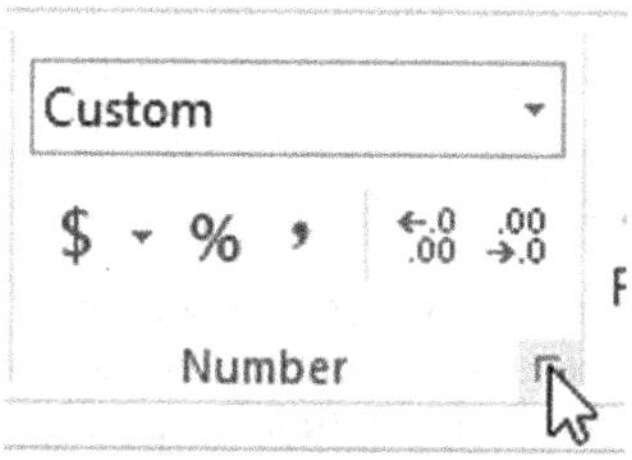

Figure 13-29. *Custom is listed in Number Format. Clicking the small button in the lower right will present the Format Cells dialog box*

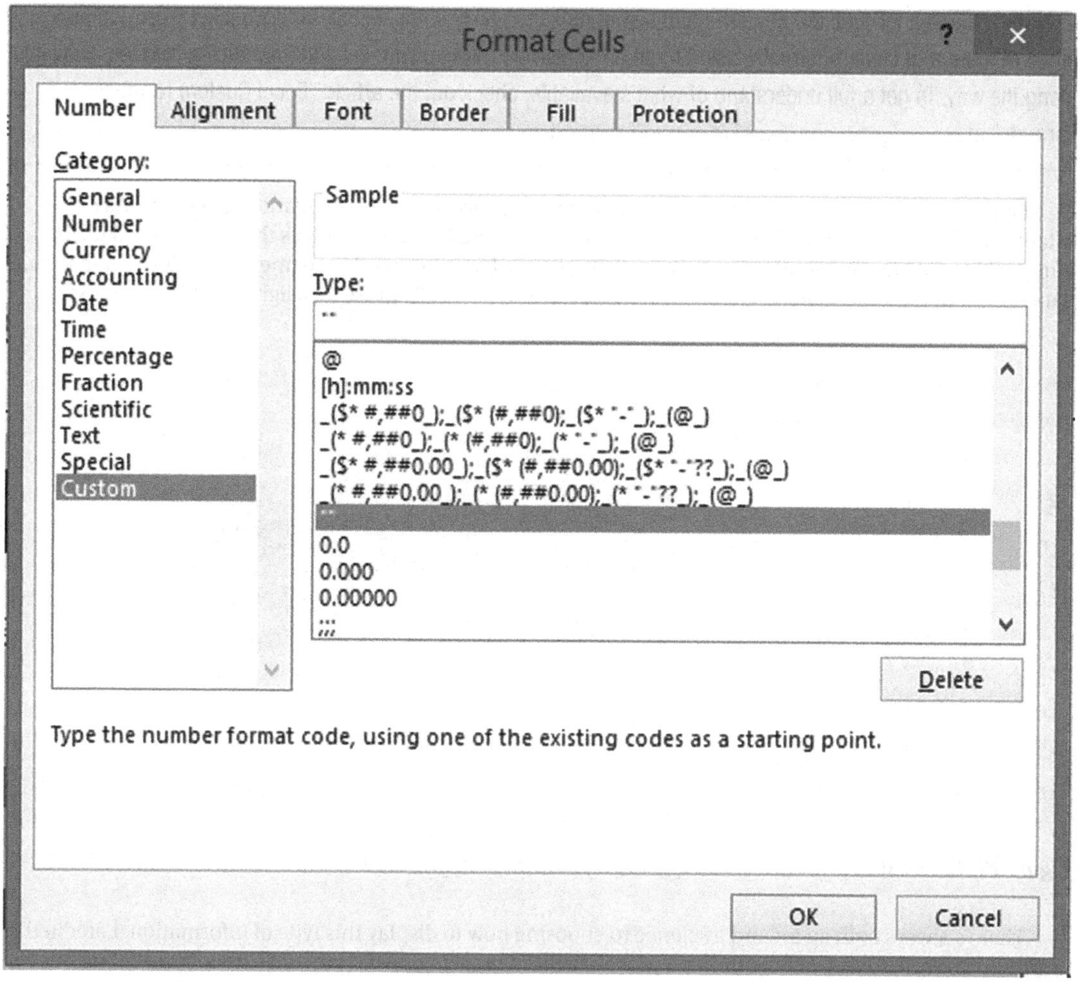

Figure 13-30. *The Format Cells dialog box*

In the Format Cells dialog box, I've defined a custom format for the selected cells. You can define your own custom format by selecting Custom in the Category listbox on the left. This will present you with an input box to define your own custom formats. As you can see in Figure 13-30, I've simply typed "" (two quotation marks), which tells Excel to replace numbers with a zero-length string. In other words, where there are numbers, you are directing Excel to show you nothing.

Why custom formats? They allow you to hide the numbers in the cell without changing the underlying values. For instance, even as you no longer see the numbers in the cells of the presented example, Excel still recognizes a value in the cell; you've simply formatted the number to appear differently. Neither formulas nor code provides this advantage of having a number both exist and not appear. Think about that one for a minute!

■ **Note** Custom formats are powerful and sometimes incredibly complicated. In this book, I'll provide only a small treatment of custom formats, using them as necessary in the examples and introducing features available along the way. To get a full understand of what's available, check out the article "Excel Custom Number Formats" at `www.ozgrid.com/Excel/CustomFormats.htm`.

Finally, I want to turn your attention to the squares that grid-off the dashboard's data range. As I established at the beginning of this book, how you present data is as important as the underlying data. In building this data range, I went through several iterations of how I wanted to segment the information in the data region. In this case, I chose a light border every five-by-five cells to create a light grid (Figure 13-31).

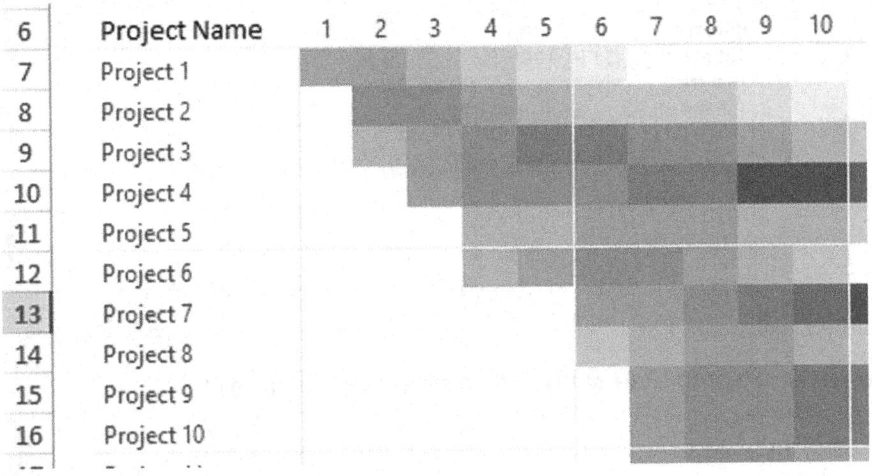

***Figure 13-31.** A subtle grid appears every five projects and every five days*

There's always both an art and a science to choosing how to display this type of information. Later in the book, you'll return to some of the thought process behind breaking up data to make it more readable. But even now there aren't any specific rules. Gridding off every cell made the entire thing look far too busy for me (Figure 13-32).

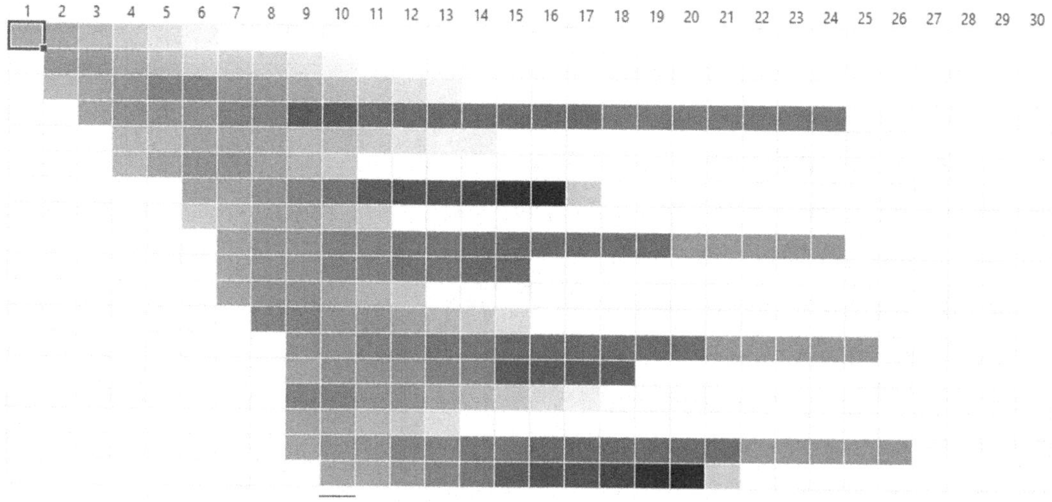

Figure 13-32. *Every cell with a border looked far too busy for my taste*

But that choice ultimately rests in your hands. It may be tempting, for instance, to place a border around every cell—certainly that would be the style most common in industry. But you should avoid all things that might inhibit data reception by the user, however small they may seem. That's thinking outside the cell.

The Last Word

In this chapter, you toured the Gantt chart dashboard, analyzing its features and how its back-end data ultimately feeds into its presentation. You traced the path of the back-end data, from how it began as a simple table on the back end and was transformed into something usable and actionable. By using formulas in place of pivot tables, you defined a living model: back-end changes to the data are always ramified up through to the presentation level.

In addition, you looked deeper into much of the underlying mechanics and presentation. You only dealt with VBA to disable a feature as you investigated the model. Indeed, it's worth noting that none of the mechanics investigated require VBA to do anything to the data. Formulas help trace the back-end data to the front, and custom formatting and conditional formatting support the visualization. To the extent possible, you let Excel features do the hard work.

In the next chapter, you'll dig deeper.

CHAPTER 14

An Interactive Gantt Chart Dashboard, Data Visualization

In the previous chapter, you investigated the Gantt chart dashboard shown in Figure 14-1. In that chapter, you took a look at the underlying mechanics, tracing how data starts from the back end and how it ultimately comes to inform the dashboard presentation. This chapter builds on the previous by digging deeper into the interactive and data visualization elements. Therefore, if you skipped the previous chapter hoping to get to this meaty bit, I strongly suggest you go back and read it, just so you'll have some clarity moving forward.

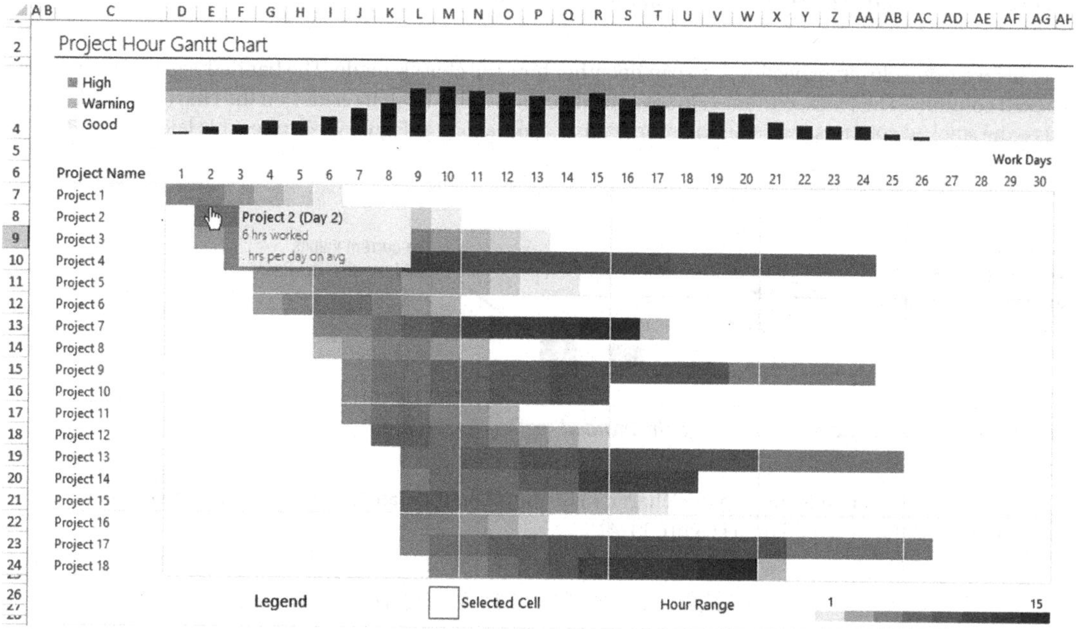

Figure 14-1. The Gantt chart dashboard

For this chapter, you'll be using `Chapter14GanttChart.xlsm`. By default, I've disabled the pop-up feature following the instructions I presented in the previous chapter. You're free to reenable it if you'd like, but I've found it distracting while working with parts of the spreadsheet. Typically I disable it while making modifications. I'll reenable it when complete.

As discussed in the preceding chapter, the front end of the dashboard is really made up of three distinct elements. First, a banded region chart at the top shows the total sum of the hours required (in black), and several graded bands let you know if far too many hours have been allocated. Next, a data region shows the actual Gantt chart project information, with an associated pop-up that provides data on demand. Finally, a dynamic legend at the bottom helps the user understand the actual ranges presented. Each item by itself represents reusable components. In this chapter, you'll reverse engineer them to discover how they work.

The Banded Region Chart

In this section, I'll discuss how to build the banded region chart. If you click into any of the bands on the banded region chart, you'll see it's actually a modified column chart (Figure 14-2).

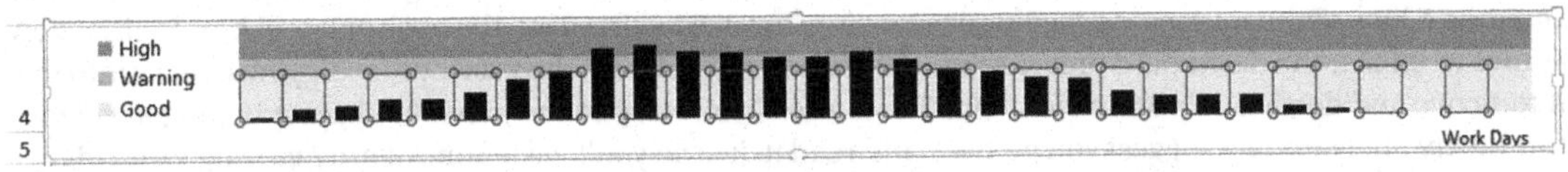
High
Warning
Good
4
5
Work Days

Figure 14-2. The banded region chart is a modified column chart

In fact, upon closer inspection, you can decipher how the chart is made. The banded regions are actually stacked columns. The black, current value is another column chart, but it resides on the chart's secondary axis—the stacked columns reside on the primary axis. Take a look at Figure 14-3 to see this laid out.

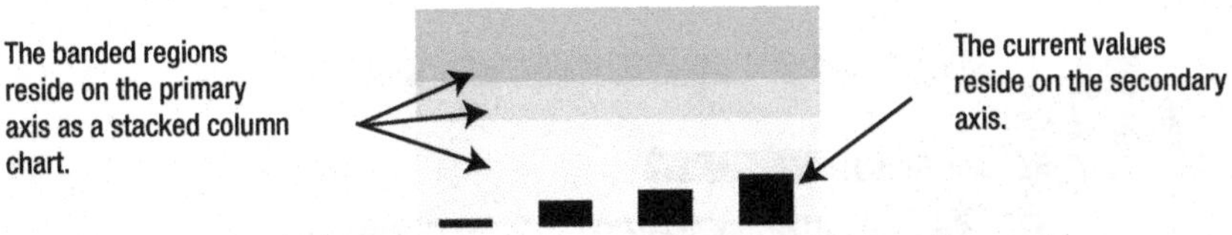
The banded regions reside on the primary axis as a stacked column chart.
The current values reside on the secondary axis.

Figure 14-3. A visual description of how the banded region chart is built

The information that feeds into this chart can be found on the Calculation tab under the tabular configuration of the back-end data (Figure 14-4).

Total	5	15	20	28	28	36	51	62	90	94	86	83	78	78	83	74	61	57	49	47	32	26	26	26	12	6	0	0	0	0
Chart Setup																														
Good	60	60	60	60	60	60	60	60	60	60	60	60	60	60	60	60	60	60	60	60	60	60	60	60	60	60	60	60	60	60
Warning	20	20	20	20	20	20	20	20	20	20	20	20	20	20	20	20	20	20	20	20	20	20	20	20	20	20	20	20	20	20
High	120	120	120	120	120	120	120	120	120	120	120	120	120	120	120	120	120	120	120	120	120	120	120	120	120	120	120	120	120	120

Figure 14-4. The data that informs the banded region chart can be found on the Calculation tab

The total row, at the top of Figure 14-4, contains the total number of hours required to work. This is the black column chart that will appear on the second axis. Below it, the next three rows define the banded regions. According to this dynamic, days with hour requirements of 60 or fewer (assume multiple people are working on projects, so these are aggregate counts among all available staff) are considered good; between 60 and 80 hours (in other words, the next 20 hours) are now in the warning territory. Anything greater than that is considered too high. That I chose 40 means the chart can show at most 120 hours. This setup is largely arbitrary. It seemed unlikely based on the data that a project count could go up that high. But for simplicity, it helps to define the legend in this way—and even picking arbitrarily high numbers forces you to think about your project and its underlying data.

Creating the Chart

To create a similar chart, you would lay out the data as I've done in Figure 14-4. Again, the numbers picked were arbitrary for this example. But for your own work, you should define what categories such as Good, Warning, and High (or any others you might think up) mean to you and your organization. In my setup, the numbers for each row are constants. But you could easily link these numbers to another input section in your own work, should you want to change the size of each region later.

To make the banded region chart, begin by selecting the banded region rows as I've done in Figure 14-5.

Chart Setup																														
Good	60	60	60	60	60	60	60	60	60	60	60	60	60	60	60	60	60	60	60	60	60	60	60	60	60	60	60	60	60	60
Warning	20	20	20	20	20	20	20	20	20	20	20	20	20	20	20	20	20	20	20	20	20	20	20	20	20	20	20	20	20	20
High	40	40	40	40	40	40	40	40	40	40	40	40	40	40	40	40	40	40	40	40	40	40	40	40	40	40	40	40	40	40

Figure 14-5. *Selecting the banded region rows*

Next, go to the Insert tab and insert a stacked column chart (from in the Charts group), as shown in Figure 14-6.

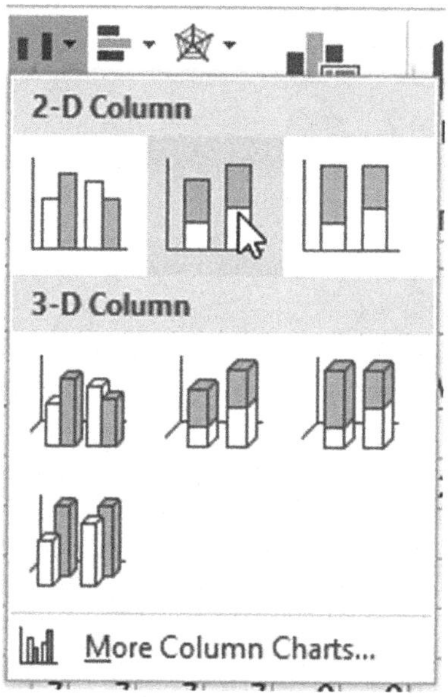

Figure 14-6. *With the rows selected, insert a stacked column chart from the Charts group on the Insert tab*

Once selected, your chart should look like the one shown in Figure 14-7.

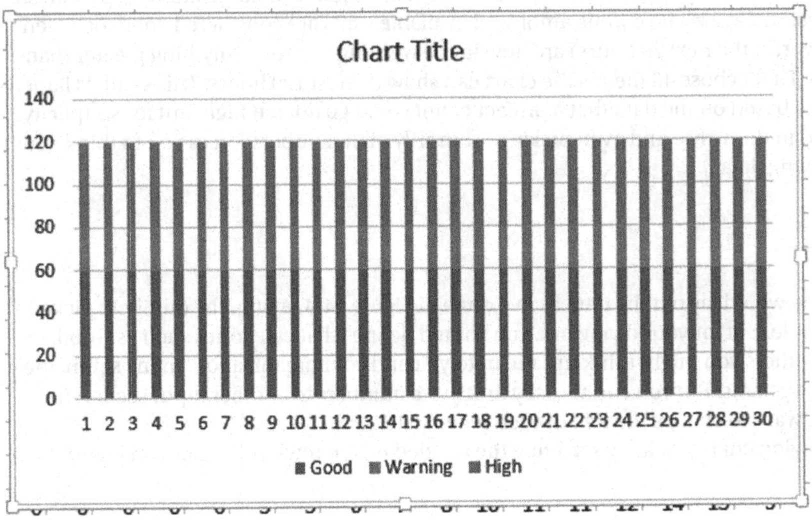

***Figure 14-7.** A stacked bar chart based on the banded regions*

Right-click any chart series and then select Format Data Series (Figure 14-8) to present the Format Data Series context pane (Figure 14-9). For Excel 2010 and earlier users, a dialog box similar to the context pane will appear.

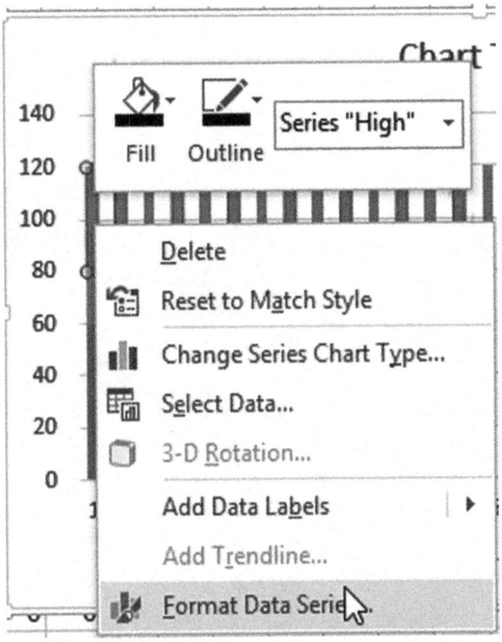

***Figure 14-8.** The context menu that appears upon right-clicking a series in the chart*

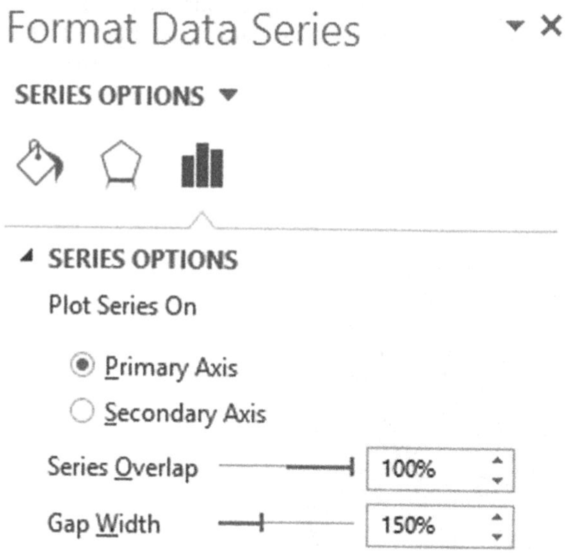

Figure 14-9. *The Format Data Series context pane*

Within the context pane (or dialog box for 2010 and earlier users), set the chart's Gap Width to zero. Once complete, the columns of the chart will touch, giving the appearance of a fluid band (Figure 14-10).

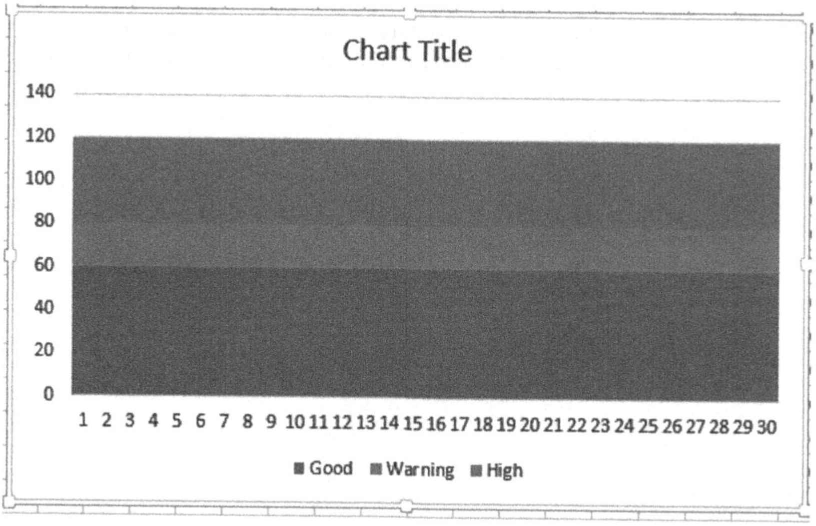

Figure 14-10. *Setting the gap width to zero*

At this point, you'll do some cleanup. If the chart title appeared on yours as it did on mine (Figure 14-10), go ahead and delete it by selecting the chart title and pressing Delete on your keyboard. (Chart titles won't appear by default in version 2010 or earlier.) Do the same with the horizontal axis and chart legend so it looks like Figure 14-11.

Figure 14-11. *A cleaned-up banded region chart*

Next, right-click the vertical axis on the left and select Format Axis. A context pane will appear on the right (Figure 14-12). Under the Axis Options, set the bounds to be a minimum of 0 and a maximum of 120.

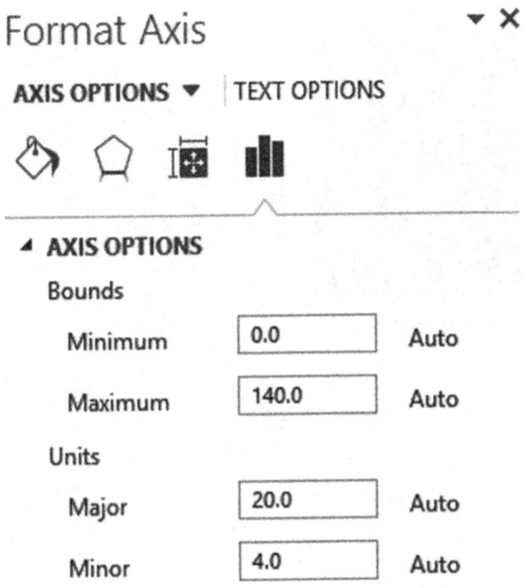

Figure 14-12. *The format axis context pane*

At this point, you're ready to add the total hours required to the chart. The easiest way to do this is to select cells B22:AF22 on the Calculation tab and then press Ctrl+C to copy (Figure 14-13).

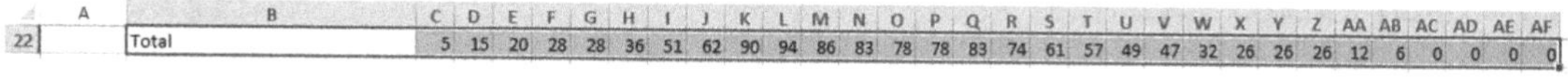
Total
5 15 20 28 28 36 51 62 90 94 86 83 78 78 83 74 61 57 49 47 32 26 26 26 12 6 0 0 0 0

Figure 14-13. *Cells B22:AF22 selected. Press Ctrl+C to copy*

Next, select anywhere in the chart and press Ctrl+V to paste. Once you've pasted this data, the chart won't look any different. That's because you set its range to 120, and as a stacked column chart, this data is not above the defined range for the chart. Though you can't see this new series, you can still modify it. With the chart still selected, go to the Format tab (that's the menu tab that pops up to the right of all the other tabs when a chart has been selected). On the left of the Format tab, there is a Chart Elements drop-down in the Current Selection group. If Series "Total" is not showing the drop-down, click the down arrow and select it (Figure 14-14).

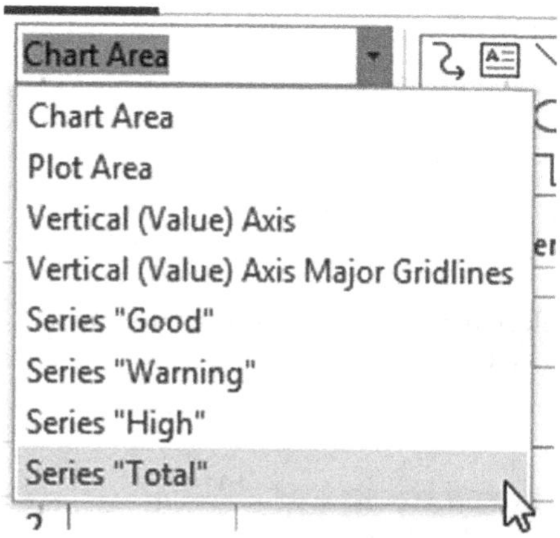

Figure 14-14. *Selecting Series "Total" from the drop-down*

Once selected, click the Format Selection button below the drop-down (Figure 14-15).

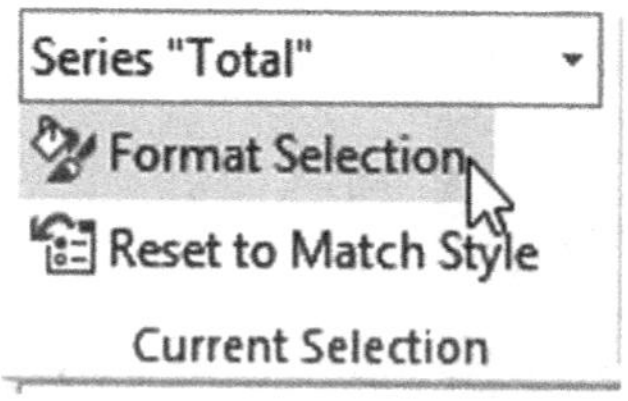

Figure 14-15. *The Format Selection button*

This will bring up the Format Data Series context pane (Figure 14-16).

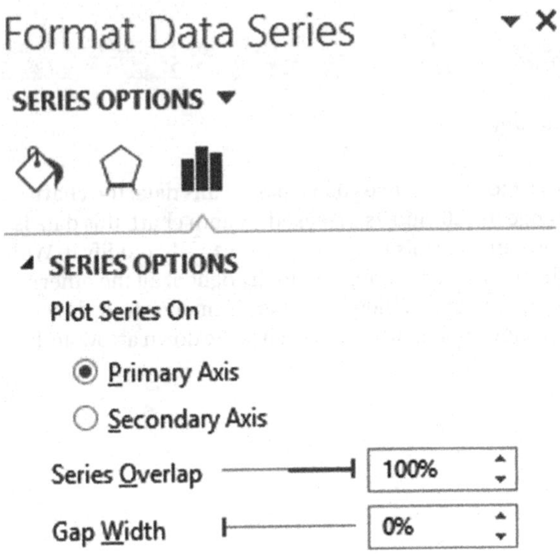

Figure 14-16. *The Format Data Series context pane*

Under Series Options, select Secondary Axis to change the selected data series to the secondary axis. Your chart should now look similar to the one displayed in Figure 14-17.

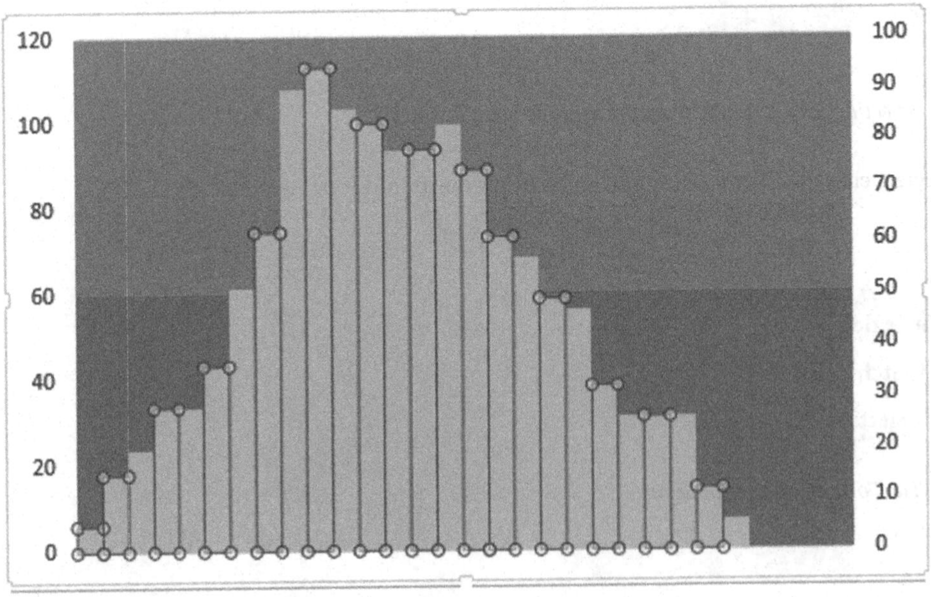

Figure 14-17. *A banded region chart not yet complete*

In Figure 14-17, you'll see you have several different series plot on different axes. However, you'll want everything to be even-steven. It wouldn't make sense to understand the total against a backdrop of a banded region plotted on a different scale. So, following the improvements you made earlier, you'll right-click the secondary axis and change the minimum and maximum to 0 and 140, respectively, as shown in Figure 14-12.

Having now set the axis, you'll need to clean everything up that you no longer need. In Figure 14-18, I've gone through and deleted both axes and the chart title.

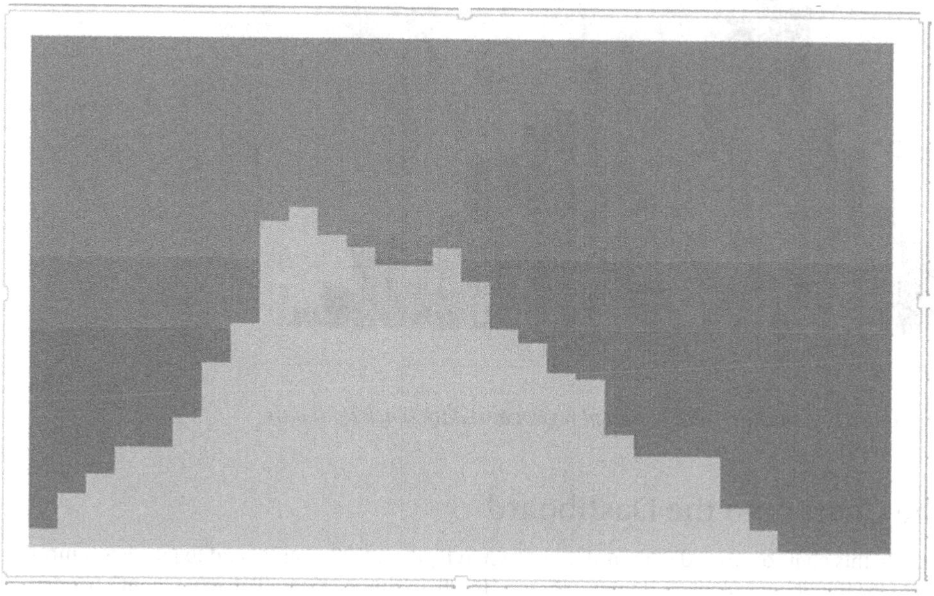

Figure 14-18. *The banded region chart without any extraneous information*

Before putting this chart on your dashboard, you'll have to set the color scale. Following the work of Stephen Few, I will always tend to prefer banded regions that follow a color scale. This is because I want to demonstrate degrees of things getting worse (or getting better). The color-fill drop-down in Excel provides several different palettes to choose from. The choice of color itself is less important than following a systematic palette that evokes the underlying nature of your data. In Figure 14-19, I chose some colors from the gray palette for the backdrop and a heavy black for the total bars.

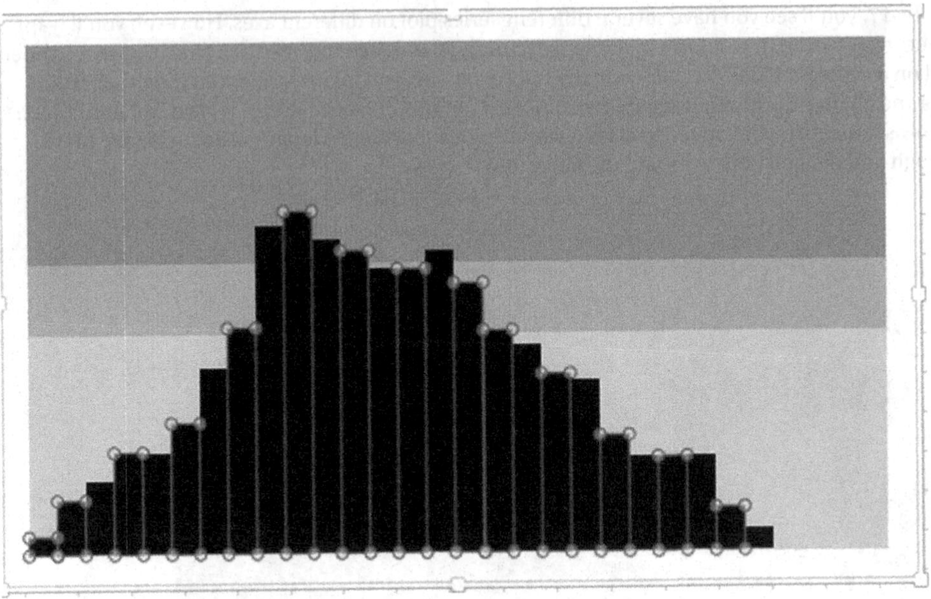

Figure 14-19. *Banded region chart with a graded region and dark black total bars*

Placing the Chart onto the Dashboard

Finally, you'll place this chart on your dashboard, as shown in Figure 14-20. You'll need to take a few more steps, however, to get it looking exactly as it does in Figure 14-20. In this section, I'll discuss what's needed.

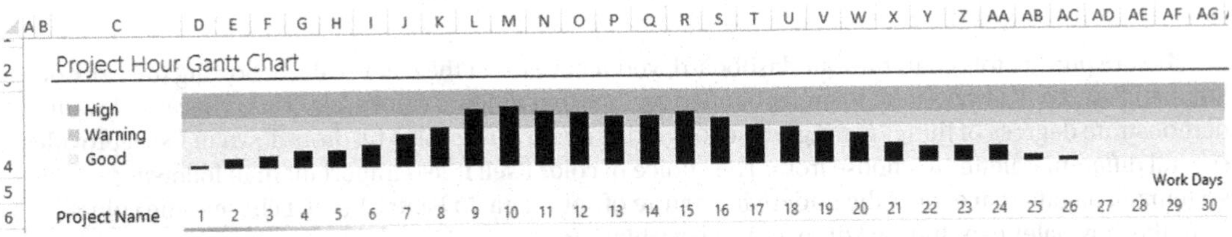

Figure 14-20. *The banded region chart placed on the dashboard*

Lining up the chart so that the bars align themselves with the dates below may seem like a hard task. However, you can make it easier on yourself by using the Snap to Grid feature. First, you place the chart on the dashboard and attempt to line it up as much as possible. Next, you select the plot area of the chart. If you're having trouble selecting the plot area (as you attempt to select it, you accidentally select a series instead), you can go to the Format context menu and select Plot Area from the Chart Elements drop-down menu (refer to Figure 14-14). Once it's selected, you can select the Snap to Grid feature from the Align drop-down menu on the Format tab (Figure 14-21).

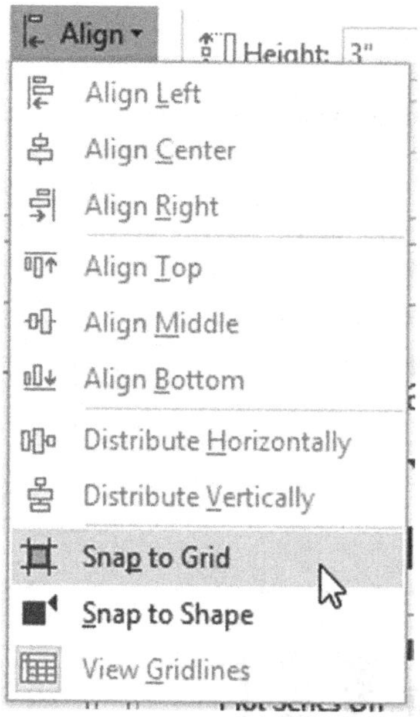

Figure 14-21. *Select Snap to Grid in the Align drop-down from the Format context tab*

The Snap to Grid feature allows you to line up any shape (in this case, the plot area) with the cell grid. You can use this feature to line up the chart with the numbers below (refer to Figure 14-19). For aesthetic reasons, I added some space between each total bar. To do this, right-click the total series on the chart and go to Format Data Series. In pop-up context pane, you'll decrease the Gap Width setting to the desired level. Figure 14-22 shows I've chosen a Gap Width setting of 91%.

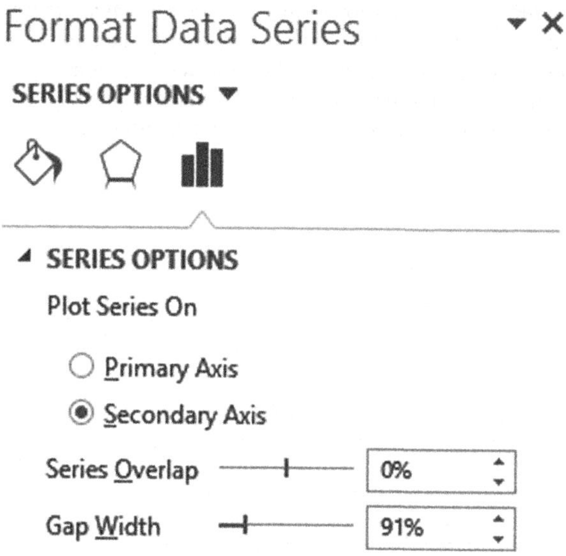

Figure 14-22. *The Format Data Series context pane showing a Gap Width setting of 91%*

Creating the Banded Chart Legend

In this section, I'll discuss creating the chart legend shown in Figure 14-23. As the figure demonstrates, this is not a chart legend that was part of the chart but rather one I created myself. Sometimes Excel's chart legends don't give you the adequate layout control needed for your dashboard, so you can make your own.

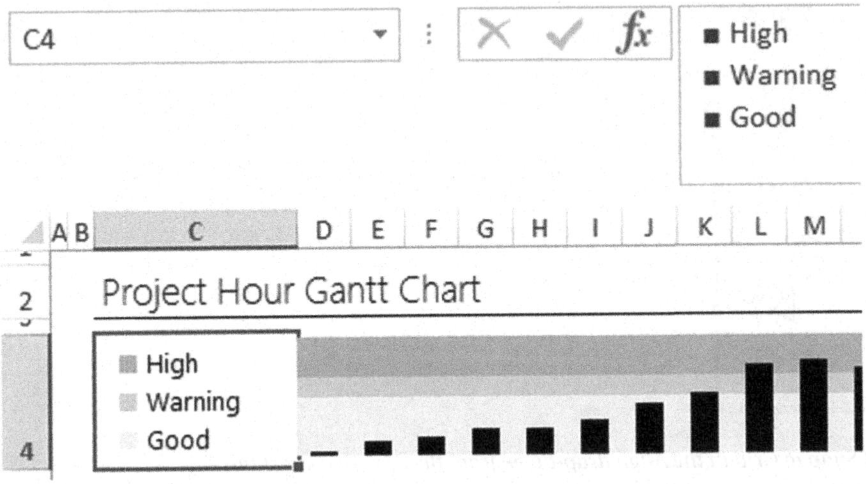

Figure 14-23. *A homemade chart legend*

Notice in Figure 14-23 that I have blocklike characters next to each text item. I inserted these block characters using the Symbol option from the Insert tab's Symbol group. When you select the Symbol option, the Symbol dialog box appears. The Symbol dialog box allows you to insert other characters available to the selected font. Notice in Figure 14-24 that the font I'm using is Segoe UI. This is the font I use across the entire dashboard. However, sometimes Excel might show Calibri in this drop-down since Calibri is the default font (unless you've changed it). Make sure the font drop-down contains the desired font since certain characters and symbols are available only to certain fonts. In the subset drop-down, notice I've selected Geometric Shapes. Many other types of symbols are available to this font, but I'm interested in that big box symbol that is part of the Geometric Shapes category. Once it's selected, I can click the Insert button to insert it into the spreadsheet.

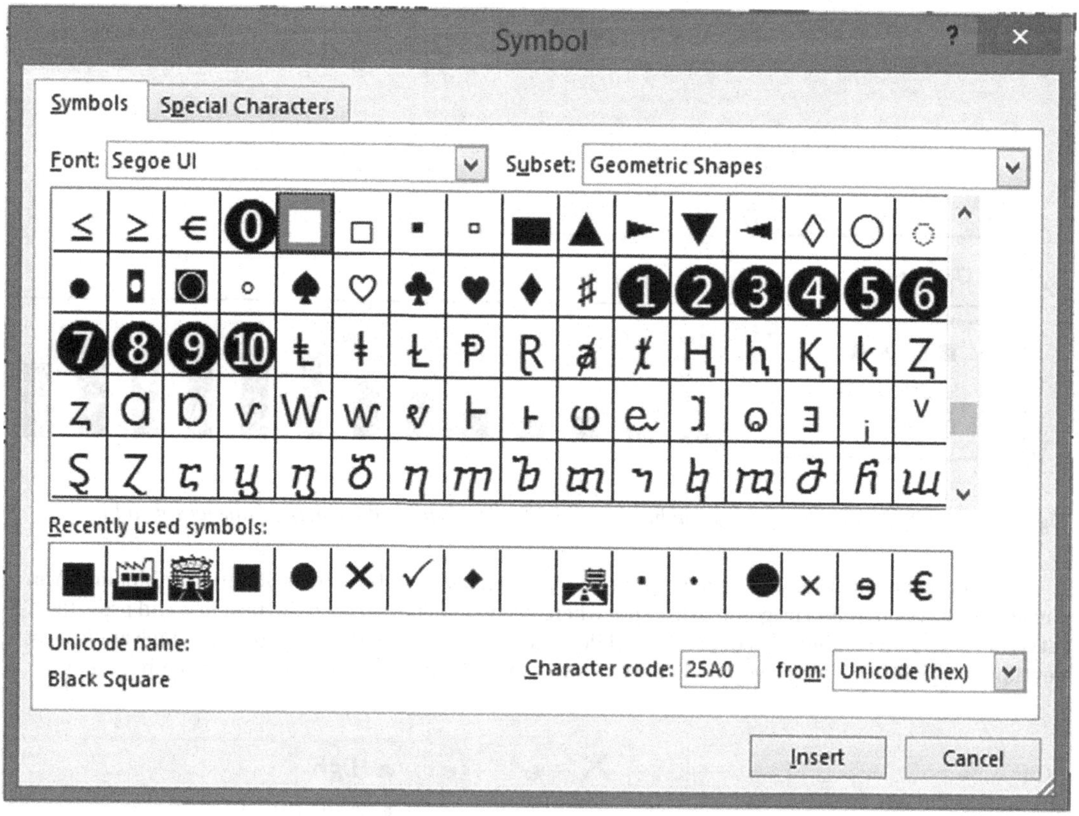

Figure 14-24. The Symbols dialog box

You may have noticed in Figure 14-22. I use the block symbol three times. You can either insert it three times now and then insert the legend labels where they need to go or, once the first one is inserted, highlight the block and press Ctrl+C to copy. Then as you need those two more times, you can press Ctrl+V to paste it.

However you choose to build the legend, you'll have to take a few more steps to make it look like the one shown in Figure 14-23. By default the squares will be black, and all the items will be on a single wrapped line. Figure 14-25 demonstrates what I'm describing.

```
ALT + ENTER
```

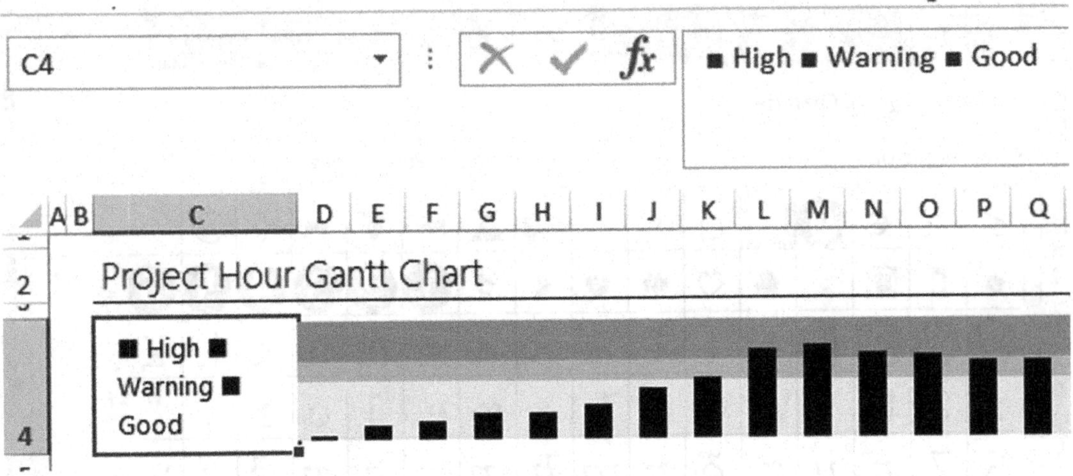

Figure 14-25. *By default the squares will be black, and the labels will all be on the same wrapped line*

To tell Excel to push something to another line, you can use the Alt+Enter keyboard combination. You can either insert a new line by going to the spot where you would like to begin the next line and press the Alt+Enter keyboard combination or create it while typing by using the combination when you want to start a new line. This will work even if you don't have word wrap enabled for the particular cell (Figure 14-26).

Figure 14-26. *Use Alt+Enter to start a new line in the formula bar*

ALTERNATIVE ALT+ENTER USES

Alt+Enter is also really useful for splitting up complex formulas. Figure 14-27 shows an `IF` function I've added some white space to, to make it more readable. You can use Alt+Enter to go to the next line and then use the spacebar to create indentations (note: you can't use the Tab key).

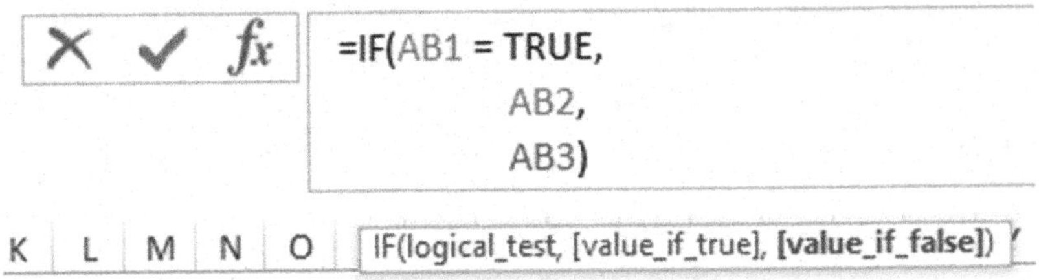

Figure 14-27. *You can use Alt+Enter plus spaces to create indentation in formulas*

To color each block individually, select the cell to put it into edit mode where your cursor is blinking in the cell. Next, select an individual block and change its font color (Figure 14-28). While this will not change the font color selected in the formula bar, it will change the color as it appears in a cell.

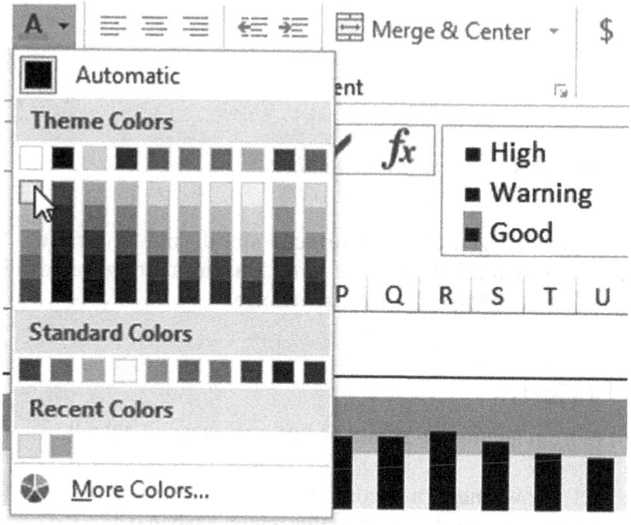

Figure 14-28. *You edit the font color within a cell by selecting the desired text and picking a new color*

So far, you've learned how to create a banded region chart that helps you understand whether you have too many hours allocated to a specific day. In the next section, I'll discuss how to create the dynamic legend.

The Dynamic Legend

This section deals with the dynamic legend shown in Figure 14-29, which appears at the bottom of the dashboard. What makes this legend dynamic is that it will adjust its range depending upon the data presented in the Gantt chart window. While the lowest value shown in Figure 14-29 is 1 and the greatest value is 15, the range will always automatically adjust to any range that exists in the underlying data. The dynamic legend is another item to have in your tool set of reusable components.

Figure 14-29. *A dynamically adjusting legend*

To understand how the dynamic legend works, you need to understand the shaded region below the numbers. In fact, the shaded region comes about through the application of conditional formatting. But take away the conditional formatting, and it's just numbers (Figure 14-30).

1							15
1.0	3.5	5.3	7.0	8.8	10.5	12.3	15.0
1	2	3	4	5	6	7	8

***Figure 14-30.** The dynamic legend uses conditional formatting applied to numbers*

There are several important features to this dynamic legend. The top row contains the minimum and maximum values displayed to the user. Below, a series of numbers help the conditional formatting create the visual legend. And below that a series of numbers (1 through 8) help create that range.

Creating the Endpoints of the Legend

First, you'll need to create the endpoints (1 and 15 from Figures 14-29 and 14-30) of this legend. I'll talk about how to do that in this section.

Let's start with the maximum first. Figure 14-31 shows the formula used to find the maximum of all values presented in the Gantt chart. Notice, for convenience, I've named this region `Dashboard.GanttChartArea`. This formula gives the maximum value shown in the Gantt chart plot. Easy enough, right?

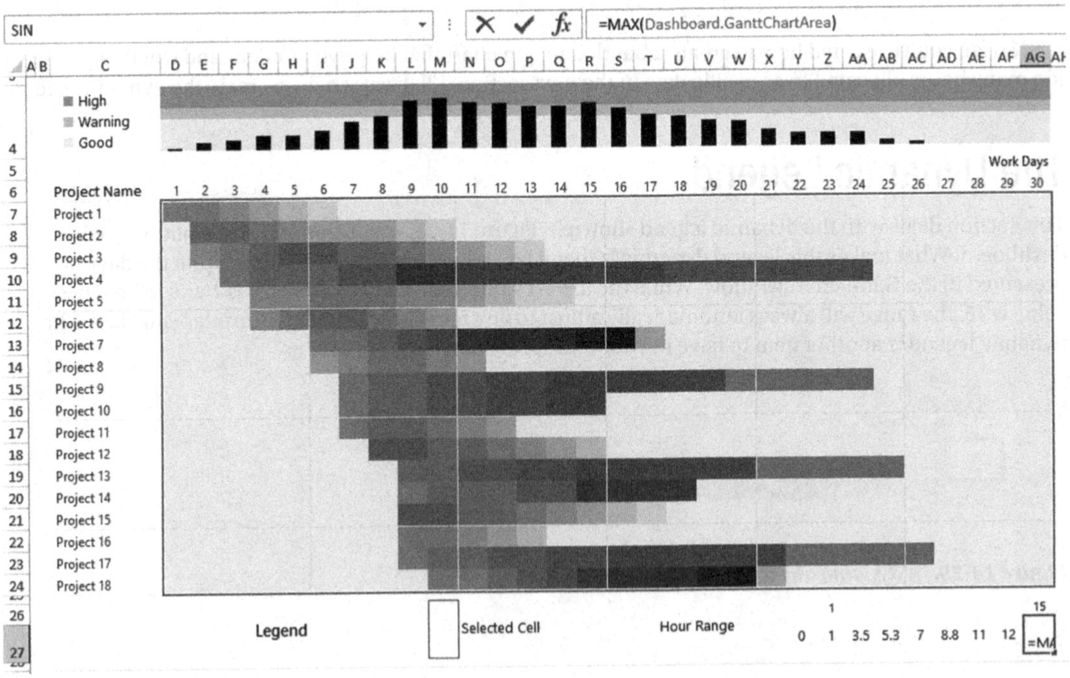

***Figure 14-31.** The maximum endpoint is derived by using the Max formula on the entire Gantt chart area region*

Getting the minimum however is a bit trickier. The problem is that the minimum for this plot will always be zero. This is because all that white space where nothing has been plotted will be treated as a zero by Excel. So, you can't simply take the minimum of the entire region because there are so many zeros. You'll need to find out what the minimum is *excluding* zeros. The formula in Figure 14-32 shows how you can do this.

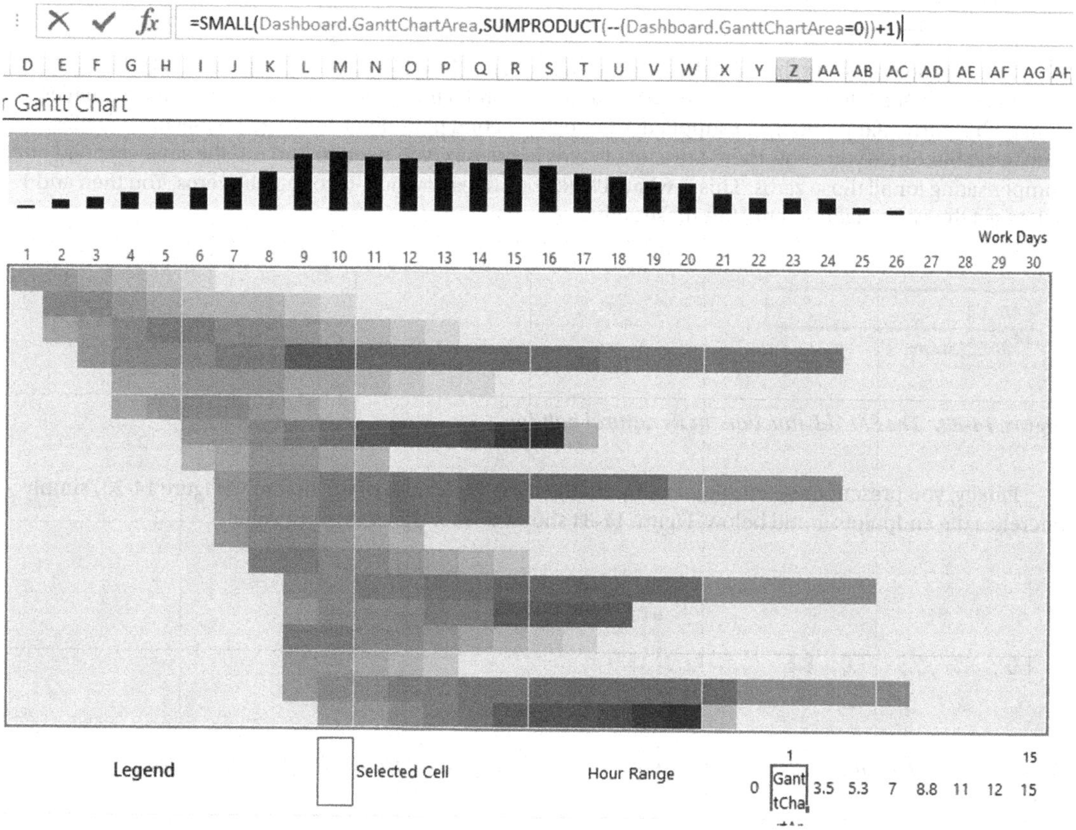

Figure 14-32. *The minimum endpoint uses a more complicated formula*

Let's take a look at how this formula works by breaking it down.

```
=SMALL(Dashboard.GanttChartArea,SUMPRODUCT(--(Dashboard.GanttChartArea=0))+1)
```

Recall from previous chapters how `SUMPRODUCT` works. `(Dashboard.GanttChartArea=0)` is the condition you want to count. By default Boolean expressions like this will not be counted in the way you want unless another mathematical application is applied to them. For instance, `(Dashboard.GanttChartArea=0)*(Dashboard.GanttChartArea=0)` will be counted (although it won't give you the answer you want, I'm just presenting it here for example), as will `(Dashboard.GanttChartArea)*1` (this will give you the correct answer). In any event, the -- is the commonly accepted shorthand to tell Excel you want it to count how many cells in `Dashboard.GanttChartArea` equal zero. (*1 will work too but is somewhat less common than --. You should choose whichever is easier to read for you.)

■ **Note** You could use `COUNTIF` here instead, but `COUNTIF` is generally slower. Plus, I wanted to show you how you can use `SUMPRODUCT` in practice. Sometimes people are scared to use `SUMPRODUCT`, but it won't bite. As always, you should choose the function that more naturally reflects the underlying nature of the problem. A reasonable argument to use `COUNTIF` could be made here.

Now let's take a look at the left side of this formula. Recall how `SMALL` works (Figure 14-33). The first parameter of `SMALL` is looking for an array of data. The second parameter allows you to return the smallest item at that particular point. If you supplied a 2 into the second parameter, you'd get the second smallest item available. Since you know there are a lot of zeros in the mix, you need to find out the smallest point after compensating for all those zeros. This is what `SUMPRODUCT` does for you—it counts the zeros. You then add 1 to it to get the *next* smallest item after those zeros.

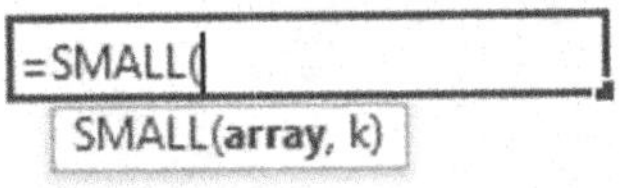

Figure 14-33. *The SMALL function, in its natural habitat*

Finally, you present these endpoint values to the user. The values of the first row (Figure 14-33) simply reference the endpoints found below. Figure 14-34 shows this for the maximum value.

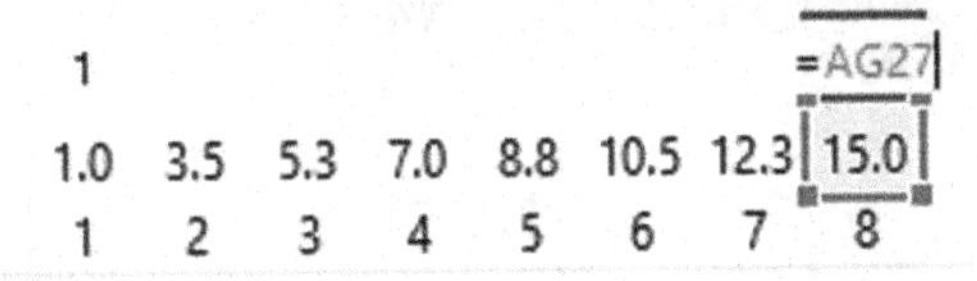

Figure 14-34. *The endpoints presented to the user are simply references to the endpoints calculated in the line below*

Interpolating Between the Endpoints

In this next section, I'll discuss how to get those values between the endpoints. Notice in Figure 14-34 that they appear to grow from the minimum endpoint to the maximum endpoint. This is called *interpolation*. Interpolation will help you create a visual scale between the endpoints.

Notice that you have eight points in total including the endpoints for the entire range. Figure 14-35 shows the formula that begins after the minimum endpoints.

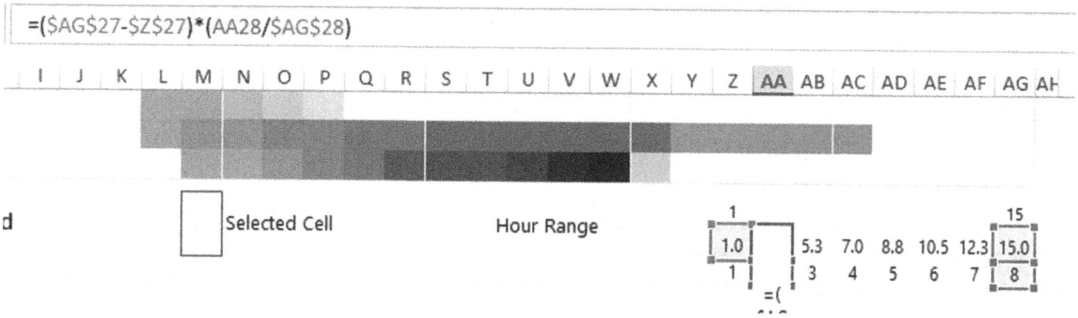

Figure 14-35. *You use the formula presented here to interpolate the values between your two endpoints*

Let's break this formula down. Look at the first half of this formula, (`$AG$27-$Z$27`). This piece of the formula is the maximum endpoint less the minimum endpoint: it finds the range. The second part of this formula is the number under the second endpoint (it's a 2, as you might imagine) divided by the total number of endpoints—8. This part of the formula is a proportion. When you multiply the entire range (15, in this case) by the proportion you want to show (2/8 = .25), the result is 3.5, in other words, at the second endpoint, 2/8ths of the entire range. At the third endpoint, you'll find 3/8ths of the entire range. You'll do this up to the seventh endpoint where you find 7/8ths of the entire range.

You can abstract this interpolation formula into the following form:

```
=[Range] * [Current point/Total Points]
```

where the Range is equal to [Maximum Endpoint - Minimum Endpoint].

Applying the Visual Effects

Once you have the numbers you need, you can apply conditional formatting to get the desired shaded effect. I'll talk about how to do that in this section.

First you highlight the interpolated region and then you apply conditional formatting (Home tab ➤ Conditional Formatting ➤ New Rule). Figure 14-35 shows the conditional formatting New Formatting Rule dialog box. In Figure 14-36 I've applied rules similar to what was done to the Gantt chart from the previous chapter. I'll be using a 2-Color Scale rule. The minimum number is .1 (which is an arbitrarily low number to create a starting point that isn't zero). I've also set the minimum to use the softest gray available in Excel's color scheme. The maximum value is derived from the data (though I could specify it if I wanted). For that you use black.

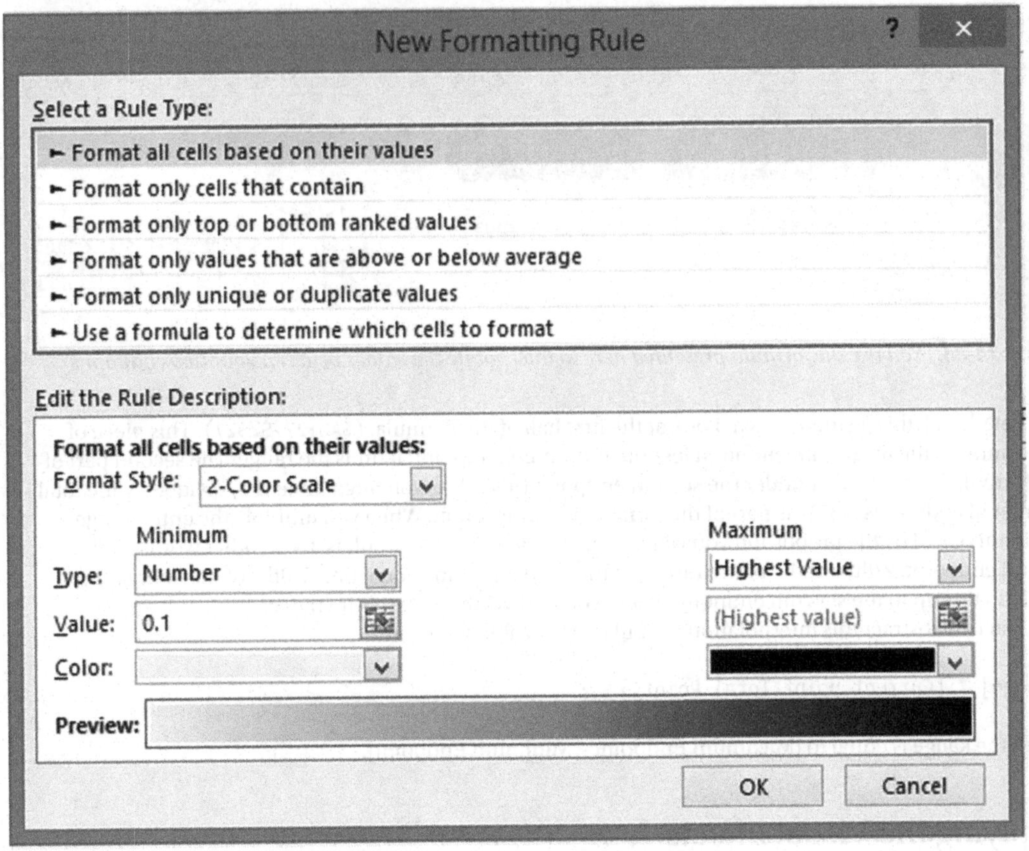

Figure 14-36. The New Formatting Rules dialog box

Once these rules are specified, you can return to the spreadsheet. Notice in Figure 14-37 the numeric values appear in the cells. However, you don't really want numeric values either in the colored cells or in the row below. To remove these numbers, you use the custom formatting trick from the previous chapter (see "The Dashboard Worksheet Tab" subsection in Chapter 13).

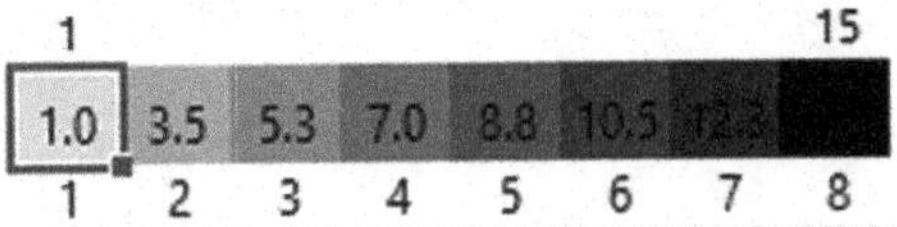

Figure 14-37. The numbers still appear once conditional formatting is applied

Once those numbers are removed, you can simply resize the row to get the slimmer effect shown at the beginning of this chapter (see Figure 14-38).

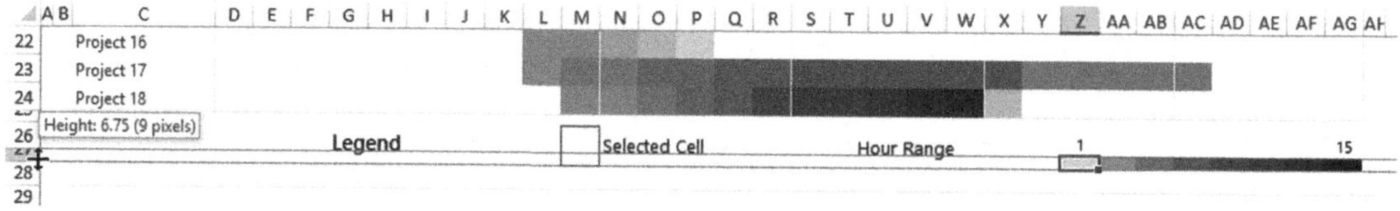

Figure 14-38. *Resizing the legend to create a slimmer effect*

The Last Word

In this chapter, you worked on a lot of the visual elements of your Gantt chart dashboard. While some of the steps may have appeared complicated at first, they become easier upon successive implementations. In your work, you can consider how you can reuse many of these components. You saw that sometimes you must make certain charts and legends yourself instead of relying on Excel's defaults. Again, once you know how to make these items, their implementation becomes straightforward.

In the next chapter, I'll discuss how to implement the dashboard pop-up feature that appears when your mouse rolls over a specific cell.

CHAPTER 15

An Interactive Gantt Chart Dashboard, Data Details on Demand

In the previous chapter, I went through the visual elements of your Gantt chart dashboard. In this chapter, I'll go through developing the interactive pop-up that presents details on demand about a specific date in time. Figure 15-1 shows this pop-up for Project 1, Day 2.

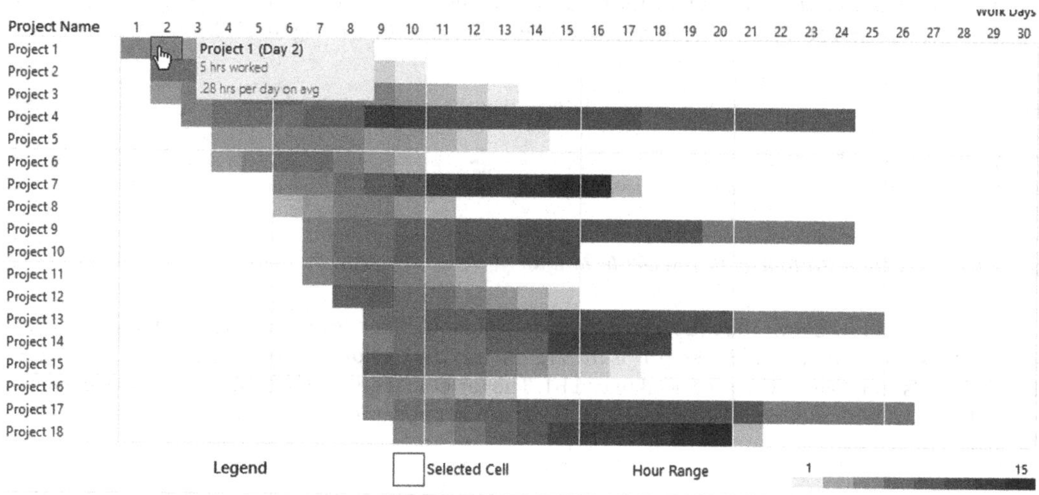

***Figure 15-1.** The details-on-demand pop-up mechanism shows details for a specific project and day*

This mechanism was first described in Chapter 5. Officially, the rollover mechanism is a bug in Excel you're exploiting to create something new. Before I go into how it's implemented in this dashboard, let's take a moment to review from a high level how it works. Therefore, this chapter is split up into two parts. First, I'll discuss the Rollover Method in more detail and demonstrate its utility as a reusable component; next, I'll show how it can be easily implemented into the Gantt chart.

The Rollover Method

In this section, I'll review how the Rollover Method works. In the first subsection, I'll review a simple example of the Rollover Method. In the following subsection, I'll go into a more advanced example and present a conceptual method for how to implement the method.

A Quick Review of the Rollover Method

As you might recall, the Rollover Method works by breaking one of the tried-and-true rules of Excel: user-defined functions (UDFs) are not allowed to make changes to the spreadsheet. However, an interesting thing happens when you place a UDF in the `HYPERLINK` function of a cell. The UDF will call the macro. Let's take a look at an example user-defined function.

Into a module I've added the code in Listing 15-1.

Listing 15-1. Sample Rollover User-Defined Function

```
Public Function MyRollover(SampleText As String)
    Sheet1.Range("B1").Value = SampleText
End Function
```

Then, on a free worksheet, I've added the following function to cell A1: `=IFERROR(HYPERLINK(MyRollover ("Hello World"),"Hover Over Me"),"Hover Over Me")`. This is shown in Figure 15-2.

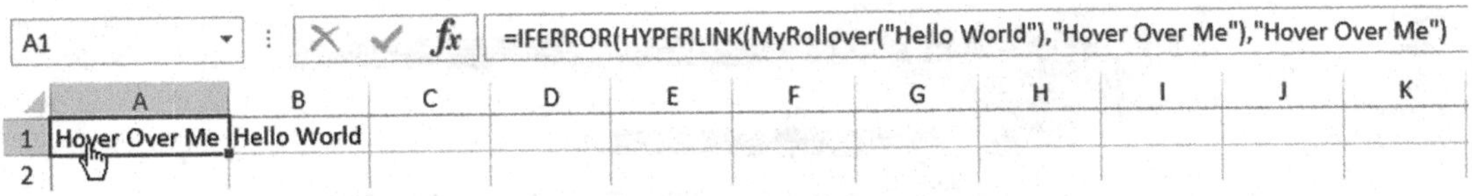

Figure 15-2. *A demonstration of the rollover technique*

Notice Figure 15-2 shows the rollover mechanism in action. When my mouse is placed over cell A1, `MyRollover` is called where `"Hello World"` is the argument. If you follow the code in Listing 15-1, you see whatever text is supplied will be produced to cell B1. The formula requires `IFERROR` surround it since it's essentially a bug. Without that `IFERROR`, a `#VALUE` error would appear in cell A1, which wouldn't look all that good.

A Conceptual Model for Rollover Method Implementation

In this section, I'll talk about a more conceptual model of how to implement the Rollover Method in your own work. While it's nice to change a cell's value, you want to add more interactivity than that. For instance, it might be nice to understand where the rollover took place. Open `Chapter15RolloverDemo.xlsm` to follow along.

Figure 15-3 shows a 5×5 grid of cells. Cells J2 and J3 are named `CurrentColumn` and `CurrentRow`, respectively.

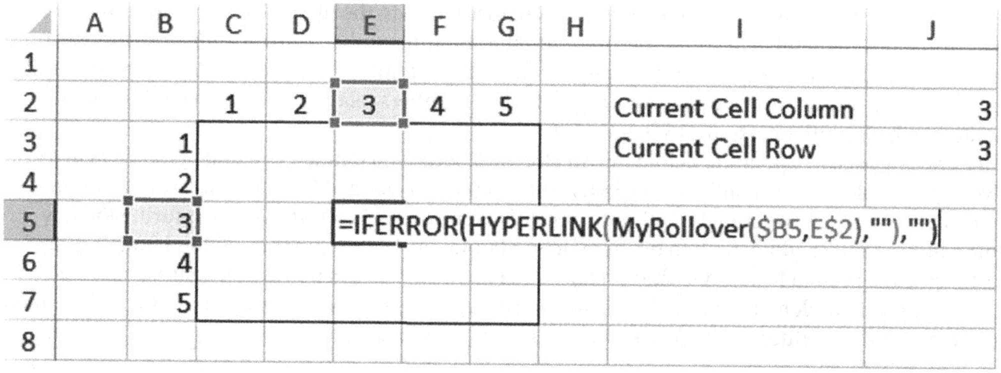

Figure 15-3. *A grid of cells where you'll implement the Rollover Method*

In Listing 15-2, I've implemented a user-defined function in a new, unused module.

Listing 15-2. A Simple Implementation of a Rollover

```
Public Function MyRollover(Row As Integer, Column As Integer)
    [CurrentRow].Value = Row
    [CurrentColumn].Value = Column
End Function
```

Finally, take a look at the formula I've implemented in each cell in Figure 15-3. In cell C3, you can see the Rollover Method formula implemented. Notice the two cell references that make up the arguments of `MyRollover`. Figure 15-4 shows this formula in the upper-left of the table at row 1 and column 1. These two cell references are set up to always pull the correct row and column coordinates for any location within the table.

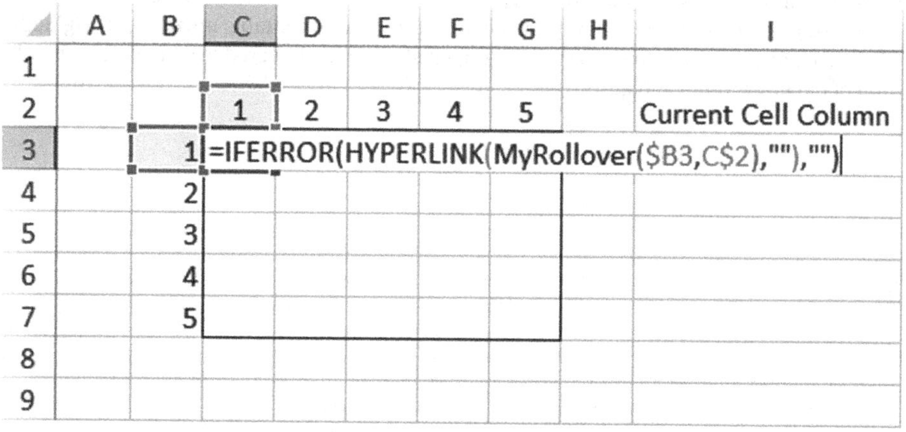

Figure 15-4. *The row and column references will always be correct no matter where the Rollover Method is in the table because of correct cell references*

To ensure the same when you implement this mechanism, start in the upper-left corner of your coordinate grid table. Remember, if you want to capture the column number, the cell address reference to the column should keep the row number absolute and leave the column letter relative; for rows, you would do the opposite: keep the column letter absolute and the row numbers relative. You can see this dynamic implemented in the formulas in Figure 15-3 and 15-4.

So, let's review what's happening before moving forward. First, you defined a region of rollovers in a grid layout. Next, you implemented a Rollover Method formula and user-defined function that would capture the location of the cell that triggered the rollover user-defined function. You did this by capturing the row and column indices and sending them to the user-defined function. Within the user-defined function, you tell Excel to write the current location to the spreadsheet. Figure 15-5 shows this mechanism working as intended. The rollover implemented in cell D6 sends the coordinates (row 4, column 2) into the user-defined function, which are then written to the spreadsheet in J3 and J2, respectively.

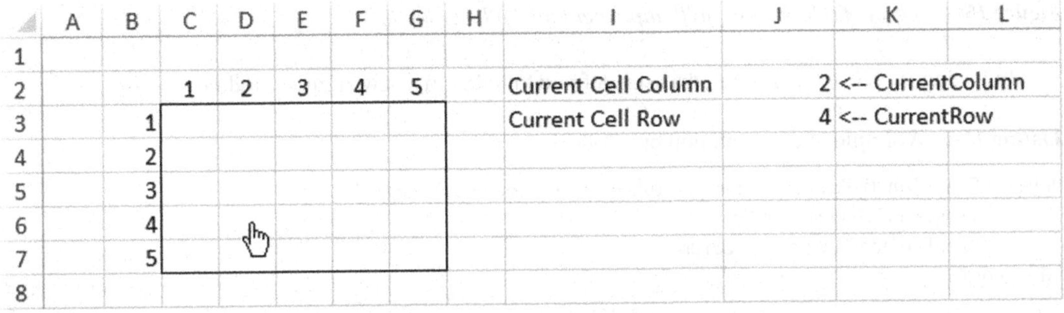

Figure 15-5. *The row and column values sent into the UDF are written to the spreadsheet*

Implementing a Hover Table

Now that you know the coordinates of the mouse location vis a vis the cell it's hovered over, you can add some interactive elements. I like to do this via what I call a *hover table*. The hover table mirrors the originally defined table grid. However, its purpose is to simply capture the cell currently hovered over. Let's take a look at an implementation of the hover table in Figure 15-6.

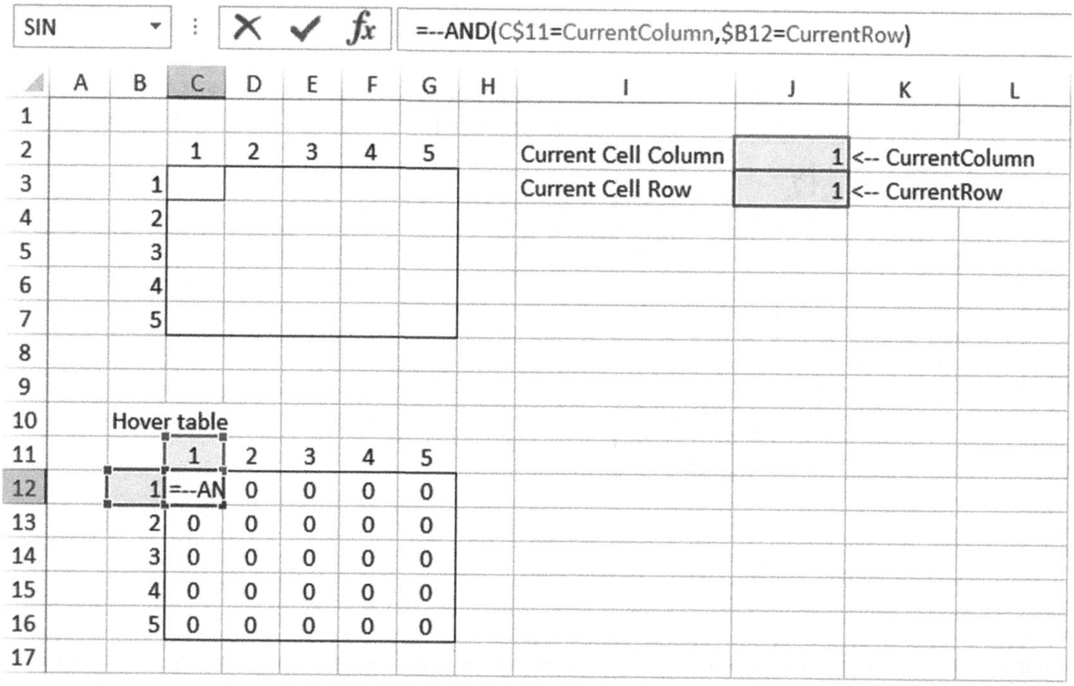

Figure 15-6. *An implementation of a hover table. The hover table parallels the rollover table by capturing the relative cell location of the cell being hovered over*

Let's take a look at the formula in Figure 15-6. Recall the AND function is a Boolean logic formula. It returns a true when all conditions specified within the AND function are true. Figure 15-6 shows the formula for the upper-left cell. But if you take a look at the relative references, you can see it is easily dragged right and then down. Because AND is by definition a Boolean function, by default it will return a TRUE and FALSE to signal whether its conditions have been satisfied. You use the shorthand -- to convert TRUE and FALSE to 1 and 0. Technically, you don't *need* to do this, but because this dynamic you've set up here treats cells as coordinates and the cells are often small, 1s and 0s are easier to read than TRUEs and FALSEs, which often appear as #### anyway given the small cell sizes.

Figure 15-7 should drive the point of all of this home. The mouse is hovering over the cell at (2,2), and the hover table has "lit up" a 1 in the same location.

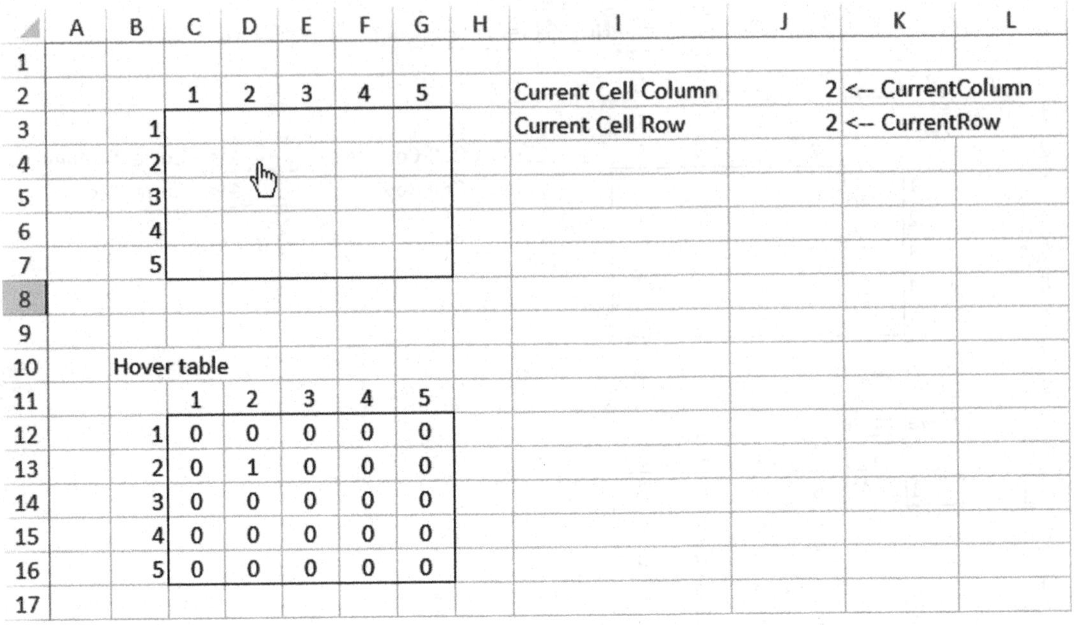

Figure 15-7. *The hover table lights up or "flags" the coordinate location where the rollover has taken place*

Implementing Conditional Formatting

With the hover table done, you can easily add all sorts of fun stuff. Let's say you want a shaded square to follow the mouse. You would do this with conditional formatting. First you would select the rollover region and implement a new conditional formatting rule (Figure 15-8).

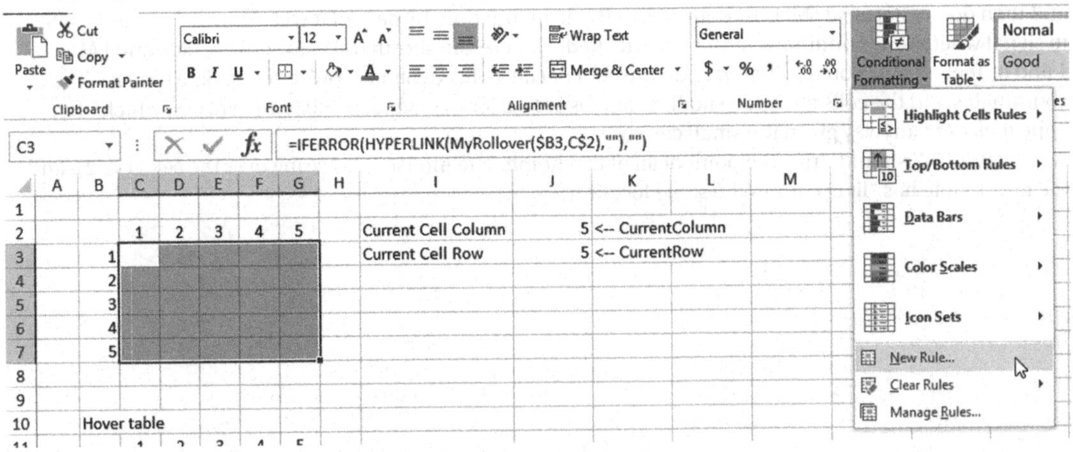

Figure 15-8. *Conditional formatting can be placed on the rollover region*

Next, in the New Formatting Rule dialog box (Figure 15-9), you set Rule Type to "Use a formula to determine which cells to format." In the "Format values where this formula is true" box, you implement the rule `=(C12=1)`. Notice C12 is the first cell in the upper-left corner of the hover table. Also, notice C12 is a relative reference. For conditional formatting, this means the rule will be test in a pairwise fashion. For instance, cell C3 from the hover table (coordinates (1,1)) will test whether cell C12 is equal to 1. Cell D3 will test whether D12 is equal to one in the hover table, and cell C4 will test against C13. Take a look at Figure 15-9 to make sure you understand this concept.

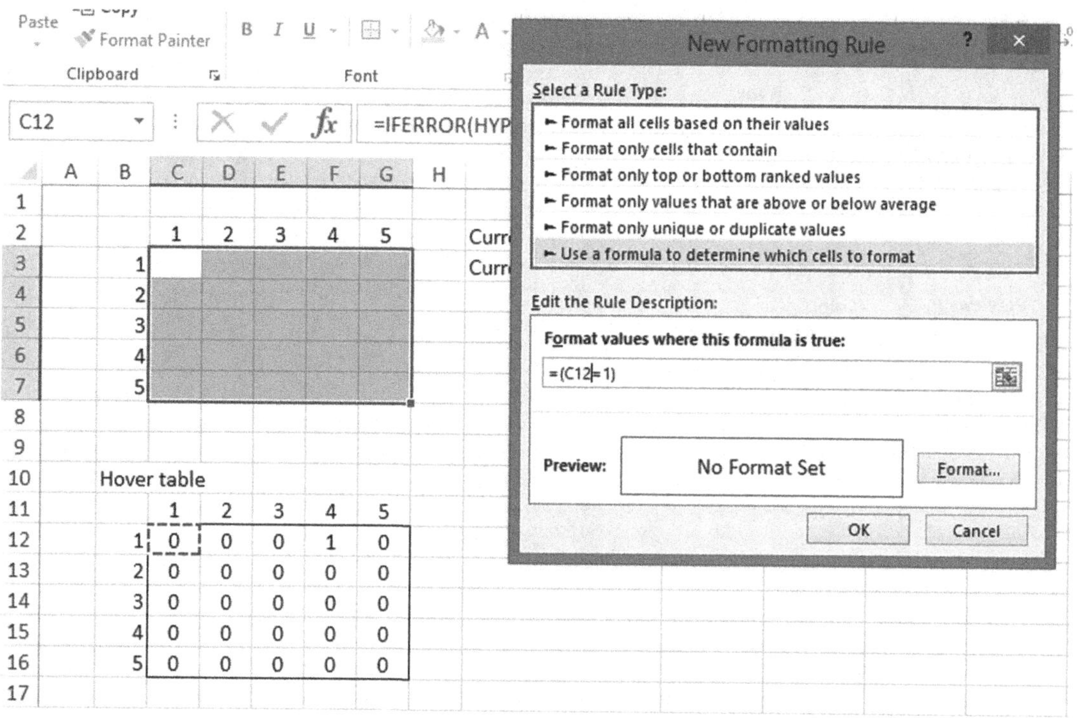

Figure 15-9. *You use a relative reference as the conditional formatting rule*

Once you've set up the rules, you can click the Format button to specify how you want a cell triggering the rollover to appear. In Figure 15-10, I've made a simple change. I've set rollover cells to show a red border wherever the mouse hovers in the region of rollovers. Once I've set this change, I'll click OK until I get back to the spreadsheet.

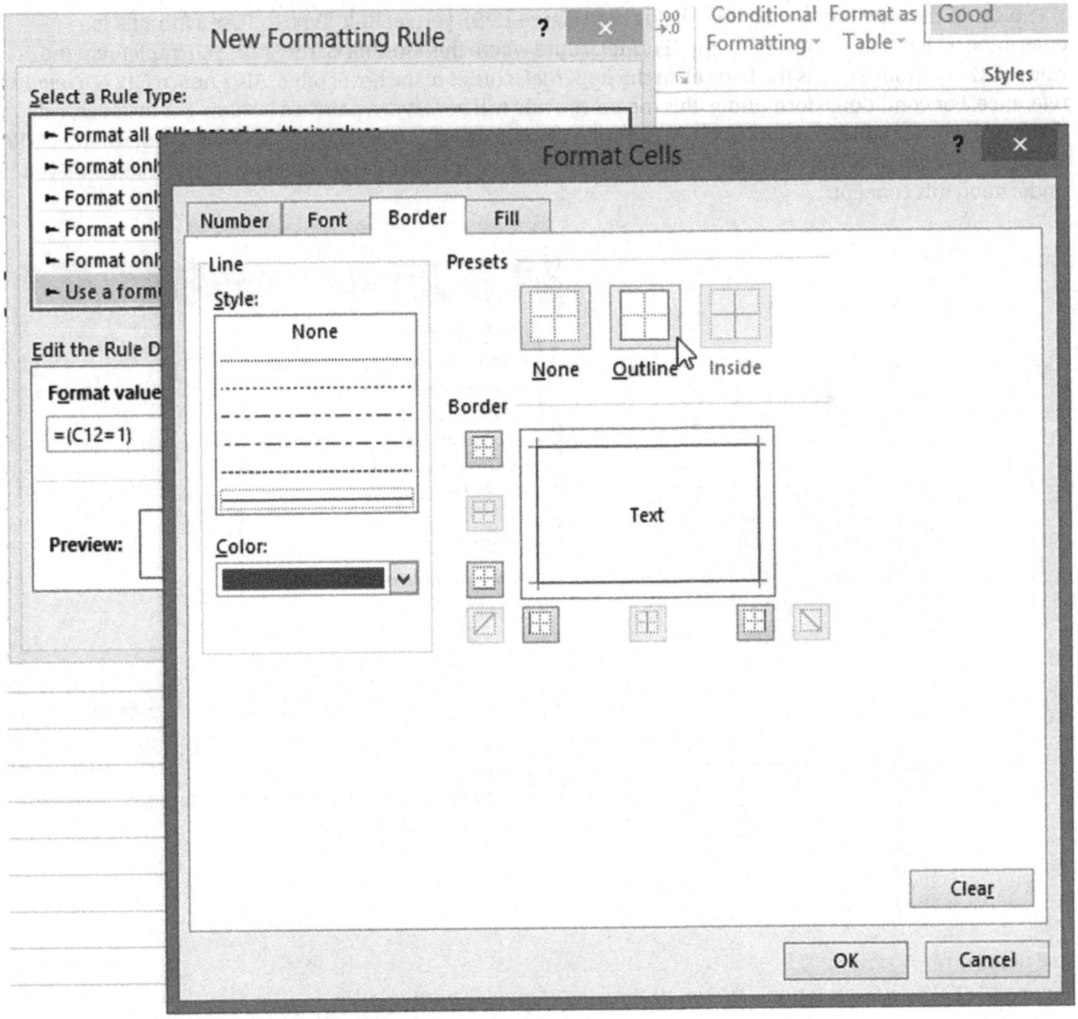

***Figure 15-10.** The Format Cells dialog box*

Figure 15-11 shows this mechanism in its final form.

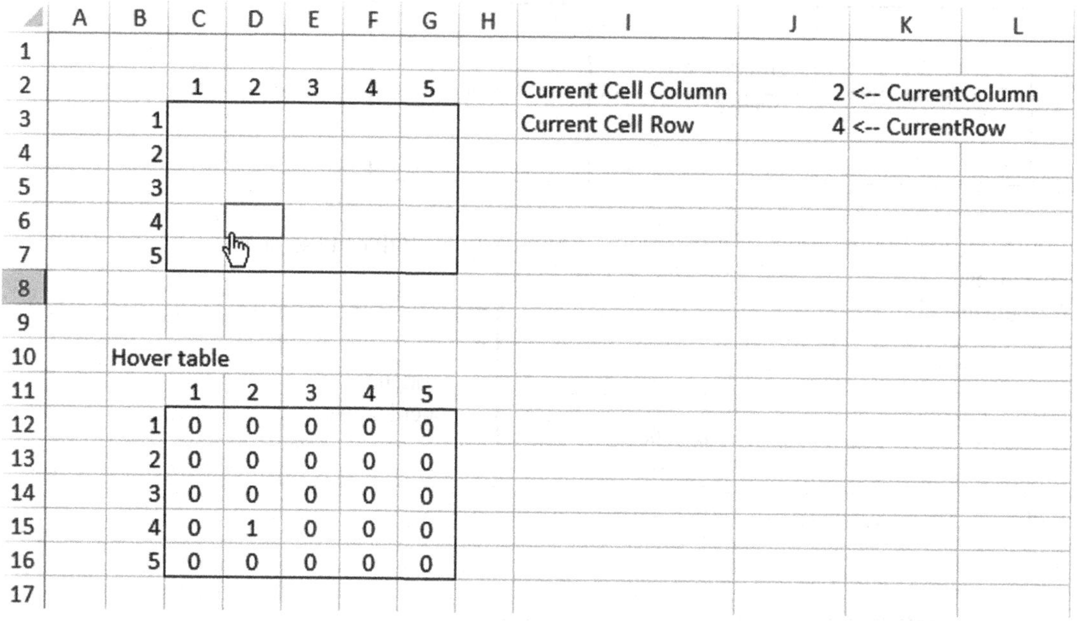

***Figure 15-11.** The red hover square follows the mouse location within the grid of rollovers*

The red square may seem like a simple implementation given all the work to create it, but there's actually a lot more available. You'll go through some even cooler uses of rollovers in the next few pages. But I wanted to present this dynamic to you at an abstract view. This simple implementation shows the basic setup of rollovers that drives the much more complex implementations.

Figure 15-12 shows a conceptual framework to understand everything you've done so far. When you abstract it to this level, its implementation makes sense. Using this framework, the rollovers become a reusable component. You can use this coordinate rollover scheme for many different types of problems you want to model. Not every implementation must follow this dynamic exactly, but it serves as a structure starting from which you can adapt and make changes. You'll be doing just that in the next section.

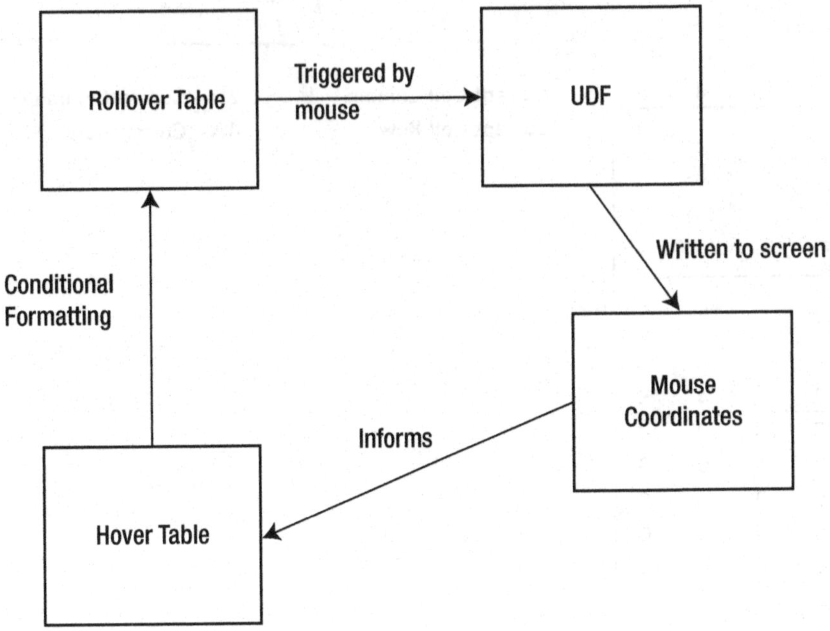

Figure 15-12. *A conceptual framework for rollovers*

Gantt Chart Rollovers

Let's go back to the Gantt chart. Open file `Chapter15GanttChart.xlsm` and ensure you're looking at the top of the spreadsheet. In this section, you'll investigate the implementation rollover in the Gantt chart. Most of the implementation draws directly from the previous section. I'll also discuss how to use rollovers to create that details-on-demand pop-up.

Rollover Implementation

In this section, I'll show you how the conceptual framework presented in the first section of this chapter has been easily implemented in the Gantt chart.

Let's start at the top of the Gantt chart. In Figure 15-13, I've clicked cell E8 to show you you're implementing rollovers.

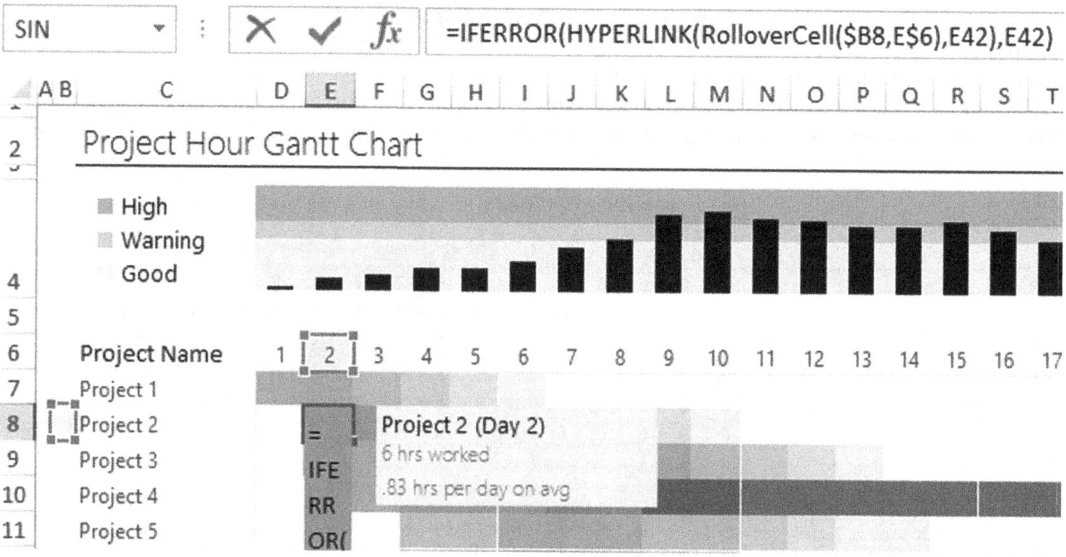

***Figure 15-13.** Notice the rollover formula follows what you investigated in the first half of this chapter*

The row of date headers serves the dual purpose of also letting you know the column index of where the column is located (cell E6). You'll notice B8 is also being referenced, but it looks empty. However, a column of coordinate numbers actually exists in column B (Figure 15-14). I've just set the font color to white to hide them. In Figure 15-14 I've temporarily made them the default color so you can see what they look like.

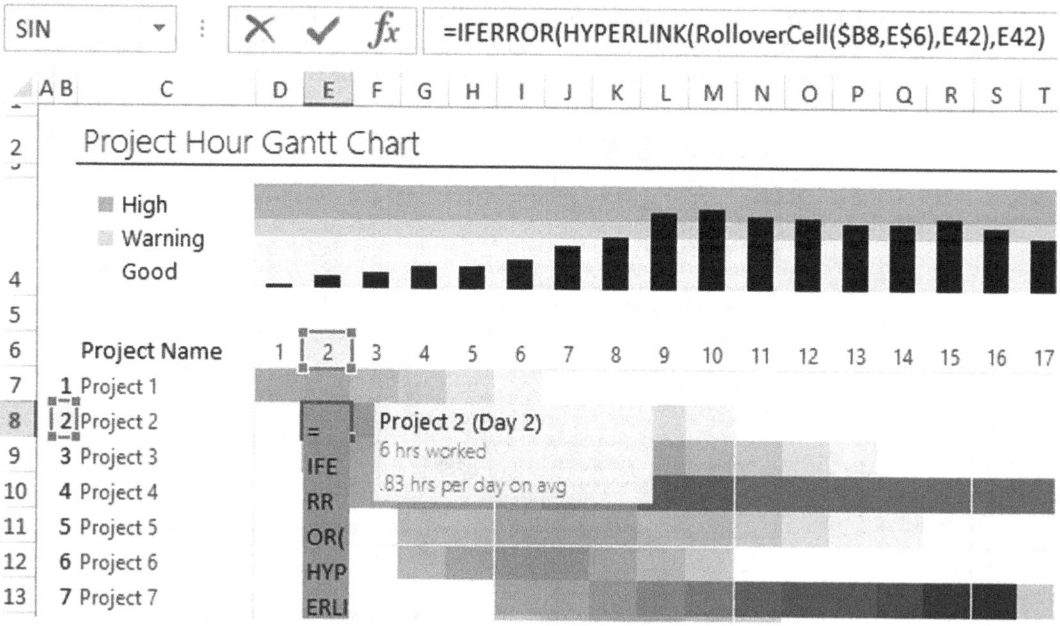

***Figure 15-14.** The row index numbers are temporarily set to black for the purpose of demonstrating to you they're there but just hidden*

Previously I discussed how information from the back end is presented in the Gantt chart. That information makes up the last two cell references of the hyperlink formula. They appear as E42 in Figure 15-14. For a refresher on how that works, take a look at "The Dashboard Worksheet Tab" in Chapter 13.

For now, let's scroll down to cell location D62. Notice in Figure 15-15 the Gantt chart implementation follows the same development pattern introduced in the first half of this chapter. Isn't it great when everything lines up?

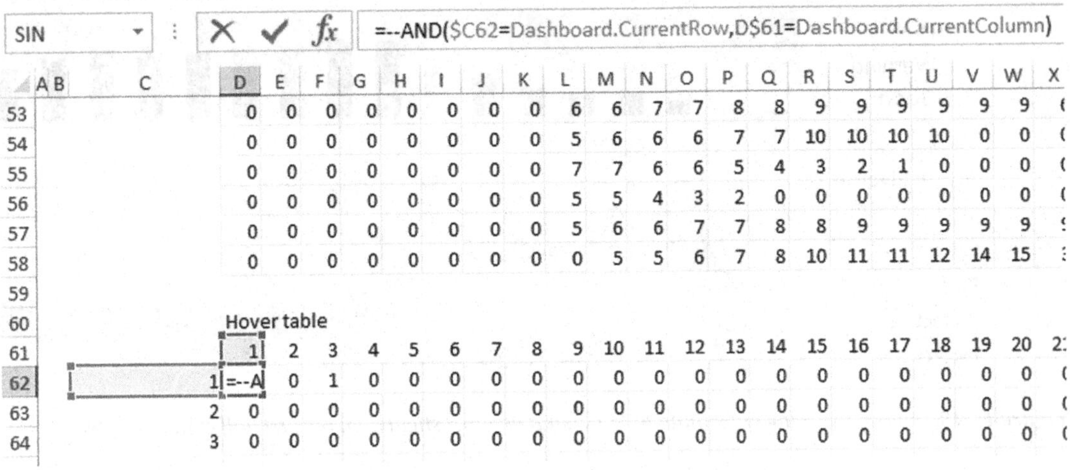

Figure 15-15. *The Rollover Method implementation follows the same development pattern that was introduced in the first half of this chapter*

The Gantt chart then uses the results from the hover table to highlight the selected cell. Figure 15-16 shows the conditional formatting rule applied to the Gantt chart. The beginning of the hover table is cell D62. Notice, again, that D62 is not an absolute reference. So, the conditional formatting rule applied to each cell in the range directly parallels with the cells in the hover table. When a cell in the corresponding hover table equals 1, the conditional formatting rule will highlight the cell on the Gantt chart.

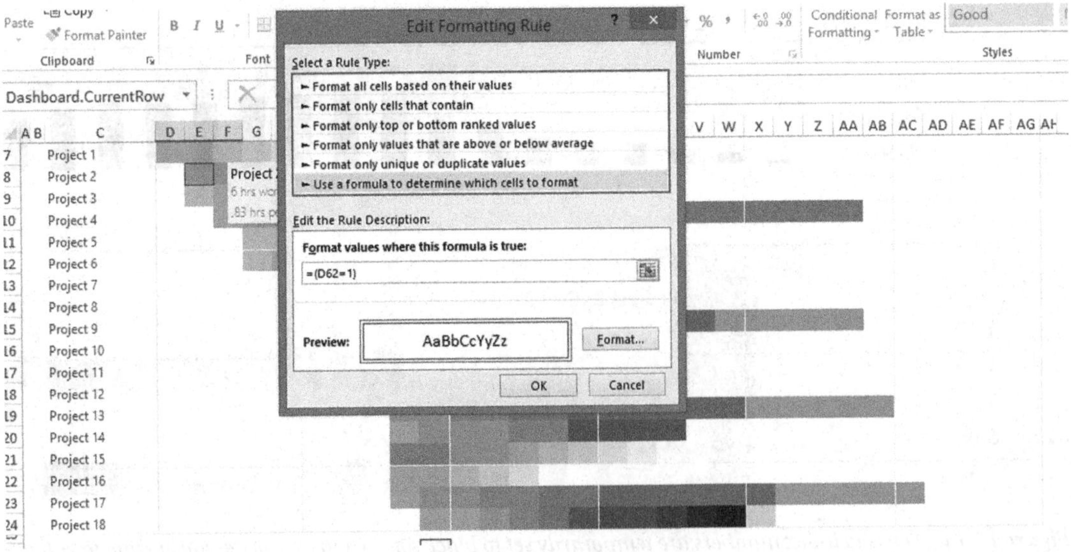

Figure 15-16. *Conditional formatting is used to highlight the cell currently hovered over by the mouse*

Now scroll to cell E36. Figure 15-16 shows the row and column values of the current cell location. Notice in Figure 15-17 the name of the cell is `Dashboard.CurrentRow`. This is where the UDF writes the current row location. Likewise, the cell underneath goes by the name `Dashboard.CurrentColumn` (not shown, but you can trust me). This is where the UDF writes the current column location.

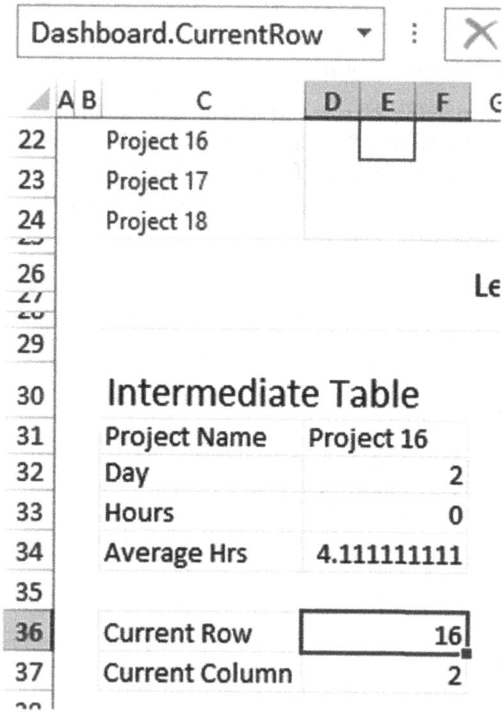

Figure 15-17. *The Rollover Method writes the current row and column location to cells Dashboard.CurrentRow and Dashboard.CurrentColumn. This is similar to the implementation from the first half of the chapter*

Now that I've shown you how the Rollover Method has been implemented in the Gantt chart, let's take a closer look at the pop-up mechanism. In the following subsections, I'll go through how to get the information you need for the pop-up, how to design it, and, finally, how to make it follow your mouse.

Getting the Information to Create the Details-on-Demand Pop-up

In this section, I'll discuss how to create the details-on-demand pop-up. In Figure 15-18 I've taken a snapshot of the pop-up.

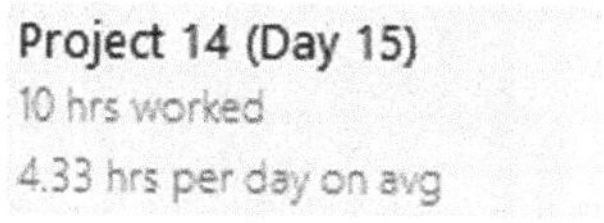

Figure 15-18. *A snapshot of the details-on-demand pop-up*

Notice you have several pieces of information you need to find out from the data based on the location of the mouse.

- The current project name (Project 14)
- The current day being hovered over
- The current value of hours worked
- The average for the entire day given by the location of the mouse

Luckily, you have the means to find this information by knowing the row and column index of the mouse cell location being hovered over. Figure 15-19 shows the intermediate table starting at C30 and going downward. To help understand what's going on, I've reproduced the formulas for each of these items to the right (the formulas won't appear in your file). Notice these all simply use the `Dashboard.CurrentRow` and `Dashboard.CurrentColumn` formulas defined in cells D36 and D37.

	C	D	E
29			
30	Intermediate Table		
31	Project Name	Project 18	=INDEX(Calculation!B4:B21,Dashboard.CurrentRow)
32	Day	13	=Dashboard.CurrentColumn
33	Hours	7	=INDEX(Calculation!C4:AF21,Dashboard.CurrentRow,Dashboard.CurrentColumn)
34	Average Hrs	4.333333333	=INDEX(Calculation!C23:AF23,Dashboard.CurrentColumn)
35			
36	Current Row	18	
37	Current Column	13	
38			

Figure 15-19. *The intermediate table with formulas shown*

Let's briefly go through each of them.

- ***Project name***: To find the project name of the currently selected project, you use the current row to find the correct name of the project in the calculations table (Figure 15-20).

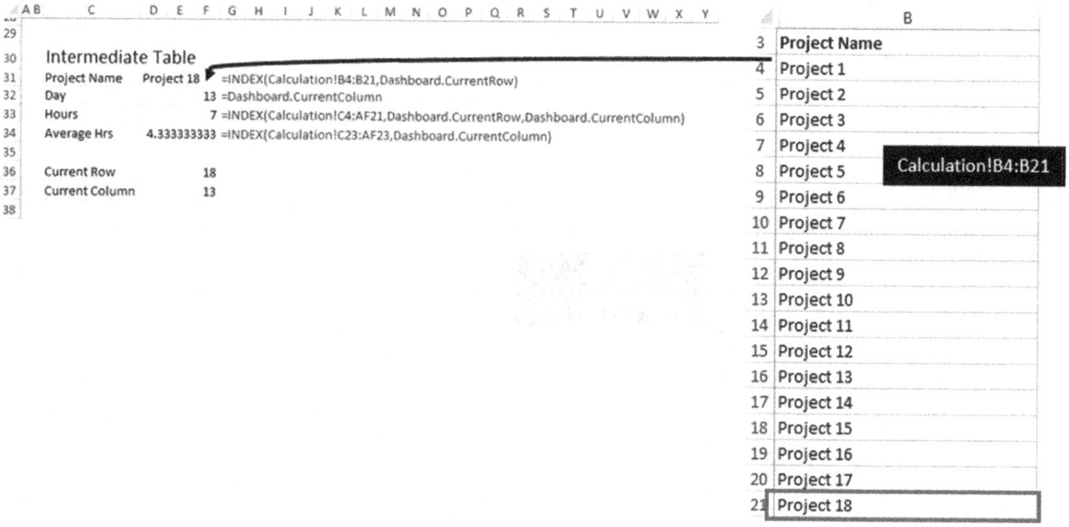

Figure 15-20. *The project name is found by looking up the current row in the list of project names on the Calculation worksheet tab*

- ***Date***: The current date is synonymous with the current column index being hovered over. As shown in Figures 15-19 and 15-20, you just reference `Dashboard.CurrentColumn`.
- ***Hours***: The hours are simply the raw data values from the data on the Calculation tab at the current row and column index. This is shown in Figure 15-21.

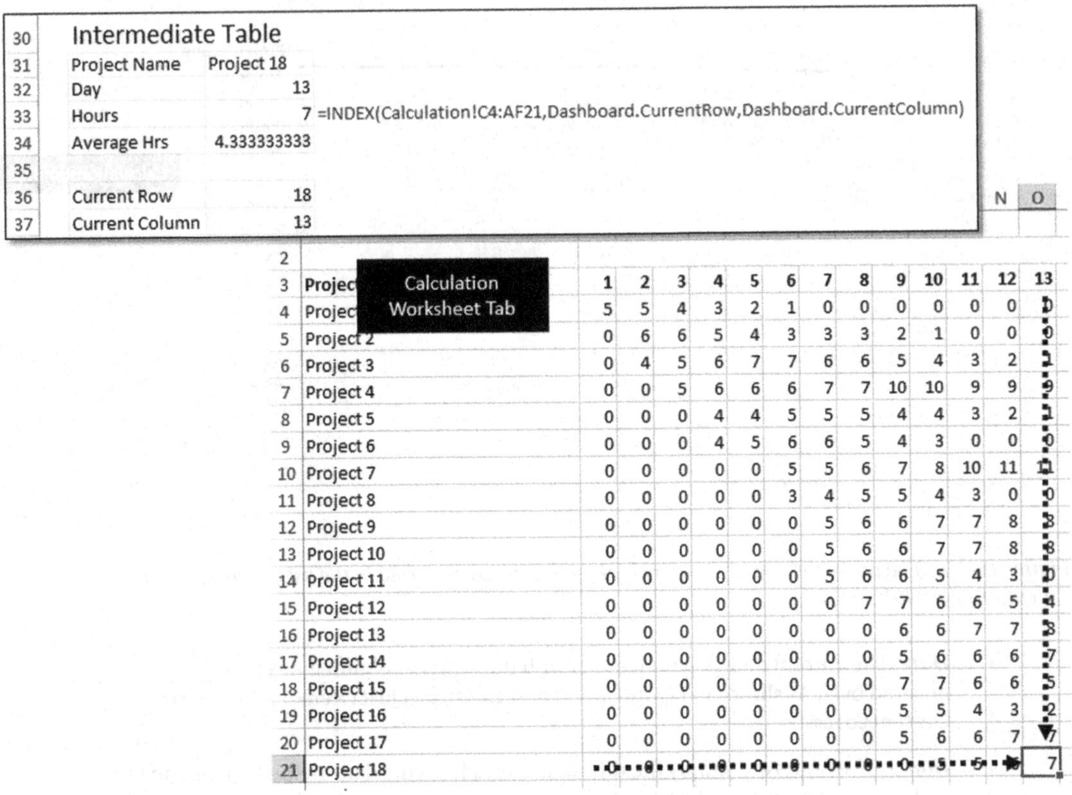

30	Intermediate Table		
31	Project Name	Project 18	
32	Day	13	
33	Hours	7	=INDEX(Calculation!C4:AF21,Dashboard.CurrentRow,Dashboard.CurrentColumn)
34	Average Hrs	4.333333333	
35			
36	Current Row	18	
37	Current Column	13	

2														
3	Projec	1	2	3	4	5	6	7	8	9	10	11	12	13
4	Projec	5	5	4	3	2	1	0	0	0	0	0	0	0
5	Project 2	0	6	6	5	4	3	3	3	2	1	0	0	0
6	Project 3	0	4	5	6	7	7	6	6	5	4	3	2	1
7	Project 4	0	0	5	6	6	6	7	7	10	10	9	9	9
8	Project 5	0	0	0	4	4	5	5	5	4	4	3	2	1
9	Project 6	0	0	0	4	5	6	6	5	4	3	0	0	0
10	Project 7	0	0	0	0	0	5	5	6	7	8	10	11	11
11	Project 8	0	0	0	0	0	3	4	5	5	4	3	0	0
12	Project 9	0	0	0	0	0	0	5	6	6	7	7	8	8
13	Project 10	0	0	0	0	0	0	5	6	6	7	7	8	8
14	Project 11	0	0	0	0	0	0	5	6	6	5	4	3	0
15	Project 12	0	0	0	0	0	0	0	7	7	6	6	5	4
16	Project 13	0	0	0	0	0	0	0	0	6	6	7	7	8
17	Project 14	0	0	0	0	0	0	0	0	5	6	6	6	7
18	Project 15	0	0	0	0	0	0	0	0	7	7	6	6	5
19	Project 16	0	0	0	0	0	0	0	0	5	5	4	3	2
20	Project 17	0	0	0	0	0	0	0	0	5	6	6	7	7
21	Project 18	0	0	0	0	0	0	0	0	0	5	5	6	7

Figure 15-21. *The hours are simply found by looking up the hours worked for a given date and project*

- ***Average hours for the given day***: Average hours for a given day are found by using the current data (the current column index) and looking up the average hours for a given date on the Calculation worksheet tab (see Figure 15-22).

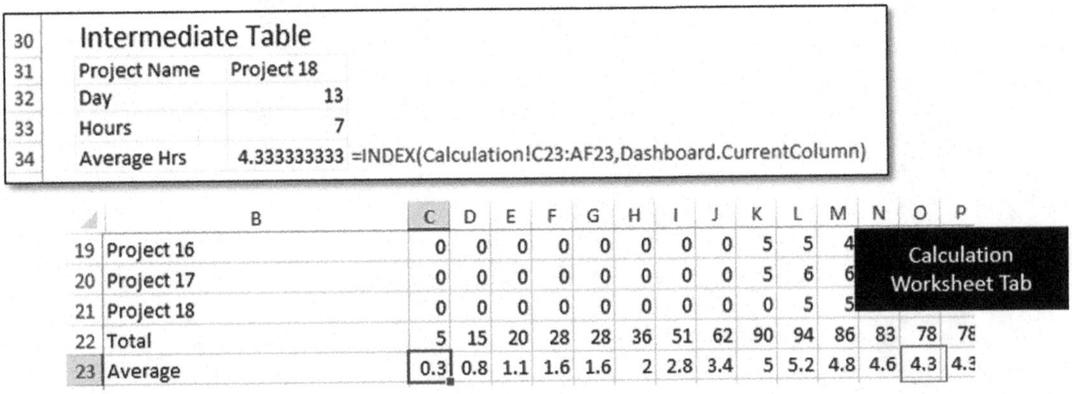

30	Intermediate Table		
31	Project Name	Project 18	
32	Day	13	
33	Hours	7	
34	Average Hrs	4.333333333	=INDEX(Calculation!C23:AF23,Dashboard.CurrentColumn)

	B	C	D	E	F	G	H	I	J	K	L	M	N	O	P
19	Project 16	0	0	0	0	0	0	0	0	5	5	4			
20	Project 17	0	0	0	0	0	0	0	0	5	6	6			
21	Project 18	0	0	0	0	0	0	0	0	0	5	5			
22	Total	5	15	20	28	28	36	51	62	90	94	86	83	78	78
23	Average	0.3	0.8	1.1	1.6	1.6	2	2.8	3.4	5	5.2	4.8	4.6	4.3	4.3

Figure 15-22. *The average hours are found by looking at the average hours calculation row on the Calculation worksheet tab*

Now that you have all the information you want to display, you need to design the pop-up.

Designing the Pop-up

If you've been following along with your worksheet open, you probably noticed there exists a formatted region in cells AI31:AI33. You can see it all the way over to the right in Figure 15-23. This is where you design the pop-up.

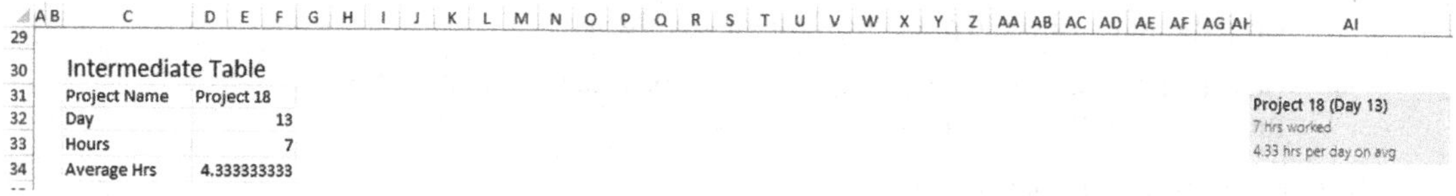

Figure 15-23. *The pop-up is designed on the spreadsheet. You can see it in cells AI31:AI34*

Let's take a closer look at the formulas for the pop-up (Figure 15-24). For the first line (cell AI31), I've simply set the cell to have a bold format. I've used the formula shown in AJ 31 to display the project name and current date highlight. For line AI32, I display the hours worked and add the text "hrs worked." In cell AI 33, I take the average hours returned for a given data and use the TEXT function to format it so that it displays the values out to the second decimal place only. I add the text "hrs per day on avg" afterward.

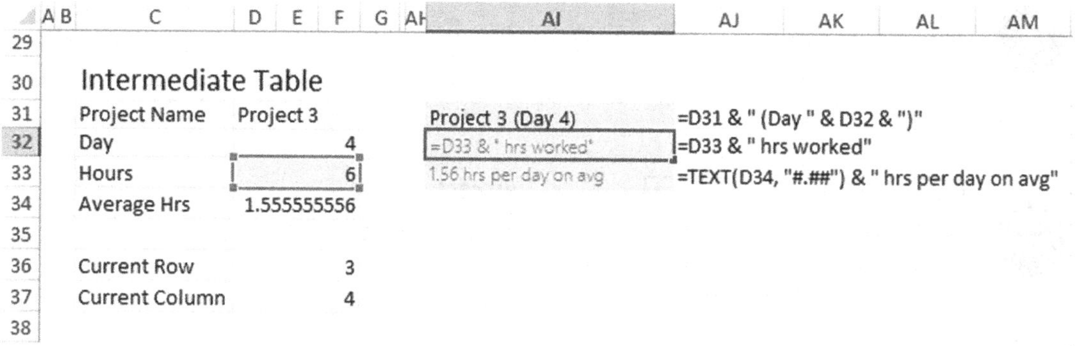

Figure 15-24. *The pop-up simply references the values from the intermediate table*

The background of the pop-up is simply a paint fill, and the border is a soft gray cell border. But you can design yours however you want. The design of the pop-up happens on the spreadsheet, so you are limited only by what Excel allows you to do to the cells.

So, I know what you're thinking: how do you get this pop-up designed on the spreadsheet to follow your mouse via the Rollover Method? I'll give you a hint on what's coming next: *say cheese!*

Making the Pop-up Follow Your Mouse

In this section, I'll talk about the last step in creating the details-on-demand pop-up. In the previous sections, I discussed how to grab the information and then how to design the pop-up. In this section, I'll show you how to create the final piece of the mechanism that will allow the pop-up to follow your mouse.

You're probably wondering how you get that information designed on the spreadsheet to follow the mouse. Well, ideally you remember the Camera tool from Chapter 5. (I always keep my camera handy!) You'll use the Camera tool to take a snapshot of the pop-up. Let's go through what you need to do.

1. Select the pop-up area.
2. Click the Camera tool.
3. Click the spreadsheet to paste the Camera tool shape.
4. Get rid of the hideous black border that appears by default (Format Context Ribbon Tab ➤ Picture Border ➤ No Outline).

Figure 15-25 shows how to do this visually.

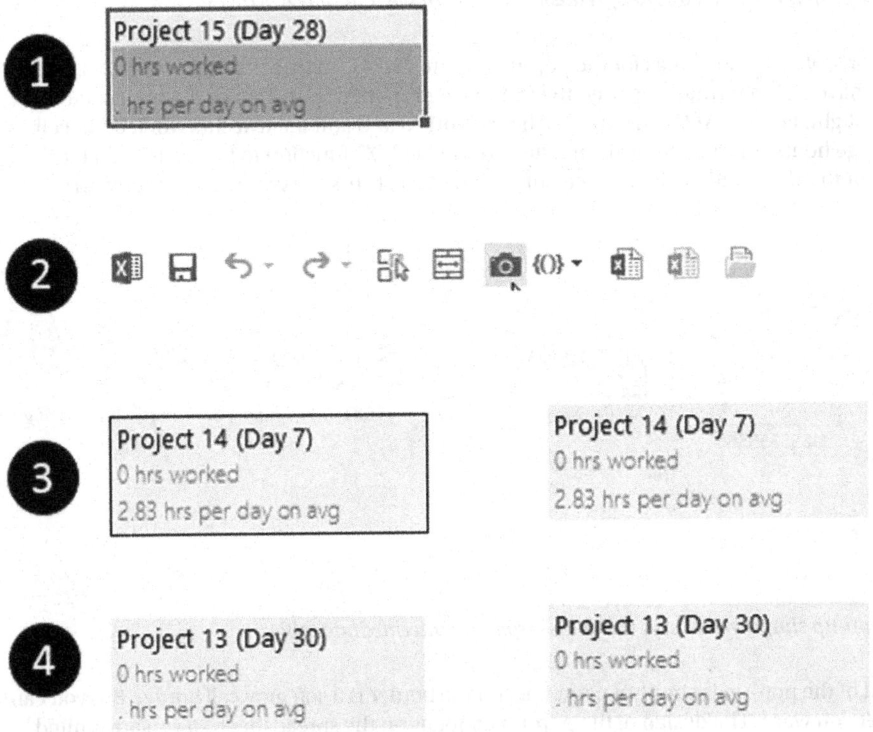

Figure 15-25. *A visual demonstration following the previous steps*

Remember the Camera tool provides a live connection to the spreadsheet. So, because the designed pop-up on the spreadsheet updates with new information, the picture created from the Camera tool will update as well.

Once you have a shape for the pop-up, you need to give it a name so you can reference it accurately in the VBA code. The easiest way to change a shape's name is to select the shape and change its name in the name box next to the formula bar. As you can see in Figure 15-26, I've given the new shape pop-up the simple name of Popup.

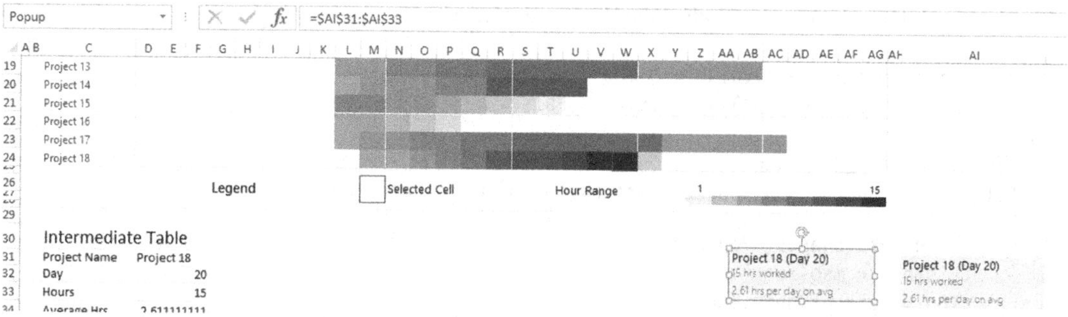

Figure 15-26. *I've named the pop-up shape Popup by replacing its default name in the name box next to the formula bar in the upper-left corner of the figure*

Next, let's turn to the rollover-based user-defined function to implement the code that will make the textbox follow the mouse. Take a look at that code in Listing 15-3.

Listing 15-3. The RolloverCell User-Defined Function

```
Public Function RolloverCell(row As Integer, column As Integer)
'Exit Function
    If Not [Dashboard.CurrentRow].Value = row Then _
        [Dashboard.CurrentRow].Value = row

    If Not [Dashboard.CurrentColumn].Value = column Then _
        [Dashboard.CurrentColumn].Value = column

    If [Dashboard.Hoursworked].Value = 0 Then
        Dashboard.Shapes("Popup").Visible = msoFalse
    Else
        Dim CurrentRange As Range
        Set CurrentRange = [Dashboard.GanttChartArea].Cells(row, column)

        With Dashboard.Shapes("Popup")
            .Visible = msoTrue
            .Top = CurrentRange.Top
            .Left = CurrentRange.Offset(0, 1).Left + CurrentRange.Offset(0, 1).Width / 2
        End With
    End If
End Function
```

Ideally this should look somewhat familiar to you by now. The row and column variables are passed into the function and then assigned to `Dashboard.CurrentRow` and `Dashboard.CurrentColumn`, respectively. I've added the additional check `If Not [Dashboard.CurrentRow].Value = row` and `If Not [Dashboard.CurrentColumn].Value = column` before the assignment of each so you don't write redundant information to the screen.

■ **Tip** Each screen write is a volatile action. In addition, as your mouse hovers over a cell, the rollover UDF will continuously fire. So, if the values aren't changing, there's no reason to continually write the same information and cause recalculation of both volatile functions and nonvolatile functions that might rely on this information.

Let's take a look at the second half of the UDF excerpted here:

```
If [Dashboard.Hoursworked].Value = 0 Then
    Dashboard.Shapes("Popup").Visible = msoFalse
Else
    Dim CurrentRange As Range
    Set CurrentRange = [Dashboard.GanttChartArea].Cells(row, column)

    With Dashboard.Shapes("Popup")
        .Visible = msoTrue
        .Top = CurrentRange.Top.
        .Left = CurrentRange.Offset(0, 1).Left + CurrentRange.Offset(0, 1).Width / 2
    End With
End If
```

The first condition, `If [Dashboard.Hoursworked].Value = 0 Then`, tests whether the mouse is hovering over a cell that has information for the given date. Remember there is white space on your Gantt chart where there is no information to report because either a project hasn't started or one has already ended. `Dashboard.Hoursworked` is captured on the spreadsheet (Figure 15-27) and reflects how many hours have been reportedly worked. If no hours are available to be reported, that means the given project for the given date has no data to report; therefore, it returns a zero. In instances where there's nothing to report, you don't want the pop-up to show. So, you set the pop-up to hidden using the following code: `Dashboard.Shapes("Popup").Visible = msoFalse` as is shown in the excerpted code.

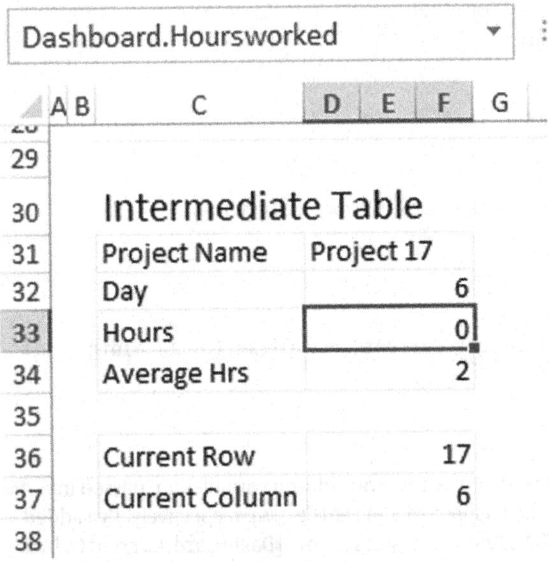

***Figure 15-27.** The Intermediate Table showing Dashboard.Hoursworked equals zero*

Now that you understand how to build rollover popups, you can use them in your own work. But before you begin implementing them, let's consider the following tips and concepts. Rollover popups can be complicated and these tips and concepts will help you avoid headaches along the way.

1. Use the Selection pane to deal with pop-ups.

   Once you've prevented the rollovers from executing, the pop-up might still be invisible. Perhaps you moved your mouse over a cell with zero hours worked, which would make the pop-up disappear. To make it reappear, go to the Find & Select drop-down on the Home tab and select Selection Pane (Figure 15-28).

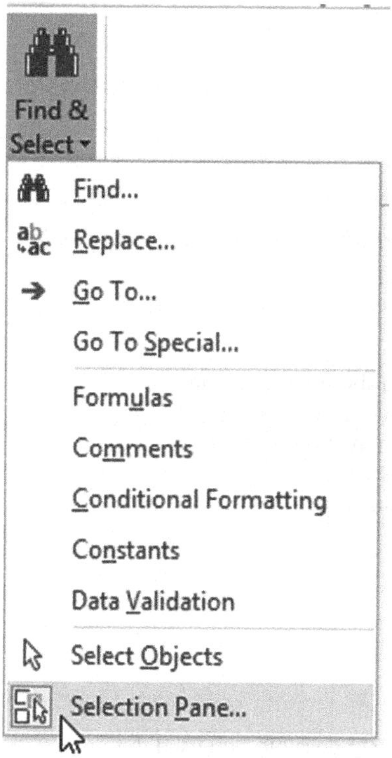

Figure 15-28. *You can find the option Selection Pane in the Find & Select drop-down on the Home ribbon tab*

In the Selection pane, find your pop-up and click the blank space next to Popup to make the eyeball icon reappear (Figure 15-29). This will signal that the item selected is now visible. You can also make it invisible by clicking the eyeball again.

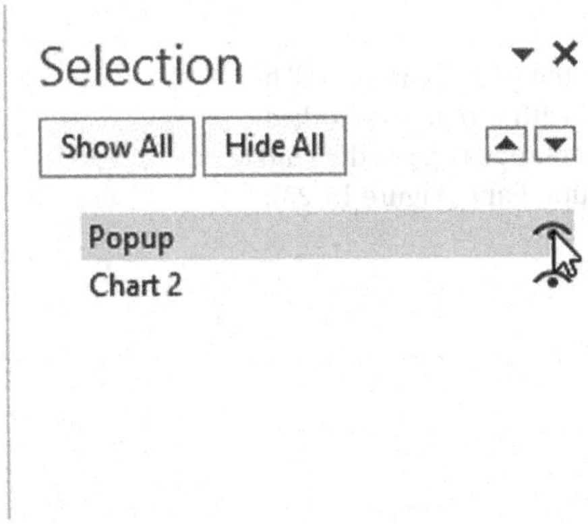

***Figure 15-29.** You can toggle the visibility of the pop-up (or any shape, really) by clicking the eyeball icon in the Selection pane*

2. Remember that you're exploiting a bug.

   If you follow the development patterns presented here, you should be just fine. That is, use the UDF to mostly write to the spreadsheet. Then, use other Excel features to go from there. Don't use the UDF to generate a new text box from scratch, design and fill it, and so on. This is asking a lot of Excel for a bug. So, keep as much as possible outside of the UDF so that you can ensure it works.

3. Save early and often.

   That's just smart.

The Last Word

In this chapter, you accomplished a lot with only a little code. To the extent possible, you used the spreadsheet to aid you in your development. You also used formulas and the Camera tool to ensure you are always dealing with live data. Finally, you saw how the Rollover Method can present you with details on demand. This mechanism represents a reusable component.

You must remember that thinking outside the cell is more than understanding the underlying mechanism. It's how you can reapply them to different scenarios. As a reusable component, the Rollover Method is extendable to many more situations than presented here. Once you understand its underlying mechanism, you can easily apply it elsewhere.

PART IV

From User Interface to Presentation

CHAPTER 16

Working with Form Controls

When introducing controls, I like to use my own technical definition. Specifically, form controls are the *whiz bangs, doodads, whatchamacallits,* and *thingamajigs* that give your spreadsheet enhanced interactivity. You may know them by their street names: check boxes, scroll bars, labels, etc. Figure 16-1 shows a group of controls lounging about in their natural habitat, the Excel spreadsheet.

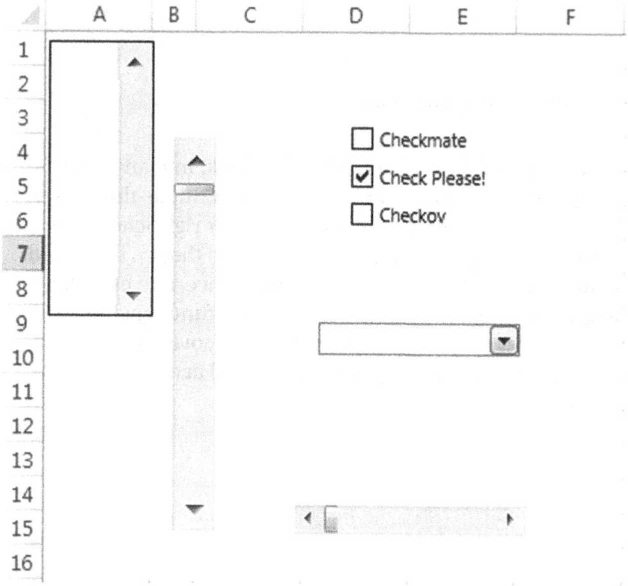

Figure 16-1. *Examples of controls on a spreadsheet*

Welcome to the Control Room

Excel contains two types of controls you can use on your spreadsheets. The first are form controls, and they are the subject of this chapter. The second are ActiveX controls, which we won't deal with in this book. There are significant differences between the two types of controls; however, they're both located in the same Insert box button, in the Controls group on the Developer tab. One important difference worth noting is that form controls are always on top, ActiveX controls are always on the bottom (see Figure 16-2).

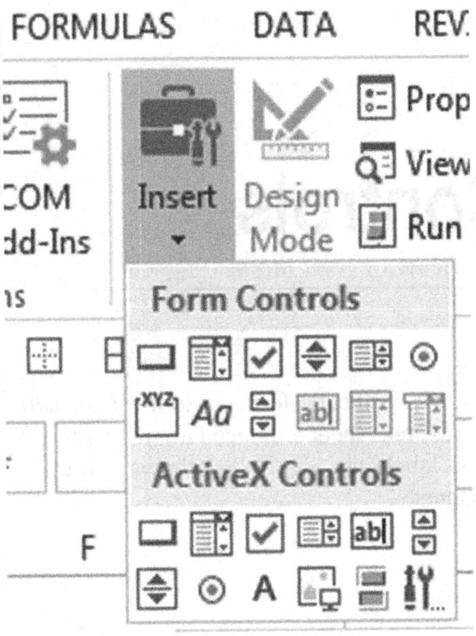

Figure 16-2. *The dropdown menu showing form controls and ActiveX controls*

Let's take a moment to discuss why ActiveX won't make an appearance in this book. In many ways, form controls are leaner, more lightweight versions of their ActiveX counterparts. For example, the ActiveX button can handle several different types of click events. It can test if you double-click or right-click, or it can fire an event the moment your mouse button is pressed down but before it's released. In theory, the added functionality may feel like a boon of capabilities has been dumped on your lap. In practice, and especially in this author's experience, rarely does your spreadsheet require that level of advanced functionality. In addition, ActiveX controls carry some baggage to your memory usage and file size; moreover, they can sometimes act unpredictably on a spreadsheet. Figure 16-3 shows the Slider Bar control acting up by appearing unexpectedly in the corner of the screen.

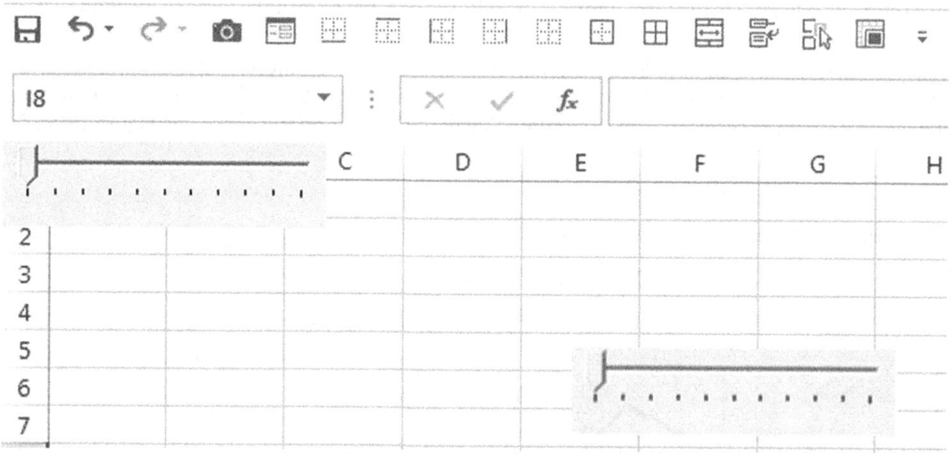

***Figure 16-3.** A very common ActiveX issue: the Slider ActiveX control appears in both the upper-right side of the sheet and its initial location on the spreadsheet*

Form controls, on the other hand, are much more lightweight. However, they are also much more limited in what they can do, at least compared to their ActiveX cousins. And, unlike ActiveX controls, form controls can do a lot without any VBA. In fact, this is one of the reasons I love form controls. Following the ideas presented in Chapter 6, if you don't need to use VBA, you shouldn't. Below, I begin with the fundamentals of form controls and present a few examples that will serve as reusable components continuing throughout the book.

Form Control Fundamentals

Think of form controls as simply an extension of the formulas you learned how to use in previous chapters. Those formulas relied strongly on the spreadsheet for the storage and manipulation of values. Figure 16-4 shows an interactive legend that lets the user check "on" and "off" for which series they want to view.

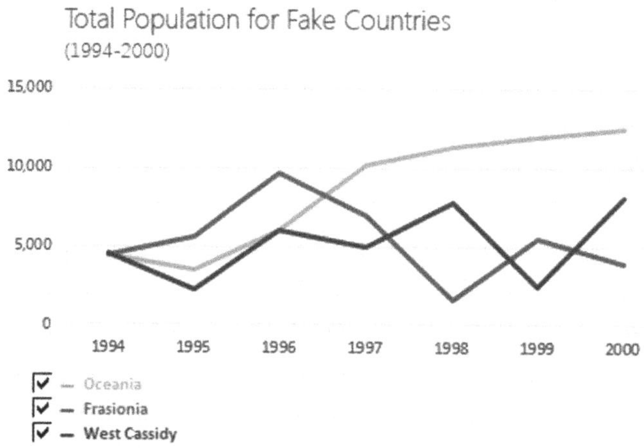

***Figure 16-4.** An interactive legend using the form control CheckBox*

Behind this interactive legend is the form control CheckBox. The CheckBox links to a cell location that either results in a TRUE or FALSE depending on whether the check box is selected or not. (TRUE = selected; FALSE = not selected.) Since TRUE and FALSE are equal to 1 and 0, you can use these response values in a formula to change the data behind the chart. When the check box is deselected, you do some work behind the scenes to change the number the series data to something that won't appear on the chart (see Figure 16-5).

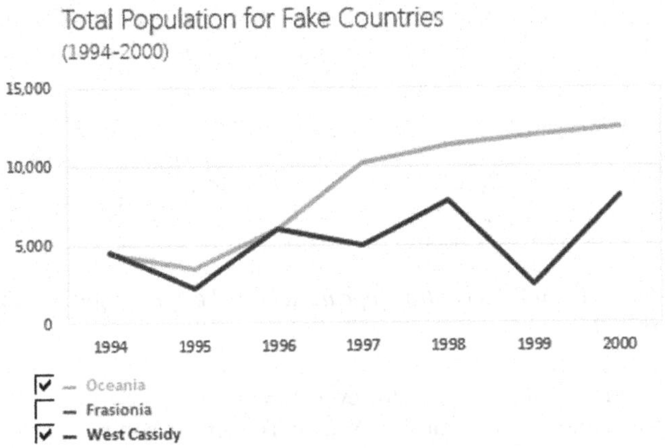

Figure 16-5. *When the check box is deselected, the line disappears from the chart*

I'll talk more about how to do something like this later in the chapter in the "The Dynamic Legend section".

As you can see from Figure 16-6, there are a total of ten form controls to choose from. Three of those form controls are grayed out. Those controls will always be grayed out for insertion into the spreadsheet. In fact, the only time they are ever available is for Excel 4.0 Macros, an older technology that Microsoft has deprecated in favor of UserForms and ActiveX controls. Officially, Excel 4.0 Macros are no longer supported so I won't spend any time on them. Tables 16-1 list all the form controls to insert.

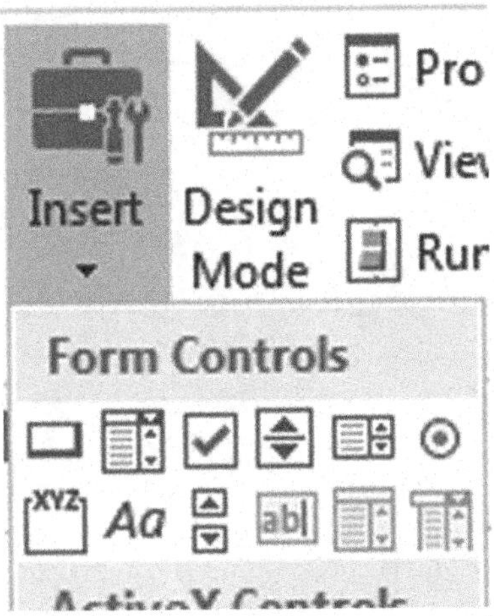

Figure 16-6. *The Form Controls dropdown showing controls that are available to insert onto the spreadsheet*

Table 16-1. *Form Control Descriptions*

Name	Icon	Description
Button		Button inserts a gray button onto your spreadsheet. You can assign a macro to be executed when the button is clicked.
ComboBox		The ComboBox is similar to the data validation dropdown you can do in a cell. You can supply the ComboBox a list of data from your spreadsheet. The ComboBox will create a dropdown from which to choose a selected item from that list.
CheckBox		The CheckBox inserts a box onto your spreadsheet that you can toggle to be checked or unchecked. You can link a CheckBox to a cell to have it display TRUE or FALSE based on whether it's checked or not.
Spinner		The Spinner allows you to insert Up and Down paddles on your spreadsheet. You can link the Spinner to a cell such that when you press up, the cell value increases, and when you press down, the cell value decreases.
ListBox		A ListBox is similar to a ComboBox. However, instead of a dropdown, the ListBox shows a larger list of items that users can scroll through.
Option Button		The Option Button is similar to the CheckBox. However, groups of Option Buttons are mutually exclusive. That means only one Option Button can be selected at a time, while no such constraints exist on Checkboxes. Similar to Checkboxes, you can link Option Buttons directly to a cell.
GroupBox		A GroupBox has no real interactivity but can surround other controls to create delineation and flow.
Label	*Aa*	A Label is a simple textbox that can be placed anywhere on a sheet. Labels are a bit limited compared to Excel's native text boxes.
Scroll Bar		The Scroll Bar is similar to the Spinner except the Scroll Bar has an area in the middle in which you can drag the value up or down. But similar to the Spinner, you can link the Scroll Bar to a cell and use the up and down (and drag) paddles to change the cell's value.

Next, we're going to go through my favorite controls. I call them my favorite because of the entire bunch, I believe they're the most useful. After we go through my favorites, we'll go through my least favorites—the ones I believe you should avoid in favor of better alternatives available.

The ComboBox Control

The ComboBox control is a useful mechanism that essentially mimics the behavior of a data validation dropdown list. But there is a difference between the two that is worth noting. Figure 16-7 shows a data validation both when a selection is being made (that is, the cell is active) and when no selection is being made.

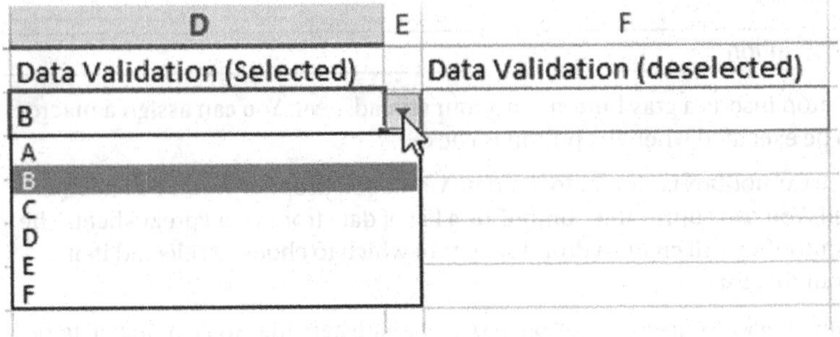

Figure 16-7. *On the left, the validation list dropdown is expanded. On the right, the cell has been deselected*

Now compare the aesthetics of the data validation dropdown in Figure 16-7 to the form control ComboBox list in Figure 16-8.

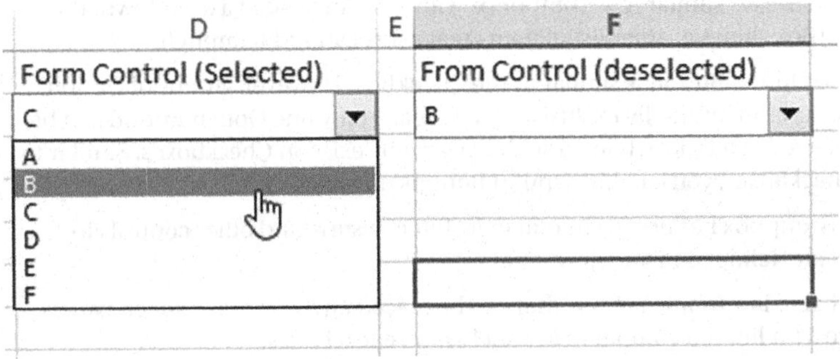

Figure 16-8. *On the left, the form control dropdown is expanded. On the right, the form control has been deseltected*

Notice the different aesthetics between the two "dropdown" lists. Generally, validation lists are better when you have a column of cells and each cell contains a dropdown, since the dropdown arrow won't appear in every cell, making for a clear appearance.

To view any control's properties, select the control and press the Properties button in the Controls group on the Developer tab shown in Figure 16-9—or, right-click a control, select Format Control, and select the Control tab.

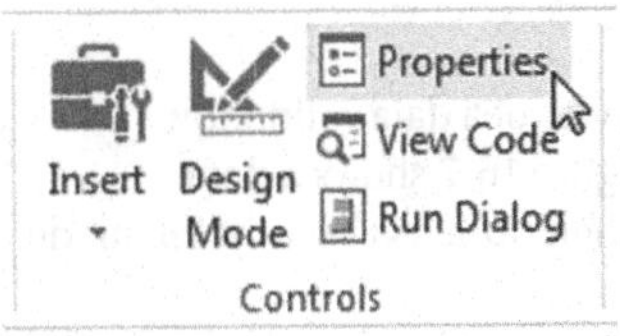

Figure 16-9. *The Properties Button in the Controls group on the Developer tab*

Figure 16-10 shows the Format Control dialog box for the ComboBox control. In this dialog box, you can change various aspects of the form control from the Control tab.

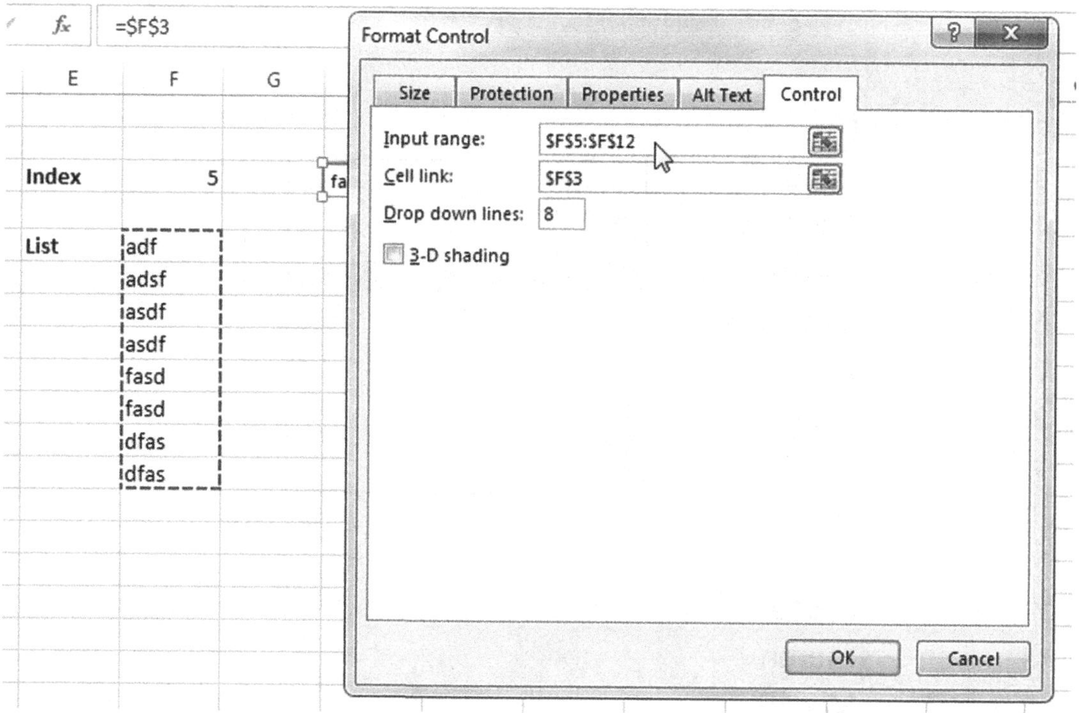

Figure 16-10. *The Format Control properties dialog box*

Note that you have two fields you can connect to the spreadsheet. The Input Range field allows you to select a desired range to fill the dropdown. The Cell link field allows you to specify a cell to display the index of the selected item.

The ListBox Control

The ListBox control is similar to the ComboBox control in that it also uses the Input range and Cell link fields. However, I believe you can better employ several mechanisms incorporated in the ListBox control, including creating a scrollable list (see Figure 16-11). So I personally don't prefer using these fields with the ListBox control.

***Figure 16-11.** The ListBox control contains a scrollable list of elements pulled from the spreadsheet*

One reason I prefer the ListBox control to the ComboBox is because I want to be able to see the data all at once. Moreover, as you'll see when you use the ComboBox, you can make the size of the control however large you want. But no matter how big that dropdown arrow becomes, the control's font and selection list underneath will always stay the same. Figure 16-12 shows a particular egregious example. Rather than fooling the viewer with these strange aesthetics, you're better off sticking to ListBox.

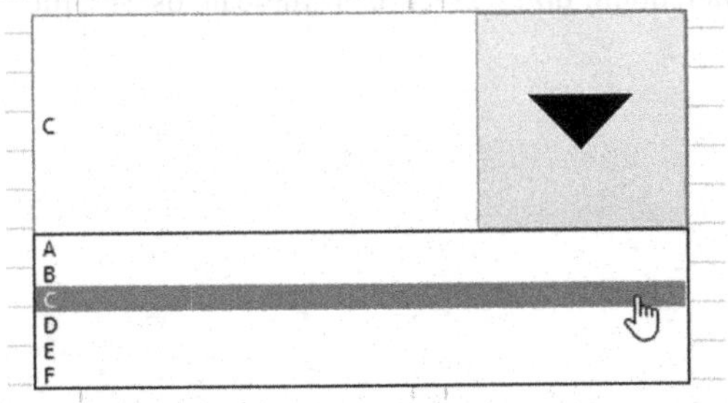

***Figure 16-12.** The combo box is sized much larger than it ever should be*

The Scroll Bar Control

The Scroll Bar is amazing and probably my favorite form control. It's simple but powerful. The basic idea is that you can link the scroll bar's value to any available cell on a spreadsheet. I've done just this in Figure 16-13. As the scroll paddle (that's the gray bar between the upper and lower paddles) increases, so does the value in C2. Similarly, as it decreases, the value in C2 decreases.

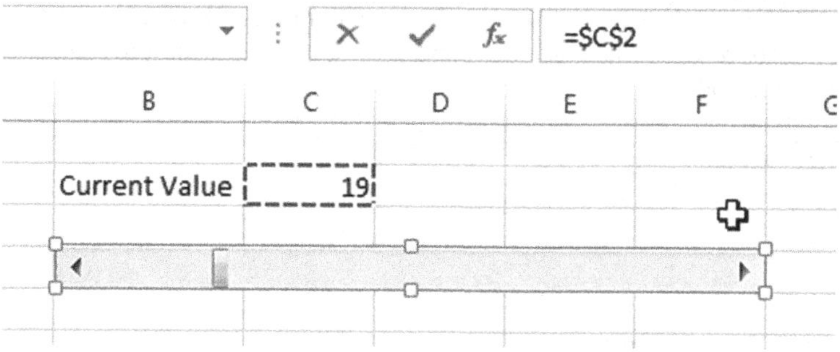

Figure 16-13. *A form control Scroll Bar linked to the cell C2*

The form control scroll bar contains some other great properties, as shown in Figure 16-14.

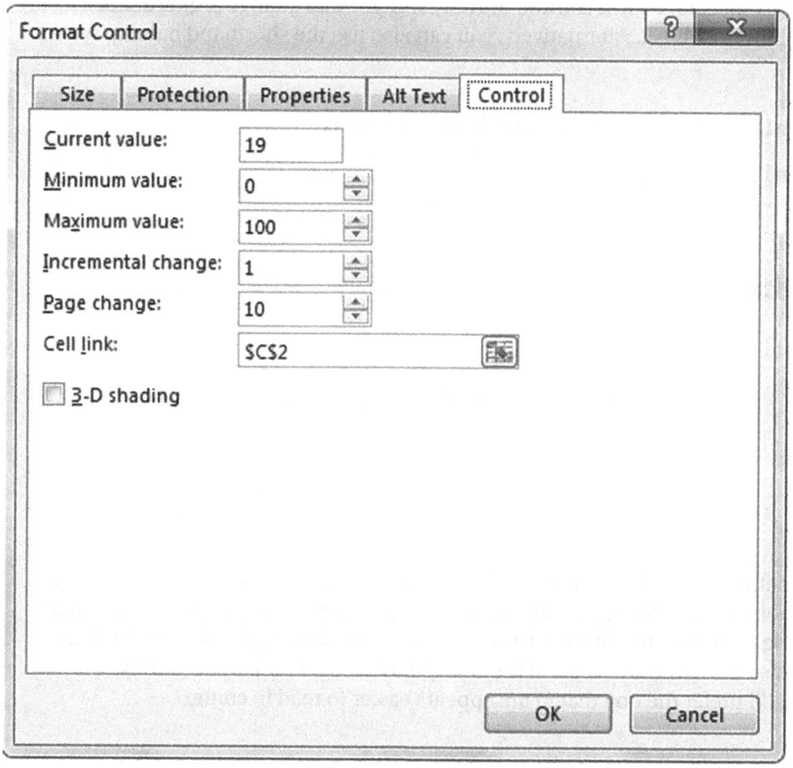

Figure 16-14. *The Format Control dialog box for the Scroll Bar*

Note that the Cell link field refers to same location in the formula bar in Figure 16-13. In Figure 16-14, you can see that the form control Scroll Bar comes with many more field properties than the ComboBox and ListBox controls. You can use the Minimum Value and Maximum Value fields to set the upper and lower bounds of the scroll bar. Indeed, you'll be doing just that in later chapters of this book. You can also use the Incremental Change field to set how much the value increases or decreases when you press the scroll bar's paddle. Finally, the Page change field refers to how much of an increase or decrease occurs when you click into the scroll bar itself and not on a upper or lower paddle.

Note that only one of the text fields in the Format Control dialog box (see Figure 16-14) can directly tie to a cell–the Cell link. The other fields shown in Figure 16-14 must be set either manually by a human (through the Format Control dialog box) or programmatically with code. Listing 16-1 shows how to change the scroll bar's Min and Max fields through code.

Listing 16-1. The SetScrollBarLimits Procedure

```
Public Sub SetScrollBarLimits()
    Const MAX_VAL = 20
    Const MIN_VAL = 3

    With Me.Shapes("Scroll Bar 1").ControlFormat
        .Min = MIN_VAL
        .Max = MAX_VAL
    End With
End Sub
```

Notice if you use the shape object on a form control, the only way you can change properties of a form control is through the `ControlFormat` object. Alternatively, you can also use the shorthand naming syntax shown in Listing 16-2.

Listing 16-2. The SetScrollBarLimits Procedure Using the Shorthand Syntax

```
Public Sub SetScrollbarLimits()

    Const MAX_VAL = 20
    Const MIN_VAL = 3
    Dim scrollbr1 As ScrollBar

    Set scrollbr1 = [Scroll Bar 1]

    With scrollbr1
        .Min = MIN_VAL
        .Max = MAX_VAL
    End With
End Sub
```

Often, I'll use the latter method as it is more easily read and intuitively understood. However, you'll notice when you type the As portion of creating your form control object, `Scroll Bar` won't appear on the list. This can become confusing as usually figuring out the correct object requires guessing at the name (e.g. typing "label," "checkbox," and "scroll bar" to see if they take). So I present both options for you to decide. Throughout the book, I'll prefer the one that to me appears easier to read in context.

The Spinner Control

The Spinner control is fairly similar to the form control Scroll Bar sans the draggable paddle and scroll region between the paddles (see Figure 16-15).

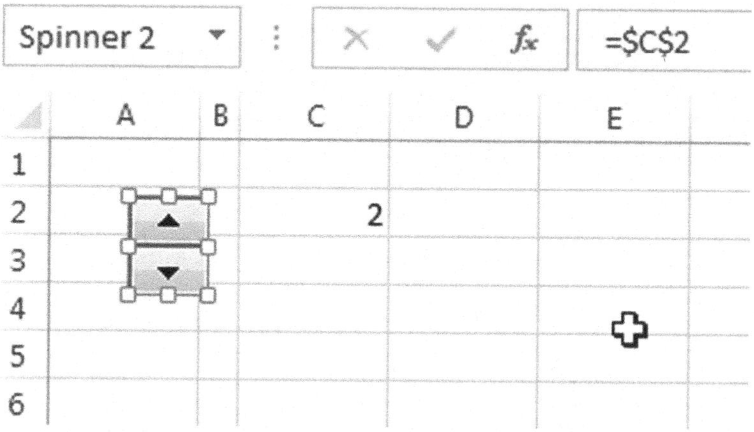

Figure 16-15. *An example Spinner control on a spreadsheet*

The Spinner control is a useful replacement for a scroll bar in a pinch. However, while the scroll bar can appear both horizontally and vertically on a sheet (see Figure 16-1), the spinner can only appear vertically, as shown in Figure 16-15. You can of course make the spinner larger (and wider, if you'd like), but those up and down paddles will always point in the same direction.

The CheckBox Control

The CheckBox control appears in the first example and it's incredibly versatile. Like the Scroll Bar, the CheckBox control links to cell whose value you can use. Unlike the Scroll Bar, the CheckBox can only take on one of three values (see Figure 16-16). The first two values you should know by heart: TRUE and FALSE. Respectively, they generate a Checked or Unchecked value in the CheckBox.

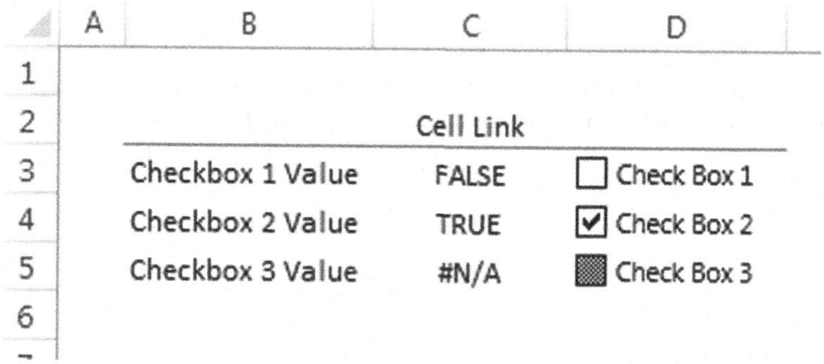

Figure 16-16. *A demonstration of the three states possible with a CheckBox*

However, check boxes can also take on a fuzzy-gray status called a "mixed" state. The mixed state cannot be set directly by toggling a CheckBox, at least not without some VBA. You can set the mixed state manually by using the =NA() formula in the CheckBox's cell link or by going into its properties dialog box and selecting the Mixed option (see Figure 16-17). You won't use the mixed state in this book, so for now let's focus on the TRUE and FALSE dynamic of the CheckBox.

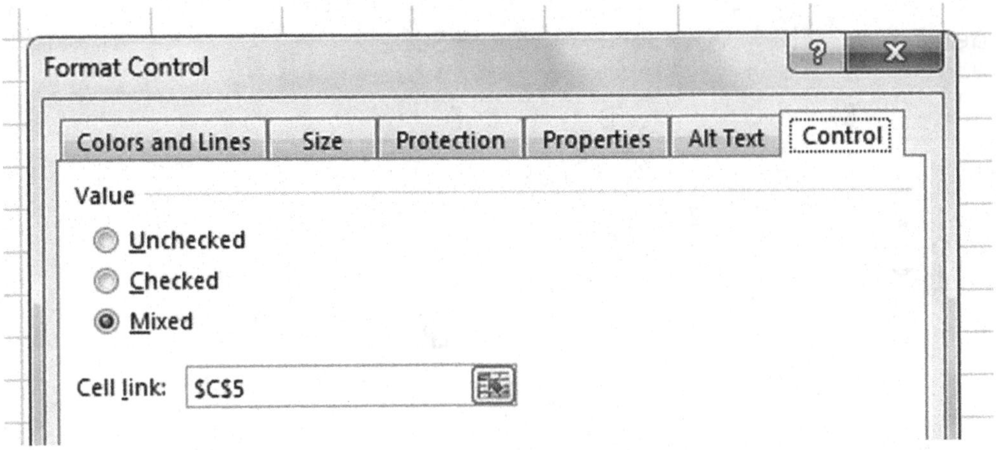

***Figure 16-17.** The Format Control dialog box for a CheckBox*

The Least Favorites: Button, Label, Option Button, and GroupBox Controls

Four controls are left:

- Button
- Label
- Option Button
- GroupBox

In this section I'll provide a little information on why I don't care much for these form controls.

The Button Control

I don't believe you should use the Button control because there are better alternatives. Let's start by taking a look at the Button control in Figure 16-18. There's not much you can do with the dated grayish aesthetic.

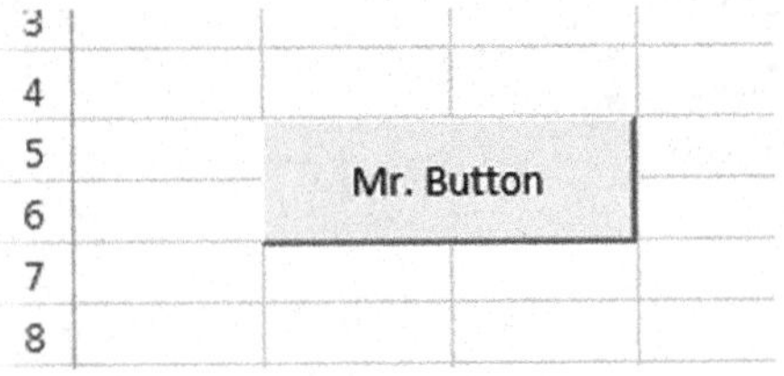

***Figure 16-18.** A form control Button*

An alternative I would suggest is to use an autoshape text box instead. You can still add interactivity to the shape the same way you would with a form control Button by assigning a macro to the shape. The text box will give you much more flexibility in terms of changing its look. In addition, there is no inherent advantage to using the form control Button that is lost when going with an Excel shape.

The Label Control

The Label control is also similarly restrictive. The font size, style, and color of a label cannot be edited directly. Notice in Figure 16-19 that the format buttons have been disabled when the label is selected.

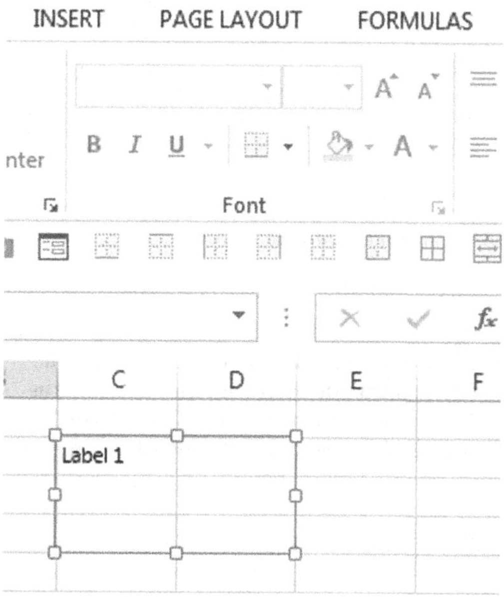

Figure 16-19. *A Label control placed on a spreadsheet*

As a matter of fact, the only way to change a label's style is to link it to a cell with the font styles already set. Take a look at Figure 16-20 to see what I mean. In cell A2, I wrote some text and then set the font color and style in the cell itself. After that, I linked the label directly to the cell. In fact, this is a workaround I discovered accidently; officially, labels aren't supposed to let you change their style. But in any event, a textbox shape does all of this without the hassle.

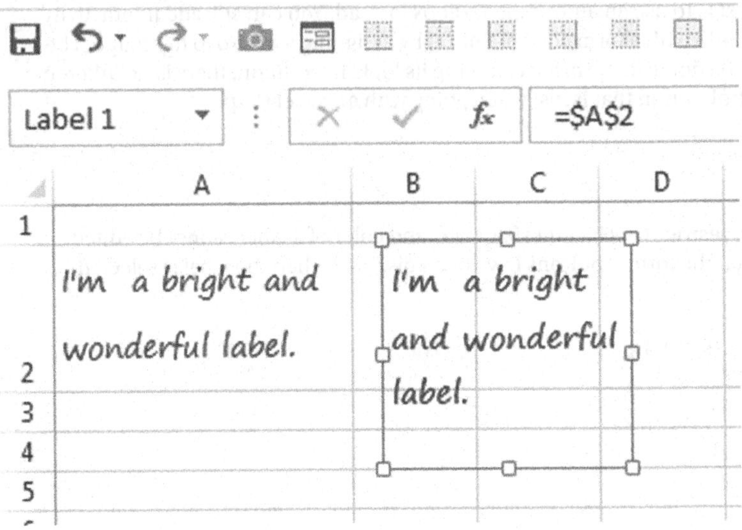

Figure 16-20. Even bright and wonderful labels can't overcome certain limitations

The Option Button Control

Option Button controls are similar to check boxes except that they allow for only one selection. In general, I find they are more trouble than they are worth. ComboBox form controls do essentially the same thing as Option Buttons and take up less screen real estate (see Figure 16-21). For situations where I would like the user to toggle between different states, I like to use text boxes instead (see Figure 16-22). The effect is much cleaner and more visually appealing.

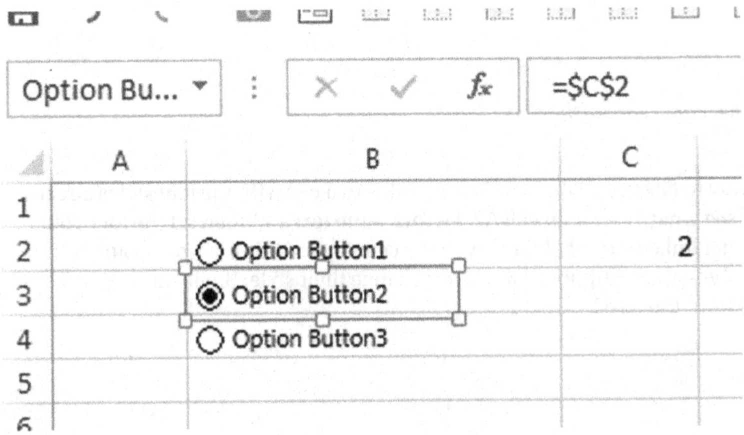

Figure 16-21. Option butttons laid out and linked to cell C2

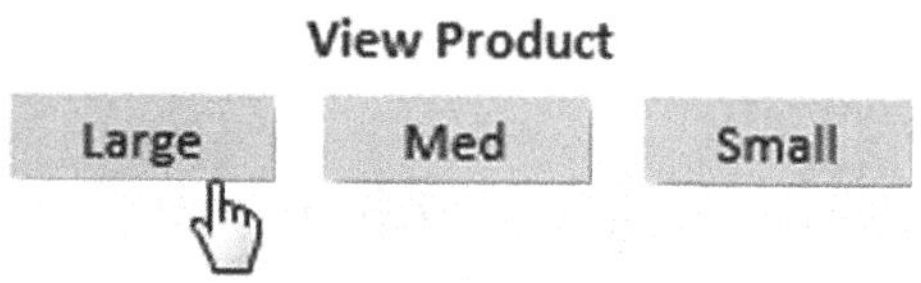

Figure 16-22. *My prefered method for toggling between options*

Figure 16-22 simply shows a group of textboxes with some extra desired formatting. When a user clicks on a textbox, a macro is called to color the textbox a reddish color and the rest a greenish color.

The GroupBox Control

Finally, form GroupBoxes, the last control left undiscussed, are not really useful for anything except grouping components together. They exist purely for aesthetic value. They're not ugly by any stretch, but I'd rather use cell formatting to create a border, especially because it delivers far more options. With the form control GroupBox you only get two options: 3D border or no 3D border. For the sake of an example, Figure 16-23 shows a GroupBox form control over the buttons from Figure 16-22.

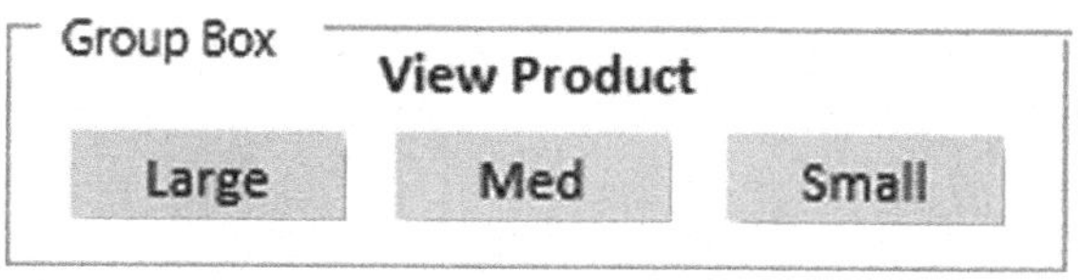

Figure 16-23. *The group box surrounds buttons with the group box's border*

Now that you know all the form controls, you'll put the useful ones to good use in a few examples, starting with the Scroll Bar.

Creating Scrollable Tables

Scrollable tables are a great form of Excel form controls. They're easy to implement and often require no VBA, assuming what you want to display isn't complicated (and usually it isn't). At the heart of these tables is the venerable scroll bar. Using the `INDEX` function and the scroll bar you can create a scrollable region from a larger table of values.

In this example, you will create a scrollable table that pulls data from a larger spreadsheet. The scrollable table will allow you to scroll through a small subset of the data a time. Figure 16-24 shows what the final product will look like. Take a look at `Chapter16ScrollableTable.xlsx` to grab the data and follow along.

Tornadoes by Year and Month

(1950-1994)

Year	Total	Jan	Feb	Mar	Apr	May	June	July	Aug	Sept	Oct	Nov	Dec
1954	550	2	17	62	113	101	107	45	49	21	14	2	17
1955	593	3	4	43	99	148	153	49	33	15	23	20	3
1956	504	2	47	31	85	79	65	92	42	16	29	7	9
1957	858	17	5	38	216	228	147	55	20	17	18	59	38
1958	564	11	20	15	76	68	128	121	46	24	9	45	1
1959	604	16	20	43	30	226	73	63	38	58	24	11	2
1960	616	9	28	28	70	201	125	42	48	21	18	25	1
1961	697	1	31	124	74	137	107	77	27	53	14	36	16
1962	657	12	25	37	41	200	171	78	51	24	11	5	2
1963	463	15	6	48	84	71	90	62	26	33	13	15	0
Avg	**760**	**13**	**21**	**51**	**102**	**163**	**160**	**88**	**58**	**37**	**23**	**28**	**17**

***Figure 16-24.** The final product of your scrollable table*

1. To start, insert a new scroll bar into the empty spreadsheet tab in the example file. After that, you must assign a scroll bar to a cell that will hold it. In this example, assign it to A4. This is shown in Figure 16-25.

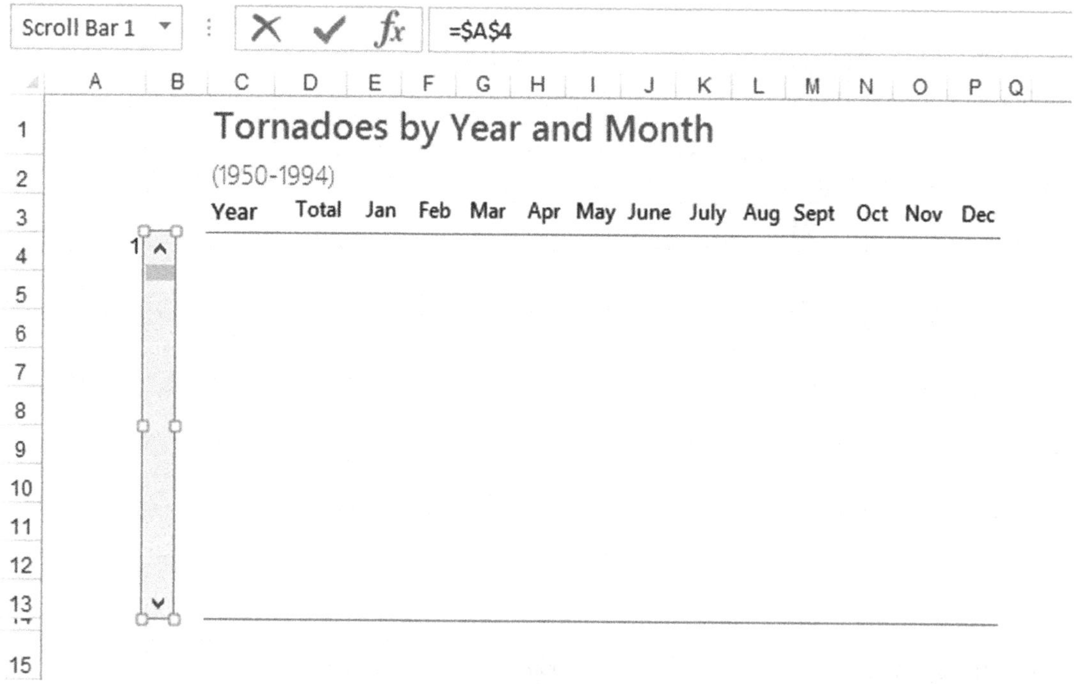

Figure 16-25. *Assiging the scroll bar to a cell value*

2. When creating a scrollable table, you'll have to decide its dimensions. In Figure 16-24, you can see ten items at a time. You'll need to set up a series of dynamic indices, so in A4, write the formula `A3 + 1` and drag down. Figure 16-26 shows this result and the formulas.

■ **Tip** To help size the scroll bar, use the Snap to Grid feature. Choose a column where you want to house the scroll bar and size the column to the width you'd like the scroll bar to be. Next, after you insert the scroll bar, go to the Format tab and select Snap to Grid from the Align dropdown in the Arrange group. Now resize the scroll bar; you'll see it easily fits to the column.

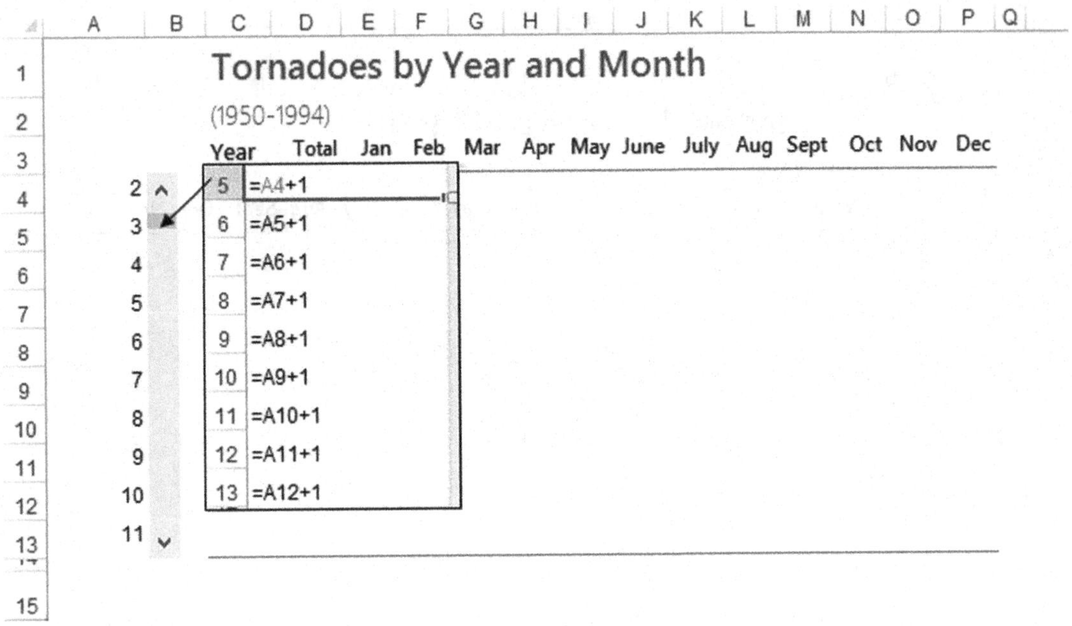

Figure 16-26. *This dynamic will increase all the numbers in the list as changes to the scroll bar are made*

If you try the scroll bar now, you'll see the dynamic indices increase and decrease with each change in the scroll bar.

3. The backend data for this exercise is on the Data tab. The series of years is named `TornadoData.Year`, the series of tornado totals is named `TornadoData.Totals`, and the data range is named `TornadoData.DataRegion`. By naming these regions you can more easily access them with the `INDEX` function.

   Specifically, you can pull the first row of the data region by using the formula `INDEX(TornadoData.DataRegion, $A4, )`. By leaving that last parameter blank, you can drag the formula across to the desired range and then press Ctrl+Shift+Enter (see Figure 16-27). The last parameter, which takes a column index argument, isn't necessary in this case. By telling Excel that you are using an array formula, Excel knows that the first cell in the region returns the first column index, the second returns the second column index, and so forth. However, for this to work, you must leave that final parameter blank. `INDEX(TornadoData.DataRegion, $A4, )` is not the same as `INDEX(TornadoData.DataRegion, $A4)`.

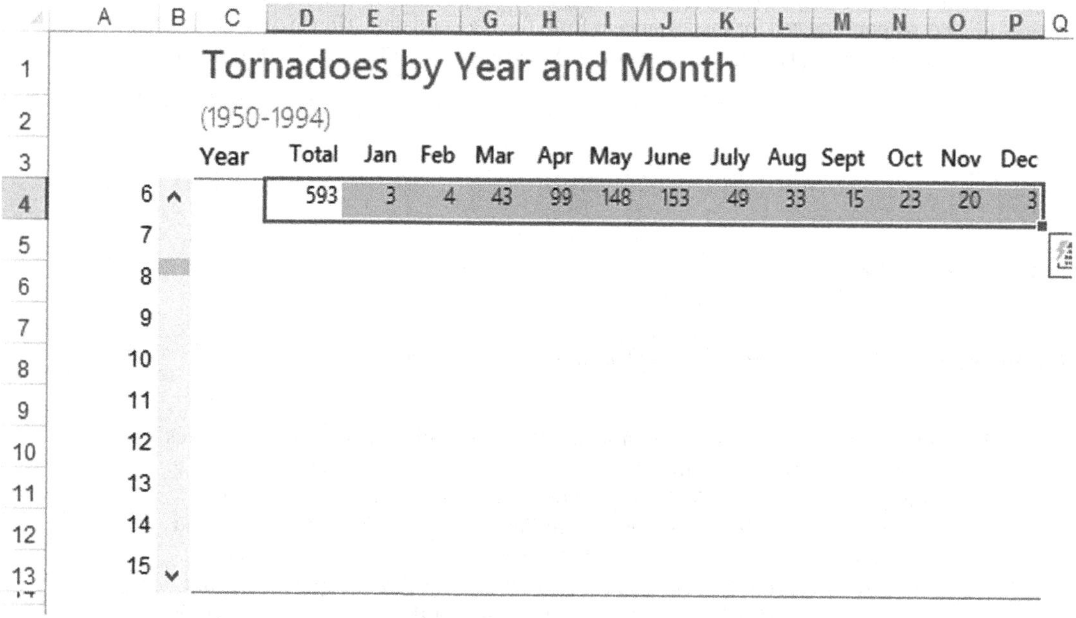

Tornadoes by Year and Month

(1950-1994)

Year	Total	Jan	Feb	Mar	Apr	May	June	July	Aug	Sept	Oct	Nov	Dec
	593	3	4	43	99	148	153	49	33	15	23	20	3

Figure 16-27. *The result of using the Array formula to pull back data*

4. Once you have the first row, you can simply drag down to fill the entire region, as shown in Figure 16-28.

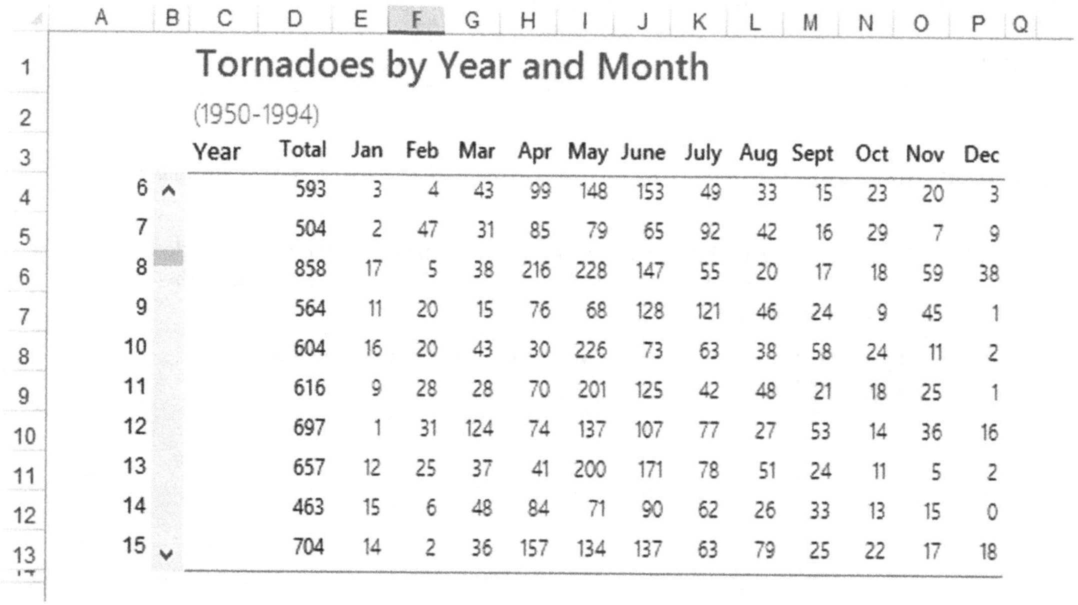

Tornadoes by Year and Month

(1950-1994)

Year	Total	Jan	Feb	Mar	Apr	May	June	July	Aug	Sept	Oct	Nov	Dec
	593	3	4	43	99	148	153	49	33	15	23	20	3
	504	2	47	31	85	79	65	92	42	16	29	7	9
	858	17	5	38	216	228	147	55	20	17	18	59	38
	564	11	20	15	76	68	128	121	46	24	9	45	1
	604	16	20	43	30	226	73	63	38	58	24	11	2
	616	9	28	28	70	201	125	42	48	21	18	25	1
	697	1	31	124	74	137	107	77	27	53	14	36	16
	657	12	25	37	41	200	171	78	51	24	11	5	2
	463	15	6	48	84	71	90	62	26	33	13	15	0
	704	14	2	36	157	134	137	63	79	25	22	17	18

Figure 16-28. *Dragging the array formula down the entire table*

5. You'll also need to do the same for the Year column. You need to pull the corresponding cell for the given year from the backend data. Here, you'll use the formula `INDEX(TornadoData.Year, A4)` (see Figure 16-29) and then drag down.

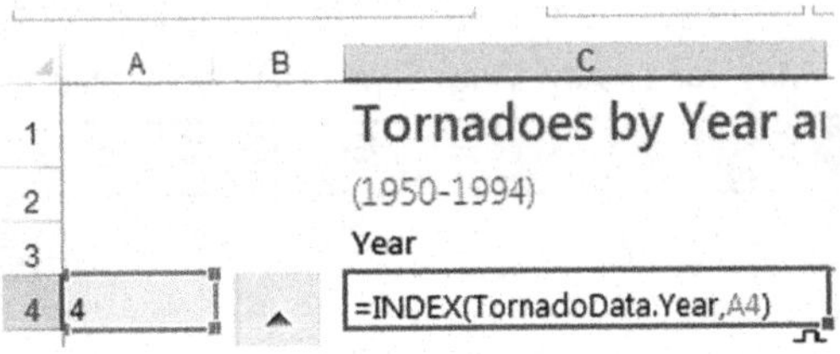

Figure 16-29. Use INDEX to retrieve the total tornados for a given year

6. Finally, you'll want to add more information to the table. This example includes the averages for each month over the entire year range by leaving the row index parameter of the `INDEX` function blank and using a static reference for the column index. This mechanism is similar to what you did above except you are pulling the entire column instead of the entire row. In addition, you are not interested in return each cell in the column; instead, you supply the entire column to an `AVERAGE` function to get the average for that year (see Figure 16-30).

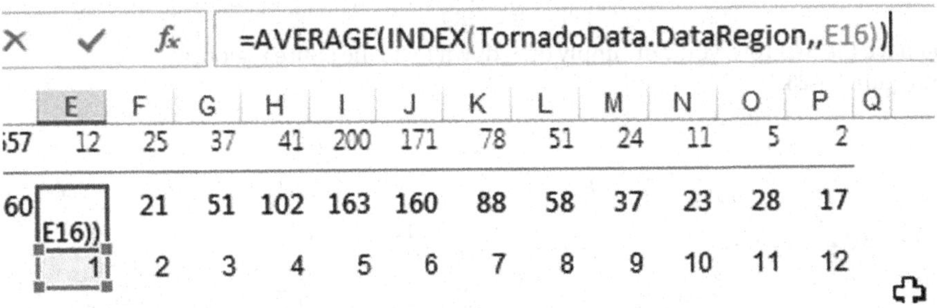

Figure 16-30. Use the AVERAGE and INDEX functions to report the average tornados for each month

7. So that the dynamic indices on the left and the static reference on the bottom do not appear in the table, change those cells to a white font, which blends in with the white background.

8. Finally, set the Minimum Value and Maximum Value fields of the scroll bar (see Figure 16-31).

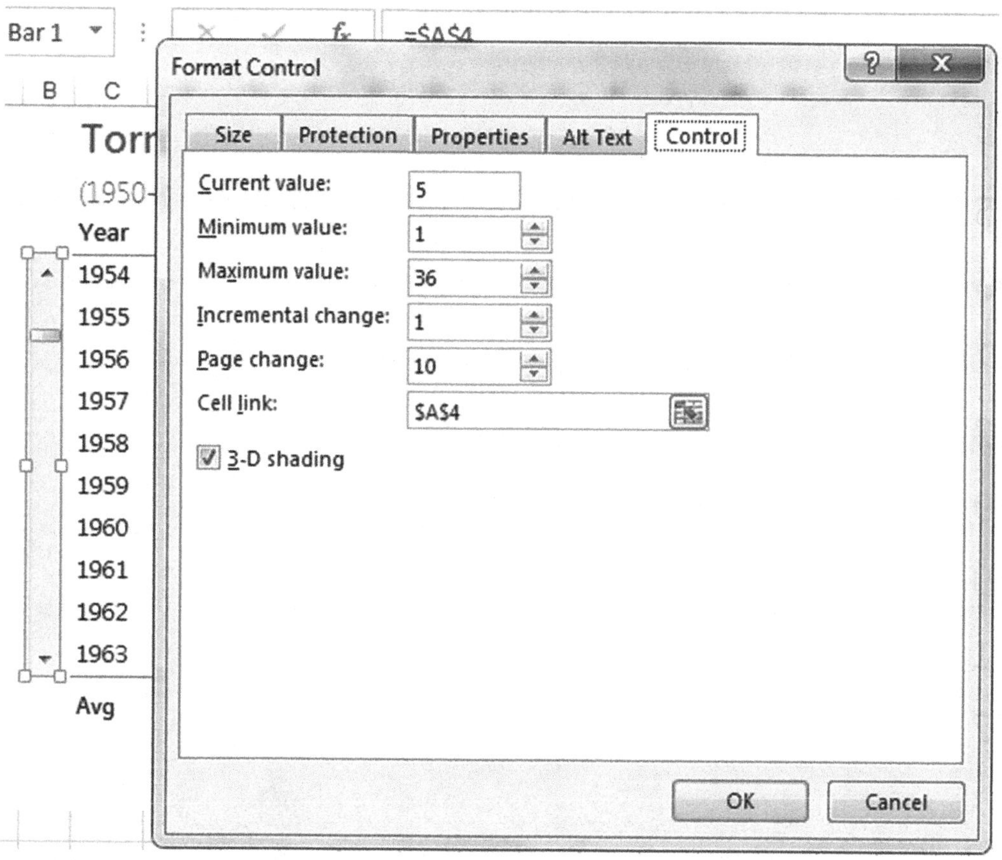

Figure 16-31. *The Format Control dialog box*

The minimum, of course, is 1. The maximum is 36. Why 36? Well, the entire year range is made up of 45 years. That's the last year in the set, 1994, minus the beginning year, 1950. (Remember, you're including 1950 in the set so it comes out to 45 years and not 44.) You show ten years in your table, and you effectively do this by adding nine years to the initial value given by the scrollbar (see Figure 16-32). So the maximum is 45 years minus 9 years, which is 36.

Year
1954
1955
1956
1957
1958
1959
1960
1961
1962
1963

Figure 16-32. *Notice that 1963 equals 1954 plus 9*

Figure 16-33 shows the final table.

Tornadoes by Year and Month

(1950-1994)

Year	Total	Jan	Feb	Mar	Apr	May	June	July	Aug	Sept	Oct	Nov	Dec
1954	550	2	17	62	113	101	107	45	49	21	14	2	17
1955	593	3	4	43	99	148	153	49	33	15	23	20	3
1956	504	2	47	31	85	79	65	92	42	16	29	7	9
1957	858	17	5	38	216	228	147	55	20	17	18	59	38
1958	564	11	20	15	76	68	128	121	46	24	9	45	1
1959	604	16	20	43	30	226	73	63	38	58	24	11	2
1960	616	9	28	28	70	201	125	42	48	21	18	25	1
1961	697	1	31	124	74	137	107	77	27	53	14	36	16
1962	657	12	25	37	41	200	171	78	51	24	11	5	2
1963	463	15	6	48	84	71	90	62	26	33	13	15	0
Avg	760	13	21	51	102	163	160	88	58	37	23	28	17

Figure 16-33. *The final table*

Highlighting Data Points on Charts

You can also use form control scrollbars to highlight a point on a chart. Figure 16-34 shows a time series of the yearly totals of tornados. Below the chart is a scroll bar that moves the black selector point left and right. As the point changes, the label changes with it.

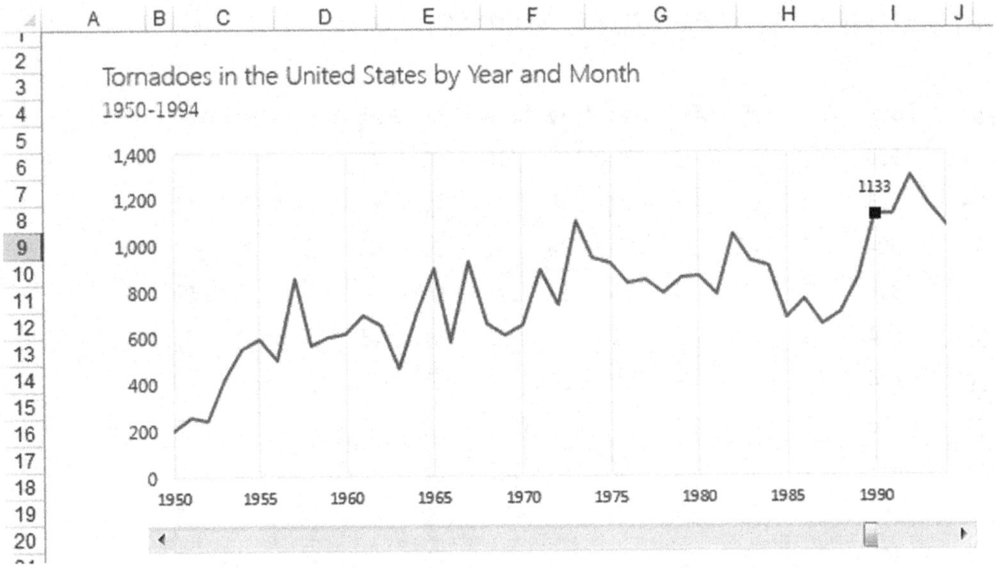

Figure 16-34. *You can highlight data points on the chart using a form control Scroll Bar*

The setup for this problem is somewhat similar to the last. You can follow along in the example file `Chapter16DataPoint.xlsx`.

First, you start with a scroll bar. This time, however, you draw it horizontally instead of vertically. Again, for precision, it's a good idea to use the Snap to Grid feature. Above, you'll see that columns that border the chart, B and C, are a bit smaller than the rest. I sized these columns about the size of the scroll bar's paddles. That way, the paddle in the scroll area lines up nicely with the selector on the chart. In addition, I was able to nicely align the plot and chart area again using the handy Snap to Grid feature.

The scroll bar is linked to a value on the side of the Excel spreadsheet. The name of the cell is `Scrollbar.Value` (gee, how creative...). Using the scroll bar's value, you pull the X and Y values using the scroll bar as an index (see Figure 16-35).

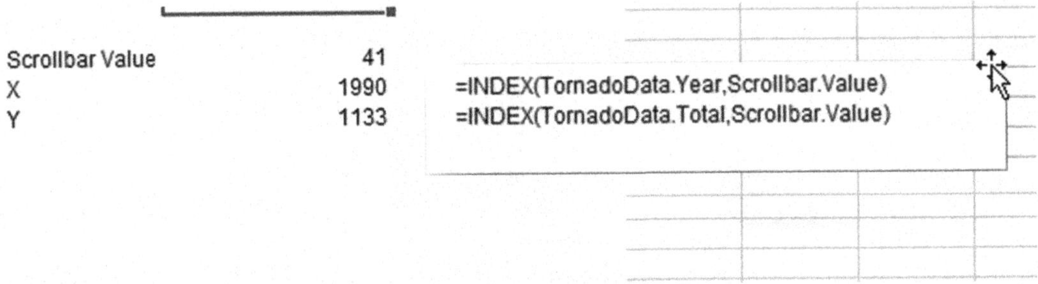

Figure 16-35. *As the scroll bar changes, the X and Y values also change*

Now, this is where the magic happens. You're using a simple scatterplot chart for your timeseries display. Because of this, you don't have to add a huge series to your chart to show the selector. You only need to add the coordinates defined in Figure 16-36. In your chart, you have a series simply named selector that points to the coordinates off to the side. Remember, those coordinates are traced to the value given by the scroll bar. So, as the scroll bar changes, the coordinates update with each change. That's how I came up with the nifty effect.

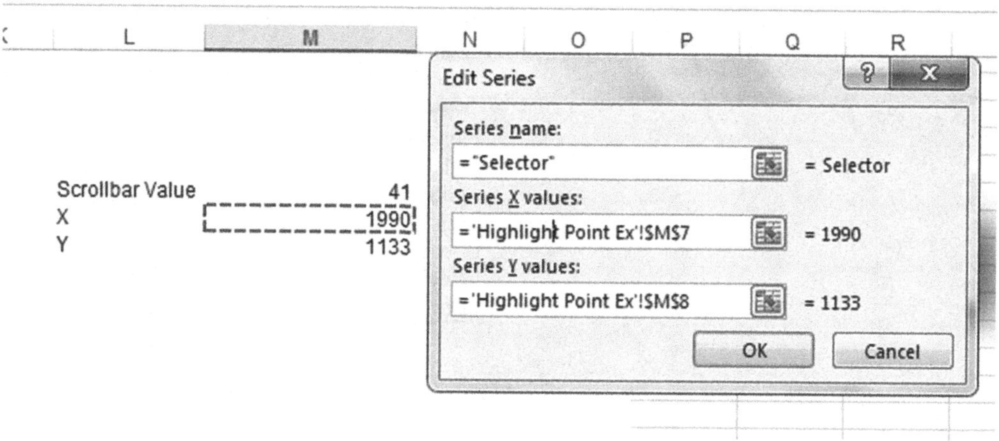

Figure 16-36. *The Edit Series dialog box*

The other series on the chart is simply the totals from your data worksheet tab (see Figure 16-37).

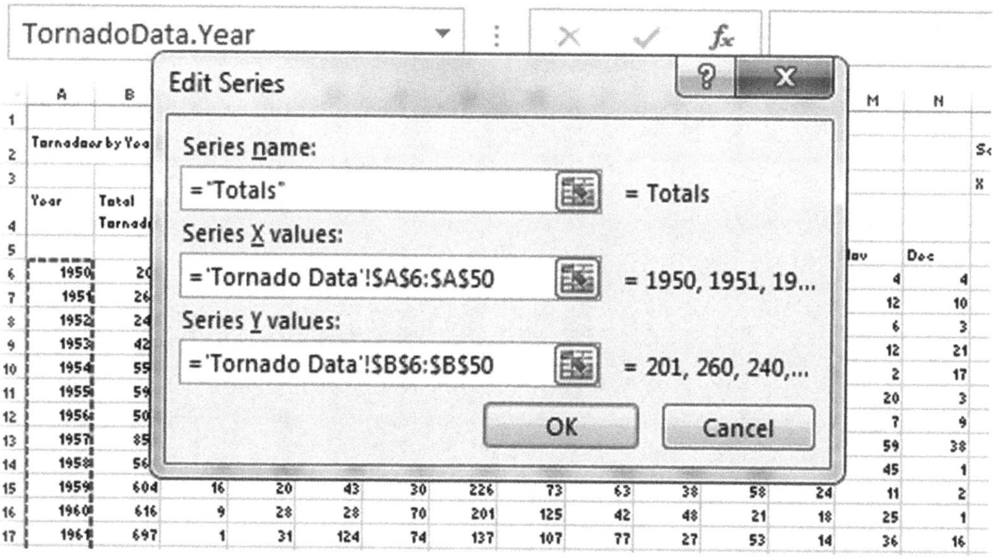

Figure 16-37. *The totals from the tornado data*

But wait! This mechanism isn't complete without grabbing information about the current year. So, let's add a small chart on the side that displays information for each month of the given year (see Figure 16-38).

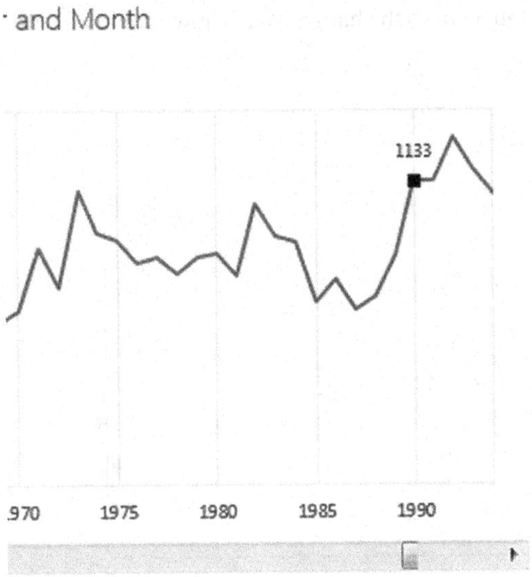

1990	
Jan	11
Feb	57
Mar	86
Apr	108
May	243
Jun	329
Jul	106
Aug	60
Sep	45
Oct	35
Nov	18
Dec	35

Figure 16-38. *An additional chart displays information for each month of the selected year*

This mechanism is not different from when you looked up rows in the table before. The difference now is that you want to flip that row into a column. So you'll wrap it in the TRANSPOSE function as shown in Figure 16-39. Once you've dragged that function down, you can press Ctrl+Shift+Enter because you're directing Excel to return a range.

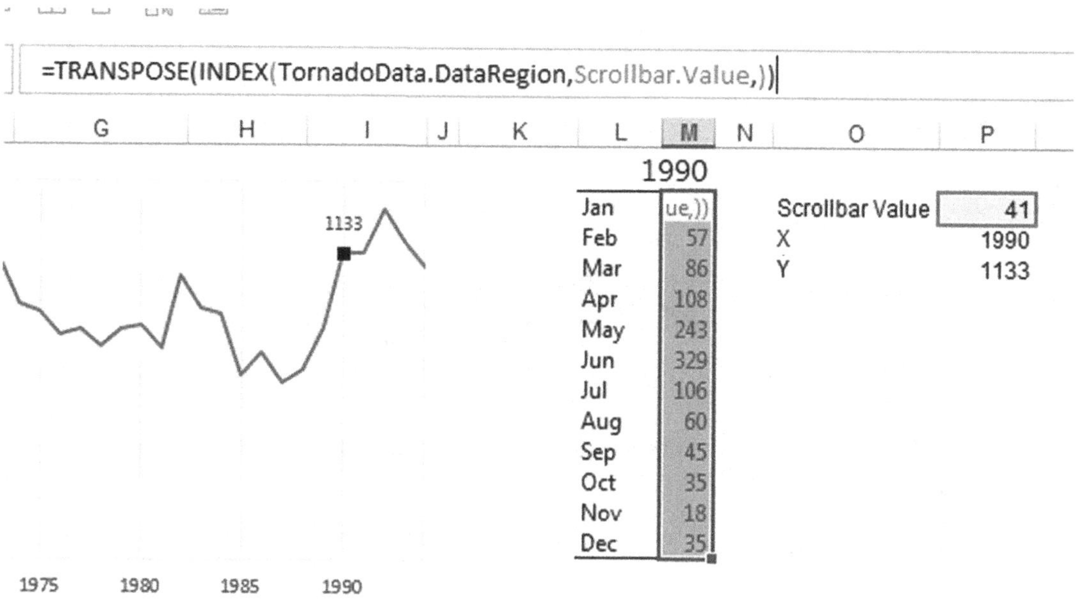

Figure 16-39. *The information table relies on the scroll bar's value to pull monthly tornado data for a selected year*

The Dynamic Legend

To make a dynamic legend, you use the CheckBox form control for a series in the chart. In this case, however, you won't use the legend Excel provides for you as a chart element. Instead, you'll create your own from scratch! Add three check boxes (clear out the default labels). In addition, write a "minus" sign and add the label next to it, both colored manually. You can see this for yourself by looking at `Chapter16DynamicLegend.xlsx` with the downloads for this chapter.

Figure 16-40 shows that the legend is simply a cell.

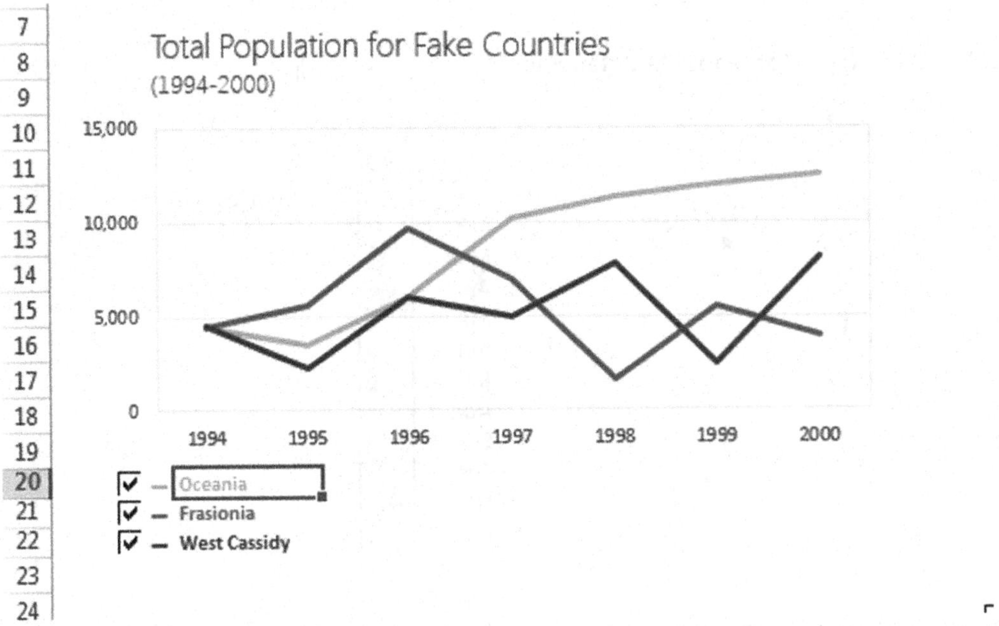

Figure 16-40. The legends here are simply cells

Here's how this mechanism works: there are essentially two tables that hold the data presented in this graph. The first table is simply static; you can think of it as a type of database. The second table is an intermediary between the database and chart. You can think of the chart as being the presentation layer. The dynamic is laid out in Figure 16-41.

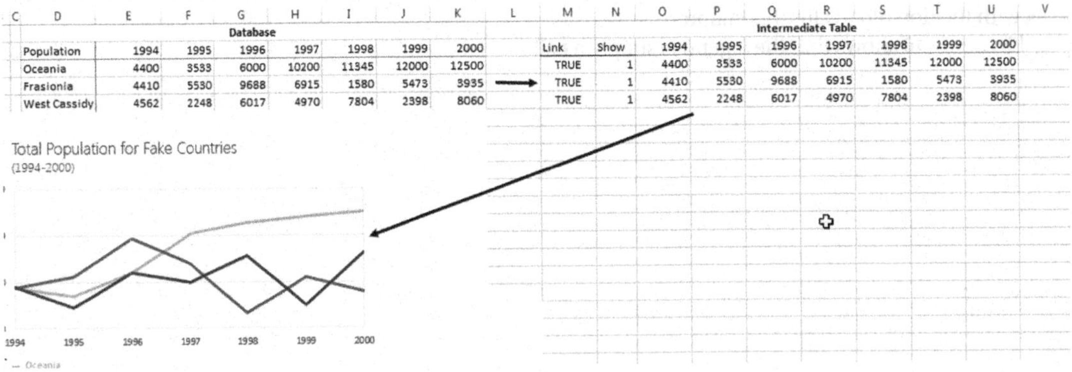

Figure 16-41. The mechanism of a dynamic legend

Let's take a closer look at the intermediate table. The first column of the table holds the linked cells of the three check boxes (see Figure 16-42).

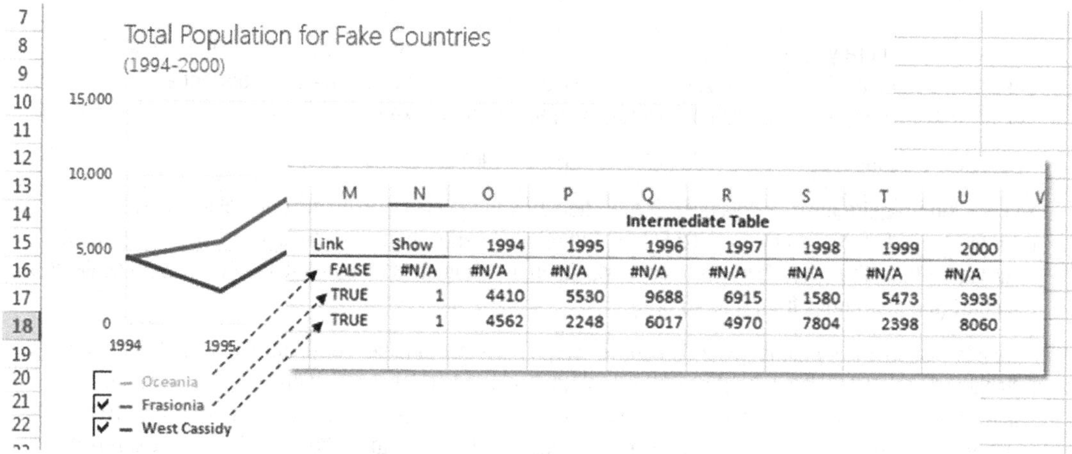

Figure 16-42. *A closer look at the intermediate table*

The next column tests whether the link has returned a TRUE or FALSE. If it returns a TRUE, Excel returns a 1; if it's a FALSE, Excel returns an `NA()` (see Figure 16-43).

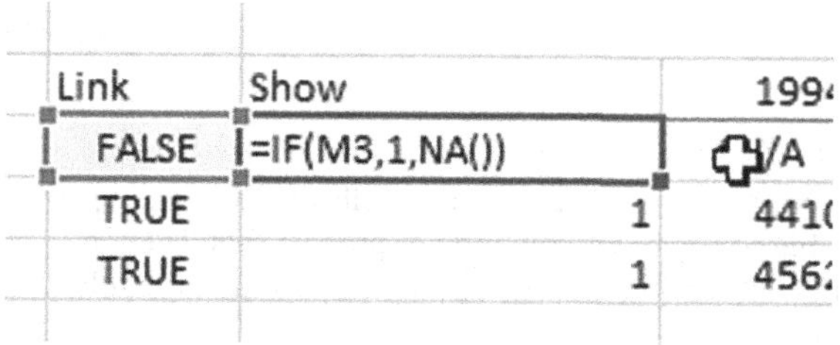

Figure 16-43. *If a CheckBox is deselected, you want to return an N/A error*

The cool thing about using `NA()` is that it returns an #N/A error, which Excel won't plot. In addition to that, anytime you multiply something by an #N/A, it also becomes an #N/A. And that's exactly what you take advantage of in your dynamic legend. The values in the intermediate table are the product of the result of the `IF` function multiplied by the original values. Figure 16-44 demonstrates this mechanism.

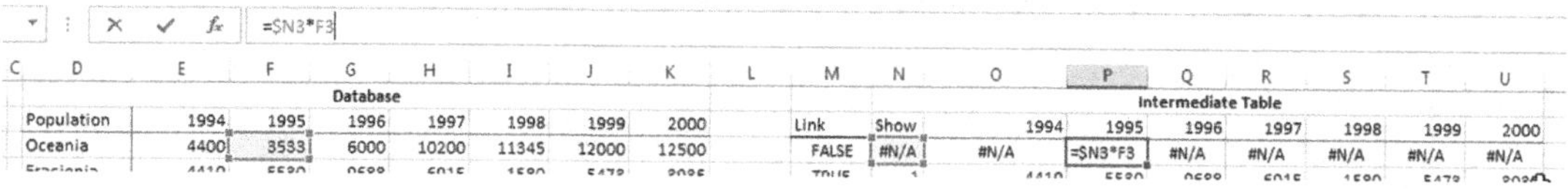

Figure 16-44. *The dynamic legend works by turning the values in a series into an #N/A error and thus removing it from the chart*

WAIT...WHY AM I USING IF()? I THOUGHT YOU SAID I SHOULDN'T USE IT?

This is a case where you couldn't get away from using `IF`. As you are likely familiar with by now, the CheckBox's value could be one or zero. Ostensibly, this response would have been perfect as the multiplier. For example, you could have simply written a formula like this:

```
=(checkbox_response) * original_series_value - NOT(checkbox_response)
```

You wouldn't require an `IF` in this case. If the CheckBox response is TRUE, the original series value is returned (or just multiplied by 1). If it's FALSE, the original series value becomes a zero and `NOT(FALSE)` returns a 1; thus, the entire formula of `=0-1` results in a -1, which is a point outside the viewing scale of the chart (the chart goes from 0 to 15,000).

Here's the issue: the dynamic described above works perfectly in Excel 2010, but it does not work as reliably in Excel 2013, at least not as of this writing. You can test for this bug on your own if you are using Excel 2013. Create a new line chart with a series of -1 and set the axis range from 0.0 to 10.0. Chances are, you won't see the line. Now, change the axis from 0.0 to 20,000. The line will reappear.

But like I said, you shouldn't necessarily *never* use `IF`; rather, you should exercise discretion. In the example, you only use one `IF` per CheckBox and the rest of the series relies on that `IF`. This is the best way to do it. You could have alternatively made each datapoint in the intermediate table also be a test against the response of the CheckBox. That would have employed far too many `IF` statements than necessary.

The Last Word

In this chapter, you learned how truly awesome form controls are. I discussed reusability briefly in Chapter 10, and form controls are an integral part of the reusable components you find on spreadsheets. They're flexible, don't often require much code, and can be moved and placed rather easily. As you can probably guess, you'll return to form controls several times through the rest of the book.

CHAPTER 17

Getting Input from Users

This chapter begins the second half of the book. From this chapter and on, you'll be creating a spreadsheet-based application using many of the principles discussed in the first few chapters. To get an idea of what you're building, you can download the completed version, `Chapter20Finished.xlsm`, from within this book's project files.

In the next four chapters, I will present you with completed work whose functions you'll reverse engineer. In that way, you're going to apply the principles from the previous chapters (as well as learn a few more along the way).

There are two good reasons for this teaching style. First, in the real world, you won't always start from scratch. Sometimes you'll receive work built by someone else. You have to reverse engineer what they've completed and also add your own features. Many of the examples files going forward are much like that inherited spreadsheet. You should know how they work, but I also want you to think creatively of how they can be extended (and tailored) for your use.

The second reason goes back to the phrase mentioned in previous chapters—that of reusable components. Many of the features I'll describe are not steps in a larger spreadsheet. Rather, they exist in their own right. They're as applicable here as they are for other spreadsheet projects. Recall from the introduction I said the most important skill to succeed in this book is creativity. That creativity will help you understand how to implement these components in your work.

The bulk of this chapter deals with creating a spreadsheet-based input wizard with Excel. But before diving into the wizard, I'll discuss creating simple spreadsheet-based forms and why they're often the better choice compared to UserForms. From there, you'll start with a completed version of the spreadsheet-based wizard. I'll walk you through several of the design components, including proper layout, input pages, and features of the user interface. By the end of the chapter, you should see how building a spreadsheet-based input wizard is consistent with building faster and leaner Excel applications.

Note You can download project files for this chapter along with the other example files for this book from the Source Code/Downloads tab at `www.apress.com/9781430249443`.

Of Input Forms and Excel

Most Excel developers would prefer UserForms to capture user input, especially when the user input has multiple steps. Indeed, conventional wisdom often argues for using UserForms and ActiveX controls. The problem is that ActiveX controls can be somewhat finicky and unpredictable, as established in Chapter 16. Remember this figure from Chapter 16 (now called Figure 17-1)?

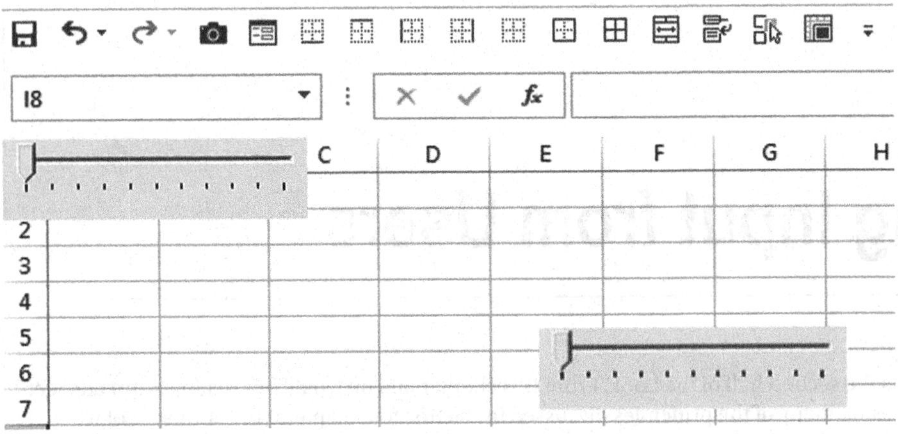

***Figure 17-1.** This is the same ActiveX shown in two different locations*

UserForms are a type of ActiveX control and they suffer from the same unpredictability. For instance, UserForms will sometimes appear different across different computers. This is the result of different internal settings and hardware. Monitor resolution, DPI, and Windows' internal font default can potentially cause these unwanted effects.

One way to get around all of this is develop input forms directly on the spreadsheet. This is what I advocate. It may seem like a hard task at first, but you will soon find it provides flexibility not found when using UserForms. In addition, the spreadsheet provides a better canvas upon which to create a more aesthetically pleasing experience. The dull grey scheme that appears by default in the UserForms feels almost anachronistic in this day and age, a relic of a bygone era. Figure 17-2 shows an example UserForm I pulled from Microsoft's Developer Network's help pages.

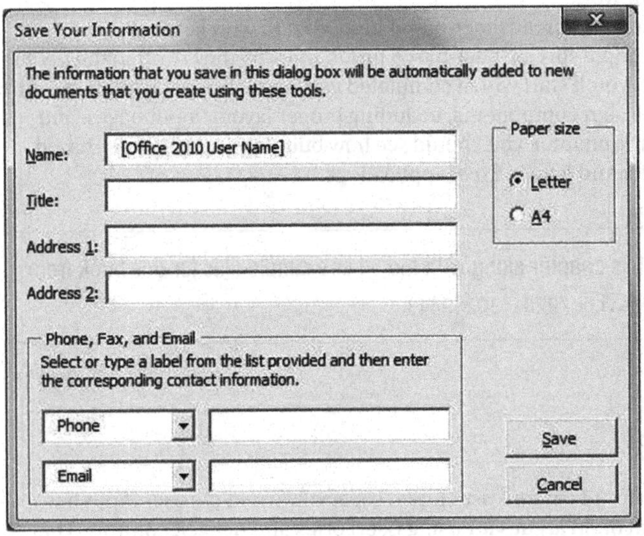

***Figure 17-2.** An example of a UserForm found in Microsoft's Excel help*

Let's take a look at what you can do when you create input forms on the spreadsheet instead.

A Simple Input Form

In this section, I'll discuss how to create a simple input form. Open `Chapter17SimpleInput.xlsm` to follow along. Figure 17-3 is a snapshot of the input form in `Chapter17SimpleInput.xlsm`.

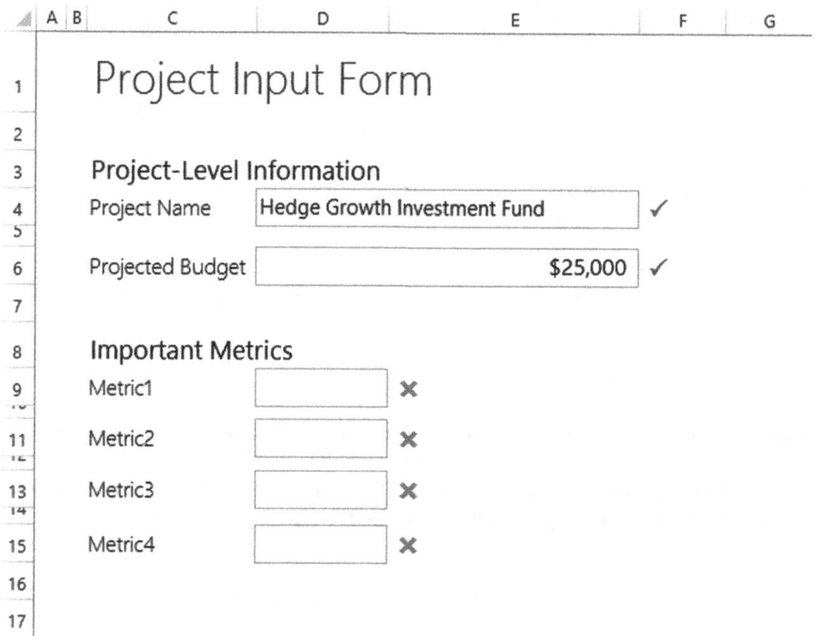

Figure 17-3. *A spreadsheet-based input form*

You can create a new input form in Excel with nothing more than an unused worksheet tab. With an idea of the information you'd like to collect at hand, it's a simple matter of laying everything out.

Nothing too fancy goes into creating something like this. Each input box is simply a named range. If you've ever created an input form on UserForm before, you know that each input TextBox is given a name. For instance, convention would tell us the name for TextBox on a UserForm that stores a Project Name would go by txtProjectName. You're doing a similar action by name each cell with a named range. The named range, as you shall see, will give you easy programmatic access to the cell's value later on down the road. Figure 17-4 shows the named ranges and the input cells they point to.

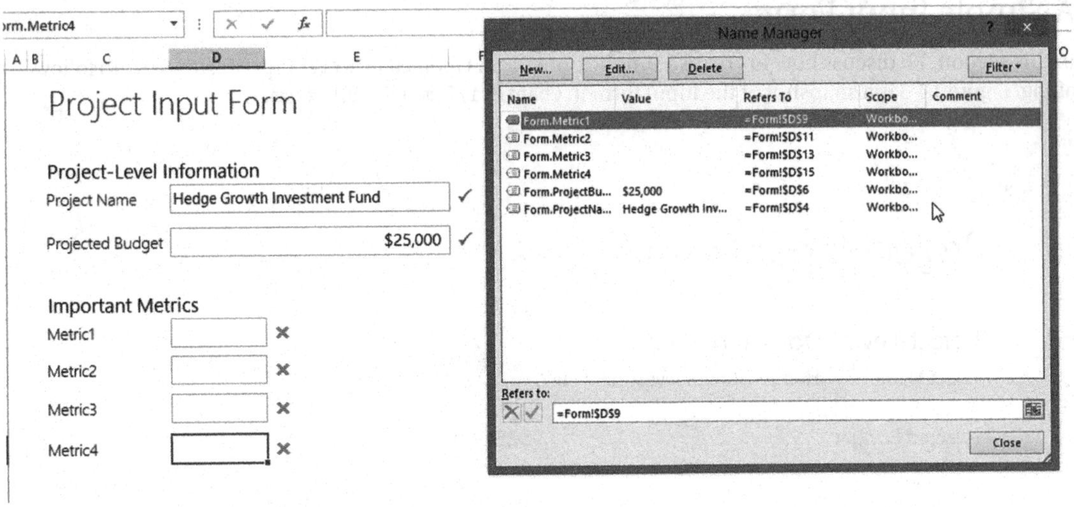

***Figure 17-4.** Input items are named ranges*

The green checks and red x glyphs in Figure 17-4 serve as data validation indicators. You probably don't need one for each and every box, but there may be inputs you want to specifically point your users' eyes toward completing. There's no fancy coding required to create these. In fact, they require no VBA code at all. It's just a simple formula and some custom formatting. Take a look at the formula in Figure 17-5.

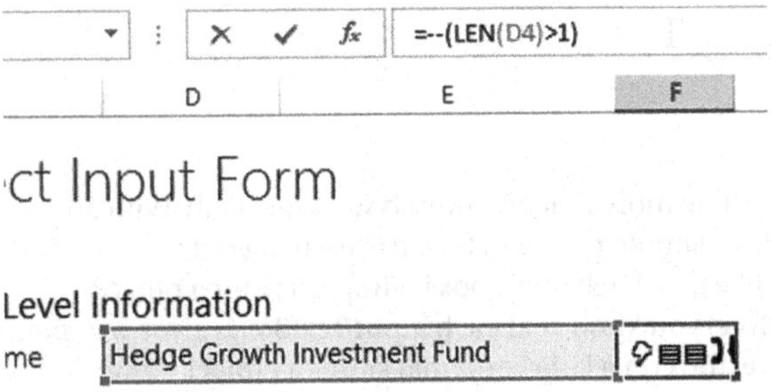

***Figure 17-5.** A visual validation formula you can use for input*

Here, you're simply testing whether the length of the text entered in the adjacent cell is greater than one. If it is, that means something has been written in the cell. If the length of text is zero, that means no input has been provided. Recall that the double-dash is shorthand for converting the Boolean values of True and False into zero and one.

If you take a closer look at Figure 17-5, you'll notice that the formula in the cell is not readable text. The reason is because to get the checkbox and x symbols, I used the Wingdings 2 font.

Custom Formats for Input Validation

In this section, I'll talk about how custom formats can help turn those zeros and ones into x's and checkmarks. It's simple; you use custom formatting. In Figure 17-6, I've used the custom formatting syntax to tell Excel what to display when the number is either a one or zero.

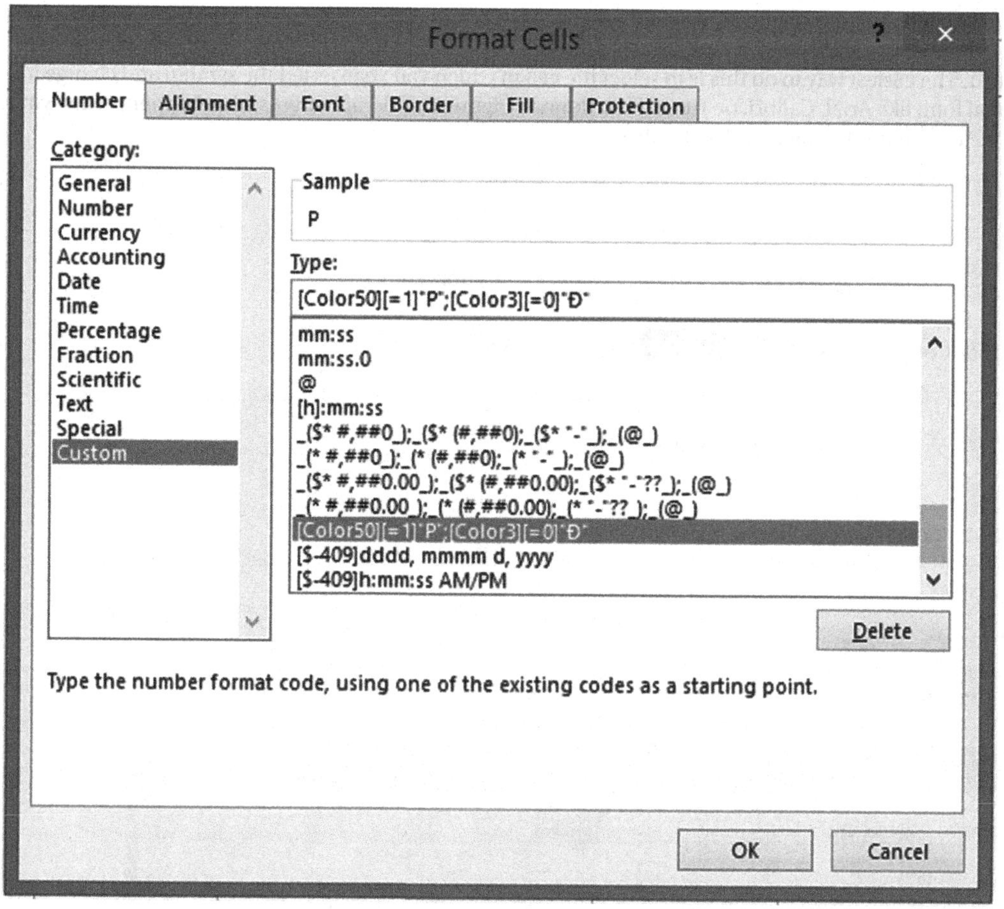

Figure 17-6. *Custom formats are shown in the Format Cells dialog box*

So let's break this down. With custom formats, I can create conditions to let Excel know when to display which symbol. For example, I have two conditions in the above formula. Can you guess what they look like? If you notice `[=1]` and `[=0]` then you're spot on! These blocks of syntax outline the conditions. Note that the semicolon separates each condition.

Now take a look at the two character symbols that are being returned. There's a "P" and a really weird looking "Đ" thing. To get these characters, I actually looked them up using the Symbol dialog box from on the Insert tab (see Figure 17-8). In this case, I selected Wingdings 2 as the font and inserted into Excel the symbols I desired. When Excel inserts these symbols into the worksheet, they'll be in the Wingdings 2 font.

But if you look again at Figure 17-6, you'll see the input box in the Format Cells dialog box is looking for regular alphanumeric characters—not symbols. So you'll need to get those Windings 2 symbols back into regular text. The easiest way to do this is to select the cell in which you've inserted the symbol and change it to a normal font, like Arial, Calibri, or Times New Roman. Figure 17-7 demonstrates what happens when you convert the output from Wingdings 2 to Calibri.

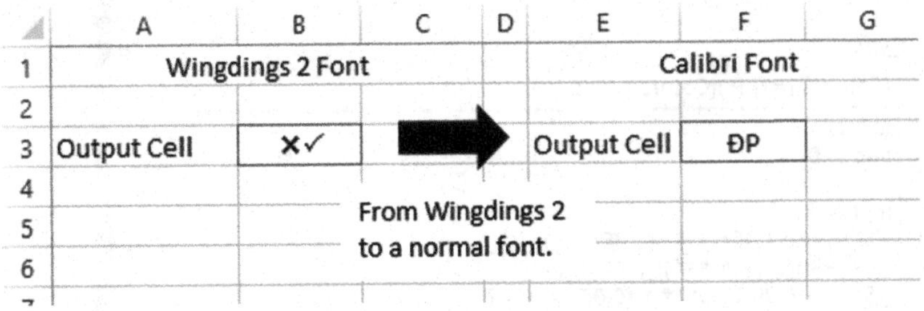

Figure 17-7. Converting the output from Wingdings 2 to Calibri

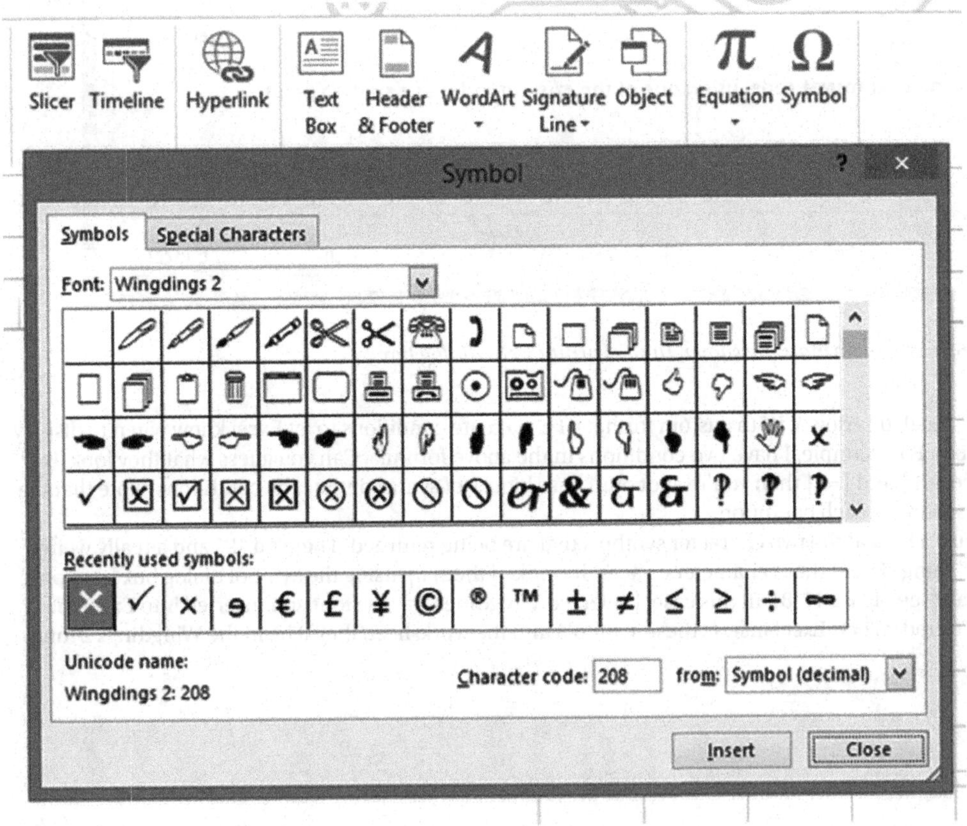

Figure 17-8. The Insert Symbol dialog box

Finally, you'll notice the other two syntax blocks in Figure 17-6 that look like [ColorXX], where XX is some number. The XX in this case is in fact a number that points to a specific color index. To see a full list of colors to choose from, go to http://dmcritchie.mvps.org/excel/colors.htm.

The basic syntax for custom formats used here is [Color XX][condition]<symbol to return>. There are other format options available, and I encourage you to take a look at them. But they are beyond the scope of this book.

Based on what you've learned so far, you're now ready to begin building a spreadsheet wizard to take input from the user. Notice that this simple input form can be created rather quickly and uses only formulas. The same form would take longer to create if made on a UserForm.

Creating a Spreadsheet-Based Wizard

In this section, you'll build off the input form created from the previous section. However, you'll also spend considerable time on the layout mechanics of a spreadsheet-based wizard. As stated in the beginning of the chapter, you'll focus on components rather than building from scratch. I recommend following along by opening Chapter17Wizard.xlsm from within the project files.

In Figure 17-9, you can see the beginnings of a spreadsheet-based wizard that will serve as the backbone for the spreadsheet application you complete in forthcoming chapters. If you have Chapter17wizard.xlsm open, I recommend going through all the interactive components.

For instance, a user can use the back and next buttons (Figure 17-9) and the current page in the middle will change to reflect the choice. Figure 17-9 shows the Introduction page of the wizard.

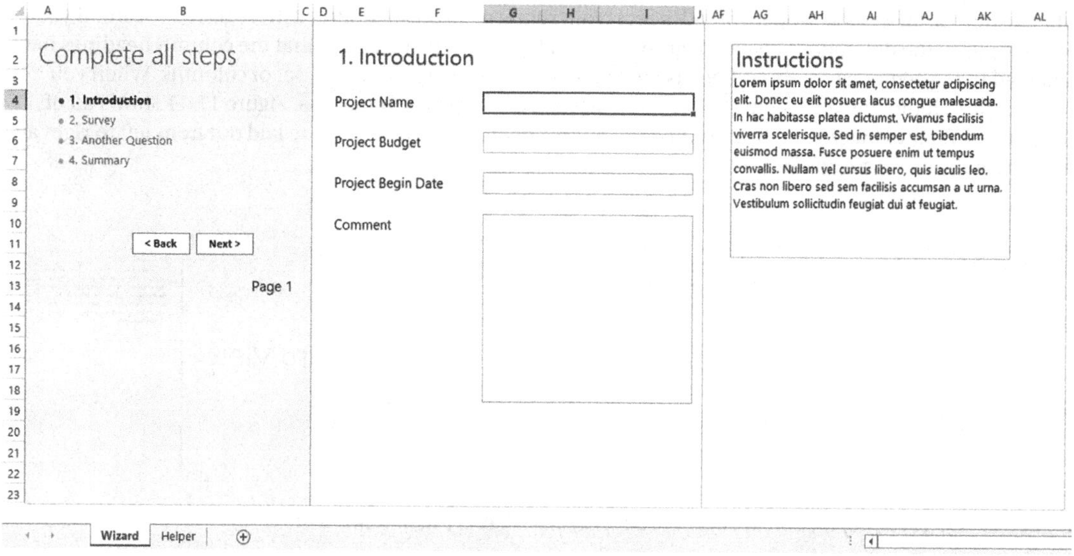

Figure 17-9. *A beautiful spreadsheet-based wizard*

Figure 17-10 shows the screen for the second page after pressing the Next button on the first page.

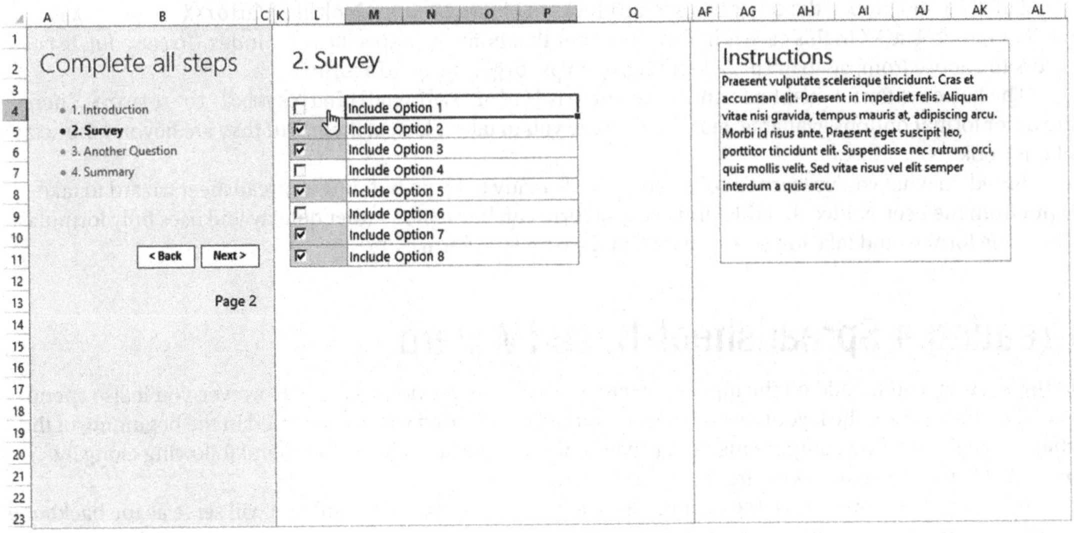

Figure 17-10. Page 2, Survey, of the spreadsheet-based wizard

Layout Patterns for the Spreadsheet-Based Wizard

This section discusses the proper spreadsheet layout required to create a spreadsheet-based wizard. If you look closely at the difference between Figure 17-9 and Figure 17-10, you'll see that the column headings have changed in the center view. This is because the first view referred to a different set of columns. When you pressed Next, it hid this set of columns and advanced to the next set of columns. Figure 17-11 shows all of the panes built into this wizard by unhiding the entire sheet. Notice that they are laid out from left to right an incrementally increasing order.

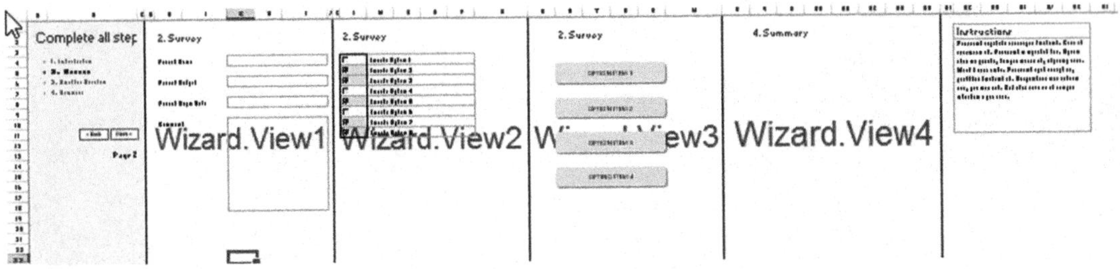

Figure 17-11. A view of the spreadsheet-based wizard with every item unhidden

The mechanism shows and hides these columns accordingly. If you unhide everything and then zoom out, you can see each of these views laid out accordingly.

Note that I've named these views successively: View1, View2, View3, etc. In this setup, it makes it easy to know which view you are currently on. As well, you can know the successive panes in the list in either direction, whether you go forward or backward. Consider, if you were on View2, you'd know the previous screen would be View1 and the next screen would be View3.

Think about the ease of this setup. If you want to make changes to each step, you simple need to make them in that step's set of columns. If you'd like to add another step, you could insert another series of columns in front of Wizard.View4 and name it Wizard.View5. The Name Manager can help you keep track of how many views you have (see Figure 17-12). In addition, you can jump to the step you want automatically by selecting its name.

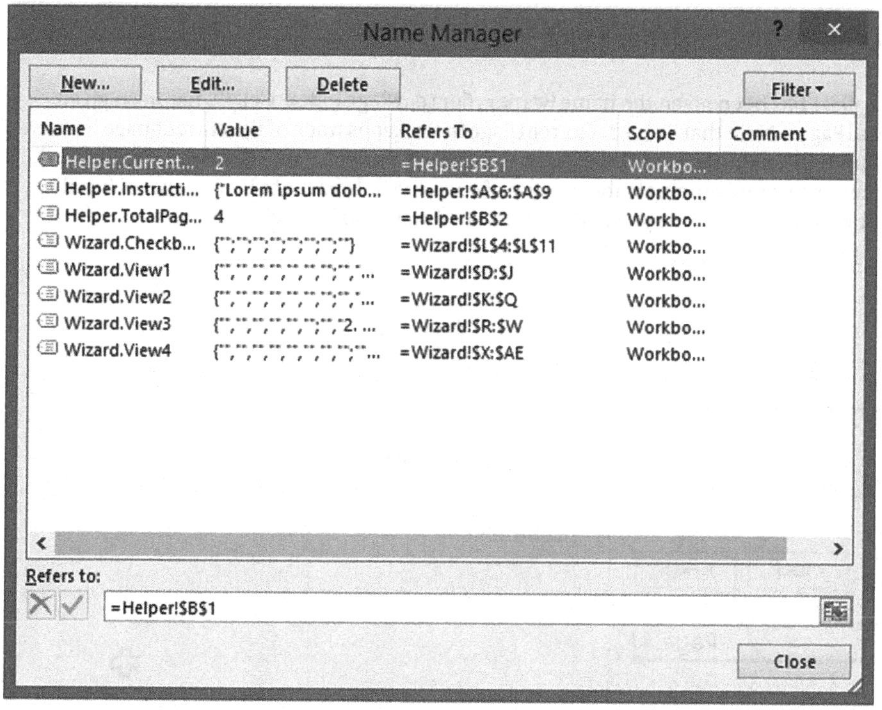

Figure 17-12. *The named range manager can help you keep track of each view*

The Helper Tab

In this section I'll talk about the Helper tab (see Figure 17-13), which is an integral part of the spreadsheet-based wizard.

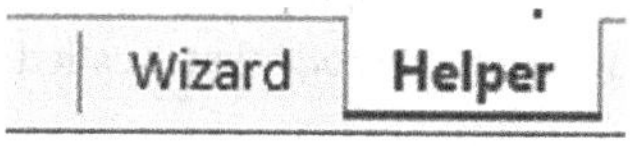

Figure 17-13. *The Helper tab keeps track of important information for the wizard*

As has been the case with previous spreadsheets, I always suggest placing extra information either in a hidden spot on the spreadsheet or in another tab. In this case, you have several items in the Helper tab (see Figure 17-14).

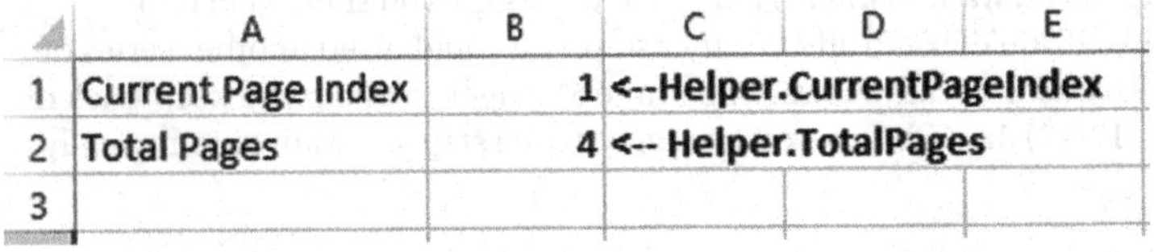

A
B
C
D
E
1 Current Page Index
1 <--Helper.CurrentPageIndex
2 Total Pages
4 <-- Helper.TotalPages
3

***Figure 17-14.** A snapshot of named ranges on the Helper tab*

In Figure 17-15, cell B1 has been given the name `Helper.CurrentPageIndex`. Cell B2 has been given the name `Helper.TotalPages`. Note that `Helper.CurrentPageIndex` keeps track of the current page in view. Its value is changed within the code. `Helper.TotalPages` is manually updated (that is, by you, the human) when you add new views. You could automate the process of ensuring `Helper.TotalPages` always has the correct total views. For now, I don't foresee you adding additional views, so let's keep it as is.

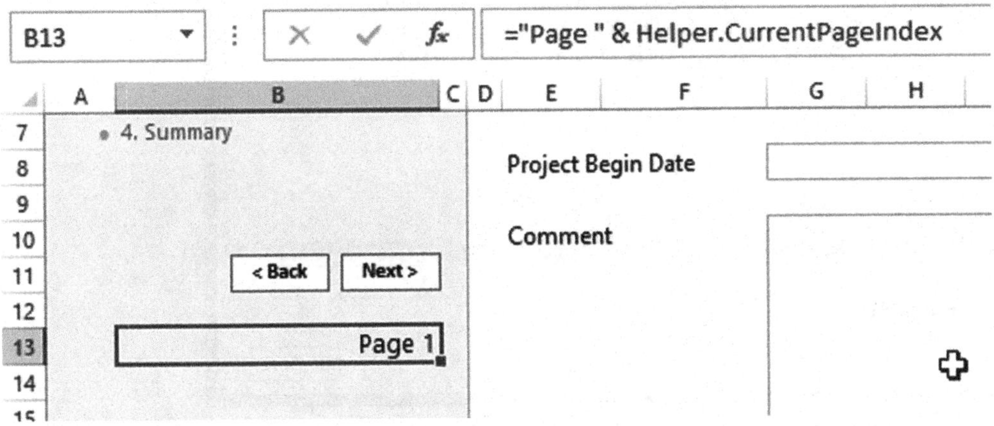

***Figure 17-15.** You can use named ranges to help you track and display information about this wizard*

Going back to the Wizard tab, you can see that `Helper.CurrentPageIndex` is referenced to let you know what page number you are on (see Figure 17-15).

Moving Between Views

For your wizard to have its full effect, you need a way to move back and forth between the views. That's what the Next and Back buttons on the wizard help you do. The following code listings show the code that is called when you press forward (Listing 17-1) and backward (Listing 17-2).

***Listing 17-1.** This Code Will Tell the Wizard to Display the Next View*

```
Public Sub GoNext()
    Dim index As Integer

    ' Read in the current page index and increment it by one
    ' to go next
    index = [Helper.CurrentPageIndex]
    index = index + 1
```

```
    ' Check if we're already on the last page
    If index > [Helper.TotalPages] Then Exit Sub

    ' Unhide the next view
    Wizard.Range("Wizard.View" & index).Columns.Hidden = False

    ' Check to see if we're on a page that requires special instructions
    If index = 2 Then
        DisplayCheckboxes
    Else
        HideCheckboxes
    End If

    ' Hide the current set of columns
    If index > 1 Then
        Wizard.Range("Wizard.View" & index - 1).Columns.Hidden = True
    End If

    'Set Helper.CurrentPageIndex equal to the next page index
    [Helper.CurrentPageIndex] = index
End Sub
```

Listing 17-2. This Code Will Tell the Wizard to Display the Previous View

```
Public Sub GoPrevious()
    Dim index As Integer

    ' Read in the current page index and decrement it by one
    ' to go previous
    index = [Helper.CurrentPageIndex]
    index = index - 1

    ' Check if we're already on the first page
    If index < 1 Then Exit Sub

    ' Unhide the previous view
    Wizard.Range("Wizard.View" & index).Columns.Hidden = False

    ' Check to see if we're on a page that requires special instructions
    If index = 2 Then
        DisplayCheckboxes
    Else
        HideCheckboxes
    End If

    ' Hide the current set of columns
    If index < [Helper.TotalPages] Then
        Wizard.Range("Wizard.View" & index + 1).Columns.Hidden = True
    End If
```

```
    'Set Helper.CurrentPageIndex equal to the previous page index
    [Helper.CurrentPageIndex] = index

End Sub
```

Take a look through both listings. Notice that they are very similar except for a few minor differences. The GoNext procedure checks to see if you've reached the end of the set of views while the GoPrevious procedure checks if you're still at the beginning. The GoNext procedure increments the current page index, while the GoPrevious procedure decrements the current page index. This is another example of a reusable component—the mechanism to go forward and backward is virtually the same, so you just need to make a few accommodations. If you think about creating a general mechanism, then reusing and adjusting the code is easy.

Views That Require Additional Instruction

Some views require extra instruction before they're displayed. For example, Figure 17-16 shows a series of check boxes, which require additional explanation.

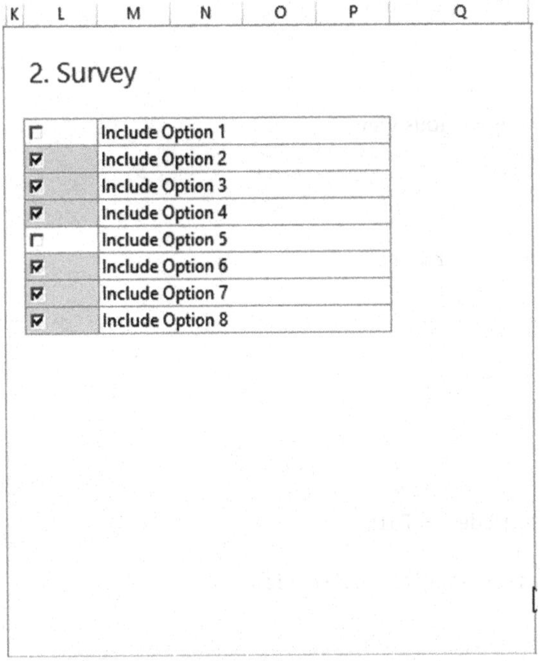

***Figure 17-16.** View2 includes a series of check boxes. These require special instructions*

Unlike input cells form on other views, the check boxes are form controls (CheckBox). They sit on top of the spreadsheet. It's not enough to simply hide the form controls by hiding the view on which they reside. The reason is that form controls don't always become hidden so cleanly when you hide a column, even when you set them to move and size with cells in their properties. So you may be wondering how to ensure that these check boxes always appear in the correct location. The answer is a technique I've come up with called *anchoring*.

Anchoring Controls

In this section, I'll talk about how to anchor your controls so they always appear in the same spot when you hide and unhide columns or rows. The first thing you need to do is name your desired controls as part of a series. Let's go back to that second view. Figure 17-17 highlights the first check box in the series.

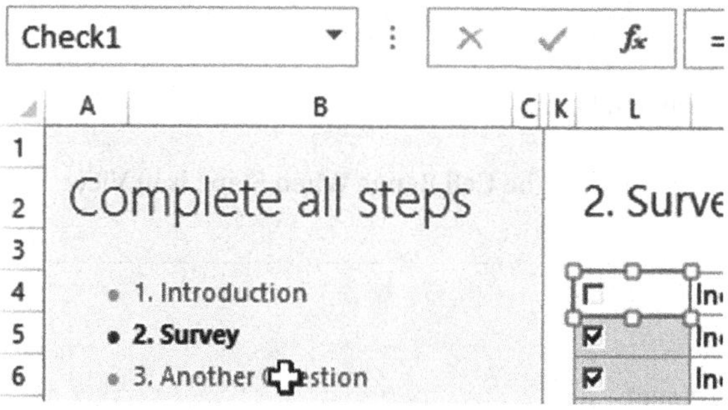

Figure 17-17. *This check box is anchored to the underlying cell*

Notice that the name of the check box is Check1. The check box below it is named Check2, and below that is Check3, all the way through to Check8. Furthermore, in Figure 17-18, I've selected the range that appears under each check box. Notice I've named it `Wizard.CheckboxAnchor`. This anchor will be your guide in placing these check boxes.

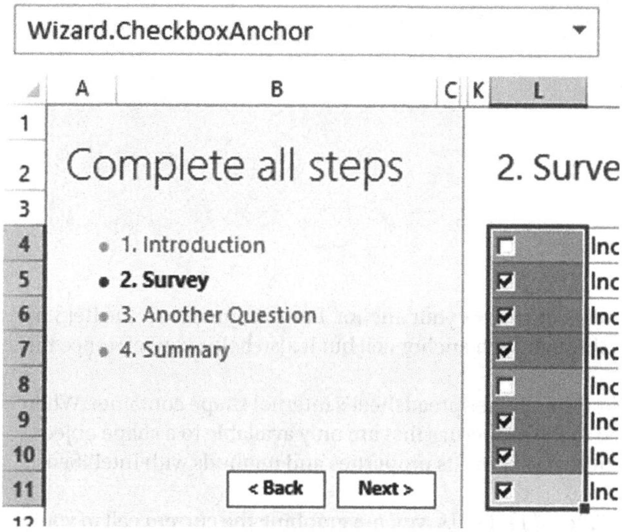

Figure 17-18. *You can create a range of anchors for a set of check boxes*

Now recall this snippet of code from `GoNext` and `GoPrevious`, shown in Listing 17-1 and Listing 17-2. When you are showing the second view, View2, you call the procedure `DisplayCheckboxes`; when you leave the second view, you call the procedure `HideCheckboxes`. Listing 17-3 excerpts this code.

Listing 17-3. An Excerpt from GoNext

```
' Check to see if we're on a page that requires special instructions
If index = 2 Then
    DisplayCheckboxes
Else
    HideCheckboxes
End If
```

Now let's take a look at the `DisplayCheckboxes` shown in Listing 17-4.

Listing 17-4. DisplayCheckboxes Will Anchor the Check Boxes to the Cell Range When Step2 Is in View

```
Private Sub DisplayCheckboxes()
    Dim i As Integer

    'Iterate through each cell in our anchor
    For i = 1 To [Wizard.CheckboxAnchor].Rows.Count

        'Create a shape object to point to our current Checkbox
        Dim CurrentCheckbox As Excel.Shape
        Set CurrentCheckbox = Me.Shapes("Check" & i)

        'Set the checkbox to be the exact same size as the
        'as the cell it sits atop
        With [Wizard.CheckboxAnchor].Rows(i).Cells
            CurrentCheckbox.Width = .Width
            CurrentCheckbox.Height = .Height
            CurrentCheckbox.Top = .Top
            CurrentCheckbox.Left = .Left
        End With

        'Ensure people can see it
        CurrentCheckbox.Visible = True
    Next i
End Sub
```

In this code, you iterate through every cell that constitutes your anchor. For your purposes, the iterator `i` not only helps you track your current location through each anchor cell but it also helps you reference the corresponding check box.

You'll notice that I reference each check box through the spreadsheet's internal shape container. When you treat check boxes as shapes, you are exposed to the properties that are only available to a shape object. This helps because the check box object does not always show its properties and methods with IntelliSense (more on that later in the chapter).

In the line `With [Wizard.CheckboxAnchor].Rows(i).Cells`, you are grabbing the current cell in your anchor given at index i. With that current cell, you can tell the check box with the same name given by index i—that is, if you are on cell 1 in `Wizard.CheckboxAnchor`, use the check box with the name Check1. You then tell that check box to be the exact same width and height, and the same top and left. This ensures the check box takes up the entire width of any cell in your anchor. You can see this effect in Figure 17-17.

When you're not on the second view, you'll want to hide these check boxes. Listing 17-5 shows how you do just that.

Listing 17-5. This Code Will Remove the Check Boxes from the Anchored Cells

```
Private Sub HideCheckboxes()

    Dim i As Integer

    'Iterate through each cell in our anchor
    For i = 1 To [Wizard.CheckboxAnchor].Rows.Count

        'Create a shape object to point to our current Checkbox
        Dim CurrentCheckbox As Excel.Shape
        Set CurrentCheckbox = Me.Shapes("Check" & i)

            CurrentCheckbox.Top = 0
            CurrentCheckbox.Left = 0
            CurrentCheckbox.Width = 0
            CurrentCheckbox.Height = 0

        'Ensure the checkbox is no longer visible
        CurrentCheckbox.Visible = False

    Next i
End Sub
```

Just as `GoPrevious` was similar to `GoNext`, but in a different direction, `HideCheckBoxes` is very similar to `DisplayCheckboxes`. It simply undoes the work performed in `DisplayCheckboxes`.

But you may be wondering, is it even necessary to change the *height, width, top, and left if you're just going to hide the check boxes?* The truth is, it may not be. You could simply hide these check boxes without doing anything else. At least, at a product level it makes no difference. However, while developing anchors on your spreadsheet, moving every unused check box to a safe location is a good idea.

Here's why. Excel acts somewhat unpredictably when working with form controls. If the above code errors out because there was a bug in the original loop, you might notice the check boxes didn't disappear as they should have. Sometimes, Excel will make several copies of the same CheckBox control (one on top of the other). What causes this is an error in your code while working with multiple form controls. By moving each control to a safe location, you can monitor when Excel has made copies of itself.

Anchoring for Large Sets of Controls

In the previous section's example, one could easily insert eight check boxes and then name them accordingly. It's not necessarily the most enjoyable of exercises, but it's a simple and quick task. What happens if you have so many controls that this take becomes incredibly burdensome? In this section, I'll talk about a quick method of anchoring for large regions.

In Figure 17-19, I've created a large check box anchor region, which I've highlighted in gray for demonstration purposes. Like the anchor region above, I've made this region a named range.

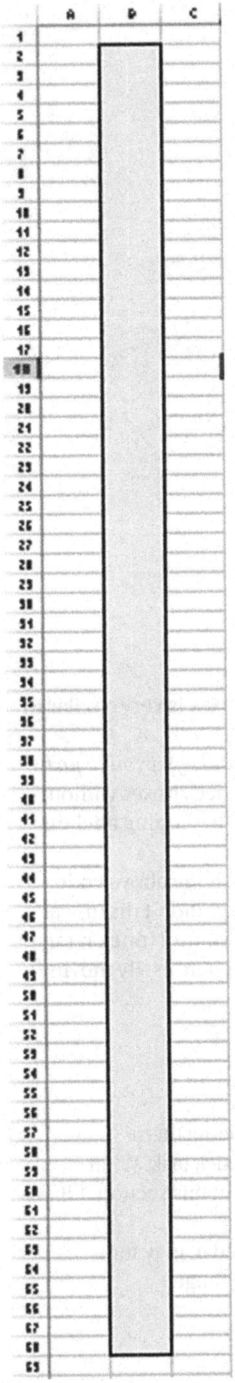

***Figure 17-19.** Inserting several check boxes and naming each one for large regions such as this is an onerous task*

You can quickly create enough check boxes for this entire region by reusing elements of the above presented code. Listing 17-6 shows the code you can use to quickly fill up the entire region with check boxes.

Listing 17-6. This Code Will Fill in a Predefined Anchor Region with Check Boxes

```
Public Sub FillCheckboxAnchorRegion()

    'Clear out any checkboxes already created.
    'This will ensure we don't duplicate checkbox
    'names.
    Me.CheckBoxes.Delete

    Dim i As Integer

    For i = 1 To [CheckboxAnchor].Rows.Count

        Dim CurrentCell As Range
        Dim NewCheckbox As CheckBox

        Set CurrentCell = [CheckboxAnchor].Cells(i)
        Set NewCheckbox = Me.CheckBoxes.Add(0, 0, 0, 0)
        With CurrentCell
            NewCheckbox.Width = .Width
            NewCheckbox.Height = .Height
            NewCheckbox.Top = .Top
            NewCheckbox.Left = .Left
        End With

        NewCheckbox.Name = "Check" & i
    Next

End Sub
```

This code is fairly straightforward. Every worksheet contains a collections object that holds all the CheckBox controls that appear on the sheet. Be careful, however; the collection is not immediately available through IntelliSense. So you need to trust that it is there, even if IntelliSense doesn't show it. When the check boxes are already created, sometimes it's easier to refer to them using the Shapes collection as you did earlier in the chapter.

The `Checkbox` collections object has an `Add` method. The parameters for this method are `left`, `top`, `width`, and `height`. Given this, you might be wondering why I would supply this argument with zeros and then adjust the checkbox's dimensions thereafter. However, in my experience, sometimes changing the `width` and `height` after setting the CheckBox control's coordinates will slightly change its position. Therefore, your best bet is to set the dimensions first and then set the coordinates.

Now, let's talk about how to provide information about the page you're on.

Components That Provide Information

This section will describe how to develop components in the spreadsheet-based wizard that provide the user with information. This includes highlighting the steps you're on, describing the page you're looking at, and including page-specific instructions to the user. Figure 17-20 highlights these components.

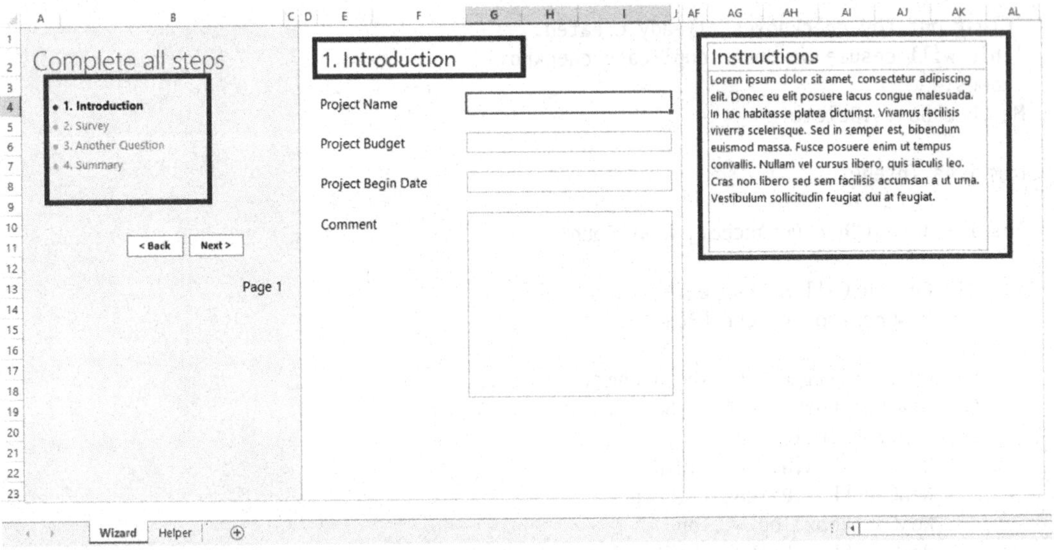

Figure 17-20. Highlighting components that provide information

Using Custom Formats to Highlight the Current Step

This section will cover how you can use custom formats (as you did in the first examples in this chapter) to help you highlight which step is currently in view. Figure 17-21 shows an excerpt of the formula. This is essentially the same formula for all the possible steps cells in Column A.

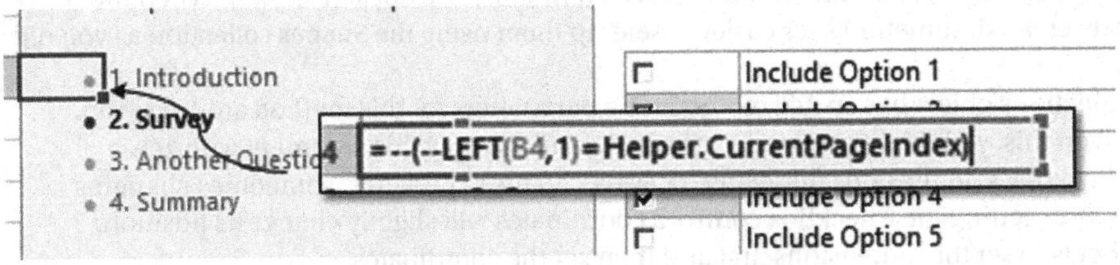

Figure 17-21. The large formula appears in the selected cell

Let's break down this formula. Recall that `--` is simply the shorthand operation to change a text string or Boolean expression into a number. Because every step starts with a given number (e.g. 1. Introduction, 2. Survey, etc), you can read in that number. Above, read in that number by looking at the first character of each step. `Left(B4, 1)` will return a 1; `Left(B5, 1)` will return a 2 and so forth. You use the shorthand value operation to turn it into a number.

Once you know the number, you can simply use a Boolean conditional to compare it to the current page you're on. In Figure 17-19, `--LEFT(B4,1)=Helper,CurrentPageIndex` would return a FALSE. This is because you are on the second page, and cell A4 refers to the first page. Cell A5 refers to the second page, so it will return a TRUE. The final `--` at the end converts the TRUE and FALSE values back to zeros and ones.

To create the dot effects above, you follow a similar custom formula described in the beginning. To all of them, I've applied this simple custom format syntax: `[Color15][=0]•;[Color9][=1]•`.

Using INDEX to Provide Step-Specific Information

This section will cover the finishing touches to your wizard. On the top of every view, I've placed the same formula throughout. You can see this formula in Figure 17-22.

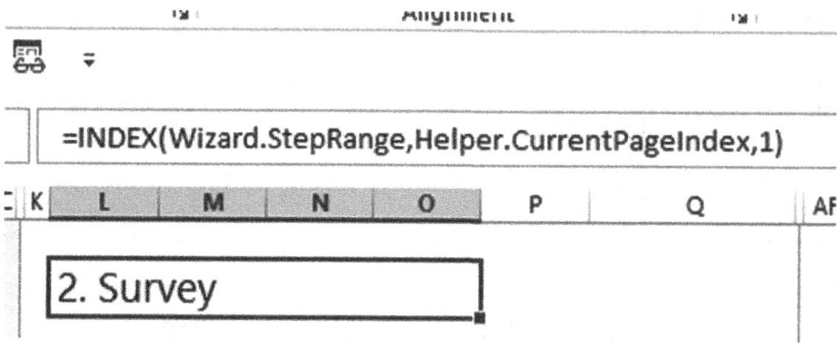

Figure 17-22. *You can use the INDEX formula to display view-specific information*

In Figure 17-23, you can see that `Wizard.StepRange` points to the list of steps on the side.

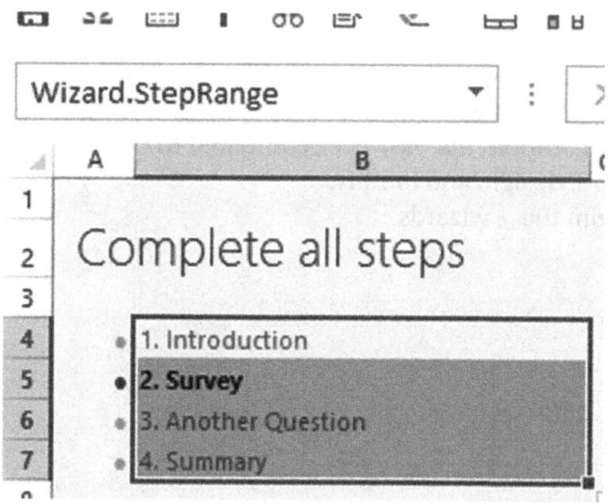

Figure 17-23. *The selected region comprises of the names of all available steps in the wizard*

Because `Wizard.CurrentPageIndex` will always refer to the current step in view, you can simply place this formula at the top of each wizard. This will ensure you always show the correct heading. In addition, you can simply change the title of the step in `Wizard.StepRange` and the change will be reflected automatically in its corresponding view.

The instructions follows a similar path. There's an Instructions Table on the Helper tab that includes instructions for each step. The Instructions Table holds particular instructions for each page in the wizard. Take a look at the instructions formula used in Figure 17-24.

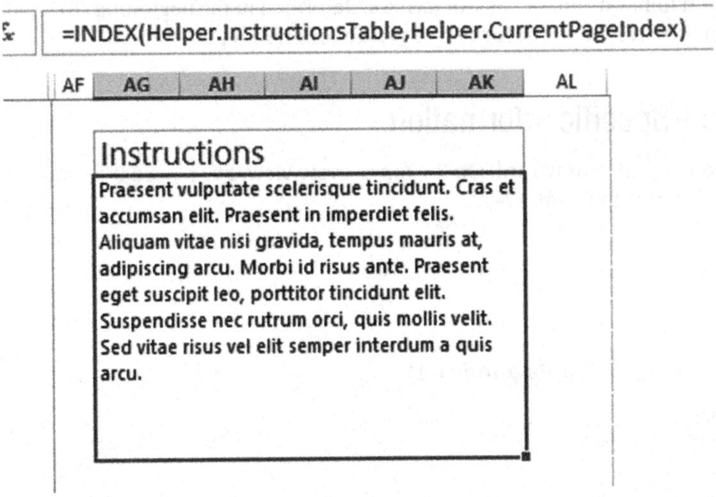

Figure 17-24. *Similar to the mechanism described in Figure 17-22, you can use INDEX to pull specific instructions*

Again, you use the current page index to help you pull relevant information for each step.

The Last Word

In this chapter, I talked about building spreadsheets that can capture user input. Spreadsheet-based wizards are particularly useful. You may not have thought that a spreadsheet was a good place to take user input. Conventional wisdom suggests that you should use ActiveX components. However, compared to UserForm-based wizards, spreadsheet-based wizards are easier to build, design, and modify.

In the next chapter, I'll talk about how to store input from these wizards.

CHAPTER 18

Storage Patterns for User Input

In the last chapter, I discussed developing the components of a spreadsheet-based wizard. The main example from last chapter had you review the infrastructure required to create a spreadsheet-based wizard. Whereas the last chapter concerned layout mechanics of creating an input interface, this chapter will deal with how to store the information once the user has finished their input. What follows builds from the previous chapter. You'll still use the spreadsheet-based wizard implementation described in the previous chapter. However, going forward, you'll make a few changes, which you'll see here soon.

In this chapter, I'll begin by describing a system of metrics that will become the inputs for your wizard. From there, I'll describe the database scheme used to store information once it's been completed. Finally, I'll discuss handling typical database functions, like inserting a new record or deleting an existing one.

The World Health Organization: An Applied Example

In 2000, the World Health Organization ranked the healthcare systems of several different industrialized nations in a study called the *World Health Report 2000 - Health systems: Improving performance.* The study used five key metrics defined here:

- **Health Level**: Measures life expectancy for a given country.
- **Responsiveness**: Measures factors such as speed to health service, access to doctors, et al.
- **Financial Fairness**: Measures the fairness of who shoulders the burden of financial costs in a country.
- **Health Distribution**: Measures the level of equitable distribution of healthcare in a country.
- **Responsiveness Distribution**: Measures the level of equitable distribution of responsiveness defined above.

I'll make some slight modifications to the original model used by the World Health Organization. For one, each country can score from 1 to 10 for a given metric. Second, I've generated a list of made-up countries. So, to be sure, all the data presented herein is notional. Except for the metrics used above (and the weights used in later chapters), the results have basically nothing to do with the actual results of the real model. That's right, all data herein is fictitious. Any resemblance to real life data is purely coincidental. No spreadsheets were harmed in the writing of this book.

In this chapter, you'll allow the user to create a new country, score each country based on metrics, and then store each result into a database. All of this will be self-contained in one spreadsheet file. In addition, you'll be following many of the themes presented in previous chapters. You'll rely heavily on named ranges and attempt to minimize unnecessary use of code.

Design of Your Spreadsheet File

You'll be using the example file `Chapter18Wizard.xlsm` for this chapter. The file is made up of five of tabs, shown in Figure 18-1.

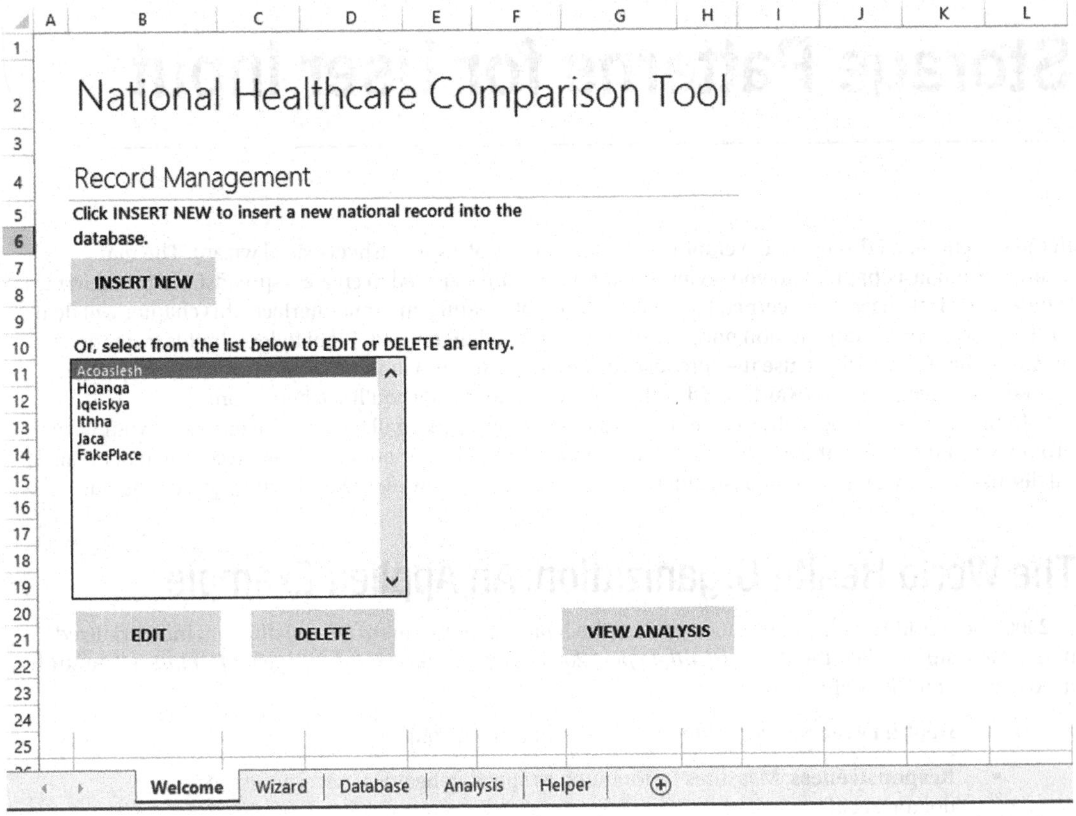

***Figure 18-1.** The five tabs you'll be using for your workbook*

Let's go through each of these tabs.

- **Welcome**: Welcome is essentially your menu. When the user first opens the spreadsheet, it's what they should see (think: "Welcome screen"). Figure 18-2 in the following section shows what the menu looks like.

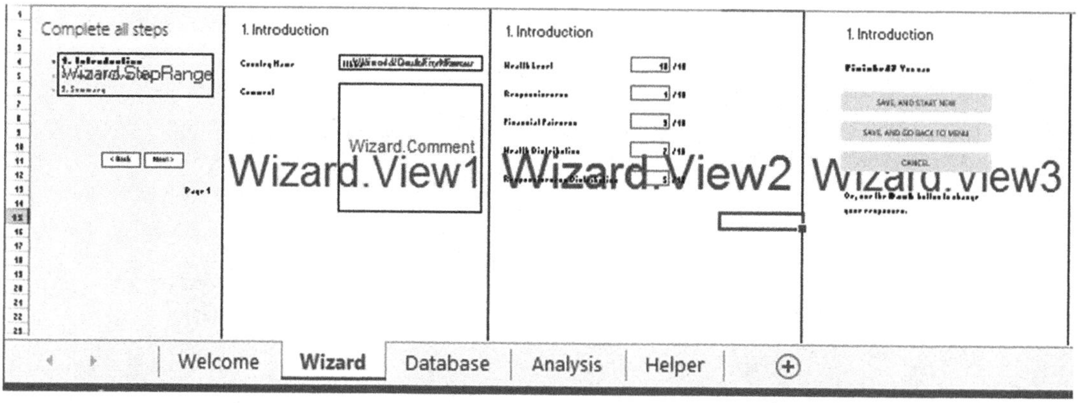

***Figure 18-2.** All the different views of your wizard*

- **Wizard**: Wizard contains your spreadsheet-based wizard.
- **Database**: Database contains the backend database you'll be using to store country record data.
- **Analysis**: Analysis contains the spreadsheet analysis system you'll be developing in the next chapter.
- **Helper**: Helper contains information about the spreadsheet application. For example, it keeps track of how many total views there are in the wizard. It also keeps track of the current wizard page. In the next few chapters, it will keep track of even more.

The Input Wizard

The wizard used here has changed substantially from the previous chapter. In this section, I'll talk about some of those changes in design plus additional design enhancements. Figure 18-2 shows what your wizard looks like with all columns unhidden and zoomed out.

■ **Tip** If you zoom out to 39%, the name of your named ranges will appear on top of the area to which they refer.

As in the previous chapter, the inputs of the wizard have each been given a name. Figure 18-3 shows the named ranges given for the inputs in the first view. Figure 18-4 shows the names for the inputs in the second view.

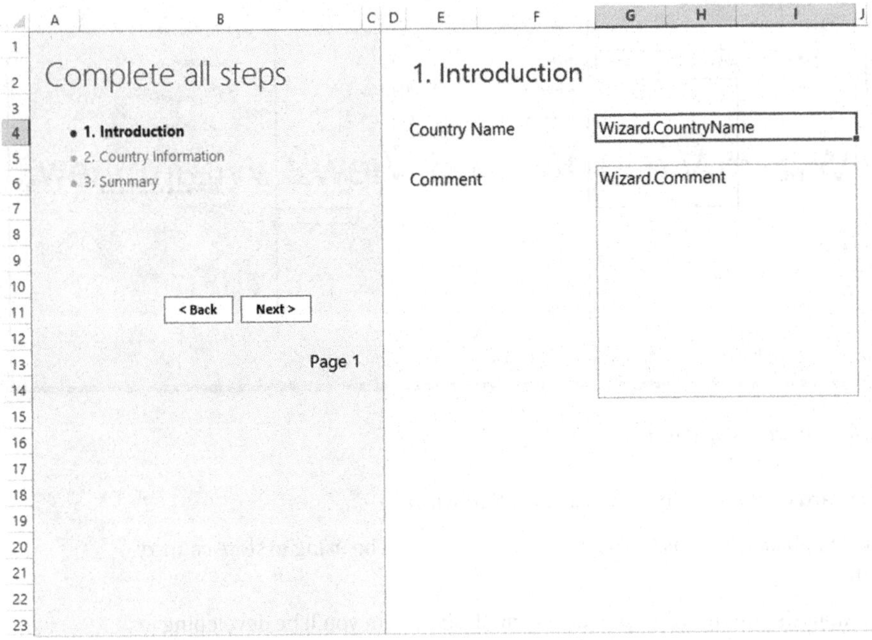

***Figure 18-3.** Inputs on the first view*

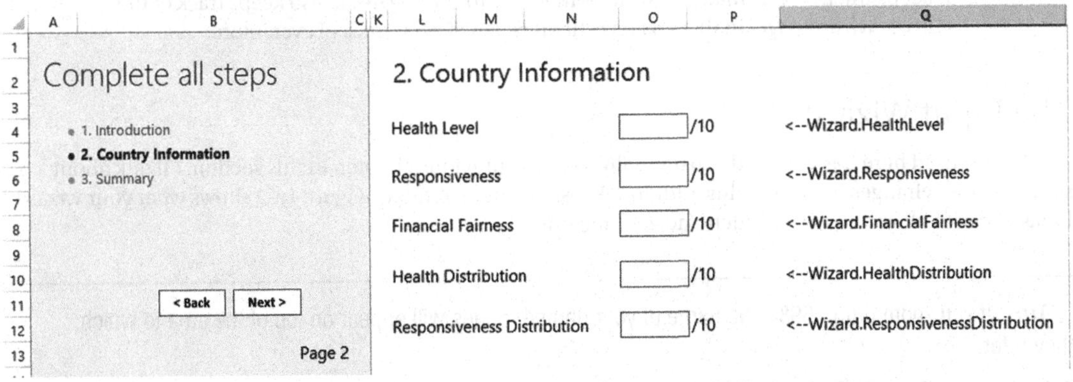

***Figure 18-4.** Inputs on the second view*

If you ever need to change the location of these named—or want to see where they are located immediately—you can use the Name Manager. Figure 18-5 shows the named ranges used to create spreadsheet-level variables. This keeps you from having to store everything in the code, which is error prone and not ideal.

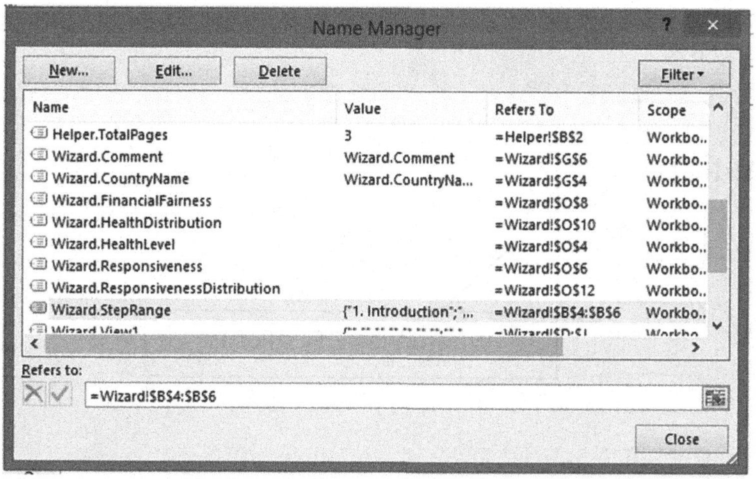

Figure 18-5. *The Name Manager showing all your spreadsheet variables*

Setting Focus to the First Input Cell

As the user clicks Next and Back in the wizard, one clear problem is that the selector doesn't move with it. For instance, if you are on the first screen, and the Comment box is selected (having just typed in some value), when you click Next, the selector will still be on the Comment box. What you want is for the selector to automatically focus on the top of each screen.

To do this, you'll set the first input box of each screen to follow the `.FirstFocus` pattern. For the first screen, you'll create a new named range called `Wizard.View1.FirstFocus` (Figure 18-6).

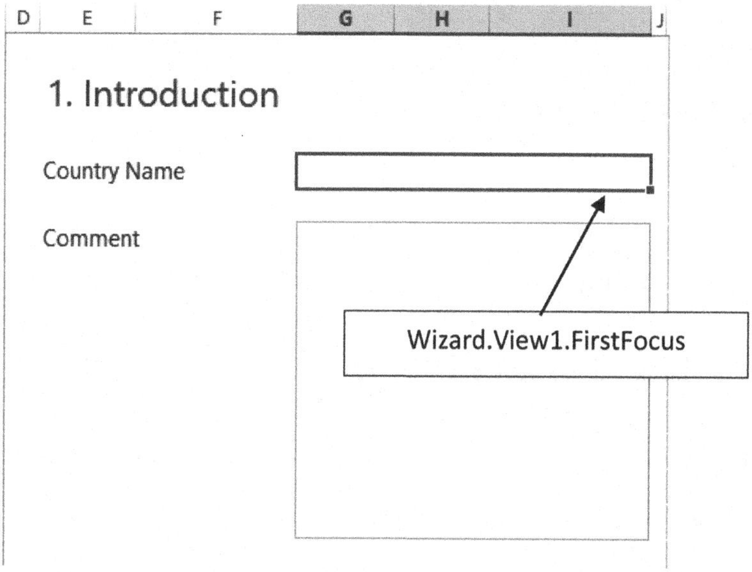

Figure 18-6. *Setting the .FirstFocus input cell of View 1*

You'll do the same for the second view (Figure 18-7).

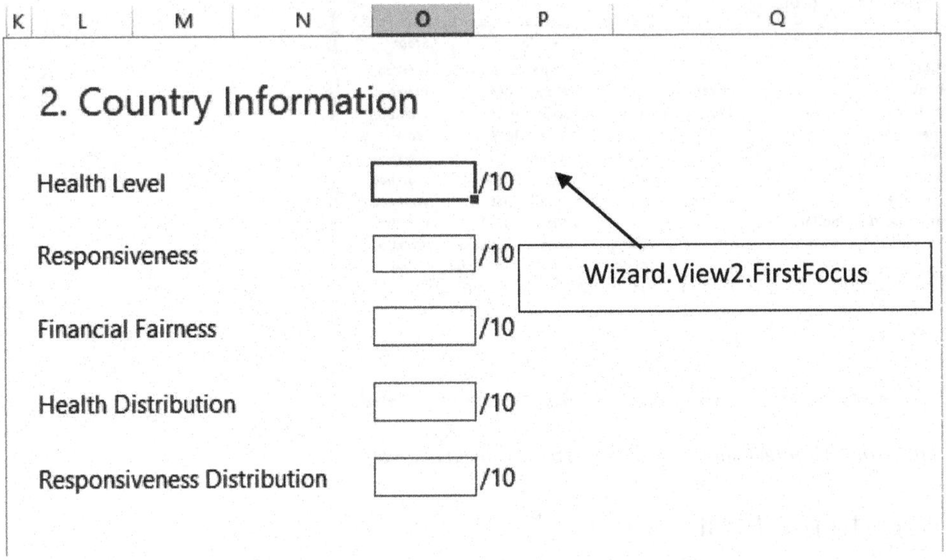

Figure 18-7. *Setting the FirstFocus for the second view*

You then need to adjust your GoNext and GoPrevious procedures, which are displayed in Listings 18-1 and 18-2.

Listing 18-1. The GoNext Procedure

```
Public Sub GoNext()
    Dim index As Integer

    ' Read in the current page index and increment it by one
    ' to go next
    index = [Helper.CurrentPageIndex]
    index = index + 1

    ' Check if we're already on the last page
    If index > [Helper.TotalPages] Then Exit Sub

    ' Unhide the next view
    Wizard.Range("Wizard.View" & index).Columns.Hidden = False
    SetFocusForView (index)

    ' Hide the current set of columns
    If index > 1 Then
        Wizard.Range("Wizard.View" & index - 1).Columns.Hidden = True
    End If

    'Set Helper.CurrentPageIndex equal to the next page index
    [Helper.CurrentPageIndex] = index
End Sub
```

Listing 18-2. The GoPrevious Procedure

```
Public Sub GoPrevious()
    Dim index As Integer

    ' Read in the current page index and decrement it by one
    ' to go previous
    index = [Helper.CurrentPageIndex]
    index = index - 1

    ' Check if we're already on the first page
    If index < 1 Then Exit Sub

    ' Unhide the previous view
    Wizard.Range("Wizard.View" & index).Columns.Hidden = False
    SetFocusForView (index)

    ' Hide the current set of columns
    If index < [Helper.TotalPages] Then
        Wizard.Range("Wizard.View" & index + 1).Columns.Hidden = True
    End If

    'Set Helper.CurrentPageIndex equal to the previous page index
    [Helper.CurrentPageIndex] = index
End Sub
```

The new procedure that helps you focus on the first input cell in each view is **SetFocusForView**, which is highlighted in bold in the code. The code for the SetFocusForView procedure is shown in Listing 18-3.

Listing 18-3. The SetFocusForView Procedure

```
Private Sub SetFocusForView(PageIndex As Integer)
    ' We test to ensure not on the last view of the wizard since
    ' there is nothing to focus in this view.
    If PageIndex < [Helper.TotalPages].Value Then
        Me.Range("Wizard.View" & PageIndex & ".FirstFocus").Activate
    End If
End Sub
```

Notice what SetFocusForView does. It takes in the current page number of the wizard. If you're looking at the first view, it looks for the string Wizard.View1.FirstFocus. If you're on the second page, it looks for Wizard.View2.FirstFocus. Obviously, since you have only two pages with input (the third page gives the user a few buttons to make a choice), you need ensure you're not looking for a .FirstFocus cell where none exists on the page. Hence, you test to ensure you're not in the last view before doing anything.

Now let's take a moment to think about what you've built. In a broad sense, the code doesn't care too much about what page you're looking at so long as there is a FirstFocus on it. Moreover, if you make changes later, and want the FirstFocus to automatically start somewhere else, it's as simple as changing where the name points in the name manager. Third, because you're following a naming convention, it's fairly clear that Wizard.View1.FirstFocus refers to the first input cell in the first View on the Wizard tab. (Compare this to other naming conventions commonly in practice, which might have used something like vw1_Focus1). Finally, you see that named ranges are super flexible. A cell can have more than one named range pointing to it at any given time.

The Database

In this section, I'll talk about the interworkings of the database that serves to store user input. Figure 18-8 provides a snapshot of the database setup you'll be working with.

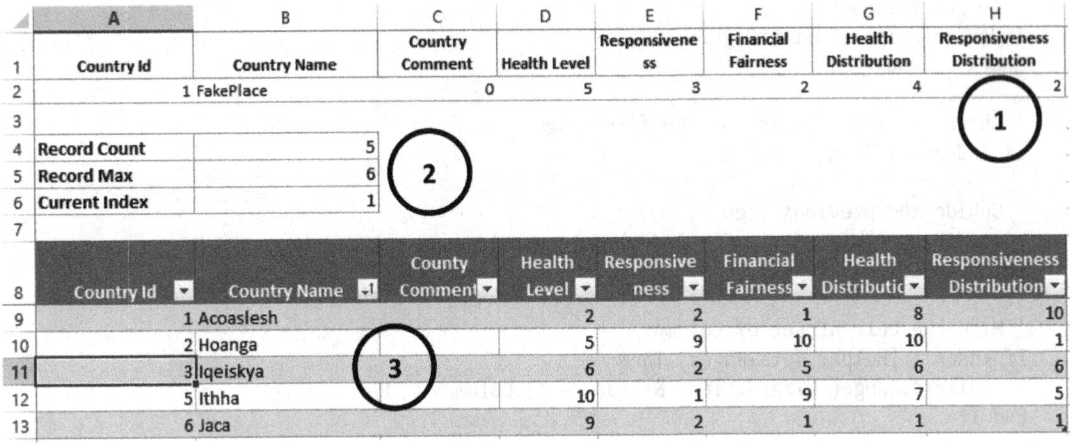

Country Id	Country Name	Country Comment	Health Level	Responsiveness	Financial Fairness	Health Distribution	Responsiveness Distribution
1	FakePlace	0	5	3	2	4	2

Record Count	5
Record Max	6
Current Index	1

Country Id	Country Name	County Comment	Health Level	Responsiveness	Financial Fairness	Health Distribution	Responsiveness Distribution
1	Acoaslesh		2	2	1	8	10
2	Hoanga		5	9	10	10	1
3	Iqeiskya		6	2	5	6	6
5	Ithha		10	1	9	7	5
6	Jaca		9	2	1	1	1

***Figure 18-8.** The backend database storing country information filled in by the user*

Figure 18-8 shows that the database is made up of three components.

1. **Input Entry table**: Serves as the "living" record of current inputs from the wizard.
2. **Database Information table**: Keeps track of the different pieces of information required to add, edit, and delete records.
3. **Database table**: Keeps a record of all information stored currently in the database. I've aptly named this table "Database," which you can see by clicking into the table and going to the Design context menu.

Let's go through each section in detail.

Input Entry Table

The `Input Entry` table is what I like to call the "living record" of the current inputs from within the wizard. Figure 18-9 shows the actual formulas for the five metrics you're capturing beneath their values. Notice that they connect directly to the named ranges found in your wizard. Unfortunately, because of the size of named ranges and page size, I wasn't able to show full names, but you can readily understand what's going on here.

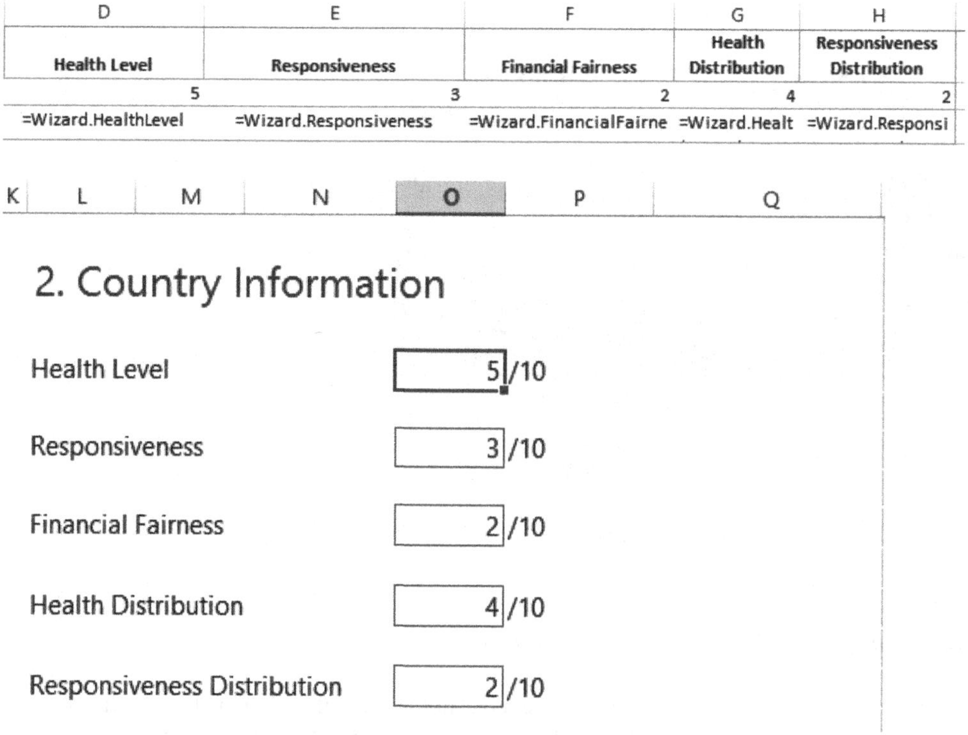

Figure 18-9. *The values in the Input Entry table link directly to the cells on the wizard*

The only cell that doesn't link directly is `Country Id` (Figure 18-10). I'll go into more detail on that in the next few sections.

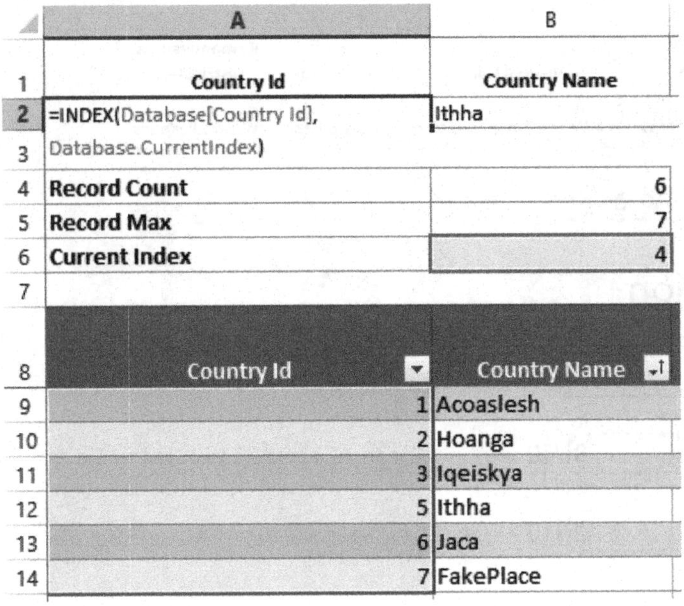

	A	B
1	Country Id	Country Name
2	=INDEX(Database[Country Id],	Ithha
3	Database.CurrentIndex)	
4	Record Count	6
5	Record Max	7
6	Current Index	4
7		
8	Country Id	Country Name
9	1	Acoaslesh
10	2	Hoanga
11	3	Iqeiskya
12	5	Ithha
13	6	Jaca
14	7	FakePlace

Figure 18-10. *Country Id uses the current index and the table*

Once you have all the inputs from the wizard in one spot, adding it into the table can be done in fell swoop. You simply need to copy the values from the `Input Entry` table into your `Database` table. Figure 18-11 shows how you're going to do this conceptually.

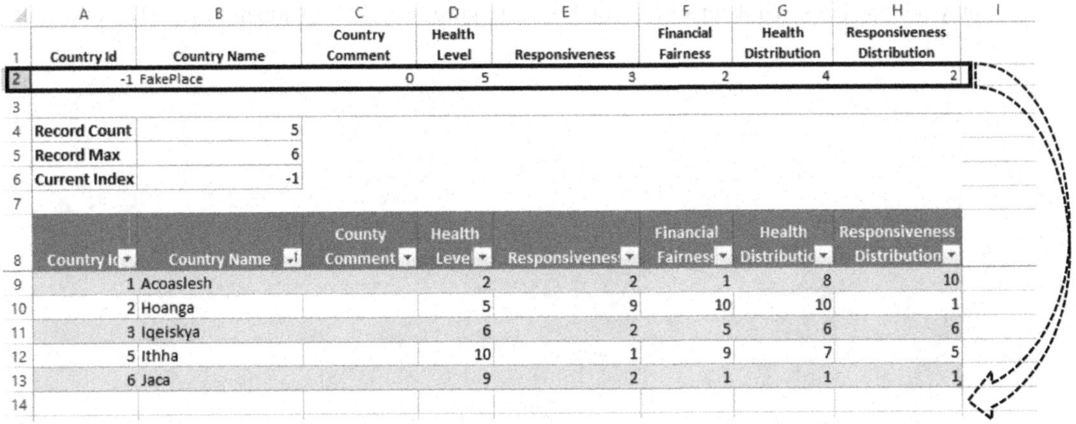

	A	B	C	D	E	F	G	H
1	Country Id	Country Name	Country Comment	Health Level	Responsiveness	Financial Fairness	Health Distribution	Responsiveness Distribution
2	-1	FakePlace	0	5	3	2	4	2
3								
4	Record Count	5						
5	Record Max	6						
6	Current Index	-1						
7								
8	Country Id	Country Name	County Comment	Health Level	Responsiveness	Financial Fairness	Health Distribution	Responsiveness Distribution
9	1	Acoaslesh		2	2	1	8	10
10	2	Hoanga		5	9	10	10	1
11	3	Iqeiskya		6	2	5	6	6
12	5	Ithha		10	1	9	7	5
13	6	Jaca		9	2	1	1	1
14								

Figure 18-11. *A conceptual visualization of how you add a new record to the database*

Because you don't want to do a lot of read/write action on the spreadsheet (since those are volatile), the best way to do this is to simply copy the information from the living record down to the bottom of the table. Figure 18-12 shows the `Input Entry` with a named range of `Database.InputEntry`. When you save a new record, the `SaveNewRecord` procedure is called. Listing 18-4 shows the code for this procedure.

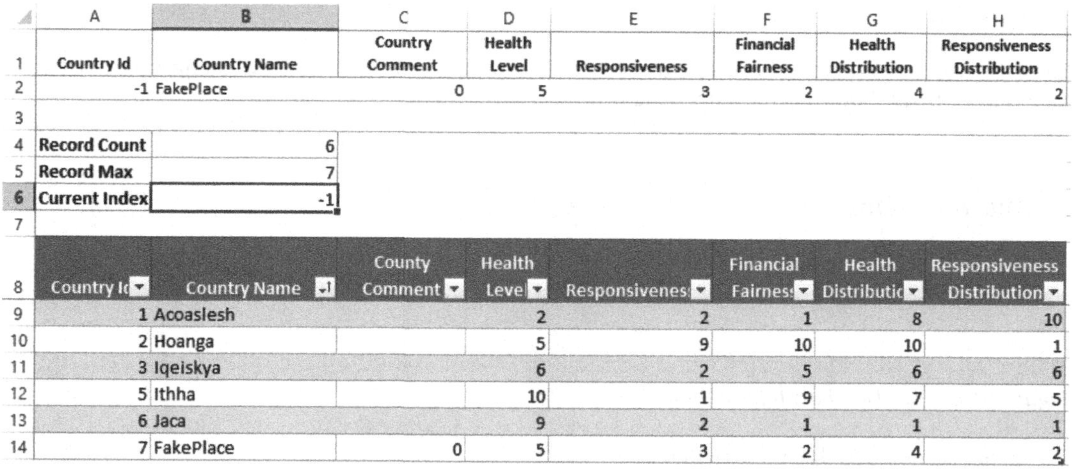

	A	B	C	D	E	F	G	H
1	Country Id	Country Name	Country Comment	Health Level	Responsiveness	Financial Fairness	Health Distribution	Responsiveness Distribution
2	-1	FakePlace	0	5	3	2	4	2
3								
4	Record Count	6						
5	Record Max	7						
6	Current Index	-1						
7								
8	Country Ic	Country Name	County Comment	Health Leve	Responsivenes	Financial Fairnes	Health Distributic	Responsiveness Distribution
9	1	Acoaslesh		2	2	1	8	10
10	2	Hoanga		5	9	10	10	1
11	3	Iqeiskya		6	2	5	6	6
12	5	Ithha		10	1	9	7	5
13	6	Jaca		9	2	1	1	1
14	7	FakePlace	0	5	3	2	4	2

Figure 18-12. *The result of adding a new record*

Listing 18-4. The SaveNewRecord Procedure

```
Public Sub SaveNewRecord()
    Dim LastRowOfData       As Range
    Dim NewRowOfData        As Range
    Dim DatabaseRowCount    As Integer

    ' Find the last row in the Database table
    DatabaseRowCount = Database.ListObjects("Database").ListRows.Count
    Set LastRowOfData = Database.ListObjects("Database").ListRows(DatabaseRowCount).Range

    ' Find the next row to place the input entry
    Set NewRowOfData = LastRowOfData.Offset(1, 0)

    ' Place the new row of data
    NewRowOfData.Value = [Database.InputEntry].Value

    ' Set the ID of the new row of data with a new ID
    NewRowOfData(1, 1).Value = [Database.RecordMax].Value + 1
End Sub
```

What allows this code to work effectively is the use of Excel tables. A feature of these tables is their dynamic growth. When you add a new row of data right below its last record, it will subsume the new record. There's no extra VBA code required for this action to take place. It happens automatically. And here you'll use it to your advantage.

Your code finds the row count for all the data in the table. It then assigns the last row in the table to `LastRowOfData`. Next, you create a new range called `NewRowOfData`, which you tell Excel to place one row below the last. Next, you simply assign the `NewRowOfData` to be the same values as that of `Database.InputEntry` (one fell swoop, right?). Finally, you assign that new row of data a unique ID, which you'll go into the next section. Figure 18-12 shows the result of running the code.

Database Information Table

The Database Information table keeps track of all the information required to make changes to the Excel table. Figure 18-13 shows that the table is made up of three elements.

3		
4	**Record Count**	6
5	**Record Max**	7
6	**Current Index**	-1
7		

Figure 18-13. *The Database Information Table*

In this section, you'll go through them.

- Record Count keeps track of the total records in the database. It uses the formula =COUNT(Database[Country Id]).
- Record Max keeps track of the maximum Country Id of all countries listed. You need to keep track of the maximum id for when you add records. The newest record will always be one plus the maximum record. This ensures each new record is always unique. The formula used is =MAX(Database[Country Id]).
- Current Index works keeps track of whether you're editing a preexisting record or a new record. When Current Index equals negative one, you're editing a new record. Otherwise, when you're editing a preexisting record, Current Index will become the row index of the record being edited.

The most important feature of Current Index is that it never refers to a Country Id. You may find this confusing at first, but it's a very important distinction. Figure 18-14 demonstrates this concept. In the Input Entry in Figure 18-13, you see you're editing the country Ithha. Notice that while Country Id is five, Current Index is four. That's because Ithha is located in the fourth row down in your database table.

	A	B	C	D	E	F	G	H
1	Country Id	Country Name	Country Comment	Health Level	Responsiveness	Financial Fairness	Health Distribution	Responsiveness Distribution
2	5	Ithha	0	10	1	9	7	5
3								
4	Record Count	6						
5	Record Max	7						
6	Current Index	4						
7								
8	Country Id	Country Name	County Comment	Health Level	Responsiveness	Financial Fairness	Health Distribution	Responsiveness Distribution
9	1	Acoaslesh		2	2	1	8	10
10	2	Hoanga		5	9	10	10	1
11	3	Iqeiskya		6	2	5	6	6
12	5	Ithha		10	1	9	7	5
13	6	Jaca		9	2	1	1	1
14	7	FakePlace	0	5	3	2	4	2

Figure 18-14. *Ithha has a Country Id of 5 but the record index is 4*

You must separate location and Id. The reason is because later on in the chapter, you'll be sorting on country name (in fact, you can see it's already being sorted alphabetically in Figure 18-14). The location of the record could change with any update. In addition, you've also included the capability to delete records. Clearly, whatever country used to have a Country Id of 4 has been deleted from this table.

The Backend Database Table

Here you use one of Excel's most powerful capabilities—the table. There are several wonderful features of Excel tables that I'll talk about in this section. For one, they allow for easy dynamic range references (there's one exception to that, which I'll get into in the next section). If I want to include the `Country Name` column in an `Index` function, I need only supply `Database[Country Name]`. That reference to the `Country Name` column is also dynamic: this means I can add or remove records—and Excel will automatically reflect these changes in the `Database[Country Name]` reference.

Another great feature is the table's ability to expand to consume new entries. If I manually type in a new value in an unused cell directly adjacent to the table headings, Excel will expand to incorporate the new column heading. Likewise, if you add any data directly below the last record, the table will expand to consume the new record. The addition of new records is a boon to your development: you're able to add records to the database by simply writing to the spreadsheet. There's no extra overhead of grabbing the table object and inserting it. It's always best to let Excel handle the heavy lifting for you. It's not worth reinventing the wheel (perhaps I should say, "don't reinvent the pie chart," which is shaped like a wheel).

One other feature, which you will use in subsequent chapters, is the table's calculated columns feature. Figure 18-15 provides an example. In the first row, I've selected the `Health Level` response for reach country and added an arbitrary amount to it (for demonstration). Notice, the syntax used is the @ symbol. You can think of that @ symbol as telling Excel that you want to do something with the values in `Health Level` *at the same row* as the current formula. Pressing Enter on the formula will automatically fill the formula down to the end of the row. You can see by the result in Figure 18-15, that each value in `Test Column` has added two to the respective values of `Health Level` in the same row.

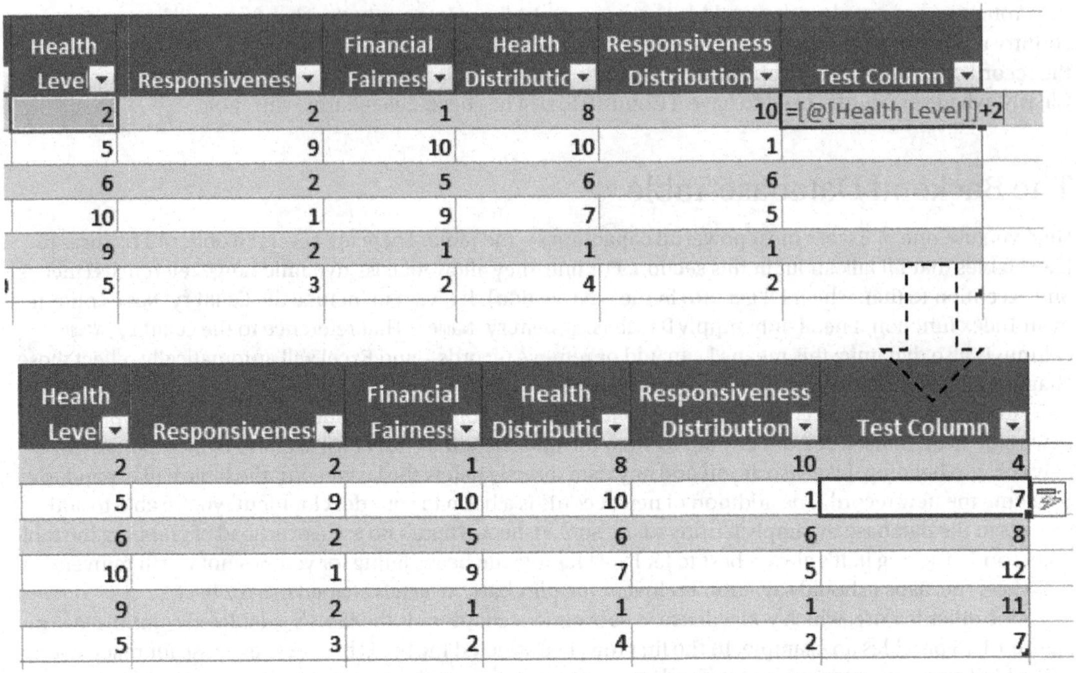
Health Level
Responsiveness
Financial Fairness
Health Distribution
Responsiveness Distribution
Test Column
=[@[Health Level]]+2
Health Level
Responsiveness
Financial Fairness
Health Distribution
Responsiveness Distribution
Test Column

***Figure 18-15.** A demonstration of calculated columns*

Menu Screen Functionality

Now let's focus on what's presented to the user when they first open the spreadsheet. Figure 18-16 shows the opening menu screen. In this section, I'll go through the different elements.

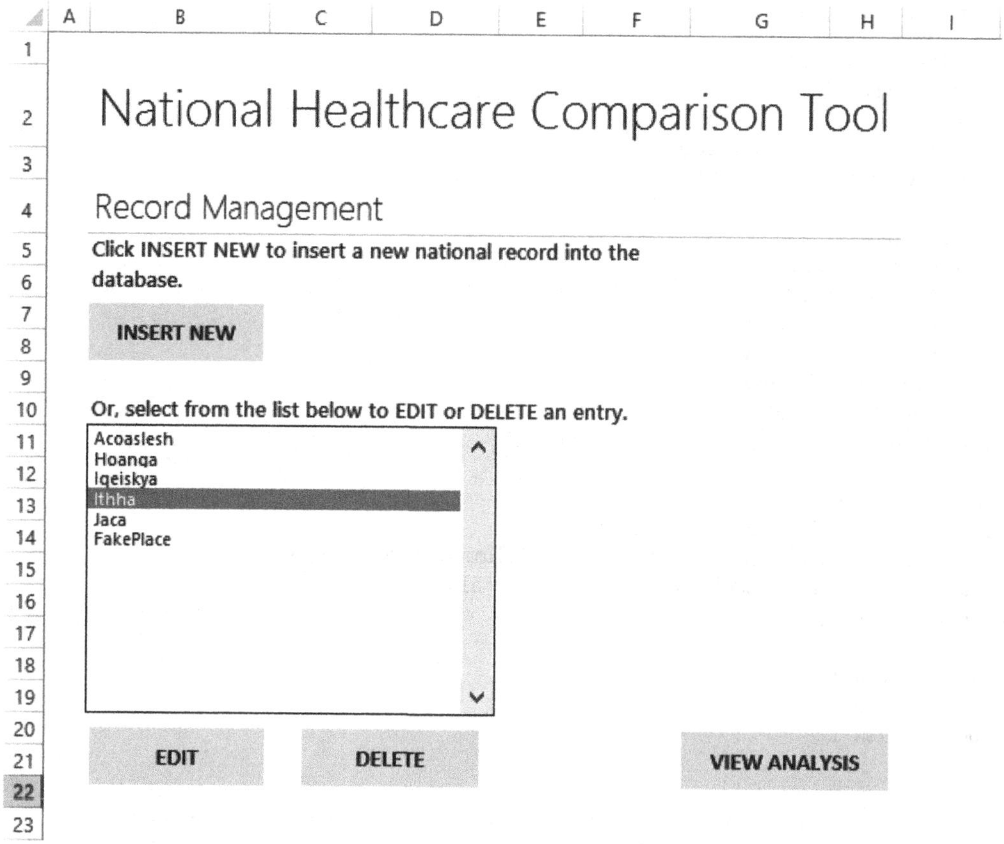

Figure 18-16. *The opening screen of your spreadsheet tool*

As you can see, the opening screen is made up of several different elements. The most prominent of those elements are Excel shapes and a list box form control. As stated earlier, I am not a fan of using form control buttons (that look like old Windows 95 buttons) on the spreadsheet. Rather, I much prefer using clean-looking Excel shapes and assigning macros to them.

Inserting a New Record

In this section, I'll talk about creating a new record *to be inserted* upon its completion. Here, I've created a button called Insert New Record. But this may be a misnomer since it doesn't insert a new record into the database; rather, it clears the wizard of its values and places the user on the wizard's first input screen. From the user's perspective, it prepares the wizard for the process of inserting a new record. See Listing 18-5.

Listing 18-5. The InsertNewRecord Procedure

```
Public Sub InsertNewRecord()
    Dim CurrentIndex As Integer

    'Set CurrentIndex to a new record
    [Database.CurrentIndex].Value = -1

    'Clear all inputs
    [Wizard.CountryName].Value = ""
    [Wizard.Comment].Value = ""
    [Wizard.HealthLevel].Value = ""
    [Wizard.Responsiveness].Value = ""
    [Wizard.FinancialFairness].Value = ""
    [Wizard.HealthDistribution].Value = ""
    [Wizard.ResponsivenessDistribution].Value = ""

    'Show the first page
    CurrentIndex = [Helper.CurrentPageIndex]
    Wizard.Range("Wizard.View" & CurrentIndex).Columns.Hidden = True
    Wizard.Range("Wizard.View1").Columns.Hidden = False
    [Helper.CurrentPageIndex].Value = 1

    'Activate the wizard
    Wizard.Activate
    SetFocusForView 1
End Sub
```

As with most of my code, I've attempted to the keep the logic fairly straightforward. You set the `CurrentIndex` to -1 to tell Excel when you're working with a new record. Next, you clear out any values in the table that may have been previously entered. Next, you tell Excel you want to start the user on the first page of entry. Finally, you activate the wizard to bring it into view.

Editing an Existing Record

In this section, I'll talk about how to edit an existing record. This is where the `Current Index` from the `Database Information` table comes in. Figure 18-17 shows the cell link for the ListBox actually pointing to `Database.CurrentIndex`. Recall the cell link tracks the row index for a selected item. Figure 18-18 shows that since you've selected the fourth row, your `Current Index` (stored as `Database.CurrentIndex`) is 4.

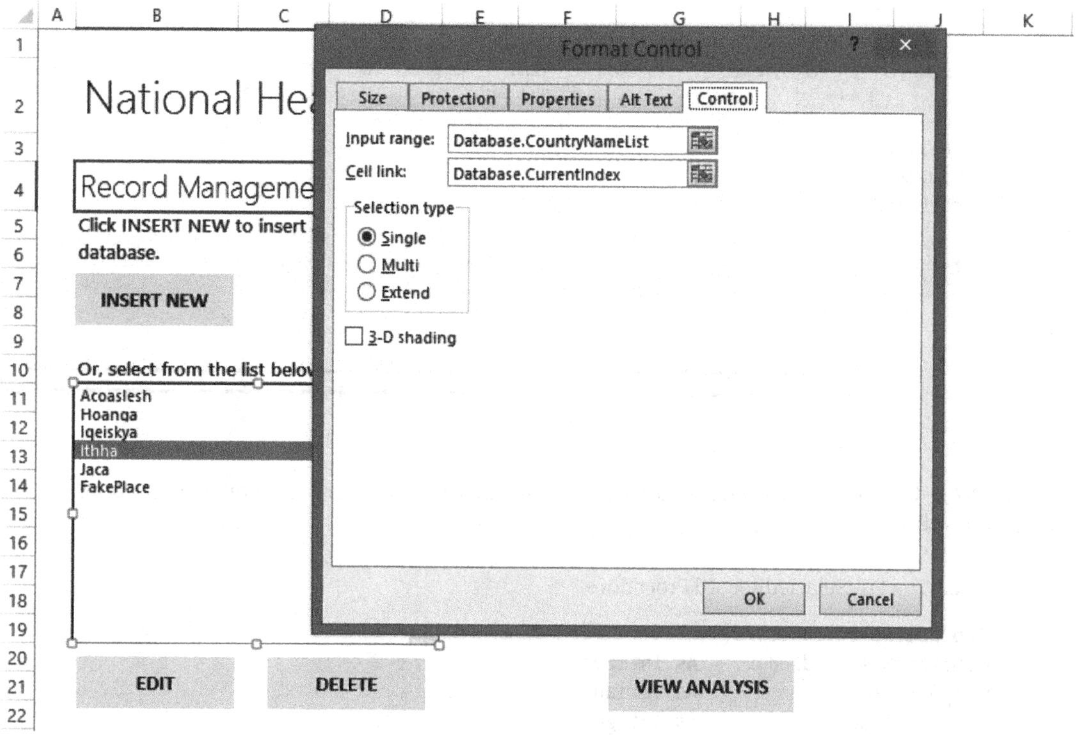

Figure 18-17. *Cell link refers to Database.CurrentIndex*

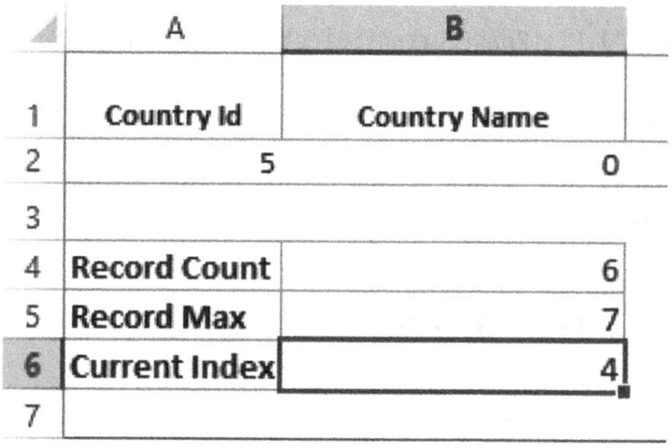

Figure 18-18. *Current Index is 4 because the list box on the front screen has the fourth row selected*

You now work in reverse of when you add a record to the table. Since you know the row location of the record you want to edit, you simply need to fill this information in your `Input Entry` table. Figure 18-19 shows what this looks like conceptually. Listing 18-6 provides the code for the procedure.

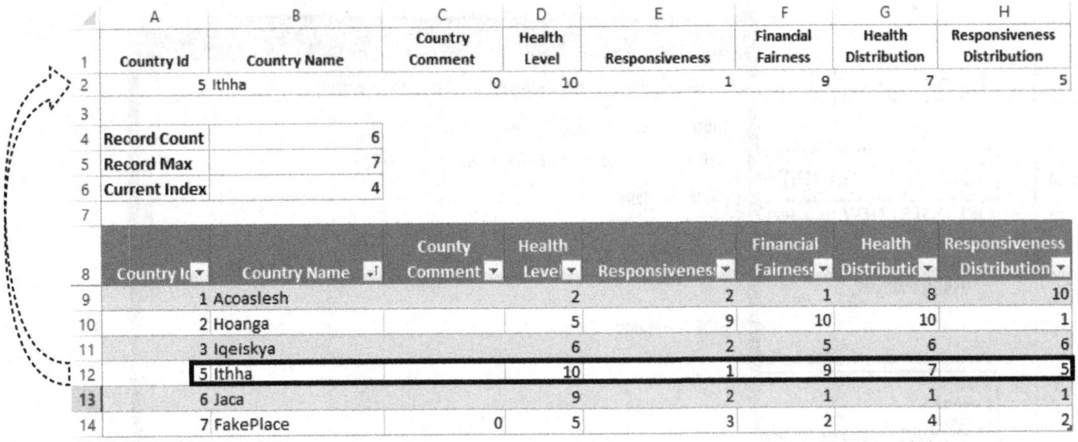

	A	B	C	D	E	F	G	H
1	Country Id	Country Name	Country Comment	Health Level	Responsiveness	Financial Fairness	Health Distribution	Responsiveness Distribution
2	5	Ithha	0	10	1	9	7	5
3								
4	Record Count	6						
5	Record Max	7						
6	Current Index	4						
7								
8	Country Id	Country Name	County Comment	Health Level	Responsiveness	Financial Fairness	Health Distribution	Responsiveness Distribution
9	1	Acoaslesh		2	2	1	8	10
10	2	Hoanga		5	9	10	10	1
11	3	Iqeiskya		6	2	5	6	6
12	5	Ithha		10	1	9	7	5
13	6	Jaca		9	2	1	1	1
14	7	FakePlace	0	5	3	2	4	2

Figure 18-19. *What happens when you edit a given record based on the user's selection in the list box from on the opening tab*

Listing 18-6. The EditSelectedRecord Procedure

```
Public Sub EditSelectedRecord()
    Dim CurrentSelectedIndex     As Integer
    Dim InputEntry               As Variant
    Dim CurrentIndex             As Integer

    'Assign the currently selected index to CurrentSelectedIndex
    CurrentSelectedIndex = [Database.CurrentIndex]

    InputEntry = Database.ListObjects("Database").ListRows(CurrentSelectedIndex).Range

    [Wizard.CountryName].Value = InputEntry(1, 2)
    [Wizard.Comment].Value = InputEntry(1, 3)
    [Wizard.HealthLevel].Value = InputEntry(1, 4)
    [Wizard.Responsiveness].Value = InputEntry(1, 5)
    [Wizard.FinancialFairness].Value = InputEntry(1, 6)
    [Wizard.HealthDistribution].Value = InputEntry(1, 7)
    [Wizard.ResponsivenessDistribution].Value = InputEntry(1, 8)

    'Show the first page
    CurrentIndex = [Helper.CurrentPageIndex]
    Wizard.Range("Wizard.View" & CurrentIndex).Columns.Hidden = True
    Wizard.Range("Wizard.View1").Columns.Hidden = False
    [Helper.CurrentPageIndex].Value = 1

    'Activate the wizard
    Wizard.Activate
    SetFocusForView 1
End Sub
```

This code is similar to the code in Listing 18-5. However, here you need to ensure that the values of the Input Entry table become that of the selected record. Notice in Listing 18-6 that you're not assigning the cells of the Input Entry table directly. This is because that would overwrite their linkages to the wizard. Rather, you assign the values to the input cells of the wizard. This is akin to the user simply typing the information in themselves.

You might also notice that you use the constant numbers for the assignment. Generally, I don't prefer this practice for other applications, but it works here in a pinch. So long as you've performed the requisite planning to ensure you won't move the column assignments around. And, in fact, even if you did end up adding input boxes into the wizard and you had to update the input table, you could simply add another column adjacent to the Input Entry table. The order of inputs the user fills in within the wizard is not the same order you must follow when storing the information. So you can add even more variables to the store without changing the order of columns above. If, in another application, you must change these numbers in your code to accommodate the insertion of another variable, it's best not to use this method (instead, go for named ranges for each cell).

Deleting a Selected Record

In this section, I'll talk about how to delete a selected record. On the opening screen, I allow the user to select a record from the list box to be deleted. Listing 18-7 shows the code to delete a selected record.

Listing 18-7. The DeleteSelectedRecord Procedure

```
Public Sub DeleteSelectedRecord()
    Dim CurrentSelectedIndex    As Integer

    ' Assign the currently selected index to CurrentSelectedIndex
    CurrentSelectedIndex = [Database.CurrentIndex]

    ' Move the ListBox Selector
    If [Database.CurrentIndex].Value = [Database.RecordCount] Then    'Last item on the list
        [Database.CurrentIndex].Value = [Database.CurrentIndex].Value - 1
    End If

    ' Delete the entry
    Database.ListObjects("Database").ListRows(CurrentSelectedIndex).Delete
End Sub
```

The code is fairly straightforward. You use the CurrentIndex to find the row location of the record you want to move. All you need to do is simply delete that row to remove it. The conditional in Listing 18-7 tests whether the selector is pointing to the last record in the table. If it is, you need to point it to the record that comes right before it since you'll be deleting that record. If you did not do this, CurrentIndex would continue to point to a record that no longer exists. You can see the problem this would cause by placing the selector on the last item in the list box. If you press Delete, the record is removed. If you pressed Delete again, an error would occur since the selector would point to a row location that is now greater than the total count of rows in the list.

Linking the Column of Country Names to the Form Control ListBox

In this section, I'll talk about how to automatically fill the list box with the list of country names from your backend database. Unfortunately, this is less straightforward than one might think. The problem stems from the ListBox's inability to accept a direct reference to the backend database. You might think you could just type `Database[Country Name]` into the `Input Range` of the form control's properties (refer to Figure 18-18). But doing this will generate a list box of blank data. Therefore, you need to create a dynamically sized named range using good ol' fashioned functions.

Look back at Figure 18-18, and you can see you've specified the named range `Database.CountryNameList`. Let's take a look at its formula.

```
=INDEX(Database[Country Name],1):INDEX(Database[Country Name],Database.RecordCount)
```

In previous chapters, I talked about creating dynamically sized functions such as these. The range operator (the colon) is what makes this formula work so seamlessly. Let's look at Figure 18-20 while attempting to go through this function. The left side of the function `INDEX(Database[Country Name],1)` will always return the first record in the `Country Name` column of your table—cell B9 in Figure 18-19. The right side, `INDEX(Database[Country Name],Database.RecordCount)`, will always return the last record in the table—cell B14 in Figure 18-20. Remember that Excel treats what `INDEX` returns as a cell reference, so behind the scenes Excel constructs the range B9:B14 on the fly based on this formula. If you added a record, Excel would construct the effective range B9:B15 on the fly.

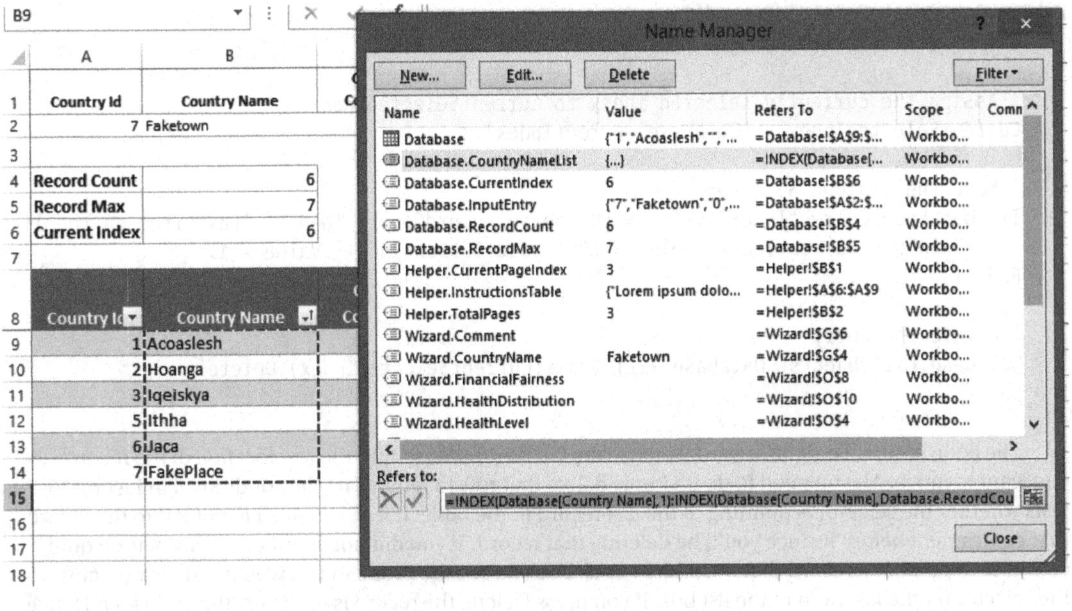

Figure 18-20. Dynamic formulas help you construct this dynamic range on the fly

Looking back to Figure 18-16, it's a matter of simply linking the ListBox's input Range to this dynamic range.

The final button on the opening menu takes users to the analysis page. I'll go over that in more detail in the next two chapters. In the meantime, look at the excerpted code in Listing 18-8. (Note this code is located in the Welcome sheet object.)

Listing 18-8. The GoToAnalysis Procedure

```
Public Sub GoToAnalysis()
    Analysis.Activate
End Sub
```

Wizard Summary Buttons

Now let's focus on the buttons that appear in the third, summary view of your wizard (see Figure 18-21). In this section, you'll go through each of these buttons. Here's a quick summary of what they do:

- **Save and Start New**: Saves the current input and begins a new record from page 1 of the wizard.
- **Save, and Go Back To Menu**: Saves the current record and returns the user to the menu screen.
- **Cancel**: Does nothing with the current record and simply returns the user to the menu screen.

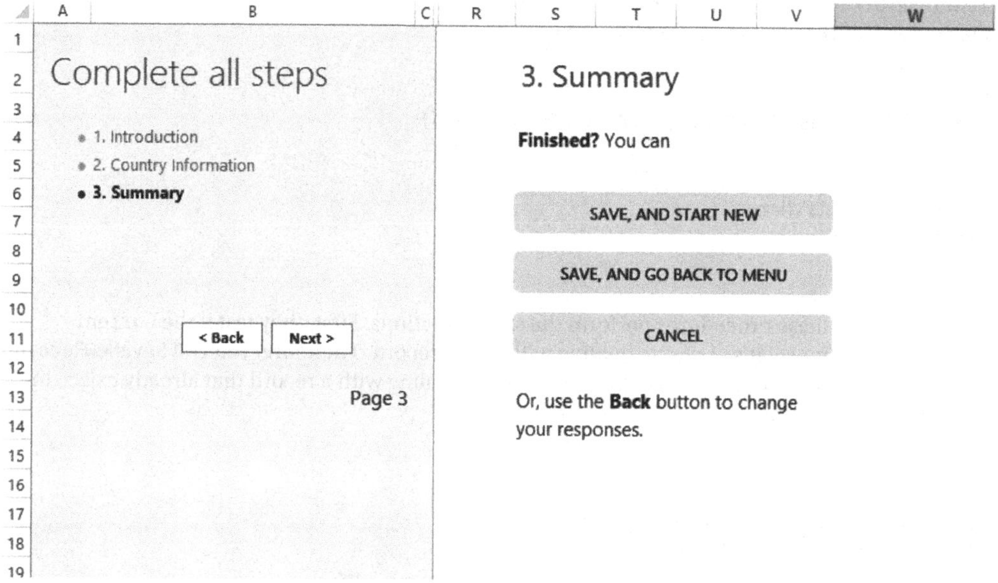

Figure 18-21. *The summary view of your wizard*

In this section, you'll go over the **Save, and Start New** and the **Save, and Go Back to Menu** buttons. Listings 18-9 and 18-10 show their code, respectively.

Listing 18-9. The SaveAndStartNew Procedure

```
Public Sub SaveAndStartNew()
    Dim CurrentIndexOfRecord As Integer

    CurrentIndexOfRecord = [Database.CurrentIndex].Value
    If CurrentIndexOfRecord = -1 Then
        Wizard.SaveNewRecord
    Else
        Wizard.SaveSelectedRecord (CurrentIndexOfRecord)
    End If
    Database.SortCountryNames
    Wizard.InsertNewRecord
End Sub
```

Listing 18-10. The SaveAndGoBackToMenu Procedure

```
Public Sub SaveAndGoBackToMenu()
    Dim CurrentIndexOfRecord As Integer

    CurrentIndexOfRecord = [Database.CurrentIndex].Value
    If CurrentIndexOfRecord = -1 Then
        Wizard.SaveNewRecord
    Else
        Wizard.SaveSelectedRecord (CurrentIndexOfRecord)
    End If

    Database.SortCountryNames
    Wizard.GoToMenu
End Sub
```

Notice that both of these procedures perform the same functions. First, they test if the `CurrentIndex` is -1. Again, you know if it's -1 you're dealing with a new record. Therefore, you call `SaveNewRecord` (Listing 18-4, from earlier in the chapter). Otherwise, you're dealing with a record that already exists. In that case, you call `SaveSelectedRecord` (Listing 18-11).

Listing 18-11. The SaveSelectedRecord Procedure

```
Public Sub SaveSelectedRecord(RecordIndex)
    Dim SelectedRowOfData As Range

    ' Assign SelectedRowOfData to the index in the database
    ' corresponding to the record we're editing
    Set SelectedRowOfData = Database.ListObjects("Database").ListRows(RecordIndex).Range

    ' Assign the updated entries back to the selected row
    SelectedRowOfData.Value = [Database.InputEntry].Value
End Sub
```

The SaveSelectedRecord procedure works similarly to that of SaveNewRecord. However, because the record already exists on the table, you need not doing anything additional except set the values in the row location to those of the Input Entry table.

Returning to Listing 18-9 and 18-10, both procedures call the Database.SortCountryNames (Listing 18-12). As you make updates to the table, you want to keep the integrity of an alphabetical sort. Here, you use a simple command to the table to resort the data using the CountryName column. Note this procedure is actually in the Database sheet object (which is why you use Database.SortCountryNames).

Listing 18-12. The SortCountryNames Procedure

```
Public Sub SortCountryNames()
    Me.ListObjects("Database").Sort.SortFields.Add Key:=[Database[Country Name]]
End Sub
```

Finally, returning once again to Listings 18-9 and 18-10, you see two both procedures differ with respect to their last line of code (which I've bolded). In Listing 18-9, you want to start the wizard over and insert another record. So you call InsertNewRecord (Listing 18-5). On the other hand, Listing 18-10 takes you back to the menu, so you call GoToMenu (Listing 18-13). Likewise, the Cancel button shown in Figure 18-21 calls GoToMenu directly.

Listing 18-13. The GoToMenuProcedure

```
Public Sub GoToMenu()
    Welcome.Activate
End Sub
```

The Last Word

In this chapter, you built upon the wizard from the previous chapter. You developed a backend database system that works seamlessly when complete. Whenever available, you let Excel do the work for you—by using formulas and features inherent to Excel's tables. You also used quite a bit of code, but you were careful to make your code simple and readable. Specifically, you avoided using code for everything. By creating a proper balance between code, formulas, and features, you've built the beginnings of a robust Excel application. And that's thinking outside the cell.

CHAPTER 19

Building for Sensitivity Analysis

In the previous chapters, you created a wizard that could take in and store user input. In this chapter, you're going to create a dashboard that allows you to perform sensitivity analysis based on the metrics described in the previous chapter. Figure 19-1 provides a preview of what's to come.

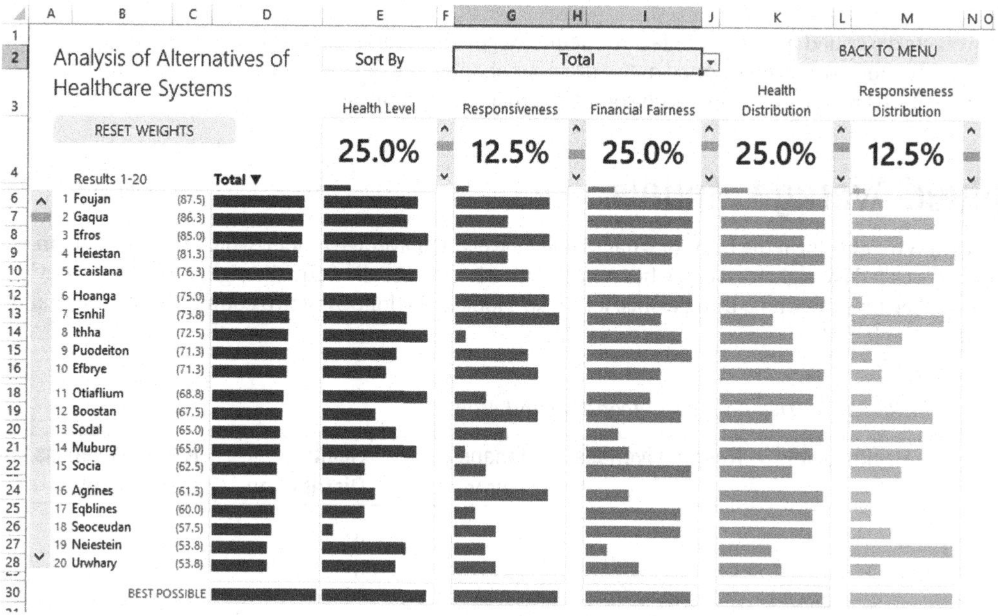

***Figure 19-1.** Analysis of alternatives decision support system*

The tool shown in Figure 19-1 allows you to do many things quickly and efficiently, much of it with only a small amount of VBA code. As you'll see, many of the mechanics are driven by Excel's built-in functions, like conditional formatting and formulas. The correct combination between formulas and code here is key. It's what allows you to make instantaneous updates to the data without the need of a "recalculate" button.

But before you do anything, let's return to the metrics described in the previous chapter. See Table 19-1.

Table 19-1. *Metrics Used by the World Health Organization's Study*

Metric	Description	Weight
Health Level	Measures life expectancy for a given country.	25.0%
Responsiveness	Measures factors such as speed to health service, access to doctors, et al.	12.5%
Financial Fairness	Measures the fairness of who shoulders the burden of financial costs in a country.	25%
Health Distribution	Measures the level of equitable distribution of healthcare in a country.	25%
Responsiveness Distribution	Measures the level of equitable distribution of responsiveness defined above.	12%
		100%

Source: The World Health Report 2000 - Health Systems: Improving Performance (`www.who.int/whr/2000/en/`)

The weights described herein are in fact the same weights the World Health Organization used in its original study. However, as mentioned in the previous chapter, the data you have is notional and the countries are fakes (I mean, they don't even sound like real county names!).

Weighted Average Models

The metrics and weights form the basis of what's called a weighted average model, which I'll talk about in this section. It's called a weighted average because the metrics are not all of equal weight (otherwise, they'd all be 20%). To see how the whole thing works, let's take a look at the following two countries, Acoaslesh and Afon, shown in Table 19-2.

Table 19-2. *The Results for Two Countries, Acoaslesh and Afon*

Country	Health Level	Responsiveness	Financial Fairness	Health Distribution	Responsiveness Distribution
Acoaslesh	2	2	1	8	10
Afon	4	2	4	2	3

As you will recall, each of these countries is scored out of 10. So, for Acoaslesh, 2 is a considerably low score given that 10 is the highest. On the other hand, a 10 for Responsiveness Distribution is the best possible score. To find the total health level (that is, the weighted average score) for Acoaslesh, you would compute as follows:

```
= [(Health Level Score/10 * Health Level Weight) +
  (Responsiveness Score/10 * Responsiveness Weight) +
  (Financial Fairness Score/10 * Financial Fairness Weight) +
  (Health Distribution Score/10 * Health Distribution Weight) +
  (Responsiveness Distribution Score/10 * Responsiveness Distribution Weight) ] * 100
```

```
=  [(.20 * 12.5%) +
    (.20 * 25.0%) +
    (.10 * 25.0%) +
    (.80 * 25.0%) +
    (1.00 * 12.5%)  ] * 100
```

```
= .425 * 100 = 42.5.
```

So for Acoaslesh, the overall health score is .425, where 1 is now the best score. That process of taking the scores and making them proportionate to the scale of 0 to 1 is called normalization.

Sometimes it's easier to understand these final scores as being out of 100 instead. So let's scale .425 to be 42.5 by multiplying the result by 100. Whether you choose .425 or 42.5, both answers are correct. It's up to you how you want to present the numbers to your audience.

Likewise, you can perform the same calculations for Afon.

```
=  [(.40 * 12.5%) +
    (.20 * 25.0%) +
    (.40 * 25.0%) +
    (.20 * 25.0%) +
    (.30 * 12.5%)   ] * 100
```

```
= 28.8
```

By scaling to 100, you make the perfect score any country could get 100 (again, if you don't scale, the perfect score is 1). You can see this yourself by assuming perfect 10s across the board and doing the calculations. When you do this for each country, you'll come up with a list like the one below. This allows you to say the countries ranking higher are better performers *according to your model* than the ones below (Figure 19-2).

8	Country Name	Total
9	Foujan	87.5
10	Efros	83.8
11	Gaqua	82.5
12	Hoanga	80.0
13	Heiestan	78.8
14	Esnhil	76.3
15	Ecaislana	73.8
16	Efbrye	73.8
17	Boostan	71.3
18	Puodeiton	71.3
19	Agrines	66.3
20	Sodal	62.5
21	Ithha	61.3
22	Seoceudan	61.3
23	Socia	61.3
24	Otiaflium	60.0
25	Eqblines	57.5
26	Muburg	55.0

Figure 19-2. *A rank of country performance based on the weighted average model*

■ **Note** The statistician George E. P. Box once remarked, "All models are wrong, some are useful." You should always remember models are simplifications (sometimes even gross over-simplifications) of reality. By their nature, they cannot capture everything. Indeed, this was a criticism of the World Health Organization regarding the these metrics; some argued that other factors were not correctly captured or weighted. Therefore, it's important to be specific when discussing model results. Rather than assert the validity of the results as being unequivocal truth, remember they are the product of a series of assumptions.

Sensitivity Analysis on a Weighted Average Model

In this section, I'll talk about sensitivity analysis with respect to the weights for a given country. The weighted sum model above is used to evaluate many different countries. Broadly, you're simply investigating a resultant list of countries whose *scores* follow directly from the *importance* of each metric (given by its weight) in your model. As such, you may want to investigate how changing the importance of inputs impacts overall scores. This is called *sensitivity analysis.*

One-Way Sensitivity Analysis

One simple, if powerful, sensitivity analysis method is to vary only one weight at a time while maintaining the proportional importance of the other weights. This is called *one-way sensitivity analysis* and it works like this. Let's say you want to see what happens if you increase Health Level by 4%. First, let's divide the weight into two theoretical groups (Figure 19-3).

WHAT WE WANT TO CHANGE	WHAT WE WANT TO MAINTAIN				
HEALTH LEVEL	HEALTH DISTRIBUTION	RESPONSIVENESS	RESPONSIVENESS DISTRIBUTION	FINANCIAL FAIRNESS	SUM TOTAL
25.0%	25.0%	12.5%	12.5%	25.0%	100.0%
=		=			
25%		75%			100.0%

Figure 19-3. *The weights split into two groups based upon which weights you want to change and which you want to maintain*

The rule here is that each group must always sum to 100%. So, if you add 4% to Health Level, you have to subtract it from the other group (see Figure 19-4).

	Beginning	Change	New%
HEALTH LEVEL	25%	4%	29%
OTHER GROUP	75%	-4%	71%
	100%		100%

Figure 19-4. *If you add 4% to one group, you must remove it from the other*

Now that the overall sum of the "other group" has changed, the weights that make up that group are adjusted while maintaining the same proportion to the group's sum as they did before. In this next stage, you find the new proportions for the group you want to maintain (Figure 19-5).

	HEALTH DISTRIBUTION	RESPONSIVENESS	RESPONSIVENESS DISTRIBUTION	FINANCIAL FAIRNESS
Original Weight	25.0%	12.5%	12.5%	25.0%
Divide by old group sum	75.0%	75.0%	75.0%	75.0%
Proportion	33.3%	16.7%	16.7%	33.3%

Figure 19-5. *Finding the new proportions for the group you want to maintain*

In the next step, you multiply each calculated proportion by the new group weight (Figure 19-6).

	HEALTH DISTRIBUTION	RESPONSIVENESS	RESPONSIVENESS DISTRIBUTION	FINANCIAL FAIRNESS
Proportion	33.3%	16.7%	16.7%	33.3%
Multiply by new group weight	71.0%	71.0%	71.0%	71.0%
New Weight	23.7%	11.8%	11.8%	23.7%

Figure 19-6. *Multiply the new proportions by the new group weight*

Finally, you reassign the new weights to their metrics (Figure 19-7). If you add all the weights together, they now once again sum to 100%.

HEALTH LEVEL	HEALTH DISTRIBUTION	RESPONSIVENESS	RESPONSIVENESS DISTRIBUTION	FINANCIAL FAIRNESS
29.0%	23.7%	11.8%	11.8%	23.7%

Figure 19-7. *New metrics weights*

In this chapter, I'll talk about how to build this mechanism into your spreadsheet. I've devised a method that I call Easy One-Way Sensitivity Analysis. You'll be surprised how easy it is to implement into your application. Indeed, you can take advantage of Excel's form controls to help you do much of the heavy lifting. That said, there are a few limitations with this method, and I'll go over them in this chapter.

Creating a Linked Values Table

In this section, I'll describe how to create the Easy One-Way Sensitivity Analysis mechanism and implement it in the spreadsheet application from the previous chapter. If you upload `Chapter19Wizard.xlsm`, we're starting on the Helper tab.

In Figure 19-8, I've placed five scroll bar form controls onto the spreadsheet, one for each metric. I've then linked each scroll bar to a cell on the right of each metric under the column `Linked Value`. Just for clarification, the left-most scroll bar links to cell B5, and the right-most links to cell B9. As you can see in Figure 19-3, the middle scroll bar is linked to `Financial Fairness`, B7.

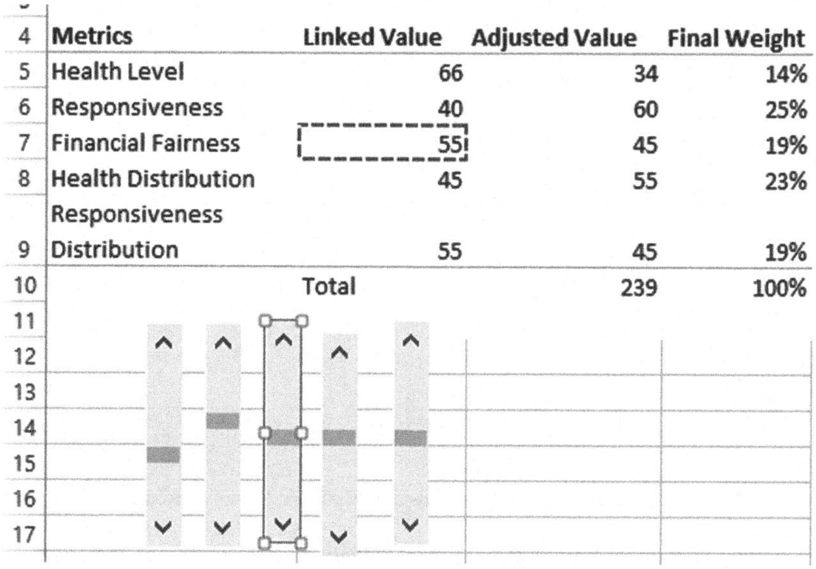

4 Metrics Linked Value Adjusted Value Final Weight
5 Health Level 66 34 14%
6 Responsiveness 40 60 25%
7 Financial Fairness 55 45 19%
8 Health Distribution 45 55 23%
Responsiveness
9 Distribution 55 45 19%
10 Total 239 100%
11
12
13
14
15
16
17

Figure 19-8. *Setting the scrollbars to the their linked cells*

For each scroll bar, I've set its minimum value to 1 and its maximum value to 100. Figure 19-9 shows an example.

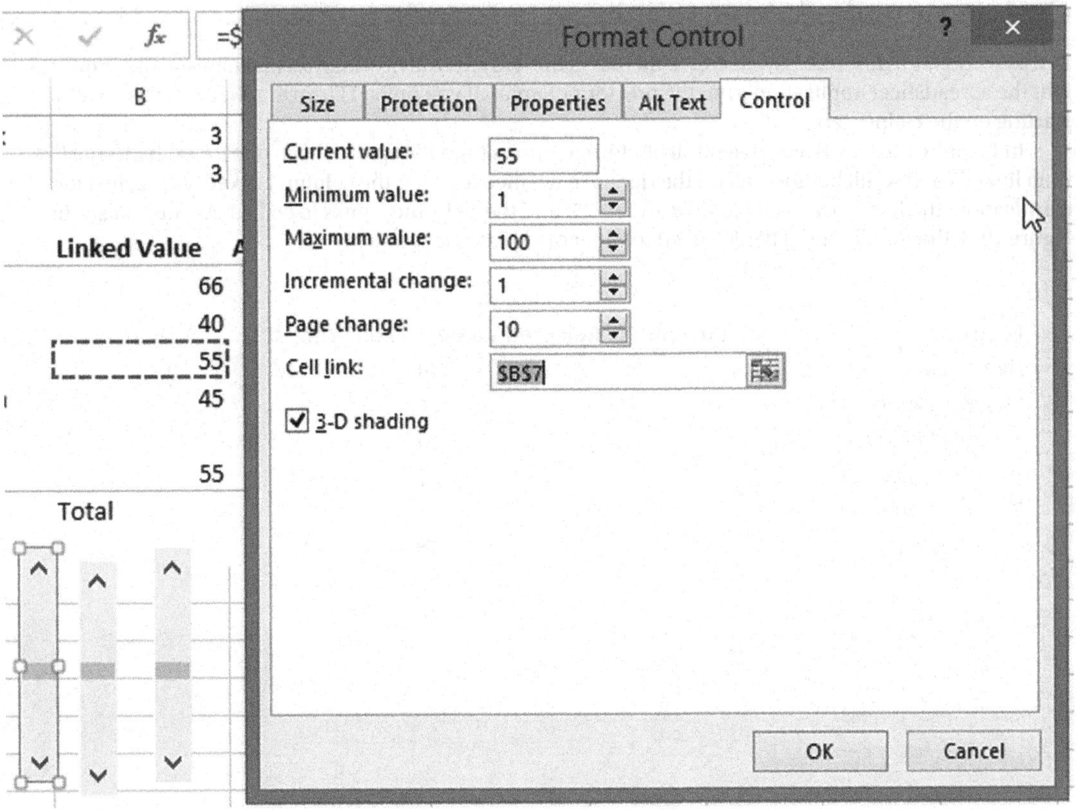

Figure 19-9. *Each scroll bar has a minimum of 1 and a maximum of 0. Right-click the scroll bar and select format control to see this property window*

Recall from previous chapters how form control scroll bars work. The more you scroll down, the greater the number in the linked cell. While there's nothing wrong with that per se, it's counterintuitive for some users. For your purposes, you'd like the action of scrolling up to actually increase the resulting value and scrolling down to decrease. So you need to adjust the values on the spreadsheet to reflect this preference.

Insert another column next to `Linked Values` and call it `Adjusted Values`. In each cell next to the linked values, you'll take the scroll bar's value and subtract it from 100 (the max value of the scroll bar). Figure 19-10 shows this formula.

	Metrics	Linked Value	Adjusted Value	Final Weight
4	Metrics	Linked Value	Adjusted Value	Final Weight
5	Health Level	66	=100-B5	14%
6	Responsiveness	40	60	25%
7	Financial Fairness	55	45	19%
8	Health Distribution	45	55	23%
9	Responsiveness Distribution	55	45	19%
10		Total	239	100%
11				

Figure 19-10. *Now, as you scroll down, the Adjusted Value decreases. As you scroll up, the Adjusted Value increases*

Next, you need to add to find the grand total of all the adjusted values. You can do that by adding a `SUM` cell at the bottom of the `Adjusted Value` column (see Figure 19-11).

	Metrics	Linked Value	Adjusted Value	Final Weight
4	Metrics	Linked Value	Adjusted Value	Final Weight
5	Health Level	66	34	14%
6	Responsiveness	40	60	25%
7	Financial Fairness	55	45	19%
8	Health Distribution	45	55	23%
9	Responsiveness Distribution	55	45	19%
10		Total	=SUM(C5:C9)	100%

Figure 19-11. *Use the SUM function to the find the total of adjusted values*

Now you want to come up with the proportion each metric's adjusted value has to the overall total. To do that, you simply need to divide each adjusted value by the total adjusted value sum, as shown in Figure 19-12.

	Metrics	Linked Value	Adjusted Value	Final Weight
4	Metrics	Linked Value	Adjusted Value	Final Weight
5	Health Level	66	34	14%
6	Responsiveness	40	60	25%
7	Financial Fairness	55	45	=C7/$C$10
8	Health Distribution	45	55	23%
9	Responsiveness Distribution	55	45	19%
10		Total	239	100%

Figure 19-12. *Find the final weight by dividing each adjusted value by the total adjusted value*

And that's it! If you play around with the scroll bars, you can change the weights as much as you want. The final weight will always equal 100%! Figure 19-13 shows an adjustment to the scroll bar assigned to `Health Level`.

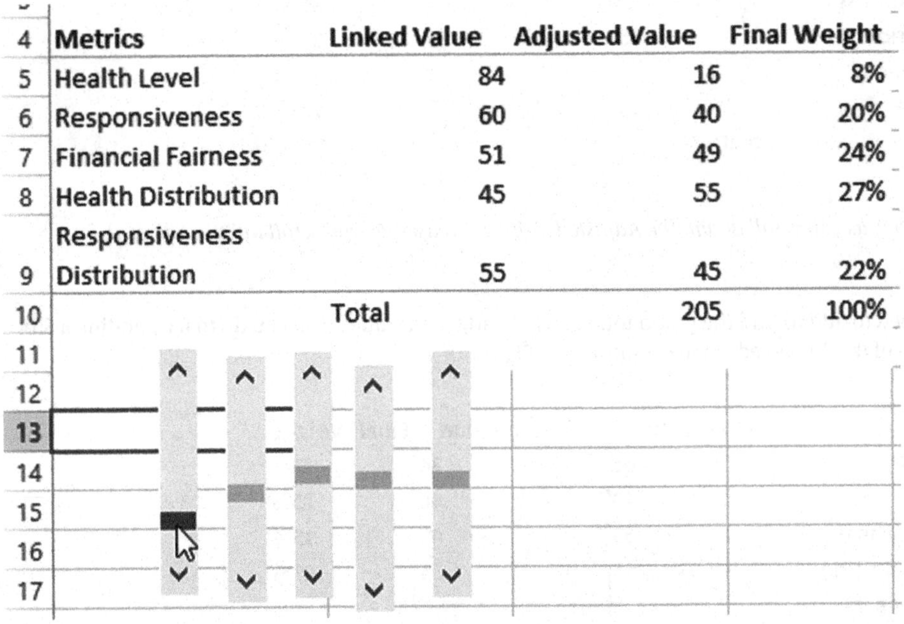

Metrics
Linked Value
Adjusted Value
Final Weight
Health Level 84 16 8%
Responsiveness 60 40 20%
Financial Fairness 51 49 24%
Health Distribution 45 55 27%
Responsiveness Distribution 55 45 22%
Total 205 100%

Figure 19-13. *No matter what values are assigned to the scroll bar, the final weights will always add up to 100%*

Linking to the Database

You're now interested in how you can link the one-way sensitivity analysis mechanism back into the database. The first thing you want to do is give each of these weights a name. Figure 19-14 shows them named following my usual conventions.

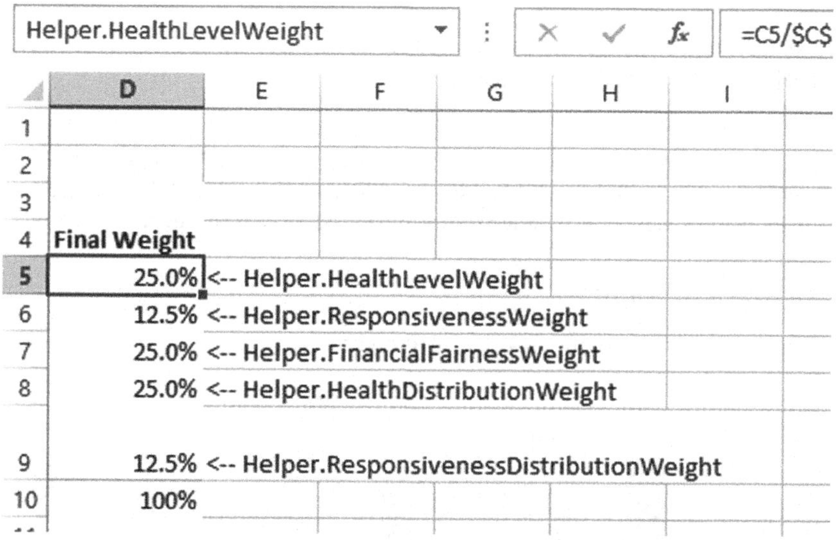

Figure 19-14. Each final weight is named in the Linked Values table

In the Database tab, I've added a few extra columns that reflect the operations you must do for each metric for each country in your list (see Figure 19-15). Across the top of the new columns, I've included a reference to the actual weight values for each metric. This isn't technically necessary, as you'll see. However, I think it provides a good reference into understanding the calculations. Anything you can do to make your work easier to understand when you come back to it is, in my opinion, always worthwhile.

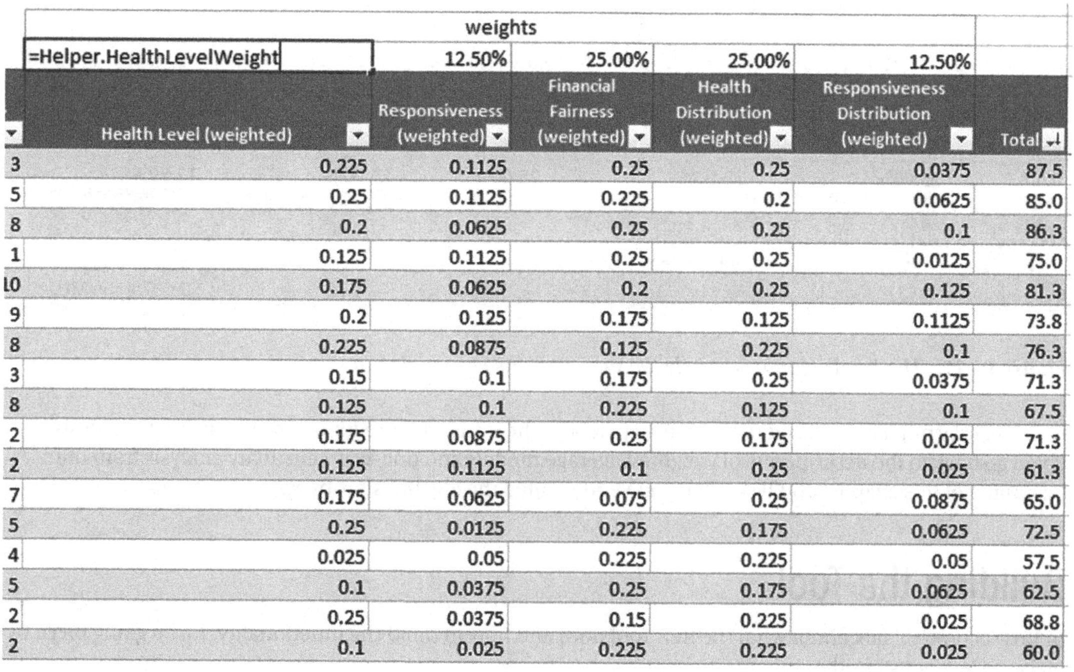

	weights					
	=Helper.HealthLevelWeight	12.50%	25.00%	25.00%	12.50%	
	Health Level (weighted)	Responsiveness (weighted)	Financial Fairness (weighted)	Health Distribution (weighted)	Responsiveness Distribution (weighted)	Total
3	0.225	0.1125	0.25	0.25	0.0375	87.5
5	0.25	0.1125	0.225	0.2	0.0625	85.0
8	0.2	0.0625	0.25	0.25	0.1	86.3
1	0.125	0.1125	0.25	0.25	0.0125	75.0
10	0.175	0.0625	0.2	0.25	0.125	81.3
9	0.2	0.125	0.175	0.125	0.1125	73.8
8	0.225	0.0875	0.125	0.225	0.1	76.3
3	0.15	0.1	0.175	0.25	0.0375	71.3
8	0.125	0.1	0.225	0.125	0.1	67.5
2	0.175	0.0875	0.25	0.175	0.025	71.3
2	0.125	0.1125	0.1	0.25	0.025	61.3
7	0.175	0.0625	0.075	0.25	0.0875	65.0
5	0.25	0.0125	0.225	0.175	0.0625	72.5
4	0.025	0.05	0.225	0.225	0.05	57.5
5	0.1	0.0375	0.25	0.175	0.0625	62.5
2	0.25	0.0375	0.15	0.225	0.025	68.8
2	0.1	0.025	0.225	0.225	0.025	60.0

Figure 19-15. The weights across the top correspond to the weights you developed on the Helper tab

■ **Tip** You should develop with the future in mind. Ask yourself, will you understand what's going on when you come back to your spreadsheet having not seen it in three months?

Note that each of the new columns corresponding to the metrics now has "(weighted)" added to the name. This is because these columns represent the individual scores divided by 10 and multiplied by their corresponding weight on the Helper tab. Figure 19-16 shows the formula used for `Health Level (weighted)`.

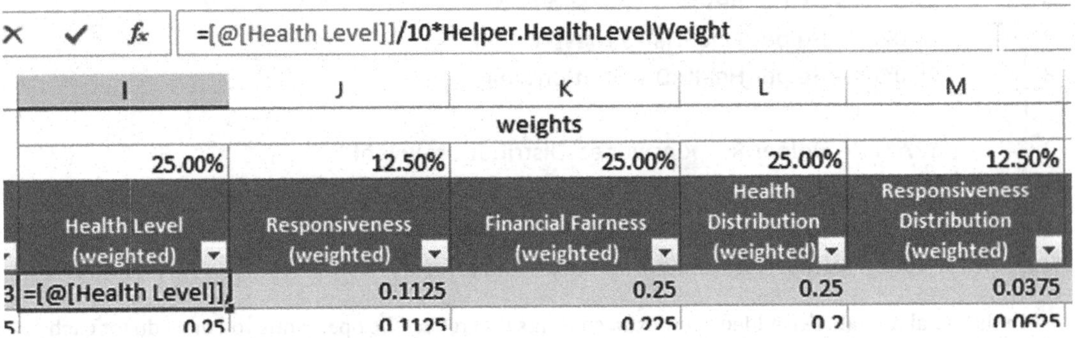

Figure 19-16. Each weighted column takes the original scored value, divides it by ten, and then multiplies it by its respective weight from the Helper tab

Finally, the `Total` column is simply the sum of all weights (see Figure 19-17).

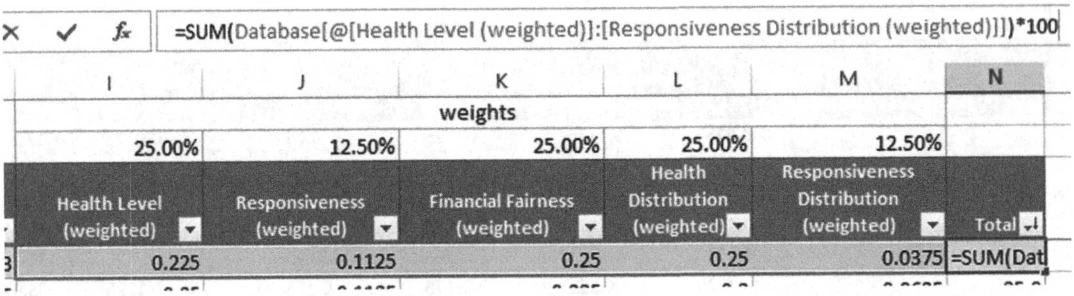

Figure 19-17. The Total column is simply the sum of all the weighted scores

You may not have realized it, but you've just built the infrastructure for one-way sensitivity analysis! If you go back to the descriptions of weighted average models and one-way sensitivity analysis from the beginning of this chapter, you'll see that you've re-created the algebra step-by-step.

Building the Tool

In this section, I'll talk about what the new tool does and how to build the functionality. I'll be going piece by piece, so let's get started.

Getting to the Backend, the Intermediate Table

As you know, I'm a huge fan of intermediate tables. We almost always need to transform (that is, do something to) the data before presenting it to the user. Obviously, where you place your intermediate tables is up to you. For many projects, I prefer placing them on a new tab. But sometimes when dealing with something that's complicated, I like to place the table in the same worksheet tab as the decision support system or dashboard. That's what I've done here.

If you look at the Analysis tab in your file, you'll see that the rows beyond 31 are hidden. That's because your intermediate table is somewhere in the hidden rows. So the first thing you'll want to do is unhide all rows to get a peek at the intermediate table. The easiest way to do that, in my opinion, is to click the grey triangle at the upper left of your worksheet to select everything (of course, there's always CTRL+A). Then from on the Home tab, go to Format ➤ Hide & Unhide ➤ Unhide rows. Figure 19-18 shows these steps.

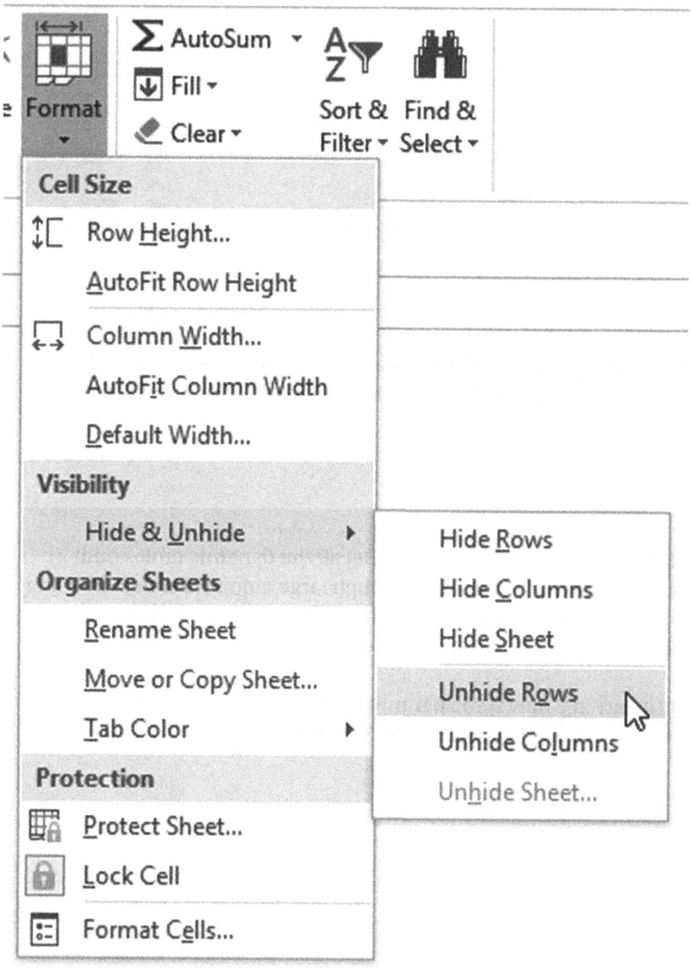

Figure 19-18. *Steps to unhide rows*

The intermediate table is shown in Figure 19-19.

Intermediate Table

Scrollbar Value	1	
Sort Column Id	6	

#	Sort Column: Total	Match Index	Country	1 Health Level	2 Responsiveness	3 Financial Fairness	4 Health Distribution	5 Responsiveness Distribution	6 Total
1	87.5027	14	Foujan	90	90	100	100	30	87.50
2	86.2533	15	Gaqua	80	50	100	100	80	86.25
3	85.0002	9	Efros	100	90	90	80	50	85.00
4	81.2525	16	Heiestan	70	50	80	100	100	81.25
5	76.2550	7	Ecaislana	90	70	50	90	80	76.25
6	75.0015	17	Hoanga	50	90	100	100	10	75.00
7	73.7548	13	Esnhil	80	100	70	50	90	73.75
8	72.5038	19	Ithha	100	10	90	70	50	72.50
9	71.2519	30	Puodeiton	70	70	100	70	20	71.25
10	71.2516	8	Efbrye	60	80	70	100	30	71.25
11	68.7510	27	Otiaflium	100	30	60	90	20	68.75
12	67.5037	5	Boostan	50	80	90	50	80	67.50
13	65.0013	37	Sodal	70	50	30	100	70	65.00
14	65.0001	22	Muburg	90	10	40	90	70	65.00
15	62.5003	36	Socia	40	30	100	70	50	62.50
16	61.2512	3	Agrines	50	90	40	100	20	61.25
17	60.0036	12	Eqblines	40	20	90	90	20	60.00
18	57.5029	35	Seoceudan	10	40	90	90	40	57.50
19	53.7535	23	Neiestein	80	30	20	50	100	53.75
20	53.7526	39	Urwhary	70	40	50	60	30	53.75
			Is Sorted On?	FALSE	FALSE	FALSE	FALSE	FALSE	TRUE

Figure 19-19. *The intermediate table*

What each element of this table does may not be immediately clear. In the next few sections, I'll go through the functionality of the dashboard. You will see where those functionalities tie in directly to the items on the intermediate table.

Scrolling Capability

In this section, I'll talk about how you achieve this scrolling capability. Recall the dynamic tables built in previous chapters. They all bring the same functionality: you scroll through large amounts of data by using the scroll bar and its ability to directly link to a cell on a spreadsheet. Hopefully, by now you're very familiar with the scroll bar (maybe even be sick of it!). In this current example decision tool, you will again use this dynamic.

As Figure 19-20 shows, you've simply inserted a new scroll bar into the sheet and linked it to the cell adjacent to `Scroll Bar Value`. This cell contains the current value of the scroll bar.

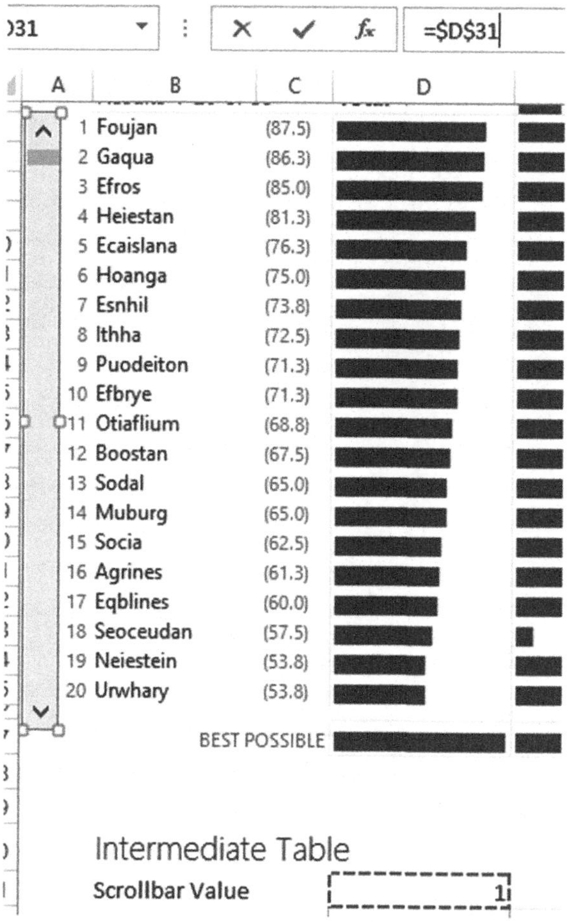

Figure 19-20. *The scroll bar for the table presented to the user is linked to a cell on your intermediate table*

As is typically the case for a scrolling table, the first cell in the table is always equal to the scroll bar value. Each cell below it is then equal to one plus the cell above. Therefore, as the scroll bar changes, each cell below changes in tandem. Figure 19-21 shows this conceptually. Figure 19-22 shows the actual formulas.

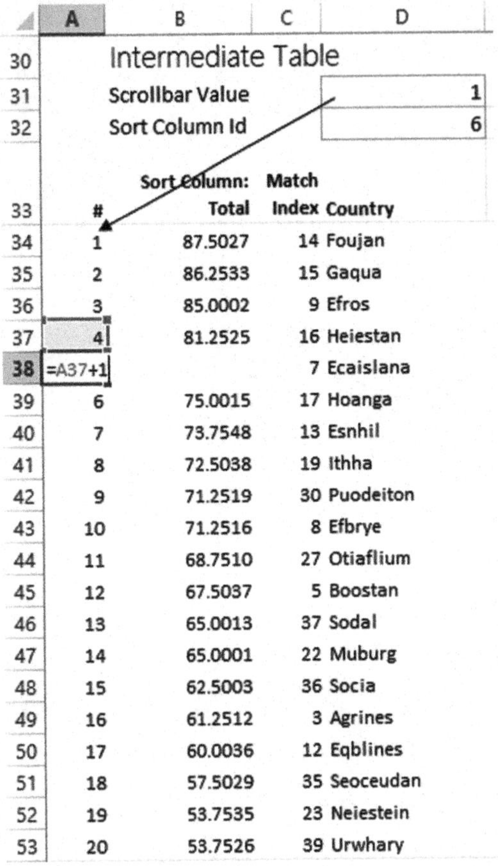

	A	B	C	D
30		Intermediate Table		
31		Scrollbar Value		1
32		Sort Column Id		6
33	#	Sort Column: Total	Match Index	Country
34	1	87.5027	14	Foujan
35	2	86.2533	15	Gaqua
36	3	85.0002	9	Efros
37	4	81.2525	16	Heiestan
38	=A37+1		7	Ecaislana
39	6	75.0015	17	Hoanga
40	7	73.7548	13	Esnhil
41	8	72.5038	19	Ithha
42	9	71.2519	30	Puodeiton
43	10	71.2516	8	Efbrye
44	11	68.7510	27	Otiaflium
45	12	67.5037	5	Boostan
46	13	65.0013	37	Sodal
47	14	65.0001	22	Muburg
48	15	62.5003	36	Socia
49	16	61.2512	3	Agrines
50	17	60.0036	12	Eqblines
51	18	57.5029	35	Seoceudan
52	19	53.7535	23	Neiestein
53	20	53.7526	39	Urwhary

Figure 19-21. *The scrolling table dynamic shown conceptually*

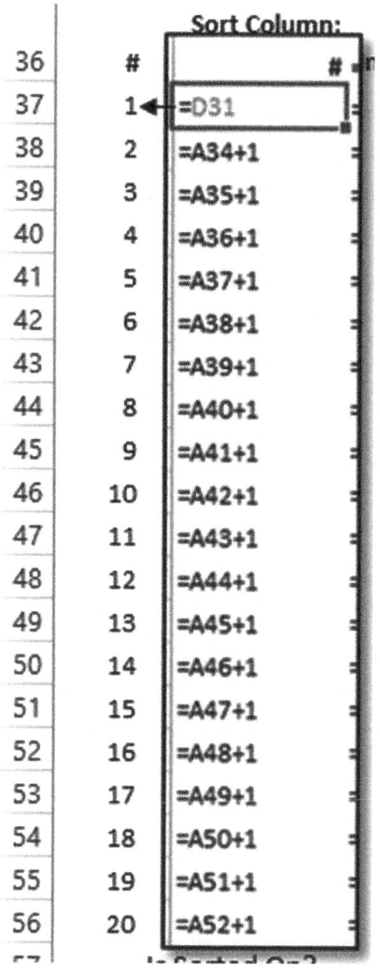

Figure 19-22. *Cells A34:A50 from above with only their formulas showing*

Notice that the index numbers from the visual presentation section of your tool are directly linked to the index numbers from below the sheet (see Figure 19-23).

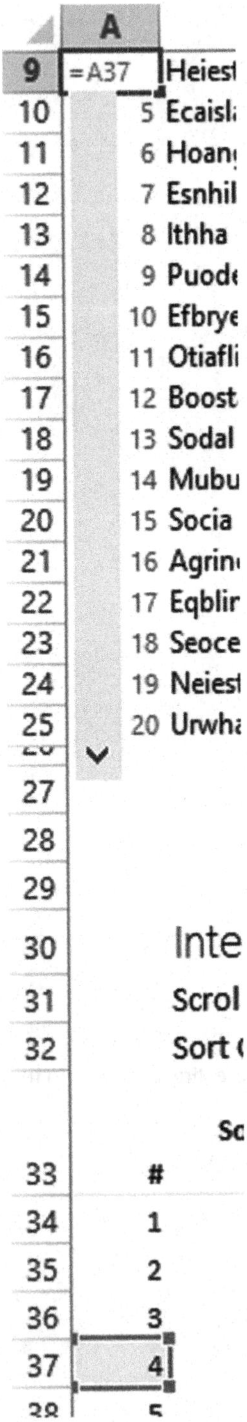

Figure 19-23. *The intermediate table links directly to the visual presentation section*

Adjusting the Scroll Bar

In this section, I'll talk about making adjustments to the scroll bar. By default, all form control scroll bars start with a minimum value of zero and go to 100. In your case, you'll never use the zero, so you need to adjust the min to always be 1. Another issue is that you expect the size of the list to change. The current example database has about 30 data items in it. But you need to accommodate an ever-changing range of data. The only instances in which you expect the amount of entries to change is when you either add or delete a new item.

At the end of both the `InsertNewRecord` and `DeleteSelectedRecord` procedures I've added a call to `SetScrollbarMax`. Listing 19-1 shows the code for this procedure.

Listing 19-1. SetScrollbarMax

```
Private Sub SetScrollbarMax()
    If [Database.RecordCount].Value <= 20 Then
        Analysis.Shapes("Analysis.Scrollbar").ControlFormat.Enabled = False
    Else
        Analysis.Shapes("Analysis.Scrollbar").ControlFormat.Enabled = True
        Analysis.Shapes("Analysis.Scrollbar").ControlFormat.Max =
            [Database.RecordCount].Value - 20 + 1
    End If

    Analysis.Shapes("Analysis.Scrollbar").ControlFormat.Value = 1
End Sub
```

The code works like this: you have 20 entries you can display on the visual layer (that's just the number I've picked, but it may be different in your own work). When the record count is greater than 20, you always want the scroll bar max to be 19 (one less than the total amount you're showing) less than that total (the chapter on form controls talks about why this is). On the other hand, if the `RecordCount` is less than 20, you won't need the scrollbar at all so you can just disable it. Finally, it's always a good idea to reset the scroll position whenever there's a change.

Formula-based Sorting Data for Analysis

In Figure 19-1, your decision support tool is sorting on total scores. (Recall that total refers to the values returned for each country from your weighted model calculations). In the previous chapter, you sent a command to your backend database table to sort each country by name. Considering the trouble you had in building the formula for the list box that was required to connect to the table, sending a command to sort the table made sense. It was an easy one-line operation.

However, in this case, you want to have the ability to sort on of any of the metrics, not just the total. But it wouldn't make sense to use VBA to sort the table directly as you did with the country names. Every time you change the sort order of the table, you lose the alphabetical order required for the list box on the menu screen. You could develop the capability to automatically sort the list box every time a user activates the menu screen, but why bother? Because you'd then have to do the same for the analysis screen (re-sort by the last option selected by the user). Clearly you need a way to sort on the data references in the backend table without changing its inherent sort order.

■ **Tip** It might help to think about the different sort types conceptually. The backend database is only sorted when you've added or deleted a record. As such, its inherent state is always that of an alphabetical sort order—and you only re-sort when changes to the underlying data are made to the table. On the other hand, here you're doing work *on top* of the data from that database to answer questions and investigate. Therefore, because you're not changing any underlying data, you want to leave the database sort order intact. In fact, it's important you do as little to the underlying data as possible lest you accidentally corrupt it.

Let's take a look at Figure 19-24. The `Sort Column Id` input cell tells you which column you're sorting. The numbers to the right of the cell are the IDs. For instance, if you're sorting by the total, the number in `Sort Column Id` is 6, consistent with what's shown in Figure 19-24. If you want to sort on `Health Level`, `Sort Column Id` would be 1. The dynamic is fairly intuitive.

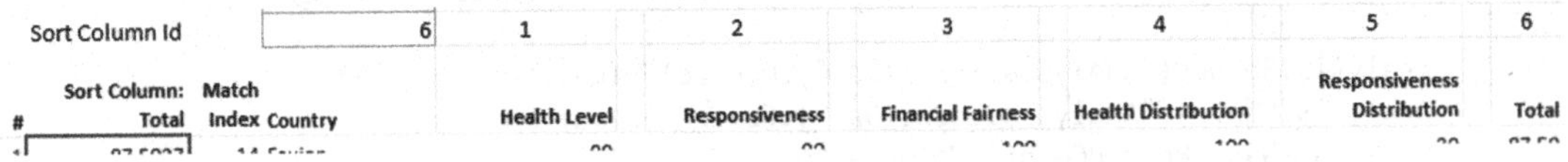

Figure 19-24. *The Sort Column Id input cell and ids corresponding to each metric*

You automatically find the `Sort Column Id` you're interested in by using the `Sort By` dropdown box from the visual portion of the tool. Figure 19-25 shows the dropdown from the `Analysis of Alternatives` table.

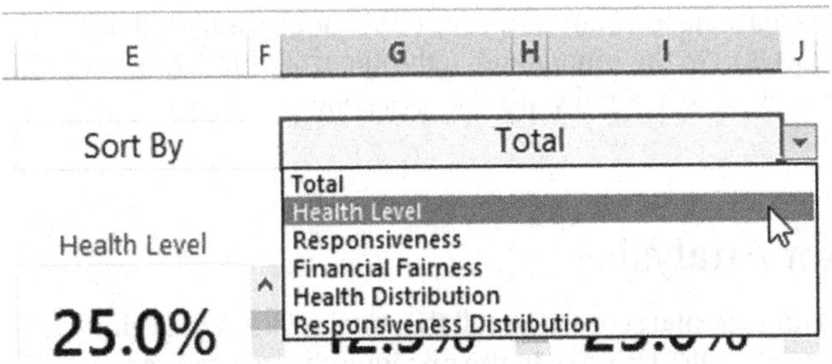

Figure 19-25. *The Sort By dropdown box*

The user response from the `Sort By` dropdown is used to lookup the correct `Column Id`, as shown in Figure 19-26.

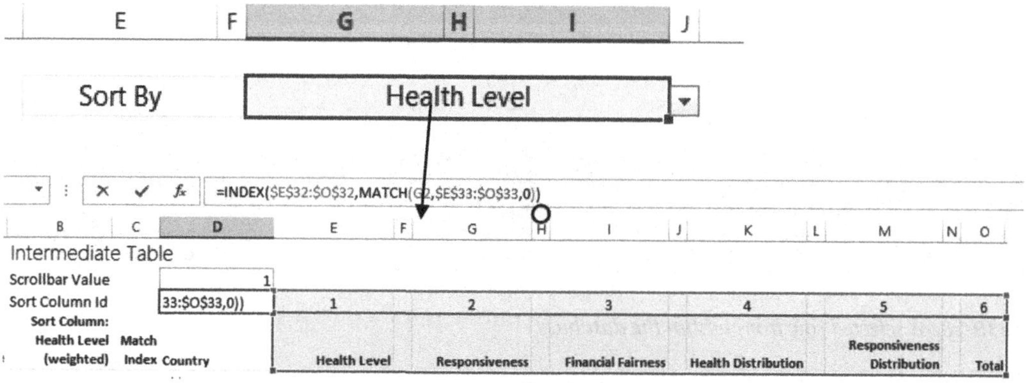

Figure 19-26. *Health Level from the dropdown is matched to the column names below*

You use the `INDEX/MATCH` dynamic to help you ultimately find the ID you're interested in. `Health Level` is matched to its location in the range E33:O33. Because it's in the first cell, Excel returns a 1. You then supply the index that matches its location (in this case, a 1) to the range above and pull out the number given by that matched location. It's like an `HLOOKUP`, but in reverse.

So let's now jump back to your database. You have this new column that's been added called the `Analysis Sort Column`.

The Sort Column, Your New Best Friend

In this section, I'll talk about using a sort column to help you sort data from multiple columns. Sort columns are necessary for whenever you want the ability to sort different fields or metrics through the use of a single mechanism. So let's take a look at the formula from the first cell in the `Analysis Sort Column` in Figure 19-27.

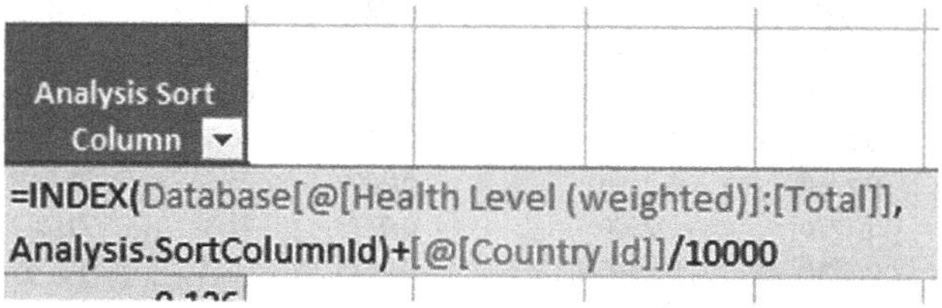

Figure 19-27. *The first cell in the Analysis Sort Column in the database*

The table expressions inside the `INDEX` may look confusing at first, so let's only deal with the left-hand side of it for now. The referent `Database[@[Health Level (weighted)]:[Total]]` is simply a row reference. Figure 19-28 shows the row reference for the first cell. I talked about the `Sort Column Id` in the previous section, but here you get to see it work its magic.

=INDEX(Database[@[Health Level (weighted)]:[Total]],Analysis.SortColumnId)

	I	J	K	L	M	N	
	Health Level (weighted)	Responsiveness (weighted)	Financial Fairness (weighted)	Health Distribution (weighted)	Responsiveness Distribution (weighted)	Total	A
0	0.0500	0.0250	0.0250	0.2000	0.1250	42.5	=IN

Figure 19-28. *A selected row from within the database*

Based on the formula above, when `Analysis.SortColumnId = 1`, then the values from within `Health Level (weighted)` are returned and placed into the `Analysis Sort Column`. When `Analysis.SortColumnId = 2`, the values from within `Responsiveness (weighted)` are returned into the `Analysis Sort Column`. And so forth up to `Total`, which is `Analysis.SortColumnId = 6`. If you take a look at Figure 19-21, you'll see your `Column IDs` line up perfectly.

For the sake of this example, let's assume `Total` has been selected from the dropdown on the visual layer of the `Analysis` tab. This would mean `Analysis.ScoreColumnId = 6`. So then you should expect the `Analysis Sort Column` to have the same values as those of `Total`. But if you look at Figure 19-29, you'll see the values in the `Analysis Sort Column` are really similar but not exactly alike.

	weights						
	25.00%	12.50%	25.00%	25.00%	12.50%		
	Health Level (weighted)	Responsiveness (weighted)	Financial Fairness (weighted)	Health Distribution (weighted)	Responsiveness Distribution (weighted)	Total	Analysis Sort Column
0	0.0500	0.0250	0.0250	0.2000	0.1250	42.5	42.503
3	0.1000	0.0250	0.1000	0.0500	0.0375	31.3	31.252
2	0.1250	0.1125	0.1000	0.2500	0.0250	61.3	61.251
1	0.1250	0.0875	0.1500	0.0250	0.0125	40.0	40.002
8	0.1250	0.1000	0.2250	0.1250	0.1000	67.5	67.504
8	0.0750	0.0125	0.2500	0.0250	0.1000	46.3	46.251
8	0.2250	0.0875	0.1250	0.2250	0.1000	76.3	76.255
3	0.1500	0.1000	0.1750	0.2500	0.0375	71.3	71.252
5	0.2500	0.1125	0.2250	0.2000	0.0625	85.0	85.000

Figure 19-29. *Analysis Sort Column is set to sort on Total values, but notice that they are slightly different than the values in the Total column*

I'll go into why they're slightly off in a moment—and why you *need* them to be slightly off. (Hint, hint: it has to do with the second half of the formula shown in Figure 19-27). But for now, you're going to execute a method called formula-based sorting. With formula-based sorting, you usually use either the `LARGE` or `SMALL` functions. Both of these functions work similarly. The prototypes for the `LARGE` and `SMALL` functions are

`LARGE(array, k)` and `SMALL(array, k)`

In either function, you supply a series of numbers in the first argument. The second argument instructs Excel to return the largest or smallest number in the list. For instance, `LARGE(A1:A10, 2)` returns the second largest number in the list of numbers stored in cells A1:A10; `SMALL(C1:C10, 4)` returns the fifth smallest number in the list of numbers stored in cells C1:C10. If you want to use these formulas to return a sorted a list of numbers from greatest to least, you use LARGE and make the K=1 in the first cell; then use LARGE again and make K=2 for the next cell. For each cell, you increment K until it equals the total size of the list.

Let's jump back to the intermediate table. You're now interested in the column with the heading starting with Sort Column:. Figure 19-30 shows the formula for the heading. Note that it's similar to the formula shown in Figure 19-27. However, in that formula, you were interested each row of data. Here, you're instead only in the headers. This formula will always bring up the header of the current row you're interested in. You won't really use the column header for anything in the visualization layer, but when you have dynamic elements, it always helps to keep track of what you're looking at!

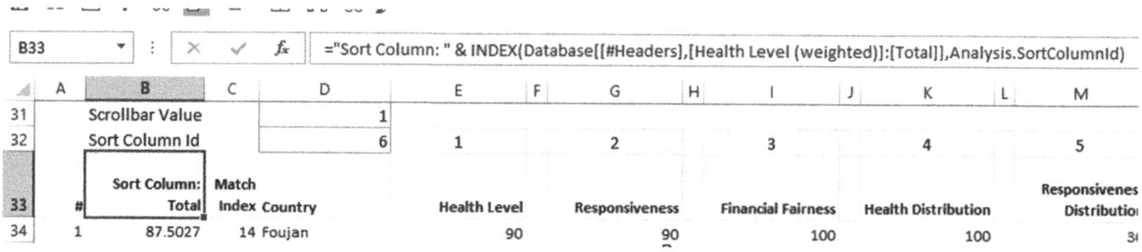

Figure 19-30. *The Sort Column always reflects the current header from within the database of the current column you're interested in sorting on*

Now you use the index list on the left of the Sort Column to return the greatest numbers in the list. Figure 19-31 shows the first cell in the Sort Column. As you can probably guess, when used supply the 1 to the LARGE function, you're returning back the first largest number in the entire column range Database[Analysis Sort Column]. In the second row, you're pulling back the second largest item; in the third row, you're pulling back the third largest item; and so forth. Figure 19-32 shows the formulas for the list.

		Sort Column:	Match	
33	#	Total	Index	Country
34	1	=LARGE(Database[Analysis Sort Column],A34)		
35	2	86.2533	15	Gaqua
36	3	85.0002	9	Efros
37	4	81.2525	16	Heiestan
38	5	76.2550	7	Ecaislana
39	6	75.0015	17	Hoanga
40	7	73.7548	13	Esnhil
41	8	72.5038	19	Ithha
42	9	71.2519	30	Puodeiton
43	10	71.2516	8	Efbrye
44	11	68.7510	27	Otiaflium
45	12	67.5037	5	Boostan
46	13	65.0013	37	Sodal
47	14	65.0001	22	Muburg
48	15	62.5003	36	Socia
49	16	61.2512	3	Agrines
50	17	60.0036	12	Eqblines
51	18	57.5029	35	Seoceudan
52	19	53.7535	23	Neiestein
53	20	53.7526	39	Urwhary

Figure 19-31. *You use LARGE to create a sorted list from the data stored in the Analysis Sort Column from the database*

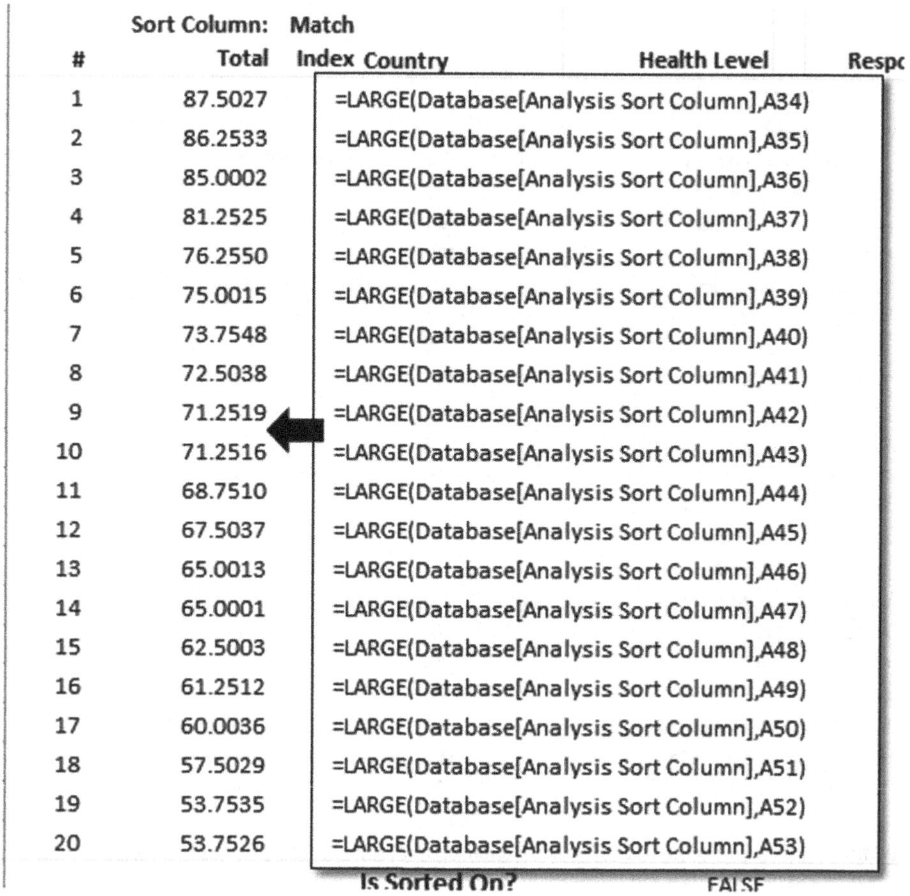

#	Sort Column: Total	Match Index Country / Health Level / Respc
1	87.5027	=LARGE(Database[Analysis Sort Column],A34)
2	86.2533	=LARGE(Database[Analysis Sort Column],A35)
3	85.0002	=LARGE(Database[Analysis Sort Column],A36)
4	81.2525	=LARGE(Database[Analysis Sort Column],A37)
5	76.2550	=LARGE(Database[Analysis Sort Column],A38)
6	75.0015	=LARGE(Database[Analysis Sort Column],A39)
7	73.7548	=LARGE(Database[Analysis Sort Column],A40)
8	72.5038	=LARGE(Database[Analysis Sort Column],A41)
9	71.2519	=LARGE(Database[Analysis Sort Column],A42)
10	71.2516	=LARGE(Database[Analysis Sort Column],A43)
11	68.7510	=LARGE(Database[Analysis Sort Column],A44)
12	67.5037	=LARGE(Database[Analysis Sort Column],A45)
13	65.0013	=LARGE(Database[Analysis Sort Column],A46)
14	65.0001	=LARGE(Database[Analysis Sort Column],A47)
15	62.5003	=LARGE(Database[Analysis Sort Column],A48)
16	61.2512	=LARGE(Database[Analysis Sort Column],A49)
17	60.0036	=LARGE(Database[Analysis Sort Column],A50)
18	57.5029	=LARGE(Database[Analysis Sort Column],A51)
19	53.7535	=LARGE(Database[Analysis Sort Column],A52)
20	53.7526	=LARGE(Database[Analysis Sort Column],A53)
		Is Sorted On? FALSE

Figure 19-32. *The formulas return a sorted list*

The Match Index Column, the Sort Column's Buddy

You now have a sorted list of data. But the obvious question is to which country do these data points belong? Having a list of sorted data tells you little if anything by itself. So now you'll need to build a Match Index (again, this follows the simple example from Chapter 17). The Match Index simply tells you the index location of where your sorted data points are located back in your database.

Figure 19-33 shows the formula you use in the `Match Index` column. You simply match the adjacent value back into the `Analysis Sort Column`. It's important to remember the `Analysis Sort Column` *isn't* sorted. Therefore, the largest values are likely to be all over the place. As you see from Figure 19-33, the second largest value is in the 15th row, the third in the 9th row, etc.

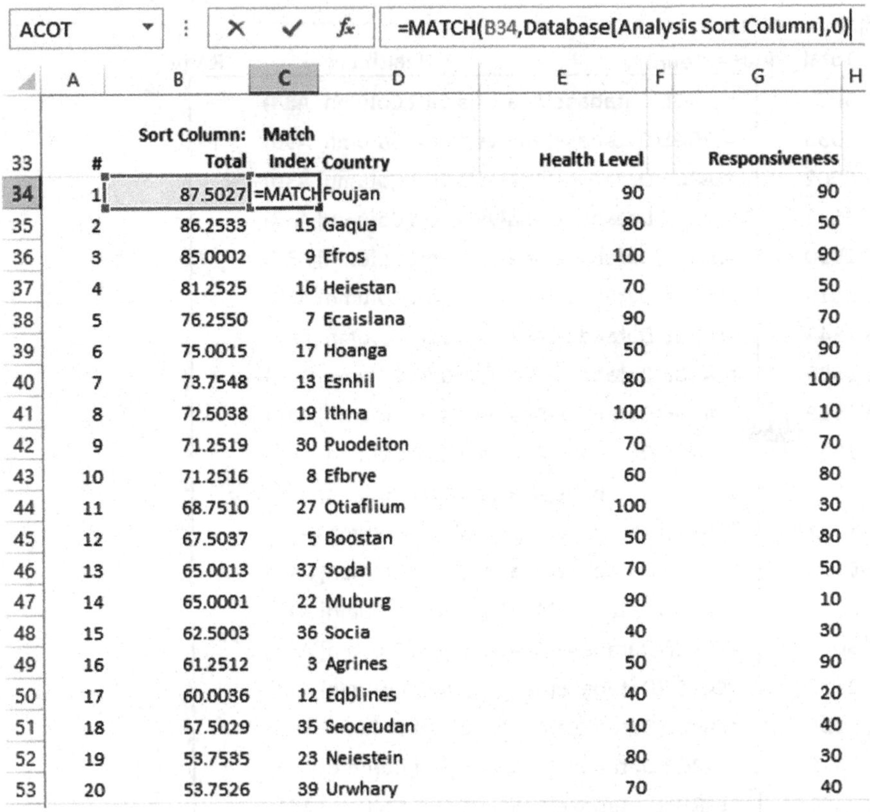

ACOT | =MATCH(B34,Database[Analysis Sort Column],0)

	A	B	C	D	E	F	G
33	#	Sort Column: Total	Match Index	Country	Health Level		Responsiveness
34	1	87.5027	=MATCH	Foujan	90		90
35	2	86.2533	15	Gaqua	80		50
36	3	85.0002	9	Efros	100		90
37	4	81.2525	16	Heiestan	70		50
38	5	76.2550	7	Ecaislana	90		70
39	6	75.0015	17	Hoanga	50		90
40	7	73.7548	13	Esnhil	80		100
41	8	72.5038	19	Ithha	100		10
42	9	71.2519	30	Puodeiton	70		70
43	10	71.2516	8	Efbrye	60		80
44	11	68.7510	27	Otiaflium	100		30
45	12	67.5037	5	Boostan	50		80
46	13	65.0013	37	Sodal	70		50
47	14	65.0001	22	Muburg	90		10
48	15	62.5003	36	Socia	40		30
49	16	61.2512	3	Agrines	50		90
50	17	60.0036	12	Eqblines	40		20
51	18	57.5029	35	Seoceudan	10		40
52	19	53.7535	23	Neiestein	80		30
53	20	53.7526	39	Urwhary	70		40

Figure 19-33. *The Match Index shows the index location each sorted value can be found back in its original column*

And once you know the row location of where the total value has been matched, you can use that information to look up the country name. Figure 19-34 shows the formula you use to look up the country name.

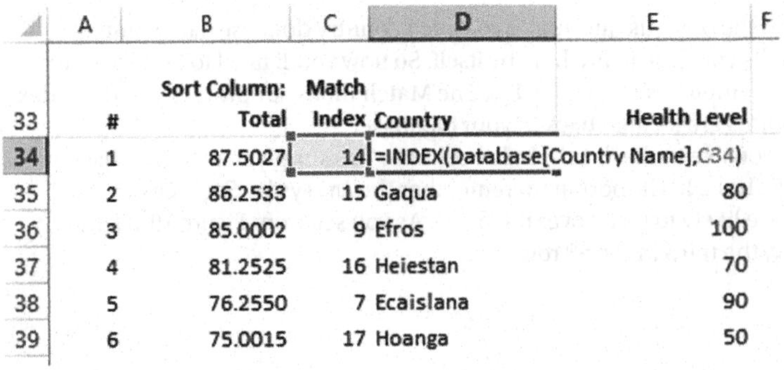

	A	B	C	D	E
33	#	Sort Column: Total	Match Index	Country	Health Level
34	1	87.5027	14	=INDEX(Database[Country Name],C34)	
35	2	86.2533	15	Gaqua	80
36	3	85.0002	9	Efros	100
37	4	81.2525	16	Heiestan	70
38	5	76.2550	7	Ecaislana	90
39	6	75.0015	17	Hoanga	50

Figure 19-34. *You simply use the Match Index to find the row location of the data you're interested in*

And you can do the same with `Health Level` (Figure 19-35), `Responsiveness`, `Financial Fairness`, `Health Distribution`, `Responsiveness Distribution`, and the `Total`. Everything displayed on the intermediate table uses the `Match Index` column.

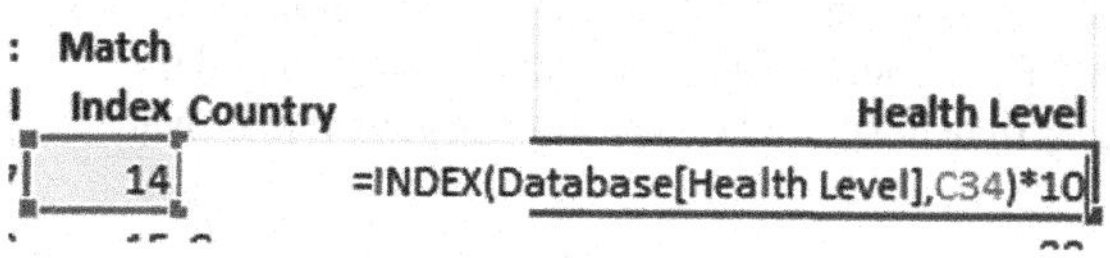

Match Index	Country	Health Level
14		=INDEX(Database[Health Level],C34)*10

Figure 19-35. Using the Match Index to find the current Health Level

You Have a "Unique" Problem

Using `MATCH` to look through the `Analysis Sort Column` works terrifically, assuming you have no duplicate values. Remember, `MATCH` will always return the index of only the first instance of the matched item in a list. (`MATCH` does not really care if there are other items in the list once it's found the value it's searching for.)

In Figure 19-36, notice that some total values do indeed repeat. In your ranking, they essentially form a tie. However, unless you do something, `MATCH` will always find that first 41.3 and return that row location. So you need some way to differentiate the first instance of 41.3 from all the instances that follow. And you do that by creating some noise in the data.

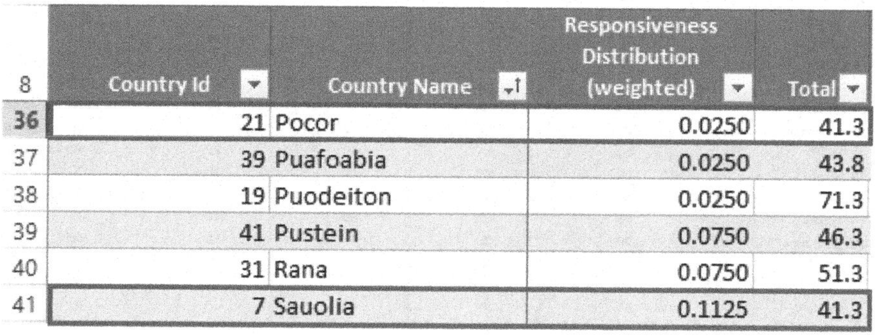

8	Country Id	Country Name	Responsiveness Distribution (weighted)	Total
36	21	Pocor	0.0250	41.3
37	39	Puafoabia	0.0250	43.8
38	19	Puodeiton	0.0250	71.3
39	41	Pustein	0.0750	46.3
40	31	Rana	0.0750	51.3
41	7	Sauolia	0.1125	41.3

Figure 19-36. Pocor and Sauolia have the same score

Remember the second half of the formula in Figure 19-37? Let's see it action (Figure 19-37).

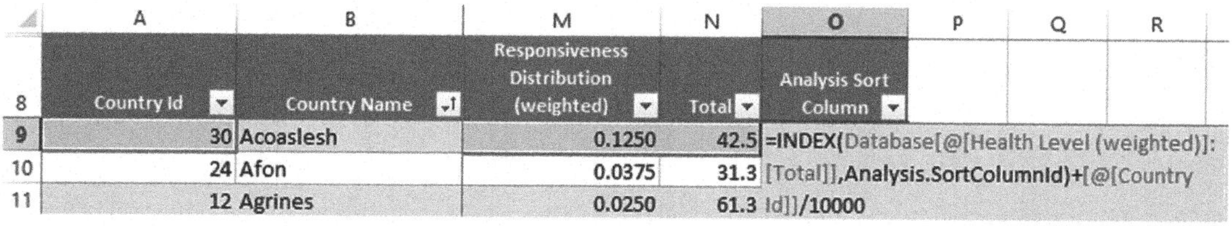

	A	B	M	N	O	P	Q	R
8	Country Id	Country Name	Responsiveness Distribution (weighted)	Total	Analysis Sort Column			
9	30	Acoaslesh	0.1250	42.5	=INDEX(Database[@[Health Level (weighted)]:			
10	24	Afon	0.0375	31.3	[Total]],Analysis.SortColumnId)+[@[Country			
11	12	Agrines	0.0250	61.3	Id]]/10000			

Figure 19-37. Focus on the second half of the Analysis Sort Column formula

The second half of that formula, `[@[County Id]]/10000`, simply adds an incredibly small amount to data returned by the `INDEX` function in the left-hand side of the formula. In Figure 19-37, you're adding the amount 30/10000. Since Country Id is always unique, you can be assured that even when you have totals that aren't unique, once you add this small amount *the results will always be unique.*

And remember, you only use the `Analysis Sort Column` from the database to help you find the locations of certain rows. That is, it helps you find the Match Index. From there, you use the Match Index to find the location of the information you're interested in. The noisy data never makes its way onto your visual layer.

Seeing It Work Altogether

The scrolling and sorting mechanisms are now complete. In fact, you can see them working together. If you adjust the scroll bar from in the visual layer, you'll see the intermediate table change. Figure 19-38 shows the scrollbar at value 19.

30		Intermediate Table								
31		Scrollbar Value	19							
32		Sort Column Id	6		1	2	3	4	5	6
33	#	Sort Column: Total	Match Index	Country	Health Level	Responsiveness	Financial Fairness	Health Distribution	Responsiveness Distribution	Total
34	19	53.7535	23	Neiestein	80	30	20	50	100	53.75
35	20	53.7526	39	Urwhary	70	40	50	60	30	53.75
36	21	52.5020	18	Iqeiskya	60	20	50	60	60	52.50
37	22	51.2531	32	Rana	20	30	70	70	60	51.25
38	23	46.2541	31	Pustein	10	30	70	60	60	46.25
39	24	46.2509	6	Dovaeria	30	10	100	10	80	46.25
40	25	45.0014	25	Opium	40	90	40	50	10	45.00
41	26	43.7539	29	Puafoabia	30	10	90	40	20	43.75
42	27	42.5032	24	Obron	10	80	50	20	100	42.50
43	28	42.5030	1	Acoaslesh	20	20	10	80	100	42.50
44	29	42.5028	11	Eprvil	20	80	60	20	60	42.50
45	30	41.2521	28	Pocor	50	30	70	20	20	41.25
46	31	41.2507	33	Sauolia	40	80	30	10	90	41.25
47	32	40.0022	4	Asnon	50	70	60	10	10	40.00
48	33	38.7551	38	Stansblink	20	30	40	50	60	38.75
49	34	36.2506	10	Elsmen	30	10	20	80	20	36.25
50	35	35.0052	21	Jordan	40	50	20	30	50	35.00
51	36	31.2524	2	Afon	40	20	40	20	30	31.25
52	37	31.2511	20	Jaca	90	20	10	10	10	31.25
53	38	30.0008	26	Osppar	30	60	20	10	60	30.00
54				Is Sorted On?	FALSE	FALSE	FALSE	FALSE	FALSE	TRUE

***Figure 19-38.** Notice that the index now starts with 19*

Notice your table now shows the country ranked in the 19th place in terms of its overall total score. Figure 19-39 shows what happens when you change the `Sort By` to `Responsiveness`.

	A	B	C	D	E	G	I	K	M	O
30		Intermediate Table								
31		Scrollbar Value		19						
32		Sort Column Id		2	1	2	3	4	5	6
33	#	Sort Column: Responsiveness (weighted)	Match Index	Country	Health Level	Responsiveness	Financial Fairness	Health Distribution	Responsiveness Distribution	Total
34	19	0.0650	16	Heiestan	70	50	80	100	100	81.25
35	20	0.0638	37	Sodal	70	50	30	100	70	65.00
36	21	0.0529	35	Seoceudan	10	40	90	90	40	57.50
37	22	0.0526	39	Urwhary	70	40	50	60	30	53.75
38	23	0.0426	38	Stansblink	20	30	40	50	60	38.75
39	24	0.0416	31	Pustein	10	30	70	60	60	46.25
40	25	0.0410	23	Neiestein	80	30	20	50	100	53.75
41	26	0.0406	32	Rana	20	30	70	70	60	51.25
42	27	0.0396	28	Pocor	50	30	70	20	20	41.25
43	28	0.0385	27	Otiaflium	100	30	60	90	20	68.75
44	29	0.0378	36	Socia	40	30	100	70	50	62.50
45	30	0.0286	12	Eqblines	40	20	90	90	20	60.00
46	31	0.0280	1	Acoaslesh	20	20	10	80	100	42.50
47	32	0.0274	2	Afon	40	20	40	20	30	31.25
48	33	0.0270	18	Iqeiskya	60	20	50	60	60	52.50
49	34	0.0261	20	Jaca	90	20	10	10	10	31.25
50	35	0.0164	29	Puafoabia	30	10	90	40	20	43.75
51	36	0.0163	19	Ithha	100	10	90	70	50	72.50
52	37	0.0134	6	Dovaeria	30	10	100	10	80	46.25
53	38	0.0131	10	Elsmen	30	10	20	80	20	36.25
54				Is Sorted On?	FALSE	TRUE	FALSE	FALSE	FALSE	FALSE

***Figure 19-39.** Responsivness is now the sort factor*

Notice that the `Sort Column Id` now shows the number 2, reflecting the column you're interested in sorting on. And the `Sort Column` shows that you are sorting on `Responsiveness (weighted)`. Your intermediate table now has a different sort order than you had previously when you were sorting on the `Total`; however, you've made no changes to the underlying data.

The Last Word

In this chapter, I talked about the type of analysis you will be performing on your data. You created the infrastructure to easily apply one-way sensitivity analysis. Further, you used formulas to create a robust sorting mechanism that can sort more than one type of metric. Finally, you used the form control scroll bar so you don't have to show all the data all at once. This work builds on what's been completed in previous chapters.

In the next chapter, you'll build the visual layer in full.

CHAPTER 20

Perfecting the Presentation

In the previous chapter, you built the intermediate table, which deals largely with transforming the raw data from the backend database. The presentation or visual layer, on the other hand, deals largely with what the user sees.

In this chapter, you'll focus on the visual layer as well as its interaction with the intermediate table. Just as before, the focus here is to create a lightweight infrastructure that isn't heavily steeped in code. You'll be using the file `Chapter20Wizard.xlsm` for this chapter. I recommend having it open as you follow along.

Implementation and Design of the Weight Adjustment System

In this section, I'll talk about implementing the weight adjustment system, shown in Figure 20-1. You'll find this across the top of your Analysis screen.

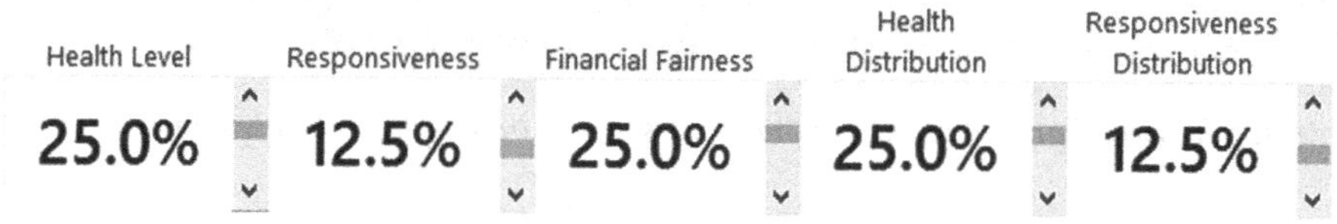

Figure 20-1. *The weight adjustment system*

Each box is simply connected to the associated weight on the Helper tab. Figure 20-2 shows the connection to `Health Level`. Note that each metric follows suit.

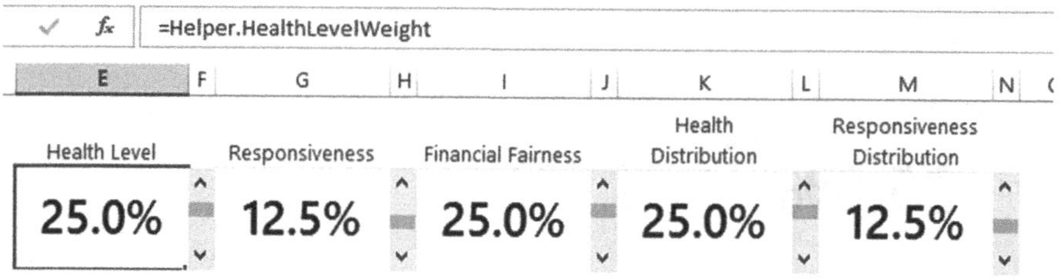

Figure 20-2. *Each weight box is connected directly to the associated weights from on the Helper tab*

Likewise, the scroll bars here are exactly like the ones on the Helper tab you built in the previous chapter (Figure 20-3). However, I don't recommend copying and pasting those scroll bars from the Helper tab and placing them on this tab. Scroll bars are usually set to relative references. If you copy and paste the scroll bars from the Helper tab, Excel will try to change the same cell address on the Analysis tab. That's not what you want.

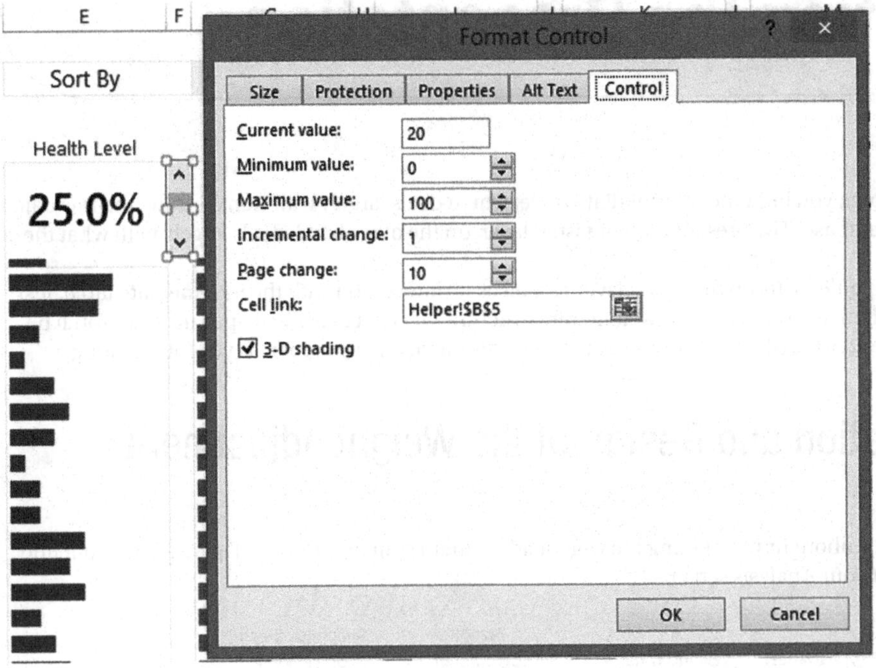

Figure 20-3. Properties for the scroll bar. Notice the cell link is the same as that of the scroll bars on the Helper tab

Your best bet is to insert each of these scroll bars manually. In Figure 20-4, you can see that I've left some space in Column F between each weight box to provide a place for a scroll bar. I used a similar space between all the weight boxes. This is similar to the process of *anchoring* described in Chapter 18.

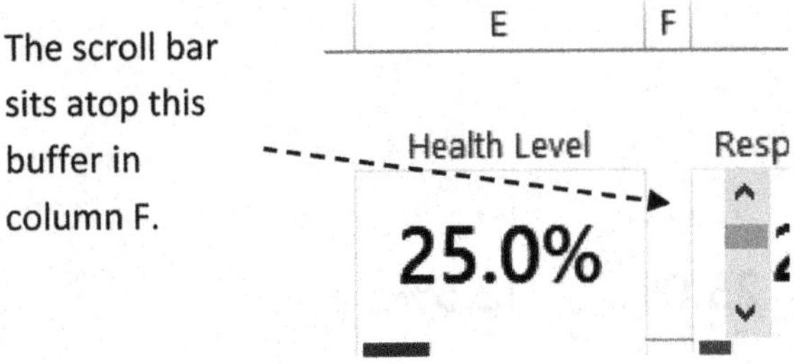

Figure 20-4. I've moved the scroll bar to the side to show the column spacer

Next, enable the Snap to Grid feature by right-clicking or Ctrl+clicking the scroll bar. From the Format context tab, pick Align and select Snap To Grid (see Figure 20-5).

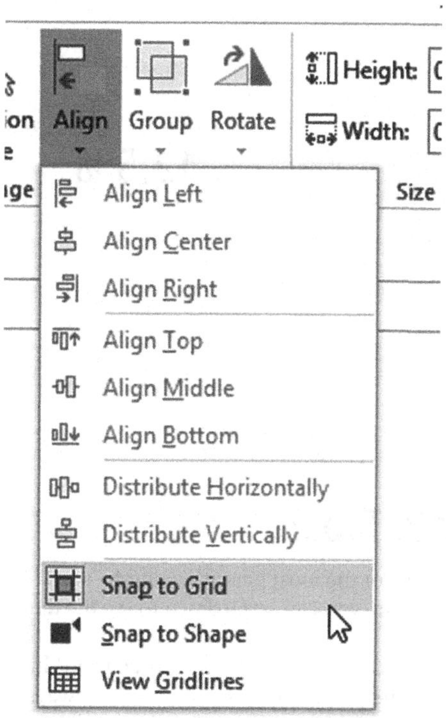

***Figure 20-5.** The Snap To Grid feature*

The Snap to Grid feature will force you to align Excel's cell grid. So if you size a spacer column as I did in Figure 20-4 in Column F, ensuring consistent alignment and size for each scroll bar is easy peasy. Of course, the "correct" size is more art than science. To make my life easier, I like to design the first scroll bar spacer. Once I like the size, I right-click the column and select column width to find out its size (Figure 20-6).

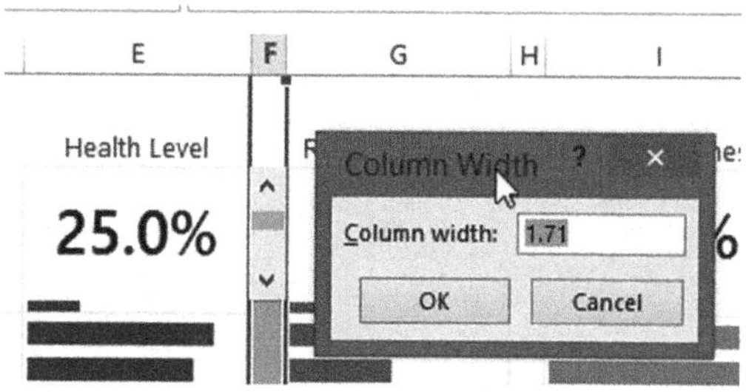

***Figure 20-6.** Column width for column F*

Then I right-click every other similar column and set its size to be the same. As you can see in Figure 20-7, 1.71 is what I liked best, but you may differ. As you may have guessed, I did the same for the weight boxes.

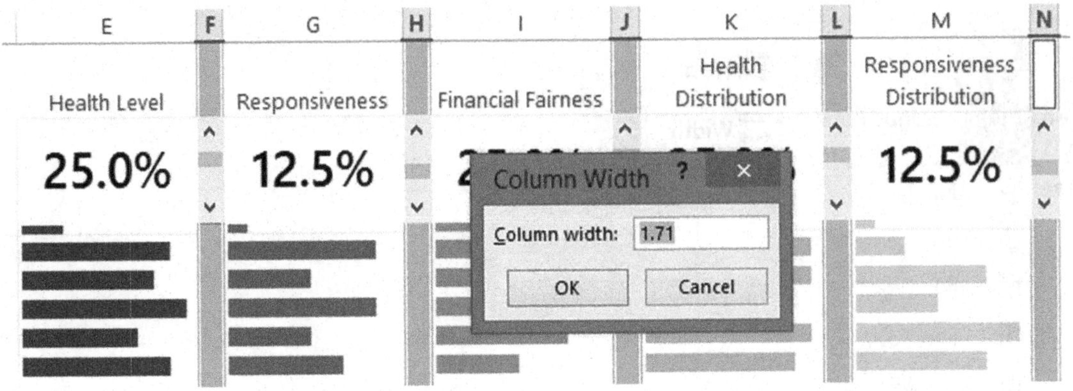

Figure 20-7. *Selecting similar columns and setting their size all at once to ensure consistency*

Displaying Data from the Intermediate Table

Now let's talk about how to display data from the intermediate table. For the most part, it's a one-to-one mapping. That is, if you look at `Health Level` in the visual presentation, you can scroll down to see the data it is visualizing directly underneath. They share the same column.

The are a few exceptions to this. Ideally, it would be great if all data items shared the same columns but sometimes the way your data is laid out constraints this ideal. (Of course, as you can see from this, I always try to align them as much as possible.) So let's go through each item.

Results Information Label

This section talks about building the results information formula. Figure 20-8 shows the results of this formula. The "7-26 of 39" means the results ranked from 7 to 26 are currently in view, out of 39 total possible items available. The formula updates as the scroll bar changes (Figure 20-9).

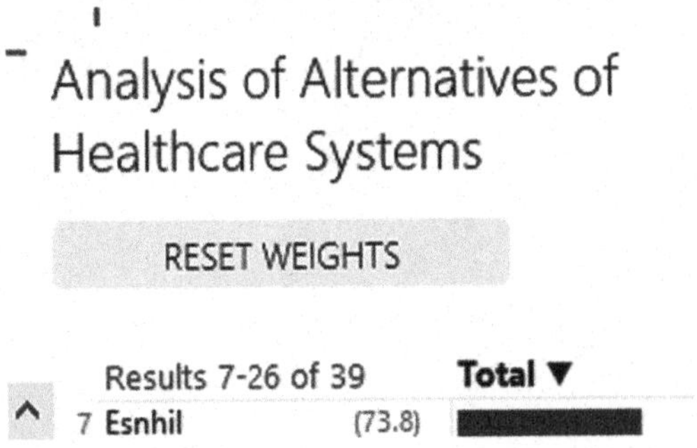

Figure 20-8. *The results information label shows the ranked items currently in view as well as the final total of items*

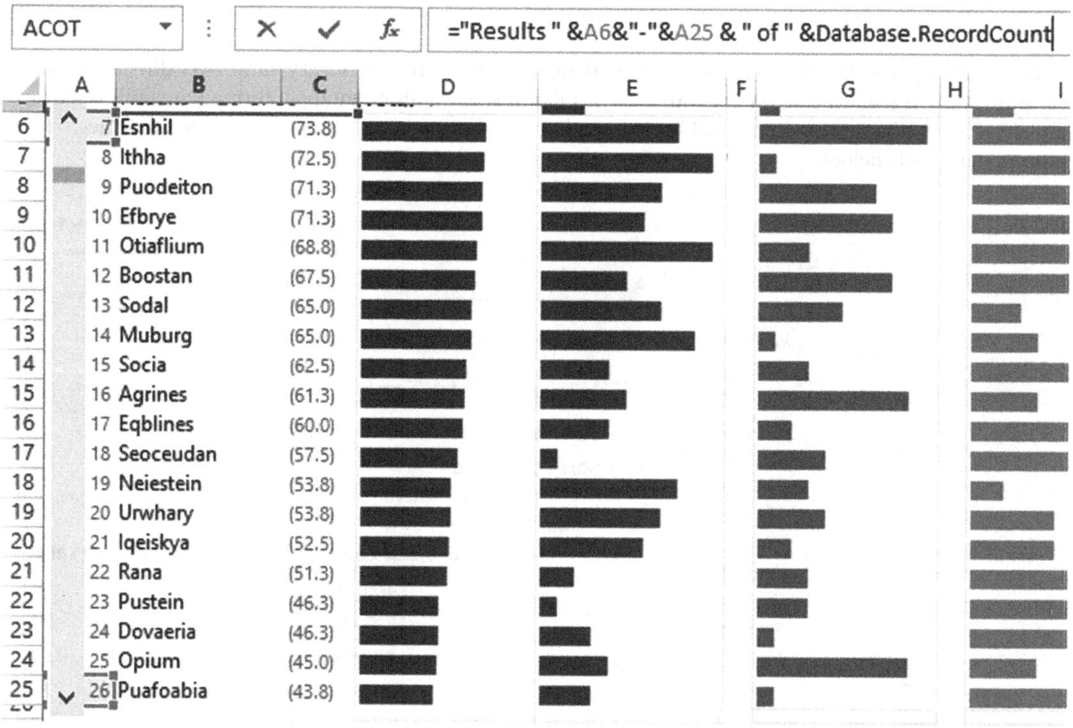

Figure 20-9. *The results information label formula*

The formula uses the first ranked item in the list and the last ranked item in the list to define the range of numbers in view. `Database.RecordCount` is used to show the total amount of records available for view (Figure 20-9).

The Current Rank of Each Country

The first item on the left is the current rank of each country shown. This value is pulled directly from the index created in the intermediate table. Figure 20-10 shows how the rank and index connect.

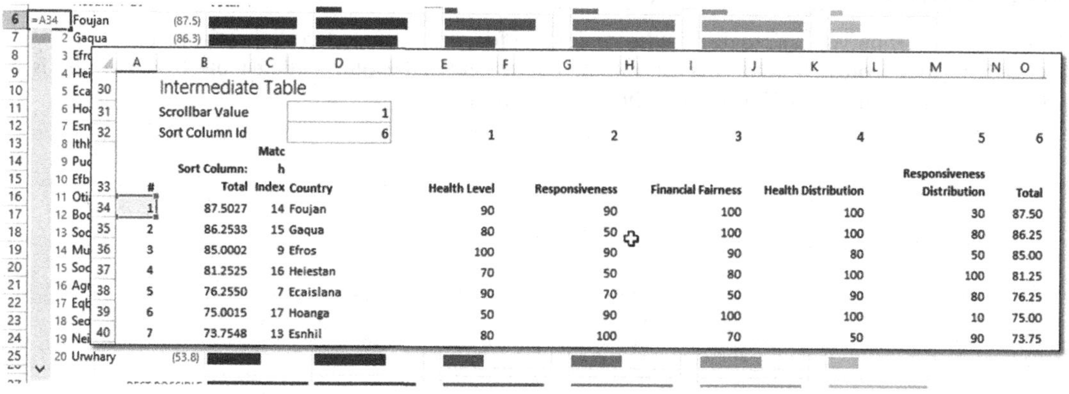

Figure 20-10. *The rank from the data visualization layer directly connects to the intermediate table*

Country Name

In this section, you're interested in the country name. Unlike the index, country name isn't directly in the column below. Again, when creating your own dashboards, remember that the intermediate table might not always be in the same columns below. Figure 20-11 shows how each country is connected to the intermediate table below.

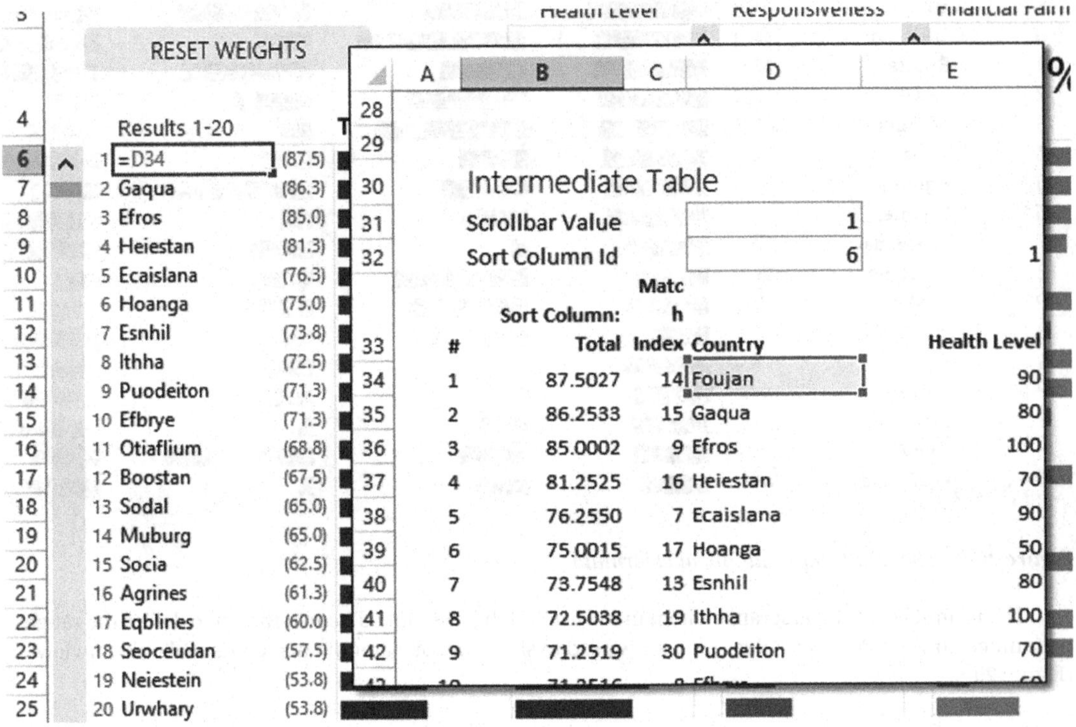

Figure 20-11. Each country name directly links to the intermediate table below, but it's not in the same column

Total Scores for Each Country

This section will show you how to display the total scores for each country. Recall that the column representing total scores is actually the last column on the right in the intermediate table. Note how this is different for your visual layer. Figure 20-12 shows the connection.

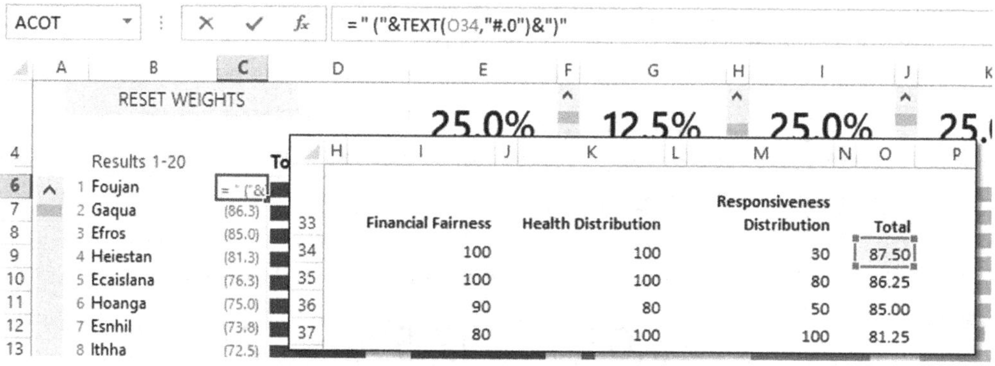

Figure 20-12. *The Total score is one of the first columns in the visual layer and one of the last columns in the intermediate table*

Let's take a moment to look at the formula. I place parentheses around the total value as a means to downplay its importance somewhat. (I'll go over why near the end of the chapter.) Since I'm using the values in the `Total` cell in a formula, I risk showing more decimal precision than required. Using the TEXT function, I've supplied a formatting rule to ensure you also see everything to the right of the decimal and always one number to the right.

In-cell Bar Charts for All Metrics

The rest of the data items in your visual layer are in-cell bar charts. As you might remember from previous chapters, you can re-create small bar charts using the REPT function and the pipe symbol. Figure 20-13 shows the formula as well as the best font selection for this type of chart. As Figure 20-13 shows, Playbill size 10 is fairly reliable. Notice the cell it refers to is O34. This is the same cell referenced to get the Total value in Figure 20-9.

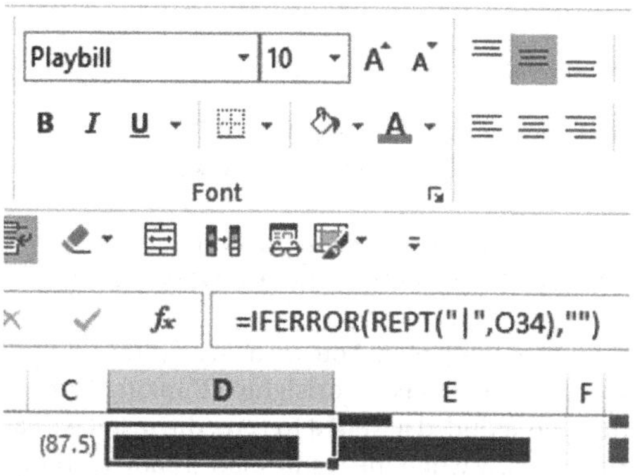

Figure 20-13. *In-cell bar chart for Total*

Figure 20-14 shows the connection for `Health Level`. It's virtually the same function setup as that used for `Total`. In this case, it refers to the `Health Level` metric from the intermediate table.

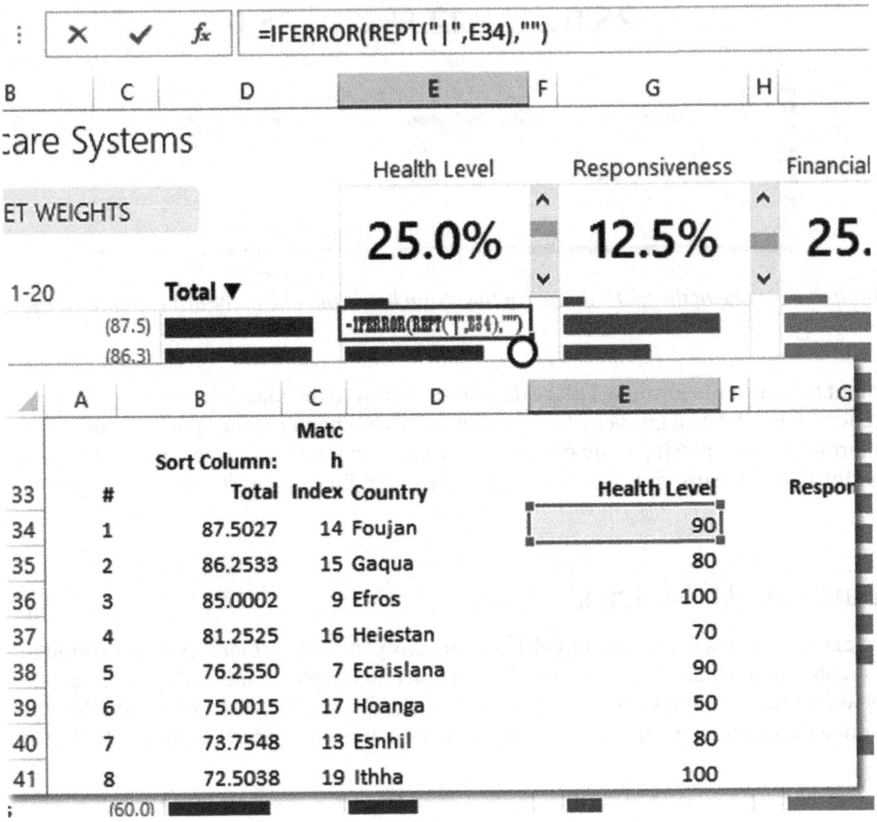

***Figure 20-14.** Formula for in-cell bar charts for metric data*

The in-cell bar charts for the rest of the metrics follow suit. `Responsiveness`, `Financial Fairness`, `Health Distribution`, and `Responsiveness Distribution` all use the `REPT` function and link to their corresponding column from the intermediate table.

You may be wondering what's going on with that `IFERROR`. Why does it appear in the function? The answer is because you need it. For one, you won't always have at least 20 entries. If there are less than 20 entries, then you need these cells to appear blank.

More importantly, however, is that you simply don't know what lies ahead. You are using a rather simple example here, so you're unlikely to see any other types of errors. But that's also shortsighted thinking. For example, in my original formulation of this spreadsheet, when you reduced a weight to zero, the result was a #DIV/0 in that metric's column. I didn't want the #DIV/0 error to show when the result should show nothing. Therefore, I used the `IFERROR` function as shown above. While subsequent changes to the model make such an error unlikely, I've kept it in just in case. However, I'm unconvinced that daring folks out there can't figure out a way to create errors I couldn't foresee. Moreover, since the proliferation of errors in cells can seriously slow down a spreadsheet, preventing them is important.

Best Possible Comparisons

At the bottom of the of the visual layer I've included the best possible scores for each metric. This allows the user to compare instantly the results against the best result. Since 100 is the best possible score, the formula for each of these cells is always `=REPT("|", 100)` (see Figure 20-15).

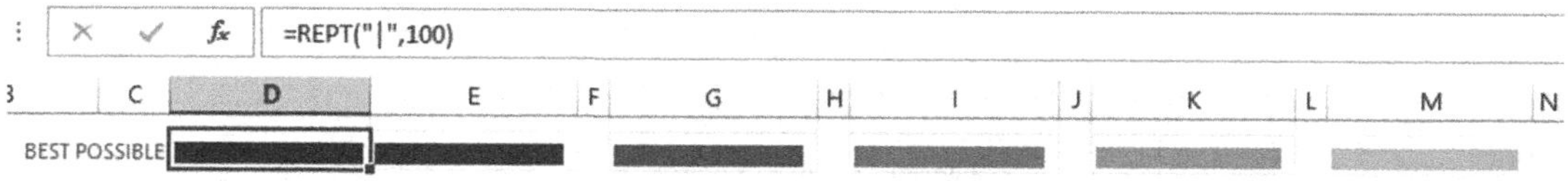

***Figure 20-15.** The formula for best possible comparisons*

Weight Box Progress Meters

Under each weight box is a progress meter that shows works exactly like the in-cell bar charts. In the Figure 20-16, you can see each small bar chart within a weight box.

***Figure 20-16.** The small lines under each weight box are progress meters*

Figure 20-17 shows the formula used for these bar charts. Notice the theme here. It's essentially the same formula. However, to make it appear smaller, I've just resized the row. This gives it the mini-field effect.

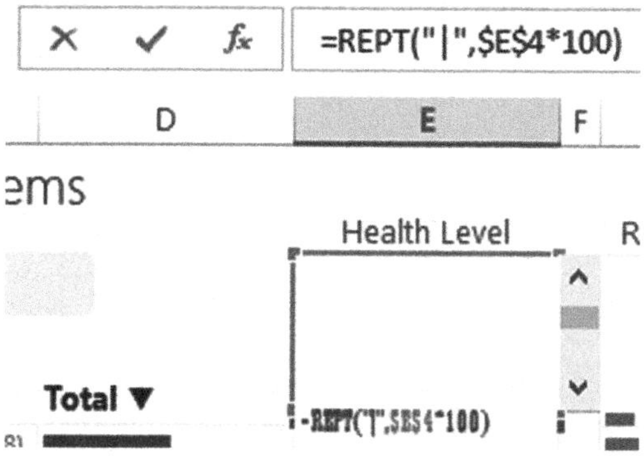

***Figure 20-17.** The progress bars under each weight value are minified versions of the same bar chart formula used previously*

"Sort By" Dropdown and Sort Labels

In the last chapter, you built the infrastructure for sorting. In this section, I'll talk about the visual elements that go along with that sorting mechanic. One of the cool features of your sorting system is that you can use the Sort By dropdown to select which metric you'd like to sort by. Once the user has made their selection, the corresponding column label becomes bold and the down arrow appears next to it (see Figure 20-18).

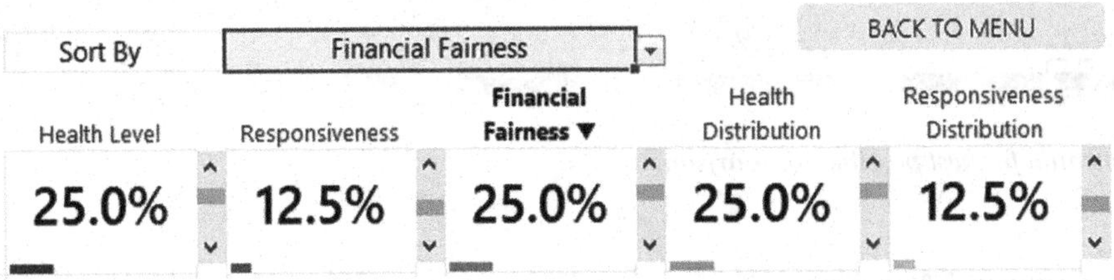

Figure 20-18. The Financial Fairness label becomes bold and a down arrow appears next to it

Following the no-code theme, this mechanism requires no VBA. However, it is a mixture of several different elements, which I'll go through in the next few sections.

Dropdown Metric Selection

In this section, I'll talk about the Sort By dropdown. It's nothing more than a data validation list (Figure 20-19), which you can insert into the spreadsheet from the Data tab. Generally, I don't like to type the list source in directly. However, the areas in which these selections appear on the spreadsheet do not appear in one contiguous region. If you look at your current sheet, you'll see that you don't have one list of data where `Total`, `Health Level`, etc. appear without any cells in between. If you were to link directly to these sources, there would be space in your dropdowns. So typing the text in directly here works best even if it's not preferred.

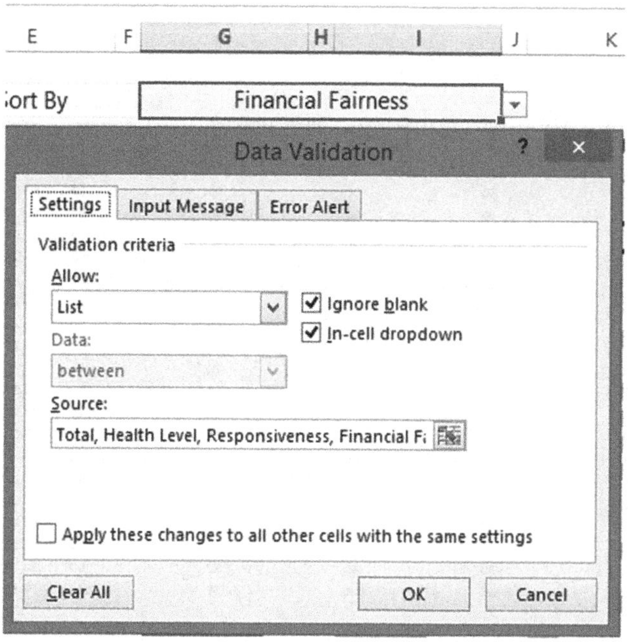

Figure 20-19. *The Data Validation dialog box showing the dropdown list you've created*

Using Boolean Formulas to Define Which Metric Has Been Selected

Recall from the previous section that changes in the dropdown change the `Sort Column Id`. Since you selected `Financial Fairness` in Figure 20-19, the `Sort Column Id` is a 3, as expected (Figure 20-20).

30	Intermediate Table									
31	Scrollbar Value		7							
32	Sort Column Id		3		1	2	3	4	5	6
33	#	Financial Fairness (weighted)	Match Index	Country	Health Level	Responsiveness	Financial Fairness	Health Distribution	Responsiveness Distribution	Total
34	7	0.2289	29	Puafoabia	30	10	90	40	20	43.75
35	8	0.2288	19	Ithha	100	10	90	70	50	72.50
36	9	0.2287	5	Boostan	50	80	90	50	80	67.50
37	10	0.2286	12	Eqblines	40	20	90	90	20	60.00
38	11	0.2279	35	Seoceudan	10	40	90	90	40	57.50
39	12	0.2252	9	Efros	100	90	90	80	50	85.00
40	13	0.2025	16	Heiestan	70	50	80	100	100	81.25
41	14	0.1798	13	Esnhil	80	100	70	50	90	73.75
42	15	0.1791	31	Pustein	10	30	70	60	60	46.25
43	16	0.1781	32	Rana	20	30	70	70	60	51.25
44	17	0.1771	28	Pocor	50	30	70	20	20	41.25
45	18	0.1766	8	Efbrye	60	80	70	100	30	71.25
46	19	0.1528	11	Eprvil	20	80	60	20	60	42.50
47	20	0.1522	4	Asnon	50	70	60	10	10	40.00
48	21	0.1510	27	Otiaflium	100	30	60	90	20	68.75
49	22	0.1300	7	Ecaislana	90	70	50	90	80	76.25
50	23	0.1282	24	Obron	10	80	50	20	100	42.50
51	24	0.1276	39	Urwhary	70	40	50	60	30	53.75
52	25	0.1270	18	Iqeiskya	60	20	50	60	60	52.50
53	26	0.1051	38	Stansblink	20	30	40	50	60	38.75
54				Is Sorted On?	FALSE	FALSE	TRUE	FALSE	FALSE	FALSE

Figure 20-20. *Sort Column Id is equal to 3*

At the bottom of Figure 20-20 is a line item that reads, “Is Sorted On?” This row highlights the row currently being sorted on. Notice for all columns except for `Financial Fairness`, the value reads FALSE. For `Financial Fairness`, the value reads TRUE. This is because you’re sorting on this metric. Figure 20-21 shows the formula you’re using in this row.

Intermediate Table

Scrollbar Value	7			
Sort Column Id	3		1	2

Financial Fairness (weighted)	Match Index	Country	Health Level	Responsiveness
0.2289	29	Puafoabia	30	10
0.2288	19	Ithha	100	10
0.2287	5	Boostan	50	80
0.2286	12	Eqblines	40	20
0.2279	35	Seoceudan	10	40
0.2252	9	Efros	100	90
0.2025	16	Heiestan	70	50
0.1798	13	Esnhil	80	100
0.1791	31	Pustein	10	30
0.1781	32	Rana	20	30
0.1771	28	Pocor	50	30
0.1766	8	Efbrye	60	80
0.1528	11	Eprvil	20	80
0.1522	4	Asnon	50	70
0.1510	27	Otiaflium	100	30
0.1300	7	Ecaislana	90	70
0.1282	24	Obron	10	80
0.1276	39	Urwhary	70	40
0.1270	18	Iqeiskya	60	20
0.1051	38	Stansblink	20	30
		Is Sorted On?	FALSE	=(G32=$D$32)

Figure 20-21. *The Boolean formula used to test whether you're sorting on a specific column*

You'll use this Boolean formula to perform conditional formatting and add the down arrow to each header.

Connecting Everything with Conditional Format Highlighting

In this section, you'll put the finishing touches on each header by conditionally formatting the selected column header as bold. This should hopefully feel somewhat familiar to you as it's a reapplication of the Highlight mechanism described in Chapter 10. (Remember, if you think of it as a reusable component, you can apply it to many different spreadsheet applications.) Figure 20-22 shows the Conditional Formatting Rules Manager for cells E3:M3. Notice I've applied conditional formatting rules to these column headers. You can see it for yourself by selecting cells E3:M3, clicking on the Conditional Formatting dropdown box from the Home tab, and selecting Manage Rules.

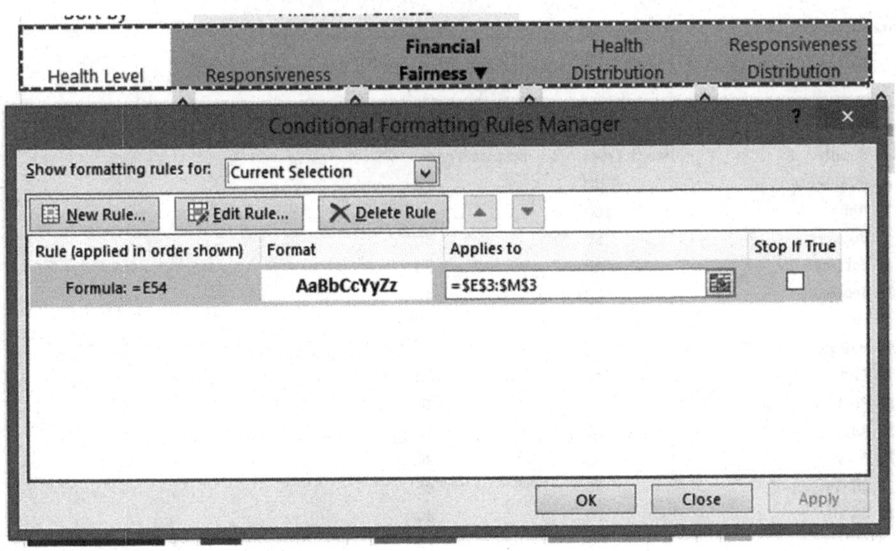

Figure 20-22. The Conditional Formatting Rules Manager dialog box

Let's take a look at the conditional formatting rules behind the scenes. If you click on Edit Rule, you will see the Edit Formatting Rule dialog box (Figure 20-23).

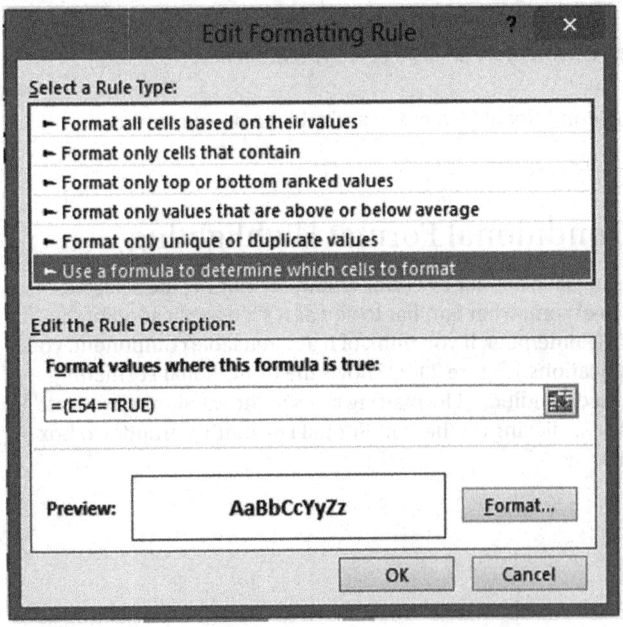

Figure 20-23. The Edit Formatting Rule dialog box

Note that I've selected "Use a formula to determine which cells to format." In the "Format values where this formula is true" rule type, I'm using the formula `=(E54=TRUE)`. This formula is what allows you to change the style of font of the sort column that's been selected. In addition, notice that I'm not using the absolute cell reference $E$54. That absolute cell reference is what appears by default. However, if you kept the absolute reference, it would only test cell E54. Instead, you want the test for conditional formatting to happen across every cell in the range. You might recall you built a similar dynamic in Chapter 10 in the "Conditional Highlight Using Formulas" section.

A QUICK NOTE ON ABSOLUTE REFERENCES AND CREATING CONDITIONAL FORMAT RULES

If you select "Use a formula to determine which cells to format" as I have in Figure 20-23, you won't start with relative references by default. What that means is, if you were to set up this formula for the first time, and you selected cell E54 from on the spreadsheet, it would look something like Figure 20-24.

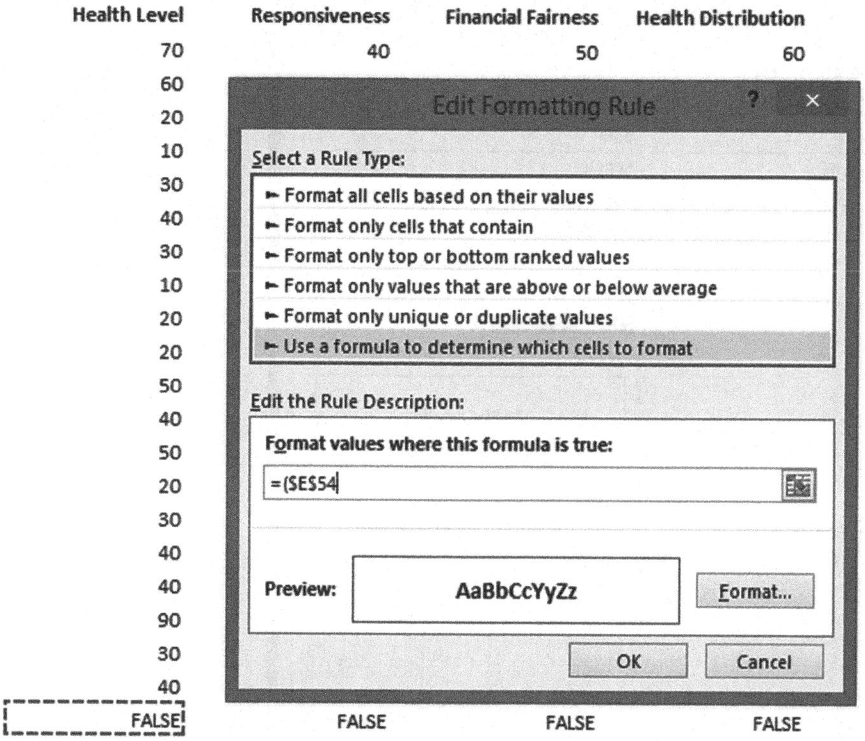

Figure 20-24. *The Edit Formatting Rule dialog box uses an absolute reference by default*

By default, all cells selected to populate the formula begin as absolute references. So the E54 in Figure 20-23 actually began as E54. You can change the absolute references manually by placing your cursor next to the dollar signs and deleting them. Or, you can cycle through the references types by pressing F4 repeatedly. This is similar to pressing F4 repeatedly in the formula box when writing a formula. In this case, if you press F4 three times, you'll arrive at the relative cell reference.

When you first set the cell, it's sometimes easy to forget the step of removing the absolute reference when it's necessary.

If you click the Format button (see Figure 20-24), you'll be taken to the Format Cells dialog box. Here, you can change the format of the cells whose sort column has been selected. For my formatting choices, I've selected a Bold font style (Figure 20-25). I've stayed away from doing any other embellishments. You don't want the selected header to take away from the data visualization portion. Nor do you want it to overwhelm the visual field. If you're not careful, you can go crazy with the formatting options. Here I am being subtle and tasteful.

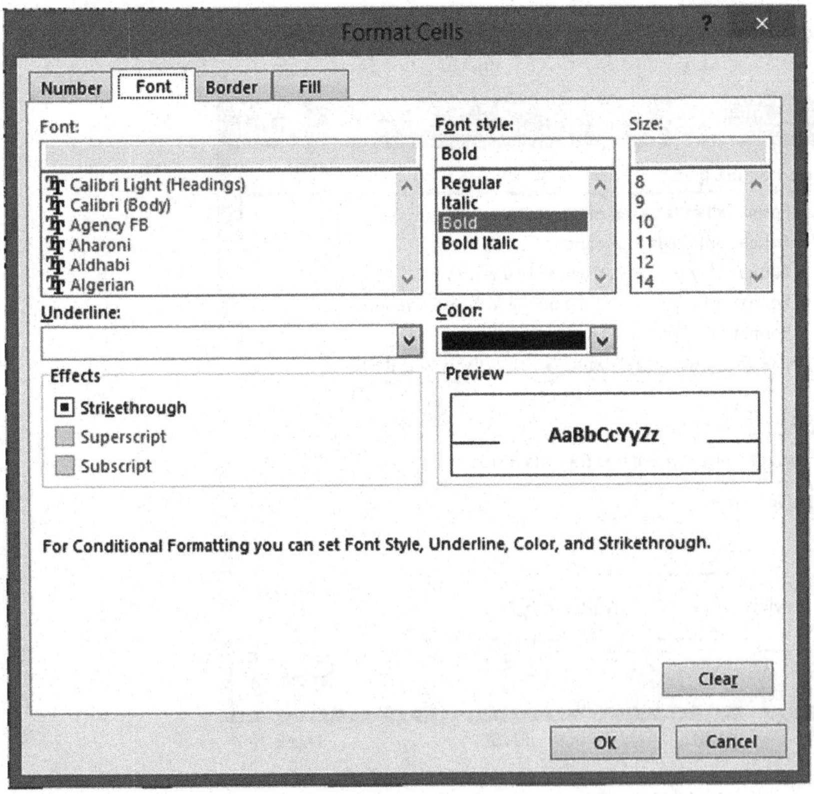

Figure 20-25. *Bold is selected in the Format Cells dialog box*

This conditional formatting rule simply takes care of the metrics across the top. It doesn't take care of `Total`, which is not part of the same row. So you'll need to make an additional rule just for the total. Remember, however, what the `Total` row refers to is in a different column on the intermediate table. Take note in Figure 20-26: the rule is set to test the cell in O45, which, unlike the other columns in the visual layer, is not directly below the `Total` on the intermediate table.

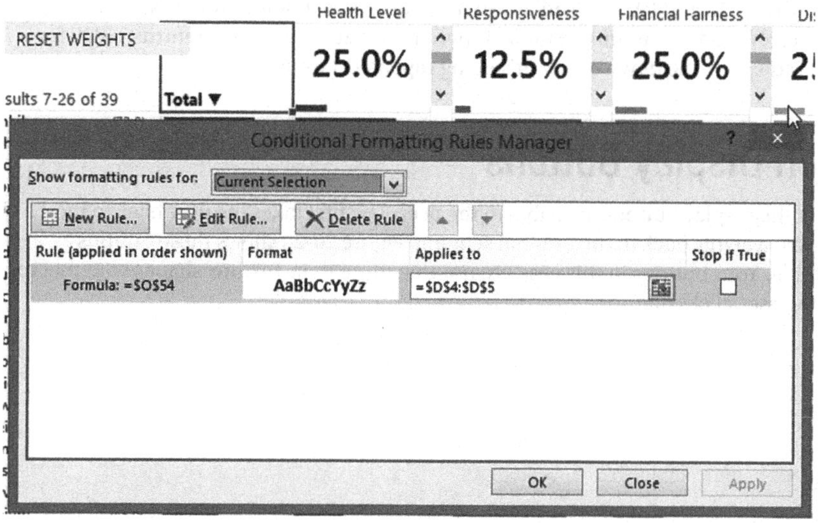

Figure 20-26. An individual rule is required for the Total header

The mechanism to display the down arrow in the weight box headings uses the same row as the conditional formatting. Let's take a look at the formulas (Figure 20-27).

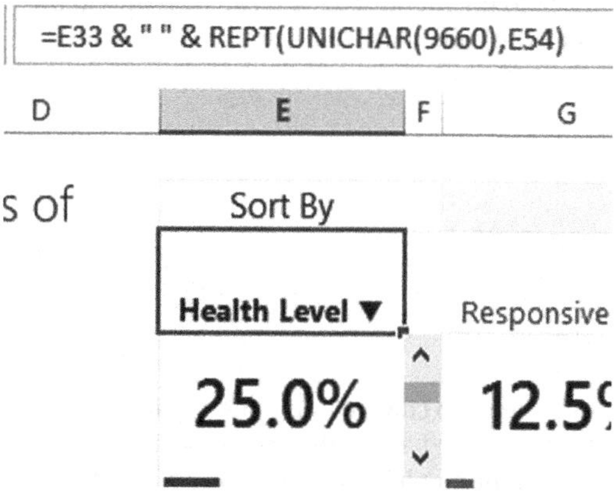

Figure 20-27. The formula used for the weight box heading

The left-side of the formula, E33, simply refers to the column header from the intermediate table. But turn your attention to the right side. In a previous chapter I talked about using Unicode characters to extend what characters we can display. The down arrow is given by the Unicode index number 9660. And we can display the character with the `UNICHAR` function. `REPT`, as you might recall, lets you specify a character in the first argument and the amount of times to repeat that character in the second argument. Here, you've specified that you want to repeat the down arrow. E54 in the formula (the value of how many times you want to repeat the formula) points to TRUE and FALSE. And, if you remember how Boolean functions work, TRUE = 1 and FALSE = 0. So each header uses this formula. When the `Is Sorted On` row returns TRUE for the corresponding column, it displays the down arrow (it's being repeated 1 time).

The Presentation Display Buttons

In this section, I'll talk about the display buttons available to the user. The first takes the user back to the menu, and the other resets the weights back to the original schema. Figure 20-28 shows these buttons placed adjacent to one another. Your buttons in this case are nothing more than TextBox shapes with macros assigned to execute when the user clicks one.

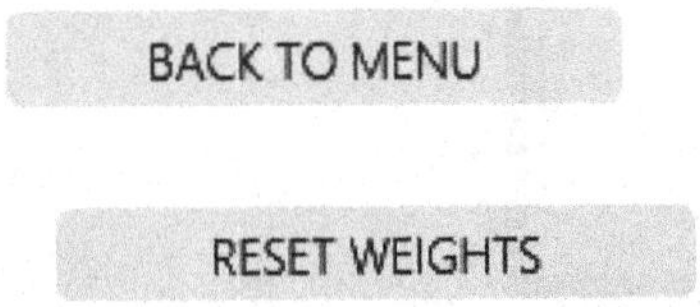

Figure 20-28. *The two buttons on your dashboard*

Going Back to the Menu

The Back To Menu button is simple. It simply takes the user back to the Menu screen. It can be found in the sheet object of the Analysis worksheet tab. Listing 20-1 shows all the code that's required.

Listing 20-1. The BackToMenu Procedure

```
Public Sub BackToMenu()
    Welcome.Activate
End Sub
```

Resetting the Weights

Because you're performing sensitivity analysis, you expect the weights to change from their original scheme. Once you've changed the weights, you might find you want to reset them back to the original scheme. Remember what dictates the weights are the ratios of the values of the scroll bars. So, one way to create this weight scheme is with the scroll bar linked value ratios shown in Figure 20-29 from the Helper tab.

4	Metrics	Linked Value	Adjusted Value	Final Weight
5	Health Level	20	80	25.0%
6	Responsiveness	60	40	12.5%
7	Financial Fairness	20	80	25.0%
8	Health Distribution	20	80	25.0%
9	Responsiveness Distribution	60	40	12.5%
10		Total	320	100%

Figure 20-29. *The Linked Value column shows the required scroll bar values to get to the original weights*

Below this table on the Helper tab is a column of data that says `Saved Weights` (Figure 20-30). Notice the values match the exact values in the `Linked Value` column in Figure 20-29. I've named this column of data as `Helper.SavedWeights`. Likewise, I've named the column of linked values in Figure 20-29 as `Helper.LinkedValues`.

19	Saved Weights	
20	20	<-- Helper.SavedWeights
21	60	
22	20	
23	20	
24	60	

Figure 20-30. *The scroll bar values that help you get to the correct weights*

The Reset Button simply copies these saved values onto the linked values. Listing 20-2 shows the code, which can be found in your file in the Analysis worksheet tab.

Listing 20-2. The ResetWeights Procedure

```
Public Sub ResetWeights()
    [Helper.LinkedValues].Value = [Helper.SavedWeights].Value
End Sub
```

Think about this dynamic for a moment. Here you've saved only schema of weights. But you could save as many weight scenarios as you'd like. It wouldn't be hard to extend this model to have the user save a weight scheme they like. Then later they could load the schema. All you would need is the simple code above to start.

Data Display and Aesthetics

In this section, I'll focus a little bit on the nature of the data you're displaying. In addition, I'll talk about some of the aesthetic choices, including color and spacing. You may have noticed that the nature of the `Total` data (column O in Figure 20-31) is different than that of the metrics (columns E, G, I, K, and M in Figure 20-31). Specifically, the metric data is all whole multiples of ten from 0 to 100, while the `Total` data can be any number from 0 to 100.

	A	B	C	D	E	F	G	H	I	J	K	L	M	N	O
30		Intermediate Table													
31		Scrollbar Value		20											
32		Sort Column Id		6	1		2		3		4		5		6
33	#	Sort Column: Total	Match Index Country		Health Level		Responsiveness		Financial Fairness		Health Distribution		Responsiveness Distribution		Total
34	20	53.7526	39 Urwhary		70		40		50		60		30		53.75
35	21	52.5020	18 Iqeiskya		60		20		50		60		60		52.50
36	22	51.2531	32 Rana		20		30		70		70		60		51.25
37	23	46.2541	31 Pustein		10		30		70		60		60		46.25
38	24	46.2509	6 Dovaeria		30		10		100		10		80		46.25
39	25	45.0014	25 Opium		40		90		40		50		10		45.00
40	26	43.7539	29 Puafoabia		30		10		90		40		20		43.75
41	27	42.5032	24 Obron		10		80		50		20		100		42.50
42	28	42.5030	1 Acoaslesh		20		20		10		80		100		42.50
43	29	42.5028	11 Eprvil		20		80		60		20		60		42.50
44	30	41.2521	28 Pocor		50		30		70		20		20		41.25
45	31	41.2507	33 Sauolia		40		80		30		10		90		41.25
46	32	40.0022	4 Asnon		50		70		60		10		10		40.00
47	33	38.7551	38 Stansblink		20		30		40		50		60		38.75
48	34	36.2506	10 Elsmen		30		10		20		80		20		36.25
49	35	35.0052	21 Jordan		40		50		20		30		50		35.00
50	36	31.2524	2 Afon		40		20		40		20		30		31.25
51	37	31.2511	20 Jaca		90		20		10		10		10		31.25
52	38	30.0008	26 Osppar		30		60		20		10		60		30.00
53	39	27.5023	34 Segro		40		70		10		10		30		27.50
54		Is Sorted On?			FALSE		FALSE		FALSE		FALSE		FALSE		TRUE

***Figure 20-31.** The intermediate table shows that the nature of the metric data differs from the total column*

Weighted vs. Not-Weighted Metrics

The reason the nature of the Total data is different from the metrics data is that the Total data is *weighted* whereas the metric data is not (Figure 20-32). Responsiveness Distribution, for example, simply uses the formula =INDEX(Database[Health Distribution],C34)*10 in its first row cell, where C34 is the Match Index. Note Database[Health Distribution] isn't a weighted column. You might be wondering why you display the weighted Total but do not display the weighted metrics (note, however, you do use the weighted metrics for your sort even if you don't display the results). I'll talk about that in this section.

5	6
Responsiveness Distribution	Total
70	65.00
90	73.75
100	53.75
80	86.25
30	53.75
100	81.25

***Figure 20-32.** You display the weighted Total but not weighted metrics*

The answer is that displaying the weighted metrics wouldn't do well to highlight the variances between metrics for a single country nor within one metric across several countries. Figure 20-33 shows how the data visualization changes when you use weighted values for the metrics.

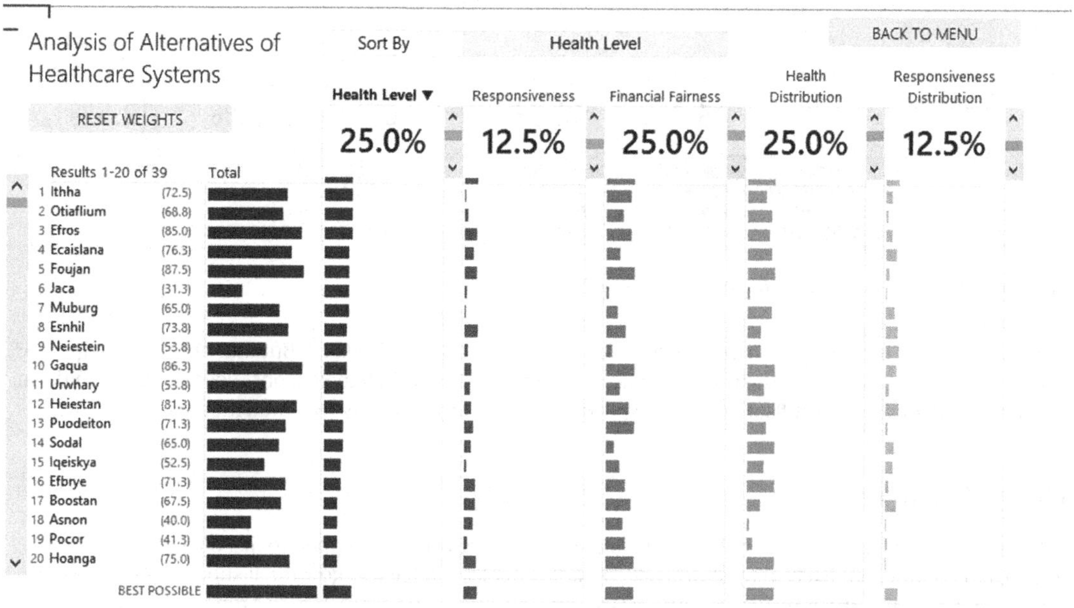

***Figure 20-33.** Using weighted values instead of raw scores*

Your ability to compare values is much harder now. This is because each metric now has a different base against which to compare a best possible score. Consider country Efros, which is ranked in the third position in Figure 20-32. It's performance in `Responsiveness` and `Financial Fairness` is, in fact, the same. But you wouldn't glean this immediately since the representation in `Responsiveness` is half that of `Financial Fairness`. Switching back to raw values shows they are the same (Figure 20-34).

***Figure 20-34.** Responsivness and Financial Fairness result in the same score for Efros*

Generally, we intuitively understand the concept of weighted models, especially when presented visually, as is the case here. In fact, this type of data visualization helps you mitigate your own bias. One common phenomenon, which I've experienced in my professional career, is the assumption that high performance in one (or two) metrics will strongly compensate for shortcomings in the rest.

In my past, I delivered a similar tool to an organization that wanted to gain insight into the performance of its different projects. Management's assumption was that because two metrics had performed well, the project should have ranked in the first or second spot. However, when presented with the tool above, they realized these two metrics were not given high weights. Indeed, you can see an example of this in Figure 20-35.

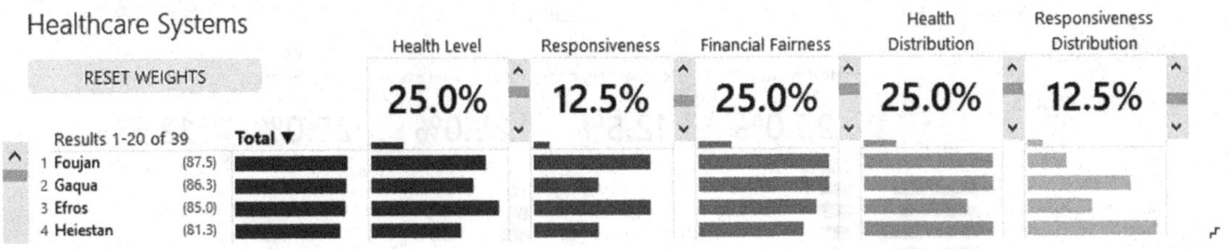

Figure 20-35. *The top four performing countries by weight*

Heiestan, for instance, ranks very well in `Responsiveness Distribution`. But that only makes up 12.5% of the overall score. Similarly, the top performer, Foujan, doesn't do well in `Responsiveness Distribution`, but that deficiency is easily offset by a strong performance in more heavily weighted metrics.

Color Choices

I chose blue as my predominant color. That choice isn't so important; I happen to like blue as color. (And it seems to go well with Excel's standard grey.) Whatever color choice you go with, it should be consistent, simple, and not overwhelming. Here, your metrics make up the total score. Varying the hue of the original blue color gives the sense of this part-to-whole relationship while similarly establishing that these metrics exist as their own measures.

Excel's color choices have gotten significantly better in terms of varying hue. But I've found for more than three metrics, the difference in color sometimes feels too strong. So for this decision support tool, I deferred my color choices to the ColorBrewer tool (`www.colorbrewer2.org`) shown in Figure 20-36. With this tool, you can define what type of data you're looking at and how many data classes you have. In my case, I chose to use a sequential hue with given data classes (based on my five metrics). ColorBrewer is a great tool to help you decide on a color palette for your work. It can even suggest color-safe alternatives that will not cause issues for those with color blindness.

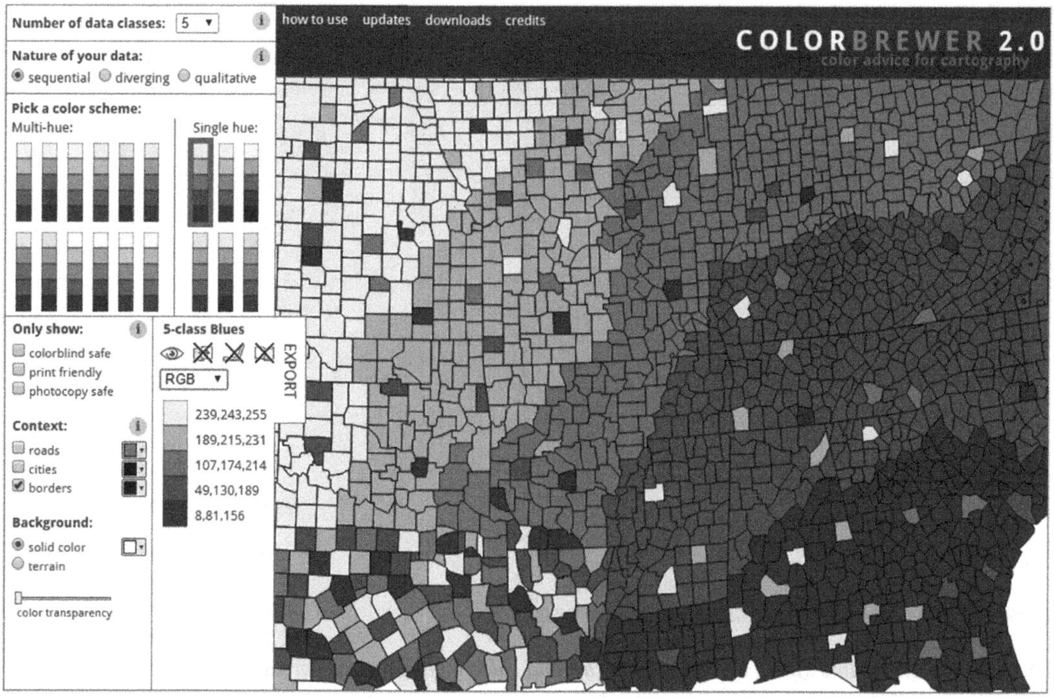

Figure 20-36. *The ColorBrewer tool (`www.colorbrewer2.org`)*

Notice in Figure 20-36, there is a dropdown box displaying RGB. By default, this dropdown box will display the Hex code color values often used for web development. However, to insert a custom color into Excel, you need to get the Red, Green, and Blue (RGB) code values. So you'll need to adjust that dropdown to say RGB.

Once you have the colors you like, you can simply type each color directly into Excel's color picker. Excel will remember these colors for later. An easy way to add these colors is to select an empty cell and then click the dropdown button next to the Fill Color icon in the Font group on the Home tab. From there, select More Colors and then click the Custom tab in the Colors dialog box that appears. You can now use those RGB code values to type in the custom color, as I have in Figure 20-37.

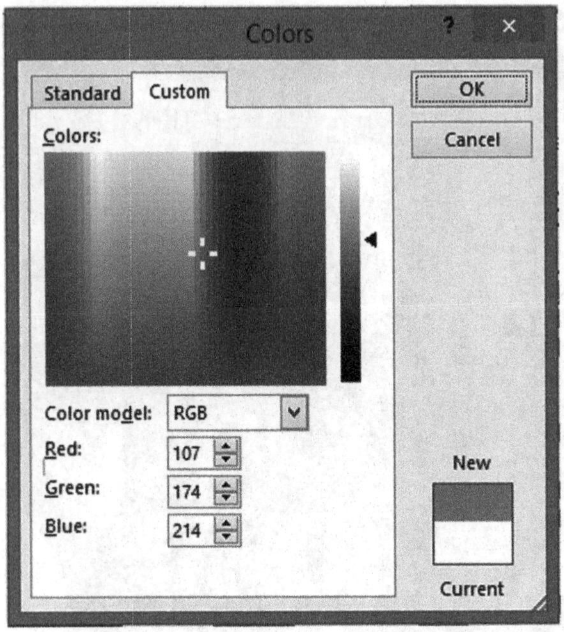

***Figure 20-37.** The Colors dialog box where you can add custom colors to the spreadsheet*

Once complete, the color will be accessible from the recent colors section in the dropdown next to the Fill Color icon (Figure 20-38).

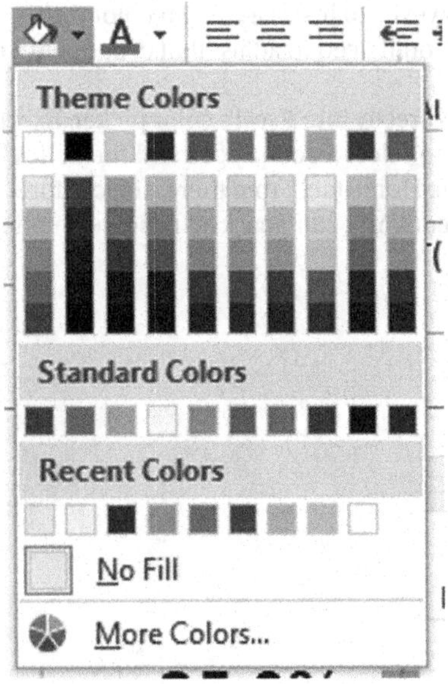

***Figure 20-38.** The Fill Color dropdown shows the custom colors that have been recently added to the spreadsheet*

Data Spacing

I've similarly kept the table borders to a minimum. Here, however, I still want to channel the notion of separation. Sometimes when there's too much data bunched together, it's hard to focus on any one data point.

Most folks, when faced with this problem, will create very strong, black borders. But a bold table border isn't needed here, and it would surely overwhelm more than it helps. Sometimes all that's required is some added white space. In Figure 20-39, I inserted a new row every five rows, and then, using the row sizing trick from above, I set them all to be a consistent size. (The project file `Chapter20Final.xlsm` includes these extra rows as my "final" touch.) There is one unfortunate drawback to this method: if you had to make a slight change to any of these columns, when you drag down from the top, the extra rows would fill in with data. The intermediate table would also be misaligned, having no spaces in it. One way around this problem is to simply add those rows to the intermediate table.

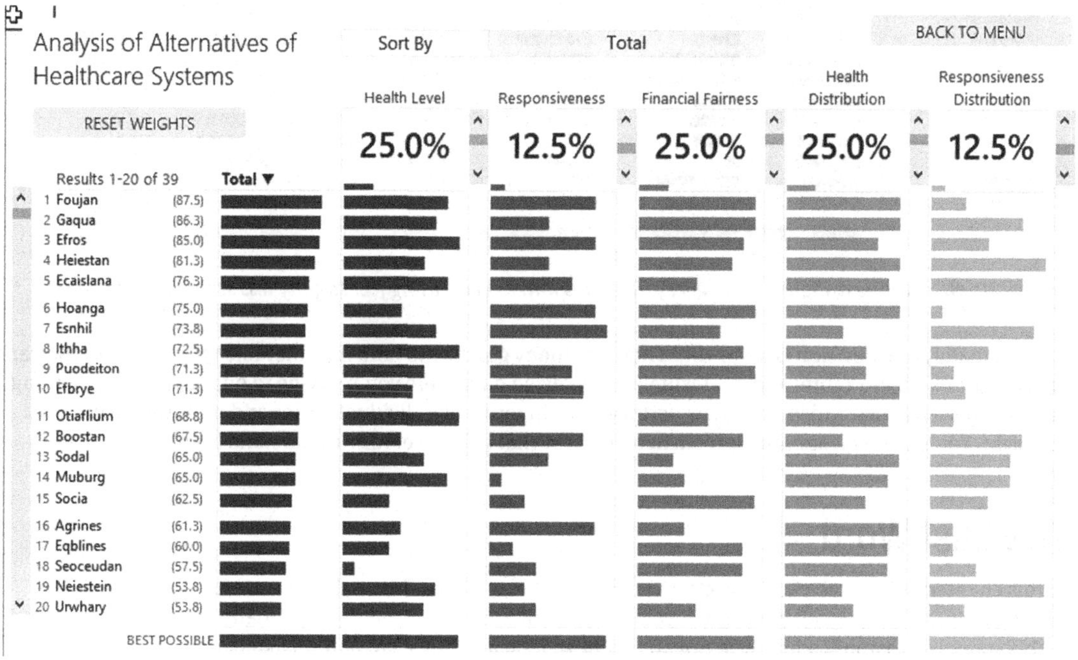

Figure 20-39. Added white space every five rows creates some seperation in our minds as we compare data across the spreadsheet

But I'm also not entirely against using borders. Another equally effective alternative is to add a light border every five metrics or so. Figure 20-40 shows an example of this.

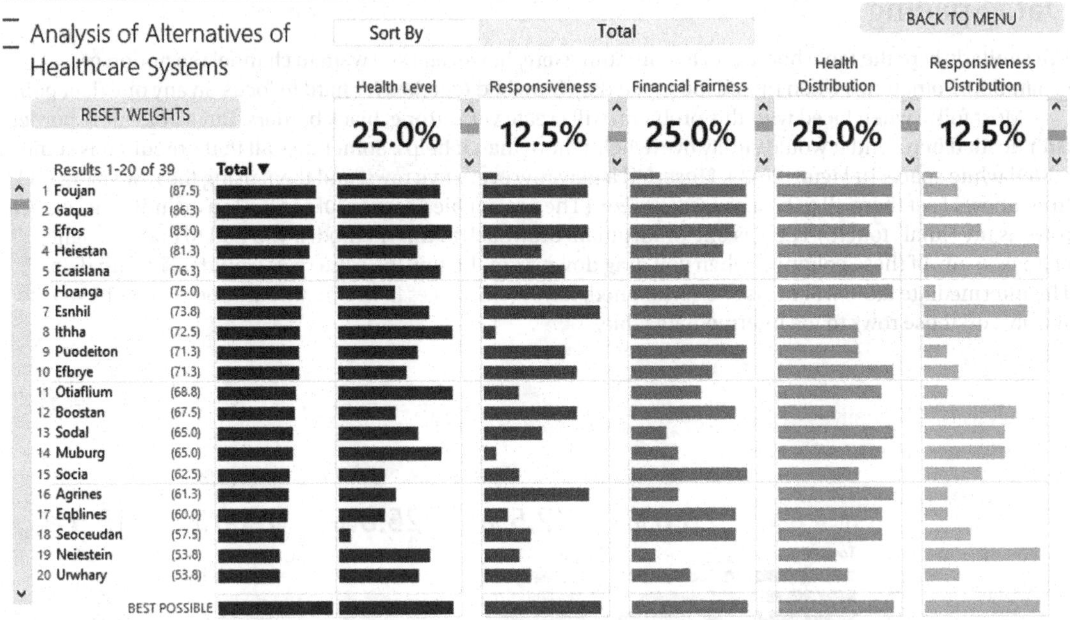

Figure 20-40. *Adding a slight border every five rows makes everything feel slightly less scrunched together*

Ultimately, the decision is up to you. There are many good ways (and innumerable terrible ways) you can help the user better interpret and contextualize visualized data. Here you're trying to optimize understanding of metric performance and importance: performance in terms of individual scores and importance in terms of weight. You should create your spreadsheet in a way that helps everyone understand both.

The Last Word

In this chapter, you perfected the link between your intermediate table and the visual layer. This included making properly sized scroll bars and developing in-cell bar charts. You saw that many of the items used in this spreadsheet application were not all that new. Instead, they were natural extensions of components built previously in this book. Finally, you saw there's a lot you can do with both code and formulas. Just as you attempt to achieve visual balance in your data displays, so too should you attempt to find the correct balance of formulas and VBA. Pursuing this balance is part of the journey.

PART V

Data Models, PowerPivot, and Power Query

CHAPTER 21

Data Model Capabilities of Excel 2013

In this chapter, I'll talk about one of the most power capabilities introduced in Excel: the data model.

Let me ask you this: what is the biggest pain faced by dashboard developers? No, it's not running out of caffeine because the office espresso machine broke. Indeed, among other things, this book assumes you have ample access to caffeine. What, then, is the biggest pain? The answer doesn't have to do with the nature of your data (although unclean and unkempt data is a pain in its own right). Even with caffeine and good data, another problem arises. *That data is all over the place: in different tables, worksheets, or workbooks.*

Disconnected data is an age-old problem. Ever since cavemen figured how to draw glyphs on inner walls, people have been asking questions like, "Is this the same symbol drawn on that cave 75 clicks south?" Those were the days before `VLOOKUP`, so our ancestors ran through forests in the heat to connect those symbols. Those were among the first data connections we humans created.

And yet we might be no better today either. We've replaced cave walls with databases, tables, workbooks, comma-separated value (CSV) files, and web sites. Instead of running through forests in the hot sun, we've employed a knotted web of `VLOOKUP`s and other crazy functions to ensure the data is connected. But when our boss asks, "Can you make a report combining sales data in SAP with customer data in our CRM and production data in ERP?" we might as well be running across that prehistoric forest for all the sweat, anxiety, and work required to fulfill this request using lookup functions and formulas.

If you've made it this far in the book, then you should know there is another class of problems dashboard developers must deal with. While the previous parts of the book dealt with creating interactive applications, there are applications that must synthesize datasets across a much broader expanse than has been presented in this book thus far. Even before you can create these dashboards, you must bring together various data sources—and those sources could come from many different systems. For these types of problems, `VLOOKUP` won't cut it. More to the point, employing many, many lookups could require your spreadsheet to become slow and unruly. Remember, part of good development is avoiding to the extent possible the option to turn off automatic calculation.

Luckily, Microsoft has saved you from slow spreadsheets—and has given you back your Friday afternoons and weekends previously spent connecting disparate data sources by way of `VLOOKUP`.

Relationship Advice

Don't worry. I am not turning this book in to relationship advice column. In this section, I'll talk about data relationships and how they are important to the data model.

Let's say you have data for sales, customer, and production. With the old method, you would have to use lookup functions to create meaningful connections between these datasets. But what if you could somehow connect everything without any formulas? Then you don't have to write a heap of `VLOOKUP`, `INDEX`, and

MATCH formulas. You could figure out questions like, "How many customers in the age group 25 to 40 bought wheat thins that were made in our factory in Nevada in July 2014?" without any formulas whatsoever.

This is where you use the *data model* feature of Excel 2013. This powerful feature helps you connect various datasets in Excel. Indeed, Excel has become even more powerful. Not only can you wrangle disparate data, but you can avoid the twisted lookup web entirely. In the next sections of this chapter, you will learn how to use the Excel 2013 data model feature.

Preparing Data for Relationships

In this section, I will explain the sample data and the setup process needed for using Excel's data model capabilities.

■ **Note** For this chapter, you'll be using `Chapter21-2013Model.xlsx`, which you can find in the source files for this book.

Imagine you are the sales manager at ACME Store and you are looking at sales transaction data for the month of December 2014. It looks like the data shown in Figure 21-1.

Sales Data

Sale ID	Time	Customer ID	Product ID	Quantity
S00001	12/1/2014 12:00:00 AM	C0001	P025	1
S00002	12/1/2014 12:00:00 AM	C0025	P025	3
S00003	12/1/2014 12:00:00 AM	C0010	P001	2
S00004	12/1/2014 12:00:00 AM	C0017	P023	4
S00005	12/1/2014 12:00:00 AM	C0018	P016	5
S00006	12/1/2014 12:00:00 AM	C0011	P018	4
S00007	12/1/2014 12:00:00 AM	C0015	P006	4
S00008	12/1/2014 12:00:00 AM	C0025	P024	4
S00009	12/1/2014 12:00:00 AM	C0016	P014	4
S00010	12/1/2014 12:00:00 AM	C0016	P012	3
S00011	12/1/2014 12:00:00 AM	C0010	P027	1
S00012	12/1/2014 12:00:00 AM	C0001	P015	1

Figure 21-1. *Sales data*

You have several questions.

- Who bought more? Male or female customers?
- What is the total revenue? What is the breakdown by product category?
- What is the sales breakdown by region of customer?
- How many large products are we selling to self-employed people?

Unfortunately, none of these questions can be answered with the data in Figure 21-1 alone. For example, looking at the first sales record, you can see that customer C0001 purchased one unit of product P025. But you don't know any other details about C0001 or P025. You need more data. So, you make a few calls and connect to some additional data sources, and now you are looking at two more datasets, as shown in Figures 21-2 and 21-3.

Customer Data

Customer ID	Customer Name	Gender	Area	Profession
C0001	Albert	Male	Middle	Retired
C0002	Barry	Male	North	Unemployed
C0003	Cindy	Female	Middle	Retired
C0004	Dorothy	Female	East	Professional
C0005	Ethan	Male	West	Self-employed
C0006	Fanah	Female	Middle	Professional
C0007	Ganesh	Male	Middle	Salaried
C0008	Harry	Male	Middle	Unemployed
C0009	Ida	Female	West	Unemployed
C0010	Jackson	Male	South	Self-employed

Figure 21-2. *Customer data*

Product Data

Product ID	Category	Name	Size	Price	Units per pack
P001	Jelly	Product 1	Large	$ 2.8	15
P002	Drinks	Product 2	Small	$ 2.8	1
P003	Drinks	Product 3	Small	$ 1.5	1
P004	Snacks	Product 4	Medium	$ 9.3	15
P005	Jelly	Product 5	Large	$ 0.5	5
P006	Drinks	Product 6	Large	$ 7.4	1
P007	Jelly	Product 7	Large	$ 2.3	15
P008	Drinks	Product 8	Medium	$ 4.0	1
P009	Biscuits	Product 9	Medium	$ 7.0	20
P010	Biscuits	Product 10	Large	$ 7.3	15
P011	Snacks	Product 11	Large	$ 3.1	10

Figure 21-3. *Product data*

Now that you know what C0001 and P025 mean, you can figure out the answers for your questions—but only after writing a gazillion VLOOKUPs. There must be a better way to set up the relationships between these different datasets. Enter the data model for Excel 2013.

Setting Up the Relationships

Now that you have all the data in one place, let's go ahead and set up the relationships between them. This process is called *data modeling*.

Before anything else, you need to ensure the data is in the Excel table format. If your data is not encased within a table, you can follow these steps:

1. Select the data you want to turn into a table.
2. Press Ctrl+T.
3. Make sure the "My table has headers" check box is selected (see Figure 21-4).

Figure 21-4. *The Create Table dialog box*

4. Click OK.
5. Give your table a name in the Design tab's Properties group (Figure 21-5).
   And that's it.

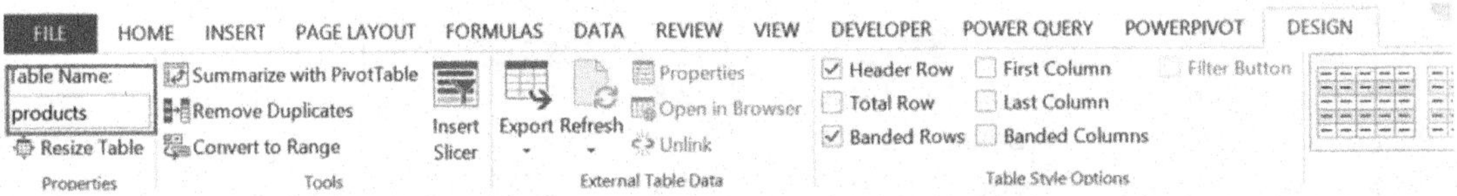

Figure 21-5. *Defining the table name on the Design tab's Properties panel*

Once all the different datasets are in tables, you can connect them with each other using the process outlined in the next few steps:

1. Click Relationships on the Data tab (Figure 21-6).

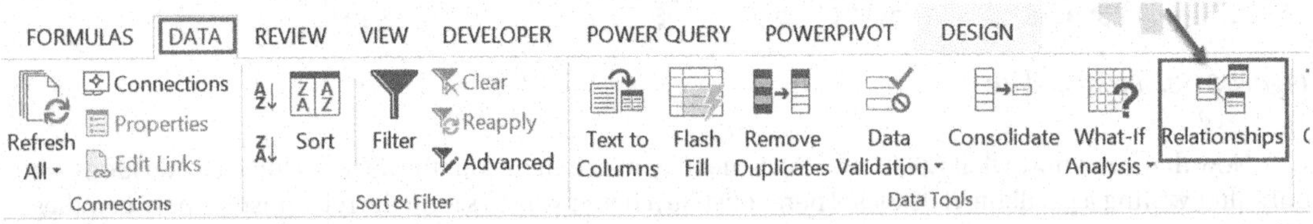

Figure 21-6. *The Relationships option on the Data tab*

2. This opens the Manage Relationships dialog box. Notice how empty and inviting it is! Let's add a few relationships. Click the New button (Figure 21-7). Where you would use VLOOKUP to look up IDs before, you can now create connections between different columns in your tables reflecting these relationships.

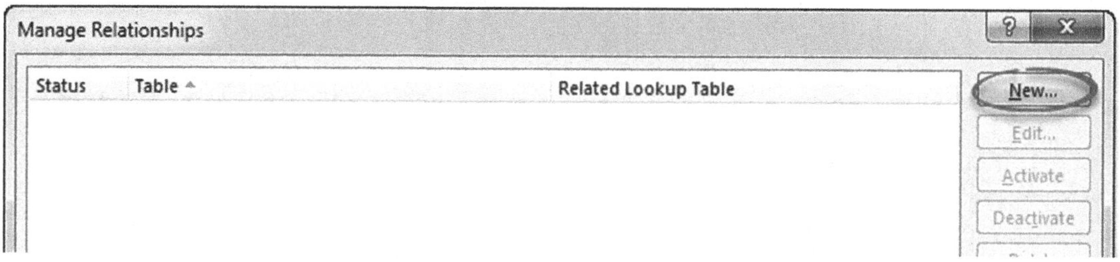

Figure 21-7. *Manage Relationships dialog: Click New to add a new relationship*

3. It doesn't matter in what order you list your relationships. Excel 2013 is smart enough to figure out the order of relationships (more on this later). So, just select both tables and columns on which the relationship should be defined. In Figure 21-8, you can see the relationship defined between the Customers[Customer ID] and sales[Customer ID] columns.

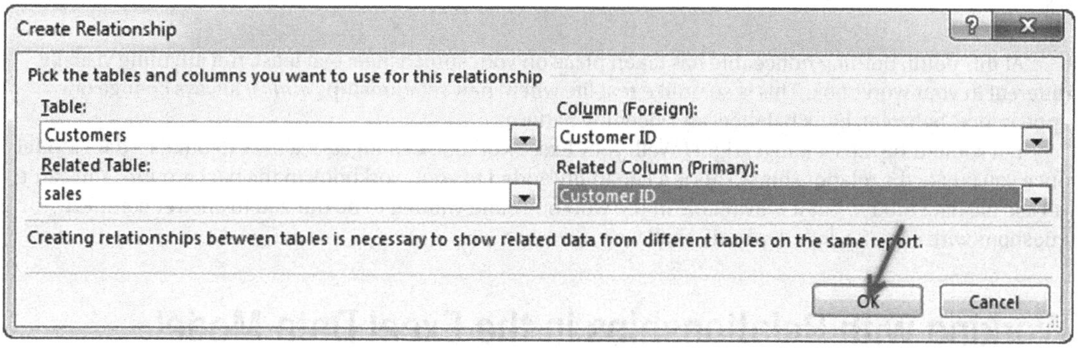

Figure 21-8. *The Create Relationship dialog box*

4. Let's add another relationship, this time between the Products and Sales tables.

5. Because the dataset is fairly simple, those are all the relationships you have. At this stage, the Manage Relationships dialog box looks like Figure 21-9.

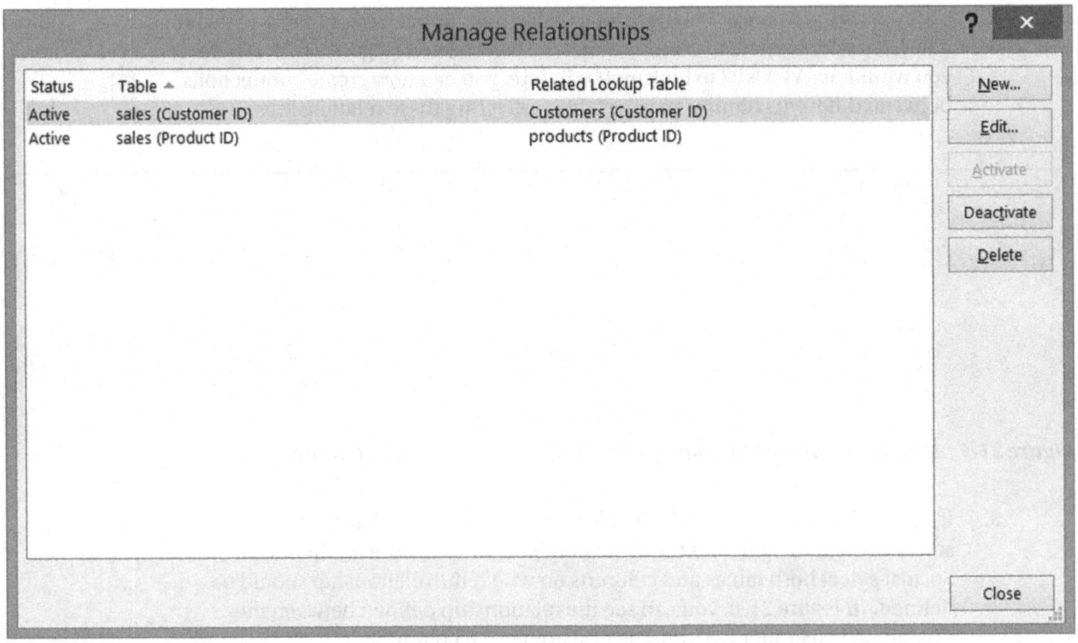

Figure 21-9. *The relationships we've just created*

At this point, nothing noticeable has taken place on your spreadsheet—at least, not anything visually different in your workbook. This is so unlike real life where new relationships *almost* always change our appearance, behavior, bank balance, and sleeping patterns.

But something must change, right? Well, your Excel workbook changes. Excel 2013 builds a data model once you create the relationships. This is a capability added to your workbook in the background. You can't yet see the data model, but it is available in the workbook and waiting to be utilized to answer complex questions with ease. So, let's deploy it, shall we?

Working with Relationships in the Excel Data Model

So far you have added some data and created relationships between them. In the next part of this chapter, let's use these relationships in pivot tables so that you can create a quick, insightful, and interactive dashboard.

Exposing Relationships with Pivot Tables

Now that your relationships are ready, let's use them. Select a cell in any of the tables and insert a pivot table from the Insert tab (see Figure 21-10). Once added, the Create PivotTable dialog box will appear (see Figure 21-11).

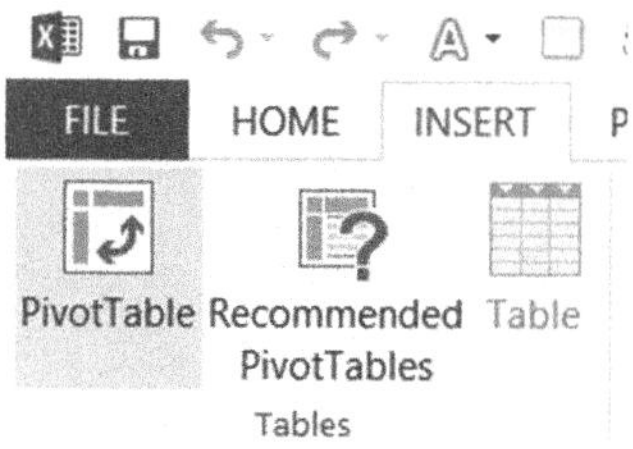

Figure 21-10. *Inserting a pivot table*

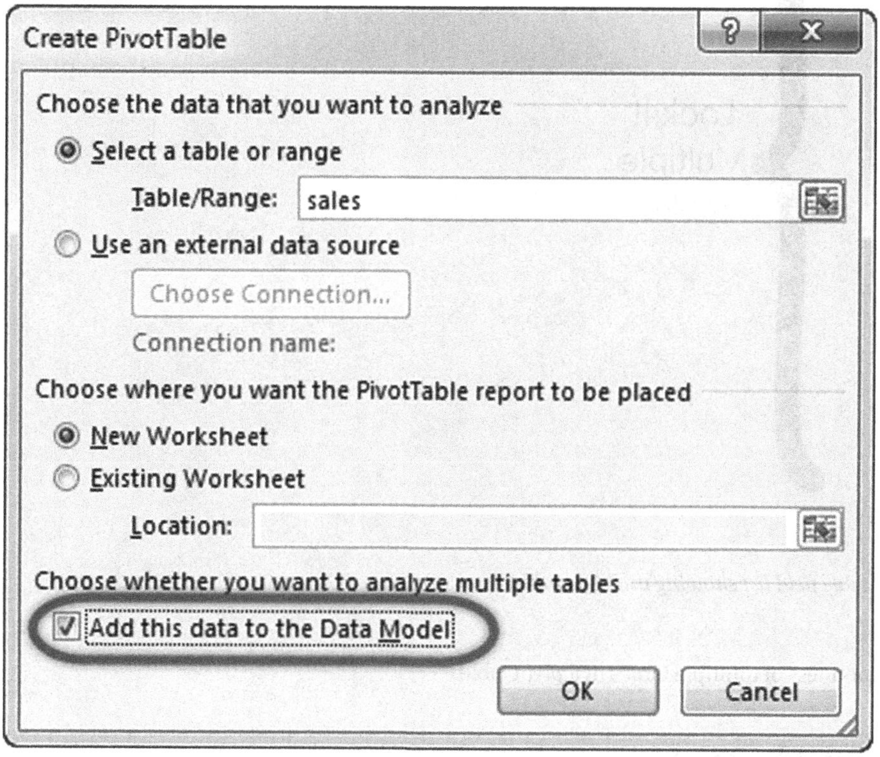

Figure 21-11. *The Create PivotTable dialog box*

Make sure you have selected the "Add this data to the Data Model" check box at the bottom before clicking OK (see Figure 21-11). This is a key step in the entire process.

Now, let's take a look in the new pivot table worksheet; look at the field list area. Do you see the difference? In Figure 21-12, you can create a pivot table by synthesizing data from multiple tables. This is the result of the tables you added to your data model.

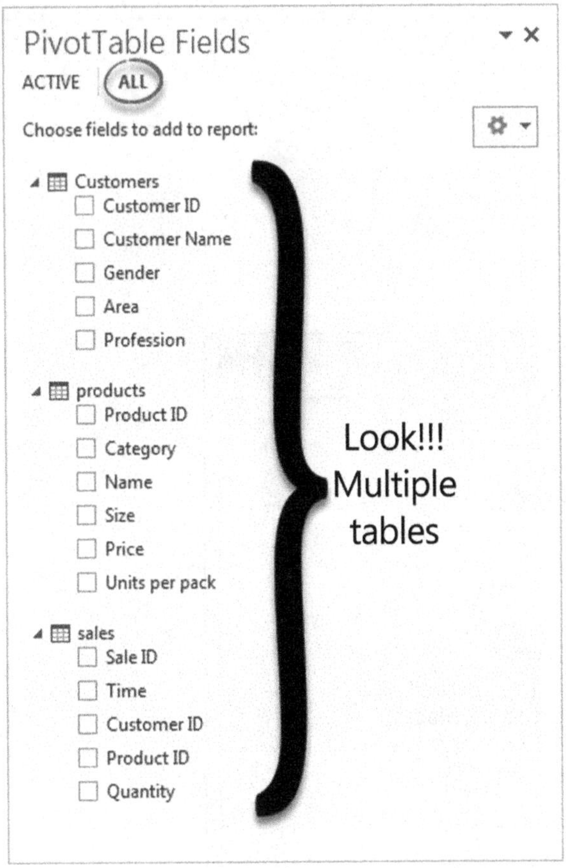

Figure 21-12. *Pivot table field list showing multiple tables*

Let's savor the goodness of multiple tables in a pivot table.

Your First Multitable Pivot

Let's answer the question, "What is the sales quantity breakdown by region of customer?" Select the Area check box in the Customers table and the Quantity check box in the sales table. And, bingo, our answer is ready. Take a look at Figure 21-13.

Row Labels	Sum of Quantity
East	2669
Middle	3844
North	2256
South	1133
West	1203
Grand Total	11105

Figure 21-13. *Example pivot table from multiple tables*

This may look like a simple report, but the mechanism that drives it is truly powerful. Excel combined the data from the Customers and sales tables using the relationship defined just a while ago and derived the regional breakdown for you, all without writing a single VLOOKUP formula.

Let's enjoy the spoils once more. This time, let's answer the question, "How many large products are we selling to self-employed people?" Add Customers[Profession] to the row label area, products[Size] to the column label area, and sales[Quantity] to the values area. Your answer is waiting for you in Figure 21-14.

Sum of Quantity	Column L			
Row Labels	Large	Medium	Small	Grand Total
Professional	796	388	565	1749
Retired	1198	605	772	2575
Salaried	836	419	482	1737
Self-employed	1559	785	991	3335
Unemployed	811	418	480	1709
Grand Total	5200	2615	3290	11105

Figure 21-14. *Understanding how multiple table pivot reports work*

Not only do you get the total for "self-employed large product units," but you get totals for every other possible combination of profession and product size. As you can see, once the relationships are in place, you can use them as per your imagination and get answers to *most* questions.

Slicing and Dicing with Relationships

Excel 2013's data model and relationships work beautifully with filtering features such as *slicers* (a feature introduced in Excel 2010) and *timelines* (a feature added in Excel 2013). I'll go through how to use each mechanism in this section.

Adding Slicers to the Pivot Report

Now that you have tied all the tables together, you can create a pivot table from two tables and "slice" it on the third table. For example, let's find out the quantity breakdown by gender and profession for only the Jelly category of products.

To do this, you need to filter the pivot table by category = Jelly. This can be accomplished by the Report Filters function of the old Excel or the more exciting *slicers* feature of the new Excel (slicers are supported in Excel 2010 and newer).

To create a slicer on the product category, locate the products table in the PivotTable Fields area, right-click the Category field, and choose Add as Slicer (refer to Figure 21-15).

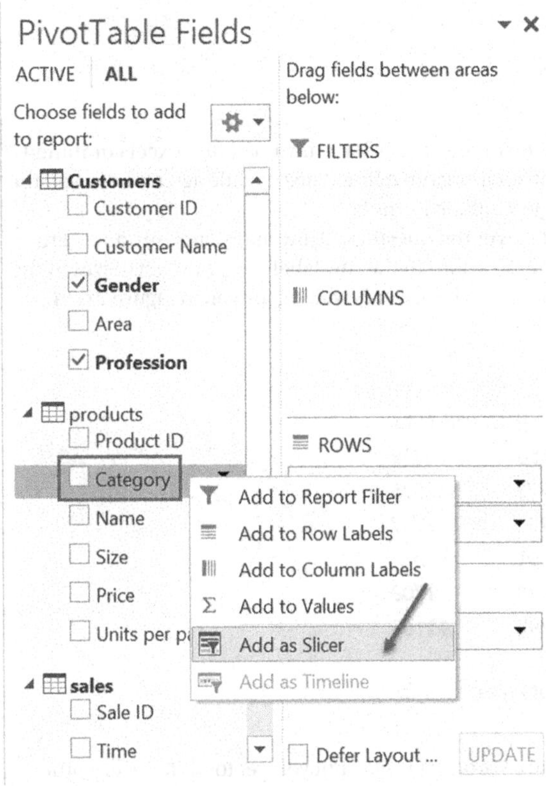

***Figure 21-15.** Adding a slicer on product category field using PivotTable Fields screen*

Once you have a slicer, just click Jelly to show the pivot report for only the Jelly category. Figure 21-16 shows the results of this.

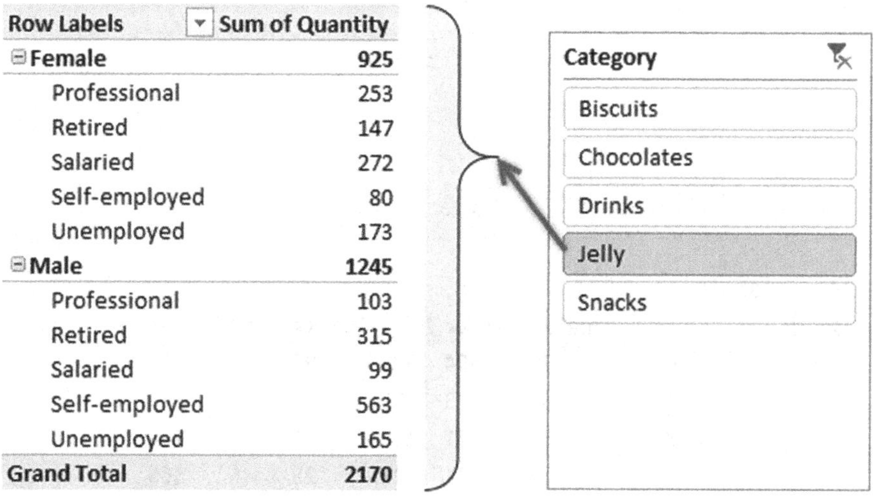

Row Labels	Sum of Quantity
⊟ Female	925
Professional	253
Retired	147
Salaried	272
Self-employed	80
Unemployed	173
⊟ Male	1245
Professional	103
Retired	315
Salaried	99
Self-employed	563
Unemployed	165
Grand Total	2170

Figure 21-16. *Quantity breakdown by gender and profession for the Jelly category of products*

■ **Note** For more information about how to create, use, and customize slicers, refer to `http://chandoo.org/wp/2015/06/24/introduction-to-slicers/`.

One More Report, Using Timelines

Figure 21-17 shows another example report employing timelines. In it you can provide a quantity breakdown by gender, region, and product category for December 4 to 12, 2014.

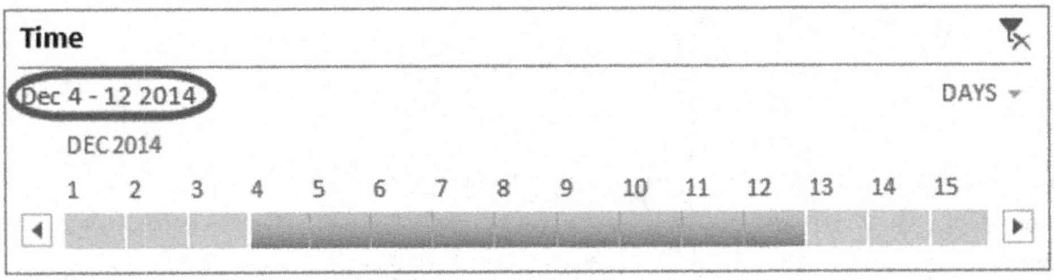

Sum of Quantity	Column Labels					
Row Labels	Biscuits	Chocolates	Drinks	Jelly	Snacks	Grand Total
⊟Female	**76**	**225**	**554**	**275**	**290**	**1420**
East	26	85	173	90	51	425
Middle	28	65	171	104	130	498
North	2	25	81	29	28	165
South	16	23	92	31	58	220
West	4	27	37	21	23	112
⊟Male	**152**	**188**	**645**	**367**	**393**	**1745**
East	31	31	110	77	89	338
Middle	47	73	210	100	175	605
North	44	54	215	136	68	517
South	9	12	26	12	25	84
West	21	18	84	42	36	201
Grand Total	**228**	**413**	**1199**	**642**	**683**	**3165**

Figure 21-17. *Timelines and pivot reports with multiple tables*

To insert a timeline, right-click the Time field in the sales table and choose Add as Timeline.

The relationships feature works seamlessly with multiple slicers, timelines, and pivot table report filters. Try them and see how easily you can answer even the most complex reporting questions. Please refer to Chapter 22 for an example dashboard constructed using multiple slicers.

Rules for Happy Relationships

As you might have guessed, relationships are at the heart of data models. They're the connections that allow you to bring datasets together. Like all relationships, there are certain rules to follow.

Let's understand them:

- ***One table must have unique values in the relationship column***: When you are connecting two tables of data, say A and B on column X, one of the tables must not have duplicate values in that column. In the database world, such a column is referred to as the *primary key*. Although Excel is not a database, the relationships feature helps you loosely mimic a database in your spreadsheet. So, the standard relationship rule of having one primary key (that is, one column with unique values) applies.

- ***No many-to-many relationships***: This is a consequence of the previous rule. In the Excel 2013 data model, you can't have many-to-many relationships. You can add one-to-one or one-to-many relationships, though.
- ***All data must be in tables (or connections that are part of the data model)***: All the data that is part of the data model and relationships should be in Excel tables or connections (that are loading data to tables or the data model automatically). If your data is not in a table, just press Ctrl+T to insert a table around it. Always give the table a meaningful name for easier referencing. Don't just use the default names such as Table1, Table2, and so on.
- ***Pivot tables should be added to the data model***: To access the power of relationships, your pivot table must be added to the data model at the time of creation.

The Last Word

The relationship capability in Excel 2013 opens doors for many possibilities. There are many things you can do with a workbook-level data model. You can create really powerful reports and dashboards using relationships, slicers, pivot tables, and charts. In the next chapter, you will examine an interactive dashboard built using these features.

In the future versions of Excel, Microsoft is likely to build more powerful features into the data model and relationships area. We will just have to wait and see.

CHAPTER 22

Advanced Modeling with Slicers, Filters, and Pivot Tables

So far in this book, you have seen really powerful and elaborate techniques to analyze data and present results in the dashboard format. You need to spend a significant amount of time when creating dashboards with these techniques. Continuing from the previous chapter, I'll provide some alternatives here.

Creating an Interactive Excel Dashboard

My goal is to create informative, interactive, and beautiful dashboard...in less than 60 minutes. You are going to create a dashboard like the one shown in Figure 22-1.

Figure 22-1. Sales dashboard using Excel

You will be using the data model feature of Excel 2013, including pivot tables, slicers, and pivot charts, to create a completely interactive dashboard from scratch in very little time.

Let's Meet the Data

Imagine you are running a set of retail stores selling various snacks. You have transaction-level data for the year 2014. There are a total of 42,684 transactions. These transactions are similar in nature to the one shown in Table 22-1. (In this chapter, you'll be using `Chapter22-AdhocDashboard.xlsx`. You can download this file from the source materials.)

Table 22-1. *Example Transaction: Sales Data*

Date	Customer ID	Product ID	Store ID	Quantity	Amount
1-Jan-2014	Xxxx	Yyyyy	Zzzzz	##	$#.##

In this example, the details for the customer, product, and store are already available in separate tables. Take a look at the Data worksheet tab in the chapter file to see them for yourself. Figures 22-2, 22-3, and 22-4 show the values in these tables.

Customer Data

Customer ID	Customer Name	Gender	Area	Profession
C0001	Albert	Male	Middle	Retired
C0002	Barry	Male	North	Unemployed
C0003	Cindy	Female	Middle	Retired
C0004	Dorothy	Female	East	Professional
C0005	Ethan	Male	West	Self-employed
C0006	Fanah	Female	Middle	Professional
C0007	Ganesh	Male	Middle	Salaried
C0008	Harry	Male	Middle	Unemployed
C0009	Ida	Female	West	Unemployed
C0010	Jackson	Male	South	Self-employed

Figure 22-2. *Customer Data table*

Product Data

Product ID	Category	Name	Size	Price	Units per pack
P001	Jelly	Product 1	Large	$ 2.8	15
P002	Drinks	Product 2	Small	$ 2.8	1
P003	Drinks	Product 3	Small	$ 1.5	1
P004	Snacks	Product 4	Medium	$ 9.3	15
P005	Jelly	Product 5	Large	$ 0.5	5
P006	Drinks	Product 6	Large	$ 7.4	1
P007	Jelly	Product 7	Large	$ 2.3	15
P008	Drinks	Product 8	Medium	$ 4.0	1
P009	Biscuits	Product 9	Medium	$ 7.0	20
P010	Biscuits	Product 10	Large	$ 7.3	15
P011	Snacks	Product 11	Large	$ 3.1	10

Figure 22-3. *Product Data table*

Store ID	Name	Parking	Hours open	Manager
STR01	Westend	Yes	24	Sam
STR02	Eastman	Yes	24	Sam
STR03	Northampton	No	24	Sam
STR04	Southie	No	16	Cynthia
STR05	Southwest	Yes	12	Cynthia
STR06	Northeast	Yes	24	Cynthia
STR07	Midwest	No	8	Jackie
STR08	Northwest	Yes	24	Jackie

Figure 22-4. *Store Data table*

As you know from previous chapters, creating a dashboard from this data requires some up-front development work. However, you can use the techniques from Chapter 21 to create this dashboard with less work. You can deploy the Excel relationships feature, pivot tables, and slicers and instantly get a beautiful report. Well, it may not be instant, but it should take 60 minutes (or less). Let's go.

Steps for Creating the Dashboard

There are nine simple steps to create this dashboard. The next sections will describe them one at a time.

Step 1: Generating Missing Data

If you look at the data, you will notice that you want to show sales by day of month for any filtered month. The raw data is at the transactional level (with 42,684 transactions). Instead of adding extra columns to this transaction table to generate month and day of month values, you can create another table that lists all the dates in the data. These types of tables are called *calendar tables*.

For the business intelligence, reporting, and data warehousing world, I define a calendar table as follows:

> *A table that contains all the dates from start to end for the reporting period, one date per row. It contains dates even when you have no reported transactions on those dates.*

Essentially, it's a calendar. Since you have data only for 2014, the calendar table will have 365 rows.

There are many ways to generate this table. If you deal with data that spans multiple years, you can autogenerate this calendar table by using SQL, by using PowerQuery, or by subscribing to calendar sources available on big data services such as Windows Azure Marketplace. All of these techniques are beyond the scope of this book. So, let's generate this data in the old-fashioned way, by typing it.

Of course, I am kidding. We all have better things to do than type 365 rows of data. You will autopopulate the calendar table using Excel's autofill feature. Just go to an empty range in your workbook, type the first two to three dates (**1-jan-2014**, **2-jan-2014**, and so on), and drag down. Excel will fill the remaining dates.

Once you have the dates, you can generate the rest of the columns using formulas. At the least, you need to create the following formulas for the new columns:

- *Day of month*: Generated using `=DAY([date]) formula`
- *Month name*: Generated using `=TEXT([date],"MMMM")`

Once these columns are added, you should have a table similar to Figure 22-5.

Date	Day of week	Day of month	Month name	Month number
1-Jan-14	Wednesday	1	01-January	1
2-Jan-14	Thursday	2	01-January	1
3-Jan-14	Friday	3	01-January	1
4-Jan-14	Saturday	4	01-January	1
5-Jan-14	Sunday	5	01-January	1
6-Jan-14	Monday	6	01-January	1
7-Jan-14	Tuesday	7	01-January	1
8-Jan-14	Wednesday	8	01-January	1
9-Jan-14	Thursday	9	01-January	1
10-Jan-14	Friday	10	01-January	1
11-Jan-14	Saturday	11	01-January	1
12-Jan-14	Sunday	12	01-January	1
13-Jan-14	Monday	13	01-January	1
14-Jan-14	Tuesday	14	01-January	1
15-Jan-14	Wednesday	15	01-January	1

Figure 22-5. *Calendar table*

OTHER COLUMNS YOU COULD ADD

In addition to the columns listed previously, there are other date columns you might consider adding depending upon the nature of your data and what you'd like to report. Here are some to consider:

- *Day of week*: `=TEXT([date],"DDDD")`
- *Month number*: `=MONTH([date])`
- *Quarter*: Can you *figure this one out?*

Step 2: Creating the Relationship Between Sales and Product

Well, you don't have to put on a robe and officiate the wedding, but you need to create the relationships between various tables. Using the instructions from Chapter 21, create the following relationships:

- sales[Customer ID] - Customers[Customer ID]
- sales[Product ID] - products[Product ID]
- sales[Store ID] - stores[Store ID]
- sales[Date] - calendar[Date]

When the relationships are created, your screen should look like Figure 22-6.

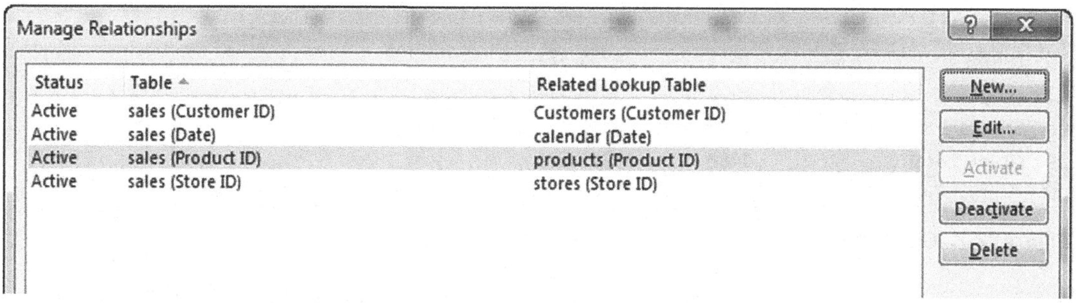

Figure 22-6. *Relationships between various tables*

Step 3: Creating Some Pivot Tables

Now that your relationships are in place, let's figure out the calculation part for your dashboard. Although I started this chapter with a preview of the dashboard you are going to construct, the correct way to do this is to define the *information needs* of this dashboard. Here are a few plausible needs:

- Which categories of products are doing better?
- Which regions are doing better in sales and quantity sold?
- What types of customers are buying your products more?
- What is the sales and quantity trend for any given month?

- What is the performance for any given manager?
- Is there any difference in purchasing patterns of male versus female customers?
- How do the sales numbers change between various SKU sizes (small, medium, and large)?

In real life, when you are creating a dashboard, this would be the first step. You'll interview the dashboard customers (your boss, client, chief executive officer, regulatory authority, and so on) to clearly understand what they want, prioritize needs, and make a rough sketch of the dashboard before collecting data and setting up relationships. Because this is a book, I am taking the shortcut of starting with a predefined vision of the dashboard and showing you how to make it.

For this example, you will create pivot tables for the first four questions and then add slicers on the calendar[Month], Customers[Gender], store[Manager], and product[Size] fields so that you can analyze the data for any combination. Refer to step 5 for instructions on creating slicers. Let's create necessary pivot tables to answer the first four questions.

■ **Note** Refer to Chapter 21 if you want to learn more about the process of creating pivot tables.

- *Quantity and sales breakdown by product category*: see Figure 22-7.

	A	B	C
3	Row Labels	Sum of Quantity	Sum of Amount
4	Biscuits	243	1654.268
5	Chocolates	669	1856.295
6	Drinks	1631	4739.373
7	Jelly	906	3376.354
8	Snacks	1039	4599.811
9	**Grand Total**	**4488**	**16226.101**
10			

Figure 22-7. *Quantity and sales breakdown by category*

- *Quantity and sales breakdown by customer's profession*: see Figure 22-8.

	A	B	C
3	Row Labels	Sum of Quantity	Sum of Amount
4	Professional	279	1110.295
5	Retired	1199	4261.885
6	Salaried	348	1174.144
7	Self-employed	2074	7454.518
8	Unemployed	588	2225.259
9	**Grand Total**	**4488**	**16226.101**

Figure 22-8. *Quantity and sales breakdown by profession*

- *Quantity and sales breakdown by region*: see Figure 22-9.

Row Labels	Sum of Quantity	Sum of Amount
Midwest	836	3186.06
Northeast	902	3285.156
Northwest	877	3067.405
Southie	906	3072.939
Southwest	967	3614.541
Grand Total	**4488**	**16226.101**

Figure 22-9. *Quantity and sales breakdown by region*

- *Quantity and sales breakdown by day of month*: see Figure 22-10.

Row Labels	Sum of Quantity	Sum of Amount
1	153	602.621
2	136	550.125
3	101	259.075
4	112	441.132
5	163	558.304
6	182	581.577
7	228	760.796
8	153	610.348
9	115	485.094
10	47	192.794
11	110	440.249
12	179	588.89

Figure 22-10. *Quantity and sales breakdown by day of month*

Once complete, you can move on to step 4.

Step 4. Creating Pivot Charts

Now that you have pivot tables, let's turn them into visualizations by using pivot charts. From each pivot, insert a pivot chart. To insert a pivot chart, complete the following process. Let's assume you want to create pivot chart for category breakdown pivot.

1. Select any cell in the pivot. This activates pivot table-specific ribbon tabs.
2. Go to the Analyze tab and click PivotChart (refer to Figure 22-11)

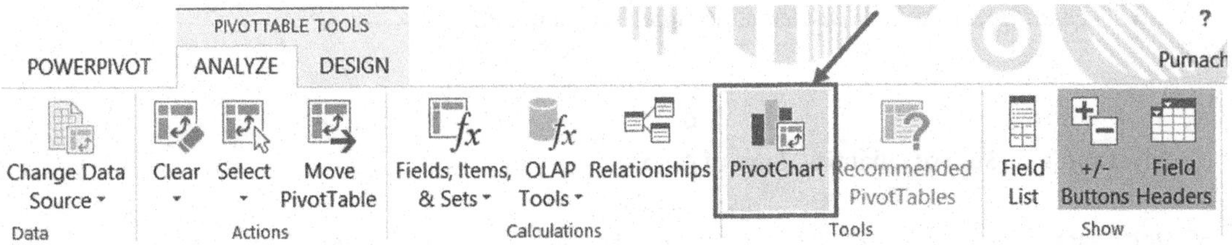

Figure 22-11. *Adding a pivot chart using the Analyze tab*

3. Set the pivot chart type to Bar (refer to Figure 22-12)

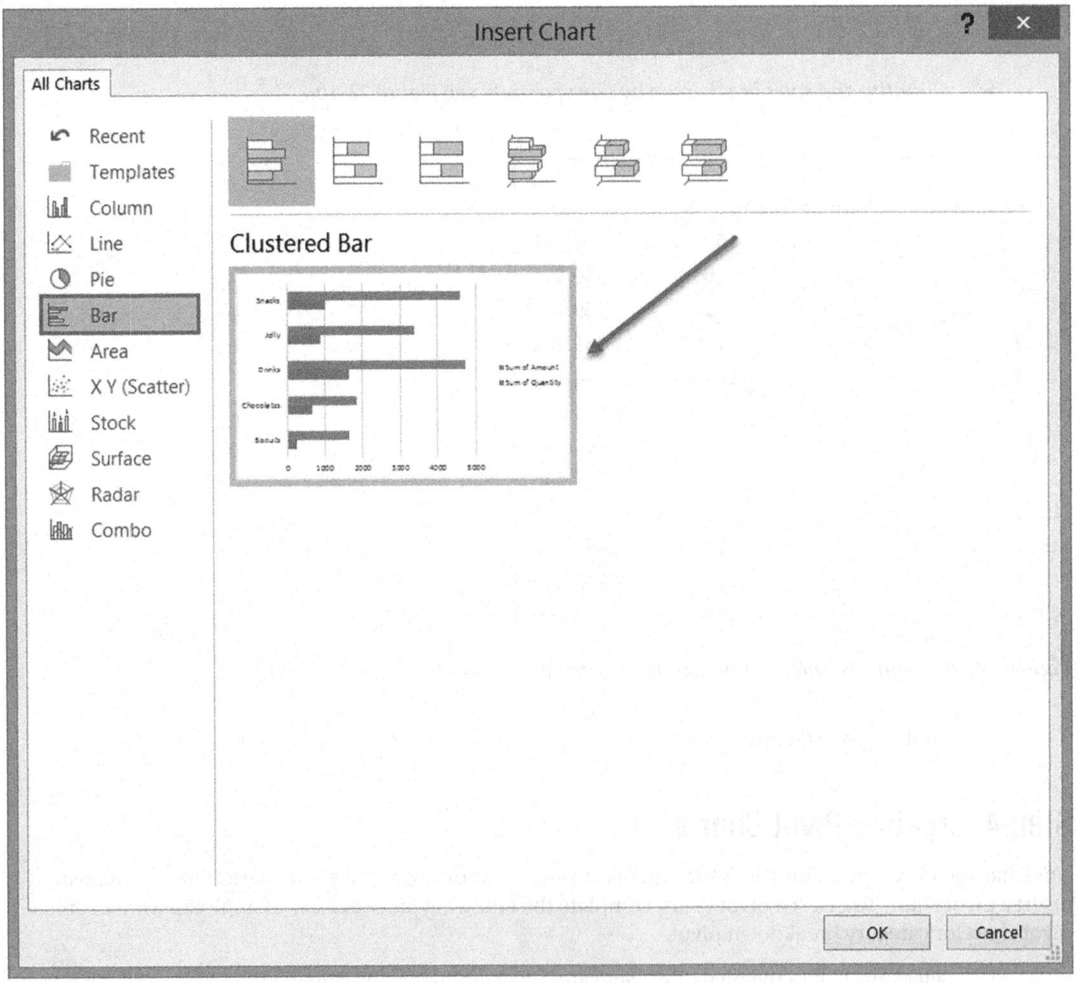

Figure 22-12. *Creating a clustered bar chart type of pivot chart*

4. Click OK.
5. To add remaining pivot charts, refer to Table 22-2.

Table 22-2. *Pivot Chart Types for Each Pivot*

Pivot	Pivot Chart Type
Category breakdown	Clustered Bar chart
Profession breakdown	Clustered Bar chart
Regional breakdown	Clustered Bar chart
Daily breakdown	Line chart

Once the pivot charts are added, move them all to one sheet using the process that follows:

1. Add a new worksheet. Call it **Dashboard**.
2. Select the first pivot chart.
3. Cut it (Ctrl+X).
4. Go to the Dashboard worksheet and paste it (Ctrl +V).
5. Repeat the process for the remaining pivot charts.

Step 5: Adding the Slicers

At this stage, your dashboard has all the necessary charts and looks like Figure 22-13. But the information displayed is for all 42,684 transactions. You wanted to analyze sales information for any given month, for a particular customer gender, for a specific store manager, and for certain product SKU sizes. In other words, you need to *filter your report to a subset of the data. This is where slicers can help.*

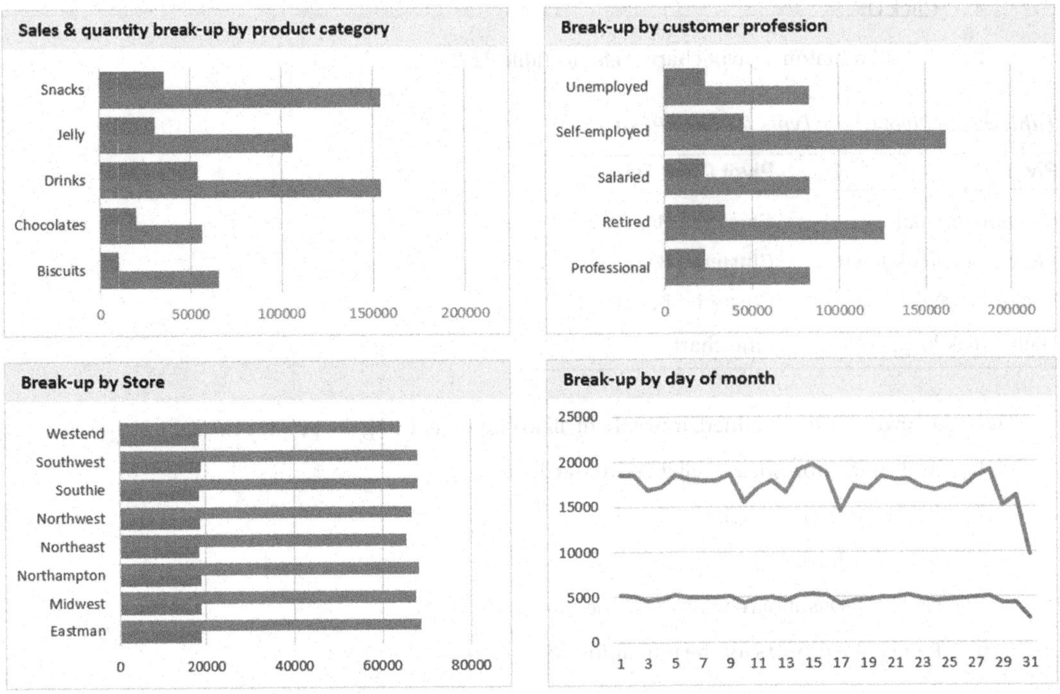

Figure 22-13. *Dashboard with pivot charts for all the data*

You'll need to create slices for the following fields (refer to Chapter 21 for instruction on how to add slicers):

- Customers[Gender]
- stores[Manager]
- calendar[month name]
- products[Size]

To insert these slicers, go to Insert tab and click the Slicer option in the Filters group (Figure 22-14).

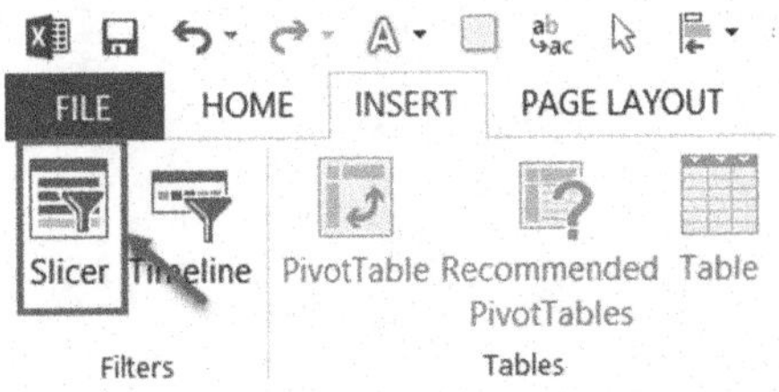

Figure 22-14. *Inserting a slicer*

■ **Caution** Make sure you are adding the slicers to the Dashboard worksheet.

Now select the slicers indicated in Figure 22-15 from the various tables in the workbook data model.

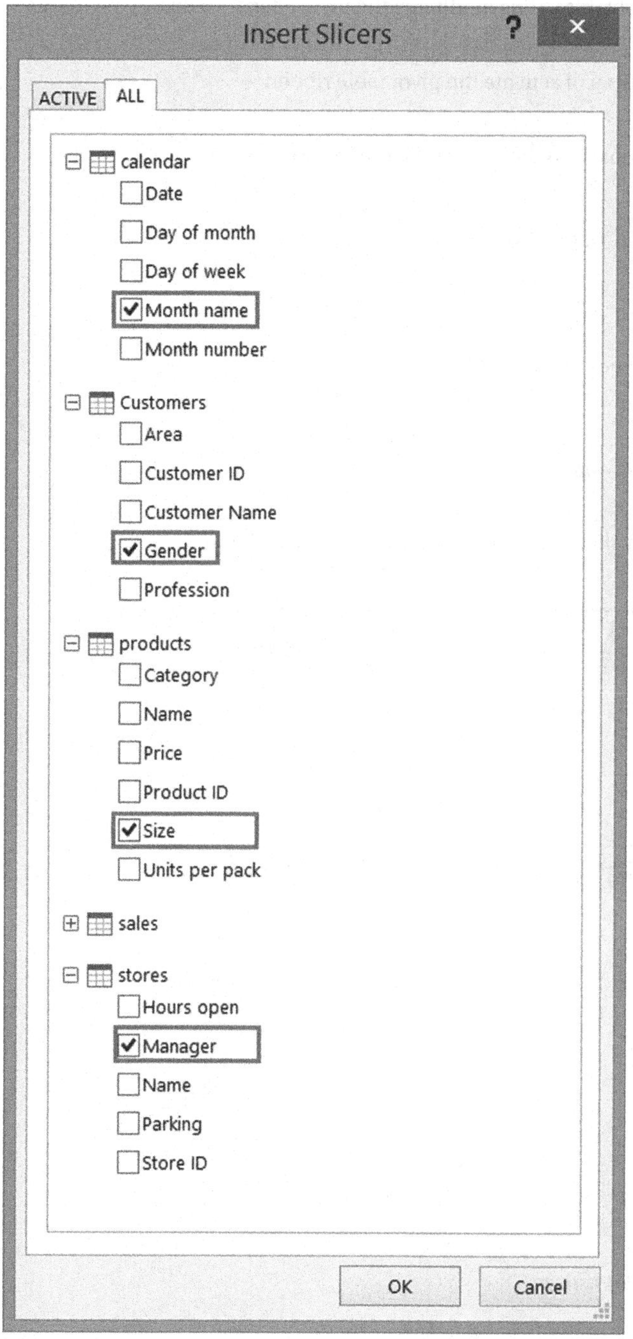

***Figure 22-15.** Inserting multiple slicers by checking table column names*

Step 6: Linking the Slicers to Pivots

Just by adding slicers, nothing will happen. You must link them to the pivot tables. Only then will the slicer selection trigger its filtering action on the pivot tables, thus modifying the pivot charts. To do this, go to each pivot table sheet and follow this process:

1. Select any cell inside the pivot. This will activate the pivot table ribbon context menu.

2. Select Analyze ➤ Filter Connections from the ribbon (Figure 22-16).

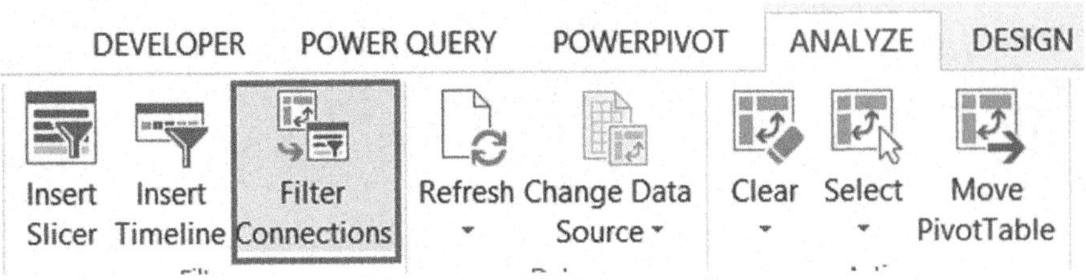

Figure 22-16. *Filter Connections option on the Analyze tab*

3. Connect the pivot table to all four slicers by selecting the boxes (Figure 22-17).

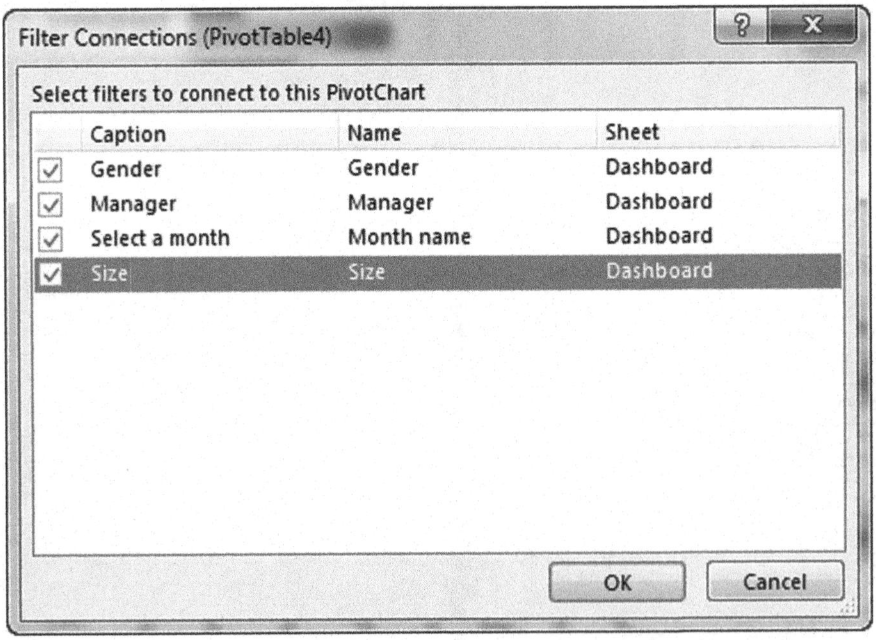

Figure 22-17. *Linking each pivot table to all four slicers*

4. Repeat the process for the remaining pivots.

Step 7: Cleaning Up the Pivot Charts

Let's agree on one thing first. Pivot charts are not the prettiest things in *any* Excel workbook. Heck, they can't even get a date with 3D pie charts. So, how can you tolerate them in a dashboard? Well, you can make them presentable. Refer to Figure 22-18 for an example default pivot chart formatted using simple guidelines.

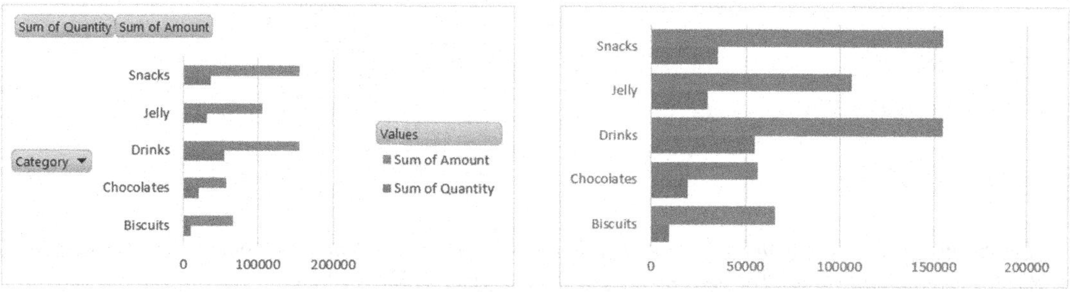

Figure 22-18. *Before and after: formatting default pivot charts (the default chart is on the left; the formatted one is on the right)*

Here are a few steps you can follow to format pivot charts to your liking:

1. Remove the filtering buttons in the pivot chart by toggling them using the Analyze ➤ Field Buttons option. See Figure 22-19.

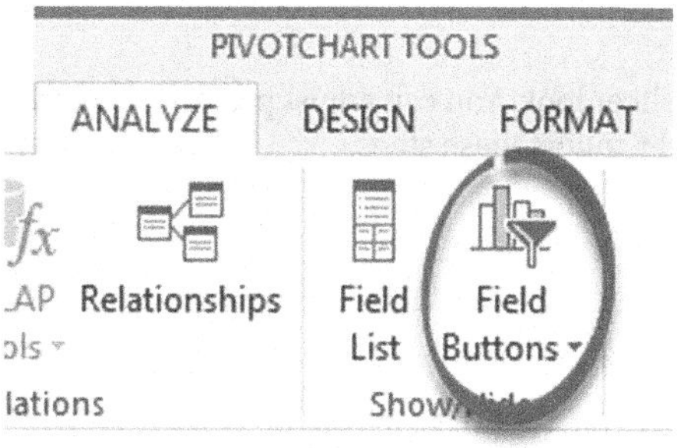

Figure 22-19. *Turning off field buttons from the Analyze tab*

2. Toggle the Field List option too (from the same Show/Hide group). This way, when you click the pivot chart, Excel won't show the field list sidebar panel.

3. Set up the colors for your pivot chart on the Format tab. Choose simple and consistent colors.

4. Adjust the gap width in the bar chart by selecting the bars, pressing Ctrl+1, and using the *Gap Width* option. Set it to 50% or similar. Refer to Figure 22-20.

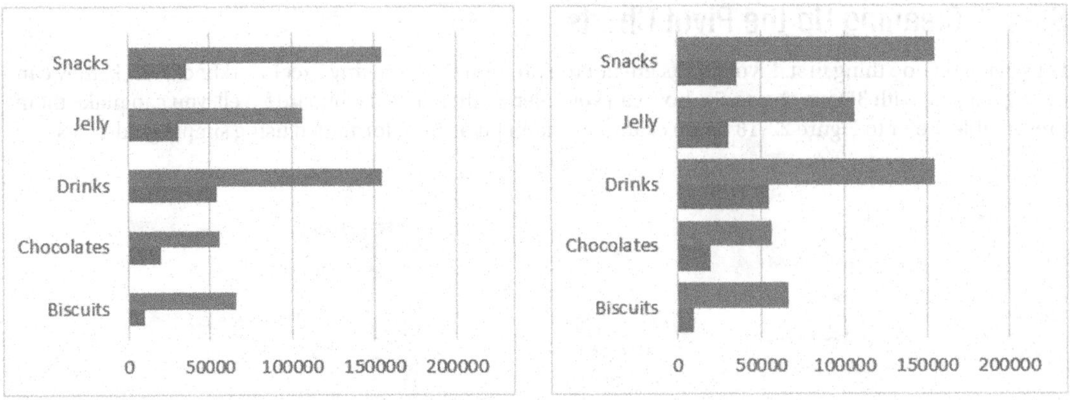

Figure 22-20. *Setting the gap width to 50% allows for a better user experience. The chart on left has a gap width of 180% (default value). The one on the right is set to a gap width of 50%*

5. Make all pivot charts same size by selecting them all (Ctrl+click each) and using the Format tab's Size option.
6. Align the charts and adjust the spacing between them, using the alignment and spacing options in the Arrange area of the Format tab.

Now that you have your pivot charts formatted the way you want them, let's turn to the slicers.

Step 8: Adjusting the Slicer Formatting

While you are formatting, you might as well clean up the default slicer look. You can adjust pretty much any aspect of slicers using custom styles. To create a custom slicer style, follow these steps:

1. Select the slicer.
2. Go to the Slicer Options tab.
3. Right-click any style in the Slicer Styles panel and choose Duplicate.
4. Set up the style you want by customizing color, border, font, font size, and so on.
5. Apply the new style to all the slicers by selecting the slicer and clicking a style option from the Slicer Styles group in the Slicer Options tab.

■ **Note** For more information about slicers, including how to format them, refer to `http://chandoo.org/wp/2015/06/24/introduction-to-slicers/`.

Step 9: Putting Everything Together

Although this step is not required to have a functioning dashboard, it adds a nice, clean look to your reports. So, you should do it anyway!

Make sure all the charts, slicer, and so on, are together and neatly aligned in the dashboard worksheet. Add titles and labels where necessary. Create a clear title and legend in the top part of your dashboard. And the final product is ready. See Figure 22-21.

Figure 22-21. *The final version of the dashboard*

Let's pause and admire the powerful dashboard you constructed in just a matter of minutes.

- The slicers can cross-filter. That's right. If you select any slicer, it filters *all* charts and other filters.
- Everything is interactive.
- Not a single formula was written to achieve this capability.
- All the data is scattered across multiple tables.
- When you have new data, just refresh the workbook (Alt+F5), and your dashboard will be up to date.
- This dashboard is viewable and interactive on the Web (using Office 365) or on Excel for tablets.

Imagine building all this using formulas or VBA. I sure will consume gallons of coffee before being able to figure out the formula for the daily sales breakdown of male customers buying large products in Cynthia's stores in August 2014.

Problems with Pivot Tables

Not all is rainbows and butterflies in the land of pivot tables. In this section, I'll talk about their drawbacks.

While there are a ton of advantages to this approach of building dashboards, it still falls short on a few fronts:

- ***Pivot tables can't calculate everything***: They are extremely good for aggregating and generating simple statistics (such as `SUM`, `AVERAGE`, `COUNT`, `MAX`, `MIN`, and so on), but they can't calculate things such as month-to-month percentage changes, target performance, and so on. You can get some of these calculations out of a pivot table, but it takes a lot of arm twisting. Often it's not worth the effort.
- ***Pivot tables and pivot charts are a pain to format***: Anytime you refresh the pivot tables and pivot charts, their formatting returns to the default settings. This can be a pain when you want to maintain a consistent and well-designed look for your dashboards.
- ***You end up with lots and lots of pivot tables***: Even a simple dashboard like the example has four pivot table (thus four separate sheets). Although you don't have to pay a tax to Microsoft for every pivot table you create, it is still a hassle. Any changes to the pivot tables or slicers must be applied across the board, and this can quickly snowball in a moderately sized business environment.
- ***Compatibility***: The pivot table, slicer, and data model–driven quick dashboard approach is compatible only with Excel 2013 or newer. So if you have a bunch of colleagues or clients who are still on Excel 2010 (or 2007 or, worse still, 2003), then you are out of luck. You must create your dashboard using traditional approaches discussed in the earlier chapters of this book.

That's enough pivot table bashing. Now that you understand some of the limitations of this approach, let's talk about how to make the best use of them.

Tips for Using Pivot Tables, Slicers, and the Data Model Effectively in Your Dashboards

Pivot table–driven dashboards are quick and easy to build. But they are a pain to format and calculate everything you want. Alternatively, the formulas and VBA-driven dashboards are comprehensive, interactive, and powerful. But they too can be difficult to build and tricky to maintain.

What if you could combine the best of both worlds and get the ease and simplicity of pivot tables, awesome interactivity of slicers, power of good old `SUMPRODUCT` and `INDEX`, and time savings of VBA automation? Now that would be awesome.

Here are few tips and guidelines to reach that level:

- ***Use slicers for interactivity***: As much as possible, use slicers in your dashboards to build interactivity. They are compatible with web/tablet versions of Excel. They look great. They can be formatted to fit your dashboard's color and font schemes. Please refer to `http://chandoo.org/wp/2015/06/24/introduction-to-slicers/` for an explanation on how to do this.

- ***Use tables***:Set up all (or as much as possible) of your raw data as Excel tables. Tables are compatible with Excel 2007 and newer. They allow you to use structural references, which are great for writing formulas. You can link tables to data sources. This way when data changes, all your formulas, charts, conditional formats, and pivot tables will remain good.
- ***Use pivot tables as the calculation engine***: Pivot tables are great for calculating totals, averages, or counts; sorting data; or filtering summaries based on slicers (or report filters). So if your dashboard has any portions that need to calculate totals or sort data automatically, use pivot tables for them. You can set up pivot tables in a separate worksheets and refer to the pivot values in your dashboard tab. This way, you don't have to deal with the formatting issues pivots present. You can format the references in the dashboard tab any way you want.
- ***Calculate things with PowerPivot***: If your calculations are too complicated, you can rely on PowerPivot to do the number-crunching part. PowerPivot is a powerful technology and allows you to build many of the calculations needed for dashboard reporting with ease. I will discuss PowerPivot at a high level in Chapter 24.
- ***Create normal charts from pivot table data***: Pivot charts are tricky to format, but you can create a regular Excel chart from the data inside a pivot table. This way you can enjoy all the goodness of regular charts and the power of pivot table number crunching in one place. This approach also allows you to combine pivot table numbers with values calculated using regular formulas (or VBA or PowerPivot) to create one chart.
- ***Use styles to format slicers***: Slicers are great for interactivity, but their default look may not turn on your boss. So, you can use custom styles to alter the way they look. My good friend Mike Alexander discusses few creative ways of doing this: `http://datapigtechnologies.com/blog/index.php/getting-fancy-with-your-excel-slicers/`

The Last Word

As you can see, you can create truly powerful, interactive, and interlinked reports using pivot tables. Many people shun pivot tables and try to do everything with formulas or VBA. I recommend you try pivot tables and harness their true power as much as possible. They will free up valuable time for you so that you can focus on other important things.

CHAPTER 23

Introduction to Power Query

I have a quick question for you: Which of the following activities takes up the majority of analysts' time when building dashboards?

a. Gathering user requirements

b. Writing formulas and building pivot tables

c. Creating and formatting charts

d. Presenting the reports to the boss/CEO and winning accolades

For me, the answer is *none of the above.* That's because most of my time is spent on collecting and cleaning data. Everything else—writing formulas, coding VBA, creating charts, presenting the dashboard—would be a breeze if I had all the data cleaned and in one place.

Microsoft Power Query for Excel, a new add-in from Microsoft, is part of the Microsoft Power BI family of tools. It is designed to mitigate this exact pain. Using Power Query, you can quickly collect data from multiple databases (or files), combine them, clean them, transform them, and bring the final set to Excel workbooks (or leave them in a workbook data model so that you can use the data in Power Pivot and elsewhere.)

Note For information about the Microsoft Power BI tool set, visit `http://bit.ly/1KQJp9v`. The Power BI service site is at `https://powerbi.microsoft.com/`.

It is a new technology, and there is so much more you can do with it. In this book, my goal is to show you at a high level how Power Query can help you. For a more detailed explanation of individual Power Query features, as well as use cases and solutions, I recommend reading *Power Query for Power BI and Excel* by Chris Webb (Apress, 2014).

POWER QUERY AVAILABILITY AND COMPATIBILITY

Availability: Power Query can be downloaded from Microsoft:

`www.microsoft.com/en-us/download/details.aspx?id=39379`.

Compatibility: It is compatible with Excel 2013 and newer.

Can colleagues and my boss open workbooks I create with Power Query? In general, yes. Think of Power Query as a SQL engine (with a friendly interface and a lot more power) built into Excel. It is an add-in. It allows you to bring, transform, combine, clean, and load data to your Excel workbook. So *technically*, others can open the files you created using Power Query, even if they do not have Power Query on their Excel.

What Is Power Query, and How Can It Help You?

As mentioned in the introduction section, Power Query is an add-in designed to help you in various stages of data collection and cleanup. Power Query offers the following key functionality.

Bringing Data to Excel

Power Query supports various data sources and lets you connect to them to bring necessary data to your workbooks. There is one key difference, though. In regular Excel, when you establish a data connection (from Data tab ➤ Get External Data tools), your data will be immediately placed in an Excel worksheet. With Power Query, the connections bring data to a staging area (called the Power Query window) so that you can perform the additional steps necessary to clean or transform the data as per your needs.

Transforming Data

That brings me to the next important feature of Power Query. When you bring external data into Excel, you usually want to perform a few operations on it before consuming the data. For example, you may want to remove all the duplicate records, sort the data, remove a few extraneous columns, merge data from two different sources, and so on. All of these steps are time-consuming if done manually or through formulas or even VBA. Power Query introduces various common transformations as simple rules that you can apply to the data connection. This way, once the connection is established, Power Query does these steps for you and gives you clean, analysis-ready data.

Loading Data to Where You Want It

Once Power Query has the data in the shape you want, you can load it either to an Excel spreadsheet or to a data model directly (refer to Chapter 21 for more information about the Excel data model). So if your analysis is done using regular formulas or VBA, you can load Power Query data to a spreadsheet table. On the other hand, if your analysis is based on pivot tables or PowerPivot (more on this in Chapter 24), you can load the data to the data model and let the corresponding Excel features pick it up.

In this chapter, you will understand all these three important aspects of Power Query in the context of five real-world problems.

Five Data Problems and How Power Query Can Solve Them

To keep this chapter simple and relevant, let's tackle five common data problems you'll encounter and how Power Query can quickly solve them.

1. Unclean data
2. Partial data sets
3. Data consolidation
4. Duplicates in data
5. Inconsistent data formats

Although Power Query can do so much more, I will limit the discussion to these five problems.

Problem 1: Unclean Data

Let's say you are the manager at Dinky's Delicious Donuts. Three months ago you launched a customer loyalty program. It involved giving a loyalty card with eight slots on it. Anytime a customer bought a donut, you punched the card. After seven punches, the customer got a free punch (not in the face, just on the card) plus a free donut and coffee. It was a great success. Customers loved getting free donuts and felt loved.

Now, you want to repeat the loyalty program next month. So, you want to e-mail the customers who participated in the earlier round and invite them to the store. Unfortunately, you went low-tech with the implementation of the loyalty program in the first round. So, you have no computerized record of customer names and e-mail addresses. You just have physical copies of the loyalty cards on which customers scribbled their names and e-mail addresses.

So, you take the stack of these cards to Jason, the cashier, and ask him to type the information into a spreadsheet. Jason loves Candy Crush Saga, coffee, and gossip. He hates typing. He is the kind of person who types with just two fingers, not ten. So, it takes him a while, but the spreadsheet is eventually ready. It has names in Column A and e-mail addresses in Column B (see Figure 23-1).

Name	Email
Ray Nikki	ray.nikki@mail.comm
Michael Julie	michael.julie@mail.com
Praveen Mohammed	praveen.mohammed@mail.com
Jeffrey Guy-Francois.	jeffrey.guy-francois@mail.com
Steven Stephanie	steven.stephanie@mail.com
Christopher Misty	christopher.misty@mail.com
Travis Kathleen M	travis.kathleen m@mail.com
Ian Kedar	ian.kedar@mail.comm
Kim Norman.	kim.norman@mail.comm
William Alison.	william.alison@mail.comm
Clay Manav	clay.manav@mail.com
Michael Leslie.	michael.leslie@mail.comm
Julie Adam	julie.adam@mail.comm

Figure 23-1. Customer data for Dinky's Delicious Donuts

After quickly eyeballing the data, you identify many issues.

- Names have inconsistent spaces in the front and middle.
- There is an occasional period at the end of names.
- Some e-mail addresses end with .com**m**, clearly a typo.

Clearly Jason was using less than two fingers to type this data. For the purposes of this example, let's assume there are no other mistakes in the data.

Although you can clean this data with good old Excel formulas, let's use Power Query because that is what this chapter is all about.

Loading the Data in to Power Query

I am assuming you have already installed Power Query. If not, just download the add-in, install it, and enable it if needed. For detailed instructions, check out the Power Query web site here:

`www.microsoft.com/en-us/download/details.aspx?id=39379`

Loading the data into Power Query is as simple as sipping a foaming, steaming, delicious latte.

1. Convert the data in to a table if not already done.
2. Select any cell inside the table.
3. Go to the Power Query tab and choose the From Table option (see Figure 23-2).

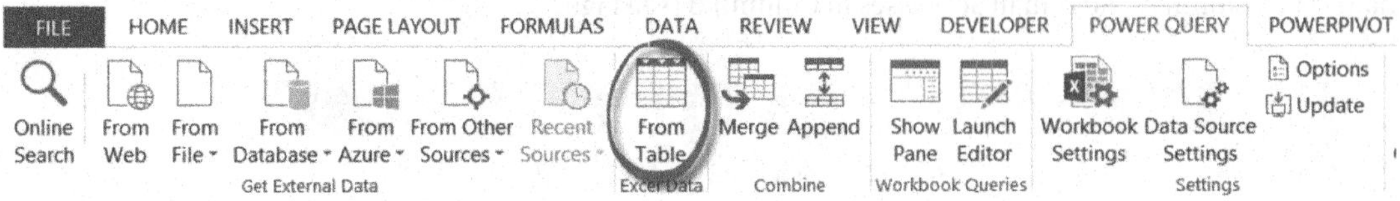

***Figure 23-2.** Adding Excel table data to Power Query*

The Power Query window will open, as shown in Figure 23-3, and your data will be loaded there.

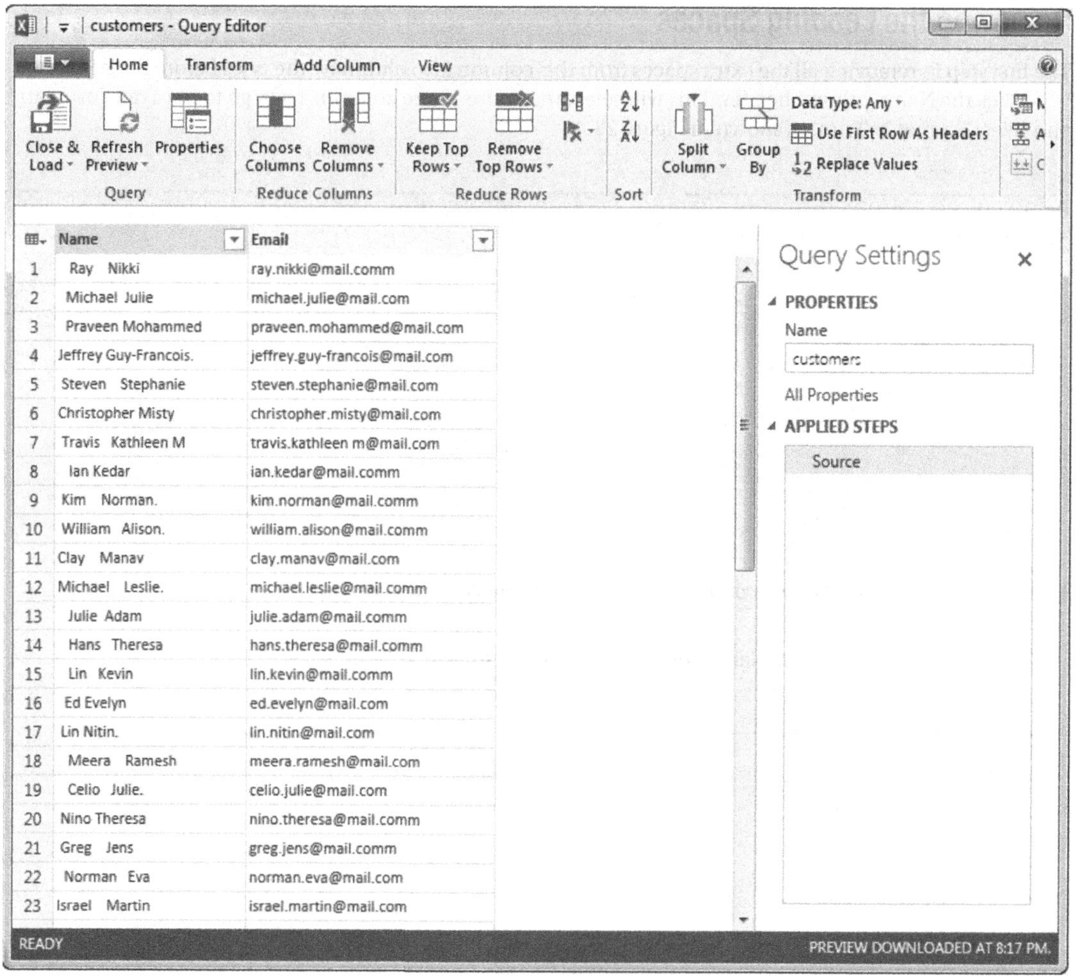

Figure 23-3. *The data loaded into the Power Query window*

That is all—your data is now ready to be scrubbed, sliced, diced, prepared, and marinated by Power Query so that you can later cook and present it any way you want.

Think of the Power Query window as a VBA window. You can access all the cleaning and transformation capabilities of Power Query from this window. A detailed explanation of this window is outside the scope of this book. So, I suggest you to explore the Power Query window on your own. Let's focus on the task at hand. Let's get cleaning.

Removing Extra Spaces from the Name Column

Let's start with the extra spaces in the Name column. First you'll eliminate the leading spaces and then the spaces between the first and last names.

Removing the Leading Spaces

The first step in removing all the extra spaces from this column is to eliminate the ones before the names.

Click the Name column header. This will select the entire Name column. Then go to the Transform tab and select Format ➤ Trim, as shown in Figure 23-4.

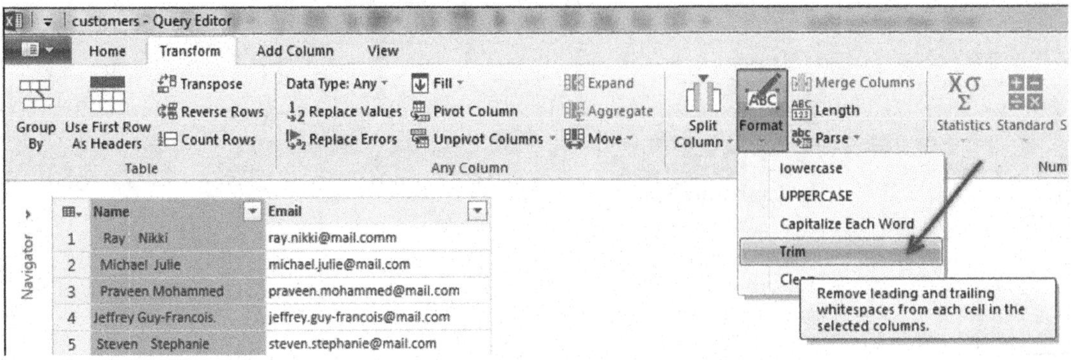

Figure 23-4. *Trimming column contents to remove extra spaces in Power Query*

At the end of this step, the Name column looks like Figure 23-5.

⊞▾	Name	▾	Email
1	Ray␣Nikki		ray.nikki
2	Michael Julie		michael.
3	Praveen Mohammed		praveen
4	Jeffrey Guy-Francois.		jeffrey.g
5	Steven␣Stephanie		steven.s
6	Christopher Misty		christop
7	Travis␣Kathleen M		travis.ka
8	Ian Kedar		ian.keda
9	Kim␣Norman.		kim.nor
10	William␣Alison.		william.i
11	Clay␣Manav		clay.mar

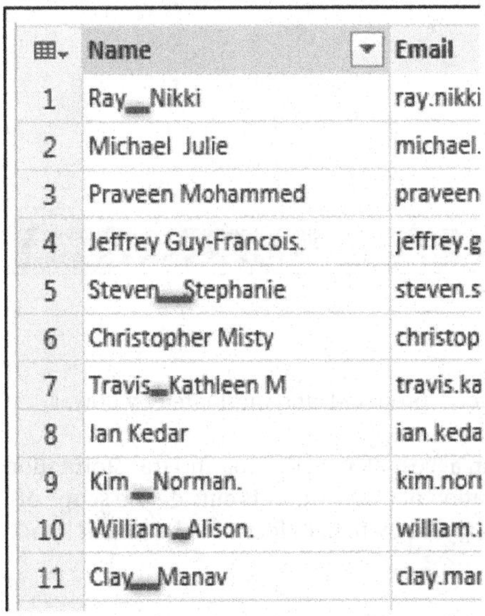

Figure 23-5. *Name column after applying trim transformation. As you can notice, there are extra spaces between parts of the names*

As you can see, while the spaces at the beginning are gone, the spaces between the first and last names are not trimmed.

So, let's perform two more transformations on this column. Note that you should perform these transformations in this order only.

1. Replace three spaces with a single space.
2. Replace two spaces with a single space.

Replacing the Spaces Between the Names

As just mentioned, you will first replace all instances of three spaces with one space and then each case of two spaces with one space.

Follow these steps to replace three spaces with one:

1. While keeping the Name column selected, go to the Transform tab and click Replace Values in the Any Column group. This opens the Replace Values dialog box shown in Figure 23-6.

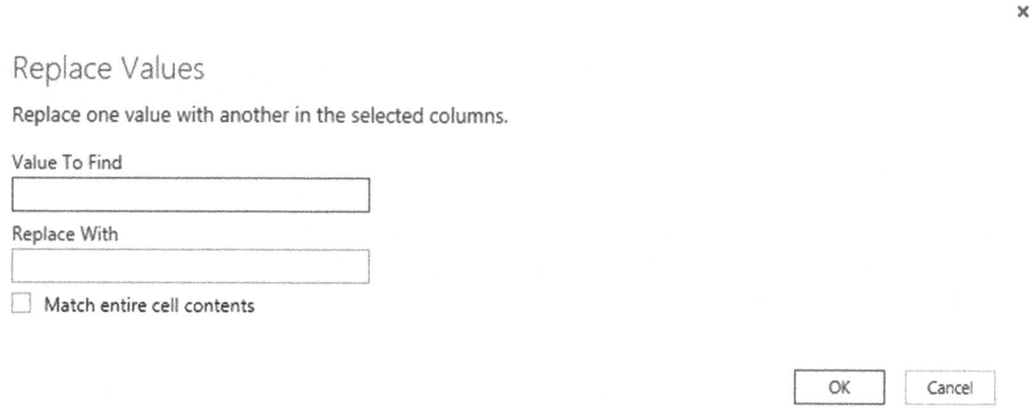

Figure 23-6. *Replacing three spaces with a single space using the Replace dialog of Power Query*

2. Now type three spaces in the Value To Find field.
3. Next, type a single space in the Value To Replace field.
4. Click OK.

Follow the same steps to replace two spaces with one, but type two spaces in the Value To Find field instead of three.

These steps should clean up the Name column.

Removing the Extra Periods

Some of the names have a period (.) at the end. To remove them, use the same steps that you used to replace multiple spaces with a single one. In step 2, type a period in the Value To Find field and then leave the Replace With field blank.

Fixing the E-mail Addresses

Fixing the e-mail addresses is simpler than the Name column. Follow these steps:

1. Select the Email column.
2. Click Replace Values on the Transform tab.
3. Replace .comm with .com, as shown in Figure 23-7.

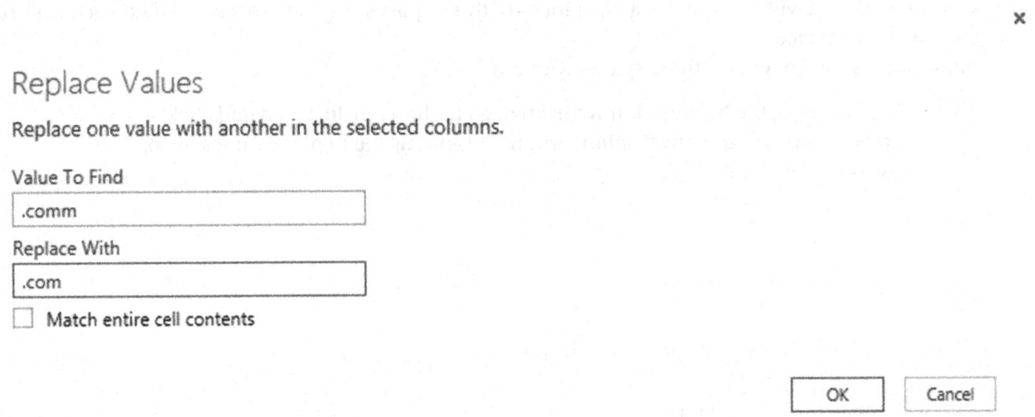

Figure 23-7. *Cleaning up the e-mail address column using the Replace dialog*

4. Click OK.

That is all. Your data is clean.

Bringing the Data Back to Excel

Once all the cleanup tasks are done, go to the Home tab and click Close & Load in the Query group (see Figure 23-8). This will load all the cleaned data as a new table to your Excel workbook, as in Figure 23-9.

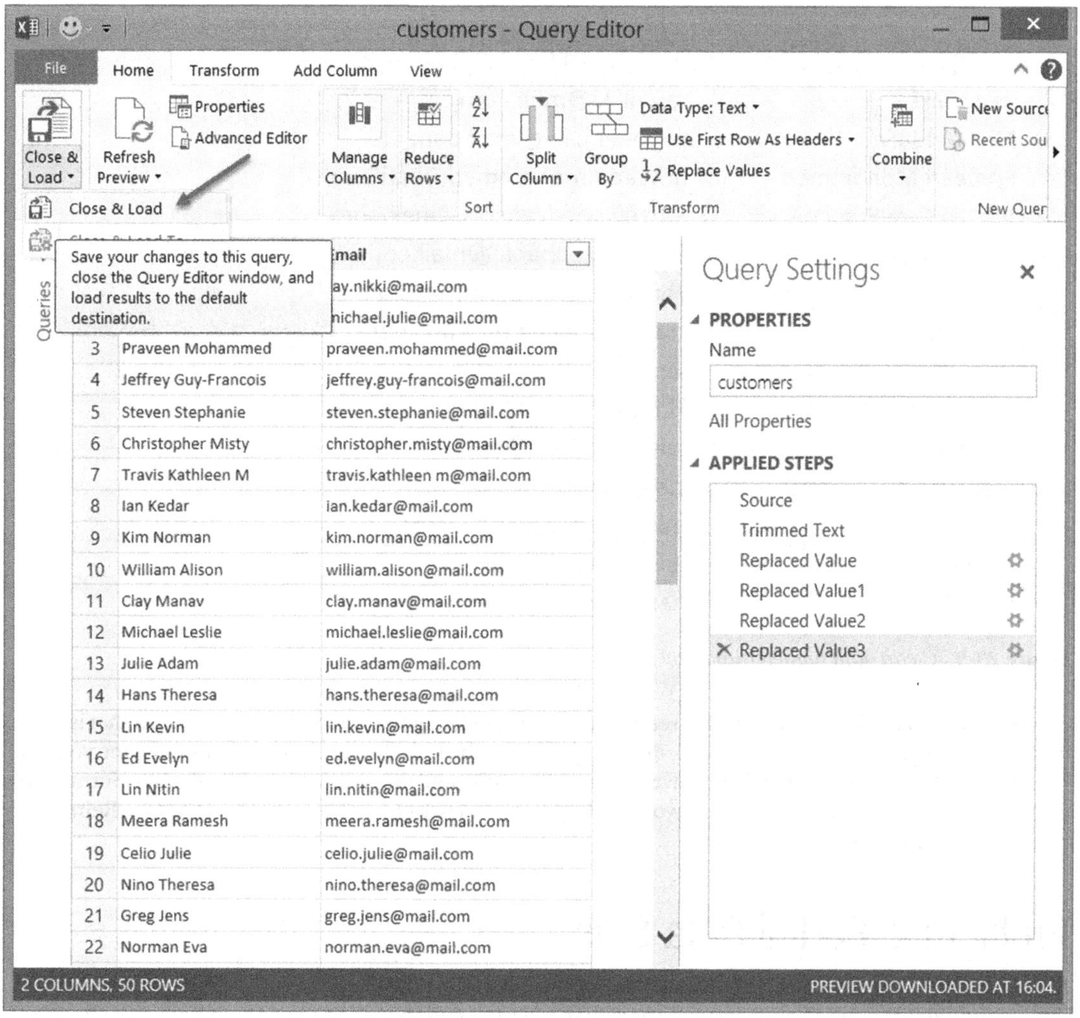

Figure 23-8. Loading clean data into Excel

	A	B
1	Name	Email
2	Ray Nikki	ray.nikki@mail.com
3	Michael Julie	michael.julie@mail.com
4	Praveen Mohammed	praveen.mohammed@mail.com
5	Jeffrey Guy-Francois	jeffrey.guy-francois@mail.com
6	Steven Stephanie	steven.stephanie@mail.com
7	Christopher Misty	christopher.misty@mail.com
8	Travis Kathleen M	travis.kathleen m@mail.com
9	Ian Kedar	ian.kedar@mail.com
10	Kim Norman	kim.norman@mail.com
11	William Alison	william.alison@mail.com
12	Clay Manav	clay.manav@mail.com
13	Michael Leslie	michael.leslie@mail.com
14	Julie Adam	julie.adam@mail.com
15	Hans Theresa	hans.theresa@mail.com

Figure 23-9. *Clean data loaded into Excel as a table*

At first glance, this approach might seem like a long-winded path to get what you want. But that is misleading. If you observe closely, you defined a set of rules to clean this data. This means any time you add new data or change the original data, Power Query will gladly (and automatically) apply the transformations on this new set of data and update your workbook, with just a click of a button. That button is the Refresh option on Excel's Data tab.

Problem 2: Partial Data Sets

Let's stay with the Dinky's Delicious Donuts example for a while. While looking at the cleaned customer data, you suddenly remembered that some customers have mentioned their phone number on the reverse side of the loyalty card. And you forgot to capture this data.

So, you go back to Jason and ask him to record all phone numbers in the same spreadsheet. By this time, Jason has realized that his true calling is not in Excel, so he is reluctant to type anything into Excel. You reach a compromise: Jason will type this phone number data into a text file using Notepad.

Quickly Jason produces all the data in a text file like the one shown in Figure 23-10.

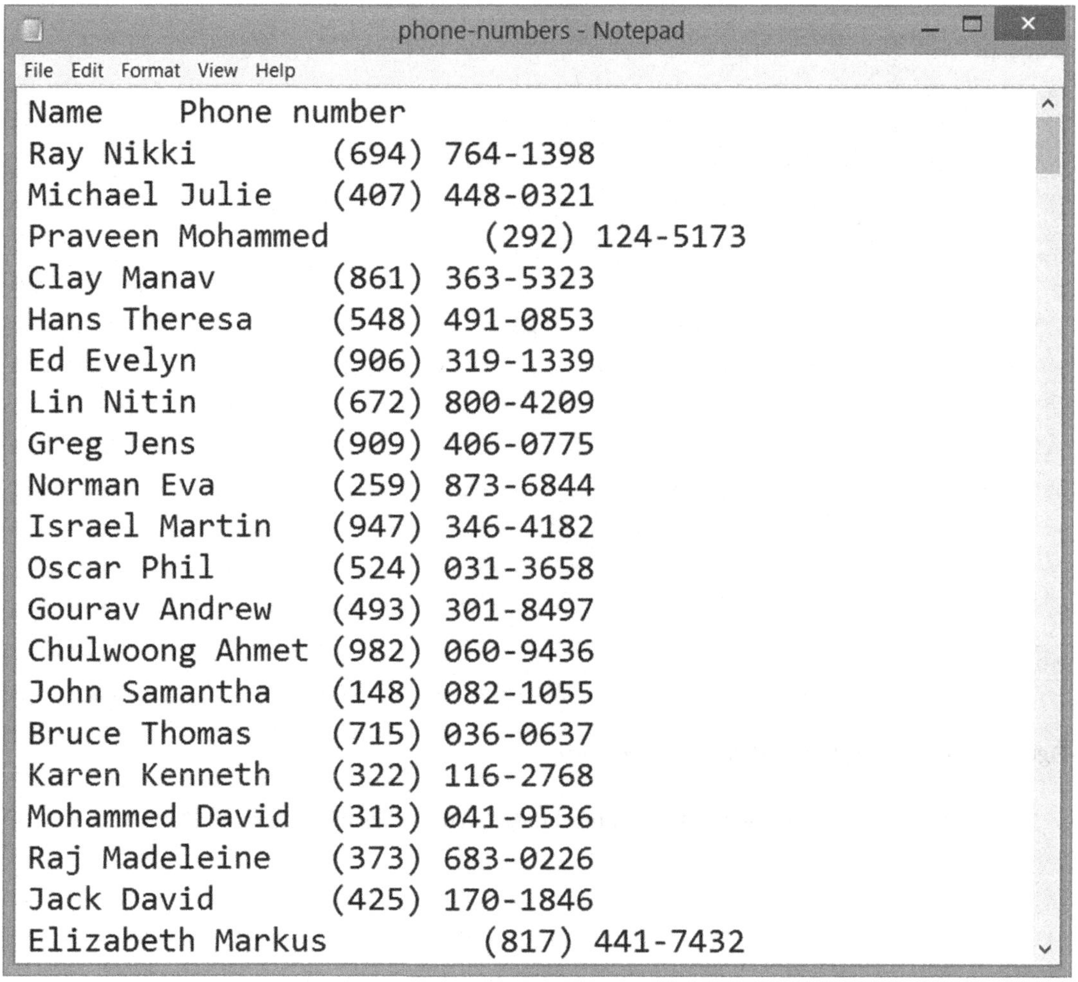


```
Name    Phone number
Ray Nikki       (694) 764-1398
Michael Julie   (407) 448-0321
Praveen Mohammed        (292) 124-5173
Clay Manav      (861) 363-5323
Hans Theresa    (548) 491-0853
Ed Evelyn       (906) 319-1339
Lin Nitin       (672) 800-4209
Greg Jens       (909) 406-0775
Norman Eva      (259) 873-6844
Israel Martin   (947) 346-4182
Oscar Phil      (524) 031-3658
Gourav Andrew   (493) 301-8497
Chulwoong Ahmet (982) 060-9436
John Samantha   (148) 082-1055
Bruce Thomas    (715) 036-0637
Karen Kenneth   (322) 116-2768
Mohammed David  (313) 041-9536
Raj Madeleine   (373) 683-0226
Jack David      (425) 170-1846
Elizabeth Markus        (817) 441-7432
```

Figure 23-10. *Customer phone number data captured in a text file*

Fortunately, there are no mistakes in the data this time, but you have a new problem. You need to merge both datasets. One is in Excel; the other is in Notepad. Again, Power Query to the rescue.

Loading the Text File Data into Power Query

First, you need to load the data from the text file. In your workbook, go to the Power Query File tab, and select From File ➤ From Text to import the text file data (see Figure 23-11).

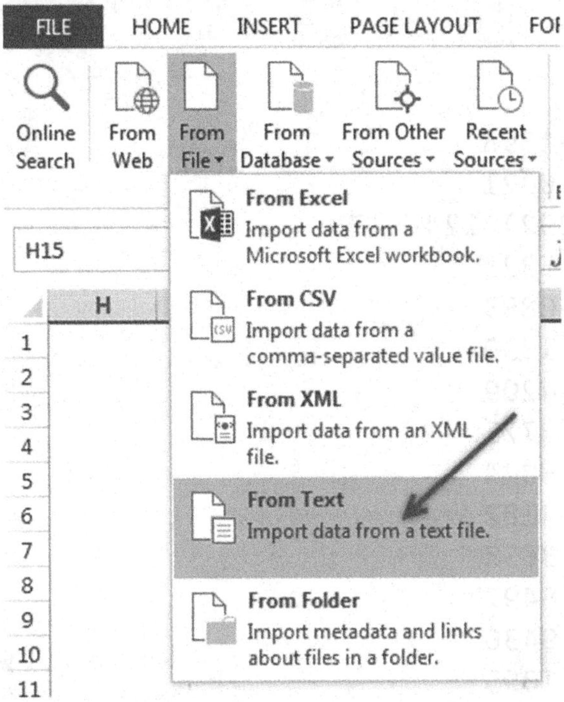

***Figure 23-11.** Loading text file data into Power Query*

Select the text file containing the phone number data and then click OK (see Figure 23-12).

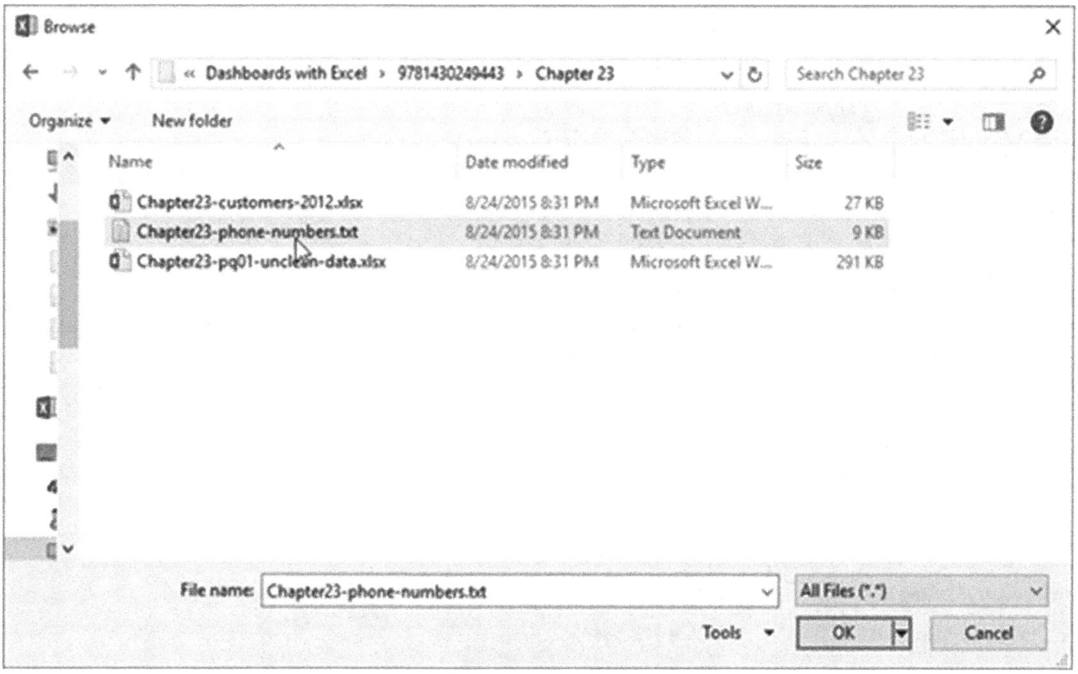

Figure 23-12. *Select the file containing text data, loading text data into Power Query*

At this stage, all the phone number data in that file is loaded into the Power Query window. It should look like Figure 23-13.

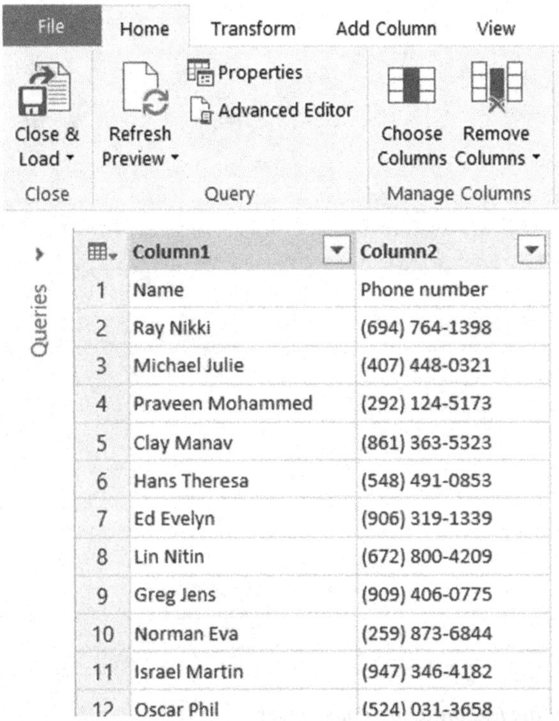

Figure 23-13. *Phone number data loaded into Power Query*

While all the data is there, you also have a new problem. *The column headers are wrong.*

No problem. You can click the Use First Row As Headers option in the Home tab's Transform group. This will clear up the problem for you (see Figure 23-14).

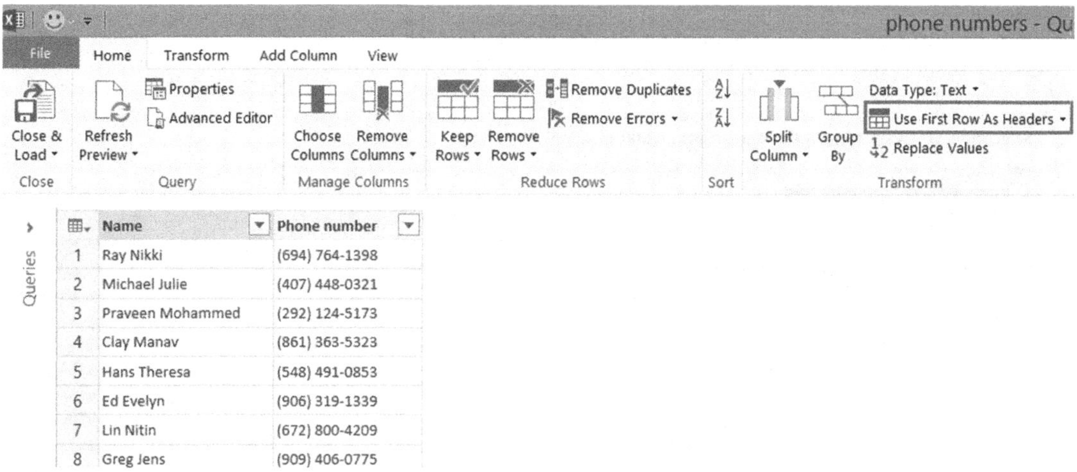

***Figure 23-14.** Setting up the first row as headers using the Use First Row as Headers option from the Transform area of the Home tab in Power Query*

Now that the first row of text file is considered a header, you need to merge the phone number data with name and e-mail address data. But before you do that, you should save your query and load the phone number data into the data model.

Saving and Loading the Query

Using the query properties pane in the Power Query window, give your new query a name. Let's call it **phone numbers**. Press Enter to save it.

Now, on the Home tab, select Close & Load ➤ Close & Load To, as in Figure 23-15. This opens the Load To window (see Figure 23-16).

***Figure 23-15.** Close & Load To button on the Home tab of Power Query*

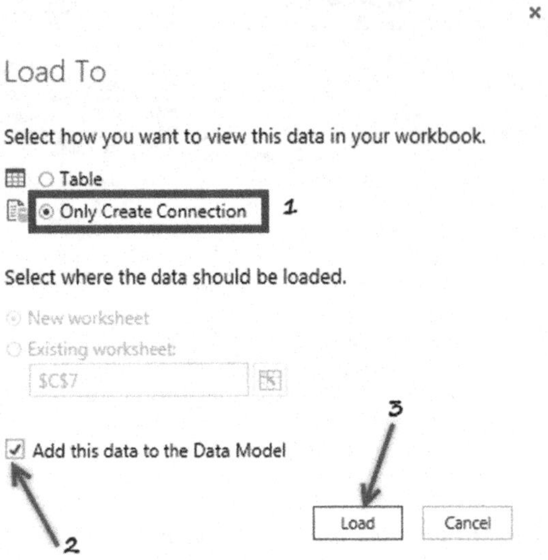

Figure 23-16. *Loading data to the data model of Excel using the Close & Load To option*

Since you want the phone numbers to be merged to existing data, select the Only Create Connection option and enable "Add this data to the Data Model," as shown in Figure 23-16. Then click Load. This will load the new phone number data into Excel's data model but not to the workbook.

Merging Customer and Phone Number Data

Now that you have both customer data (loaded from Excel table) and phone number data (loaded from text file), you now need to merge them to create a consolidated table. Follow these steps to accomplish this task:

1. Go to the Power Query ribbon in Excel and click Merge in the Combine group (see Figure 23-17). This will open the Merge window, as shown in Figure 23-18.

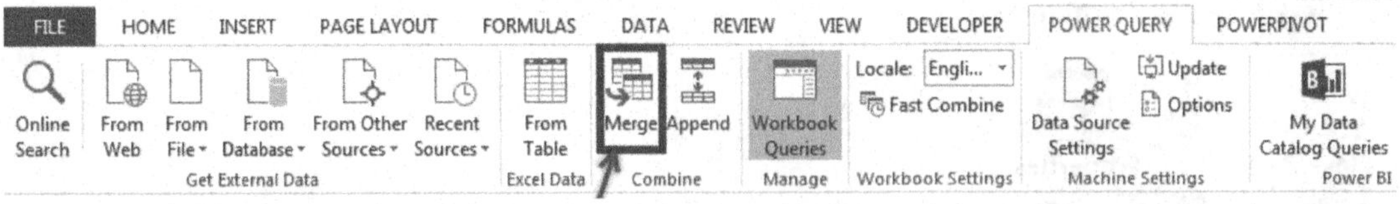

Figure 23-17. *Merging two queries using the Merge button on the Power Query tab in Excel*

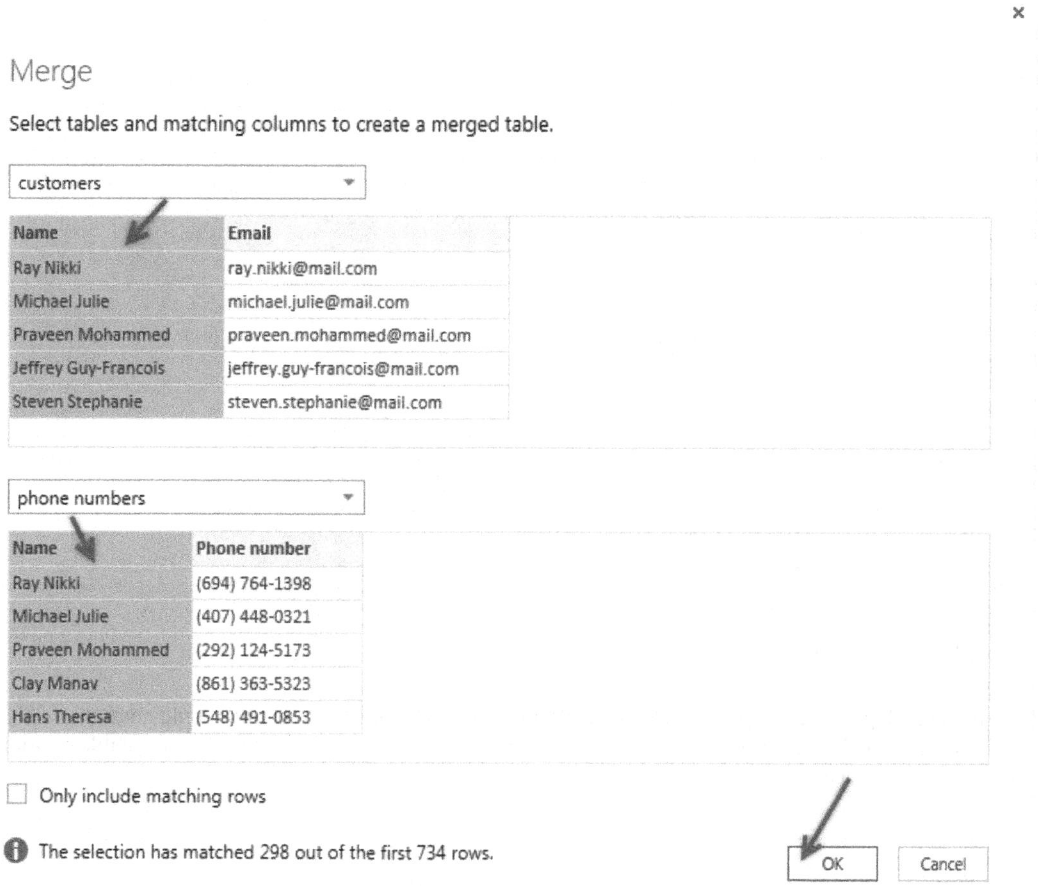

Figure 23-18. *Merging two queries based on common column*

2. Select the customers query from the first drop-down.
3. Select the phone numbers query from the second drop-down.
4. Highlight the customer Name column in both lists.
5. Click OK.

This will load the merged data into the Power Query window. You can't see the merged data yet, although it is there. To expose the phone number data, just click the two-sided arrow button next to the NewColumn header (see Figure 23-19).

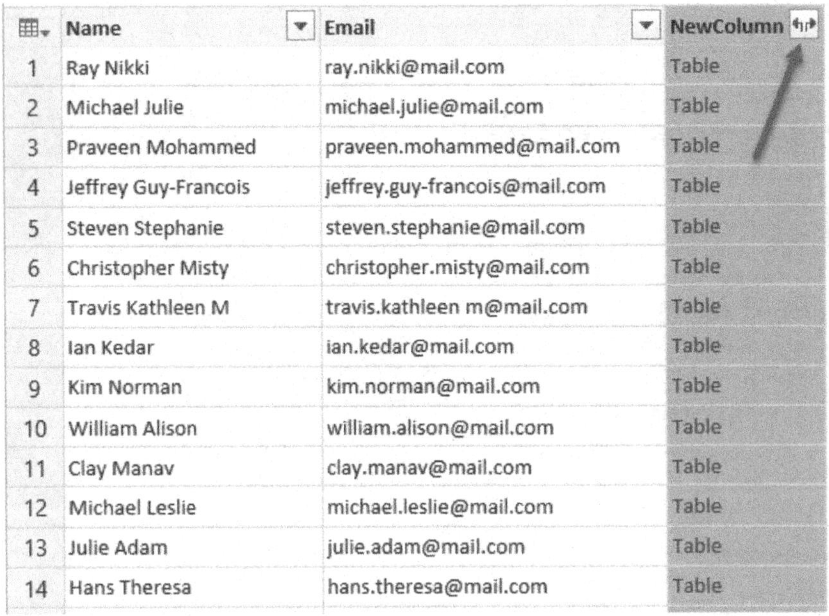
Name
Email
NewColumn
1 Ray Nikki ray.nikki@mail.com Table
2 Michael Julie michael.julie@mail.com Table
3 Praveen Mohammed praveen.mohammed@mail.com Table
4 Jeffrey Guy-Francois jeffrey.guy-francois@mail.com Table
5 Steven Stephanie steven.stephanie@mail.com Table
6 Christopher Misty christopher.misty@mail.com Table
7 Travis Kathleen M travis.kathleen m@mail.com Table
8 Ian Kedar ian.kedar@mail.com Table
9 Kim Norman kim.norman@mail.com Table
10 William Alison william.alison@mail.com Table
11 Clay Manav clay.manav@mail.com Table
12 Michael Leslie michael.leslie@mail.com Table
13 Julie Adam julie.adam@mail.com Table
14 Hans Theresa hans.theresa@mail.com Table

Figure 23-19. *Expanding the new column, merging two queries*

In the dialog box that appears, just select "Phone number" alone because you already have the customer Name column (see Figure 23-20). This will load the phone numbers for all the available customers, as you can see in Figure 23-21.

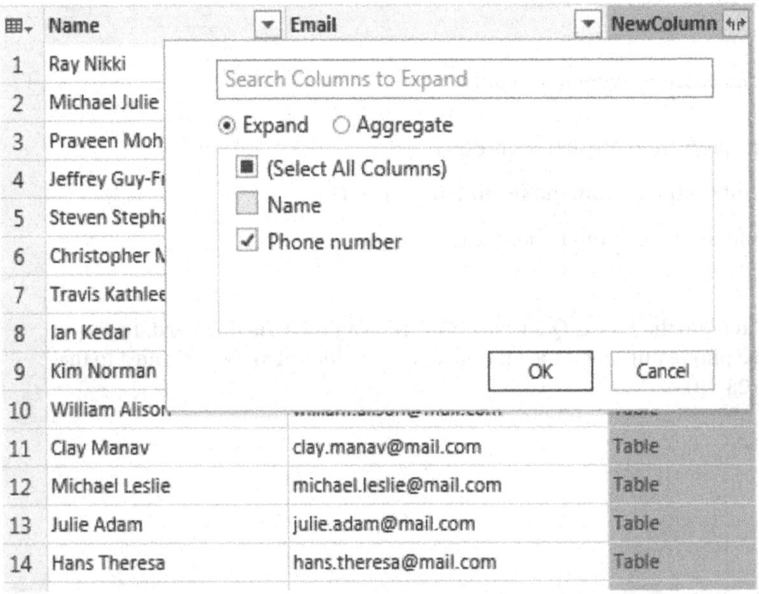

Figure 23-20. *Expanding phone number column*

	Name	Email	NewColumn.Phone num...
1	Ray Nikki	ray.nikki@mail.com	(694) 764-1398
2	Michael Julie	michael.julie@mail.com	(407) 448-0321
3	Praveen Mohammed	praveen.mohammed@mail.com	(292) 124-5173
4	Jeffrey Guy-Francois	jeffrey.guy-francois@mail.com	*null*
5	Clay Manav	clay.manav@mail.com	(861) 363-5323
6	Steven Stephanie	steven.stephanie@mail.com	*null*
7	Hans Theresa	hans.theresa@mail.com	(548) 491-0853
8	Christopher Misty	christopher.misty@mail.com	*null*
9	Ed Evelyn	ed.evelyn@mail.com	(906) 319-1339
10	Travis Kathleen M	travis.kathleen m@mail.com	*null*
11	Lin Nitin	lin.nitin@mail.com	(672) 800-4209
12	Ian Kedar	ian.kedar@mail.com	*null*
13	Greg Jens	greg.jens@mail.com	(909) 406-0775
14	Kim Norman	kim.norman@mail.com	*null*

Figure 23-21. *Phone number column expanded and showing phone numbers for customers who have the data*

You might ask what "null" is doing in the phone number column. Because you don't have phone number data for all customers, when Power Query tries to merge a customer with their nonexistent phone number, it gets *empty* as answer. This *empty* is shown as *null* in Power Query. These nulls will become blank cells when you load the data into the Excel workbook.

Giving a Proper Name to the Phone Number Column

By default the phone number column would have a name like "NewColumn.Phone number." This is uncool. Every other column would make fun of this new column. Let's give it a normal name.

Double-click the column header and type whatever name you fancy. I like the name Phone Number. There is a nice ring to it.

Loading the Merged Data in to Excel

Now that the data is in the shape you want, let's load it into Excel. To load it in to Excel, follow these steps:

1. Click Close & Load on the Power Query Home tab (see Figure 23-22).

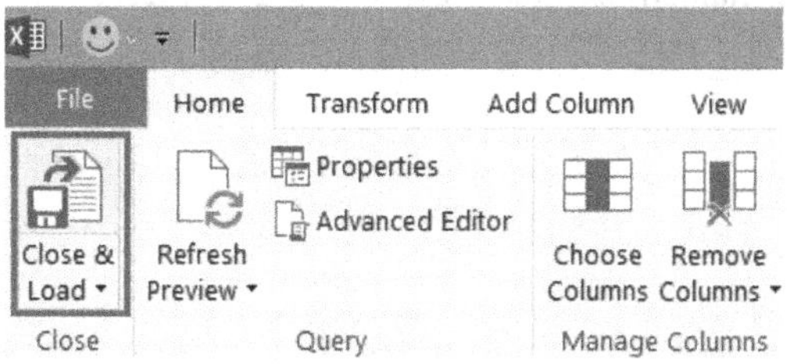

Figure 23-22. *Click Close & Load to load the data into an Excel workbook*

2. This will create a new worksheet in your workbook and load the merged data there as an Excel table (as shown in Figure 23-23).

	A	B	C
1	Name	Email	Phone Number
2	Ray Nikki	ray.nikki@mail.com	(694) 764-1398
3	Michael Julie	michael.julie@mail.com	(407) 448-0321
4	Praveen Mohammed	praveen.mohammed@mail.com	(292) 124-5173
5	Jeffrey Guy-Francois	jeffrey.guy-francois@mail.com	
6	Clay Manav	clay.manav@mail.com	(861) 363-5323
7	Steven Stephanie	steven.stephanie@mail.com	
8	Hans Theresa	hans.theresa@mail.com	(548) 491-0853
9	Christopher Misty	christopher.misty@mail.com	
10	Ed Evelyn	ed.evelyn@mail.com	(906) 319-1339
11	Travis Kathleen M	travis.kathleen m@mail.com	
12	Lin Nitin	lin.nitin@mail.com	(672) 800-4209
13	Ian Kedar	ian.kedar@mail.com	
14	Greg Jens	greg.jens@mail.com	(909) 406-0775
15	Kim Norman	kim.norman@mail.com	

Figure 23-23. *Merged data with customer names, e-mail addresses, and phone numbers where available*

As you can see in Figure 23-23, when the data is loaded in to Excel, *nulls* are replaced by blank cells.

Problem 3: Data Consolidation

Let's again stick with Dinky's Delicious Donut enterprise problems. Imagine a new scenario. You suddenly remembered that exactly two years ago there was a similar customer loyalty program. At that time, you gathered contact details from a few hundred customers (names, e-mail addresses, and phone numbers). For upcoming marketing efforts, you would like to combine both these lists and create one unified table of customers.

Fortunately, the earlier customer data is in a workbook. You just need to combine this with new data. Again, Power Query to the rescue.

Taking a Look at the Old Data

Let's imagine that all the old customer data is in a workbook named `Chapter23-customers-2012.xlsx`. Figure 23-24 shows a snapshot of this data.

Name	Email	Phone Number
Nguyen Joseph	nguyen.joseph@mail.com	
Randy Dante	randy.dante@mail.com	
Joseph Jeff	joseph.jeff@mail.comm	7265236034
Caroline Saurov	caroline.saurov@mail.com	
Eylem Ray	eylem.ray@mail.com	
Harold Randy	harold.randy@mail.comm	
Daryl Kathleen M	daryl.kathleen m@mail.com	
Manishankar Alvaro	manishankar.alvaro@mail.comm	
Michael Lori	michael.lori@mail.com	
Ian Geary	ian.geary@mail.com	
Navin Michael	navin.michael@mail.com	3836841537
David Nikolaos	david.nikolaos@mail.com	7100305750
Christopher Silvio	christopher.silvio@mail.comm	8530138828
Richard William	richard.william@mail.comm	
Catherine Sridevi	catherine.sridevi@mail.com	9257369189
Yan Alexander	yan.alexander@mail.com	
Joseph Michael	joseph.michael@mail.comm	
Sandylee Bee	sandylee.bee@mail.com	

Figure 23-24. *Customer data from 2012. You want to append this data to the latest customer data*

Fortunately, the workbook uses the same columns as the current workbook.

Setting Up a New Connection

First, you need to set up a new connection.

1. Go to the workbook that contains all the latest customer data. Navigate to the Power Query tab, and in the Get External Data group, click From File ➤ From Excel to get the data.

2. Select the workbook using From File ➤ From Text as earlier in the chapter. This looks the same as Figure 23-12 in the section "Loading the Text File Data into Power Query."

3. At this stage, Power Query opens the Navigator pane where you have to select the data that needs to be loaded. The Navigator pane (refer to Figure 23-25) shows all tables and worksheets of the `Chapter23-customers-2012.xlsx` file. Please select the table containing customer data (named `customers_2012`) and click Load to load this data to data model alone.

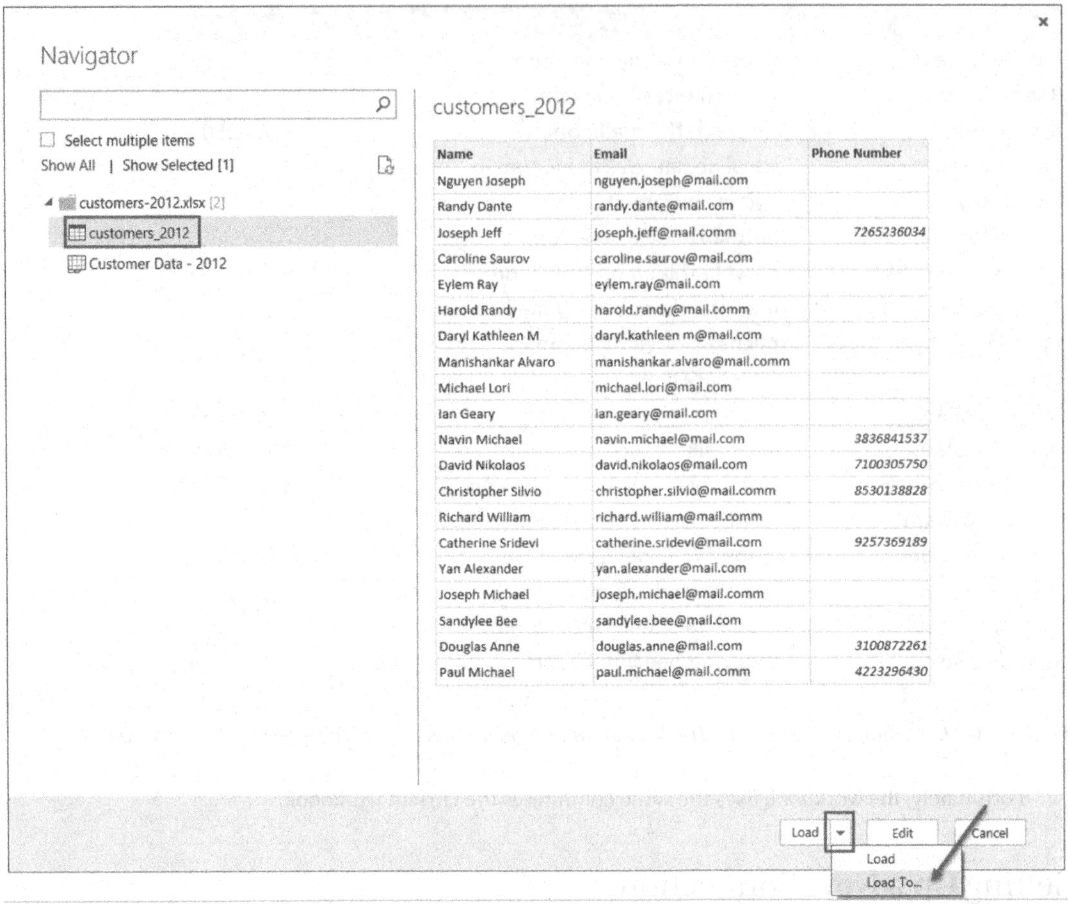

Figure 23-25. *Using the Navigator pane, select the customers_2012 table and load it into the data model*

Appending Data

Once the old customer data is in the data model, you can append it to the new customer data using the Append query feature of Power Query.

1. To do this, go to the Power Query tab and click Append in the Combine group (see Figure 23-26).

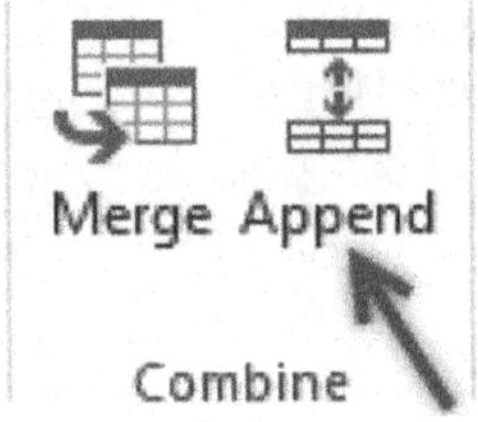

Figure 23-26. *Appending two queries using the Append feature of Power Query*

2. Select both tables that you want to append, as shown in Figure 23-27.

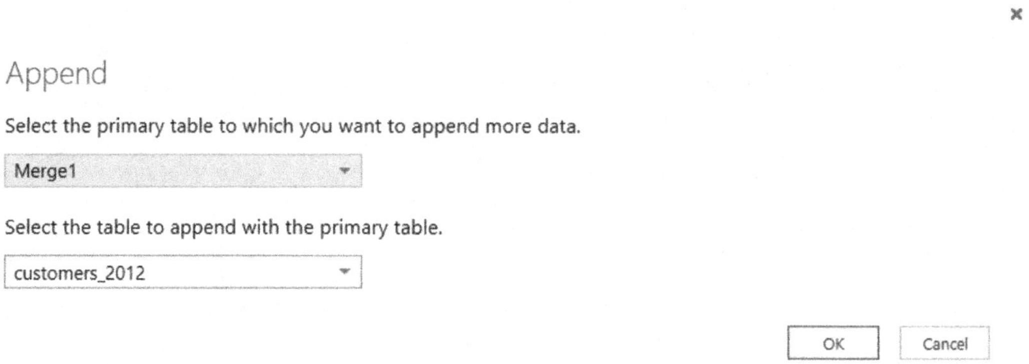

Figure 23-27. *Appending 2012 customer data with the latest data using the Append feature of Power Query*

3. Click OK.
4. This will open the Power Query window (see Figure 23-28). Here you can make any additional changes to the merged data, such as cleaning up a column, removing duplicates, and so on. You need to give this new query a name. Let's call it All Customer Data.

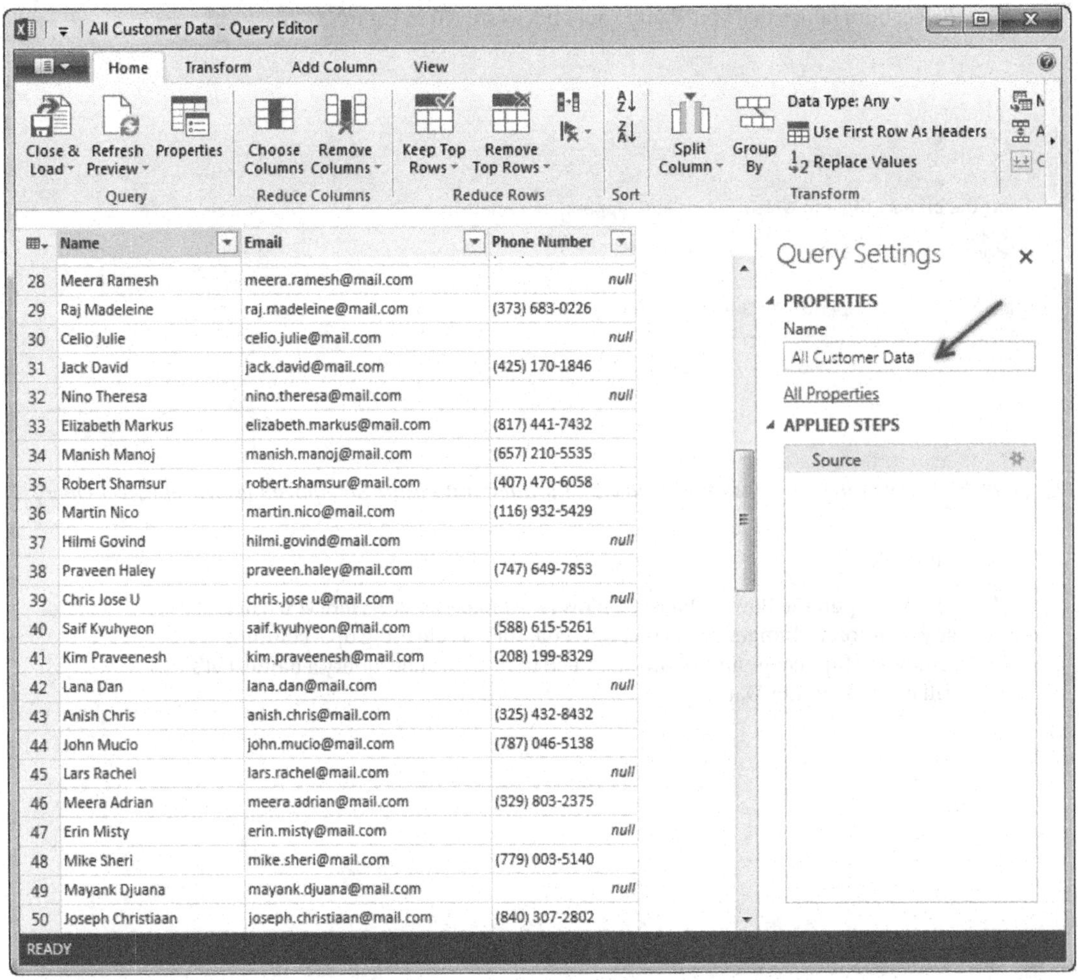

Figure 23-28. *Naming the appended query will make it easy for editing or referring to it later*

5. Close the Power Query window and load this data to your workbook. Please refer to the section "Loading the Merged Data in to Excel" for instructions on how to load data to Excel. Once you load the data, the Workbook Queries pane will look like Figure 23-29.

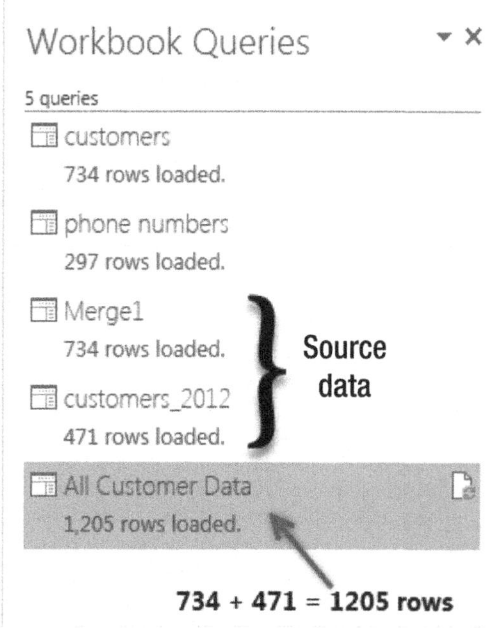

***Figure 23-29.** The data is loaded*

WHY CAN'T WE COPY/PASTE THE DATA? WHY BOTHER APPENDING?

Copying and pasting is so 1997. Well, the real reason is, Power Query saves the append configuration for you. This means if, at a later date, the `Chapter23-customers-2012.xlsx` file changes, then you just need to refresh your query to bring in the new data. While such a scenario may not be realistic for your customer data, it is an everyday occurrence in many companies. Data is dislocated all the time, and you are expected to combine two or more sets of data to generate reports. This is where the Append feature really comes in handy.

So, say good-bye to manic copying and pasting.

Problem 4: Duplicates in Your Data

Now that you have all the data in one place, you are about to embark on your genius marketing plan. But as you look at the list, you realize that there a few duplicates. Some customer e-mail addresses are repeated in the All Customer Data query. Well, again Power Query to the rescue.

You can set up a rule in Power Query to remove all the duplicates from the combined data.

To do this, edit the All Customer Data query (right-click the query and choose Edit, as depicted in Figure 23-30) and use the following steps.

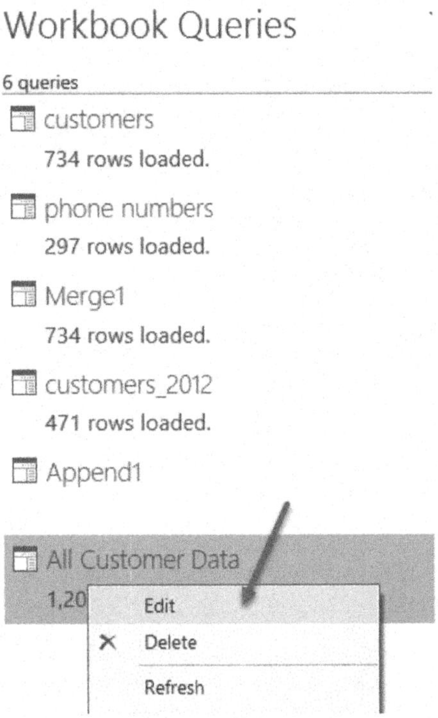

***Figure 23-30.** To edit a query, right-click the query name and choose Edit. This opens the Power Query window and loads the query there*

1. Select the Email address column.
2. On the Power Query Home tab, click Remove Duplicates in the Reduce Rows group (see Figure 23-31).

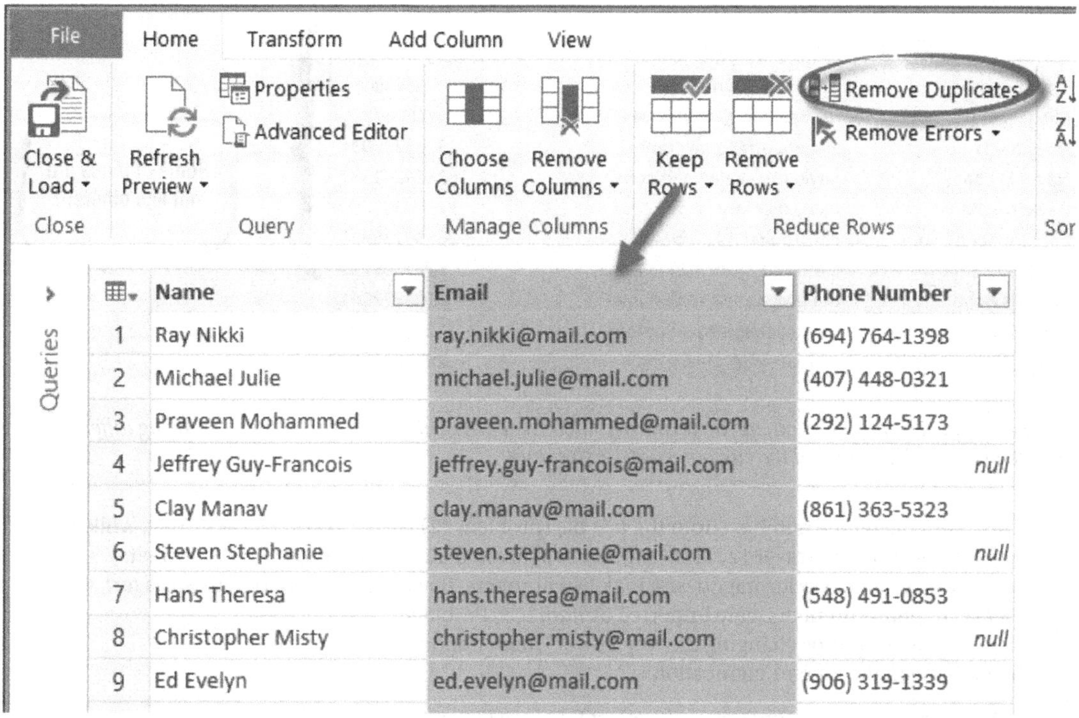

Figure 23-31. *Removing duplicate customer e-mail addresses using the Remove Duplicates feature from the Home ➤ Reduce Rows area of Power Query*

3. Save and load the query.

And you are done!

WHY CAN'T YOU USE THE REMOVE DUPLICATES BUTTON IN EXCEL?

While the Remove Duplicates button in Excel (on the Data tab) is powerful, it is a manual process. That means any time your data changes, you must remove the duplicates *again*. This where Power Query shines. You can simply set up a rule in Power Query to remove duplicates from data. Every time your data changes, you just refresh the connection and Power Query will bring clean data to you, almost like a *genie*, plus you don't need to rub the magic lamp.

Problem 5: Inconsistent Data Formats

Let's stay in the Dinky's Delicious Donut land for some more time. As you are about to thump your chest with pride and satisfaction for the fact that you have cleaned, merged, appended, and removed the duplicates from the data, all before finishing your first cup of coffee in the morning, you notice one little problem. Some of the phone numbers are messed up (see Figure 23-32).

Gil Jeffrey	gil.jeffrey@mail.com	(234) 928-8508
Lori Keshav	lori.keshav@mail.com	(282) 859-4178
Eylem Zach	eylem.zach@mail.com	(963) 814-3438
Michael Kim	michael.kim@mail.com	(217) 498-6667
Joseph Jeff	joseph.jeff@mail.comm	7265236034
Navin Michael	navin.michael@mail.com	3836841537
David Nikolaos	david.nikolaos@mail.com	7100305750
Christopher Silvio	christopher.silvio@mail.comm	8530138828
Catherine Sridevi	catherine.sridevi@mail.com	9257369189
Douglas Anne	douglas.anne@mail.com	3100872261
Paul Michael	paul.michael@mail.comm	4223296430
Adam Hilah	adam.hilah@mail.comm	2857134502

Some of these are not like others!!!

Figure 23-32. *The phone numbers are formatted inconsistently. This is because of the formatting differences between the text file data and the customers-2012.xlsx data*

It turns out the phone numbers from the text file (problem #2) are in (xxx) xxx-xxxx format, while the phone numbers in `customers-2012.xlsx` (problem #3) are in plain-old ten-digit number format.

Since the (xxx) xxx-xxxx format doesn't look like numbers, Power Query imported them as *text*, while the other set of phone numbers were imported as *numbers.* Problem!

Well, you can fix this by changing the way Power Query imports data from a text file.

To do this, edit the Merge1 connection:

1. Right-click the connection and select Edit (see Figure 23-33).

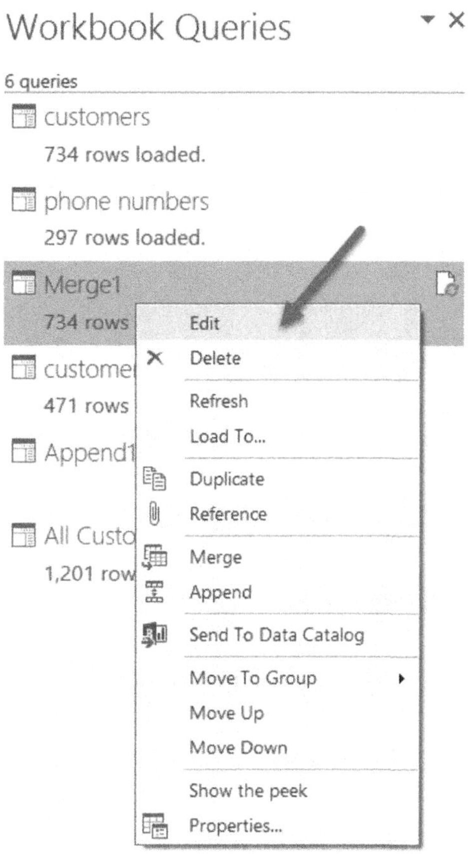

Figure 23-33. *Edit and merge the data query (Merge1) by right-clicking it and choosing the Edit option*

2. Select the Phone Number column.
3. Using the Replace Values option on the Power Query Home tab, replace spaces, commas, and hyphens with nothing.

At this stage, the data looks like Figure 23-34.

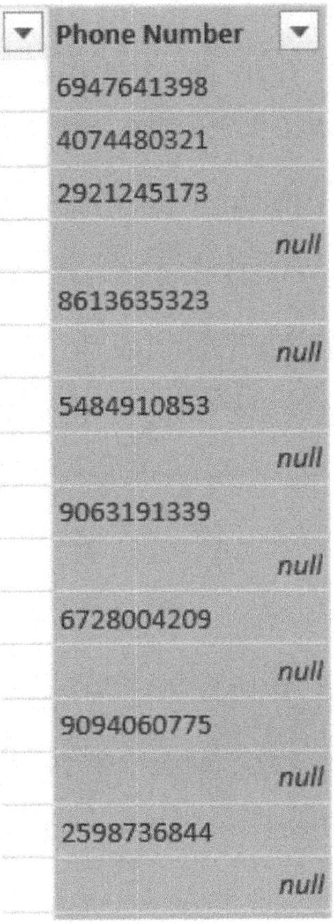
Phone Number
6947641398
4074480321
2921245173
null
8613635323
null
5484910853
null
9063191339
null
6728004209
null
9094060775
null
2598736844
null

Figure 23-34. *Reformatted Phone Number column by removing brackets, spaces, and hyphen symbols*

4. Keep the Phone Number column selected and go to the Transform tab.
5. Click Data Type and change it to Whole Number, as shown in Figure 23-35.

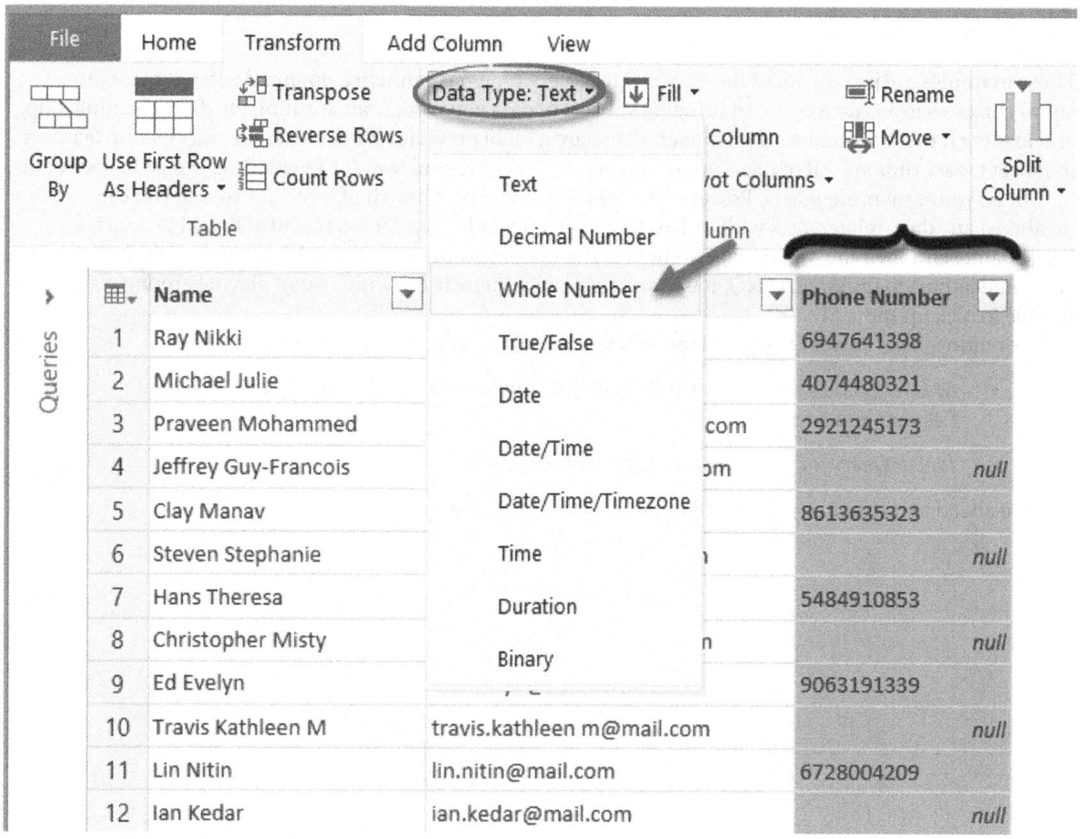

Figure 23-35. *Changing the data type of a query column using the Transform ➤ Any Column area*

6. Save your query.
7. Refresh the All Customer Data query, and there is your uniformly formatted Phone Number column.

WAIT…DID YOU NOTICE WHAT POWER QUERY DID?

You edited the Merge1 query, but when you refreshed your All Customer Data query, you got cleaned phone numbers in *that query*.

That's right, when you change one of the intermediate steps in Power Query, the subsequent steps (and queries) will automatically change too.

The Last Word

These examples are just the tip of the Power Query iceberg. It has immense potential when it comes to connecting to various data sources, bringing subsets of data you want, transforming the data, cleaning it up, and loading it to the workbook data model. There are a lot of powerful transformation and cleanup features in Power Query ribbons. All of these are simple to use. Just click and wait for Power Query to go at your data.

But if you want more *power,* Power Query offers a whole new bunch of formulas so that you can do almost any data-related task with it. This language is called M, and it is a mix of SQL and JavaScript. Don't panic; although the M language sounds like something James Bond would use to send coded communications to his London HQ, it is *almost* like plain English. So, with a bit of playing around, you may be able to pick up some M.

For more about Power Query and the M language, please refer to the following books:

- *M Is for (Data) Monkey: A Guide to the M Language in Excel Power Query* by Miguel Escobar and Ken Puls
- *Power Query for Power BI and Excel* by Chris Webb

Go ahead and conquer your data problems with Power Query.

CHAPTER 24

Introduction to PowerPivot

So far you have learned various techniques and advanced concepts when it comes to using formulas (and VBA) to build dashboards. Let me ask you one question.

> *What are some of the limitations of formula-driven (or VBA-driven) dashboard development?*

Go ahead and think about it.

For all its glory and power, it turns out that formula-driven dashboard development suffers from a few key limitations, such as the following:

- **Not scalable:** As you bring more data into your dashboard world, suddenly you realize that the `SUMIFS`, `SUMPRODUCT`, and `LOOKUP` formulas are taking forever to calculate. Even if you are willing to compromise on speed, you will eventually reach the theoretical limit of 1 million rows at which point either you have to crunch *less* data or come up with some clever mechanism to work with data split into multiple ranges.
- **Not easy:** Although you are at the tad end of a fairly advanced Excel book, you may still be wondering how to calculate certain values using the data you got. This is because some of the most commonly asked business questions are hard to answer with simple Excel formulas. Sample these questions:
  - "How many unique customers visited our store in Columbus, Ohio?"
  - "What is the longest duration for which production was stopped in the month of May 2015?"
  - "How many patients visited our hospital this month and last month too?"
  - "What are the names of top three products by sales in our best five stores?"

  Although it is possible to answer these questions with Excel formulas, these formulas tend to be long, complicated, and often tricky to modify when business requirements change.
- **Disconnected:** One of the key things you notice when you look at any business data is that different kinds of data are maintained in different places. Take, for example, separate tables for customer data and sales data, separate databases for CRM data and manufacturing data, and so on. This creates additional challenges for analysts, when you try to combine all this data to answer even simple questions. Occasionally you may end up weaving a complex web of formulas just to bring everything to one place even before starting the work on the dashboard.

If you seem to be nodding along while reading the previous reasons, then you are going to love PowerPivot. This new technology (well, it has been around for five years now, but you could argue that for a majority of Excel users, PowerPivot is still new) overcomes many of the limitations of Excel and can truly transform Excel into a powerful business intelligence application.

What Is PowerPivot?

PowerPivot is an Excel add-in from Microsoft. It is part of the Power BI family of tools. PowerPivot is designed to help you (data analysts, managers, report creators, data nerds, and so on) answer complex questions about your data with ease. In a nutshell, the process for using PowerPivot to go from raw data to insights is like this:

1. Feed raw data to PowerPivot (you can bring data from *almost* anywhere, such as from text files, Excel workbooks, databases, Azure data stores, Power Query connections, workbook data models, and so on).
2. Set up the data model by connecting tables with each other (just like how you connected tables in Chapter 21 using Excel 2013; in PowerPivot too you can connect tables.)
3. Create measures (formulas that tell PowerPivot how to calculate numbers you want).
4. Create a regular pivot table and use measures as *value fields*.
5. Done!

A Note About How to Get PowerPivot

PowerPivot is compatible with Excel 2010 and newer for Windows.

- If you are using Excel 2010, you can download PowerPivot from the Microsoft web site.
- If you are using Excel 2013 or 2016, you can activate PowerPivot in Excel by using the COM Add-ins option.

■ **Note** If you don't see the PowerPivot add-in, that means your version of Excel 2013/2016 does not have PowerPivot. You may have to upgrade your Excel version to the Professional Plus package.

- If you are using Office 365, you may add Power BI to your subscription.

For more about PowerPivot compatibility, availability, and installation, please visit the official PowerPivot web site at `http://bit.ly/1MfBdSl`.

What to Expect from This Chapter

Because PowerPivot is a vast technology, it is not possible to cover it at any length in one chapter. So, in this chapter, I will limit the discussion to the following topics:

- Getting started with PowerPivot
- Loading sample data into PowerPivot
- Setting up the data model
- Creating simple measures using the PowerPivot DAX language
- Inserting a simple PowerPivot table into an Excel file
- Finding out more about PowerPivot

Getting Started with PowerPivot

First, download and install PowerPivot for your respective version of Excel. For more, refer to `http://bit.ly/1MfBdSl`. Once you install PowerPivot, you should see a new tab, called *PowerPivot,* in Excel (see Figure 24-1). This is your gateway into the world of PowerPivot.

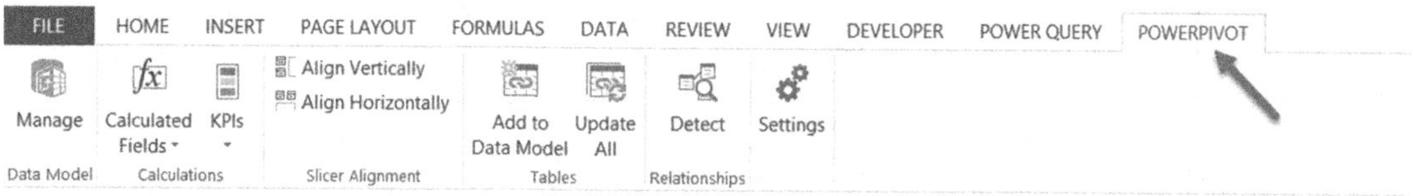

Figure 24-1. *The PowerPivot tab*

You can now create PowerPivot tables (they are like regular pivot tables but can do so much more). But first, you need to load some data into PowerPivot. After all, PowerPivot needs data to do analysis.

Loading Sample Data into PowerPivot

PowerPivot accepts various data sources. You can load data from *almost* any database and from text files, CSV files, Excel workbooks, SQL Server Analysis Services, tables in current workbook, and connections created in Power Query.

The process for loading data into PowerPivot will differ based on the type of connection. In this chapter, you will learn how to load data from Excel tables into PowerPivot. For other types of data, refer to the "The Last Word" section at the end of this chapter or visit `http://bit.ly/1MfBdSl`.

Imagine you have three tables in Excel, containing customer, product, and sales data, as shown in Figures 24-2, 24-3, and 24-4.

Customer ID	Customer Name	Gender	Area	Profession
C0001	Albert	Male	Middle	Retired
C0002	Barry	Male	North	Unemployed
C0003	Cindy	Female	Middle	Retired
C0004	Dorothy	Female	East	Professional
C0005	Ethan	Male	West	Self-employed
C0006	Fanah	Female	Middle	Professional
C0007	Ganesh	Male	Middle	Salaried
C0008	Harry	Male	Middle	Unemployed
C0009	Ida	Female	West	Unemployed
C0010	Jackson	Male	South	Self-employed
C0011	Kurt	Male	East	Self-employed
C0012	Linda	Female	East	Salaried
C0013	Mindy	Female	Middle	Professional

Figure 24-2. *Customer data*

Product ID	Category	Name	Size	Price	Units per pack
P001	Jelly	Product 1	Large	$ 2.8	15
P002	Drinks	Product 2	Small	$ 2.8	1
P003	Drinks	Product 3	Small	$ 1.5	1
P004	Snacks	Product 4	Medium	$ 9.3	15
P005	Jelly	Product 5	Large	$ 0.5	5
P006	Drinks	Product 6	Large	$ 7.4	1
P007	Jelly	Product 7	Large	$ 2.3	15
P008	Drinks	Product 8	Medium	$ 4.0	1
P009	Biscuits	Product 9	Medium	$ 7.0	20
P010	Biscuits	Product 10	Large	$ 7.3	15
P011	Snacks	Product 11	Large	$ 3.1	10
P012	Jelly	Product 12	Small	$ 0.6	15
P013	Snacks	Product 13	Small	$ 1.6	15

Figure 24-3. *Product data*

Sale ID	Time	Customer ID	Product ID	Quantity
S00001	12-1-2014 12:00:00 AM	C0001	P025	1
S00002	12-1-2014 12:00:00 AM	C0025	P025	3
S00003	12-1-2014 12:00:00 AM	C0010	P001	2
S00004	12-1-2014 12:00:00 AM	C0017	P023	4
S00005	12-1-2014 12:00:00 AM	C0018	P016	5
S00006	12-1-2014 12:00:00 AM	C0011	P018	4
S00007	12-1-2014 12:00:00 AM	C0015	P006	4
S00008	12-1-2014 12:00:00 AM	C0025	P024	4
S00009	12-1-2014 12:00:00 AM	C0016	P014	4
S00010	12-1-2014 12:00:00 AM	C0016	P012	3
S00011	12-1-2014 12:00:00 AM	C0010	P027	1
S00012	12-1-2014 12:00:00 AM	C0001	P015	1

Figure 24-4. *Sales data*

To load these tables into PowerPivot, follow these steps:

1. Select one table. (You'll load one table at a time.)
2. Click Add to Data Model in the Tables group (see Figure 24-5).

   This loads the table to the PowerPivot data model (more on this later) and opens the PowerPivot window.

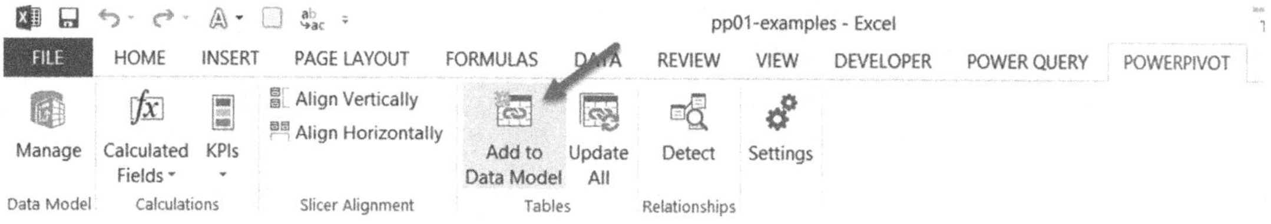

Figure 24-5. *Adding tables to the data model through the PowerPivot tab*

3. Close the PowerPivot window to return to Excel.
4. Repeat the process for the other tables of data you have.

What Is the PowerPivot Data Model?

For PowerPivot to process your data, analyze it, and calculate the numbers you want, it must construct a data model. This consists of nothing but the following:

- A collection of your data tables and connection settings
- Relationships between various tables defined as rules
- Measures and calculations you build on top of these tables

A key difference between the data model introduced in Chapter 21 and the data model used by PowerPivot is that when you use PowerPivot, the relationship-building process happens in PowerPivot. For more about the data modeling capabilities of Excel 2013, refer to Chapter 21.

Let's Enter the World of PowerPivot

Now that you have added three tables to the workbook's data model, let's get into the world of PowerPivot and start exploring.

Click the Manage button on the PowerPivot tab. This opens the PowerPivot window, which looks like Figure 24-6.

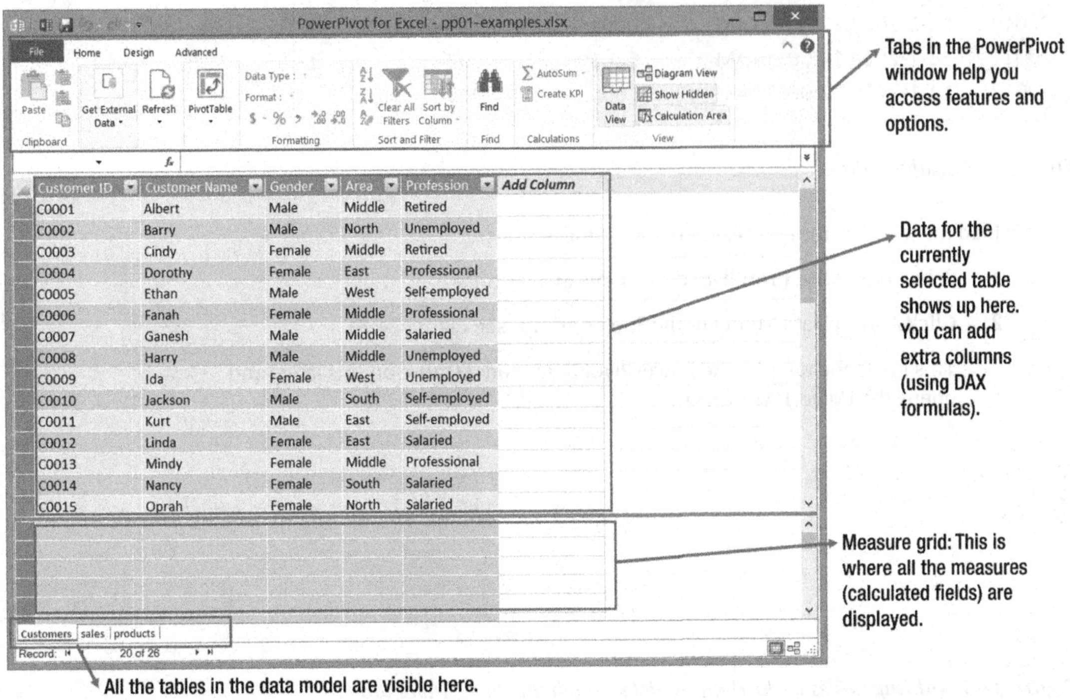

***Figure 24-6.** The PowerPivot window, explained*

The PowerPivot window offers a lot of features and functionalities. Because the aim for this chapter is to provide a brief overview of what you can do with PowerPivot, let's skip the discussion of these features. You can review the features in detail at the URL provided earlier in the "Getting Started with PowerPivot" section.

As a first step, now that the data is in PowerPivot, let's set up relationships between tables. Click Diagram View on the Home tab of the PowerPivot window (see Figure 24-7).

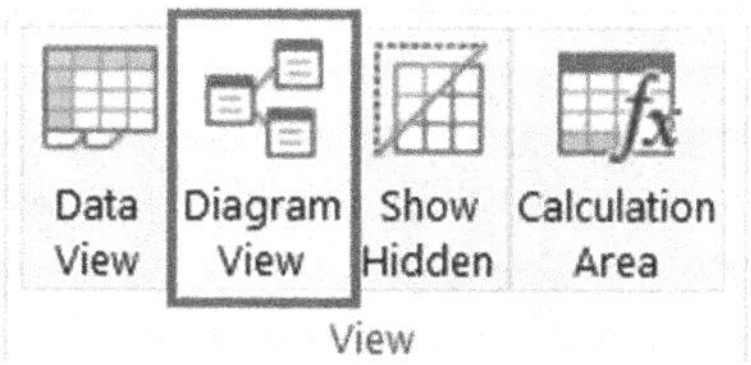

Figure 24-7. *The Diagram View option in the View group on the Home tab in PowerPivot*

This will open the diagram view where each table is represented by a box (with the columns of the table listed as separate items in the box), as shown in Figure 24-8.

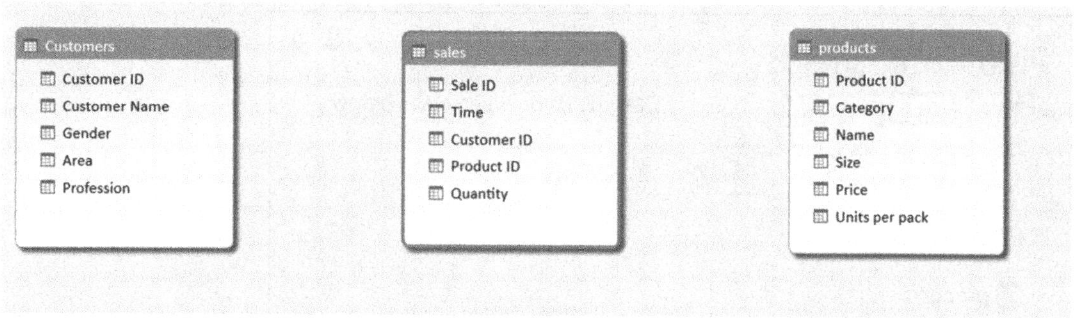

Figure 24-8. *Diagram view of tables, PowerPivot window*

To set up the relationships between tables, follow these steps:

1. First identify which relationships are needed. For this example, you have two relationships.
    - Customers[Customer ID] related to sales[Customer ID]
    - products[Product ID] related to sales[Product ID]
2. Select the Customer ID field in the Customers table and drag and drop it on the Customer ID field of the sales table.
3. Select the Product ID field in the products table and drag and drop it on the Product ID field of the sales table.

    Done! Your relationships are now set up.

Creating Your First PowerPivot Table

Now that you have loaded some data and created the necessary relationships, let's create a PowerPivot table so that you can see what this is all about.

To create a PowerPivot table, click PivotTable on the Home tab of the PowerPivot window (see Figure 24-9). This opens the Create PivotTable dialog box and prompts you for the location of the PowerPivot table. By default the new PowerPivot table will be inserted in a new worksheet. Click OK.

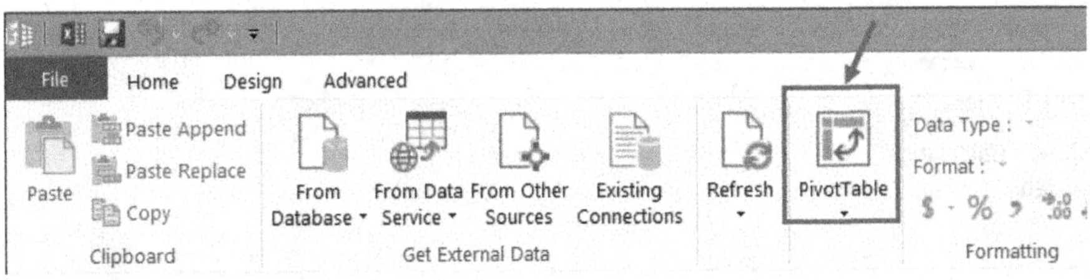

Figure 24-9. *Inserting a pivot table from a PowerPivot window*

At this point, the PivotTable Fields list will show all three tables (if you see only one table, switch to the ALL view from the ACTIVE view). Please refer to Figure 24-10.

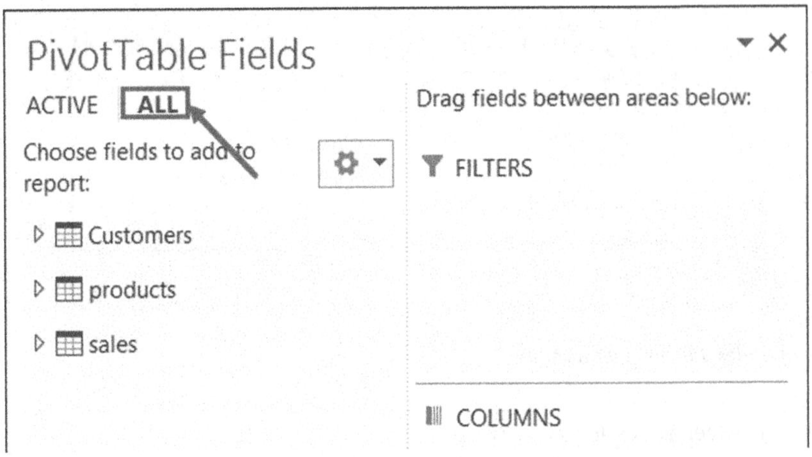

Figure 24-10. *The PowerPivotTable Fields list shows all the tables in your data model*

You can mix and match any fields from any of the tables to create a combined pivot report. For example, see the "Quantity Breakdown PowerPivot by Product Category & Customer Gender" PowerPivot table, as shown in Figure 24-11.

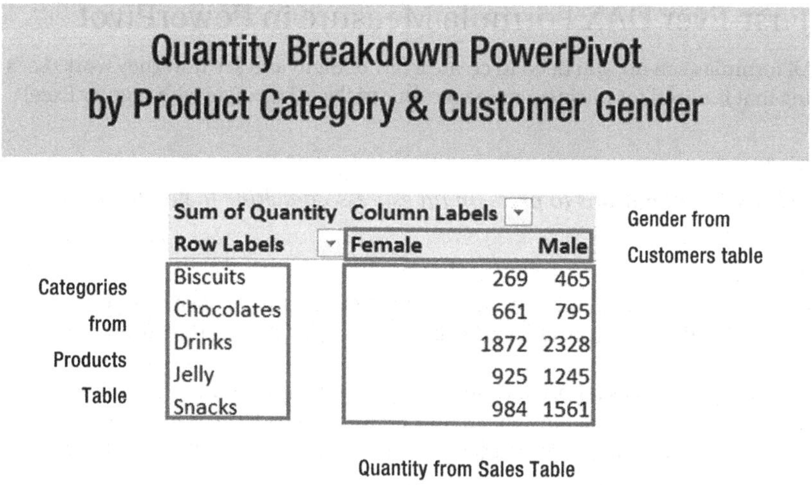

Sum of Quantity	Column Labels	
Row Labels	Female	Male
Biscuits	269	465
Chocolates	661	795
Drinks	1872	2328
Jelly	925	1245
Snacks	984	1561

Figure 24-11. *Example PowerPivot table, quantity by category and gender*

Since you are familiar with this process (refer to Chapter 21), let's talk about the *Power* part of PowerPivot.

The Real Power of PowerPivot: DAX Formulas

When you drag a field to the values area of the pivot table, by default Excel will either sum or count that field. Using the pivot table calculation options, you can calculate a few other summaries such as average, minimum, maximum, and so on.

In other words, there are only a few ways in which you can summarize (or analyze) data with regular pivot tables.

PowerPivot gives you Data Analysis Expressions (DAX) formulas, which you can use to calculate a lot of different numbers easily. Here are a few sample numbers that can be easily calculated in PowerPivot using DAX formulas:

- "How many unique customers visited our store in Columbus, Ohio?"
- "What is the longest duration for which production was stopped in the month of May 2015?"
- "How many patients visited our hospital this month and last month too?"
- "What are the names of the top three products by sales in our best five stores?"
- "What is the growth rate in sales this month compared to last year for the same month?"
- "What is the three-month moving average trend in customer footfalls across our stores in the United States?"

Think of DAX formulas as a mix of Excel formulas, pivot tables, pixie dust, and your favorite superhero (for me it's the Flash).

Let's Create Your First-Ever DAX Formula Measure in PowerPivot

To truly appreciate what DAX formulas can do, you need to create a few of them and see how they work. Let's start by calculating something that is useful for business managers but tricky to calculate with regular Excel formulas.

> *Finding the right combination of buttons to press on an espresso machine to get the most awesome coffee ever!*

Of course, I am kidding. PowerPivot can't tell you how to make the perfect cup of coffee. Not yet.

Instead, let's calculate something that is truly useful for business managers: finding the distinct customer count.

Let's say you are looking at a monthly sales report and wondering how many customers bought from you in this month. Although you had 6,000 transactions, that doesn't mean you had 6,000 customers. Because a few customers might have made multiple purchases, the customer count could be less. But how do you calculate it?

The Process for Creating a DAX Formula to Calculate Distinct Customer Count

To create a new measure, you will be using the Calculations area of the PowerPivot tab in Excel.

1. Start by inserting a new PowerPivot table. (You need to go to the PowerPivot window and click PivotTable on the Home tab.)
2. Let's say you want to find the distinct customer count for each product category and gender combination. So, add the product categories as row labels and make "Row Labels" and the two genders the column headings. At this stage, the PowerPivot table looks like Figure 24-12.

	Column Labels		
Row Labels	**Female**	**Male**	**Grand Total**
Biscuits			
Chocolates			
Drinks			
Jelly			
Snacks			
Grand Total			

Figure 24-12. *Blank pivot table with categories and genders*

3. Go to the PowerPivot tab and click Calculated Fields ➤ New Calculated Field. See Figure 24-13.

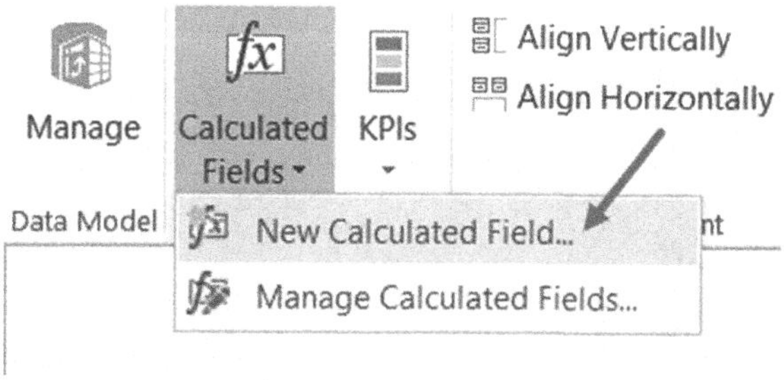

Figure 24-13. Inserting the calculated field from the PowerPivot tab

4. This opens the Add Calculated Field dialog. Let's give the calculated field a name such as Distinct Customer Count.

5. In the Formula area, type the formula `=DISTINCTCOUNT(Sales[Customer ID])`.

6. Set Format to Whole Number with a thousands separator. See Figure 24-14.

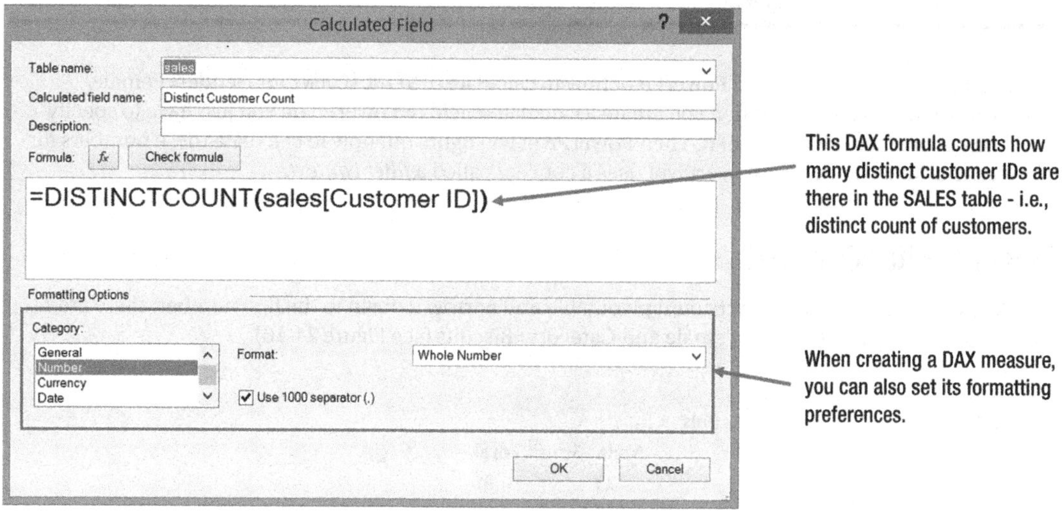

Figure 24-14. DISTINCTCOUNT() PowerPivot measure, explained

7. Click OK.

At this stage, PowerPivot calculates the distinct count for each of the category and gender combinations and loads them into the pivot table. The output looks like Figure 24-15.

Distinct Customer Count	Column Labels		
Row Labels	Female	Male	Grand Total
Biscuits	11	15	26
Chocolates	11	12	23
Drinks	11	12	23
Jelly	11	15	26
Snacks	9	14	23
Grand Total	**11**	**15**	**26**

Figure 24-15. *Distinct count of customers by category and gender, PowerPivot example report*

DISTINCTCOUNT(), I LIKE THE SOUND OF IT

`DISTINCTCOUNT()` is one of the hundreds of formulas available in PowerPivot to calculate what you want. As the name suggests, `DISTINCTCOUNT` counts how many unique (or distinct) values are present in a table column. In this case, `DISCINCTCOUNT` is looking at the Customer ID column of the sales table and finding the count of customers.

Oh! Wait a second, I never told PowerPivot how to calculate `DISTINCTCOUNT` for Gender=Female, Category=Biscuits. That's right. When you create a calculated field in PowerPivot, you just have to specify the abstract or business definition of it. Then PowerPivot will figure out how to calculate these numbers for every scenario. To facilitate this, PowerPivot uses a concept called a *filter context.*

What Is a Filter Context?

Let's take a closer look at the distinct count pivot table and narrow it down to the first number; there are 11 distinct customers where Gender=Female and Category=Biscuits (see Figure 24-16).

Distinct Customer Count	Column Labels		
Row Labels	Female	Male	Grand Total
Biscuits	11	15	26
Chocolates	11	12	23
Drinks	11	12	23
Jelly	11	15	26
Snacks	9	14	23
Grand Total	**11**	**15**	**26**

Figure 24-16. *Understanding PowerPivot filter contexts*

In that situation, the filter context is nothing but Gender=Female and Category=Biscuits. Once PowerPivot determines the filter context for each cell of the pivot table, it will calculate the measure (distinct customer count) for only that filter context.

Everything you add to a PowerPivot table will have a role in defining the filter context.

- If you add a slicer on the customer profession and select "Self-employed," that will be added as another filter context.
- If you add a report filter on the product size and select the Large and Medium sizes, they will be added as another filter context.

The filter context helps PowerPivot narrow down to the subset of data on which it calculates the measures.

MEASURES VS. CALCULATED FIELDS

Both of these refer to the same idea. In Excel 2010 PowerPivot, they were called *measures*. In Excel 2013 PowerPivot, they were called *calculated fields*. Who knows what Microsoft will call them in Excel 2016? In this chapter, I will use both words so that you get used to them.

Let's Create a Few More DAX Measures

Now that you are familiar with the process of creating DAX measures (or calculated fields), let's create a few more of them for the data model.

To create these measures, use Calculated Fields ➤ New Calculated Field from the PowerPivot tab.

You will create measures for calculating Total Quantity and Average Quantity per Customer using simple DAX formulas.

Total Quantity Measure

The total quantity is nothing but the sum of the Quantity column in the Sales table. The measure definition looks like this:

```
Total Quantity = sum(sales[Quantity])
```

You can see this in Figure 24-17.

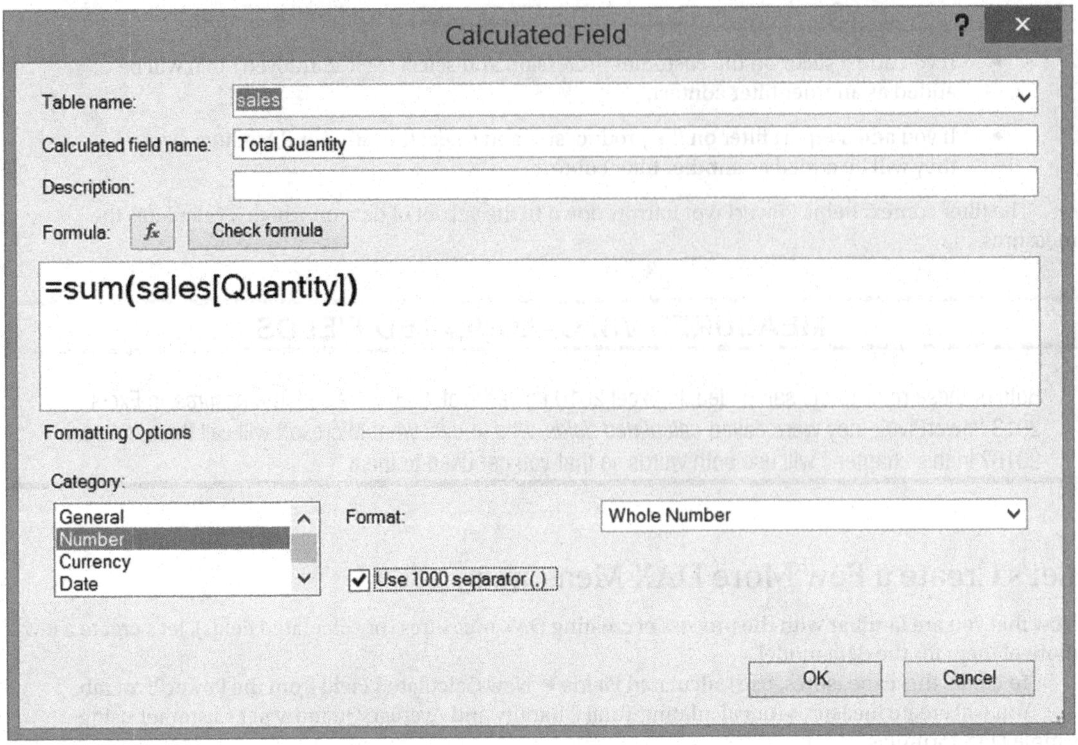

Figure 24-17. *Adding the Total Quantity measure using the SUM DAX formula*

Average Quantity per Customer

Since you know both the total quantity and the customer count, you can calculate the average quantity per customer. This is defined as follows:

Average Quantity per Customer = `[Total Quantity] / [Distinct Customer Count]`

Figure 24-18 shows the Average Quantity per Customer measure.

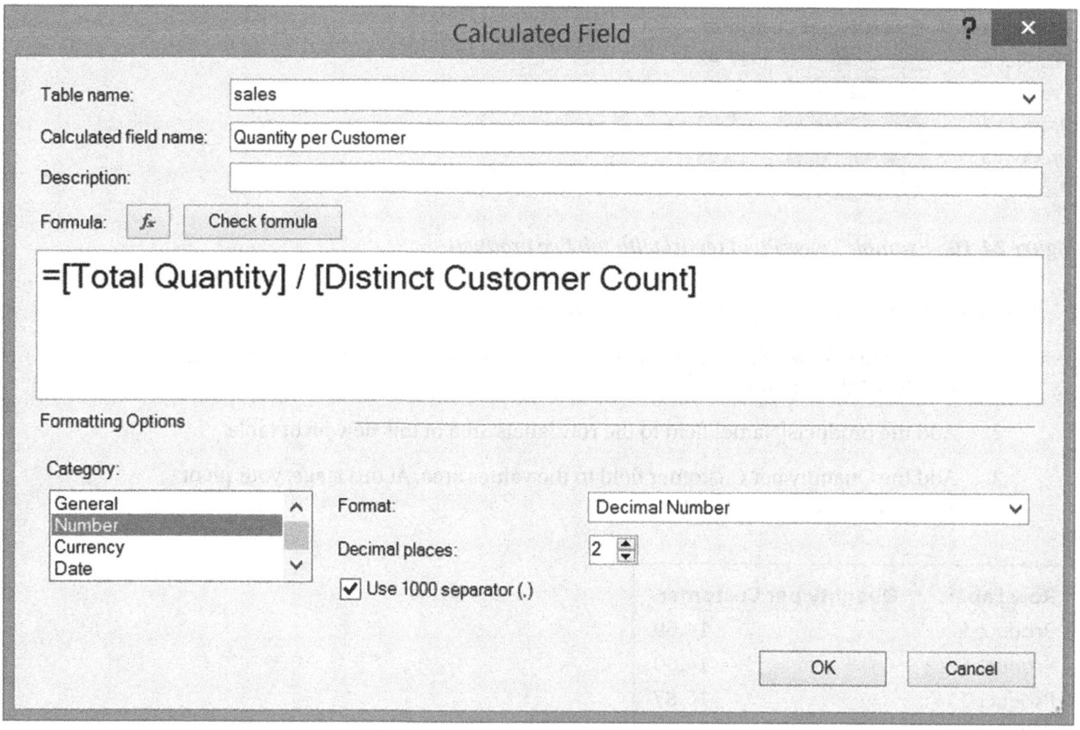

Figure 24-18. *Adding the Average Quantity per Customer DAX measure*

THAT'S RIGHT, POWERPIVOT MEASURES ARE REUSABLE

Once you create a few measures, you can use them in constructing other measures.

Think of each measure as a LEGO block. Once you have a bunch of them, you can creatively mix them to come up with a new kinds of measures.

Example PowerPivot Report: Top Five Products Based on Average Quantity per Customer

Now that you have the Quantity per Customer measure, you can use it to find the top five products based on how much customers buy them. Essentially, you are trying to create something like Figure 24-19.

Row Labels	Quantity per Customer
Product 8	17.48
Product 11	16.87
Product 29	15.82
Product 3	15.68
Product 6	15.43

Figure 24-19. *Example PowerPivot report with top five products*

To create this PowerPivot report, follow these steps:

1. Insert a new PowerPivot table by going to the PowerPivot window and clicking the PivotTable option.
2. Add the products[Name] field to the row labels area of this new pivot table.
3. Add the Quantity per Customer field to the values area. At this stage, your pivot table looks like Figure 24-20.

Row Labels	Quantity per Customer
Product 1	14.69
Product 10	14.50
Product 11	16.87
Product 12	14.35
Product 13	12.57
Product 14	15.39
Product 15	14.35
Product 16	14.22
Product 17	14.73
Product 18	12.12
Product 19	14.39
Product 2	11.91
Product 20	14.00
Product 21	11.41

Figure 24-20. *Quantity per Customer for all products*

4. Right-click any Quantity per Customer value and choose Sort ➤ Largest to Smallest. See Figure 24-21.

   Now that product names are sorted by Quantity per Customer, let's filter down to the top five products alone.

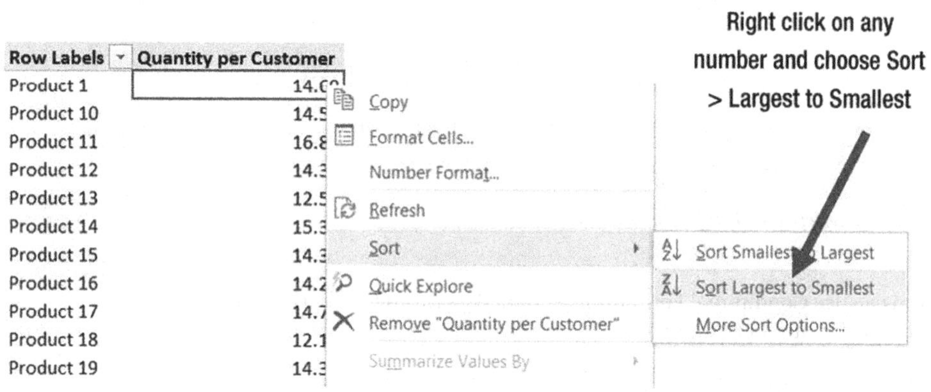

Figure 24-21. *Sorting the pivot table by Quantity per Customer measure*

5. To do that, right-click any product name and choose Filter ➤ Top 10. See Figure 24-22.

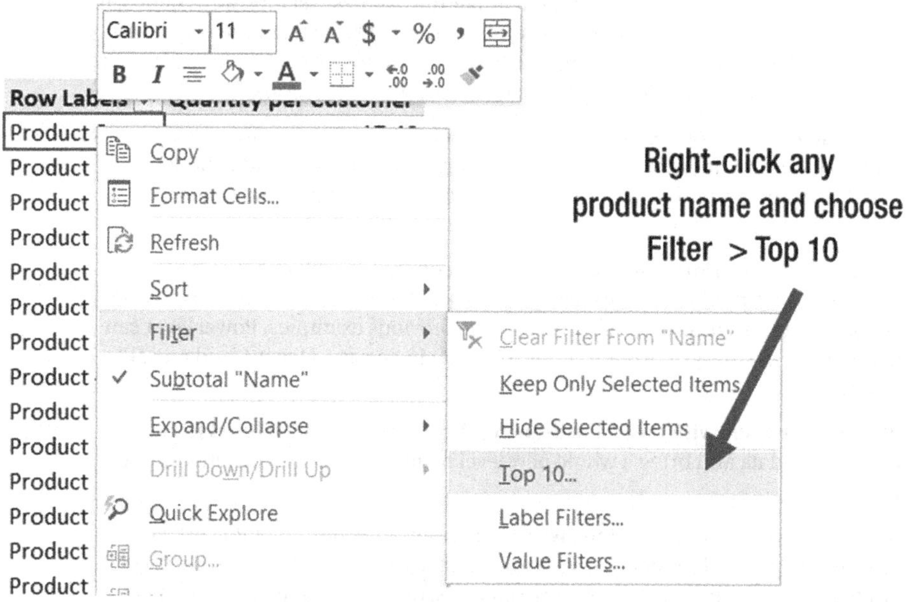

Figure 24-22. *Filtering top five products using the Top 10 value filter*

6. Specify 5 as the number of items, as shown in Figure 24-23, and click OK.

   Your pivot report with the top five products based on quantity per customer is ready.

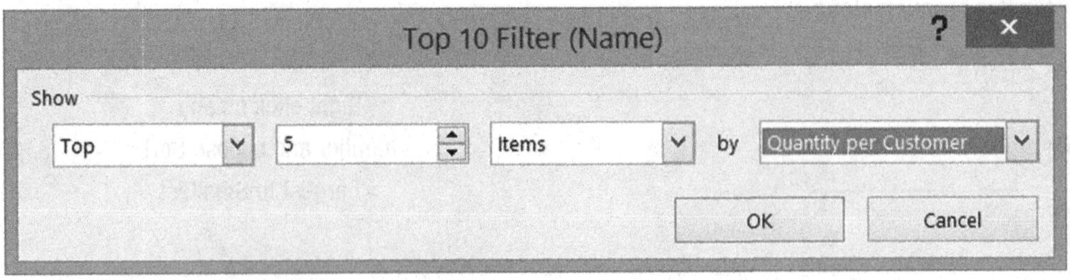

Figure 24-23. *Filter criteria for top five products*

7. You can use Conditional Formatting ➤ Data Bars (from Excel's Home tab) to make these numbers stand out.

PowerPivot and Excel Dashboards

PowerPivot is like a powerful processing engine for analyzing data. Since dashboards often involve analyzing huge amounts of data, PowerPivot fits naturally into this world. Here is how you can use PowerPivot to speed up your dashboard development:

- **Use PowerPivot for connecting datasets:** PowerPivot allows you to bring data from multiple sources and connect them as per the business relationships between each of those datasets. This means no more lengthy `VLOOKUP` statements or clumsy `INDEX+MATCH` formulas. You can simply use PowerPivot to connect tables with each other and generate PowerPivot tables to answer business questions.
- **Overcome Excel's processing limitations:** Whenever you have more than a few hundred thousand data points, regular Excel formulas (or VBA) tend to be slow. PowerPivot handles fairly large datasets (up to a few million data points) with ease on normal office computers.
- **Answer tough questions with ease:** Instead of coming up with complex array formulas or lengthy `SUMIFS` formulas, you can use PowerPivot measures to answer complex business questions. As you saw in the previous examples, PowerPivot can answer many business questions about your data in an easy, elegant, and reusable fashion.
- **Let your users play with dashboards using slicers:** You can add slicers to any fields in your data and bring a whole new level of interactivity and insights to the dashboards.
- **Mix PowerPivot with everything else in Excel:** Since the output of PowerPivot will be either pivot tables or cells, you can mix them with everything else in Excel, like conditional formatting, charts, form controls, or VBA to come up with totally impressive and detailed dashboards.

Figure 24-24 shows an example dashboard that depicts product performance based on the dataset introduced at the start of this chapter.

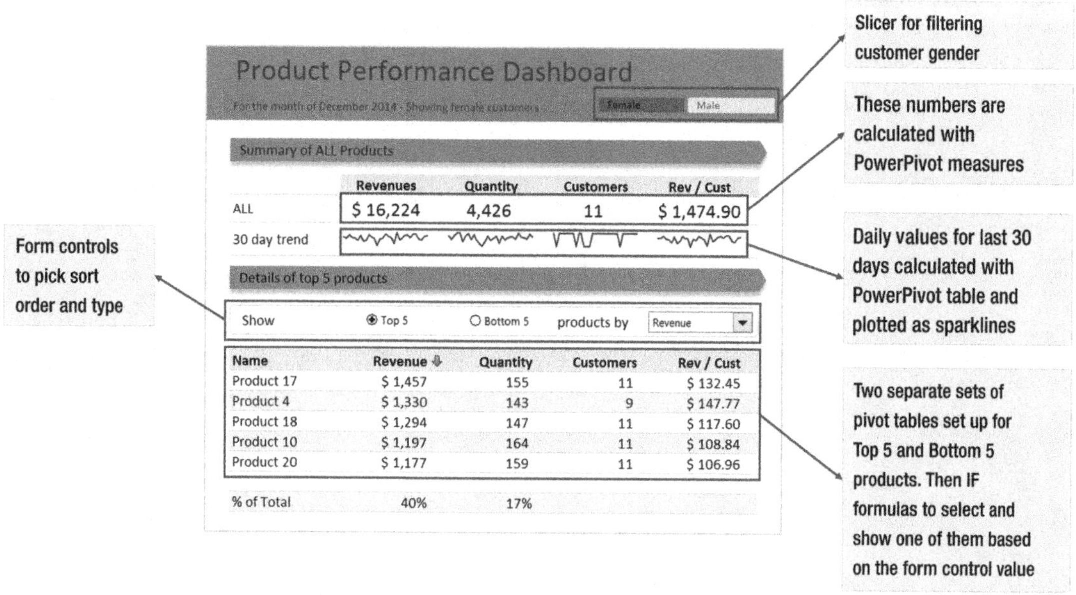

Figure 24-24. *Example Product Performance Dashboard made with PowerPivot, explained*

Explaining the construction of this dashboard is beyond the scope for this discussion on PowerPivot. If you are feeling curious, you may refer to this chapter's workbook, `Chapter24-pp01-examples.xlsx`, and learn by breaking it apart.

The Last Word

I am sure you are feeling curious about PowerPivot and its possibilities. If so, please check out the following resources:

- **PowerPivotPro.com** by Rob Collie offers a lot of tutorials, discussion, examples, books, and material on PowerPivot.
- At Chandoo.org, I have been running an online course on PowerPivot, teaching people how to use this technology to solve real-life business problems and build awesome dashboards. Check it out at `http://chandoo.org/powerpivot/`.

Index

■ D

E

F

G

H

N

O

P, Q

R

Printed in the United States
By Bookmasters